Gifted

CHALLENGE AND RESPONSE FOR EDUCATION

Joe Khatena

F. E. PEACOCK PUBLISHERS, INC.
ITASCA, ILLINOIS

Dedication

In the following lines I dedicate this book to my dear grandchildren Paul, Joshua and Jessica, and all children of the world who must strive to actualize gifted potential for transformation to eminence.

SPRING TO LIFE

The excited twitter of a bluejay
Preparing for the stir of spring,
The leaping rainbow-trout
Shivering beaded radiance,
The myriad flashings
Of a dawning day,
Autumn gold in rage promises
Icy adaptation to green,
A billion busy bees
Murmur from flower to comb:
Indomitable you struggle—
Life and conquest are yours.

Source: J. Khatena (1981). *Images of the Inward Eye: Selected Poems.* Starkville, M.S.: Allan Associates. Copyright © 1981 by Joseph Khatena. Reprinted by permission.

Contents

CHAPTER 9

Nurturing Creative Intellect

CHAPTER 10

Learning for Excellence

Preface

For me, the writing of a book on the gifted has been both a delight and challenge. My first book on the subject, written more than a decade ago, deals with the gifted from the perspective of creativity. The goal of that book was to fashion a caring and nontechnical discussion of what parents and teachers can do for their creatively gifted children. I urged them to be the catalyst of the mystery and magic of existence, for it is my view that fostering the creativity of gifted children provides the foundation of a magnificent future for all.

My continued efforts to encourage the educated community to provide the best for the gifted, led to discussions of the many facets and complex nature of giftedness and to the steps we can take to maximize its fullest development. So much has been said to date by many committed to the task of discovering and facilitating the proper educational direction of gifted children that to design yet another work on superior children becomes a veritable challenge. My response to that challenge is the present book. Its intent is to put in one place, for easy access to the professional and general community, a representative sample of the most significant theory and practice on the subject of gifted education.

The book is substantial and solidly based on research and practice. It gives appropriate attention to such subjects on the gifted and talented as (1) their special abilities, (2) their developmental characteristics, (3) the problems they face and how they may be assisted to overcome them, (4) the nature of their intellectual processes, (5) methods that have been successfully tried to nurture them towards more effective productivity, (6) various educational models designed for better learning, and (7) motivational approaches and their relevance for gifted education. In addition, there is emphasis on the need to understand gifted and talented children and to regard their education in terms of the past, present, and future.

As an unusually comprehensive treatment of diverse contributions to the field, this text captures the essences and essentials of the most innovative ideas, instructional materials, measurement approaches, theories in historical perspective, and modern technological correlates of giftedness. Rich in both psychological theory and educational philosophy and technology, this text fairly represents the many ideas and issues that have made gifted education an exciting one in recent years. In so doing it prepares the way for further advances in the field.

Each chapter of the book introduces the reader to its contents by way of an introduction and ends with a conclusion. A comprehensive list of references places the work in proper context. Apart from its function as an extensive and challenging reference to the educated and curious reader, the book is designed for graduate and undergraduate students seeking professional qualification and state certification. Furthermore, the book may be used as a text for a single course, or its components are applicable as supplementary readings in related courses.

The components of the book have been organized into a holistic model of education. The five parameters of the model consist of environment, individual, intervention, outcome, and communication. These are interconnected to the multitudinous details and complex nature of the subject of giftedness. It presents the reader with a gestalt that serves as framework for a more universal grasp and coherent understanding of the subject. In this way, it is expected that the reader will not be lost in the detail of exposition, but will experience an emergent coherent understanding of the subject. The reader will find the model illustrated and discussed in the third chapter of the book.

I am indebted to so many people who have in one way or another brought this work to fruition. Among them are my talented children and my wife, Nelly Khatena, whose creative imagination in art strengthens and refreshes me; the community of children and educators who shape my understanding of educational process and technology giving me the reason to write; and several eminent scholars, Dr. H. C. Chang of Cambridge University, the late Paul Torrance of the University of Georgia, who have served, and continue to serve, as my mentors. I am also grateful to Kathleen Ermitage and the staff at Proof Positive/Farrowlyne Associates, Inc., for editorial design and production of the text.

Let me close by wishing my readers *bon voyage*, as they recognize their own gifts and those of others in preparation for the journey of excellence designated for eminence.

ABOUT THE AUTHOR

Dr. Joe Khatena is professor and head of the Department of Educational Psychology and professor of psychology at Mississippi State University. He earned his B.A. and M.A. (Honors) at the University of Malaya with a major in English. He holds an M.Ed. from the University of Singapore and a Ph.D. in psychology from the University of Georgia.

Dr. Khatena was a teacher in the Singapore public schools (1950–56), part-time lecturer at the University of Singapore (1965–66), and lecturer of English at the Singapore Teachers Training College (1961–65). Furthermore, he was assistant professor of psychology at East Carolina University (1968–69) before joining Marshall University where he served as associate professor (1969–72) and professor of educational foundations (1972–77).

His interest in giftedness and creativity led to the development of several measures and books related to the identification and nurture of creativity, talent, and giftedness, among which are the *Khatena-Torrance Creative Perception Inventory* (1976), *The Creatively Gifted Child: Suggestions for Parents and Teachers* (1978), *Educational Psychology of the Gifted* (1982), *Imagery and Creative Imagination* (1984), and the *Khatena-Morse Multitalent Perception Inventory* (1991). Journals which have published his works include the *Gifted Child Quarterly, Journal of Creative Behavior, Journal of Educational Psychology, Psychological Reports, Perceptual and Motor Skills, Art Psychotherapy, Humanitas, Journal of Mental Imagery,* and *Metaphor and Symbolic Activity.* Further he has lectured extensively on these subjects both nationally and internationally.

Dr. Khatena is a member of Phi Kappa Phi, Kappa Delta Phi, and the American Educational Research Association, a fellow of the American Psychological Association, a colleague of the Creative Education Foundation, and a past president of the National Association for Gifted Children (NAGC). He is listed in many biographical works including *Men and Women of Science, Men of Achievement, International Who's Who in Education, Who's Who in Frontier Science and Technology, Who's Who in America, Directory of Distinguished Americans, the Encyclopaedia of Special Education,* and the *International Authors and Writers Who's Who.* In addition he is the recipient of several awards including the NAGC Distinguished Scholar Award and Distinguished Service Award, Distinguished Summer Lecturer of Texas Women's University, and Fulbright Senior Lecturerships to India.

CHAPTER ONE

Ready to Take Off

*I*NTRODUCTION

Formal schooling for the gifted is a twentieth-century phenomenon that has developed due to events of the past 30 years or so. Although there was some recognition of excellence at various times in the history of civilization, this recognition was idiosyncratic and occasional, more often occurring after than during the lifetime of the gifted individual. For the most part, those who were different or those who did not follow the norm met with resistance. Society saw the gifted as a threat to the accustomed way of life and, in defense of that life-style, would react in ways that would squelch talent. The few who recognized importance and value in sustaining talent acted as patrons or mentors, and, in so doing, supported, protected, and facilitated the emergence of numerous great works to the continued delight of the many generations that followed. There were also those less fortunate individuals who, despite the lack of patronage or mentorship, succeeded in the face of impossible odds by sheer brilliance and grit. But there were those, too, who, overcome by adverse conditions, never made their mark in this world.

There were all kinds of gifted people, but few consciously fostered and developed their talent during their formative years. The compelling urgency of these talents directed the energies of the gifted individual, allowing the talents to surface and gain some recognition. Gifted people often did not know the real reasons why they found more problems than

1

their fellows; they were nagged by the spirit of genius to actualize, even in the face of almost insurmountable difficulties; they prepared themselves for the eminence that was to follow; and they left behind a true wealth of accomplishment that is now ours to share. They were brilliant politicians and statespersons; eminent orators, thinkers, musicians, and artists; literary giants; engineers; inventors of excellence; and others who, by their achievements and performance, have made a difference in the lives of their fellows and in the world. They became known and recognized as gifted people, but little was known about the nature and function of giftedness, the variety of abilities related to it, or the extent to which the environment held influence over talent and its expression until the development of mental testing and the exploration of its theoretical origins.

Before being more intensely studied by Lewis M. Terman's researchers in the early years of this century, the intellectually gifted were considered something of a genetic curiosity. We now understand that the creativity of gifted and talented children is a valuable resource. Indeed, we are interested in them nowadays for precisely this reason; it is the creative potential of the gifted and talented that excites us. Their education is no longer a fringe issue. It involves the central question of whether or not our society can maximize creative performance in its adults. Not all gifted or talented children reach actualization. The task for teachers, parents, and others is to be found in the answer to the question: What kinds of parental, educational, and other interventions will promote the maximization of creativity in such children?

Yet, if we are to do what we must to bring this actualization about, we have to keep in mind that there are varieties of giftedness—intellectual and talent resources that differ markedly from those of the general population. Identifying the gifted is only the first of a number of interrelated concerns. After they have been identified, the question that springs to mind is, What do we do for the gifted now that we have begun to know who they are? It may appear that their education is of primary concern and, by and large, this must be true; so we busy ourselves planning for their formal education and deciding on suitable curriculum content and the best methodology to implement it. This is not to say that the effectiveness and significance of informal education can be omitted from consideration; to some extent, its admission as a facet of formal learning may be a key direction. The keen recognition that the gifted are highly individualistic and even idiosyncratic in their learning needs and styles must ensure a greater use of individualized learning approaches, ranging from teacher to student control. Creative learning must receive the attention it deserves, for it is the key to the development of the intellect and talent. Ferment can only preface the occurrence of eminence.

The influence of environmental factors on intellectual and creative development and the factors that hinder or facilitate giftedness must also be of concern. To think of giftedness only in terms of those unique attributes possessed by an individual is an incomplete approach to the concept. One must take into account interactive sociocultural and economic conditions that have so much to do with the emergence of talent. It was once thought that gifted individuals were less likely to have problems than their nongifted peers, but it is now recognized that the gifted, too, have problems and are also in need of guidance. The task of nurturing the gifted is complex. What once appeared to be the responsibility of the educator must now become the concern of all. This responsibility manifests itself in more deliberate parental involvement, both personally and publicly; in legislation that has been and continues to be widely enacted in the United States; and in the efforts of national, regional, and local groups who champion and. even provide opportunities for the gifted. Hopefully, all this is prologue to universal educational opportunities for the gifted and their teachers—opportunities propelled by public and private support.

ONE IN A MILLION GIFTED

Marilyn vos Savant, listed in the *Guinness Book of World Records* as having the world's highest intelligence quotient (I.Q. of 230 on the Stanford-Binet), was interviewed by the *National Forum* in 1988 about her opinions on several aspects of intelligence testing. Though not an authority on the subject, her answers to questions posed by the interviewer are of some interest to us and are presented as follows:

NF. Do you believe that our society places too much emphasis on testing for talent identification?

MVS. I believe that our society places too much emphasis on testing for talent identification, but for a reason that is not widely accepted. I suspect that "talent" may be surprisingly easy to develop in nearly all people and that we are mistakenly concentrating our efforts on locating them "after the fact." In other words, I think that perhaps the "talent" we are finding may actually be "talent achievement."

If this is true, a great disservice is being done to the large proportion of the population labelled "untalented."

NF. Do you think that I.Q. tests isolate important abilities?

MVS. I believe that I.Q. tests may isolate some important abilities, although not to the extent that the public believes. Ideally, the tests would isolate abilities to profit from the different avenues of learning, such as through language or mathematics, to name two particularly large boulevards. However, I feel that the tests lack the ability to discriminate effectively in more subtle but extremely important areas, such as insight and intuition—the latter being not at all mystical. I suspect that good spelling, for example, may be correlated with intuition.

NF. Does it surprise you to find that often high I.Q. is not correlated with success in school or success in life?

MVS. It does not surprise me to find that a high I.Q. is not as well correlated with success in life as we might have expected, because I feel that success in life is, to a great extent, dependent upon social skills rather than on intellectual skills. Social skills are an area sadly neglected by many bright people—always to their peril. Too much time is spent with books and not enough time with people.

NF. Do you think that I.Q. test scores can be improved with study?

MVS. I'm sorry to say that I suspect I.Q. test scores can be improved with study. Many of those we consider bright are merely intellectually skilled, and vice versa.

NF. By all measures, you fit into the category of "gifted child." Do you have any special advice to give to those who would attempt to educate "gifted children"?

MVS. My advice to those who educate "gifted" children is the same as my advice to those who educate all other children, only "more so": concentrate on teaching them how to think rather than what to think. Inundating people with information doesn't help them to learn how to handle it.

NF. A lot is made of the distinction between the genetic and environmental basis of intelligence. How do you weigh in on this issue?

MVS. I don't think there is much doubt that heredity defines the parameters of our intellectual capacity. We inherited a human brain. A dog inherited a dog's brain. If you take your dog to college with you—even if he's a good student, sits in the front row, and never barks at his neighbors—he will be unable to explore the subtleties of even "The Brady Bunch." On the other hand, environmental factors weigh very heavily on whether we ever fulfill what potential we have. [1]

Marilyn vos Savant, although not a professional educator or psychologist, insightfully anticipates some of the major issues that will be dealt with in this book. She contends that there is an overemphasis on the use of tests to discover talent and achievement rather than talent potential. The implication that talent, occurring after the fact, can be identified by nontest approaches reflects what E. Paul Torrance (1973) advocates about

---

[1] From "One in a Million—An Interview with the Smartest Woman in the World," *National Forum*, LXVIII, 2, p. 17. Copyright © 1988 by *National Forum*. Reprinted by permission.

observing creative positives of culturally different children to discover their talent.

Although I.Q. tests isolate certain important abilities, such as those involved in learning language or mathematics, they lack the power of discriminating other major abilities involved in insightful thinking and intuition. This observation reflects the thinking of those like J. P. Guilford and E. Paul Torrance who speak strongly for the inclusion of the dimension of transformative thinking, as found in creativity, when assessing mental potential.

Vos Savant attributes life success to a strong dependence on social skills in addition to intellectual skills. In so doing, she echoes the views of both E. L. Thorndike on social intelligence and J. P. Guilford on the behavioral component of the Structure of Intellect.

That I.Q. can be improved with study is a view that is supported by those scholars such as J. McVicker Hunt who place great emphasis on the significant influence of the environment in developing intelligence. Such a view is implicit in the informational-theoretical model known as the Structure of Intellect.

Marilyn vos Savant's emphasis on teaching children how to think rather than what to think is congruent with current thought on the education of the gifted (e.g., E. de Bono, M. N. Meeker, and J. S. Renzulli), which will be reiterated in numerous places in this book.

Touching on the inheritance-environment controversy of intellectual capacity, she observes that heredity defines the parameters, and environment determines the extent to which development and actualization takes place. This is consistent with the best thought on the subject and reflects the positions taken by scholars such as A. Anastasi, J. P. Guilford, and J. McVicker Hunt.

MEANING OF BEING GIFTED

It is not uncommon to hear people talk about the exceptional person as gifted, as if there were no differences between one gifted person and another. The following definitions add further dimension to the concept of giftedness and support the concept's multidimensional origins.

Webster's (1980) defines gifted as, "having a natural ability or aptitude; talented." When we look up the definition of talented, we find it to be "having talent; gifted." The implications shown here are that giftedness is inherited and that gifted and talented are synonymous terms.

When used in the medieval sense, to be gifted is to provide evidence of accomplishment in some creative endeavor; this, in turn, is supposed to predict further accomplishments. There is no concept of potential to accomplish included.

Giftedness is culture bound, not easily recognized as such (Gallagher, 1985), and highly dependent on societal needs (Newland, 1976).

There are two important approaches for looking at giftedness: (a) relating giftedness to the universe of exceptional and extraordinary characteristics or qualities of the individual, either acquired through inheritance (avoiding the nature–nurture controversy) or as a result of the interaction of inheritance and environment; and (b) seeing giftedness as determined by the needs and biases of the cultural group of which the individual is a member.

Newland (1976) attempted to give some coherence and clarity to the word *gifted* and redefined gifted in terms of societal needs. Thus, a society would have to determine how many individuals were needed to carry out high-level operations and differentiate the essential characteristics required for these operations so that schools could locate such individuals and prepare them for their respective roles in society.

Gallagher (1985) described this subject as an unresolved issue.

If our definition of gifted changes as the values of our society change, what will the definition look like in 1990? What values will be downgraded and what values more highly regarded? (p. 28)

Let us remember the important observation by Ruth Benedict (1935) that culture shapes man, but, although more slowly, man shapes culture as well. No definition of the gifted is adequate if it does not regard the interactive nature of individual excellence and society's needs and requirements.

In attempting to define the term *gifted*, we must first recognize its complexity not only for its denotative but also for its connotative meanings. The term *gifted* is multidimensional, acquiring a variety of meanings from various fields of inquiry. Of particular relevance are the changing conceptions of intelligence when different emphasis is placed on general mental ability or g (Spearman, 1927). General mental ability is conceived by some as dominant in a hierarchical structure of human abilities (Vernon, 1951). By others, the existence of g is denied, as in the cube model of the Structure of Intellect (Guilford, 1967).

Sir Cyril Burt (1962) cited Leta Hollingworth and Lewis Terman as examples of those who accept Francis Galton's assumption that potential achievement is primarily determined by an individual's allowance of general ability and who base their definitions of the gifted on I.Q., as assessed by tests of intelligence. A gifted person has an I.Q. of 130 and above according to the Stanford-Binet (Terman & Merrill, 1960). However, it is interesting to note that, in practice, cutoff scores based on the Stanford-Binet I.Q. fluctuate between 110 and 150, depending on who uses it, where in the country a need was found to identify giftedness, and for what project the identification was needed.

Definitions of gifted that included more than I.Q., as we shall see in Chapter 3, stemmed from the early work of L. L. Thurstone (1938) on primary mental abilities and J. P. Guilford (1967) as expressed in his Structure of Intellect model. However, the multivariate conception of intellect goes beyond intellectual ability and admits abilities to excel in music, in the creative arts, and in the psychomotor areas. Giftedness in these areas is more appropriately termed *talent*.

An eclectic point of view recognizes the all-round gifted and those who are gifted in some special way (Burt, 1962). This would identify those highly intelligent people of I.Q. 125 and above as gifted; and those of average and above average in academic ability, endowed with poetic, musical, artistic, or mechanical ability, as talented. This way of looking at the gifted does not present the kind of problem that the term *academically talented* does.

Newland (1976) suggested that "academically talented" is a euphemism to avoid disturbing connotations of mental superiority, explicitly anchored to intelligence testing. He sharply distinguished the gifted and talented by suggesting that

> those children who anticipated superior social contribution as primarily a function of their superior conceptualization capacity be regarded as gifted and those whose promise is not primarily so based be regarded as talented. (p. 24)

Paul Witty proposed a broad definition of the term *gifted*. According to him "the gifted or talented child is one who shows consistently remarkable performance in any worthwhile line of endeavor" (Henry, 1958, p. 19). N. E. Cutts and N. Moseley (1957), sensitive to the problem of using I.Q. alone to identify the gifted—because it does not make allowances for character, motivation, art or music talent, leadership, and the like—consider Witty's definition a wise one.

Newland, however, questions the validity of a definition that would depend on demonstrated achievement for identification and the debatable nature of "worthwhile endeavor."

Thus we have presented an approach to define giftedness in terms of performance, and commentary that regards this approach as weak relative to the need to identify potential. In any case, there is a certain looseness in the definition that contributes to ambiguity rather than clarity. We need to recognize that people can be gifted in a variety of ways and the variety of giftedness needs to be more carefully specified in operational terms.

In attempting to bring together the many and varied definitions of the term, the United States Office of Education (USOE) sponsored a series of conferences held in Washington, D.C., which were attended by many leading experts in the field of the gifted (Marland, 1972a). From these conferences emerged a broadened concept of the gifted or talented child. Such a child can be identified by professionally qualified persons as one with outstanding abilities who is capable of high performance and demonstrated achievement in any one of six areas, namely, general intellectual ability, creative or productive thinking, specific academic aptitude, leadership ability, visual and performing arts ability, and psychomotor abilities. The last category has been excluded by the United States Congress (PL95-561) in 1978 as unnecessary since artistic psychomotor abilities can be included in the performing arts category, and the athletically gifted are taken care of very well.

Thus, we have recognition, at the federal level, of the complex nature of giftedness and an acceptance of a theoretical orientation that subscribes to general intelligence as well as creative or productive thinking. The inclusion of specific academic aptitude, leadership ability, and visual performing arts ability recognizes both the complexity and multiplicity of giftedness. The roots of these abilities can be traced by using a variety of models of which the Structure of Intellect is but one, group dynamics another, and artistic creation in the domain of thinking-feeling interaction, a third.

The United States Office of Education's attempt to delineate giftedness as multiple is a very significant step forward. This office's insistence that attention be paid to categories of giftedness in planning educational intervention for the purpose of obtaining funds that have now become available affected a transition in educational practices from the dark ages to modern times.

Renzulli (1979b, 1986), however, stated that the United States Office of Education definition, despite its usefulness, fails to include nonintellective or motivational factors. He indicated that this definition presents categories of giftedness that are by nature nonparallel (i.e., specific academic aptitude, and visual performing arts abilities call attention to performance, as do leadership and psychomotor abilities; whereas the remaining categories, like general intellectual abilities and creative or productive thinking, call attention to processes that can be applied to performance). Besides, such a definition may be misinterpreted and misused by practitioners. Renzulli attempted to get around these and related problems by proposing a product definition model of giftedness that includes three interactive areas of abilities, creativity, and task commitment. This three-ring interaction conception of giftedness defines students as gifted relative to the specific projects they undertake, and to their productivity and commitment to these projects.

Such a definition is attractive in that it moves from identifying potential superiority as developmental to excellence requiring the operation of creativity and commitment. According to Renzulli, giftedness is identified by results. This means that subjects must perform (i.e., produce within the framework of time).

Renzulli's approach, graphically presented in Figure 1.1, focuses our

Figure 1.1 Graphic Representation of Renzulli's Definition of Giftedness

General Performance Areas

Mathematics	Social Sciences	Religion
Philosophy	Music	Movement Arts
Language Arts	Physical Sciences	Life Sciences
Visual Arts	Law	

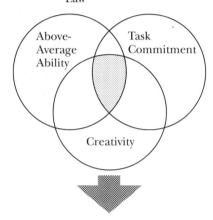

Above-Average Ability

Task Commitment

Creativity

Specific Performance Areas

Advertising	Electronics	Musical Composition
Agricultural Research	Fashion Design	Navigation
Animal Learning	Film Criticism	Ornithology
Astromony	Film Making	Play Writing
Biography	Furniture Design	Poetry
Cartooning	Game Design	Pollution Control
Chemistry	Genealogy	Public Opinion Polling
Child Care	Jewelry Design	Puppetry
Choreography	Journalism	Sculpture
City Planning	Landscape Architecture	Set Design
Consumer Protection	Local History	Statistics
Cooking	Map Making	Weaving
Costume Design	Marketing	Wildlife Management
Demography	Meteorology	
Electronic Music	Microphotography	

From *What Makes Giftedness?* (p. 24) by J.S. Renzulli, 1979, Los Angeles: N/S LTI on the Gifted and Talented. Copyright © 1979 by J.S. Renzulli. Reprinted by permission.

attention on the importance of motivational and creative factors that can make all the difference between mediocrity and excellence, and as such must be taken into account in our identification and educational facilitation of the highly gifted.

Renzulli's definition suggests that some careful rethinking and operationalizing of the USOE categories of giftedness designed to develop appropriate screening procedures appear necessary. In fact, critical comment relating to the adoption of these categories by various educational agencies for purposes of identification or programming without regard to their ambiguous, undefinable, or overlapping nature (e.g., Treffinger & Renzulli, 1986) appears to support this view.

It should be noted, however, that the USOE definition of giftedness attempts to provide several generic categories as directional to the development and implementation of screening procedures whose ultimate goal would be to identify those deserving of special educational opportunities. So while Treffinger and Renzulli's criticism has some relevance, it should not suggest to those involved in gifted education that they abandon the generic definitions provided by the USOE, but rather that they regard them as having enough latitude to encompass more specifically defined giftedness within each of the particular categories.

STORIES OF GIFTED CHILDREN

The literature is teeming with stories of children gifted in many ways. There are those who are highly intelligent (even extremely superior), highly creative and talented, and those gifted who are beset with problems owing to physical or emotional disabilities and sociocultural hindering factors that relate to their underachievement and lack of fulfillment. Of the many stories available, a few are presented here to prepare for a more serious discussion about gifted children and what can be done for them (Khatena, 1978a, pp. 1–7).

Ike — The High-Creative Kid

One such person was a seven-year-old boy named Ike, who lived in Kentucky. He was brought to my notice by parents who did not see Ike getting the best out of schooling. I found Ike to be highly creative but with little opportunity for the development of his creative thinking abilities. The parents were willing to do what they could to help the boy, so they were often open to suggestion. This [procedure] involved them working with Ike's teacher on the matter, and providing opportunities at home for the growth of his creative talent.

Mary — The High-I.Q. Kid

Mary was a superior student [well] liked by her teacher. She consistently obtained good grades and got along well with her classmates. Identified as one with a *Stanford-Binet* I.Q. of 158, Mary did not receive a challenging education that would have accelerated the development of her intellect. On being assessed for creative potential by the Torrance measures of creative thinking, Mary was found to have quite average scores on fluency, flexibility, originality, and elaboration. The information disappointed her parents, but this was to be expected since children with high I.Q.'s did not necessarily do as well on measures of creativity. Being accepted for a newly begun gifted program three years later, Mary blossomed in the years that followed to become one of the brightest students in her school, making straight A's, [being] elected president of an honors society, with every indication [that she would be eligible] for early admission to the university.

Jim — The High-I.Q., Creative, Problem Kid

One referral was the son of a distressed parent. [The family] lived in Ohio and Jim, the nine-year [-old] boy was doing poorly in school although he was very bright. His underachievement frustrated both his teacher and parent. Jim was a pain in the neck to his teacher, for he insisted on doing things his own way, looking up [information in] the encyclopaedia ever so often; reading widely out of classroom texts; inventing, among other things, a more efficient clothes rack; and designing a system of pulleys to prevent his mother, who had a back condition, from climbing two flights of stairs, burdened with groceries. Screened by the Wechsler intelligence scale, Jim was found to have an overall I.Q. of 140. His creative thinking abilities were also high on the Torrance creative thinking measures. Jim did not lack ability but was not challenged in school. Class work bored him, and when he did get good grades, he was distressed by peer reaction. He found it better to pretend that he was not smart so that he would be accepted by his age mates. The fact that there were no special provisions for children like him [in the school] aggravated the situation. Not recognized, understood, or counseled, Jim continued to have problems until a discerning teacher trained to handle kids like Jim took him under her wing and changed the course of his life.

John — Growing Up Gifted

Then there was John. Like Jim, he was highly intelligent and creative but not understood by his teachers. John was miserable as a student but survived as some highly gifted students do, despite adverse conditions of the system, to achieve at the highest levels of learning; to distinguish himself as a professor in a university; and to become a make-up artist, poet, scientist, and musician. John's reminiscence of his school life, as he grew to adulthood, is presented as follows:

> Like a billion others I was shaped by formal schooling. When I was little, I remember my mother dressing me for school. I entered into grade one and sweated [my schooling] out for twelve years.

I used to dream quite a lot even at seven, and this annoyed my teachers. I often found myself wearing a dunce cap or a basket—not that I minded the ignoble costume, but to have to face the rest with eyes peeping sheepishly through that intricately woven contraption was upsetting in no small way. I was convinced my teacher did not understand me, but that was not unusual because I didn't understand myself.

I was easily bored and punished for being naughty. The years slipped by and so did I—from one grade to the next.

Once a week I had to sing as [did] the other boys. I tried to tell my teacher it wouldn't work but at the point of her piercing eyes I croaked, in a voice better silent, the lovely lines, 'All things bright and beautiful. . . .' At thirteen I tried not to be heard, and by fourteen definitely hated music. However, I found myself a professional musician at sixteen and loving every bit of it.

The only lesson I really liked in school was Spoken English, and that was because we had a teacher of vitality with a booming voice, a kindly gentleman who spoke faultlessly except for an occasional 'umph!', a deep breath, and the inevitable boom. But I loved him and the familiar crunch of boot on gravel. The entry made, the furniture moved, and we along with it. Then followed an hour of pure delight in the drama of the court house, the marketplace, the nobleman's castle enacting scenes of real life and fantasy.

Of course I disliked grade eight history. I had a teacher whose target was the chair, with foot thrust in bottom drawer of desk, a subtle clicking of the tongue and smooth oscillation of the head in quick survey of forty cringing devils. 'Turn to Chapter 3 . . . and read the next eleven pages.' Sixteen minutes later, a thump or two delivered with precision on two or three backs hunched in pretended industry, and we knew at once the prowler was at large again. A week before the exams, a fog of chalk dust emerged from the green board, and with tired inky fingers we were painfully scratching the forty-ninth page of notes. It took me the better part of ten years to get rid of that gritty historical chalk dust to major in college history.

I almost learned mathematics in school. But mathematical relations were slapped into me. For instance, one teacher who taught me geometry thought that proximity to him and the figural representation of two isosceles triangles would aid my understanding of their relationship. He made significant feet movements as he manipulated his palm, and I like many others learned to anticipate a right slap when the left foot was raised. I saw, ducked, and felt the impact of both hands on my face. Pythagoras must have squirmed!

The geography teacher was in contrast good, but between church and scouting activities I had little of him or geography.

Oddly enough it was not until I was 35 years old that I found myself, and why I behaved the way I did. I never could do as well as my classmates when it came to remembering facts and repeating them when called upon to do so in the many examinations our teachers devised for us—of course this did not mean that I could not remember those things I wanted to remember! But when it came to writing a dramatic sequence or story, I did quite as well if not better than most of my classmates. But then, we were not asked to use our imagination too much in school; we were being prepared for the real hard facts of life!

I became interested in poetry a few years after high school. Somehow I never really enjoyed poetry lessons. I guess because my teachers were too concerned with giving lessons and missed the whole point about poetic experience and its appeal to the intellect, emotion, and imagination. We learned lines by heart but forgot them even quicker. Recitation was for the most part boring and painful, and somehow quite embarrassing to me as I crunched my way through the stony path of words.

When I played the guitar, I enjoyed ad-lib more than I did the tune itself. Somehow the school had inhibited the development of my talents. I noticed this even more when, at the age of 26, I began writing many poems, some of which have since been published.

Stage make-up excited me quite a bit and what I enjoyed most was to create faces for fantasy characters like Caliban or do unusual and difficult character make-up requiring the use of invention. Now that I look back, I realize the poverty of my school experience in the realm of the imagination. If only my teachers had been sensitive enough to spot me out as a dreamer or troubled to provide experiences that were rich, stimulating, and challenging both to the intellect and imagination, my heartaches, wasted energies and time could have been prevented.

CULTURALLY DIVERSE GIFTED CHILDREN

The importance of cultural diversity as it influences the shaping and development of gifted children is better understood and recognized today than it was many years ago. In fact Henry H. Goddard's (1908, 1911) attempt to develop the Simon-Binet scale for Americans by translation was doomed to failure because he had not taken into account the effects of cultural differences. And although Lewis Terman (1916) approached the development of the Stanford-Binet scale with cultural differences of American and French people in mind, he paid little or no attention to sociocultural variables within the United States. This omission led to the serious questioning of the validity of the Stanford-Binet for African Americans and new migrant populations that have added to the cultural diversity of this country.

Alexinia Baldwin (1978) focused additional attention on environmental influences by citing factors like cultural diversity as well as socioeconomic deprivation and geographical isolation, which share an inter-

Figure 1.2 Baldwin's Matrix of Cultural Diversity

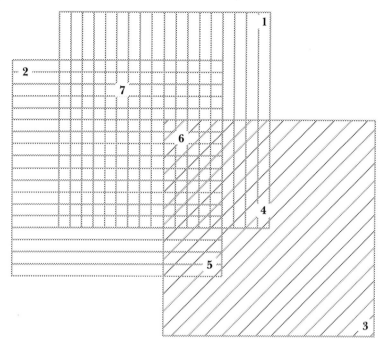

Key: From Educational Planning for the Gifted (p. 4) by A.Y. Baldwin, G.H. Gear, & L.J. Lucito, 1978, Reston, Va.: Council for Exceptional Children.

Area 1 — Culturally diverse children
Area 2 — Socioeconomically deprived children
Area 3 — Geographically isolated children
Area 4 — Culturally diverse children affected by geographic isolation
Area 5 — Socioeconomically deprived children affected by geographic isolation
Area 6 — Culturally diverse children affected by socioeconomic deprivation and
           geographic isolation
Area 7 — Culturally diverse children affected by socioeconomic deprivation

active relationship. These influences tend to conceal the talent potential of a large number of gifted children and in the event of identification, hinder true readings of measures.

Baldwin's examples serve as a brief illustration and are cited in Figure 1.2. Depending on how the three variables interrelate each individual case requires different attention. Carmen, a Puerto Rican student, is culturally diverse but is also socioeconomically deprived, so her problems are different from Jose who has a language difference along with his cultural diversity but whose parents are not economically destitute. Tommy lives on a farm, is poor, and is from a different culture. Plans for identifying and planning for individuals in his situation should include consideration of all three of the variables. Lon is an Asian student who has just come to this country to escape the political problems of his native land; he cannot speak English but his family is able to live moderately well. Therefore, he falls in the category of cultural diversity. Elain is a black student whose parents have just moved back to America after serving the government in Europe and Africa. She is culturally diverse but other support systems have diminished the effects of this variable on her functioning level (p. 4).

A PHYSICALLY DISABLED AND GIFTED CHILD

M. L. K. Pringle's (1970) case study of Toby provides an interesting example of a gifted but physically handicapped boy. Toby had an I.Q. of 133 at the age of 9 years and 9 months. A cleft palate at birth left him with a bad speech defect. Weak verbally and severely retarded educationally, he was regarded by the principal as a slow learner.

Toby was timid, well-behaved, and often anxious. He had few friends, feared his teacher, and disliked school. Often, he would pretend to have various ailments to avoid going to school. However, Toby's parents were generally supportive and loving, although the mother was torn with keeping him in school and letting him remain at home.

His plight changed when a discerning young teacher took interest and arranged for the correction of his deafness and defective vision with needed aids. Her understanding and attention contributed to his general well-being, by providing positive attitudes to learning and developing a determination to succeed. Against all odds and with great industry, Toby overcame the debilitating effects of his problems. At the age of 21, Toby's educational attainments included the passing of all accountancy exams. As a result he became an associate of the Institute of Chartered Accountants. Later, he was honored with the Duke of Edinburg award for his outstanding achievements.

A profile of these 10 gifted students is presented in Figure 1.3.

INTELLECTUAL PRODIGIES

Several years ago, Kathleen Montour (Stanley, George, & Solano, 1978) presented accounts of a number of intellectual prodigies. These included the poet Thomas Chatterton and the mathematician Evariste Galois, both of whom died young. Chatterton was barely 10 when he published his first poem and committed suicide 3 months before his 18th birthday.

Figure 1.3 A Profile of Ten Gifted Children

| Name | | | | Individual and Sociocultural Factors | | | | | |
	Intelligence	Creativity	Academic Achieve-ment	Talent	Under-achievement	Cultural Diversity/ Socio-economic Factors	Physical Handicap	Emotional Difficulties	Lack of Oppor-tunity/ Challenge	Other Problems
Ike		■							■	
Mary	■		■						■	
Jim		■						■	■	■
John				■	■					
Carmen										
Jose						■				■
Tommy						■				
Lon						■				■
Elain						■				
Toby	■							■		■

Galois, who was a match for the best mathematicians in France by 17, was killed in a treacherous duel at 20.

Phillipa Duke Schuyler, poet, composer of music, and journalist, was an intellectually versatile woman, who at the age of 9 was said to have a mental age of 16 or I.Q. of 185.

Three other examples were Joel Kupperman and George Van Dyke Tiers who were known in the forties as the "quiz kids," and Charles Louis Fetterman who at 22 became the youngest American full professor of the University of Chicago.

However, one prodigy of particular interest is William James Sidis. He is an exception to Lewis Terman's research findings about gifted children growing up to be healthy and successful adults. Sidis exemplifies the familiar case of an individual who experiences a brilliant and precocious beginning, a burnout of talent, and a decline into unhappy obscurity. Montour (Stanley, George & Solano, 1978) reported the following:

> William Sidis was both a brilliant and maladjusted young man who completed his baccalaureate at Harvard while still 16 years old. As a baby he would amuse himself by spelling words with toy blocks. One woman tested him by spelling out "Prince Maurocordatos, a friend of Byron," and asked the baby a week later to give her the name of Byron's friend. William did this with ease. But already his inability to cope with everyday life was showing itself. On one occasion, after having read on the menu that breakfast was to be served from 8 to 9 o'clock, he had to be carried away shrieking when he was brought to be fed at 7:45 A.M. He knew algebra, trigonometry, geometry, and calculus by age 10 and was finally admitted to Harvard at age 11 after being refused at age 9 because he was thought to be too young.
>
> At Harvard young Sidis was said to have begun by specializing in a mathematical topic called quaternions. In January of 1910 he gave a lecture about "Four-Dimensional Bodies" to professors and advanced graduate students in mathematics. Still, his phenomenal accomplishments were tempered by his social ineptitude. He would distract a class whenever he was bored and had been rude to his questioners when he gave his famous lecture.
>
> Though extremely troubled otherwise, William always seemed to be able to cope intellectually—he was granted his A.B., cum laude in 1914. But, as he grew older, interviews showed him to be quite warped in his outlook. He refused ever to consider marrying and thought being totally cut off from people was the perfect life.
>
> Sidis spent a year at Harvard in graduate school and three years in Law School without ever taking a degree. He wrote two books before dropping out of sight. When he resurfaced in 1924, it was now as a routine computational clerk, whereas he had once been an instructor at Rice Institute.
>
> Sidis always expressed great animosity towards his father for parading his accomplishments and having him branded as a freak. As a result, he strenu-

ously avoided academic life and all publicity until his death in 1946 at age 46. Although it meant dying penniless and alone, Sidis managed to thwart his father's aim to produce the ideal man in his son. (p. 52)

ADULT ROLES

Gifted children depend on adults to facilitate the blossoming and realization of their potential. Hence it is important for adults to become informed about the varieties of giftedness to provide appropriate conditions that allow for effective development. To do this, adults play different roles, among which are included parenting, teaching, and counseling.

Parenting

In a recent letter to the editor of the *Gifted Child Quarterly*, a journal produced by the National Association for Gifted Children, a parent expressed her concern for her gifted child. She anticipated the impact this news would have on others in her community if she were to talk about it.

> If I were to say that I had a retarded or physically handicapped child, people would believe me. No one would resent me, and most reactions would be sympathetic. Having a gifted child, however, I know I do better keeping quiet. People wouldn't believe me. "Another bragging mother," I would be called. . . . In a small town, especially, it is wiser not to mention it. (Oppen, 1970, p. 92)

This mother is not alone in anticipating the complications of having the gifted child recognized in the community. Instead of enjoying the opportunity to share a community resource, she feels the need to hide it from others for fear of being scorned, envied, and even hurt.

Parents of the gifted are the most significant people in the child's life and by far the most potent force for realizing a child's potential. The proper attitude and knowledge is essential for developing the attributes of the gifted child.

McCall's carried a story entitled "Living with People" which described the relationship of Gail Sheehy and her daughter, Gabby, whose teamwork led to the writing of their novel *Love-Sounds*.

Gabby Florensia was a gifted girl who suffered from cerebral palsy. Gabby was not depressed by her condition but positive in her approach and found expression and realization in her talent. Despite her paralysis, she learned (with parental help and encouragement) to type with her right toe that was spared, and communicated greatly with her eyes. Gabby was a wheelchair writer who became a novelist, and much of her miraculous success can be attributed not only to her will and grit but also to the love and support of her parents and the facilities they provided to make her achievement possible.

Recall another true story (depicted in the movie *My Left Foot*) of an Irish writer, Christy Brown. As a child, he began writing a novel of great quality, which took 12 years to complete because he suffered from cerebral palsy. Much of his success can be attributed to his mother who showed him love and understanding, made him feel significant, gave meaning to his life, and showed great appreciation for his talent. The mother had done for the Irish novelist at home what Plato had advocated the state should do for the young when he said that "What is honored in one's own country is what will be cultivated."

The amount of information written on the parent effort to mobilize forces for change in the education of gifted and talented children has been increasing. Most of what has been published serves to inform parents about the subject, and direct them to possible actions that they might take to facilitate needed changes (Hildreth, 1966; Khatena, 1978a; Nathan, 1979; Strang, 1960). Current information about gifted education in the United States reaches parents through the news media or magazine and journal articles. These sources usually simplify the material for general readership (often in a cursory way), as do conferences and training sessions conducted by various associations, National/State Leadership Training Institutes, and local district efforts. There is no doubt that in recent years, parents have been more sensitized to giftedness, more cognizant of approaches that are needed for many kinds of giftedness, more aware of the state's responsibility to establish adequate provisions, and more pointed in their demands for the realization of their children's potential.

Many parents have recognized that they can play a number of roles to effectively develop and facilitate opportunities for their gifted children to grow and achieve excellence. First is their role as responsible surveyors of current advances and information. Abundant information about gifted children and what parents can do to enhance talent is becoming increasingly accessible. In addition, pertinent parent-oriented material can be found in the various issues of the *Gifted Child Today*, and the *Roeper Review*. In addition, a special newspaper for parents of gifted children attending the Roeper School is also available. The *National/State Leadership Training Institute Gifted and Talented Bulletin* also carries a brief section for parents in addition to informational sketches on national events and notes on useful materials that are currently available. In these ways, parents can effectively complement formal schooling efforts.

Where no facilities are available in school, they can, as an interim measure, create the kind of climate at home that nurtures and invigorates talent growth.

The second major role parents can play is by developing a cooperative partnership with the school and its professionals. As individuals, parents serve as an informational base for those who are involved in the education of their children; as effective follow-up service of the school providing continuity to the work done in the classroom; as resource persons for gifted students in and out of school, depending on the measure of their expertise; and as the driving force for funds and related advantages.

Third, organized in local parent groups, especially as affiliates of gifted and talented national or state groups, parents become one of the strongest forces in initiating legislation. They also can act in an advisory capacity to the school board, state and local agencies, principals of schools, and other administrators to make changes in curricula consistent with the best thought and practice on gifted education. Besides, they have some say in the selection of procedures that qualify their children for special educational opportunities.

Organized efforts can be parent-shaped and may take the form of local district and state parent groups. The formation of a national organization of parents on behalf of gifted and talented interests will take time, effort, money, commitment, and a more stable economy to allow for sufficient and consistent funding of gifted programs.

A more powerful approach would be for parents, either individually or as local groups, to belong or affiliate themselves to existing national associations for the gifted, the most viable of which, at present, is the National Association for Gifted Children. Another important and active organization is the Association for the Gifted—a component of a larger professional organization, the Council for Exceptional Children—which has a totally professional educator membership. The membership thrusts of these associations have led to the formation of many state chapters.

Finally, parents, in the role of taxpayer, have the right to see that laws of the land pertaining to the gifted are properly implemented. As we know, Public Law 94-142 (which, in essence, established the right to a free appropriate public education for all the physically disabled children in the nation), Public Law-230 Section 806c (which established the right to free public educational provision for the gifted and talented), and Public Law 95-561 (a confirmation and refinement of the first two), give parents the legal bases for demanding the opportunities that are rightly due to their gifted children. Where legislation, relative to provisions for gifted and talented, exists in their states, parents have access to due process of law to obtain their rights.

Teaching

The primary role of the teacher is to educate. To do this, the teacher needs appropriate professional preparation and a command of knowledge areas that is consistent with demands of the curricula at all levels of schooling ranging from the preschool to the secondary school. Subject area emphases of the secondary school, unlike other levels of schooling, will require specialized knowledge of certain content areas. The teacher will need to acquire methodological skills to increase effectiveness of communication and instruction as learners become involved in acquisition of knowledge and development of thinking skills.

A survey of 14 books on the gifted (Khatena, 1982a) generated a list of personal and professional characteristics expected of teachers of gifted students. However, some of the characteristics listed were common virtues of all good teachers (e.g., alertness, common sense, understanding, admired, consistent behavior, knowledge of theories of learning, and various categories of teaching proficiency). How, then, can we distinguish traits of the good teacher from the teacher of the gifted? This is not an easy matter and may prove impractical to verify. Yet, if pressed to identify, one might emphasize "inspiration" as the key to educating gifted students.

According to the findings of the study (Khatena, 1982a, pp. 382–383), ten of the most frequently identified *professional qualities* of the teacher of the gifted follow:

1. Proficient (course content well-known, interesting, well-organized and stimulating)
2. Fair and impartial in dealing with the learner
3. Caring, sympathetic, and sensitive to student problems
4. Able to direct the achievement of full potential
5. Able to encourage students to want to learn
6. Establishes and maintains a democratic atmosphere
7. Communicating an enjoyment for teaching
8. Experienced in the art and science of teaching
9. Fair and impartial
10. Encouragement of individual development

Another important role of the teacher relates to the understanding of students. This sometimes involves the evaluation of gifted students using multiple nonpsychometric approaches—in the form of observation, completing inventories, sociometric analyses—to direct and nominate students for special educational opportunities. The teacher's role also involves matching students' abilities and interests with relevant educational experiences that foster the best manifestation of potential.

In this role, the teacher has to have or needs to develop personal and professional qualities that provide "psychological freedom" and "psychological safety" (Rogers, 1967), challenges, stimulation, and mentorship for the realization of children's potential gifts.

The findings of the same study (Khatena, 1982a, pp. 382–383) indicate that the 10 most frequently identified *personal qualities* of the teacher are as follows:

1. Consideration for others
2. Friendliness
3. Kindliness
4. Creativity, generally, and originality and flexibility, in particular
5. Decisiveness
6. A good sense of humor
7. Intellectual superiority
8. Understanding
9. Versatility
10. A wide variety of interests

Yet another role involves the teacher with the parent. In the first instance, the teacher has been delegated certain parental responsibilities for the intellectual development, social adjustment, emotional health, and ethical well-being of the student. This role requires the teacher to be a resource person, conferring with and advising parents on all matters pertaining to their children. The teacher, as an essential counterpart of the parent in the parent-teacher association, provides educated judgment of professional matters and interacts with parents in a way that is conducive to the proper enhancement and advancement of gifted education.

The teacher who is well-known and popular with students is approachable and can serve as counselor in a number of ways. Students frequently bring their problems to the teacher, sometimes just to unburden themselves and at other times seeking advice. Sensitive to their needs, being more experienced, and perhaps even possessing wisdom, the teacher is in a good position to assist students who call for help. The teacher in this role is not formally trained as a therapist, but, like some parents, can be therapeutic. However, if a situation is out of the teacher's range, students can be referred to others better trained to help them.

The teacher has the important role of being an agent of change. Primarily as educator, the teacher is most closely involved in the shaping of student minds, arranging appropriate curricula and delivery systems to maximize the full growth of gifted potential. A teacher that throws out challenges for effective response, prepares students to meet challenges, and creates new challenges is providing a never ending chain of growth towards higher levels of achievement. As model, the teacher can direct student behaviors towards productive consequences for themselves and society, using historical and contemporary models as facilitative shaping agents for individual growth and progress.

Not long ago, E. Paul Torrance (Torrance, 1975d) indicated that there are too few great teachers because of the grave risks involved. What characteristics are essential to the great teacher? They perform miracles and inspire creative and independent thinking and action even if these actions get them into trouble or lead them to the danger of "crucifixion." One would expect a "Great Teacher" to find most of these characteristics personally applicable (pp. 453–454).

> My enemies and exploiters twist every word around some other way.
> I am anxious to see my students "going" while I can still support and encourage them.
> I am considered dangerous to the "public."
> I am considered by some as a wonder person or hero or fool.
> Authority does not dare to leave me to my own devices.
> Many of my associates fear their own elimination.
> People frequently feel that "there are too many of me but too few of themselves."
> My closest friends and loved ones are helpless to protect me.
> Ultimately, some of my admirers and disciples despise me and betray me.
> I am blamed for letting any followers get out of hand and I am held responsible for the independent action of my followers.
> I reach a point when I lose my inspiration at least temporarily and feel sad and tired.
> There are times when I feel scared to finish what I started, but I go ahead and do it anyway.
> My fans not only demand miracles, they demand inappropriate miracles.
> I am always in danger of being crucified.

Perhaps the more these characteristics relate to a person the closer the individual may approximate someone who is willing to risk much to attain the stature of "Great Teacher." We must not be disappointed if we do not qualify, for it is unlikely that most do.

Counseling

In recent years we have come to recognize that gifted children, like all other children, are in need of guidance. Their need for guidance can be more pressing because they face, in addition to the problems that all children face in day-to-day living, intellectual demands that go beyond what they know well or what society is prepared to support. In addition, the highly creative gifted often have more difficulty satisfying their needs and relating to others as they attempt to form an identity and realize their potential.

One of the most insightful appraisals of counselor roles can be found in Torrance's (1962a) classical work *Guiding Creative Talent*. By reading the many imaginative stories written by children, you will become sensitive to creative children and the many problems they face. Take for instance the story of Lippy, "A Lion That Won't Roar" that illustrates society's coercive influence against divergence.

> Lippy Lion, a friend of mine, has a little problem. He won't roar! He used to roar, but now he won't. His name used to be Roarer, too. I'll tell you why.
>
> When Roarer was about your age, he would always roar and scare people. Now this made his mother and father worry. Everybody was always complaining. So they decided they should talk to Roarer.
>
> They went to his bedroom. . . . But when they started talking he roared and scared them downstairs. So finally they went to a magician. They talked things over until he had an idea. Then the three went home together.
>
> The magician said his words and said, "He'll never want to roar again."
>
> The next morning he went to scare his mother by roaring, but all that came out was a little squeak. He tried again but only a little squeak came out. But he pled and pled to get his roar back, so the magician made it so he could roar. But Roarer didn't believe him. So now that he can roar he won't.
>
> Soon they had to name him Lippy. (pp. 105–106)

A counselor of the creatively gifted, according to Torrance, has at least six major roles: (a) to provide highly creative individuals with a "refuge," (b) to be a sponsor or patron to them, (c) to help them understand their divergence, (d) to let them communicate their ideas, (e) to see to it that creative talent is recognized, and (f) to help parents and others understand them (p. 15).

Related counseling roles (Khatena, 1982a) involve assisting the gifted in the following ways:

1. To attain higher levels of creative functioning
2. To overcome those times of their lives in school that lower their level of creativity
3. To foster love that makes the preconscious accessible to creative thinking and expression
4. To reduce the cramping influences of stress
5. To use their imagination to think in analogy and imagery
6. To give appropriate feedback that will move them in directions of better achievements
7. To counteract adverse effects of formal education that make it difficult for the gifted to be themselves and think independently

8. To guide them to emulate historical and contemporary models
9. To make materials and equipment available to advance their creative development
10. To make them more aware of the diversity and richness of cultural offerings that can assist them to realize their potential
11. To strive to be the best, and in so doing accrue rich rewards for themselves.

CONCLUSIONS

Although systematic study of the gifted began with Lewis Terman's *Genetic Studies of Genius* (Terman & Oden, 1947, 1959) in the first quarter of the century, it was not until federal legislation in the 1970s coupled with efforts of parents, and educators at all levels of the profession, that special opportunities for the gifted were legitimated nationally. The spread of such opportunities took place slowly but surely so that today, all states have at least some provisions for gifted children. Earlier contributions by educators, and educational and state agencies, were made with relatively limited resources or support, and where none was available, parents and teachers acted to provide gifted children with informal educational nurture to enhance regular school experience.

Our knowledge of individual differences and the technology for identification of gifted children have improved tremendously, so that now we not only know that children can be gifted in many ways, but also have available a number of techniques to discover this. The tests that Binet, Terman, and others have developed to measure intelligence in terms of I.Q. have been quite useful for predicting how well students can do in the basic academic subjects. This has led many to assume erroneously that I.Q. represents everything we need to know about a person's mental capacity. As the term *gifted* becomes more diversified and identifies a variety of talents, the limitations of I.Q. tests surface and it becomes necessary to question the infallibility of measures of intelligence.

A large body of information is available on the nature of creativity showing how creativity contributes to eminence and progress as well as creates conflicts between individuals and society with consequent emotional and psychological problems. Understanding these variables allows teachers and parents to assist gifted children to become creative adults who will contribute to the betterment of society. There are available good measures of creativity, like those constructed by J. P. Guilford (1973), E. P. Torrance (1974), and Joe Khatena with E. P. Torrance (1990ab), and methods to maintain, cultivate and enhance creativity, like those developed by Sidney J. Parnes (1967a), William J. J. Gordon (1961),

Frank E. Williams (1972), E. P. Torrance and R. E. Myers (1970), and Joe Khatena (1984).

Generally, instruments will continue to be developed and refined for the purpose of identifying gifted children. The need for such instrumentation is directly related to the need to discover ways to predict giftedness so as to provide special educational opportunities for the fuller development and realization of giftedness. More and more we are thinking of identification as inseparable from its twin, education. The main reason we identify gifted children is to determine those to be selected for education appropriate to their talent potential, and to provide related counseling services to facilitate their fullest and healthiest development to become productive adults.

We have, at a certain time of our history, assigned the responsibility of educating our children to the professional educator, or guided our children to the professional counselor. While this perhaps became necessary by the increasing complexity of society and serves us well, we should not neglect to recognize that the parent, teacher, and counselor are in fact single fractions of a counseling whole. A certain flexibility of shifting roles is essential to the effective functioning of the adult assisting the child generally and the gifted child particularly in the growing up process.

CHAPTER TWO

Sixty Years of Activity

INTRODUCTION

Historically, the serious inception of the gifted movement began with the efforts of Terman in the early twentieth century. For many years, study of the gifted was dominated by Terman's work—particularly the basic concepts of giftedness derived from his construction and use of the Stanford-Binet and *Genetic Studies of Genius*. The latter is a monumental five-volume longitudinal study by Terman and his associates of 1,528 gifted urban children in California who were followed from kindergarten through high school, and then on through mid-life (e.g., Terman, 1925; Terman & Oden, 1959). Terman refers to the discovery and encouragement of exceptional talent in the concluding remarks of his valedictory address (Terman, 1954).

> To identify the internal and external factors that help or hinder the fruition of exceptional talent, and to measure the extent of their influences, are surely among the major problems of our time. These problems are not new; their existence has been recognized by countless men from Plato to Francis Galton. What is new is the general awareness of them caused by the manpower shortage of scientists, engineers, moral leaders, statesmen, scholars, engineers, and teachers that the country must have if it is to survive in a threatened world. (p. 41)

EARLY SOURCES

Contributions to thought on the gifted have come to us from many sources. Those by M. H. Oden (1968), J. W. Birch (1954), P. Brandwein (1955), E. K. Brown and P. G. Johnson (1952), J. C. Gowan (1955), L. S. Hollingsworth (1926), and P. A. Witty (1951) are among the most thoughtful (Bish, 1975).

Structure of Intellect

One of the most significant and germane contributions on the nature of human intelligence came from J. P. Guilford's (1967) Structure of Intellect, first presented in his presidential address at the American Psychological Association in 1950. For the first time in the history of the testing movement a theoretical model was designed that emphasized a variety of abilities that included divergent production or creative thinking and regarded the activity of intellect in an informational and problem-solving setting.

Creativity

The subject of creativity found expression in E. P. Torrance's (1962a) works on the measurement, nurture, and guidance of creative talent, and A. F. Osborn's work (1963) on the cultivation of the creative imagination. This was followed, soon after, by the founding of the Creative Education Foundation in Buffalo, New York with its annual Creative Problem-Solving Institute. There were also several Utah conferences on creativity, organized by C. W. Taylor during 1955–57.

Sputnik

The Russians successfully launched *Sputnik* in 1957. Bish refers to *Sputnik* as the successful launching of a 184-pound ball in space that "caught the attention of more Americans than the blast of the H-bomb and also stung their national pride" (Bish, 1975, p. 282). This dissatisfaction found focus in the call for curriculum reforms by the Physical Science Study Group headed by J. R. Zacharias of the Massachusetts Institute of Technology and the School Mathematics Group directed by E. G. Begle of Stanford University and others. This type of attention led to the development of more rigorous curricula in science and mathematics for gifted students. The federal government's response to *Sputnik* was the passage of the National Defense Act in 1957. Following in its wake were (a) the first National Education Association Invitational Conference on the Academically Talented Pupil held in February, 1958; (b) the publication of the conference report, 8,000 copies of which were sold in three months; (c) the establishment of the three-year Academically Talented Project designed to prepare the teacher (through publication, conference, and consultation) to better serve the needs of the gifted and talented, with Bish as its director.

Psychology

Advances in psychology over the past 40 years have served to expand the concept of giftedness. In recent years, information from psychometrics, personality, human development, guidance, learning, cognition, and computer technology research has persuaded us to think afresh about giftedness and how this potential quality in individuals can be cultivated for individual good and for the good of the community.

Other Sources

Khatena (1977a, 1982a) presented some important advances in thought on the gifted, giving particular focus to conceptions of intelligence that move from the unitary and global to the multiple and complex. Further, he addressed approaches of identification on a continuum from formal to less formal procedures, which have roots in good measurement theory and practice. Khatena also connected educational facilitation to theoretical constructs of accelerative enrichment. In addition, he reminded us of our increasing awareness of the significance of creativity for the gifted, and our realization that gifted people too have problems, many of which are developmental, and need guidance.

ORIGINS OF GIFTED AND CREATIVE MOVEMENTS

The gifted child movement initiated by Terman's studies in the 1920s and the creativity movement, launched particularly by Guilford and Torrance's works in the 1950s and 1960s, have enhanced our understanding of the gifted enormously. Gowan (1978a) perceived that these two movements cannot be regarded as separate and independent disciplines. He suggested that these advances are only two of several that can be appropriately and meaningfully subsumed under the heading of *humanistic psychology*, which can be traced to William James, his colleagues, and their students—John Dewey, Erik Erikson, Arnold Gesell, G. H. Hall,

Joseph Jastrow, F. Kuhlman, D. W. MacKinnon, William McDougall, W. R. Rhine, and Lewis M. Terman.

Gowan (1978a) presented a chart (Figure 2.1) that illustrates the interrelatedness of these and other contributors to seven areas of development that are pertinent to humanistic psychology and that have influenced thought on the gifted today. The seven areas are identified as broad humanism, measurement of individual differences, intelligence/gifted children, creativity, development, and parapsychology. In brief, here are Gowan's comments about each of these areas (pp. 2–4).

Broad humanism establishes that each individual has intrinsic value with potential for development, process, and self-actualization, with rights irrespective of sex and ethnic group. To this may be added the value of individual differences and recognizing the idiosyncratic talents of the exceptional person.

Measurement of individual differences apprizes their worth and asserts that different talents can be measured, are of social value, and should be cultivated.

Intelligence/gifted children points to a relationship between high intelligence and gifted children that is characterized by changing views of intelligence from unifactor (general intelligence) to multifactor (e.g., structure of intellect) conceptions. Gifted children, in this model, represent a pool for potential creativity, not abnormal geniuses. From a mechanistic concept of intelligence—consisting of cognition and memory, as in most measures of intelligence—views change to a concept of intelligence that emphasizes transformations, implications, and a more creative consciousness (expressed by Guilford, Maslow, and Torrance).

Creativity is a phenomenon that has transformed from a religious to a psychological concept, from an unknown to a turn-on variable, from connectedness (Thorndikian) to psychological openness (Rogerian), from a neurotic trait to an early dividend of mental health, and from a curiosity to an end in itself or correlate of self-actualization (Maslovian).

Development is an aspect that shows change from continuous growth to discontinuous development concepts; from separate views of development to fused views on concurrent development of psychomotor, affective, and cognitive processes; and from tests that do not measure developmental processes to those that do.

Parapsychology has been used by quacks and psychics as well as for scientific investigation of the unknown. Unverifiable reports characterized its early application and now it is a valuable resource to examine physical effects. Parapsychology has grown from superstitious epiphenomena to a niche in humanistic psychology that can explain some aspects of the power of the human mind. All phenomena, of whatever kind, are natural and we can account for them although we may not be in possession of all knowledge.

Figure 2.1 A Brief Intellectual Genealogy of Humanistic Psychologists

Broad Humanism	Measurement of Individual Differences	Intelligence/Gifted Children	Creativity	Development	Parapsychology
James					
	Peirce				McDougall
				Freud	
Hall	E. Thorndike	Pressey		Gesell	Rhine
Dewey	Jastrow Kuhlman Cattell (J.K.)	Terman		Erikson	
	Otis Goodenough	Worcester	Burt		
Rogers	Bernreuter	Ward	Allport		
	Kelley	Seagoe	MacKinnon		
	Flanagan Davis	Rulon	Getzels		
	Sears	Stanley Snedden	Gowan		
			Bruch Khatena		
		Feldhusen			
		Renzulli Treffinger			
(Other psychologists in area)	Thorndike, Thurstone, R. Michael, Roe, Lehman	Binet, Guilford, Hollingworth, Spearman	Kubie, Torrance, Osborn, Parnes, Taylor	Piaget, Maslow, Sullivan	Crookes, Lodge, Krippner

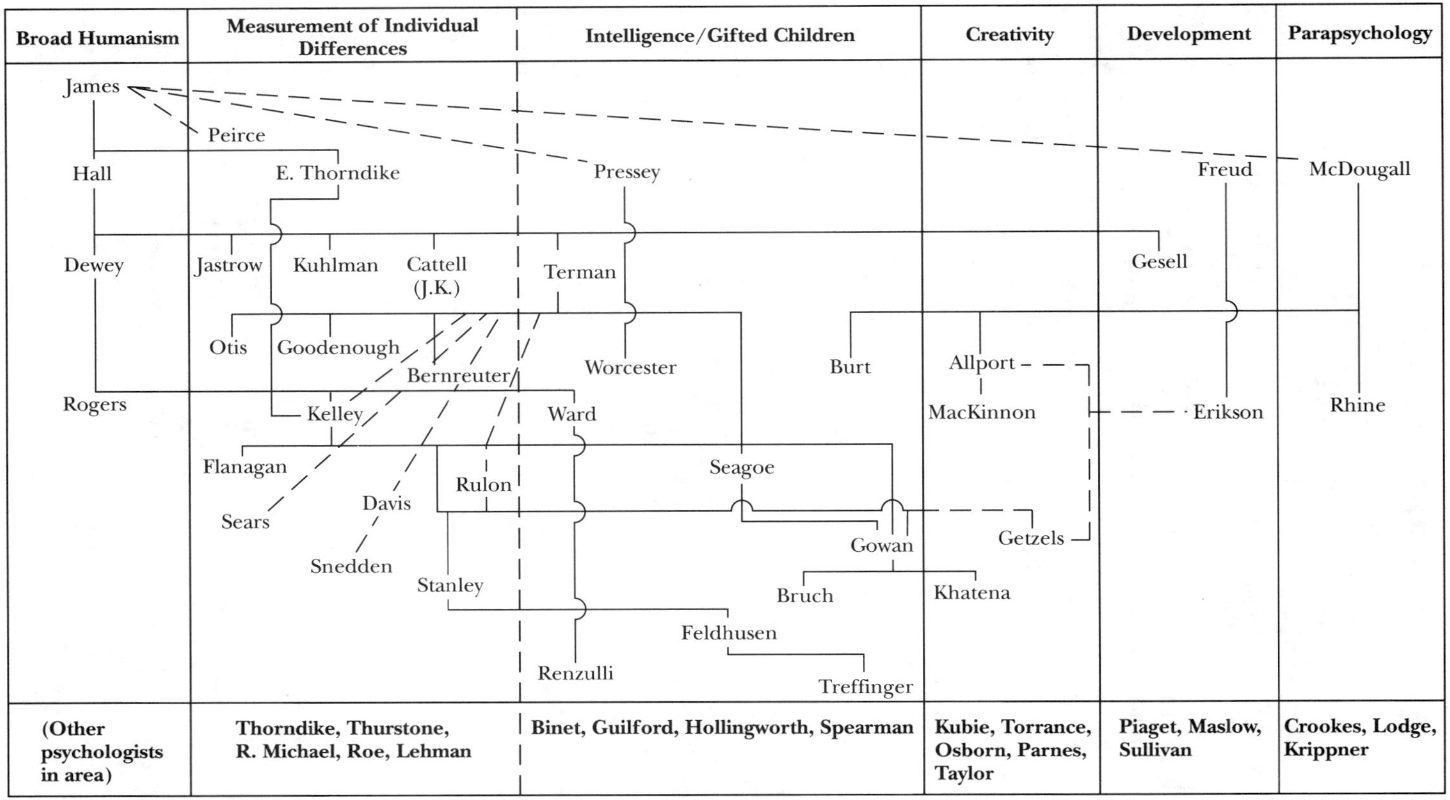

From "A Brief Intellectual Genealogy of Humanistic Psychologists" by J.C. Gowan, 1975. Unpublished manuscript. Copyright © 1975 by J.C. Gowan. Reprinted by permission.

TERMAN AND HIGH I.Q. CHILDREN

Terman became interested in the gifted after he read a report by Francis Galton and another by Alfred Binet, while at Clark University. Terman's interest in mental tests and exceptional children led to a doctoral dissertation that explored the intellectual processes of seven of the brightest and seven of the dullest boys of a large city school. The study, he explained, did not contribute as much to science as it did to his future studies.

With a grant from the Commonwealth Fund of New York City in 1921, Terman located 1,000 subjects of I.Q. 140 or higher. Thus, his study of highly gifted children began (Terman & Oden, 1959). His gifted group came from school children in California, and the sole criterion for selecting his sample was I.Q.—as measured by the Stanford-Binet (1916 revision) or the Terman Concept Mastery Test (Terman, 1916) relative to the top 1% of the school population selected for the purpose.

Terman used a two-step procedure in kindergarten, primary grades, and high school, and a three-step procedure in grades 3 to 8 for the identification of gifted children. Each classroom teacher was asked to nominate the first-, second-, and third-brightest child, and the youngest student in the class. A group intelligence test was administered to all nominated children of grades 3 to 8. Those who showed promise were then administered the Stanford-Binet. Because there was no group test suitable for those below grade 3 at the time, nominated children in kindergarten and the first two primary grades were administered only the Stanford-Binet. At the high school level, children were tested by the Terman Concept Mastery Test. The group identified as gifted comprised 851 boys and 671 girls, and with some additions made in 1928, numbered 1,528 subjects. The mean I.Q. on the Stanford-Binet was 151 and on the Terman Concept Mastery Test was 142.6.

Additional information regarding characteristics of this group of identified gifted children was obtained. Evidence from the three follow-up studies presented by Terman and his associates in Genetic Studies of Genius (Burks, Jensen, & Terman, 1930; Terman & Oden, 1947, 1959) concerning the intellectually gifted as they grew up to mid-life provides the following portrait:

> Intellectually gifted children were born of intellectually and physically superior parents, and either because of better endowment or physical care or both, are as a group slightly superior to the general population in health and physique and tend to remain so. They generally maintained their relative intellectual superiority at least through adolescence at which time or soon after girls more often than boys showed a drop in I.Q. Their children showed regression towards the mean on traits measured.
>
> As a group, they were not intellectually one-sided, emotionally unstable or

lacking of social adaptability and other types of maladjustments. In fact they showed themselves to be superior on traits of emotional stability and social adjustment though to a less marked degree on intellectual and volitional traits. Their personal adjustments and emotional stability continued to be good as expected with below-normal incidence of serious personality problems, insanity, deliquency, alcoholism and homosexuality.

Incidence of marriage was about equal to that of the general population though the death rate after 35 years for them was lower. Their health ratings were in the main good, and physically they were above average.

Further, they were found to be either normal or superior in social interests, and play activities, averaging much better than the general population in practically every personality trait.

In educational achievement they were well in advance of their age mates but often found in grades two or three years below their level of curriculum attainment. When they received rapid promotion they were found equal or superior to gifted non-accelerates in health and general adjustment, did better school work and had greater success in later careers. Those with above 170 I.Q. were more accelerated in school and received better grades and more schooling.

They continued to achieve well through high school with almost no occurrence of failure in school subjects, and with nearly three-quarters of the total marks earned by girls and half of those earned by boys being A grades. In their senior year they averaged above the 90th percentile on the *Iowa High School Content Examination.* Though this superiority continued into college there were many who lost interest and showed records of mediocre performance. However, educationally they were superior with about 70 percent graduating from college (a third of whom achieved academic distinction), 63 percent going to graduate school (67 percent men and 60 percent women), and 18 percent (14 percent men and 4 percent women) graduating with doctoral degrees.

In summing up the findings on the characteristics of the initial sample, Terman and Oden (1959) observed the following:

> The deviation of gifted children from the generality [i.e., the population at large] is in the upward direction for nearly all traits; there is no law of compensation whereby the intellectual superiority of the gifted is offset by inferiorities along non-intellectual lines; the amount of upward deviation of the gifted is not the same for all traits; and the unevenness of abilities is no greater for gifted than for average children, but is different in direction— whereas the gifted are at their best in the "thought" subjects, average children are at their best in subjects that make the least demands upon the formation and manipulation of concepts. (pp. 15–16)

Terman and Oden also point to the wide range of variability that exists within their sample group on every trait investigated. They caution that descriptions of the gifted in terms of the typical, although useful as a basis for generalization, should not blind us to the fact that gifted children represent an almost infinite variety of patterns.

Terman (1954) was also aware of and concerned about the fact that some of his gifted group were highly successful, whereas others were not. He observed that intelligence, although an important determinant of success, was not the only determinant, and that motivational factors had a great deal to do with success.

In attempting to identify the nonintellectual factors that influence life success among the men in the gifted group, Terman and Oden (1947) had three judges working independently to examine the records (from 1922 to 1940) of 730 men who were 25 years old or older and rate each one of them on life success. Based on the extent to which a subject had made use of his superior intellectual ability, giving little weight to earned income, two groups of 150 each were rated either highest or lowest for success. These were identified as the A and C groups, respectively, and they were compared on about 200 items of information obtained from childhood onward to find out how they differed.

During the elementary school years, the two groups were almost equally successful. However, differences in achievement and scholarship in favor of the A group became evident as they passed into high school. By the end of high school, the gap was marked. Terman found that these differences were not due to extracurricular activities or intelligence, but to family background. Interesting differences between A's and C's were found (from the childhood data) on their emotional stability, social adjustments, and various traits of personality—generally in favor of the A's. Furthermore, in 1940, it was found that A's and C's differed most widely on items such as "persistence in the accomplishment of ends" and "integration toward goals" but did not differ much in categories such as "drifting," "self-confidence," and "freedom from inferiority feelings" (Terman & Oden, 1947, pp. 349–352). The greatest contrast between the A's and C's was in drive to achieve and in all-round mental and social adjustment.

In 1959, Terman and Oden followed up their investigation with another study, using a biographical questionnaire, that explored what constitutes life success for gifted men and women. The final question read: "From your point of view, what constitutes success in life?"

The replies showed a wide range of variability and lack of agreement. However, Terman and Oden (1959) placed the most frequently given definitions of life success, as perceived by intellectually gifted people, into the following five categories (p. 152):

1. Realization of goals, vocational satisfaction, a sense of achievement
2. A happy marriage and home life, bringing up a family satisfactorily

3. Adequate income for comfortable living (but this was mentioned by only 20 percent of women)
4. Contributing to knowledge or welfare of mankind, helping others, leaving the world a better place
5. Peace of mind, well-adjusted, adaptability, emotional maturity

Terman and Oden observed that many people considered happiness, contentment, emotional maturity, and integrity as the most important achievements in life. Success was not necessarily limited to occupational advancement, but had much to do with heroic sacrifices, uncommon judgment in handling the little things of daily life, countless acts of kindness, loyal friendships, and the conscientious discharge of social and civic responsibility.

There is no doubt that Terman's seminal work prepared the way for thought and research on the gifted. He made unique contributions to our understanding of the intellectually gifted by constructing I.Q. measures for their identification and by collecting substantial, comprehensive longitudinal evidence that described their behaviors and achievements from childhood to midlife. In these respects, he is unrivaled by anyone except perhaps Torrance in his longitudinal studies of the creatively gifted (1980, 1981).

The *Genetic Studies of Genius*, however, is not without flaws. Because Terman chose to select his subjects on the I.Q. criterion, it is appropriate to consider his findings about the gifted as primarily relevant to the population of high-I.Q. people and not to all gifted people. The Stanford-Binet is known to favor the highly verbal subject; this automatically disqualifies many nonverbal and low socioeconomically gifted students from participating. In addition, it should be recognized that although I.Q. is a valuable global, one-dimensional model of intelligence, it does not tell us enough about the specific abilities of the child (Edwards, 1971; Gowan, 1978a; Sattler, 1988; Stanley, 1974; Sternberg, 1988). Hence this study fails to provide information about gifted children in areas like music and drawing where their relationship with abstract intelligence is only slightly above zero (Carroll, 1940, p. 205).

The sampling subjects that Terman selected as gifted cannot really be considered as representative of the gifted American population. At best, they can be considered representative of urban Californians who attended large or medium-sized schools. Terman's sample included a strong Jewish component in the gifted school population, which was disproportionate to the total population of Californians at the time. Furthermore, the schools that were chosen were predominantly white, excluding black students and other minorities from the study. Ideally, the Stanford-Binet or the Terman Concept Mastery Test should have been administered to all Californians to identify those who would qualify as gifted. Of course, this would have been prohibitive in terms of money and time. Relative to the location of his study, the next best thing would have been for Terman to select randomly a manageable number of subjects from the total number of Californians attending school and to administer the measures of I.Q. for the purpose of identifying the gifted. He chose, however, to do the initial screening by means of teacher nominations, which is an unreliable method because many gifted children must have been eliminated from participation right from the start.

In addition to these factors, Terman, as he later realized, should have depended on school records rather than on the teacher to identify the brightest children in the class for his initial screening process. The children that were identified as gifted and labeled "genius" may have been treated more respectfully both at home and in school and this could have affected their performance; the full extent of such influence cannot be known. Although Terman recognized the importance of nonintellectual factors, such as *will* and *motivation* to life success, in his A and C studies (Terman & Oden, 1947) he paid nearly no attention to socioeconomic variables—an omission that can be traced back to sampling bias and the selection procedure used to determine his gifted group. In all fairness, the adverse effects of socioeconomic influences were not well documented at the time of his study. Terman also did not consider the interactive effects of heredity and environment and paid little attention to the influence that creativity and self-actualization often have on life success or the attainment of goals set for a successful and fulfilled life. Finally, the *Genetic Studies of Genius* is a work that is descriptive and factual rather than speculative and theoretical; there was no attempt to generate hypotheses about gifted people for investigation.

CREATIVE INDIVIDUALS

In a paper (C. W. Taylor, 1958) presented at two conferences (the Fifth American Society for Child Development Research Institute—Eastern Section, Washington, D.C., and the Second Minnesota Conference on Gifted Children), C. W. Taylor stressed the importance of reconsidering the significance of the I.Q. measure as the only index of the gifted individual. He indicated that any legitimate concept of giftedness would have to include alternative measures of nonintellectual ability because the I.Q. measure does not do an adequate job of identifying creative talent.

> In factor analysis studies by many research workers across the country, the factors which get at the ability to sense problem areas, to be flexible, and to produce new and original ideas tend to be unrelated or to have only low rela-

tions with the types of tests entering into our current measures of intelligence. Getzels and Jackson, in the College of Education at the University of Chicago, as well as Torrance, in the Bureau of Educational Research at [the University of] Minnesota, have reported that if an I.Q. test is used to select top level talent, about 70 percent of the persons who have the highest 20 percent of the scores on a creativity test battery will be missed. Or stated otherwise, more cases with high creativity scores are missed than are identified by using an I.Q. test to locate creative talent. (p. 174)

C. W. Taylor pointed to the findings of three University of Utah Research Conferences on Creativity that have emphasized the need for a broader approach to the identification of creative talent than *a single measuring device* such as an I.Q. Taylor also called for alternate ways of identifying nonintellectual characteristics of creative individuals.

Elsewhere in the paper, C. W. Taylor drew from his own research and that of others, such as J. P. Guilford, F. Barron, J. W. Getzels, and P. W. Jackson, to identify some of the more salient intellectual and personality characteristics of creative individuals.

Originality
Redefinition
Adaptive flexibility
Spontaneous flexibility
Associational fluency
Expressional fluency
Word fluency
Ideational fluency
Elaborative
Ability to sense problems
Capacity to be puzzled
Power to reject superficial explanations of one's own as well as others
Ability to sense ambiguities
Effective questioning ability
Ability to manipulate, restructure, and rework ideas
Ability and tendency to strive for more comprehensive answers, solutions, or products
Capacity to work intermittently across long periods of time below the conscious level
Observant (seeing both what others do and what they do not)
Values truthful reporting and testifying of observations and able to make them explicit
Makes rich syntheses and notes their impulses more
Curiosity
Thoughtful
Likes to manipulate and toy with ideas

Intellectually persistent

Likes recognition for achievement

Likes variety

Needs autonomy

Needs preference, complex order, and challenges therein

Tolerant of ambiguity

Resistant to closing up and crystallizing things prematurely coupled with a strong need for ultimate closure

Enjoys mastering problems

Insatiable for intellectual ordering

Needs to improve currently accepted orders and systems

Highly energetic with vast work output through disciplined work habits

Willing to take greater and more long range risk for greater gain

Often accumulates an overabundance of raw stuff as well as willing ultimately to discard some of it in forming final products

Intensely esthetic and morally committed to work

Enjoys much greater variety of occupational choices, greater interest and awareness of unconventional careers

Senses that personal views are not the predominant ones of what success in adult life is

Willing to be nonconforming and consequently to be in the small minority

More devoted to autonomy

More self-sufficient

More independent in judgment

More open to the irrational in themselves

More stable

More capable of taking greater risks in the hope for greater gains

More feminine in interests and characteristics (especially in awareness of one's impulses)

More dominant and self-assertive

More complex as a person

More self-accepting

More resourceful

More adventurous (bohemian)

More controlling of their own behavior by self-concepts

More emotionally sensitive

More introverted and bold

The psychologist who probably has done more work than anyone else in the area of developing measures of creativity is Torrance (e.g., 1974b, 1988). His work has contributed to the understanding of creative children and how we can help them realize their potential (1962a, 1965c,

1972a, 1979b, 1984). He indicated the great importance of parental, teacher, and societal influences on the development of a child's creative behaviors. Torrance suggested that certain characteristics that parents and teachers encourage or discourage would help us understand and predict the behavior of children under their guidance. In addition, to know the characteristics children, by selecting from a checklist of items, consider ideal would help us predict their creative achievements more accurately.

The rest of the paper summarizes some of the work Torrance had done over 15 years in developing the Ideal Pupil Checklist, which is of particular interest to us. The checklist was developed from a survey of over 50 empirical studies that attempted to differentiate the personality characteristics of a group of highly productive creative people from a similar group of less creative people. According to this checklist, the most salient characteristics of creative individuals are as follows (pp. 138–139):

Adventurous, testing limits	Prefers complex tasks
Asks questions about puzzling things	Regresses occasionally, may be playful, childlike
Attempts difficult tasks	Remembers well
Becomes preoccupied with tasks	Self-assertive
Courageous in convictions	Self-confident
Curious, searching	Self-starting, initiating
Determined, unflinching	Self-sufficient
Expresses emotions strongly	Sense of beauty
Emotionally aware, sensitive	Sense of humor
Energetic, virtuous	Sincere, earnest
Guesses, hypothesizes	Strives for distant goals
Independent in judgment	Thorough, exhaustive
Independent in thinking	Truthful even when it hurts
Industrious, busy	Unwilling to accept things on mere say-so
Intuitive, insightful	Visionary, idealistic
Likes to work alone	Willing to take risks
Never bored, always interested	
Persistent, persevering	

Khatena's study (1977b) related creative perceptions to components of the creative personality using the Khatena-Torrance Creative Perception Inventory (Khatena & Torrance, 1990a). A summary of these findings are presented as follows (pp. 521–523):

People who perceive themselves as high creatives are experimentally and power oriented, have less need for structure and possess relatively high intuition.

On the matter of past experiences, highly gifted adolescent girls who perceived themselves as creative regularly read news magazines and other non-required reading materials, watched television news and special reports frequently, enjoyed courses in the sciences, music or art and were active in dramatic and musical groups, liked their teachers and generally felt that their high school education was adequate, dated more infrequently than their less creative peers in high school and went steady at an older age, not close to another and did not discuss intimate and/or important matters with them, did not often suffer "attacks of conscience" when they felt that they had done wrong by the standards of society, church or parent, and did not want to become more socially acceptable or better prepared as a responsible family member, daydreamed a lot, felt downcast, dejected and sensitive to criticism, brooded over the meaning of life to a greater extent, and overtly expressed anger toward friends and tried to get even when someone close hurt or upset them.

Creative adolescent boys, however, disliked school and their teachers, did fewer hours of homework, had teachers who were not very successful in arousing academic interests, disliked physical education courses and seldom engaged in team sports and physical activities, did not particularly like science, enjoyed discussion courses often questioning teachers about subject matter; were regarded as radical or unconventional often wanting to be alone to pursue their own thoughts and their own interests, had parents of high school educational income and occupational levels who were less strict, critical, or punitive, generally allowing them greater freedom than parents of less creative peers, and where this was not the case creative boys would express anger, and they did participate in church, religious, or charitable organizations' activities.

When adults perceived themselves as creative, they tended to be more verbally original and imaginative.

Teachers who perceived themselves as high creatives were low value-centered, and low creatives were high value-centered, where value-centeredness was the extent to which judgment of behavior was based on subjective approval or disapproval.

BETWEEN TERMAN AND GUILFORD

Since Terman, the contributions and advances of many scholars have propelled us to the position we are in today. In attempting to explain pertinent contributions to advances in thought relative to the subject, Gowan (1977b), selects the following 12 significant research milestones (pp. 19–20):

1. The factor analytic advance of the Structure of Intellect and its identification and curriculum intervention correlates (Guilford, 1967, 1972)

2. The Terman and Oden (1959) mid-life follow-up study of their gifted group that provided, among other information, evidence of the increase of mental age through age 50
3. The importance of predisposing guidance and the trainability of scientific talent (Brandwein, 1955)
4. The direct influence of socioeconomic class on personality differences that hitherto were attributed to intelligence (Bonsall & Stefflre, 1955)
5. The identification-procedures research of Pegnato and Birch (1959) that shows that both the efficiency and effectiveness of various identification measures are less than has been assumed
6. The development of creativity in children and the attempts to measure effects of this development by the Torrance Tests of Creative Thinking (Torrance, 1974b)
7. The use of the Structure of Intellect for curriculum development in the classroom (e.g., Meeker, 1969; F. E. Williams, 1971a, 1972)
8. The interrelationship between creativity and intelligence (Getzels & Jackson, 1962; Torrance, 1962a), and the issue of dimensionality (e.g., Khatena, 1971b; Treffinger & Poggio, 1972)
9. The work of Goldberg and Passow (1959) at De Witt Clinton High School in New York City that showed underachievers required assistance with learning skills and identification with a supportive teacher
10. The study of facilitation of mathematically precocious youth through educational acceleration longitudinally (e.g., Stanley, Keating, & Fox, 1974)
11. The developmental theories of Erik Erikson and Jean Piaget fused by Gowan into the periodic developmental stages theory with its implications for creative development (Gowan, 1972, 1974)
12. The progression of identification procedures from the Stanford-Binet to biographical information measures (e.g., Khatena & Morse, 1990; Khatena & Torrance, 1990; Schaefer, 1970; Taylor & Ellison, 1966)

General Intelligence to Multitalent

Although there are still some issues to resolve on the validity of Guilford's tests relative to the Structure of Intellect, there is no doubt that his model is the most comprehensive explanation of intellectual abilities and their significant educational implications. These have been explored by his associates (e.g., Meeker, 1979a, 1979b) and others (e.g., Gray & Young, 1975). Discussing this question, Torrance (1970) stated that, in England, the Education Act of 1944 shows recognition of many talents (e.g., abstract, mechanical, concrete-practical). Torrance cited Guilford's Structure of Intellect and C. W. Taylor's (1978) multitalent model of giftedness, which is based on world-of-work needs that specify talent areas as they relate to academic ability, creative-productive abilities, evaluation, planning, forecasting, and communication. C. W. Taylor (1978, 1986) emphasized that basic research has shown the existence of many different kinds of talents, not just one academic ability or general intelligence. Typical group intelligence tests, he says, attempt to measure no more than eight talents, which is less than one-tenth of those now known; that is, nine-tenths of current measurable talents are not covered by intelligence tests (e.g., artistic, creative, musical, social talents). This finds support in recent discussions and commentary that advocate the need to go beyond testing for intelligence (*National Forum*, 1988).

Dimensionality

These theories on the intellect have led to expansion of the field of measurement. When this relates to measures of creativity and intelligence, there is the problem of dimensionality or convergent-discriminant validation (Campbell & Fiske, 1959). For example, measures of the construct *creativity* are expected to yield high intercorrelations with other creativity measures (i.e., convergent validation), and low intercorrelations with measures of a different construct such as *intelligence* (i.e., discriminant validation) (Treffinger & Poggio, 1972).

Although measures of intelligence were not found to identify highly creative abilities (Getzels & Jackson, 1962) or to correlate highly with talented achievements outside the classroom (Wallach & Wing, 1969), I.Q. measures were found to yield substantial correlations with divergent production tests, which require many different responses to a given problem (Guilford, 1967). And creativity measures, like the Torrance Tests of Creative Thinking (Torrance, 1974b), were found to correlate substantially with intelligence and could serve as alternate measures of general intelligence (Wallach, 1968). There is still lack of agreement concerning these issues (Feldhusen, Treffinger, van Mondfrans, & Ferris, 1971; Guilford, 1971; R. L. Thorndike, 1966; Wallach & Kogan, 1965; T. M. Williams & Fleming, 1969). This, in fact, has prevented the emergence of a commonly accepted construct of creativity.

Intelligence and Culture

Terman's studies of the gifted did not consider the socioeconomic variable as an influence on personality differences. Gowan, however, indicated the importance of this dimension as a milestone in the development of the gifted and creative movements. This led Torrance, for instance, to suggest that the identification process of talent should account for the positive talents of culturally disadvantaged children—for whom he and his associates have attempted to develop nontest measures that would tap the hidden giftedness of these children (Torrance, 1973, 1977b)—as well as plan for the construction of special programs designed to satisfy these needs (Torrance, 1977b).

Educational Intervention

On the matter of educational intervention procedures, a federal government report identified learning conditions provided for gifted and talented children (Marland, 1972a). These conditions were categorized as enrichment of curriculum and physical surroundings, methods of instruction, psychological climates conducive to learning, administrative arrangements to facilitate learning, and acceleration or advanced placement.

Over the past 20 years, *process learning* has re-emerged as a significant agent of educational facilitation. Jerome S. Bruner's (1961) approach to process learning advocates generic learning as a means of leaping over the barrier of specific event and information to thinking. Generic learning involves the grasp of a principle that allows the recognition of new problems one encounters as exemplars of old principles mastered. As such, it is essential to significant intellectual activity involved in processing information. In a discussion on the facilitation of significant learning, Carl R. Rogers (1969) stressed the nurture of the discovery process, whereby learning how to learn and involvement in a process of change become the primary aims of education.

A more recent expression of process learning, with the gifted in mind, can be found in the Enrichment Triad Model (Renzulli, 1979a). The model presents three levels of enrichment: Type I deals with general exploratory activities, Type II involves group training activities, and Type III relates to individual and small group investigations of real problems. The first two types of enrichment are said to be appropriate for all learners while the third type is considered appropriate for gifted learners. Whereas Type I and Type II enrichment deal with strategies for expanding student interests and developing thinking and feeling processes thereby acting as logical input and support systems, Type III enrichment consists of activities that require actual investigation of real problems by using proper methods of inquiry.

The Structure of Intellect model initiates several other approaches to educational facilitation (Guilford, 1972). Mary N. Meeker is primarily responsible for the production of workbook materials for developing numerous abilities identified by this model: cognition, memory, convergent production, divergent production, and evaluation (Meeker, Sexton, & Richardson, 1970).

The lack of a shared conception of how to facilitate creativity has led to the production of diverse training approaches and materials by many (e.g., Khatena, 1978a, 1984; Renzulli, 1973; Torrance & Myers, 1970; F. E. Williams, 1972), to encourage the use of the creative potential in the classroom. The model proposed by F. E. Williams attributes importance to the affective domain while Khatena's model (1984) places strong emphasis on the interactive effects of emotion and intellect in the realm of imagery and creative imagination.

Creative problem-solving approaches to learning provide yet other important models for productive education. The most important of these are the materials developed by Osborn (1963), Parnes, Noller, and Biondi (1977), Torrance and Myers (1970), Feldhusen and his associates (e.g., Feldhusen & Treffinger, 1980), W. J. J. Gordon (1961), and Prince (1968).

Development

Nearly no attention has been given to developmental features of the gifted and talented by those concerned with educating them. A starting point from which to examine the developmental characteristics of gifted children is the evidence derived from the Terman longitudinal study, reported in five volumes. The 1,528 gifted urban children of California were followed from kindergarten through high school, and then on through midlife. Extrapolating from these findings, it can be said that gifted children generally maintain their intellectual superiority and versatility, emotional stability, social-adjustment capabilities, and educational achievement and carry these traits into adulthood (Terman & Oden, 1959).

Most of what we know about developmental patterns of intellect and creativity, however, has come from studies of the general population through the intelligence and factor components of the Wechsler scales. Relative to the Structure of Intellect, no systematic attempts have been made to study developmental patterns, except Guilford's inferences about those based on the factor analytic work of L. L. Thurstone and T. L. Kelley. As for the study of complex intellectual abilities of gifted children as they grow older, nearly nothing exists. It is interesting to note Guilford's (1967) rejection of the Garrett (1946) hypothesis stating that multiple abilities develop from a single, general intellectual ability prevailing in infancy and early childhood and becoming differentiated with increasing age. Guilford considered the Garrett hypothesis to be akin to a hierarchical model of intellect like the one proposed by P. E. Vernon. The factors of intelligence that are differentiated for adults that give rise to the Structure of Intellect, according to Guilford, may also apply to children at various ages, though the evidence of extensive differentiation is very sketchy and generally lacking for the very young. Perhaps his morphological model may not be the same for very young children. The fact that there are as yet no studies on the direct rate of growth of Structure of Intellect abilities is indicative of the need for much research in the area of intellectual development.

The use of the Torrance Tests of Creative Thinking to study developmental patterns of creative thinking abilities in the United States and abroad has produced interesting thoughts on the creative development of children. Torrance (1967b) focused on what he called the *fourth-grade slump* or drop in creative thinking abilities. This concept hypothesizes that development of creative thinking abilities is continuous; that is, creative thinking abilities are expected to increase with age. Some of Torrance's later thoughts on the subject (Torrance, 1978a) reiterate his position that, although intelligence is less likely to be affected by stimulation, creative thinking abilities are affected by stimulation and show significant increments. This conception of continuous growth is closely related to measurement research.

Gowan—drawing on Sigmund Freud, Jean Piaget, Erik Erikson, and others—considers development to occur in discrete stages. He grouped these into three major periods in a person's life, namely, infancy, youth, and adulthood. During each of these three periods, an individual passes through three developmental stages, but each time at a higher level. Gowan stated that this development or growth sequence is an important natural occurrence in human life and is related to a transformation of energy called *periodicity*, which "occurs when the same pattern of events is seen to run through higher development as has been contained in a corresponding pattern from a lower sequence" (Gowan, 1971, p. 158).

Two other concepts with essential implications for the gifted are escalation and dysplasia (Gowan, 1974). By analogy, he defined *escalation* as the step-by-step development of five interrelated aspects: discontinuity, succession, emergence or the debut of new powers, differentiation, and integration. *Dysplasia*, he explains, occurs when one aspect of the psyche (e.g., the affective) continues to escalate although another aspect (e.g., the cognitive) becomes arrested at a given stage—a condition that produces block or *anomie*, and eventual neurosis.

Problems

More information has surfaced to show the problems that highly gifted children have as they grow up. Oden (1968) assessed the relationships of vocational achievement and genius. In this assessment, she compared 100 of the most successful and least successful male geniuses and found that the most successful men came from families that had higher socioeconomic status and who were given more encouragement to succeed. They also ranked higher as adolescents in volitional, intellectual, moral, and social traits, and they had more self-confidence, perseverance, and integration toward goals. In addition, although scholastic achievement had been similar for both groups in grade school, half of the successful men had graduated from college. The male geniuses were also found to be more prone to emotional and social difficulties. The concern that most of these problems are culture bound and arise from negative attitudes of our society toward creative, disadvantaged, physically handicapped, emotionally disturbed, and underachieving gifted individuals has been expressed by many prominent thinkers in the field (Barron, 1963; Gallagher, 1985; Getzels & Jackson, 1962; Gowan & Bruch, 1971; Khatena, 1973b; Krippner, 1967; Kubie, 1958; Torrance, 1962a, 1965a, 1970).

Many problems that gifted children face stem from the conflicts they have with people who are around them. These conflicts may be between a gifted child and a single person, or several people, or the representatives of education, government, and so forth. Torrance convincingly argues that many of the problems people encounter involve damming or distorting their creative energies (Torrance, 1962a). This situation applies as well to gifted children who are often dominated by the inner forces of their creativity. These forces sometimes make them do things beyond their control, acts that are in conflict with traditional modes of behavior and that call for adjustments. Effecting these adjustments satisfactorily leads gifted children to mental health and productivity. If these adjustments are not made, repression occurs with consequent personality problems and possible breakdown or mental illness. In addition, interest has increased in approaches for promoting adjustment or constructive behavior (Torrance, 1965a) and the realization has developed that the gifted child, too, needs guidance, both in the areas of personal development and career plans (Gowan, 1972; Torrance, 1976a; Zaffrann & Colangelo, 1977).

PUBLIC INTEREST AND SUPPORT

Although our knowledge of the gifted and what could be done for them has increased over the years, it has not been without considerable frustration owing to the obstructionism of the public education system that essentially is geared to a philosophy of egalitarianism (Conant, 1977; Silberman, 1970). It was the achievement of a foreign power and its threatening implications in the form of *Sputnik* that shook Americans out of their complacency and skepticism concerning the gifted (Bish, 1975). There was a definite turn of thought that separated pre- from post-Sputnik times. Americans, at first, blamed the education system for curriculum and instructional weakness in mathematics and science; so reforms were sought. At about the same time, the National Defense and Education Act was passed.

Bish (1975), speaking of the American reaction to *Sputnik*, describes the early efforts of the National Education Association. With the assistance of grants from the Carnegie Corporation, the association designed and supported a project whose major function was to inform the American public about the urgent need to attend to the education of the gifted and talented. During its lifetime (1958–69), the project acted as a clearinghouse and center for the dissemination of information by way of various publications and organized conferences all over the country. It also provided consultant services. As Bish (1975) observed, "It bridged a gap between the apathy of the post-war Fifties and the demands of the Seventies" (p. 288).

Serious initiatory and supportive efforts of federal and state legislation and funding became noticeable in the 1970s. However, the proposed budget cuts in education by the Reagan administration in 1981 introduced an ominous note in what otherwise might be considered an unprecedented period of growth in gifted education. The establishment of the Office of the Gifted and Talented in 1972 initiated major thrusts for better educational opportunities for the gifted. The computer services of the Council for Exceptional Children and the Association for the Gifted/ Educational Resource Information Center (Reston, Virginia) served to bring information on the gifted to those who needed it rapidly. Dissemination of information and provision of in-service leadership activities by the National/State Leadership Training Institute helped to create better opportunities for the gifted all over the country. To these must be added the significant efforts of parent and other organized groups and the contributions of the universities and colleges in preparing teachers to assume the role and responsibility of facilitators of gifted and talented education.

Federal Efforts

The challenge of the 1950s and the response by Bish (1975) prepared the way for a truly significant step to counteract the problem (Khatena, 1976a). This took the form of an act of the United States Congress, which included provisions for gifted and talented children in its amendments to the Education Act of 1969. The act was made law on April 13, 1970 (Marland, 1972a). The law required the Commissioner of Education (a) to determine the extent to which special educational assistance programs were necessary or useful to meet the needs of gifted and talented children; (b) to evaluate how existing federal educational assistance programs could be more effectively used to meet these needs; and (c) to recommend new programs, if any, that were necessary to meet these needs. Further, the commissioner was to report the findings and make recommendations no later than one year after the enactment of the act (Section 806c of Public Law 91-230).

This led Commissioner Marland to define the immediate steps the Office of Education was to take for launching the federal program for the gifted and talented without further legislation. At the same time it was to provide long-range planning at the federal, state, and local levels by both the public and private sectors to alleviate systematically the problems identified by the study. These provisions would take the form of the following:

1. A planning report on the federal role in education of gifted and talented children
2. An assignment of program responsibility and establishment of a Gifted and Talented Program Group
3. A nationwide inventory and assessment of current programs for the gifted and talented
4. Strengthening of state educational agencies for establishing more effective provisions of educational programs for the gifted and talented through Title V of the Elementary and Secondary Education Act
5. Leadership development and training of representatives from the states at institutes whose programs would aim at the development of a strategic plan for the education of the gifted and talented
6. Career education models in line with the existing ones developed by the National Center for Educational Research and Development
7. Experimental schools devoted to the individualization of programs to benefit gifted and talented students as a comprehensive design to effect education reform
8. Supplementary plans and centers relative to encouragement of Title III Elementary and Secondary Education Act in cooperation with the Office of Education-Gifted and Talented Program Group to support still further the agencies within the states to provide special programs for the gifted and talented
9. Ten regional offices with a part-time staff member to be identified as responsible for gifted and talented education, and who would act as liaison with the national office of the Office of Education, provide developmental assistance to state agencies, effect continuous dissemination of information, and give management assistance to specialized regional activities as they arise
10. Higher educational opportunities for the gifted and talented, which would be determined and implemented by the Office of Education-Gifted and Talented Program Group

Three years after formulation, these objectives found realization in the establishment of the Office of the Gifted and Talented, Office of Education Regional Part-time Directors, the Educational Resource and Information Center Clearinghouse on the Gifted and Talented, and the National/State Leadership Training Institute, Internships in the Office of the Gifted and Talented, cooperative interstate projects supported by Title V (Section 505) funds, a gifted students symposium, and many state projects on the gifted and talented.

Office of the Gifted and Talented

Discussions of federal responsibilities and efforts (e.g., Jackson, 1979; Lyon, 1976; Marland, 1972b) point out that the Office of the Gifted and Talented began with preparation of the Marland report. It had no funds with which to operate. Under the leadership of Harold C. Lyon, Jr., assisted by Jane Case Williams, this office set itself up in an advocacy role to champion the cause of the gifted and talented, using the needs-assessment-survey information included in the Marland report (1972a) as a guideline. The information in the report supported the following conclusions:

1. Federal, state, and local funds for differential educational provisions had low priority for gifted and talented students.
2. Fewer than 4% of gifted children were receiving services commensurate with their needs.
3. Fifty-seven percent of the school administrators said they had no gifted or talented students in their classrooms.
4. Minority and culturally diverse gifted were hardly reached.
5. Although legislative or regulatory provisions existed for these students in 21 states, only 10 states having full-time personnel were assigned to gifted-child education.
6. Such children needed special opportunities and were not, in fact, doing well on their own.
7. The belief that gifted children came exclusively from upper middle class and wealthy families was a prevailing myth.
8. Identification procedures were poor; funds were lacking; and, frequently, teachers and administrators were apathetic and even hostile to the needs of the gifted.
9. Only 12 American universities were training teachers at the graduate level for gifted and talented students.
10. The expected federal role in the delivery services to gifted and talented students was practically nonexistent.

Because the Office of the Gifted and Talented was faced with an enormous task and had meager resources, it moved in a number of directions.

1. It adopted the strategy of sustained advocacy.
2. It used the leadership-training approach (with funds from the Education Professions Development Act) (a) to further support professionals already interested in the gifted and talented; (b) to

reach key educators, opinion shapers, and legislators; (c) to begin developing potential parent constituency; and (d) to provide concrete skills in planning and program building at the state level.

3. It called on private foundation, business, industry, and community groups to provide special benefits to gifted and talented students, using the national news media, extensive travel to speak to various groups, and writings in popular and professional publications.

4. It found a great deal of publicity for the gifted and talented through such programs as exploration scholarships (funds for which came from the Explorers Club and Expeditions International), scholarships provided by the Bureau of Indian Affairs, and a national symposium for gifted high school students (jointly sponsored by the American Association for Gifted Children and the Presidential Scholar Program initiated by President Lyndon B. Johnson in 1964).

5. It alerted local and state education agencies to use creative grantsmanship techniques to obtain funds for programs via various Elementary and Secondary Education Act title categories.

6. It also sought support from the National Endowment for the Arts and Humanities, the National Science Foundation, the Robert Clark-Sterling Foundation, and other related funding agencies.

Harold C. Lyon, Jr., wrote a letter on February 19, 1975, to Friends of the Gifted and Talented noting that the Special Project's Act (Public Law 93-380, Section 404) gave his office statutory authority to administer programs for this group. So, for the first time, funds amounting to $2.56 million could be made available. He indicated that a call for proposals would shortly be forthcoming with the expectation that funds could be awarded for state comprehensive programs, for a consortium of academic institutions and internships carrying graduate credit and degree status to potential leaders, for a technical assistance project, for exemplary projects relative to special groups of gifted and talented youth, and for an analysis of requirements for the gifted and talented and their dissemination to practitioners.

Although these funds were scarce because they were spread over 50 states for as many as one million potentially gifted students, for the first time in the history of the United States, commitment to implement legislation for the gifted and talented was made. This must be recognized as the significant precursor to escalating support. Using the successful strategy adopted by the National/State Leadership Training Institute, the Office of the Gifted and Talented diverted half of its money to state educational agencies for professional staff development and to local projects and model programs with replication potential in their design, foreseeing the great possibility of contagion and rapid spread.

The initial allocation of $2.56 million in 1976 for gifted programs increased in 1979 to $3.78 million, and Public Law 95-561, as projected for fiscal year 1980, had an escalated amount of funds available from $6.3 million to $25 million over a five-year period (Sisk, 1979). Of course, with the Reagan administration's proposed cuts in education at the time, such funds did not materialize. However, this new legislation, had it been allowed to become operational, would have directed 75% of the federal appropriation to the states, 90% of which was expected to flow through competition to the local district of each state, with the requirement that 50% of the money must serve culturally disadvantaged gifted children (Lyon, 1979; Sisk, 1979). In addition, 25% of the commissioner's discretionary funds would have been distributed according to the commissioner's priorities, namely, graduate-level training, statewide planning, contracts for research, information products, and model products (Lyon, 1979). To these must be included Lyon's second communication (1979) that announced up to 100 monetary awards for young people for study in the humanities under the Gifts for Youth Projects Program and the National Endowment for the Arts and Humanities.

Apart from describing the new legislation that continued to provide special provisions for the gifted and talented, Sisk (1979) reviewed the events during her term (1976–79) as acting director of the Office of the Gifted and Talented, and made the following observations and comments:

1. The increases in federal funds resulted from a greater awareness of gifted children's needs brought about through the efforts of state and local agencies and a variety of news media coverage.
2. The strengthening and funded support of nearly all education agencies has found expression in a multitude of innovative programs.
3. There has been a tripling of the number of funded local projects since 1976 and their positive efforts in terms of the dissemination of materials and local replications.
4. A call for proposals went out in 1979 for models addressing the minority or disadvantaged gifted and talented program with emphasis on mathematics and science and visual and performing arts.
5. There has been funding of a university consortium graduate-training program in the gifted that has trained over 45 leaders, which allows them to occupy positions in various universities around the country.
6. Since 1979, there has been continued emphasis on building leadership in the minority areas to work with minority gifted and talented, as reflected in awards to black colleges for training teachers.

7. Funds have also been allocated to the National/State Leadership Training Institute and regional effort for a mentor/teacher-training program with emphasis on creative problem-solving.
8. Relative to future trends and needs, it was perceived that greater emphasis had to be placed on teacher training and in-service training to serve the regular classroom teacher who teaches gifted and talented students, that gifted curriculum institutes were needed, and that continued development of measures to identify all kinds of gifted and talented had to have priority.

However, the Reagan administration reduced funding for education, and even abolished the Office of the Gifted and Talented a few years ago, so that no dollars needed for gifted children of public school age flowed from Washington (Ballard, Ramirez, & Weintraub, 1977). But Gallagher's (1986) recent proposal for a more active federal role in the education of gifted children, if implemented, may correct the poor financial support given at the federal level—less than $7 million was provided for gifted education since the passage of Public Law 91-230 (Section 806c). However, it must be noted though that the Jacob K. Javits Gifted and Talented Children and Youth Education Act of 1987, passed by the United States Congress, can be expected to invigorate state and local provisions for the gifted through Title IV of the Elementary and Secondary Education Act funds.

Council for Exceptional Children Computer Service

An important component of the national effort, which far exceeds the potential of the National Education Association's effort to disseminate information on the gifted in the 1960s, is the Council for Exceptional Children's official tie-in (1972) with the computer services of the Educational Resource Information Center. Although supported by federal dollars, it was not perceived at the time as directly related to the federal approach of initiating and maintaining changes in education that would give special opportunities to American gifted children. Its major functions include the gathering, abstracting, and disseminating of information on the many aspects of gifted children and their education; the production of monographs, manuals, reports, and various studies; the computer search of special topics on an individual basis; the sponsorship of information related to research on gifted children and the best practices available for dealing with these children.

Over the past 14 years, this computer information resource has performed these important functions most effectively. It is recognized as a significant vehicle for the establishment and operation of a communication network that has the capability of reaching everyone in the country who is concerned with the gifted. In the clearinghouse facility, we have a power no country in the world has to date that shares information in all matters pertaining to the gifted with maximum economy and efficiency. The fact that researchers, educators, parents, and others interested in and concerned about the gifted have extensively used the Council for Exceptional Children-Educational Resource Information Center facilities is testimony to its great need and success.

National/State Leadership Training Institute

The highest priority perceived by the Office of the Gifted and Talented in 1972 was the need to strengthen national and state leadership. To this end, the National/State Leadership Training Institute was created. It was funded primarily by the Education Professions Development Act for a period of 3 years and administered by the Superintendent of Ventura County, California. The mission of this group was to train five leaders in every state so that they would have significant input in making state education policy. Each team was to consist of one state-level leader, one local education representative, two teachers or parents from the academic community, and one noneducator. The director of this effort has been Irving Sato. He and his staff develop sensitivity to the educational needs of the gifted, train educators in specialized teaching techniques, and help plan for the special educational needs of gifted children at the state and local levels.

In the first 3 years of its operation, the National/State Leadership Training Institute trained 48 state teams who developed state plans. It also trained the teams to plan long-term programs for the gifted, which they would implement on their return to their respective states. The teams would also provide the leadership for relevant legislation, funding, community support, and media coverage in their respective states. In addition, the group set up a national network of persons and agencies committed to gifted education; keeps people informed nationally through a monthly bulletin, visits, conferences, consultation, on-site technical assistance, and the like; and offers many important publications on various topics of interest. The continued activities of the group have trained a large number of educators, administrators, parents, and others. The frequency of their meetings can be seen in the rather comprehensive agenda listed in their monthly bulletin as well as in the quality of the institute's leadership program. All this is testimony to the fact that they have fulfilled the goals initially set for them by the Office of the Gifted and Talented.

State Efforts

The many projects and differential programs for gifted and talented students that have been, or are still, in existence around the country—as reported in a special issue of the *Gifted Child Quarterly* (1979a) and in related sources (Cox, Daniel, & Boston, 1985; Passow, 1979)—are indicative of the spread of interest in providing special opportunities for such students. Stimulated by the efforts of federal legislation that expressed itself not only in terms of money (though not a great deal) for various innovative projects but also in leadership training, conferences, the issuance of relevant information, and so on, many states have enacted legislation and allocated some of the state resources to formalize provisions of special educational opportunities for their gifted students. As yet, not all states have legislation and funds for the implementation of special educational opportunities, but many of those that do not have this advantage have set up (or are setting up) the machinery necessary to attain this end.

We now have state provisions for the gifted along a continuum from relatively informal to quite formal support funds that vary from state to state. Of course, there is room for considerable improvement. Several states had their own financed programs even before federal recognition and facilitation. In fact, they served as models to many states initiating programs for the gifted and talented. Among those states serving as models were California, Connecticut, Florida, Illinois, Kansas, Maryland, New York, North Carolina, Ohio, Oregon, and Pennsylvania (Gallagher, 1985; Gowan & Demos, 1964; Laird, 1971; Laird & Kowalski, 1972).

Program provisions have emerged not only from state conceptualizations but also from local school districts whose initiatives have helped, in many instances, to establish a framework for planning at the state level. Thus, there is, on the one hand, the state-mandated provisions for the gifted in California and, on the other hand, the emergent provisions that derive their force from local efforts in Illinois (Newland, 1976).

A number of studies by Lary Laird (1971), D. M. Jackson (1979), J. Zettel (1979), and Khatena (1982a), surveyed state educational provisions for gifted children. Taken together, these studies show a significant increase in legislation, funding, program development, teacher training, state personnel assigned to the gifted and talented, and organized teacher-parent groups.

Whereas very little was done for gifted and talented students before federal legislation and funding, strides made for gifted education tended to be more by way of local and less formalized efforts (except for a few states, like California, Connecticut, Florida, Illinois, and Pennsylvania). Federal legislation invigorated states to work on legislation of their own and to formalize their provisions for gifted education. Whatever federal monies that were made available, either directly or through state agencies complemented by state financial support, have activated the several thrusts to provide for better gifted education.

The barriers that were perceived by Gallagher (1972, 1985, 1986), insufficient financial support, inadequately trained personnel, inadequate curriculum development, inadequate referral and diagnostic techniques, lack of public interest, inadequate legal base, insufficient physical space, and other limitations, still persist but not all are at the same level of severity. Other priorities will command our attention, but federal and state legislation is having an impact.

The number of trained personnel has sharply increased over the past few years. This increase was facilitated by many conferences, workshops, and related activities held at the state and local level; by the contributions of the leadership training institutes; by state certification requirements; and by the formalized offerings in colleges and universities that fulfill certification needs and provide training leading to advanced degrees. There are strong indications that curriculum development has made and can continue to make significant strides. The greater awareness of many kinds of giftedness that is finding application in identification and screening procedures has taken off some of the edge of this problem although by no means removed it. In this area, there is so much more that needs to be done, including the construction of new instruments, the refinement of those that exist, and more competent and extensive referral services. There is certainly more public interest than there was before, and this has been facilitated by the news media, advocacy groups, parent-teacher associations, lawsuits, and the like.

The problem of having an adequate legal base was established by passage of Public Law 94-1421 and Public Law 91-230 (Section 806c). These appear to be recently confirmed by the Jacob K. Javits Gifted and Talented Children and Youths Education Act of 1987. Furthermore, most states have legislation with the expectation that other states will follow suit before long.

As for the problem of physical space, various administrators have helped by making special classrooms available by sharing several schools in a district, demonstration and resource centers, and project facilities.

D. M. Jackson (1979), in reviewing the activities for gifted and talented, identifies five major developments.

1. The presence of better trained and equipped personnel in gifted education, many of whom possess a master's or doctor's degree in the field
2. The occurrence of significant policy changes at the state level as well as legislative advances and developments in state departments of education
3. The movement from a dominant cognitively oriented program to a diversification of programs that subscribe to the needs of five

United States Office of Education categories of giftedness by way of model projects of the Office of the Gifted and Talented (e.g., visual and performing arts, creativity, early childhood, disadvantaged gifted, rural and community-based mentor programs)
4. A variety of pedagogical styles that have emerged from the diversification of programs (e.g., resource rooms, acceleration, enrichment, intensive one-to-one relationships with mentors)
5. The propensity to "piggyback" on community and private sector resources

CONCLUSIONS

Early efforts to find appropriate means for the identification of the intellectually gifted led to the development of increasingly more sophisticated I.Q. tests and the continued study of the characteristics of gifted persons. However, the effort to provide special opportunities for all gifted children has not been a nationwide one. Rather, these efforts are the sporadic attempts of inspired and dedicated professionals who saw the importance of assisting the academic acceleration of gifted students who received very little, if any, support. The impetus for advances in thought on the gifted came from several directions that today have converted what were largely individually inspired efforts to federal and national thrusts for the educational enhancement of the gifted.

Subsumed under humanism are those influences that have broadened our perspectives of special students; we no longer judge giftedness within the narrow confines of I.Q. Rather, we see giftedness as multidimensional and inclusive of all kinds of abilities and talents. We regard creativity as subject to enhancement by means of educational intervention through which the gifted can be prepared to be productive. Understanding creative development of the individual can better prepare us to provide those facilitative agents for the most productive interaction among the creativity peaks in the developmental cycles of gifted students. Gifted students can perceive and benefit from guidance, and socioeconomic factors can be given proper attention in the screening procedures that are designed to provide special opportunities. And the new force of parapsychology can be used to derive fresh dimension and significance in educational planning for the gifted and talented.

Terman and his associates engaged in sustained research of a single large Californian group of gifted students relative to their abilities, behavior, development, and fortunes, following them into midlife. Creativity research began in earnest in the 1960s and, unlike the Terman studies, derived its information from many investigators using various groups of subjects of different ages and ethnic origins living all over the

United States. One exception is the recently reported longitudinal studies of creative individuals by Torrance.

Generally, the data obtained from creativity research were generated by a multiplicity of techniques, ranging from the historical to the experimental. Overwhelming evidence suggests that I.Q. measures identify only one kind of giftedness and that other measures are needed to measure special abilities and talent in a number of different areas of giftedness. In general, measures for these many kinds of giftedness were not really available in the early stages of gifted research. Some are not yet available in effective form today. However, in the 1960s, the attention of many researchers shifted to the development of instruments to measure creative potential. The great strides that have been made to accomplish the production of reliable and valid measures still leave some issues unsettled.

The post-*Sputnik* response and the national expression for the need of special educational opportunities precipitated legislation in the past 18 years with slow but increasing funding for gifted education in the United States. National and state efforts have invigorated various dimensions of gifted and talented education all over the country. The inclusion of professional educators and parents in interactive support roles and state and federal attention to achieve an American dream toward excellence will continue to prepare the way for one of the richest harvests of talent in this century before long.

The agency that provided both the thrust and momentum at the federal level was the Office of the Gifted and Talented. Through the National/State Leadership Training Institute and the Council for Exceptional Children Educational Research Information Centers computer based services, the agency has not only disseminated information rapidly and effectively to reach an interested American public but has also created leaders organized in a national network that has undoubtedly ordered local opinion and effort to inaugurate and sustain special opportunities for the gifted and talented. Experience has confirmed that if a program is to be successful, it must be the result of the combined efforts, commitment, and press of both local initiatives (including professionals, educators, parents and local education agencies) and state agencies (voluntarily or, if necessary, compelled by legislation to enact financial appropriations) to support attempts to provide special opportunities for gifted and talented children at the local levels.

CHAPTER THREE

Understanding Abilities of the Gifted

*I*NTRODUCTION

Gifted education can be explained in a holistic way to illustrate several interrelated dimensions of human functioning. To this end, a holistic model is presented to define five interconnected parameters: the environment, individual, interventions, outcomes, and communication. The model (Figure 3.1) is an extension of one developed earlier (Khatena, 1983, 1984) to describe the multidimensional and interactive nature of imagery and creative imagination.

Environment

The *environment* is everything external to the individual, including all of the physical and sociocultural universe. It provides the primary source of all information received through the senses (e.g., sight, hearing, touch, smell, taste). Such information is transmitted to the brain via processes of the neurophysiological pathways, it is recorded, in the first instance, as electrochemical impulses that take the shape of images. Images are then coded in one language form or another (e.g., verbal, numerical, musical). In addition, information may reach the individual, not only in its raw state, but also secondhand. Secondhand information had to have been processed at least once before it could be presented in a language form.

Not all information is accepted by the brain. A mechanism called *mental set* acts as a filter system that accepts or rejects information reaching the senses before it is transmitted to the brain. It is a mechanism that is primarily programmed to protect the individual and is directly or indirectly related to survival. Because it is, in part, based on previous experience, it is able to watch incoming information with prior reactions to the same information.

Individual

All that relates to the human being comprises the *individual* dimension. As the model indicates, this dimension consists of content and process areas.

Content

Information reaches the brain as images. They are coded in language and stored for future use. In the act of communication, individuals may receive informational content in either its image or language form. These two kinds of content are interrelated and interactive and are called integrative functions, because either or both can be called to use. If the connections are properly made at the beginning, a dual storage system of images and language is installed. Layers of meaning are directly related to experience, so that the richer and more comprehensive the experience with either images or language, the greater the depth of meaning informational content processes (Khatena, 1984, pp. 38–39).

Process

The process component of the individual dimension incorporates the capability of all forms of human informational processing. These forms include hereditary-based intellectual operations, creative thinking and problem solving, and imagination. Such processing capabilities correspond to different stages of development. They also engage the various levels of awareness, from deliberate mental control to the autonomous mental functioning of the different states of consciousness—past, present, and future. Process activity stores and retrieves information that is the direct function of memory. Feeling-motivational states may enter the informational processing capacity affecting various levels of awareness and energizing creative thinking and imagination.

Interventions

The *interventions* dimension involves information organized in certain ways for learning, behavioral change, and growth. Although it provides information to the individual, as in the environment dimension, this in-

Figure 3.1 Holistic Model for Educating Gifted Children

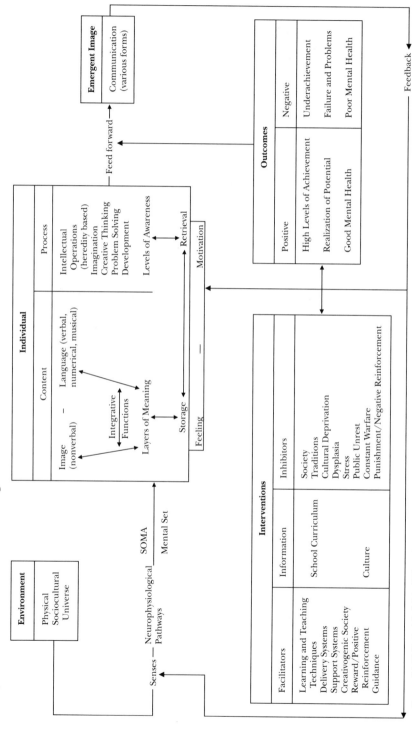

From "A Holistic Model for Educating Gifted Children" by J. Khatena, 1988. Unpublished manuscript.

formation is structured for input in particular ways. Two such major sources of information are (a) formalized content of the school curriculum categorized as subjects like literature, mathematics, science, and art; and (b) the broader content of culture.

Facilitators of interventions include learning and teaching techniques; delivery systems that relate to different organized methods of schooling; and support systems provided by the federal, state, and local governments or by the school and home. Other facilitators are what Silvano Arieti (1976) has called the "creativogenic society." Such a society supports the creative individual in various ways, including the provision of rewards or reinforcements and guidance. *Information* is an aspect of interventions concerned with the transmission of knowledge and skills constituting the school curriculum and its cultural correlates. *Inhibitors* include the following: conformity required by a society's traditions and customs; deprivation of cultural stimulation, facilities, and opportunities; developmental arrest of cognitive or affective growth or both that John C. Gowan (1972) calls "dysplasia"; public unrest or disturbances, and constant warfare (Simonton, 1978); and a system of punishments or negative reinforcements.

Outcomes

The *outcomes* dimension takes into account the environment and interventions input processed by the individual that lead to positive or negative results. Positive outcomes are those associated with high levels of achievement, the actualization of potential, and the realization of good mental health by individuals. If the outcomes are negative, they relate to individuals' underachievements, failures, and problems with consequent poor mental health.

Communication

Eventually, the product of all these activities manifests itself through *communication*. The images that emerge must be labeled in one language form or another for expression to others, otherwise the mental activity will not be detected. Such information may be the result of processing without deliberate interventions. However, in educational settings, interventions are arranged so that all four dimensions—the environment, individual, interventions, and outcomes—become involved and eventually get directed to communication. Once communication occurs, information received by others will evoke responses that activate the feedforward-feedback loop for continued functioning of the whole system.

In conclusion, the model will provide the conceptual basis for the discussion of various aspects of gifted education. Each chapter of this text will be developed relative to one or more of these five dimensions either singly or in interactive relationships. As the reader progresses, the holistic approach of gifted education will give a total view of the subject and set in motion future directions to be taken. The reader is encouraged to refer frequently to the model to keep the total picture in mind.

INTELLECT

The *individual* dimension is useful for understanding the conceptual changes of intellect of the gifted individual. Many researchers offer explanations of the intellect and its many mental functions, creativity and problem solving, academic aptitude or abilities involved in school learning, leadership ability, and abilities in the visual and performing arts.

I.Q. has been the measure used to identify gifted children in terms of intelligence and their ability to learn in school. Often, labeling the child is a definitive measure that is taken without realizing that I.Q. is nothing more than an index of the child's performance on a particular test, and at best, a predictor of academic achievement. Such a position has been recently reiterated, for instance, by Howard Gardner (1987), Robert J. Sternberg (1988), and Stephen W. White (1988), among others.

At this point, it would be useful to note two views of intelligence advanced some years ago. One regards intelligence as innate, and the other regards intelligence as a construct.

Two Views of Intelligence

Simmons (1968) explains that a single psychological approach to intelligence is difficult to determine because psychologists tend to divide into two camps. Psychologists believe intelligence is either (a) something *innate* that limits how people experience and the ways they behave, and is transmitted by heredity in the same manner as physiological characteristics; or (b) a synthetic *construct* defined by a culture or subculture that explains the great variety of human behaviors, which are highly dependent on experience and knowledge for their manifestations.

Intelligence as Innate
Those who assume that intelligence is innate and global, attempt to measure true intelligence (i.e., intelligence free from cultural contamination, commonly known as culture fair). Testing procedures are standardized to control for cultural and situational differences. It is assumed that intelligence is real and constant over time and that deviations or declines in intelligence are pathological (e.g., brain damage or anxiety). Measures of intelligence tend to encapsulate the knowledge of an individual in

I.Q. and ignore important behaviors (e.g., verbal and motor behaviors, reaction time to success and failure, reaction to time press) that are observable during test taking and that would give valuable information about the individual beyond the assigned I.Q. number index. In practice, the intelligence test does very little beyond predicting academic success; it is probably only a general measure of academic achievement that is not much different from a school achievement test—except in degree of specificity—or a general aptitude test.

Intelligence as Construct

Psychologists who take the construct view regard intelligence not as a single function or something fixed or predetermined, but as culture or experience bound. They develop measures of specific abilities and regard variation in performance as the result of prior learning experience. More attention is paid to what the individual says and does during the testing session. Such information is most likely incorporated in the appraisal of the individual. Deviations in intellectual functioning are attributed to changing conditions in life, interests, and values of the individual, especially as they relate to test taking.

CHANGING CONCEPTS OF INTELLIGENCE

Guilford (1967) suggested that tests have been developed ahead of an understanding of what they measure and that definition of intelligence is far from settled. Common to the two views of intelligence described is the fact that intelligence is an intangible and abstract phenomenon. At best, it manifests itself in behaviors of the individual. What a test does is sample some behaviors to derive evidence of intelligence. However, the lack of agreement on what behaviors constitute intelligence and the related problems of instrumentation have contributed to the difficulties of reaching a general consensus regarding theoretical formulations of intelligence. However, tests of intelligence that go beyond the appraisal of intelligence as sensory and motor functions or mental traits have moved from a *univariate* approach (giving a single score) to a *multivariate* approach (giving multiple scores).

Univariate Approach to Intelligence

Although the Binet scale was relatively neglected in France, it caught the interest of American psychologists and was soon applied to the study of mental retardates and normal children. The first American to use the Simon-Binet scale was Henry H. Goddard (1908, 1911) who translated the 1905 version of the Binet scale into English (1908). However, both

Binet and Goddard used the scales for either average or mentally re-tarded children.

General Intelligence

Unlike Binet and Goddard, Terman and his associates at Stanford University adapted the Binet scale in 1916 for white Americans and modestly called their revision the Stanford-Binet (Terman, 1916). Two other revisions of the Stanford-Binet followed. The 1937 version consisted of two forms of the test (Forms L and M), and the 1960 version essentially combined and refined the 1937 L and M forms and updated the measure (Terman & Merrill, 1937, 1960). Yet another revision of the measure was produced in 1986 by R. L. Thorndike, R. P. Hagen, and J. M. Statler. It was not only a further refinement of the 1960 version but also an expansion of its theoretical rationale presented as a three-level hierarchical model of intelligence.

The first two revisions of the Stanford-Binet attempted to measure the intellectual performance of children from age 3 to young adulthood or age 16. An individual's intellectual performance on the test was determined by comparison with the performance of normal children at different age levels. As in the Binet scale, the Stanford-Binet of 1916 expressed the scores in terms of mental age. Therefore, persons would be considered *normal* if they could solve the test items of persons their age; *retarded* if they could only solve those items of younger persons; and *superior* if they exceeded the performance of persons of their age. Terman has defined mental age or M.A. as the degree of general mental ability possessed by the average child of corresponding chronological age. The conversion of M.A. to I.Q. (the idea for which has been attributed to Wilhelm Stern, a German professor) was included in the 1937 and 1960 revisions of the Stanford-Binet.

The 1986 revision of the Stanford-Binet maintains continuity with the 1960 scale, building upon its strengths. Changes were implemented to make the instrument more effective for appraising, in a continuous scale, the cognitive skills of individuals from age 2 to adulthood. The theoretical rationale of the 1986 revision draws from two advances in cognitive psychology: Charles Spearman's thinking on intelligence and the hierarchical expansion of intelligence by P. E. Vernon and Sir Cyril Burt, whose models will receive attention later in the discussion. The formulation of the revision was influenced by clinicians and educators who had used the earlier editions of the Stanford-Binet. They frequently used the measure to identify gifted and mentally retarded students, and to assess the cognitive abilities of mainstream students having learning difficulties.

Neither Binet nor Terman concerned themselves with theoretical models for the intelligence scales they developed, unlike R. L. Thorn-

Figure 3.2 Theoretical Model of the Stanford-Binet

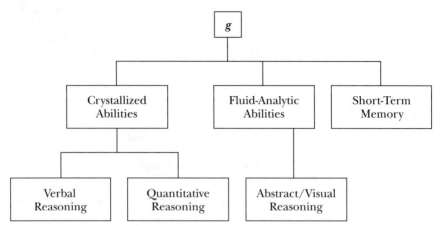

From *Stanford-Binet Intelligence Scale (4th ed.): Technical Manual.* (p. 4) by R.L. Thorndike, E.P. Hagen, & J.M. Sattler, 1986, Chicago: Riverside Publishing. Copyright © 1986 by Riverside Publishing Company. Reprinted by permission.

dike and his associates who presented a hierarchical model as the basis for the selection of items of the 1986 revision (see Figure 3.2).

Stanford-Binet as a Hierarchical Model of Intelligence

Thorndike, Hagen and Sattler (1986) followed the example of P. E. Vernon by formulating a hierarchical structure of the Stanford-Binet. Figure 3.2 is a three-level hierarchical model of intelligence presented as cognitive abilities. At the top level is g or a general reasoning factor below which are *crystallized abilities, fluid-analytic abilities,* and *short-term memory.* The third level expands crystallized abilities to *verbal reasoning* and *quantitative reasoning.* It also expands fluid-analytic abilities to *abstract/ visual reasoning.*

Intelligence as Global

David Wechsler (1939) described three factors of intelligence: *intellectual abilities; nonintellective* forces, such as drive, energy, impulsiveness, will, and persistence; and *temperament* variables, such as interest and achievement, which are functions of total personality. Like Binet, Wechsler subscribed to the concept of general intelligence. He was careful to point out, however, that intelligence is some kind of mental energy, which enters into all human behavior in some way or other, and that intellectual abilities reflect a person's potential through test performance.

General intelligence, then, is the expression of an individual's personality in a *global* sense. It is a potential energy whose nature is not known but whose use is for the good of society. General intelligence allows individuals to cope effectively with their environment. Inferences about the nature of intelligence may be drawn from the behavior exhibited. An individual exhibiting *intelligent* behavior engages in activities requiring reasoning, abstract thinking, observation of appropriate relations among things, drawing inferences, understanding words literally and figuratively, problem solving, and the like.

A variety of abilities manifest themselves through this global capacity. These intellectual abilities may be defined and measured quite precisely. The scores obtained that measure these abilities provide the means for inferring a person's global capacity or general intelligence.

The original Binet was commissioned early in this century by the French government to discover some way of identifying children who could benefit from schooling and those who could not. As a scientist, Binet relied heavily on empirical data to carry out this task. He believed that theory was important only insofar as it provided direction to the empiricism that must follow. Nowhere in his writings does he state a clearly defined theory of intelligence. He recognized that intellectual competency has to be identified by means of highly complex mental processes without specifically defining these processes. Because this was difficult to do, and until it could be done, Binet considered that some measure of general intelligence reflecting the operation of higher complex mental processes would be sufficient.

Binet admitted the existence of multiple abilities as a unitary function that permeated all of behavior. He called this unitary function *general intelligence*. His search for a measure of general intelligence, in which he was assisted by Theodore Simon, led to the construction of a developmental scale. Such a scale would tell how well children could understand, reason, and judge; how adaptable and persistent they could be; and the extent to which they could apply self-criticism (Binet & Simon, 1905).

This research led to the brilliant idea that if children could do the tasks relative to the abilities of other children their own age they would be of average intelligence. For example, a 6-year-old child who could do the tasks of other 6-year-old children would have a mental age (M.A.) of 6 years; that is, this child would be of average intelligence. If a 6-year-old child could do the tasks of 7-year-old children, the child would have an M.A. of 7 years; that is, this child would be brighter than other children of the same age.

These theoretical notions about the nature of intelligence led Wechsler (1966) to define intelligence as "the aggregate or global capacity of the individual to act purposefully, to think rationally and to deal effectively with his environment" (p. 7).

Although Wechsler's theoretical notion about the nature of intelligence is not completely implemented in the tests he consequently constructed, he does focus on the operation of nonintellective and temperament factors in the intellectual functioning of an individual that relate to the global capacity concept of intelligence. However, he does indicate that, generally, intelligence may only be inferred from measures of a person's intellectual abilities.

Wechsler was the first to publish an individual test of intelligence for adults. Later he extended the concepts involved in the construction of a test to include youth and children. His tests are listed as follows:

1. Wechsler Adult Intelligence Scale (1955)
2. Wechsler Intelligence Scale for Children—prepared as an extension of the original Wechsler-Bellevue Scale (1939), designed for use with children whose ages range from 5 to 15 years, and now revised as the Wechsler Intelligence Scale for Children-R (1974) for children from 6 through 16 1/2 years old
3. Wechsler Preschool and Primary Scale of Intelligence (1967)—designed to test children whose ages range from 4 to 6 1/2 years. All scales contain verbal and performance subscales that yield a verbal I.Q., a performance I.Q., and a full-scale or composite I.Q.

Mental Age and I.Q. as a Ratio

Mental age (M.A.) is a term coined by Binet to represent different degrees or levels of intelligence as measured by his tests. The measure assembled a series of intellectual tasks of varying difficulty for different age groups. There are six intellectual tasks at each level of the test. Successful performance on each task earns a credit of 2 months, with a maximum credit of 12 months obtainable per level. An M.A. is a score expressed in months and years that is derived by adding the number of months credit obtained by successful performance of the tasks at each level to the number of months credit before the level at which the subject gets all items correct, which is known as the *basal age*. For example, John, a child of 6 years, passes all six tests at year 7, five tests at year 8, three tests at year 9, and one test at year 10. He has a basal age of 6 years and is awarded a credit of 72 months to which is added 12 + 10 + 2 months for a total of 102 months. This total represents his M.A.

An M.A. can then be converted into an I.Q. The formula proposed by Terman, which is no longer used, was:

$$I.Q. = \frac{M.A.}{C.A.} \times 100$$

Wechsler explains that chronological age (C.A.) should not be thought of as the life age of an individual at the time of testing but in terms of the I.Q. formula. Like mental age, chronological age is just a score that the examiner assumes individuals of a given age would attain if their abilities were exactly the same as that of the average individual who has the same life age. This formulation makes test scores in M.A. and C.A. identical units; that is, if 8-year-old individuals were average for their age group, their C.A.'s would also be 8 years. Wechsler suggests that it would be more appropriate to state the old I.Q. formula as follows:

$$\text{I.Q.} = \frac{\text{Attained or actual score}}{\text{Expected mean score for age}}$$

He defines I.Q. as the ratio between a particular score obtained by a person on a measure of intelligence and the score in identical units obtained by an average individual of the same life age.

In the example, John's M.A. is 102 months and his life age or C.A. is 72 months. To obtain his I.Q., enter the following information:

$$\text{I.Q.} = \frac{102}{72} \times 100 = 141.6 \text{ or } 142$$

Wechsler suggests that an I.Q. provides a way of defining relative intelligence, tells us how bright persons are as compared with those of their own age, and remains relatively constant throughout life. However, this method of calculating I.Q. is inadequate because, depending on the age at which individuals are tested, they may obtain different I.Q.s even though their relative brightness remains the same. Furthermore, intellectual growth does not proceed by equal amounts throughout its development. Children's I.Q. scores tend to decrease as they grow older and progressively decline until ultimate arrest of growth. For these and other related reasons, psychologists believe that the I.Q. as a measure of intelligence should be abandoned. Wechsler suggests that there is nothing intrinsically wrong with the I.Q. *concept,* but fault rests with the *method* by which I.Q. is calculated.

Deviation I.Q.

An I.Q. was first derived by dividing M.A. by C.A. and multiplying by 100 so that a 5-year-old child with an M.A. of 6 would have an I.Q. of 120. This process was used to compute I.Q. values in the 1916 and 1937 revisions of the Stanford-Binet. However, an I.Q. obtained in this way did not allow for a comparison of one I.Q. with another at a specific age level or with I.Q.'s of different age levels. To get around this problem, the procedure used to compute standard scores was used to compute I.Q.'s. The I.Q.'s obtained in this way are called *deviation I.Q.'s* and are actually standard scores derived from an assumed mean of 100 and a standard deviation of 16 (on the Stanford-Binet 1960 revision) or 15 (on the Wechsler scales). Of course, deviation I.Q.'s have been computed and are presented in norm tables found in the test manuals.

Thus deviation I.Q. values are given for each age level from 2 years to 18 years in the 1960 revision of the Stanford-Binet as are the values of each age level 4 years through 75 years and above, depending on which of the Wechsler scales is used. The average or mean I.Q. on the Stanford-Binet is 100, with a standard deviation of 16. These values indicate that for persons to be considered highly intelligent their I.Q.'s must be at least two standard deviations above the mean (i.e., $100 + 2(16) = 132$). On the Wechsler scales, because the standard deviation is 15, persons must have I.Q.s of at least 130 to be considered highly intelligent.

In this way, the inadequacies of the earlier method of computing I.Q. are avoided, so that an I.Q. indicates relative ability at different ages and remains (except for chance errors) the same from one age to another, provided no change in ability occurs. For example, John's deviation I.Q. of 130 at age 10 can be compared with his deviation I.Q. at age 12, or John's deviation I.Q. can be compared to Donna's deviation I.Q. of 140 at age 10 or at another age.

Standard Age Scores

The 1986 revision of the Stanford-Binet provides *standard age scores* as indices of cognitive abilities with an I.Q. conversion procedure for making the scale comparable to the earlier two revisions of the scale. Raw scores are converted into standard scores for each of the subtests (e.g., vocabulary, absurdities, number series, memory for objects). For this conversion, the mean is 50 and the standard deviation is 8. The *area scores* (e.g., verbal reasoning, abstract/visual reasoning) and the *composite score* have a mean of 100 and a standard deviation of 16 (similar to the mean and standard deviation of the old scales and therefore comparable with them). A composite score is obtained by combining an individual's performance on the subtests, as instructed in the test's technical manual. Conversion tables are provided in the scoring and administration guide to assist the examiner to determine indices of cognitive abilities and general reasoning ability, and to facilitate interpretation of results.

Constancy or Stability of I.Q.

Wechsler (1966) indicated that consistency of I.Q. is a basic assumption of all scales of intelligence. If a measure of intelligence is to have practical value, for purposes of prediction and diagnosis, it must assume and eventually demonstrate that I.Q. remains invariant over a considerable period of time. Without this assumption, no permanent scheme of classifying intelligence is possible. If they are close to the means, I.Q.'s tend to remain constant. Those individuals identified as having average intelligence will generally show little, if any, difference in I.Q. at various age levels. However, I.Q.'s that are one to two standard deviations above or below the mean tend to show more fluctuations at different age levels. For example, if an individual obtained an I.Q. of 130 at age 10, we can expect that person to obtain an I.Q. of between 135 and 140 or between 120 and 125 at age 12. It must be realized, however, that I.Q. differences relate to the scores obtained on a test and not to differences in true intelligence, the nature of which we do not really know and can only infer from test performance. Wechsler points out that, depending on the age at which an individual is tested, the I.Q. may vary although the subject's actual brightness (i.e., "true" intelligence) remains unchanged.

N. Bayley (1949) suggested that test results in the first two years of life tend to be inconsistent, that there is an increase in the predictive power of intelligence tests between the ages of 2 and 6 years, and that, after the age of 6, test scores tend to be relatively stable for most individuals. The study also reports that average changes in I.Q. tend to be about 5 points, although individual variations can be as much as 30 points from one test to the next. Extreme changes in I.Q. scores are not unusual, for instance, when very highly gifted individuals are tested at different age levels.

The constancy of I.Q. depends on the measures used and the nature of the individual's capacity. Much of the variance hinges on the reliability of the measures used and the scores they give. Where equivalent or alternate forms of tests are used, the problem hinges on the sameness of the two measuring instruments. And, because the constancy of I.Q. is determined by repeated administrations of a test at different age levels, variations in I.Q. may be due to instrument discrepancies. Another important consideration is that of other extraneous variables that affect an individual during and between testing sessions. However, it must be remembered that, if changes in I.Q. do occur, they are changes in test scores and not in the level of native intelligence, which by definition, is independent of age.

Multivariate Approach to Intelligence

Once factor analysis became available to researchers interested in understanding the nature and measurement of intelligence, the conception of intelligence changed from univariate to multivariate. Factor analysis is a statistical technique that uses correlation coefficients to discover psychological functions that are basic to test performance and are used to differentiate fundamental intellectual abilities. By a complicated process of intercorrelating scores achieved on a number of tests by a group of people, certain common elements or attributes among the tests are identified. These common elements or attributes group together to form clusters. Each cluster, called a factor, is then given a name for the ability required to do the several related items of a test.

Some test items, for instance, require memorizing lines, and the factor identified is *visual memory*. Other test items may require the manipulation of numbers, and a *numerical* factor is then identified. A factor score tells how much of a certain attribute a person may have, whereas a composite or total score on a test may tell how well a person has done on the whole test (Guilford, 1967). Identification of these elements or attributes through factor analyses makes it possible to theorize about the structure of intelligence. Factor analyses facilitated the development of several multivariate theories of intelligence: the *two-factor* theory, the *hierarchical* theory, the *multifactor* theory, and the *Structure of Intellect.*

Two-Factor Theory of Intelligence

Charles Spearman (1927) was one of the first to use factor analysis in psychology to explain the nature of intelligence. Using a simple factor analysis model, Spearman derived evidence that led him to believe that intelligence is composed of two factors: (a) a general factor or mental energy (labeled g) that enters all intellectual activity and is possessed by everyone in varying degrees, and (b) a large number of specific factors (labeled s) that are highly relevant to particular tasks.

Spearman suggested that, unlike the theory of general intelligence, the two-factor theory provides a satisfactory explanation of the tendency for all abilities to show—not only overlap to some extent but also considerable unevenness. He suggests that g represents the general mental energy that is part of an individual's natural endowment, and he compares the s factors to many mechanisms or "engines" capable of being set in motion by this energy. Whereas s factors depend on the influences of education and training, g, being innate and ineducable, does not. Much of Spearman's theory of intelligence can be traced to his three famous neogenetic principles of cognition: *apprehension of experiences, eduction of relations, and eduction of correlates.*

Hierarchical Models

Both Sir Cyril Burt and P. E. Vernon were followers of Spearman and firmly subscribed to the concept of g, although they gave more attention to group factors and specific factors.

The Burt Model   Burt's (1949) conception of intelligence, which applied to the whole of the human mind, distinguishes between abilities that are intellectual in nature (Spearman's g) and practical or behavioral in nature (e.g., psychomotor, mechanical, and spatial abilities). He placed these factors in a hierarchical order with each higher level factor subdividing into two immediately lower levels in a series of successive dichotomies. The first dichotomy emerges from the head of the hierarchy, the *human*

Figure 3.3 Burt's Hierarchical Model

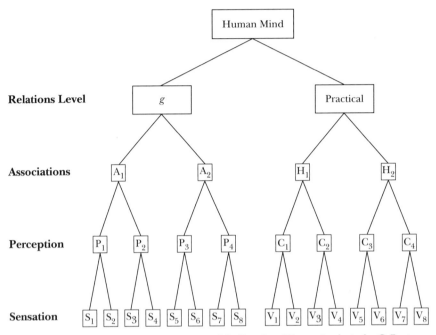

From "The Structure of the Mind: A Review of the Results of Factor Analysis, by C. Burt, 1949, *British Journal of Educational Psychology*, 19, p. 103. Copyright © 1949 British Journal of Educational Psychology. Reprinted by permission.

mind, as the *relations* level (g) and the *practical* level. The next lower level, the *associations* level subdivides and forms the dichotomy of *perception* and *sensation* (see Figure 3.3).

The Vernon Model   Vernon (1951) also described intelligence in terms of a hierarchical model headed by g, which subdivides into two sets of *major group factors:* verbal-educational (*v:ed*) and kinesthetic-motor (*k:m*) factors. The latter is equivalent to Burt's practical factor. The major group factors subdivide into *minor factors: v:ed* subdivides into verbal, numerical, and educational factors; *k:m* subdivides into practical, spatial, mechanical, and physical factors. These smaller categories then subdivide still further into *specific factors* (Figure 3.4).

According to Vernon (1960), intelligence corresponds to the general level of complexity and flexibility of a person's schemata accumulated during a lifetime, the acquisition of which is limited by innate ability. Furthermore, the emergence of higher order schemata is dependent on the acquisition of specific perceptual schemata; the higher the level of schemata, the more of the g factor it will contain. Vernon maintains that

Figure 3.4 Vernon's Hierarchical Model

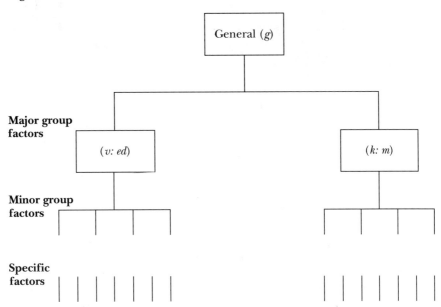

the complexity and flexibility of schemata are contingent on a stimulating environment.

Multifactor Theory of Intelligence

Other factor approaches found in America moved away from the English two-factor and hierarchical models to multifactor models that do not subscribe to the *g* factor. In particular, the contributions of L. L. Thurstone and J. P. Guilford are important.

Thurstone and Primary Mental Abilities   Thurstone (1924) described intelligence as operating at four major levels of *trial and error*. The least intelligent level is *overt trial and error* behavior. At the next level, *perceptual trial and error* intelligence, individuals may experience mentally what they would otherwise achieve by contact experience. Percepts are imaginal for the most part, and when their sensory cues are dropped, corresponding ideas remain. At the *ideational* level of intelligence, experience can be anticipated without direct encounter. Thurstone illustrates the difference between perceptual and ideational intelligence using an everyday situation. If a person should have an impulse to walk along a street and remembers that it is under construction, perceptual intelligence would allow the person to walk until a street-closed sign is seen, whereas ideational intelligence will help the person anticipate the situation in advance.

The highest level of intelligence is *conceptual intelligence*, where trial and error continues among quite crude, loosely organized, tentative, and incomplete actions or concepts. It is the conceptual level of intelligence that Thurstone focused on to measure intelligent behavior.

By using factor analysis to manipulate test results, he discovered that certain groupings of these tests occurred. Although Thurstone (1938) found no presence of g, he did find a limited number of elementary factors. This finding led him to state that intelligence consists of about a dozen or so group factors that he called *primary mental abilities*. The most important of these were verbal comprehension, number, spatial relations, word fluency, memory, and reasoning. He described these as follows:

Verbal comprehension (V)—measured by vocabulary and reading comprehension tests

Number (N)—measured by arithmetic word problems

Spatial relations (S)—measured by tests requiring mental manipulation of symbols or geometric designs

Word fluency (W)—measured by tests requiring rapid production of words

Memory (M)—measured by tests requiring recall of words, sentences, and paired associates

Reasoning (R)—measured by tests of analogies and series of completions

However, Thurstone's factor analysis did not find that primary factors related to each other. However, as a result of further work with these tests he did find some relationship among the factors. He describes this relationship as a second-order factor.

Guilford and the Structure of Intellect   Guilford (1967) was dissatisfied with the various models that evolved from factor analysis. Following extensive research in measurement, he conceived a model that he named the *Structure of Intellect*. The model is a theoretical one that is psychometric and information-processing based.

The Structure of Intellect is a comprehensive extension of the *multifactor* theory that takes the form of a three-dimensional or cubelike model. It consists of five *mental operations* (cognition, memory, divergent production, convergent production, and evaluation); four kinds of *contents* (figural, symbolic, semantic, and behavioral); and six kinds of informational forms or *products* (units, classes, relations, systems, transformations, and implications). In all there are a total of 120 (or 5 x 4 x 6) intellectual abilities. These were recently increased to 150 abilities by breaking figural content into visual and auditory dimensions (Guilford,

Figure 3.5 The Structure of Intellect

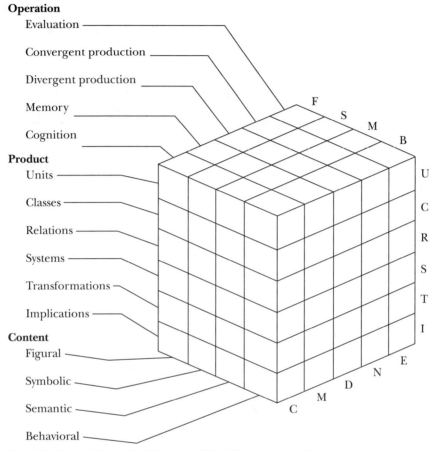

From *The Nature of Human Intelligence* (p. 63) by J.P. Guilford, 1967, New York: McGraw-Hill. Copyright © 1967 McGraw-Hill. Reprinted by permission.

1982). Each of the abilities is distinguished from the rest by its unique interactive combination of mental operation, content, and product (Figure 3.5).

1. Operation The five major kinds of intellectual activities involved in the processing of raw materials of information are included in the *operation* dimension. Briefly, the operation of *cognition* is knowing. In terms of information-processing psychology, cognition is a matter of coding or constructing items of information. The operation of *memory* stores (or fixes) and retrieves information in the brain. The operations of *divergent production* and *convergent production* are similar in that each depends on retrieval of information from storage. They differ in the following way:

in divergent production, the information is more or less open and a number of different or alternative productions are logically possible and may occur, and in convergent production the given information is restrictive to one fully acceptable response. The operation of *evaluation* involves comparison and judgment relative to certain criteria.

2. Content   The content dimension consists of five broad classes of information. *Figural* (visual, auditory, and kinesthetic) content refers to concrete forms of information perceived as images. *Symbolic* content relates to information in the form of denotative signs that have no significance (e.g., letters, numbers, and words) when the things for which they stand are not considered. *Semantic* content relates to information that is meaningful and may occur in verbal, numerical, musical, or pictorial form. *Behavioral* content relates to essentially nonverbal information that involves the attitudes, needs, desires, moods, intentions, perceptions, thoughts, and the like, that occur in human interactions.

3. Product   After an individual processes information, it takes the form of products. There are six kinds of products. *Units* are taken as wholes and without analysis; through their various combinations the remaining five product forms are derived. *Classes* are three or more units of information categorized or grouped together by their common properties. *Relations* are associated units of information that are meaningfully connected. *Systems* are organized sets of units of information that comprise interrelated or interacting parts. *Transformations* are changes in the form or the functioning of information and involve redefinition, revision, and modification. *Implications* are extrapolations of information that take the form of expectancies, predictions, or known or suspected consequences.

Triarchic Intelligence

Robert J. Sternberg (1981, 1984a) designed an information-processing model that he called a *componential* or *triarchic theory of human intelligence*. In making a case for his theory, Sternberg suggested that the psychometric approach has not produced measures that adequately differentiate among mental processes, in terms of content (e.g., verbal from spatial) and knowledge. Hence, he suggested the need for a theory of intelligence based on information-processing.

According to his model, the basic unit of analysis is found in information-processing and is not found in common factor or psychometric theory. Sternberg makes this distinction between a component and a factor: a *component* emphasizes the activity of elementary information-processing; a *factor* comprises latent sources of individual differences. Single factors may contain multiple components that can be organized to generate similar patterns of individual differences (Sternberg, 1980). Other differences between the psychometric approach and the Sternberg model relate to (a) *stimulus* variation (component) versus *subject* or individual variation (factor), and (b) the ease with which intelligent behavior can be falsified.

In his triarchy of intelligence, Sternberg describes three broad, information processing components for characterizing gifted individuals.

1. Metacomponents—higher-order executive processes used for deciding on the nature of the problem and selecting a strategy for solving it
2. Performance components—nonexecutive processes used for executing a problem-solving strategy
3. Knowledge acquisition—the process of acquiring new information, retention, and transfer components or skills involved in learning, retrieval, and generalization of information

The components are a highly interactive system such that they can activate one another with metacomponents as central elements in the system. These processes should adequately account for intellectual tasks used in the laboratory or in tests of intelligence.

Sternberg asserted that gifted individuals have easier access to components and the quality and quantity of the interactions. Gifted individuals are also more sensitive to the feedback provided by the component. Furthermore, the gifted have these processes organized in ways that lead to novel and insightful thinking (Sternberg, 1984b).

Sternberg makes a valid case for the componential theory of intelligence but points out that it is different from the factor approach. Although both are information-processing based, Sternberg's view is especially different from Guilford's view. Guilford conceptualizes intelligence more broadly, thereby providing more ways for understanding it. However, Sternberg's research findings provide support for both approaches.

Multiple Intelligence

Unlike the statistical techniques of factor analysis used by L. L. Thorndike and J. P. Guilford, Howard Gardner (1987, 1988) used *subjective factoring of information*, considering the various ways people can be bright. Furthermore, Gardner believes the I.Q. concept must not only be challenged but replaced. In its place, he suggests a list of *seven intelligences* as a preliminary attempt to subjectively factor or organize a mass of information that is not in a form for computer assimilation and analyses.

1. Linguistic intelligence—the ability to use language in a literary sense
2. Logical mathematical intelligence—logical, mathematical, and scientific ability

3. Spatial intelligence—the ability to form a mental model of a spatial world including the ability to maneuver and operate it according to the model
4. Musical intelligence—the ability to use the language of music
5. Bodily-kinesthetic intelligence—the ability to solve problems or to fashion them using parts of the body or the whole body
6. Interpersonal intelligence—the ability to understand other people and their motivations, and to know how to work alone or cooperatively with others
7. Intrapersonal intelligence—a correlative ability turned inward, and a capacity to form an accurate and truthful model of self that can be used to operate effectively in life

In this way, Gardner makes a strong case for the plurality of intelligence whose seven dimensions work together to solve problems. His conceptual contributions do not differ from the intellectual categories advanced by factor analysts, but the approach he has taken is unique. Like Guilford's Structure of Intellect, Gardner's seven intelligences are capable of development and facilitated by formal schooling. He is currently involved with David Feldman in two programs—Project Spectrum and Arts Propel—to further his goals in developing procedures for testing and educational facilitation.

CREATIVE THINKING

Until recently, the main method of identifying gifted children was by means of their general intelligence. Theories of general mental ability have expanded, becoming a multifaceted phenomenon rather than a unitary one. This reached prime articulation in the Structure of Intellect (Guilford, 1950, 1967). The model provided the rationale for considering gifted individuals in many different ways. Particularly important is the focus that Guilford gave to *divergent production* abilities within the operations face of his cube model. These abilities are sometimes referred to as *creativity.*

Theory of Creativity

Creativity is recognized as a very complex concept (e.g., Gowan, 1972; Roweton, 1973; Torrance, 1974b, 1988). In terms of its measurement correlates, this complexity is a great source of apprehension. Considerable lack of agreement exists over the definition of creativity (Torda, 1970) because, through usage, the term has become associated with various aspects of creative behavior and mental functioning that range along a cognitive-emotive continuum. This lack of agreement has been further complicated by the great number of definitions concerning the energy source for creativity—depending on which theoretical model of human functioning serves as the frame of reference.

Two theoretical classifications of creativity, one by J. C. Gowan and the other by W. E. Roweton, provide useful generic categories of the subject.

Gowan's Classification of Creativity
Gowan (1972) has classified creativity theory along a rational-psychedelic continuum as follows:

Creativity as cognitive, rational, and semantic This classification places creativity within the realm of problem solving and recalls the studies of S. J. Parnes, J. P. Guilford, and others who were interested in creativity as a component of intellect.

Creativity as personal and environmental relative to child-rearing practices This concern expressed, for instance, by R. J. Hallman and E. P. Torrance is more heavily weighted toward personality correlates that hinge on originality, energy, and, in particular, self-concept.

Creativity as a high degree of mental health Studies with this orientation were produced by figures such as A. H. Maslow and C. R. Rogers. They emphasize openness to experience and antiauthoritarian influences.

Creativity as Freudian Sigmund Freud described creativity as the sublimation of the sexual urge, which is a source of artistic activity and the main source of cultural energy, compensation, and the collective unconscious. From this has sprung the candid neo-Freudian view that the *oedipal crisis*, which occurs during the narcissistic stage, is the genesis of creative functioning. A variation of this theme views creative accomplishments as sublimations of aggressive, phallic, or incestuous desires, and hence, as refinements of basic drives and primary processes. The preconscious is viewed as the source of creativity, and its development is considered central.

Creativity as psychedelic This classification traces the connections among creativity and hypnotism, extrasensory perception, and other paranormal aspects, such as precognition.

Much of what Gowan suggested about creativity and the way we draw on it is related to opening up the preconscious and bringing that material to the conscious level. He intimates that this activity is both governable and ungovernable; creativity can be called on at will and also act as a latent force that rises to the surface on its own.

Roweton's Classification of Creativity

Roweton (1973) suggested six theoretical approaches to the interpretation of creativity: *definitional, behavioristic, dispositional, humanistic, psychoanalytic,* and *operational.* The psychoanalytic, humanistic, and operational approaches are quite similar to Gowan's classifications of Freudian, mental health, and cognitive-rational-semantic approaches, respectively. The dispositional approach is similar to Gowan's mental health and cognitive-rational-semantic classifications.

According to Roweton, the *definitional* approach attempts to conceptualize creativity, and although this is not easily verified empirically, it often provides psychologists with a rich source of testable hypotheses.

The *behavioristic* approach to creativity recognizes association and reinforcement theories and the effects of incubation and transfer. This perspective is valuable because it embodies a more parsimonious expression of creativity, for it is based on observable behaviors and performances. Although inferences are not easily drawn or deductions easily made, the data are at least concrete.

Definition of Creativity

The term *creativity* is defined by its theoretical source and has to be thought of in a relevant context. Lack of agreement concerning definition of this term can be traced not only to the many different ways people can be creative (Torrance, 1988), but also to the fact that explanations of these behaviors derive meaning in part from referential theoretical models. Hence, it is necessary to describe and define operationally the particular abilities that people possess.

Among the many cogent earlier definitions relative to creative thinking as a *process* are the following:

Thinking by analogy (Ribot, 1906)

The initiative to break away from the usual sequence of thought into an altogether different pattern of thought (M. Simpson, 1922)

The process of seeing relationships with both conscious and subconscious processes operating for the eduction of relations and correlates (Spearman, 1930)

The distinction between *cogito,* or the ability to shake and throw things together, and *intelligo,* or the ability to choose and discriminate among many possibilities for synthesizing and binding together elements in original ways (Barchillon, 1961)

At no other time in the history of measurement have we had so many attempts to operationalize creativity for its scientific identification. Following are some of the definitions of creativity that have led to the production of measures of creativity:

> Intellectual operations relative to divergent production, transformation, and redefinition; and abilities set in motion by a sensitivity to problems (Guilford, 1967)
>
> The process of sensing gaps or disturbing missing elements and forming hypotheses concerning them, testing these hypotheses, communicating the results, and possibly modifying and retesting the hypotheses (Torrance, 1962a)
>
> The ability to generate or produce within some criterion of relevance many cognitive associates, many of which are unique (Wallach & Kogan, 1965)
>
> The power of the imagination to break away from perceptual set to structure ideas, thoughts, and feelings into novel and meaningful associative bonds (Khatena & Torrance, 1990)
>
> Creativity operationalized as traits of a person, products generated, thinking process involved, and functioning under conditions of stress or press (Rhodes, 1961)

Guilford and Divergent Production

Guilford's definition of intelligence—as a systematic collection of abilities or functions for processing different kinds of information in different ways using *contents* and *products*—includes creativity and fits within the realm of the Structure of Intellect. The mental operation involved in the informational processing component of the model is divergent production (Guilford, 1975).

Guilford defined *divergent production* as a set of factors or intellectual abilities that pertain primarily to information retrieval, which, in testing, calls for varied responses to each test item. Testees of divergent production are required to produce their own answers and not to choose from alternatives given to them. Of special relevance to creative thinking are abilities having to do with fluency, flexibility, originality, and elaboration.

Fluency
Fluency is an ability measured by the ready flow of ideas and relating to all divergent production tests. In particular, these production tests apply to three traditional kinds of tests in the semantic category that have parallel abilities in the figural and other content areas—*ideational fluency*

(divergent production of semantic units or DMU), *associational fluency* (divergent production of meaningful relations or DMR), and *expressional fluency* (divergent production of meaningful systems or DMS).

Flexibility

Flexibility involves *spontaneous flexibility*, or changes in an individual's direction of thinking without instruction or requirements to do so. Flexibility also involves *adaptive flexibility* or changes in an individual's direction of thinking to solve problems.

Originality

Originality is the ability to produce responses that are statistically rare in the population and remotely related and clever.

Elaboration

Elaboration is the ability to add details to basic ideas produced. Guilford (1967) attempted to measure creative thinking by applying the mental operation category of *divergent production* and the product category of *transformation*. Either or both of these are involved in the thinking episode and are the source of novel ideas. He used a test format that generally requires a person to respond to many stimuli, each of which measures a specific ability that simultaneously requires the interactive involvement of thinking operation, content, and product.

Torrance and Creative Thinking

Torrance (1974b) approached creativity quite differently. He attempted to measure creative thinking through the presentation of several complex tasks designed to trigger the expression of several creative thinking abilities. Like Guilford, he gave major roles to *fluency, flexibility, originality,* and *elaboration*.

Torrance's (1989a) scoring and interpretive manual, relative to the Torrance figural tests, has identified five norm-referenced measures: *fluency, originality, abstractness of titles, elaboration,* and *resistance to premature closure*. In addition, 13 criterion-referenced measures are identified.

Expression of feeling/emotion in drawings/titles
Articulateness in telling a story; context and environment
Movement/action (running, dancing, flying, falling, etc.)
Expressiveness of titles
Combination of two or more incomplete figures
Combination of two or more repeated figures
Unusual visual perspective (as seen from above, below, etc.)
Internal visual perspective (inside, cross section, etc.)

Extending/breaking boundaries
Humor in titles/captions/drawings
Richness of imagery (variety, vividness, strength, etc.)
Colorfulness of imagery (excitingness, earthiness, etc.)
Fantasy (figures in myths, fables, fairy tales, science fiction, etc.)

Torrance's definition of creativity given earlier in the chapter is central to his measures of creative mental functioning. He annotates the definition in terms of strong human needs.

> If we sense some incompleteness or disharmony, tension is aroused. We are uncomfortable and want to relieve the tension. Since learned ways of behaving are inadequate, we begin trying to avoid the commonplace and obvious (but incorrect) solutions by investigating, diagnosing, manipulating, and making guesses or estimates. Until the guesses or hypotheses have been tested, modified, and retested, we are still uncomfortable. The tension is unrelieved, however, until we tell somebody of our discovery. (Torrance, 1974b, p. 8)

INTELLIGENCE AND CREATIVITY

The selection of gifted students in the Terman studies was done solely on the basis of general intelligence defined by I.Q. and measured by the Stanford-Binet or Terman Concept Mastery Test. Of course, at the time the Terman studies began (1925), there were no effective intellectual measures that could yield a better index of superior abilities than the Stanford-Binet I.Q. In fact at the first Minnesota Conference on Gifted Children, it was pointed out that Terman's proposed genius or near-genius category challenged educators, sociologists, and psychologists to produce, if they could, "another concept as effective as I.Q., for delimiting of a group of talent to include the most successful students, the best achievers in the academic world, and, as he (Terman) believed, in the world of human relationships and human endeavor generally" (Miles, 1960, p. 51).

The assumption underlying the validity of a prestigious individual measure of intelligence, like the Stanford-Binet or a Wechsler scale, as the sole criterion for identifying the gifted went unchallenged (Torrance, 1962a). If any dissent was heard, it related to the measurement of special talents, for instance, art, music, and drama (Gallagher, 1966).

Some very pertinent questions were asked about the content validity of I.Q. measures as adequate identifiers of all kinds of giftedness. For example, Spearman (1927) brought to our notice that, in addition to general mental ability (g), there were specific abilities (s) in human mental functioning. Others, like Guilford (1950) and Thurstone (1924), were telling us that we should consider an intellect that comprised many abilities rather than a single general mental ability. Guilford's presidential address at the American Psychological Association 1950 Annual Convention on the Structure of Intellect presented the intellect as a complex three-dimensional model of abilities. The questions that arose found focus in investigations that attempted to differentiate other mental functioning than the functioning tested by I.Q. measures. For instance, I.Q. measures were found to be deficient in items that called for divergent or creative thinking. It was not that Terman was unaware of the existence of this dimension of mental functioning—as can be seen in two of his tests constructed for his first study of seven bright and seven dull boys, namely, tests for *inventiveness, imagination,* and *insight*—but his conceptions of these tended to border close to *convergent production.*

The most obvious emphasis of I.Q. measures was on *cognition, memory,* and *convergent production.* It led C. W. Taylor to state that intelligence is a concept created by Western culture that stresses important Western values. He maintains that tests of intelligence in our culture

> essentially concerned themselves with how fast relatively unimportant problems can be solved without making errors [whereas in another culture] intelligence might be a measure more in terms of how adequately important problems can be solved making all the errors necessary and without regard for time. (Taylor, 1959, p. 54)

Guilford (1950) had remarked that if we were to study the domain of creativity, we need to look far beyond the boundaries of I.Q. He also stated that the conception of "creative talent, to be accounted for in terms of high intelligence or I.Q. . . . is not only inadequate but has been largely responsible for lack of progress in the understanding of creative people" (p. 454). His predictions that correlations of scores on intelligence and creativity tests would be moderate or low and that the highly creative could probably not be highly intelligent sparked a series of studies in the 1960s that tended to support these predictions.

The well-known Getzels and Jackson (1962) study was one attempt to look at the relationship between creativity and intelligence as well as at a number of other variables that related to these two areas. They administered creativity tests to 533 students (292 boys and 241 girls) whose average I.Q. was 130, but depended on school records for intelligence test scores as derived from the Henmon-Nelson Tests of Mental Ability, the Stanford-Binet, and, to a lesser extent, the Wechsler Intelligence Scale for Children. Using this information, they selected the top 20% on creativity tests and the top 20% on I.Q. tests (matched for sex and age), excluding those students who were in the top 20% on both measures of creativity and intelligence. Comparing the performance of 24 highly creative and 28 highly intelligent students on total scholastic achievement, they found that, although there was a difference of 23 I.Q. points between the high creative group and the high I.Q. group, both groups performed equally well on scholastic achievement. This led them to conclude that creativity was just as important as, if not more important than, intelligence for scholastic achievement.

They also found relatively low correlations between I.Q. and performance tests that required the use of creative thinking abilities, and attributed these low correlations to the high mean I.Q. bias of their sample. Similar findings were obtained with less extreme groups as well.

Torrance (1962a), in eight partial replications of this study, arrived at similar conclusions about the relationship between intelligence and creativity. His findings led him to conclude that the selection of the top 20% on I.Q. measures would exclude 70% of the top 20% on creativity measures, implying that correlations between intelligence and creativity are low, and that creativity tests identify the gifted better than intelligence tests.

Although these findings were considered a breakthrough by some for understanding the *intelligence-creativity* distinction, they were not so considered by others (e.g., McNemar, 1964; Wallach, 1970). Among the deficiencies of the Getzels and Jackson (1962) study are:

1. The authors failed to administer a single intelligence test to all subjects at the time creativity tests were administered and, therefore, failed to control for the variance introduced by use of old information derived from multiple-test data records.
2. The study excluded the top 20% of subjects on both intelligence and creativity measures.
3. The researchers failed to report basic correlations between creativity, intelligence, and achievement.

Some of these disagreements concerning the *intelligence-creativity* distinction can be traced to the more basic problem of the validity of creativity measures or how much these measures identify actual creativity, which is prized by our society. McNemar (1964) in an article entitled "Lost: Our Intelligence? Why?" expressed concern over the changing emphasis placed on I.Q. that resulted from factor analytic research. He concluded that general intelligence has not been lost in the trend to test for more and more abilities; it has been misplaced by the expectation that factor analysis can identify those factors that, when and if measured, are socially useful.

On the matter of creativity research findings, McNemar observed that creativity tests do not yield high correlations with I.Q. measures whose uncurtailed scatter would be bivariate normal. McNemar also suggested that, if suitable criterion measures of literary, architectural, or scientific creativity were available, the relationship between I.Q. and creativity, as shown by a scattergram, would be triangular in shape.

This would explain why a wide range of creativity exists at high I.Q. levels whereas the scatter for creativity is less and less as I.Q. levels go down to average or low. McNemar also concluded that having a high I.Q. does not guarantee creativity, whereas having a low I.Q. means creativity is impossible.

Michael A. Wallach (1970), in his appraisal of the study of the relationship between creativity and intelligence, concluded that the kind of creativity measures used in a study like the ones used by Getzels and Jackson show much higher relations than were earlier reported (e.g., Hassan & Butcher, 1966). Wallach also noted that these creativity measures do nothing but measure general intelligence. Both these observations are consistent with the issues raised by Wallach and Kogan (1965) who make a case against the Torrance Tests of Creative Thinking and for the instruments that they constructed to measure creative thinking abilities.

Finally, Anne Anastasi and Charles E. Schaefer (1971) also pointed out that it is erroneous to regard intelligence and creativity as independent and distinct entities. They state that, generally, intelligence and creativity test scores correlate with each other almost as highly as individual intelligence test scores correlate with each other.

Wallach and H. D. Wing (1969), exploring the creativity-intelligence problem, make it quite clear that an intelligence measure, although useful for predicting academic success, is useless for predicting talented accomplishments outside the classroom. These accomplishments require measures that elicit ideational productivity and uniqueness of ideas. They say that alternative bases for talent identification are essential, and suggest that substantive guidelines need to be set for the purpose.

An interesting focus on the relationship of intelligence and creativity was given by Wallach and Kogan (1965) when 151 fifth grade pupils (70 boys and 81 girls) were classified as intelligent and creative above or below the median on the basis of their test scores. They fell into four groups: high-intelligent/high-creative, high-intelligent/low-creative, low-intelligent/high-creative, and low-intelligent/low-creative. In this way, Wallach and Kogan presented a model that brought into sharp focus the interactive effects of both dimensions of intellect—intelligence and creativity. Behaviors of each of the four groups were defined and included in a 2 x 2 model (Table 3.1).

T. E. Newland (1976), commenting on Wallach and Kogan's model, suggests that an analysis of a comparable grade level relative to different socioeconomic levels would add further meaning to it, and that a longitudinal study of similar dimensions would also be appropriate. Perhaps a study of these interactive elements relative to different ethnic groups (beginning at earlier grade levels and going up to the senior high school grades), living in rural and urban areas, would provide fuller and more valuable evidence.

We have to note that intelligence measures do not set out to appraise a person's ability to be creative, imaginative, inventive, and original. Hence, when intelligence measures are administered to groups these measures will only identify individuals who have the ability to memorize, to generalize and evaluate, to give a single solution to a problem, to show understanding of factual information and meaning of words, and to comprehend certain kinds of verbal and numerical relationships that call for single right answers. People who think beyond these dimensions are, therefore, incorrectly assessed and often appear to be less bright or gifted than they really are. If we want to identify producers of knowledge as well as conservers of knowledge, we need to heed the caution that I.Q. is not a universal measure of giftedness.

Other insights into the relationship of intelligence and creativity are offered by Getzels and Jackson (1958, 1960, 1961). Their studies differentiate between highly creative and highly intelligent adolescents of Grades 7 through 12 as follows:

1. Highly creative and highly intelligent adolescents were equally superior on achievement tests, in spite of a difference of 23 mean I.Q. points.
2. Teachers considered high-I.Q. adolescents more desirable students than their high-creative peers.
3. High-creatives showed a predisposition to take greater risks, to be independent, and to enjoy the uncertainty of the unknown.
4. High-creatives were more proficient at producing new forms and more willing to combine elements that appear independent and dissimilar than were high-I.Q. adolescents.
5. More high-I.Q. adolescents preferred conventional occupations, such as medicine, law, engineering, and so on, whereas high-creative adolescents preferred unconventional occupations, such as those relative to invention, writing, and so on.

Following interviews with parents of both groups of adolescents, Getzels and Jackson (1961) found that when compared to parents of high-I.Q. adolescents parents of high-creative adolescents showed the following characteristics:

1. They did not appear to make much mention of their financial troubles.
2. They were less inclined to convey their present feelings of personal insecurity, whether real or imagined.
3. They were less conscious and alert to their children's academic achievement.

Table 3.1 Personality Traits of Fifth Grade Boys and Girls Scoring High and Low in Intelligence and Creativity

| | Creativity | | | |
| | High | | Low | |
	Boys	Girls	Boys	Girls
High Intelligence	Acute degree of interpersonal sensitivity Sharp awareness of own identity and integrity in midst of adults and peers Sense of warmth, but sense of objectivity in relations with others Earnestness and seriousness in matters concerning human beings Maturity coupled with tolerance for being boylike—a simultaneous awareness of adult and peer group frames of reference and capacity to remain in contact with both	Strong powers of integration and structuring in combination with ability to range freely and imaginatively with rich affect and enthusiastic involvement Come to grips with these and more controlled ways of functioning Display social awareness and sensitivity to emotional expression in others	Overriding concern with academic success Strong desire for academic excellence Sense of competition with peers or siblings for status in eyes of adults Intellective success perceived as critically important determinant of their standing with significant adults Preoccupied with how such adults view them Narrowing down and rigidifying of intellectual behavior as consequence of their so sedulous pursuit of success Exceptionally low levels of general and test anxiety High defensiveness suggesting presence of coping mechanisms for adequate handling of failure stresses in pursuit of success	Rather mechanical use of academic achievement as means of attaining status and success with impression that such achievement has more the meaning of reducing pain than increasing pleasure To get this achievement, may work long hours at their studies for fear of criticism Affectively, hold themselves carefully within bounds relative to their own expression and their perceptions of others Inhibit themselves emotionally to do well in school

TABLE 5.1 (continued)

| | Creativity | | | |
| | High | | Low | |
	Boys	Girls	Boys	Girls
Low Intelligence	Give the impression of being engaged in battle against others and/or themselves Sensitivity to and therefore anger over own inadequacies Angry lashing out at the world and supersensitivity to signs of rejection from others Confidence appears shattered Engaged in various defensive and constructive maneuvers aimed at establishing self-worth Magnitudes of forces involved in these battles great because of their articulated sensitivities Detailed exploration of what other people think of them Introspective exploration of themselves, artistic ability	React negatively to school pressure Anger and resentment toward school setting, regressive listlessness and/or mischief in response to academic demands Social shyness and withdrawal prominent Free and even wild imaginings—possibly more extreme because tinged with rebelliousness and even revealed in strongly nurturant adult environment that invokes no sanctions of academic failure and success	Simple avoidance or giving up, of resignations to a sour fate relative to academic activities Blustering hyperactivity Basic sense of bewilderment, tend to seek comfort by some means or other (e.g., through melting into peer group, through protection from sympathetic adults, or through mischief)	Try to deal with poor intellectual performance Do not seem to know how to cope successfully with academic tasks and at least resort to imitating surface behaviors that reflect successful coping by others (e.g., trying to appear assertive, and being neat in one's work) Fear and depression over academic failure present at worst Frustration over academic work leads to use of relatively infantile defenses (e.g., being cruel and vengeful toward children who are weak, being passive and unresponsive in classroom, or developing psychosomatic complaints)

Note. From Modes of Thinking in Young Children (p. 269–285) by M. A. Wallach & N. Kogan, 1965, New York: John Wiley & Sons, Inc.

4. They were less critical of the school and their children.
5. They expressed greater concern for their children's values, interests, enthusiasms, and were open to their experiences.

SPECIFIC ACADEMIC APTITUDE

Gifted children may also be identified by their superior capacity in one or more academic areas, such as language, mathematics, science, and social studies. In terms of the various models of intelligence, specific academic aptitude would relate, for instance, to the specific verbal-educational abilities of Vernon's hierarchical model or the symbolic and semantic dimensions of Guilford's Structure of Intellect.

In terms of the Vernon model, the mental energy at work is g, whereas in the Guilford model, there would be the five mental operations of *cognition, memory, convergent production, divergent production,* and *evaluation.* Of the two models, Guilford's tends to be highly operational. He defines the mental operations and content (symbolic and semantic) with which they work and the product form to be processed and the eventual form it takes (units, classes, relations, systems, transformations, and implications). In this way, we have at least 60 (5 x 2 x 6) intellectual abilities that may be involved in the learning of academic subjects.

If *specific academic aptitude* means the potential to do better in certain subject areas than in others, then measures of intellectual abilities, generally, and the subtests of these measures, specifically, may be used to predict aptitude. However, if *specific academic aptitude* means performance in the academic subject areas, then abilities should be measured with respect to the specific areas such as language or mathematics. Predicting excellence in an academic subject could be done by administering tests to measure ability in a subject area rather than just knowledge of the subject.

Language capacity, for example, may be determined by measuring a child's understanding of factual, emotive, tonal, and intentional forms of language. Ability could also be measured by testing the use of language that involves analogy and the use of language for productive thinking and evaluation. Briefly, testing should determine the ability to handle the symbolic and semantic systems of language.

In mathematics, the aim should be to test for capacity to use the symbolic and semantic systems of numbers. This may involve children's exhibition of their ability to handle number sets, probability, deductive and inductive thinking, and the like.

Measures are available to test for achievement levels in the various academic subject areas. Achievement scores obtained can be used to interpolate a specific academic aptitude. Where a measure of academic aptitude is available, for instance on an intelligence test, this may also be used.

LEADERSHIP ABILITY

The ability to manage and represent people and initiate events and situations on behalf of others is defined as *leadership ability*. Such ability requires a person to be bright; to understand people; to know the mechanics of behavior in groups; to be aware of strategies of individual and group managements; to be sensitive to changes; and to possess the creativity to handle the dynamics of human behavior, interaction, and change. Leadership ability draws its energy from intellectual and affective sources of human functioning.

The Structure of Intellect model offers one explanation of this dimension of giftedness, particularly in terms of the *behavioral* component. Behavioral content relates essentially to nonverbal information that involves attitudes, needs, desires, moods, intentions, perceptions, and thoughts that occur in human interactions. The behavioral component of intellect, the five mental operations (cognition, memory, convergent production, divergent production and evaluation), and the six products (units, classes, relations, systems, transformations and implications) offer a reasonably good model for the assessment of abilities for leadership roles. Other explanations of leadership are offered by Gardner's (1988) interpersonal and intrapersonal intelligence and Sternberg's (1988) practical intelligence.

However, leadership studies over the years have revealed that ability of an individual is one of several dimensions. Other dimensions relate to the group of which the individual is a member, the task or situation at hand, the motivational and reinforcement variables of the relationships, and interaction effects of all of these. Each of these and their interactions have important parts to play in leadership.

Unlike the other four USOE categories of giftedness, the attributes of leadership cannot be considered entirely personal. Furthermore, leadership ability is not something inherited, although certain ability predispositions appear to be present. Rather, leadership appears to be emergent, depending on the sociocultural group context and the specific situation.

Leadership has been defined, for instance, as the interaction of personality traits and situations (Fiedler, 1964), as a complex social phenomena of personal and social factors (Gowan & Demos, 1962), or as a product of functional relationships with specific individuals in specific situations (Knickerbocker, 1948). Leadership has also been described as an emergent phenomenon created through interaction of leaders and followers where an individual's status in a group is a joint function of a person's personality, the particular group setting, and the perceptions of followers (Mann, 1959).

Research evidence (e.g., Fiedler, 1964; Stogdill, 1974) is not without contradiction. However, the current view favors the concept of leadership as emergent within the context of individual-group-situation interactions. One early theory on the subject regards the leader as a *great man*, someone endowed with outstanding characteristics that impel him to direct the affairs of others. Another, the *times theory*, defines leadership in terms of a social situation where a leader is needed for a particular task at a particular time. Leadership as *effective influence* (Gibb, 1947) involves interactions of the individual and the social situation so that the group allows for the expression of this ability. In such a circumstance, the influence exerted by the individual must be voluntarily accepted by the group for it to become effective. Where influence is one of domination, leadership is accepted with resentment. Where the influence is symbolic, leadership is not powerful enough to influence the group.

The *trait theory* approach requires the identification of qualities or characteristics of leadership potential. However, a review of this approach (Gibb, 1947; Mann, 1959; Stogdill, 1948) indicated that, in itself, the trait theory approach is insufficient. To have any relevance, a trait or pattern of traits had to be considered in the context of situations. And when the situations differed radically, the qualities and characteristics for different situations varied accordingly.

The *interaction theory* of leadership draws from earlier theories and includes studies of personality variables. Leadership behavior is related to such attributes as intelligence and formal education, extroversion, assertiveness, and social maturity (Fleishman, 1973; McGarth & Altman, 1966). Interpersonal sensitivity to interaction approaches to leadership were also recognized (e.g., Fiedler, 1967; Mann, 1959; Stogdill, 1974).

One of the interaction theoretical approaches is the *interaction-expectation theory* that has three versions: the *expectation-reinforcement theory* of role attainment (Stogdill, 1959), the *path-goal theory* of leadership (Evans, 1970), and *motivational theory* (House & Dressler, 1974). An *interaction-expectation* theory of leadership includes three basic components: action, interaction, and sentiments. The increase in one component is accompanied by a proportionate increase in the other two. The leader's role is to originate interaction and maintain structure until the group matches its expectations. The leader also determines the path for the group by providing guidance, direction, support, and rewards.

Another approach to interaction theory is *contingency theory* (Fiedler, 1964). *Contingency theoretical models* generally assume that no universally good leaders exist, and that there are a variety of leadership styles that are effective according to particular situations (Chemers & Rice, 1974). Fiedler (1964) developed the most widely accepted contingency model of leadership that specified that the effectiveness of leadership performance depends on the leader's motivational pattern, which is contingent on *situational favorableness*—the extent to which situations are favorable or advantageous.

The three important ingredients of situational favorableness are as follows: followers' acceptance of the leader; a clear outline by the leader of the task and procedures for completing it, which outline must be accurately perceived by the followers; and the leader's power to reward or punish followers. A leader possesses certain attributes that are stable, enduring, and determined by situations. However, although these attributes may *appear* to change with changes in a situation, actually the attributes—which are more organized toward group activity and are relatively central to the individual—do not change.

The theories and research about leadership suggest that a number of important variables have to be taken into account to identify leadership. These variables relate to personal qualities of the individual leader in the context of the dynamics of the group, the interactive relationship in different situations, and the perceived goals, rewards, or punishment of followers. All in all, leadership is a complex of many variables, which is succinctly summarized by Stogdill's extensive review of the research and theory on the subject.

> The findings suggest that leadership is not a matter of passive status, or of the mere possession of some combination of traits. It appears rather to be a working relationship among members of a group, in which the leader acquires status through active participation and demonstration of his capacity for carrying cooperative tasks through completion. Significant aspects of this capacity for organizing and expediting cooperative effort appear to be intelligence, alertness to the needs and motives of others, and insight into situations, further reinforced by such habits as responsibility, initiative, persistence, and self-confidence. (Stogdill, 1974, p. 65)

VISUAL AND PERFORMING ARTS ABILITY

Ability in the visual and performing arts is more appropriately considered an ability in one or more of the fine arts. *Visual arts*, in the context of the gifted, mean drawing, painting, sculpturing, designing, composing music, and all other related forms of art whose products are tangibles and can be observed. *Performing arts* comprise music, dance, oratory, drama, and all other related forms of art that require performance.

Abilities required for superior production or performance are not easy to measure. Few, if any, adequate psychological measures are available for this purpose. Although there are many methods available to measure musical ability, they are generally regarded as incomplete identifiers or as technically inadequate (Lehman, 1968). Measures of art ability are fewer and even less appropriate as identifiers of talent. Measures of dramatic ability are almost nonexistent. Researchers may have to rely on the observable behaviors and products of individuals to determine potential talent in the visual and performing arts when psychometry cannot help.

Intelligence has been recognized as having some relevance for the visual and performing arts. Changing conceptions of intelligence have not left these specialized areas of talent unaffected. Measurements of music ability, for instance, reflect some of this change. Some test constructors of music tend to reflect a *g* factor in their measures (e.g., Kwalwasser & Dykema, 1930; Wing, 1961), whereas others tend to reflect the multi-abilities model (e.g., E. Gordon, 1965; Seashore, Lewis & Saetveit, 1960). Generally, however, those individuals who show themselves to have extraordinary talent in the arts tend to be highly gifted intellectually (e.g., Passow, Goldberg, Tannenbaum, & French, 1955) although they may not necessarily show this superiority on an I.Q. test.

Another aspect of importance is the *symbolic system* that is acquired and used by individuals in special fields of talent. Musical notation provides the basis for the communication of music (although some have attempted to substitute a number system for it, for instance, in the Far East and Southeast Asia). Nonverbal systems are the substitute for the verbal in the visual arts and dance, unlike oratory and drama, which are dependent on the verbal language system for communication. Dance, acting, and oratory, use body language or symbols in performance.

Mental imagery is also an important component of thinking and expression in the visual and performing arts. In the various theoretical models of intellect, imagery lies in the nonverbal domain. Its role in art, music, dance, and acting is significant because imagery overcomes the barriers of intermediary symbolic systems to present visions that eventually find themselves expressed in one art form or another.

Common to all these art forms is *creativity*, a processing and energizing agent that differs in degree of operation, depending on the form of art used. On the subject of creativity and the visual arts, Guilford (1968) focused attention on the importance of three divergent production abilities in the figural dimension of the Structure of Intellect: fluency, flexibility, and elaboration. Communicating meaning in the visual arts is nonverbal and often involves these three divergent thinking abilities. Fluency in the figural information area is broken down into *ideational fluency* (or the ability to generate many ideas), *analogy fluency* (or the ability to produce many analogues), and *expressional fluency* (or the ability to organize figural information as systems rapidly). Two kinds of abilities relate to a shift in thinking from one category to another—*spontaneous flexibility* (or automatic shifts in thinking) and *adaptive flexibility* (or shifts in thinking owing to the need for different solutions to a single problem). Guilford considers *elaboration* very important to art when, early in a creative production, a general schema, motif, or plan develops that is psychologically a system that adds details as the system becomes distinct.

Other abilities have importance and relevance for creative artistic production. These abilities include the ability to visualize changes in figural information (or *transformation ability* outside the divergent production category), the ability to *evaluate* individual total production of an art object, and the ability in the behavioral category to transform semantic or behavioral information to figural information.

V. Lowenfield and W. L. Brittain (1964) discuss the creative and mental growth of talented children as related to art and identify five major characteristics. The first is *fluency of imagination and expression* (i.e., ideas spontaneously flow and imagery expands with the creative process as in a chain reaction). The second is a highly developed *sensibility toward movement, rhythm, content, and organization* (i.e., integration of thinking, feeling, and perceiving is experienced to a high degree by the talented person). The third is the *intuitive quality of imagination,* which is possessed to a high degree by the talented individual and is a source of imagery for the creative act. The fourth, *directness of expression,* relates to the self-confidence expressed by the gifted individual in the act of artistic creation. The fifth is a high degree of *self-identification* with the depicted experience that is exhibited by the gifted individual.

Highly specialized knowledge and skill, specific to each art form, must be acquired by individuals before they can express themselves in that medium. Because it takes time to acquire this knowledge and skill, it is not unusual to find that screening of young children for talent in the arts is difficult. However, this may be more a function of psychometrics than a real problem. A. Capurso (1961), citing two studies on the subject of emergence of musical giftedness, suggests that the talents of musically gifted children generally reveal themselves during early childhood: "With the exception of a few masters such as Berlioz, Tschaikovsky and Wagner, most of the great musicians revealed their artistic gifts before their teen years" (p. 318).

However, K. Sward's (1933) study of musicians who have performed in the New York Philharmonic and in the Boston, Chicago, and Philadelphia symphony orchestras showed that these musicians received instruction between the ages of 3 and 16, either under a master-teacher or in a conservatory. A few examples of this are Arthur Rubenstein (age 3); Jascha Heifetz (age 5); Harold Samuel and Gregor Piatigorsky (age 15); and Ossip Gabrilowitsch, Walter Gieseking, and Mischa Mischakoff (age

16). These examples suggest that, although musical talent may manifest itself through the whole range of the school years, maturation, environment, and other related variables do play significant roles in the emergence of musical talent, as they do in other forms of talent as well.

CONCLUSIONS

The five-dimensional Holistic Model for Educating Gifted Children should have provided a coherent understanding of the subject. Properly used it should explain the interrelations of each of the dimensions as the discussion of the subject of educating gifted children continues.

The first of the USOE categories of giftedness, general intellectual ability, suggests a single mental ability related to Binet's conception of general intelligence and, to a lesser extent, to Wechsler's conception of global capacity, and to Spearman, Burt, and Vernon's g factor. This category of giftedness can be traced to the strong influence of I.Q. and its extensive and dominant position over the years as the major criterion for the identification of the intellectually gifted.

General intellectual ability does not include the changing conceptions of the construct "intelligence" or the measures that have developed with it. However, the remaining five USOE categories of giftedness—creative or productive thinking, specific academic aptitude, leadership ability, visual and performing arts ability, and psychomotor ability—do bear relationship to the construct, although they are not clearly delineated as mental ability. Creative or productive thinking, for instance, can be identified in the Structure of Intellect model mainly as divergent thinking abilities.

Although overwhelming evidence suggests that pure intelligence is not measurable, intellectual activity is reflected by test tasks. Other evidence suggests that many different abilities are available, with one or more retrieved for handling an intellectual assignment on different occasions, and intelligence does not depend on learning. It would seem to be more appropriate to modify the term *general mental ability* or general intelligence to read many *intellectual abilities,* and to measure this by a general intelligence index and indices of intellectual excellence similar to those of the Guilford model.

The observation that 70% of the top 20% of subjects ranked on creativity tests are excluded from I.Q. tests suggests that I.Q. measures are not adequate as the sole criterion for identifying giftedness. The same may be said of creativity measures, which do not identify the conservers of knowledge at the upper levels of I.Q. This phenomenon seems to be more a function of measurement than of intellectual potential. If we are to accept Guilford's Structure of Intellect model, either kind of measure should contain items that require the use of mental operations of cognition, memory, convergent production, divergent production, and evaluation for any kind of approximate identification of intellectual functioning.

There is an increasing tendency to move away from a unidimensional index to multidimensional indices of intellectual functioning. In particular, if we want to know the function of specific abilities excluded from I.Q. measures, we must go to those measures that do deal with the functions of specific abilities. Only in this way can we derive reasonably appropriate clues concerning the identification of talent, for instance, in the areas of mechanical aptitude, mathematics, music, and art. Of course, we do know that more of the Spearman g is required for mathematics than for art, and that I.Q. measures give us a better prediction of mathematical ability. However, an appropriate special abilities test will more accurately differentiate those who can handle the symbol systems of the area at a superior level from those who cannot. This is not to say that we have available measures for all special abilities; for instance, we lack good measures in music and art. However, for music and art, the available measures of creativity may be helpful to differentiate between those who can develop great skill and those who can generate new skills and compose and innovate within the disciplines.

Academic aptitude, or the capacity to do well in school subjects, can best be approached by determining the level of achievement through standardized achievement tests. Although tests made by teachers can be used to measure the level of school learning at a particular point of time, their highly local and specific nature will not adequately serve the purpose. Besides, even standardized achievement tests are not designed and intended for superior students and may not have sufficient ceiling to discriminate the really top students from the rest.

Much is known about leadership and the qualities that are involved in it, but, as yet, research data that is helpful in designing procedures for the identification of leadership talent is lacking. The difficulty in obtaining such data is largely due to the complexity of this facet of ability, especially because it involves the possession of intellectual and creative thinking abilities, personality traits peculiar to the individual, and the dynamics of the individual and group as they interact relative to task and situational variables. Hence, any attempt to identify leadership talent must pivot on a multimodal approach.

At the highest levels of functioning in the visual and performing arts, intelligence, creativity, and feeling play important roles, apart from the language system that is unique to the art form used for communication. It has generally been found that the more musically talented child tends to show this in the earlier rather than the later school years. However, to speak in the language of music with fluency, originality, and maturity requires some mastery of the fundamentals of the language of music. This is more noticeable in the middle and later school years through early adulthood, although exceptions to this may be found in the precocity of music child prodigies.

It is more common to understand abilities as plural and multiple in dimension than to understand them as categorically singular. Even those who still subscribe to the concept of general intelligence, in terms of the Spearman g, have recognized other levels of mental functioning that are operationally subsumed below it. Besides, as has been pointed out, psychometric measures are not always available or appropriate to identify many kinds of abilities, nor do they tell everything about the human intellect. We have to rely on observation and subjective judgment to group the many forms of abilities or intelligences. Further, factor analyses, which have confirmed the presence of many abilities, may not be the final approach to take in adequately differentiating content and knowledge among mental processes as explained, for example, by the triarchic theory of human intelligence. Perhaps the important work of cognitive psychologists interested in developing measures of the intellect may provide the answers to more effective ways to identify our gifted. Yet, until this breakthrough occurs the best resources are the Structure of Intellect, the measures that in revised form identify many abilities, and the nonpsychometric approaches used to determine certain areas of abilities and talents.

CHAPTER FOUR

Identifying Intellectual and Creative Children

*I*NTRODUCTION

One of the chief concerns of educators and psychologists over recent years has been the proper identification of the gifted child. This concern found expression in the writing and research of many scholars, in numerous conferences on the gifted, and in the federal government's recognition of six categories of giftedness. The earlier chapters reflected on the fact that people may be gifted in a number of different ways and that to regard a person with a high I.Q. as gifted to the exclusion of other classes of giftedness is to ignore the greater gifted population. It is now necessary to include among the gifted people who are creative and productive thinkers, high achievers in school subjects, exceptional leaders, and talented in the visual and performing arts.

The major theoretical orientations of the five United States Office of Education (USOE) categories of giftedness, discussed in the previous chapter, have been the bases for the construction and use of instruments to measure intellectual potential. However, dissatisfaction with this approach at categorizing gifted individuals has been expressed by several scholars, particularly by Renzulli and Treffinger (Renzulli, 1979b, 1986; Treffinger & Renzulli, 1986). For example, they criticized the USOE model for not including motivation as part of their categorical definition of the gifted, and for the nonparallel nature of its categories. They also noted that specific academic aptitude, leadership, and visual and performing arts relate to the expression of specific areas of talents; abilities, intelligence, and creativity, (with the exclusion of the psychomotor dimension) relate to areas of general mental capacity or abilities (Renzulli, 1979b). As a result Renzulli presented an alternative way of regarding the gifted and talented and the way they functioned relative to schooling. In the wake of Renzulli's presentation other models that attempted, according to their authors, to improve conceptually upon the USOE model followed.

The Renzulli Model

The Renzulli Model, cited in Chapter 1, attempts to illustrate the interrelatedness of ability, creativity, and task commitment and how they affect general and specific performance of the curriculum and learning. (See Figure 1.1). In other words, definition, identification, and educational programming presented as interlocking domains are important considerations in any attempt to select gifted children for special educational opportunities (Treffinger & Renzulli, 1986).

Francoys Gagne's (1985) critique of Renzulli's model (1979b) suggested that the motivational aspect, embedded in the task commitment component, is inapplicable to underachievers. If it were to be applicable to underachievers, assuming they are gifted, motivation has to perform a different role. Furthermore, according to Gagne, the basis for including creativity as an essential component of giftedness is questioned. While creativity appears to be applicable to certain fields of achievement (e.g., architects) requiring originality, novelty, or uniqueness, it is not applicable to those fields of achievement requiring interpretative performance or other skills (e.g., musicians, teachers, professors, and so forth). In addition, Gagne says that Renzulli's model does not differentiate above-average ability into separate ability domains, leaving us with the impression that these abilities are intellectual in nature.

The Cohn Model

S. J. Cohn's (1981) hierarchical model of giftedness presents three major categories of abilities: intellectual, artistic, social. Each of these domains subdivide with the capability of further differentiation (Figure 4.1). It is interesting to note that Cohn includes talent dimensions in each of the four major domains.

Francoys Gagne's (1985) critique of Cohn's model approves of its parsimonious taxonomy of human abilities, but considers its hierarchical structure, with the insertion of diverse subcategories of talent in each of the four ability domains, a major problem. The implication that talent excellence is restricted to one governing ability domain at a time is false,

Figure 4.1 Graphic Representation of Cohn's Model of Giftedness

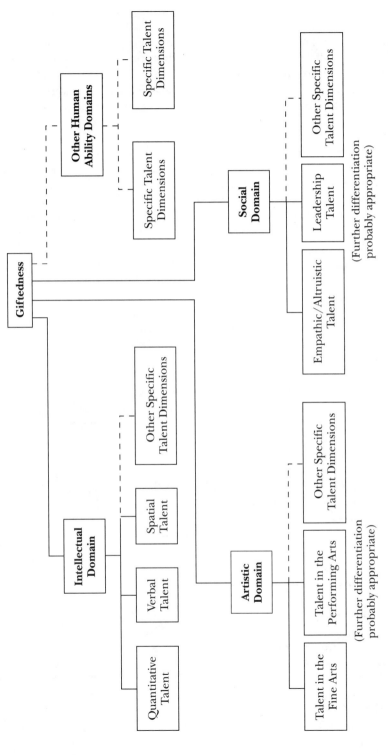

From "What Is Giftedness? A Multidimensional Approach" (p. 37) by S.J. Cohn in A.H. Kramer *Gifted Children: Changing Their Potential*, 1981. New York: Trillium. Copyright © by Third International Conference on Gifted Children Organizing Committee (1979) and World Council for Gifted and Talented Children. Reprinted by permission.

because several abilities may be involved in any one talent, and successful expression of talent can take a number of different forms. Such a model, if it is to be adequate, must have multidirectional rather than bidirectional connections between abilities and talents; that is, an ability can contribute to excellence in several talent areas or a talent is the result of the activity of several abilities.

The Gagne Model

W. Foster (1981) integrated the Renzulli and Cohn models to illustrate its relevance to leadership but Gagne considered it little different from the two models upon which it is based. Following his appraisal of these models, Gagne proposes one of his own in which *giftedness* is associated with ability, and *talent* is associated with performance (Figure 4.2). Gagne defines *giftedness* as competence and *talent* as performance distinctly above average in one or more ability and performance domains.

The model presents four major domains of abilities (intellectual, creative, socio-emotional, sensori-motor, and others), with sensori-motor preferred to psychomotor. Because of the existence of differences in theorizing, research, and opinion about the intellectual domain, Gagne does not specify the specific domains of ability. In his model, creativity is just one of several general domains of ability and consequently not an essential factor of giftedness or talent. Specific fields of talent are listed rather than grouped into general and specific fields or ordered in a hierarchy so as to emphasize the multidirectional relationship between talents and giftedness. Each specific talent is expressed by a profile of abilities differing somewhat from the profile characteristics of another talent.

At the center of the model are catalytic variables for talent expression such that interests, personality traits, and the environment fixes the orientation of an individual to a particular talent area while motivation, together with ability, contribute to talent intensity. Furthermore, Gagne indicates that the environment has a greater influence on talent than giftedness. In principle, the Gagne model is closely tied to the purpose of identification for education of gifted *or* talented rather than gifted *and* talented individuals.

Appraisal of Definitions and Models

Francoys Gagne emphasized the need to remove the conceptual ambiguity of the terms *gifted* and *talented* that are currently used synonymously. John Gowan's (1979a) distinction—intellectually gifted as forming the best current identifiable source of potential verbal creativity, and talented children as the best current identifiable source of nonverbal creativity—is but marginal to Gagne. So too is M. C. Robeck's (1968), which

Figure 4.2 Graphic Representation of a Differentiated Model of Giftedness and Talent

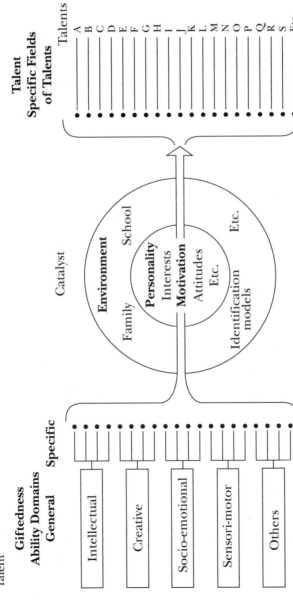

From "Giftedness and Talent: Reexamining a Reexamination of the Definitions" by F. Gagne, 1985, *Gifted Child Quarterly, 29,* pp. 103-112. Copyright © 1985 by Gifted Child Quarterly. Reprinted by permission.

distinguishes gifted individuals as those scoring I.Q.s of 145 to 160 and talented individuals as those scoring I.Q.'s of 130 to 145. However, we need to note that according to the Stanford-Binet and Wechsler scales, these I.Q. indices in the genius levels are not necessarily considered appropriate distinctions.

Gagne cites J. Zettel's (1979) distinction of *gifted* and *talented* as follows:

> *Gifted Children* mean children . . . who are endowed by nature with high intellectual capacity and who have a native capacity for high potential intellectual attainment and scholastic achievement. *Talented Children* mean children . . . who have demonstrated superior talents, aptitudes or abilities, outstanding leadership qualities and abilities, or consistently remarkable performance in the mechanics [sic], manipulative skills, the art of expression of ideas, oral or written, music, art, human relations or any other worthwhile line of human achievement. (p. 63)

According to Gagne, Zettel's distinction is the only one that goes beyond making a singular contrast between intellectual and other kinds of ability, to imply a distinction between innate versus acquired abilities, and capacity versus performance.

Another approach (Tannenbaum, 1986) suggests that giftedness is *psychosocial* in origin. In this understanding people consider giftedness not as one thing, but four different kinds of talent.

There are talents that are *scarce* or forever in short supply like those of Jonas Salk, the discoverer of a vaccine to conquer polio.

Then there are *surplus* talents that enhance people's sensibilities and sensitivities, taking them to new heights, as found in Bach's music or Michelangelo's art.

Quota talents are those associated with specialized, high-level skills needed for the provision of goods and services for which there is a limited market, only to emerge in response to popular demand.

And then there are *anomalous* talents that reflect the extent to which powers of the human mind and body can be stretched though not recognized for excellence. These are to be found, for instance, in the mastery of mountains of trivia, performance of complex mathematical calculations faster than a computer, gourmet cooking, and trapeze artistry.

In this conceptual framework, any definition of giftedness asserts that talent, in its developed form, exists only in adults. Giftedness in children denotes potential for becoming performers or producers of ideas that enhance the moral, physical, emotional, social, intellectual, or aesthetic life of humanity. Furthermore, five factors have to mesh together if a child is to become truly gifted: superior general intellect, distinctive special aptitudes, the right blending of nonintellective traits, a challenging environment, and good fortune at crucial periods of life. Interaction within separate talent domains reiterates that the five factors are all represented in every form of giftedness. As far as creativity is concerned, it is not additive but integrated in each of the several dimensions of giftedness.

Another approach (Feldhusen, 1986) proposed that giftedness comprises four components: *general intellectual ability, positive self-concept, achievement motivation,* and *special talents.*

P. Haensly, C. R. Reynolds, and W. R. Nash (1986) provided another model that is more ecologically than individually based. This model comprised four components. *Coalescence* defines abilities that come together to work in producing significant products. *Context* describes situational factors determining the worth of a product. *Conflict* shapes and hones the development of the gifted individual. *Commitment* identifies an individual's willingness to preserve and stick to the development of excellence.

Yet another approach (Gallagher & Courtright, 1986) makes a distinction between *psychological* conceptions of giftedness (based primarily on individual differences), and educational *conceptions* of giftedness (based primarily on school performance and assessment). They do not confine themselves to any one theoretical domain but compare existing definitions within and across the two.

Robert J. Sternberg and Janet E. Davidson (1986) appraised these four contributions (with the fifth offered by Renzulli and described earlier) and focused attention on several important and common themes.

1. The domain that serves as the basis of definition needs to be defined, whether it is individual or societal.
2. Cognitive abilities are essential to giftedness whether they are domain-general or domain-specific.
3. Motivation, as task commitment, is an essential prerequisite for giftedness.
4. The developmental course of various talents, no matter if or how they are expressed, are rewarded, ignored, or punished by society throughout the life span of individuals. The extent to which individuals are identified as gifted will depend on their reaction to rewards, negligence, or punishment.
5. Combination or "coalescence" of abilities in a motivated way is affected by social forces that channel their expression.

The perceived differences in the meaning of giftedness is a problem in semantics. The dictionary provides meanings of the words *gifted* and *talented* and distinguishes between the factual meanings of each word and their recent operational usage; these definitions often cloud rather than

Table 4.1 Major Dictionary Definitions of *Gifted* and *Talented*

Words	Oxford English Dictionary	Webster's Dictionary
Gifted	Endowed with gifts	Endowed with a natural ability or aptitude
	Talented	Talented
Giftedness	The condition, quality or state of being gifted	The state of being gifted
Talent	Mental endowment	A gift committed to one's trust to use and improve
	Natural ability	
	Power or ability of mind	A special superior ability in an art, mechanics, learning, and so forth
	A special natural ability or aptitude, usually for something expressed or implied	
	A natural capacity for success in some department of mental or physical activity	
Talented	Endowed with talent	Having talent
	Possessing talent	Possessing skill
	Gifted	Highly gifted
	Clever	
	Accomplished	

clarify the meaning. Reference to two major works (*Oxford English Dictionary*, 1980; *Webster's New Twentieth Century Dictionary of the English Language*, 1980) provides us with many definitions, most relevant of which are presented in Table 4.1.

It becomes quite clear from this information that the terms *gifted* and *talented* are used interchangeably; refer to endowment, either by divinity or nature—a semantic prerequisite—for use or improvement; and refer to the condition, quality, or state of having talent or being gifted or talented. *Factual* meanings of words are the vocabulary of our language and must be used so, unless we designate them for special use. The problem we face lies not in the use of these terms but in the interpretation we give to them. The *inferential* meanings we assign to them are what causes the problem.

It is not that we need more theoretical models to make our position clear, but we need to provide operational definitions of the words to give individual focus to their meanings. Without these definitions, we get tangled in the web of theoretical models—whose foundations lie in the controversy of heredity, environment, and their interactions—and in the conceptual differences—advanced by the hierarchical and multidimensional models of intellect and their ramifications in diverse human abilities.

The terms *gifted* or *talented* can be used interchangeably as the dictionary defines them but each term needs a qualifier to indicate more precisely what is meant. Qualifying words could include the following: *musically* gifted or talented, *poetically* gifted or talented, gifted or talented in the *sciences*, and gifted or talented *leader*. The terms *gifted* and *talented* in this text will be used interchangeably and will be qualified when necessary.

Motivation and related variables in the nonintellectual domain of human functioning, although they sensitize and even activate the innate and/or acquired propensities to operate in superior ways, must be thrown in to contaminate the struggle involved in the identification problem. Unlike gifted and talented, motivation is a state or condition arising from individual transactions with the environment and most closely relates to various homeostatic imbalances and need levels (Maslow, 1954), or with cultivated or shaped needs (W. W. White, 1959). In harnessing motivation to mental functioning for productivity, we can best lead the gifted or talented to actualize themselves.

The potential to be *creative* is the inheritance of all human beings, whether it is called to use or not. It should be quite obvious that not all human activities require the use of creativity. Many activities, especially those routine in nature (e.g., survival activities), require none. However, if there is interference in the common flow of the routine, creativity becomes necessary to cope with the interference, and new ways of doing things are found and established as routine. Creativity becomes essential when activities—physical, or intellectual (as it relates to the individual) and social (as it relates to others)—challenge the emergence of new and relevant events.

Several *models* on the gifted are different expressions of the same need to establish, with a high degree of specificity, alternative ways of defining what constitutes giftedness. The models are in themselves interesting though incomplete, and certainly suggestive of the complexity of giftedness that must be taken into account if we are to adequately identify the gifted.

Philosophical and procedural differences, as they relate to a category of giftedness, present some difficulty. When one deals with intangibles, such as intellectual potential, one can expect views about it to be quite different. The issues on the nature of human *intelligence* are far from settled. More is known today than in the time of Alfred Binet and Lewis M. Terman, but more will be learned about it in years to come. There is a tendency today to accept the multidimensional nature of intelligence proposed by J. P. Guilford. His model, the Structure of Intellect, is considered by many researchers as the apex of thought on intellectual functioning, despite some scholarly disagreements concerning his factor-based conceptual framework. Yet, with the continued refinement of available tools and procedures—to which may be added the invention of others (Gardner, 1987; Sternberg, 1988)—we may see changes in thought in the near future that may not seem possible now.

To identify the gifted child, the identification process should be versatile enough to pick out qualities of mental functioning that can indicate the potential to extend as well as to conserve the boundaries of human existence. Although one of the five United States Office of Education categories of giftedness is creative or productive thinking abilities, the potential to be creative or productive may enter into the categories of leadership and visual and performing arts abilities. If we were to attempt to simplify these five categories of giftedness, we could regard general intellectual ability as the capacity to function at a high level of mental effectiveness relative to all kinds of verbal and nonverbal performance. The term echoes the theoretical models of Charles Spearman, Sir Cyril Burt, P. E. Vernon, and E. L. Thorndike and associates, relative to the g factor; or David Wechsler's global capacity of intellectual functioning. In terms of its measurement correlates, general intellectual ability implies identification by I.Q. tests. Creative or productive thinking does not belong to this model but relates to Guilford's Structure of Intellect model with divergent production, redefinition, and transformation abilities as integral components of it.

Academic aptitude, the potential to achieve at high levels of success in school subjects, relates closely to general intellectual ability and I.Q. tests modeled to predict its potential. Guilford's analysis of test items on I.Q. tests indicate that no attention is given to divergent production and little to evaluative thinking abilities. Aptitude to perform well in academic subjects necessitates the use of cognition, memory, convergent production, and evaluative thinking abilities. The extent to which academic aptitude can contain creative components is worthy of some thought.

On the matter of *visual and performing arts*, high levels of performance should necessitate at least above average to bright levels of general ability as well as above average to high levels of creative functioning, contrary to F. Gagne's opinion. If the special skills and knowledge involved in these two areas of exceptional talent relate to performing what is known well, with little use for innovation, then high levels of creative functioning may not have to be identified as well. However, exceptional talent in the visual and performing arts should reflect ability to go beyond technical skill and individual knowledge.

A high level of *leadership* potential requires the possession of high intellectual abilities and creative thinking abilities with an understanding of people and sensitivity to the needs of others. Again, we are faced with the problem of differentiating between the administrator who maintains the status quo, perceiving and using the rules slavishly, and the manager of human relations who functions in a dynamic and innovative way, as changing circumstances and events allow.

Identification of these kinds of giftedness may take the form of *more formal* to *less formal* approaches. Although measures are available for some components of giftedness, these measures are not applicable to all categories and subcategories of giftedness. Where measures are available, we may arrange to use them. They should provide the objective evidence needed for the purpose of appropriate identification. Where measures are not available, identification procedures have to be less formal. According to certain criteria relative to a category of giftedness, direct observation is used. The problem of identification can be alleviated considerably by using this approach. Some treatment of the variables associated with each of the USOE five categories of giftedness was given in the previous chapter. In this chapter, formal approaches for identifying giftedness, especially as they relate to teacher accessibility and use, will receive attention. In the next chapter, less formal identification approaches will be examined.

GENERAL INTELLECTUAL ABILITY

To identify the general intellectual ability of a child, it is common to determine the child's intelligence or I.Q. and, according to the fourth edition of the Stanford-Binet, its equivalent in Standard Age Scores (SAS). Both the Wechsler Scales and the Stanford-Binet can be used for the purpose of identifying intellectual ability represented by I.Q. or SAS, and can be expected to provide the best evidence of this kind of giftedness.

An Individual Intelligence Test

For instance, the fourth edition of the Stanford-Binet Intelligence Scale was redesigned for use with individuals between the ages of 2 and 23 years. The measure consists, in a hierarchical model, of three levels of *cognitive abilities* that provide information about a person's general intellectual capacity or g (Level 1); crystalized, fluid-analytic, short-term memory abilites (Level 2); and verbal, quantitative, and abstract/visual reasoning abilities (Level 3).

General intellectual capacity or g (similar to the Spearman or Vernon g), the first level of the structure, provides information on how well a person responds to a problem that he or she has not been taught to solve.

The second level consists of *crystalized abilities, fluid-analytic abilities,* and *short-term memory. Crystalized abilities* (i.e., scholastic or academic abilities) indicate the extent to which a person has cognitive skills necessary for acquiring and using information about verbal and quantitative concepts to solve problems. These abilities are not only greatly influenced by schooling, but also developed by more general outside-school experiences (similar to Vernon's *v:ed* or verbal-educational abilities).

Fluid-analytic abilities represent cognitive skills needed for solving new problems involving figural or other nonverbal stimuli, and call for the invention of new cognitive strategies or the flexible reassembly of known strategies to cope with novel situations (similar to Vernon's *k:m* or kinesthetic-motor abilities).

Short-term memory, a third set of abilities of the second level, relates to complex aspects of cognitive performance. It serves to retain temporarily newly perceived information prior to storage in long-term memory, but also holds information from long-term memory needed to handle an ongoing task. Furthermore, information about short-term memory activity is indicative of the efficiency of an individual's storage-retrieval system.

Level 3 comprises *verbal reasoning, quantitative reasoning,* and *abstract/ visual reasoning.* These abilities are more specific and more content-dependent than those of Levels 1 and 2.

Items of the fourth edition of the Stanford-Binet comprise 15 subtest areas as follows:

Verbal reasoning—vocabulary, comprehension, absurdities, verbal relations
Quantitative reasoning—quantitative, number series, equation building
Abstract/visual reasoning—pattern analysis, copying, matrices, paper folding and cutting
Short-term memory—bead memory, memory for sentences, memory for digits, memory for objects

No one is required to take all 15 subtest areas of the battery. Those taking the test are required to take only those tests that correspond to an entry level based on individual performance upon the vocabulary test and chronological age. Administration of the full battery of tests may take from 30 to 90 minutes. Each raw score recorded on the test booklet is converted to a SAS for each subtest from which a composite SAS is derived. The same procedure is followed to determine subtests and composite SASs for each of the four ability areas: verbal reasoning, quantitative reasoning, abstract/visual reasoning, and short-term memory.

Separate items are not included to measure capacity at Levels 1 and 2. But it is understood that these levels are called into action to deal with problems posed by specific items. Level 1 function is implied in the composite score, and Level 2, in the area indices.

Within each age group, each test has an SAS mean of 50 and a standard deviation of 8. However, SASs for the *area scores* and the *overall composite score* are based on a mean of 100 and a standard deviation of 16 or 15; conversion tables are available for comparison of SASs with I.Q.'s obtained on Form L-M of the Stanford-Binet (Terman, 1960) and the Wechsler scales, respectively. In addition, tables for the conversion of SASs to percentile ranks are available. The flexibility of the measure may permit the combination of SASs of several subtests, but at present, a partial composite of the verbal and numerical subtests, (whose correlation with school grades is high) is recommended. Information on reliability and validity is good. Details of this and related information, as well as interpretative data, can be found in two technical manuals (Delaney & Hopkins, 1987; Thorndike, Hagen, & Sattler, 1986).

The fourth edition of the measure is valuable for two additional reasons. First, its hierarchical structure provides not only an overall index of intellectual capacity, but also subindices that represent many different kinds of abilities. Second, the measure has been used with special populations, including the gifted population. Therefore, the measure is consistent with current thought on the multidimensional nature of abilities, and can be used to identify many abilities of gifted children.

Group Intelligence Tests

Administering individual intelligence tests such as the Stanford-Binet is time consuming and relatively expensive. Besides, individual intelligence tests are inaccessible to teachers and must be managed by trained psychologists.

An alternative to the individual intelligence test is group intelligence tests that claim to do relatively the same job. As such, they have been widely used. Among the better group measures available are the California Test of Mental Maturity, the Lorge-Thorndike Intelligence Test, the Henmon-Nelson Tests of Mental Ability, the Otis-Lennon Mental Ability Test, the Pinter General Ability Tests, the Primary Mental Abilities Test, the California Test of Mental Maturity (Short Form), the College Qualification Test, the Kuhlmann-Anderson Test, and the Raven's Progressive Matrices.

Terman (1919), recognizing the problem of using the Stanford-Binet in a school setting, advocated the use of the group test as an initial screening device. He believed that scores on group tests should not be considered substitutes for information derived from an individual measure of intelligence. In other words, gifted children can best be identified by group tests in initial screenings and by individual measures of intelligence for more accurate identification in later screenings. Of course, this is a less expensive and time-consuming approach because fewer children will be involved in the final identification process.

Support for Terman's approach comes from several studies (e.g., Martinson, 1961, 1974; Pegnato, 1958). Group measures of intelligence have been found to misidentify children, usually showing children scoring lower I.Q.'s on group measures of intelligence than on individual measures, such as Form L-M of the Stanford-Binet (Terman & Merrill, 1960), with differences of as much as 30 I.Q. points. These differences are attributed to a number of factors relative to the composition and ceiling effects of group intelligence tests.

It is important to note that most tests of intellectual potential have not been particularly designed with the gifted in mind but for the general population. An exception, for instance, can be found in the Concept Mastery Test developed by Terman for the identification of gifted children of his famous longitudinal study. In content, group tests of intelligence are limited, and hence do not provide suitable challenge to those children of superior intellect. Furthermore, because of the limited number of test items on such measures, overall indices of intellectual capacity are depressed and inaccurate readings follow. In addition, group measures of intelligence do not provide information about levels of abilities as does the fourth edition of the Stanford-Binet.

Of the many group measures available (e.g., Keyser & Sweetland, 1987; Sweetland & Keyser, 1986), three measures are selected for discussion here as the most representative and most commonly used instruments that educators with some background in psychometrics find accessible. It is important, though, that the measures appropriately interpret the scores obtained. The selected measures are the California Test of Mental Maturity (Short Form), the Otis-Lennon Intelligence Tests, and the Scholastic Aptitude Test.

California Test of Mental Maturity

The California Test of Mental Maturity (Sullivan, Clark, & Tiegs, 1963) is a group measure of intelligence intended to parallel Form L-M of the Stanford-Binet. It measures functional capacities basic to learning, problem solving, and responses to new situations. The 1963 revision of the Short Form of the measure consists of seven subtests, each of which is expected to measure a different component of general ability.

Test 1:   Opposites
Test 2:   Similarities
Test 3:   Analogies
Test 4:   Numerical Values
Test 5:   Numerical Problems

Test 6:   Verbal Comprehension
Test 7:   Delayed Recall

The items on each of these subtests are both *verbal* and *nonverbal*, and multiple choice in structure. They are grouped according to four areas of abilities as follows:

Factor I—Logical Reasoning (opposites, similarities, and analogies tests)
Factor II—Numerical Reasoning (numerical values, and numerical problems tests)
Factor III—Verbal Concepts (verbal comprehension test)
Factor IV—Memory (delayed recall test)

The Short Form of the measure has eight articulated test levels that cover the grade and age range from preschool to adulthood. Directions are read verbatim to the examinee and time limits for each of the subtests are prescribed, with total actual testing time varying from 39 to 43 minutes, depending on the level of the measure used. Details concerning the construction, reliability, validity, normative, and other relevant data can be found in the examiner's manual and several other supplementary publications.

Besides, deviation I.Q., M.A., standard score, and percentile ranks are provided for the verbal and nonverbal areas as well as for the composite score. To these may be added the provision of standard scores and percentile ranks for factor scores.

An assessment of the relative merits of the California Test of Mental Maturity (Short Form) shows the need for some improvement of the examiner's manual, especially to clarify what the norms represent in the section describing the scaling procedures. Information on concurrent and predictive validity of the four factors also helps in the interpretation of factor scores. Because there is a lack of such information, it would be best to use the total test I.Q. for identification and the language and non-language I.Q. for differentiating the mode of intellectual strength. All in all, however, the value of the measure relates to its identification of both a verbal and nonverbal I.Q. as well as a composite I.Q.

Otis-Lennon Mental Ability Test
The Otis-Lennon Mental Ability Test (Otis & Lennon, 1967) is a revision of the earlier Otis Tests (Otis Self-Administering Tests of Mental Ability and Otis Quick-Scoring Mental Ability Tests). Consistent with the earlier versions, the present Otis-Lennon test comprises a variety of items aimed at measuring general mental ability. The measure is designed for use from kindergarten to Grade 12.

There are two primary levels of the test, each containing 55 items and all of which are pictorial. The purpose of these is to measure the following mental processes: classification, quantitative reasoning, following directions, and comprehension of verbal concepts.

There are three elementary levels and one advanced level of the measure. The first of the elementary levels has 80 items. It measures reasoning by analogy in addition to the mental processes of the elementary levels. The other levels contain 80 verbal and nonverbal items (synonyms, opposites, verbal and figural analogies, and number series), each structured in a spiral omnibus fashion that measures a number of mental processes, with emphasis on abstract reasoning.

Testing time varies from 30 to 50 minutes, depending on the level of the test. A single score is obtained to measure the verbal-educational (*v:ed*) component of *g* relative to Vernon's hierarchical structure of intellect. The measure provides norms in terms of deviation I.Q.'s, percentile ranks, and stanines. The technical manual for the test reports respectable reliability and validity information with standardization data based on a population of about 150,000 students (about 6,000 students at the kindergarten level, and 12,000 students for each of Grade 1 to Grade 12) selected from 117 school systems from all 50 states so as to provide representative and sound norms. In addition, the manual provides guidelines for appropriate interpretation that can be used by a teacher who has preparation in basic psychometrics. The technical information provided by the manual is stated with clarity.

Scholastic Aptitude Test

The Scholastic Aptitude Test of the College Entrance Examination Board is one of several tests developed for the selection of students for college admission. It is generally taken in the senior year of high school. Students who need to take such an examination in their junior year are administered a shorter but comparable form, the Preliminary Scholastic Aptitude Test. This shorter version can be used most appropriately to identify intellectually gifted students, and may even be administered to them in their first year of secondary school.

The measure consists of a *verbal* and a *mathematical* section, and scores are provided for each of these two ability areas. Items of the measure are constructed in a best-answer multiple-choice format, with 3 hours allowed for taking the test. The mathematics section attempts to measure ability for dealing with concepts rather than mathematical achievement, although some knowledge of elementary mathematics is necessary to solve problems given. The verbal section measures reading comprehension and perception of analogical relations where a wide reading background has developed vocabulary and reading skill over a period of years. The measure has been most carefully developed and the extensive research and ongoing refinements of the instrument have produced a technically sound instrument. Achievement on the verbal and mathematics sections of the Scholastic Aptitude Test is reported in standard score units. Additional technical information on the measure may be found in a technical report prepared for the college board by Angoff (1971).

Using These Group Measures

The three group measures, briefly described, are examples of instruments that can be used to identify general and related abilities of gifted children and youth. The California Test of Mental Maturity (Short Form), and the Otis-Lennon Mental Ability Test are generally more appropriate for the screening of gifted elementary and secondary students because test-ceiling effects are quite noticeable with highly precocious youth. In selecting test levels for screening, the ones recommended by the test publisher may be followed. However, if there is reason to believe that the subjects to be tested are highly able, it might be more appropriate to administer the test at a higher level than recommended. This approach was successfully applied in Project Talented and Gifted, an experiment conducted in West Virginia by the author (Khatena, 1977a). In this instance, the California Test of Mental Maturity (Short Form) was used to identify gifted students nominated by their schools for the project.

The Scholastic Aptitude Test has a ceiling high enough to discriminate among able students and is best suited for identification of highly gifted students in their junior and senior high school years. Stanley (1977b) and his associates have been using the mathematics section of the Scholastic Aptitude Test for the identification of mathematically precocious youth to participate in the Educational Acceleration Program at Johns Hopkins University. Students as young as 10 and 13 years have been identified in this way.

Other variables that may interfere with the more effective functioning of group intelligence tests generally include heavy verbal loading of items, time limitations, and lower reliability and validity than individual intelligence tests. However, use of group intelligence measures for identifying the gifted has recently received further endorsement (Van Tassel-Baska, 1986).

A Measure of Structure of Intellect Abilities

Guilford's monumental work on the *Nature of Human Intelligence* (1967), which found expression in the Structure of Intellect, was generally based on information derived from adults. Although test items relative to the identifiable Structure of Intellect abilities are to be found in this book, they are primarily designed for adults. An exception is Guilford's (1973) Creativity Tests for Children, though the items in this measure are adaptations of the adult ones and will be described in the section on creative talent.

Mary N. Meeker (1979b) and her associates developed a measure for school children entitled Structure of Intellect Learning Abilities Test (Meeker, M. N., Meeker, R., & Roid, 1985). This measure incorporates 24 Structure of Intellect subtests, which were selected from the model's 90 known abilities because of their established relationship to school subjects, such as reading, arithmetic, writing, and creativity.

The Structure of Intellect Learning Abilities Test consists of items related to the five mental operations areas: cognition, memory, convergent production, divergent production, and evaluation.

Cognition

Cognition or comprehension involves immediate discovery, awareness, rediscovery, or recognition of information in various content areas identified as

CFU—Visual closure
CFC—Visual conceptualization
CFS—Constancy of object in space (Piaget)
CST—Spatial conservation (Piaget)
CSR—Comprehension of abstract relations
CSS—Comprehension of numerical progressions
CMU—Vocabulary of mathematical and language concepts
CMR—Ability to comprehend extended verbal information

Memory

The memory operation involves processes that store and retrieve information. There are six memory tests in the visual-auditory (figural) dimension of the content areas.

MFU—Visual memory for details
MSU—Visual and auditory attending
MSS—Visual and auditory sequencing, serialization, and
    conservation
MSI—Inferential memory

Convergent Production

Convergent production is the mental operation that works on informational content to produce single correct answers. It generates conventionally accepted best answers from given information and defines successful school achievement. There are four tests of convergent production as follows:

NFU—Psychomotor skills
NSS—Application of mathematical facts
NST—Speed of word recognition
NSI—Formal reasoning (logic)

Divergent Production

Divergent production is the mental operation that acts upon informational content to generate a variety of quality answers. It illustrates fluency, flexibility, and originality of thinking and sometimes is referred to as creativity of a limited kind because transformations in the product domain are also indicators of creativity. There are three tests of divergent production as follows:

DFS—Creativity with things (figural)
DSR—Creativity with arithmetic facts
DMU—Creativity with words and ideas

Evaluation

Evaluation is the mental operation of judging, effective planning, decision making, and foresight. This mental operation is measured by four tests.

EFU—Visual discrimination
EFC—Judging similarities and matching concepts
ESC—Judgment of arithmetic similarities
ESS—Judgment of correctness of numerical facts

Conclusion

The Structure of Intellect Learning Abilities Test can be used to measure the Structure of Intellect abilities of students in Grades 1 to 8 and comes in alternate forms. Technical information on reliability, validity, and norms can be found in two manuals (Meeker, M. N. 1979b; Meeker, M. N., Meeker, R., & Roid, 1985). Norming of the test involved Caucasians, African Americans, and Hispanics of inner city and suburban schools, as well as other sources in the United States. Conversion tables for each ability (24 subtests) and the general dimension of the Structure of Intellect model at each grade level is provided in terms of normal score equivalents derived from percentage scores. In addition, an evaluation table presents normal score equivalent data for all grade levels in one summary sheet with five cut-off levels for each grade: the median score, 84th percentile for superior-level performance, 94th percentile for gifted-level performance, and the 16th and 6th percentiles. The lowest levels (16th and 6th percentiles) are presented as criteria for determining limiting-level and disabled-level performance respectively. This summary table allows intergrade comparisons for each of the five levels presented, particularly among median scores.

The Structure of Intellect Learning Abilities Test is also designed to provide information to the teacher for developing Structure of Intellect abilities. To apply the test to the school curriculum, end lessons have been designed but shall be dealt with in a later chapter.

ACADEMIC ACHIEVEMENT

Another way to identify the intellectually gifted is by evaluating their academic achievement. Often, such an identification approach has gone hand in hand with measures of intelligence. It has been established that those who do well on intelligence tests have been found to do well on achievement tests. Where intelligence measures attempt to measure capacity to achieve well in school, academic achievement tests attempt to measure learning in terms of knowledge of facts and principles, and their application in complex and frequently lifelike situations.

Attainment in learning may be measured relative to performance on school subjects in a specific class. In this case, it is often teacher-made tests that are administered. Learning may also be measured relative to the learning expected of pupils of certain grade levels located all over the country, in which case, a standardized test is administered. In the latter case, a pupil's academic achievement in one place may be compared to the performance of others of the general population taking the test. To evaluate gifted pupils, the standardized test best serves the purpose of identifying gifted pupils in academic subjects.

In selecting an instrument, consideration must be given to the effectiveness of the measure as an identifier of academically gifted pupils. The same problem of ceiling effects also exists for measures of academic achievement because most measures have not been specifically constructed with the gifted in mind. There is no single instrument available to measure effectively the academic achievement of pupils at all grade levels because specialization in different school subjects increases with advancement of grade level. In the lower grades, a measure evaluating the achievement in many school subjects seems appropriate, whereas in junior and senior high school, achievement tests in each subject area appear to be more appropriate for identifying the academically gifted pupil.

Sometimes a combination of both kinds of measures serve individual needs best.

Another issue relates to the lack of appropriate reliability and validity data, even though other considerations, such as item analyses, content selecting, and the size of the norm population, are handled with care. This situation adds to the difficulty of picking just the right measure for the purpose of identifying gifted students. It must be assumed, because the gifted student is several grades above grade-placement level, that it would be more appropriate to begin administering a form of the measure, two or even three grades above the one recommended. This procedure is especially the case when tests that measure a number of different subject areas have been constructed relative to recommended grade levels. It is especially useful for the teacher involved in identifying academic achievement to make some educated guesses about the level of attainment of the children.

For an account of available measures, test users should consult *Test Critiques* (Keyser & Sweetland, 1987) and *Tests* (Sweetland & Keyser, 1986). Among the many achievement tests accessible to educators are the California Achievement Test, the Iowa Tests of Basic Skills, the Metropolitan Achievement Test, the Stanford Achievement Test, the High School Arts and Humanities Test, and the American College Test. Three of the most representative and commonly used instruments are selected for discussion.

Stanford Achievement Test

The Stanford Achievement Test (Kelley, Madden, Gardner, & Rudman, 1965) was designed to measure the knowledge, skills, and understanding that are considered important and desirable outcomes of the major branches of the elementary school curriculum. The current edition of the measure is organized in five batteries for use with students in Grades 1 to 9 as follows: Primary Batteries I and II, Intermediate Batteries I and II, and Advanced Batteries. Each test comes in four forms (W, X, Y, and Z) matched for content and difficulty with slight overlapping of content between adjacent batteries.

Nine subtests of the Intermediate Battery Level II measure the content areas of word meaning, paragraph meaning, spelling, language, arithmetic computation, arithmetic concepts, arithmetic applications, social studies, and science. Eight subtests of the Advanced Battery measure the same content areas except for word meaning. The tests are fundamentally power and not speed tests, although all subtests are timed for ease of administration because time limits are calculated to give nearly all students sufficient time to attempt all questions that they are capable of answering correctly.

High School Arts and Humanities Test

There is also a test, limited in scope, for students in Grades 9 to 12 called the High School Arts and Humanities Test (Buros, 1972). The publisher describes this test as measuring knowledge and understanding in the areas of classical and contemporary literature, music, art, drama, and philosophy. The test consists of 65 multiple-choice items and comes in Forms W and X. It takes 40 minutes to complete.

Responses to test items can be hand or machine scored. Information on construction, reliability, validity, and related data may be found in the administration directions and technical report of the measure. Merenda (1965) questioned the reliability and validity data of this test. But he commented that the Stanford Achievement Test batteries remain available to school personnel for use below the senior high school level, and he recommends its continued adoption and use.

American College Test

The American College Test (Buros, 1972) like the Scholastic Aptitude Test is one of the most widely used measures for college entrance purposes. It is administered five times a year to high school seniors. The latter consists of four tests: English usage, mathematics usage, social studies reading, and natural sciences reading. In addition, a biographical inventory of nonacademic achievements, aspirations, special campus needs, and perceptions of college is also included in its test booklet.

The English usage test consists of 75 items related to fairly long reading samples and has a time limit of 40 minutes. The mathematics usage test is made up of 40 items in arithmetic, algebra, and plane geometry with a 50-minute time limit. The social studies reading test contains 52 items and has a time limit of 35 minutes; it calls for information based on four reading passages and miscellaneous facts from the social studies area. The natural sciences reading test contains 52 items based on four reading passages of scientific and general science content with a time limit of 35 minutes.

These tests are all multiple choice in form. Scores in each of the subject areas as well as a composite score are provided. Scores are presented in scaled score units form 1 to 36. Item analyses show that construction and selection of item content need improvement. Information on the reliability of the measure needs to be better. Validation of the test is extensive, and it consistently achieves good results. Although the measure is not free from criticism, its chief strength lies in its predictive validities vis-à-vis criteria of college success. Various guides, such as a supervisor's manual, a counselor's handbook, and an interpretive booklet for students are available. A technical report produced in 1965 is also available. The American College Test is a measure that can be used to advantage to identify gifted high school students.

Using Academic Achievement Measures

The standardized achievement tests described can be used for the screening of the academically gifted student. The Stanford Achievement Test batteries are appropriate for students in the elementary and junior high school, whereas the American College Test is appropriate for senior high school screening purposes. Where ceiling effects are anticipated for the Stanford Achievement Test, it may be necessary to screen at a level or two above that recommended by the test publisher. This approach was successfully used in an experiment conducted in West Virginia called Project Talented and Gifted (Khatena, 1977a) using the Stanford Achievement Test.

Standardized tests, although helpful in the identification of academically gifted students, do not tell us everything about the individual screened. Turnbull (1978), president of Educational Testing Service, has pointed out that we are prone to have fallacious assumptions of three kinds about standardized tests. The *micrometer fallacy* attributes too much precision to test scores. The *whole-person fallacy* is the tendency to apply inappropriate significance to achievement test scores, for scores simply represent the amount a student has learned in a given subject. The *preparation fallacy* is the expectation that the test will compensate somehow for the differences in the academic development of children whose learning opportunities have differed dramatically.

CREATIVE TALENT

Creativity is a complex construct. It is a source of apprehension and misgivings, especially in terms of its measurement correlates. There is considerable lack of agreement over the definition of the term because the word has, through usage, become associated with many aspects of creative behavior and mental functioning. It ranges along a cognitive and emotive continuum. Hence, any attempt to construct measures to identify creative talent must begin with a precise definition of the term. That is to say that we must provide an *operational definition* of creativity so that the user of the measure will know what we are attempting to measure.

Among the foremost psychologists in the field of creativity measurement are J. P. Guilford and E. P. Torrance. Generally their measures give major roles to abilities known as fluency, flexibility, originality and elaboration; however, their approaches to measurement differ. Guilford (1967) attempts to measure divergent thinking by using a test format that generally requires the subject to respond to many stimuli, each of which measures a specific component of the Structure of Intellect. Torrance (1974b) attempts to measure these abilities through the presentation of several complex tasks designed to trigger the expression of several abilities at one and the same time.

Others like Mary N. Meeker and this author have given additional perspective to the measurement of creativity and have constructed instruments for the identification of the creatively gifted (Khatena & Torrance, 1990a, 1990b; Meeker, 1979b).

As to the associative conception of creativity, several measures have been constructed. These include measures constructed by a number of scholars in the field.

1. M. A. Wallach and N. Kogan (1965) constructed an instrument that attempts to arrange associative conditions for the production of many unique associates not very different from the concepts of fluency and originality.
2. S. A. Mednick and M. T. Mednick (1967) constructed the Remote Associates Test whose items present three associative stimuli for the production of a single remote associate scored as original.
3. E. P. Torrance, J. Khatena, and B. F. Cunnington designed Thinking Creatively with Sounds and Words (Khatena & Torrance, 1990b) that provides conditions of free association for the production of original (i.e., statistically infrequent and relevant) responses.
4. C. E. Schaefer (1975) developed the Similes Test which calls for free association to produce original responses.
5. E. K. Starkweather (1971) designed measures for preschool children that require free association for the production of original responses.

Instruments that identify the creative individual are listed as follows:

1. Biographical or creative perception instruments—Alpha Biographical Inventory (IBRIC, 1968; Taylor & Ellison, 1967), Biographical Inventory: Creativity (Schaefer, 1970), Khatena-Torrance Creative Perception Inventory (Khatena & Torrance, 1990a), and Group Inventory for Finding Creative Talent (Rimm & Davis, 1976, 1980)
2. Motivational-attitude type instruments—How Do You Think Inventory? (Davis, 1975) and Personal-Social Motivational Inventory (Torrance, 1958)
3. A creative self-concept measure—How Do You Really Feel About Yourself? (F. E. Williams, 1971b)
4. Measures of conformity, nonconformity, and willingness to try the difficult—Form Board Test, Social Conformity Test, and Target Game (Starkweather, 1971)

5. Creative transactualization and communication—Creative Behavior Disposition Scale (I. A. Taylor, 1972) Social Interaction and Creativity in Communication System (D. L., Johnson, 1979)
6. Thinking style involving right, left, and both cerebral hemispheric functioning—Style of Learning and Thinking (Torrance, 1988)
7. Creativity expressed by action and movement—Thinking Creatively in Action and Movement (Torrance, 1981a; Torrance & Gibbs, 1979d)

A variety of personality inventories have been used rather successfully in studying creative personalities although not primarily measures of creativity. Among the best of them are the Allport-Vernon-Lindzey Study of Values (Allport, Vernon & Lindzey, 1951), California Psychological Inventory (Gough, 1956), Omnibus Personality Inventory (Heist & Yonge, 1968), Myers-Briggs Type Indicator (Myers, 1962), Runner Studies of Attitude Patterns (Runner & Runner, 1965), and Gough Adjective Checklist (Gough, 1960).

Several effective approaches for identifying the characteristics of creative individuals have emerged from the Institute of Personality Assessment and Research of the University of California at Berkeley. These approaches include the following (Barron, 1958, 1969; Crutchfield, 1951; MacKinnon, 1978): life history interviews, personality-trait ratings, adjective checklists, q-sort method, multiple regression analyses predictive of creativity, capacity for metaphor, mosaic construction, and insight test puzzles. To this list of approaches must be added the informal interview process (Walkup, 1971) as a method of identifying creative individuals.

Few instruments are available on the assessment of creative achievement. A variety of techniques have been used by researchers to assess creative achievement, for instance, checklists and indicators of real-life creative achievements (Khatena, 1982a). There has been little, if any, sustained effort to develop measures for the purpose of assessing creative achievement relative to school subjects (Torrance, 1977a) or to objectives of courses in teacher education and certification (Torrance & Hall, 1980).

Anne Anastasi (1988) has indicated that more than divergent thinking is involved in the assessment of creative achievement because the critical evaluation phase follows the uninhibited divergent-production phase for genuine creative achievement to occur. The brainstorming approach of Alex F. Osborn and Sidney J. Parnes appears to be related to this perception—where delayed judgment and free-wheeling, followed by evaluation against some set criteria of value and usefulness, are steps in the creative thinking process.

One of the closest approaches to the measurement of creative problem-solving—although it does not measure creative achievement in areas of school subject matter—is the Purdue Elementary Problem-Solving Inventory (Feldhusen, Houtz, & Ringenbach, 1972); there is also a measure of future problem-solving performance (Torrance & Horng, 1978). The measurement of creative achievement—whether in science, engineering, art, music, or other fields of human endeavor—requires a complex pattern of aptitudes and personality traits peculiar, appropriate, and specific to these special areas of knowledge. In the same vein, Frank Barron and D. M. Harrington (1981) indicate that the domain-specific nature of creativity in different fields is becoming increasingly evident (Anastasi, 1988). Another approach taken by Teresa M. Amabile (1983) measures creative products via a consensual assessment technique. It should also be noted that biographical measures of creativity (Taylor & Ellison, 1967) and measures of creative self-perception (Khatena & Torrance, 1990b) requesting information regarding the generation of products (though not necessarily related to schooling) are other viable ways of measuring achievement.

CREATIVE THINKING ABILITIES

Identification of creative talents have been approached in a number of ways that include the measurement of divergent production, creative thinking abilities, originality, creative imagination imagery, and creative self-perceptions.

Divergent Production Abilities

The geometric representation of mental function conceived by Guilford as the Structure of Intellect comprises three dimensions of abilities. These are five kinds of mental operations, four kinds of content, and six products or information forms. One of the five mental operations is *divergent production* (see Figure 4.3).

Divergent production processes four kinds of content organized in six product categories. It requires the examinees to produce their own answers and they cannot choose from the alternatives given to them. Divergent production calls for the use of several creative thinking abilities that include *fluency, flexibility, originality,* and *elaboration.*

The various measures of creative thinking produced by Guilford and his associates relate to the divergent production abilities of the Structure of Intellect. These measures, largely, have been used with adult and adolescent populations, although some of their work has involved younger children (Guilford, 1967, 1973). However, Guilford (1975) indicates that the creativity measures for children between Grades 4 and 6

Figure 4.3 Divergent Production Abilities

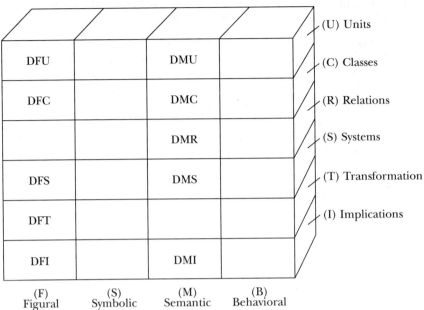

(U) Units
(C) Classes
(R) Relations
(S) Systems
(T) Transformation
(I) Implications

DFU   DMU
DFC   DMC
       DMR
DFS   DMS
DFT
DFI   DMI

(F)   (S)   (M)   (B)
Figural   Symbolic   Semantic   Behavioral

From *The Creatively Gifted Child: Suggestions for Parents and Teachers* (p. 29) by J. Khatena, 1978, New York: Vantage Press. Copyright © 1978 by J. Khatena. Reprinted by permission.

are revisions of the adult forms. The instructions were rewritten to make them appropriate for children.

Guilford's Test of Creativity for Children

Guilford's tests of creativity for children are made up of 10 tasks, each measuring 1 of 10 of the identified 24 divergent production abilities. The 10 divergent production tests for children are Names for Stories, What to Do With It?, Similar Meanings, Writing Sentences, Kinds of People, Making Something Out of It, Different Groups, Making Objects, Hidden Letters, and Adding Decorations.

The first five tasks are verbal, the remaining five tasks are nonverbal. Details about these tasks can be found in the test manual. However, one verbal and one figural task are given as examples.

Verbal Task: *Names for Stories (Divergent Semantic Units)*
The plot of a story is given with a few sample titles. The child is asked to write as many titles as possible in the few minutes given. A score is then

derived from the total number of acceptable clever and nonclever titles. Take for instance the following story given for the purpose of generating names to describe it (Khatena, 1978c, p. 30):

> One day three friends found a box of gold coins. As they did not want others to know about it, they decided to wait for nightfall before taking it into the nearby village. One of them went for food and drink while the two remained to watch over the gold and each other. Soon after, they planned to kill their friend when he returned so that each could have more gold coins. The man who went for food and drink wanted all the money for himself, so he put poison in the wine. On his return his two friends attacked him. They then ate the food and drank the wine and soon died. Whatever became of the box of gold coins no one knows to this day!

Several names can be given to the story like:

Riches Make Men Bad
The Lost Treasure
Gold Is Poison
False Friends
Death Wins After All

Figural Task: *Hidden Letters* (*Divergent Figural Transformation*)

A page of repeated and somewhat complex figures is given to the child. He is to find letters of the alphabet hidden in each of them. This ability requires the child to tear down the lines that make the figure and recombine a few of them into a letter of the alphabet, an ability to transform information that is commonly known into something original. Many inventions have resulted from the use of this kind of ability. Each non-repeated capital letter so obtained receives credit. See, for instance, Figure 4.4 (Khatena, 1978c, p. 34).

Measures relevant to 18 of the 24 divergent production abilities, as they relate to adults, are described in The Nature of Human Intelligence (Guilford, 1967). However, these measures do not include divergent symbolic transformations. Measures of the four behavioral component's of divergent production abilities are described in a paper by Guilford and his associates (Guilford, Hendricks, & Hoepfner, 1976).

Guilford's measures of divergent production abilities are timed tests, based on the rationale that timing is critical to accurate testing. Scoring of each task is not difficult and, with some practice, gives consistent results. Guilford recommended that scoring by an inexperienced scorer be checked by another person. Should disagreement occur, an expert should act as moderator. Information on reliability, validity, norms, and related matters can be found in the norms-technical manuals. It is appro-

Figure 4.4 Adding Decorations (Divergent Figural Implications or DFI)

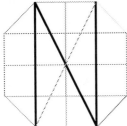
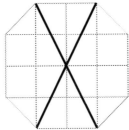
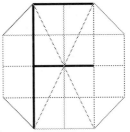

Note: From *The Creatively Gifted Child: Suggestions for Parents and Teachers* (p. 34) by J. Khatena, 1978, New York: Vantage Press. Copyright © 1978 by J. Khatena. Reprinted by permission.

priate to note Guilford's observation that high reliability indices for tests of divergent production are not to be expected because of fluctuations in motivation and dependence on a number of irrelevant determining circumstances.

According to Guilford, factorial validity is the best evidence of construct validity. Extensive research prior to the publication of the measures identify each test as a component of the Structure of Intellect. However, evidence of criterion-related validity for his measures is generally lacking, although some is available in a few scattered independent studies.

Relative to predictive validity for the Creativity Tests for Children (Guilford, 1973), the manual reports some evidence of validity derived from correlations of test scores with teacher judgments. However, Guilford has cautioned that validity indices obtained on the basis of teacher judgments can be questioned.

Further, the concurrent validity evidence that Guilford attempted to generate, by using total scores of the verbal and figural batteries of Torrance Tests of Creative Thinking (1974b) as correlates, did not turn out as expected. Significant correlation indices were found for three of the test tasks—one with the figural and two with the verbal Torrance measures. Tentative norms are given in C scores or percentile equivalents that relate to groups of adults and ninth-graders for most of the tests and to fourth-, fifth-, and sixth-graders for all the children's tests.

Torrance and Creative Thinking Abilities

Guilford (1967) measured creative thinking abilities by way of divergent production so that a person is required to respond to many stimuli, each of which sets out to measure a specific ability. Torrance measured creative thinking abilities by presenting several complex tasks designed to trigger simultaneous expression of several creative mental operations that give major roles to *fluency, flexibility, originality,* and *elaboration* (Torrance, 1974b). A recently developed streamlined scoring and interpretive manual for his figural tests expands the scoring dimensions of these measures (Torrance, 1989a).

Torrance defined creativity as

a process of becoming sensitive to problems, deficiencies, gaps in knowledge, missing elements, disharmonies, and so on; identifying the difficult; searching for solutions, making guesses or formulating hypotheses about the deficiencies; testing and retesting these hypotheses and possibly modifying and retesting them; and finally communicating the results. (Torrance, 1974b, p. 8)

This construct is central to the Torrance Tests of Creative Thinking (Torrance, 1974b).

Torrance Tests of Creative Thinking

The Torrance Tests of Creative Thinking consist of alternate forms of verbal and figural measures, both of which present activities in the visual modality that relate to the creative process and involve different kinds of thinking. The measures were carefully constructed to make the activities interesting and challenging for individuals at all educational levels, from kindergarten through graduate school.

These measures can be either individually or group administered. The *verbal* forms consist of seven subtests, and the *figural* forms consist of three subtests.

Verbal Test
The seven subtests of the verbal battery are given as follows: Asking Questions, Guessing Causes, Guessing Consequences, Product Improvement, Unusual Uses, Unusual Questions, and Just Suppose.

The first three activities all have a common stimulus in the form of a picture. They are included in the test battery to allow the expression of curiosity and to assess the ability to make hypotheses and to think of many possibilities. A person is given a picture and encouraged to *ask questions* about what is happening in the picture, to *guess causes* or give reasons for what is taking place, and to *guess consequences* or the results of the activity in the picture. All questions and statements are guesses that cannot be generated by merely looking at the picture.

Figural Tests

The three subtests comprising the figural battery are given are Picture Construction, Incomplete Figures, and Repeated Figures.

In the *Picture Construction* task a shape, such as a tear drop or jelly bean made of colored paper with an adhesive side, was given to a person. (This shape has since been replaced by a printed darkened shape to cut publication costs.) The individual is told to use the shape as an important part of a picture about to be made with encouragement to add details to give it more meaning. The task is expected to prompt the tendency for finding a purpose for something that has no definite purpose and to elaborate on it in such a way that a purpose is achieved.

In the standard scoring guides, the verbal measures are scored for *fluency*, *flexibility*, and *originality*, whereas the figural measures are scored for the same three abilities and *elaboration*. However, the streamlined scoring procedure for the figural forms (Torrance, 1989a) identifies 5 norm-referenced measures: fluency, flexibility, originality, abstractness of titles, elaboration, and resistence to premature closure. In addition 13 criterion-referenced measures are identified:

> Expression or feeling/emotion in drawing/titles
> Articulateness in telling a story; context, environment
> Movement/action (running, dancing, flying, falling, etc.)
> Expressiveness of titles
> Combination of two or more incomplete figures
> Combination of two or more repeated figures
> Unusual visual perspective (as seen from above, below, etc.)
> Internal visual perspective (as seen from above, below, etc.)
> Extending/breaking boundaries
> Humor in titles/captions/drawings
> Richness of imagery (variety, vividness, strength, etc.)
> Colorfulness of imagery (excitingness, earthiness, etc.)
> Fantasy (figures in myths, fables, fairy tales, science fiction, etc.)

Scores on the standard scoring procedure for these abilities are obtained for each subtest and then combined to give *total creativity indices* for each of the three verbal abilities and four figural abilities. These raw scores are then converted into standard scores. No composite single creative index is recommended although a few test users have chosen to generate this. However, it appears that such a score may give a rather stable index of the total amount of creative energy a person has available (Torrance, 1974b, p. 56).

The Torrance Tests of Creative Thinking are timed tests built on the premise that a certain degree of pressure is required to provoke creative mental functioning within a framework of encouragement aimed at making legitimate divergent thinking. Awarding credit for creative productions has never been easy. Any attempt to do so brings a certain element of subjectivity. With the Torrance Tests of Creative Thinking, a good measure of success has been attained toward establishing objectivity by quantifying responses. Counting the *number* of relevant responses, the different *categories* of response, the *statistically infrequent* but *relevant* response, and the *number of new ideas or details* added to the basic idea produced, allows for the determination of fluency, flexibility, originality, and elaboration scores, respectively.

Information on reliability, validity, norms and so on, can be found in the norms-technical manual (Torrance, 1974b). Torrance explains that the most difficult ability to score is *originality,* whether it be verbal or figural, which explains why lower *interscorer reliability* coefficients can be expected although Torrance will not accept anything less than an $r = .90$. Torrance indicates that lower interscorer reliabilities for originality result most often from "failure to scan adequately the listed originality weights," and that those for elaboration result most often from "failure to give credit for subtle forms of elaboration such as shading, unusual uses of a line, and symbols that express feeling or emotional tone" (Torrance, 1974b, p. 18).

Few studies of test-retest reliability, where the complete batteries of the alternate forms of the Torrance measures were administered to the same individuals, have been done. Reliability indices obtained from these few studies range from .70 to .90, with indices for the verbal tests being higher than for the figural tests.

Torrance has paid attention to content, concurrent, and predictive *validity* relative to creativity as a process. Such an approach relates to the kinds of abilities necessary "for successful operation of the process in various situations or for the production of various kinds of products [or] of personality characteristics, group dynamic variables, and other environmental characteristics that facilitate or impede the kind of functioning described by the process definition" (Torrance, 1974b, p. 21). Hence, Torrance uses this general approach for the validation of his measures of creative thinking abilities.

For *content validity,* the tasks' instruction and scoring procedures are based on the best theory and research available. Selection of task items was made on the basis of information drawn from the theory and research on the functioning of the human mind. Great care was taken to exclude technical or subject matter content from the tasks. Several studies involve the comparison of personality characteristics of high and low scorers on the Torrance tests, while others involve simple correlations between test scores and related measures.

Still other validity studies, conducted mainly with high school children, assess growth in creative thinking relative to experiments and provide evidence on the *construct validity* of the measures (Torrance, 1974b).

Evidence of *concurrent validity* presented and the finer points of its relations discussed relate to peer and teacher nominations, sales productivity, and educational achievement.

Attention to *predictive validity* is also given by Torrance, and this relates to evidence obtained from short-range and long-range predictive validity studies that set out to determine whether scores obtained on the Torrance Tests of Creative Thinking at different stages of education predict socially relevant creative behavior in adult life. Positive results are reported.

Norms are given in *T*-score units (mean = 50 and standard deviation = 10), based on data collected on students from a variety of localities and at different educational levels. A careful attempt has been made to exclude samples having special characteristics that might be expected to influence performance on the tests. The current norm group is multiracial and multiethnic, and is intended to be representative of the midrange of most school populations. The author provides conversion tables constructed on the basis of fifth grade elementary school children, and college students. To convert raw scores of elementary school children to *T* scores, the user uses the fifth grade conversion table, and of adults, the college conversion table. With reference to special needs, the user can construct other similar conversion tables. The manual also provides a section on interpretation of scores.

Thinking Creatively with Sounds and Words

Another measure of creative talent as it relates to originality and creative analogy is Thinking Creatively with Sounds and Words (Khatena & Torrance, 1990b; Torrance, Khatena, & Cunnington, 1990). This battery is made up of two measures of verbal originality entitled, Onomatopoeia and Images constructed by Joe Khatena, and Sounds and Images constructed by E. P. Torrance and B. F. Cunnington. Both components come in two forms, one set for children (Forms 1A and 1B), and the other for adults (Forms 2A and 2B). The logic of both measures hinges on the operation of the creative imagination to effect a break away from the perceptual set of audio or verbal stimuli to bring about the production of original responses. *Originality* is defined by Khatena as the power of the imagination to break away from the perceptual set so as to restructure or structure anew ideas, thoughts and feelings into novel and meaningful associate bonds (Khatena & Torrance, 1990b).

Onomatopoeia and Images presents verbal-auditory stimuli in the form of onomatopoeic words. The *verbal* components have semantic and sound elements that are tied to associative bonds of *referential* and *inferential* meanings established through usage. When presented to the listener, these words act as sets from which the listener must break away by using what Samuel Taylor Coleridge (1956) refers to as the *secondary imagination* to produce new combinations of meaning. The *auditory* component of the words subtly strikes the listener and stirs the emotional base of intellect, providing a tendency toward the irrational response. It is in the intellectual-emotive interaction that the mechanisms of the creative process function most effectively to produce the original.

Sounds and Images presents auditory stimuli in the form of sounds that range from the simple to the complex. Built on the same rationale as Onomatopoeia and Images, these sounds also act as mental sets when presented to the listener who must break away from them to produce original verbal images. Like onomatopoeic words, these sounds require that the intellect interact with emotion to evoke an imaginative response.

Both measures have certain *built-in conditions* that help listeners use their creative imagination. The measures

allow for progressive warm-up.
stress the legitimacy of divergent thinking.
provide freedom from threat and evaluation.
invite listeners to regress for the purpose of breaking away from inhibiting meaning and sounds sets, and of producing original verbal images.

The administration of tests is standardized by presenting all instructions on long-playing records or cassette tapes. A narrator prepares subjects for the test by explaining its nature and purpose, calling for the use of the imagination to create original verbal images. Take, for instance, an excerpt of the recorded narrative of Sounds and Images as given in a demonstration record and printed in the Directions Manual and Scoring Guide of the Measure (Torrance, Khatena, & Cunnington, 1990, pp. 4–5):

> Have you ever given much though to the world of sound, that mysterious region just beyond your eardrums? It's as close as the ring of your telephone, the rustle of the wind through the trees in your backyard, or the rumble of thunder on a warm summer afternoon.
>
> In just a moment you're going to take a journey into the most fantastic corners of the world, and there hear things you've never heard before. Although the first sound you'll meet along the way should be familiar enough, the

others are going to be somewhat strange to your ears, and you'll most likely scratch your head a bit as you wonder what on earth they might be. . . . Remember, write down your impression of each sound as it occurs in the recording. . . . All set? Here we go, then, into the mysterious world of sound.

In Sounds and Images, four sounds (simple to complex) are presented three times, with a 30-second interval (children's version) or 15-second interval (adult version) between one sound and the next. In Onomatopoeia and Images, onomatopoeic stimuli (5 for the children's version and 10 for the adult version) are presented four times with a 30-second (children's version) or 15-second (adult version) interval between one onomatopoeic word stimulus and the next.

Verbal images produced are scored for originality, much like the Torrance Tests of Creative Thinking. This scoring is based on the principal of statistical infrequency and relevance so that credits from 0 to 4 points may be awarded to a response. A scoring manual that accompanies the measures provides detailed scoring information with many examples.

A norms-technical manual (Khatena & Torrance, 1990b) provides interscorer reliability and other reliability information as well as validity and normative data. Interscorer, odd-even, split-half, and test-retest (with varying time intervals) *reliability* coefficients are reported. In addition, construct, content, and criterion-related *validity* indices derived from studies of personality, attitudes, biographical information, experimental manipulation, and the like, provide the necessary support.

Norms are given in standard scores with mean = 50 and a standard deviation of 10. The norm population is representative of regular school and gifted children of all age-grade levels measured by the tests, as well as, college adults. Furthermore, means and standard deviations for students from Grade 3 to the college graduate level are also provided for comparison so that test users may construct local norms where these are needed.

Research on creative imagination imagery with these instruments (Khatena, 1978b, 1984) led to the development of a scoring procedure that identifies the production of *creative analogies* (Khatena, 1983b). Studies on analogy production (Khatena, 1984, 1987) show that *direct* analogies are most frequently produced, that self-involvement in analogy production is less frequent so that fewer *personal* analogies are produced, that *fantasy* analogy production is even more infrequent, and that there is very little occurrence of *symbolic* analogy. Preference for the production of analogies with simple image structure rather than complex image structure is also evident (e.g., "John sings like a crow" rather than "John sings like a featherless crow on a winter's day.") Highest credit is given to the less frequently produced kind of analogy and image with scores ranging from 0 to 3 for the kind of analogy produced, 0 or 1 for the image structure given, and a combined score that ranges from 0 to 4 points. As yet, the scoring guide for creative analogies is in unpublished form, but further work on the guide will produce a technical manual.

Khatena-Torrance Creative Perception Inventory

Considerable evidence has accumulated to support the use of the *autobiographical instrument* as a screening device for giftedness and creativity. Instruments to measure an individual's perception of himself or herself in the form of checklists, questionnaires, and inventories have been found to be an efficient way of identifying creative talent (e.g., Roe, 1963; C. W. Taylor, 1958). One such inventory that serves this purpose effectively is the Khatena-Torrance Creative Perception Inventory (Khatena & Torrance, 1990a). It consists of two measures: What Kind of Person Are You? and Something About Myself. The battery is primarily designed to identify creative children and adults beginning from the age of 10.

What Kind of Person Are You?
What Kind of Person Are You? is based on the rationale that the individual has a psychological self structured to have incorporated creative and noncreative ways of behaving. The purpose of this measure is to present verbal stimuli to trigger those subselves that would yield an index of the individual's disposition or motivation to function in creative ways.

It contains 50 items of paired characteristics randomly arranged in a forced-choice format so that an item may call for a choice between a socially desirable and a socially undesirable characteristic or between a creative and noncreative characteristic. The subject is asked to choose one of each pair and mark an X for this on an answer sheet as, for instance, in the two following sample items:

___X___ Works hard

_____ Neat and tidy

_____ Care for others

___X___ Having courage for what you believe

The test is easily administered and interpreted and yields a creative index obtained by counting the number of correct responses out of 50. In addition to a creative perception index, What Kind of Person Are You? yields five factors or orientations (Bledsoe & Khatena, 1974) as follows:

Factor I: *Acceptance of Authority* relates to being obedient, courteous, conforming, and accepting the judgments of authorities.

Factor II: *Self-confidence* relates to being socially well-adjusted, self-confident, energetic, curious, thorough, and having a good memory.

Factor III: *Inquisitiveness* relates to always asking questions, being self-assertive, feeling strong emotions, and being talkative and obedient.

Factor IV: *Awareness of Others* relates to being courteous, socially well-adjusted, popular or well-liked, considerate of others, and preferring to work in a group.

Factor V: *Disciplined Imagination* relates to being energetic, persistent, thorough, industrious, imaginative, adventurous, never bored, attempting difficult tasks, and preferring complex tasks.

Something About Myself

Something About Myself is based on the rationale that creativity is reflected in the personality characteristics of individuals, in the kind of thinking strategies they employ, and in the products that emerge as a result of their creative strivings. The purpose of the measure is to obtain an index of a person's creativity by the number of positive choices made relative to the items in the three categories.

Something About Myself consists of 50 statements. The subject is asked to indicate on an answer sheet with an X whether or not the statement is applicable as, for instance, in the following sample items:

____X____ I am imaginative.

_____ I like adding to an idea.

_____ I have made a new dance or song.

____X____ I like taking risks.

____X____ I can make new things.

The test is easily administered and interpreted. It yields a creative index obtained by counting the number of positive responses out of 50.

Something About Myself, in addition to a creative perception index, yields six factors or creative orientations (Bledsoe & Khatena, 1973).

Factor I: *Environmental Sensitivity* involves openness to ideas of others; relating ideas to what can be seen, touched, or heard; interest in the beautiful and humorous aspects of experiences; and sensitivity to meaningful relations.

Factor II: *Initiative* relates to directing, producing, or playing leads in dramatic and musical productions; producing new formulas or new products; and bringing about changes in procedures or organization.

Factor III: *Self-strength* relates to self-confidence in matching talents against others, resourcefulness, versatility, willingness to take risks, the desire to excel, and organizational ability.

Factor IV: *Intellectuality* relates to intellectual curiosity, enjoyment of challenging tasks, imagination, preference for adventure over routine, a liking for the reconstruction of things and ideas to form something different, and a dislike for doing things in a prescribed routine.

Factor V: *Individuality* relates to preference for working by oneself rather than in a group, seeing oneself as a self-starter and as somewhat of an eccentric, being critical of others' work, thinking for oneself, and working for long periods without getting tired.

Factor VI: *Artistry* relates to production of objects, models, paintings, and carvings; musical compositions; receiving awards, prizes, or having exhibits; and production of stories, plays, poems, and other literary pieces.

Both components of the Khatena-Torrance Creative Perception Inventory are untimed tests. Designed for quick and easy administration, the measures can be administered either individually or in group settings. It generally requires from 10 to 20 minutes to complete. Scoring is simple and rapid. A credit of 1 point is awarded for each positive response on Something About Myself according to a scoring key with scores ranging from 0 to 50. Scoring keys are also provided for factor orientations.

The test manual provides information on interscorer, odd-even, split-half, and test-retest *reliability*. Careful attention is given to *item selection* and content *validity*. Construct validity is derived from factor analyses, attitudinal relationships, personality characteristics of high intelligence and creativity, sociometric analyses, and the like. Criterion-related validity coefficients are derived from studies of personality variables, biographical information, creative ratings, experimental manipulations, and other criteria.

The norm population of the 1990 edition of the manual is representative of regular and gifted children and adolescents, and college adults beginning from Grade 1 or age 6. Conversion tables allow for the conversion of total and factor raw scores to T scores, stanines, and standard scores (mean = 5 and standard deviation = 1). In addition, profile charts are provided for each test component.

Style of Learning and Thinking

Another measure of creativity in the Torrance family of instruments is the Style of Learning and Thinking (Torrance, 1988), developed from thought on the subject of cerebral hemisphericity. Such thought recognizes that each hemisphere has independent specialized functions. The *left cerebral hemisphere* or left brain appears to handle logical analytic and propositional thought. It is regarded as the center for nearly all language information, ordering, and time sense, operating linearly and sequentially. The *right cerebral hemisphere* or right brain appears to handle visuospatial and appositional thought, and imagination. It is virtually nonverbal and frequently makes itself known through dreams and fantasy. Unlike the left brain that processes information logically and systematically, the right brain processes information nonlinearly, simultaneously relating and associating a variety of information. With respect to *creative thinking*, both right and left brain processing are required.

Early research to discover a suitable instrument that could measure creativity via cerebral hemispheric functioning, led finally to the development of the Elementary and Youth Forms of Style of Learning and Thinking. The Elementary version of the measure consists of 25 items while the Youth version consists of 28 items. The former is designed for students in Grades 1 to 5, and although it can be administered to kindergarteners it is not recommended since children at this age level have barely begun to lateralize. The Youth Form is intended for students in Grades 6 to 12.

Both forms have a simple response format and can be administered individually or in groups. Take, for instance, two items of the Elementary Form:

1. _____ I like make-believe stories.

    __X__ I like stories about real people and things.

2. __X__ I like to work on lots of things at one time.

    __X__ I like to work on only one thing at a time.

The student taking the test is required to place an X if the statement is true, or two Xs if both of the pair of statements are true. The responses are then scored by counting the number of times both blanks are marked (W or Whole), and then the number of times left brain (L) or right brain (R) were selected according to a scoring procedure provided. Furthermore, a *strategy profile* can also be developed from the information of a person's Left, Whole, and Right response patterns. Such a profile provides data on brain specialization and/or integration in information processing, relative strengths and weaknesses in such functioning, and the basis for planning activities to emphasize the strengths or correct weaknesses. The test manual provides technical information on test-retest *reliability*, content and construct *validity*, *norms*, and how profile information can be used.

CONCLUSIONS

The widespread recognition that there are many kinds of giftedness found expression in the five USOE categories of giftedness. Identification approaches have fluctuated between the formal and less formal, depending on the availability of psychometric resources and appropriate instrumentation. On the matter of intellectual functioning, Guilford's model, the Structure of Intellect, with its inclusion of divergent production specifically and creativity generally, has provided the best logic and direction for thought and instrumentation design for more than one category of giftedness, although R. L. Thorndike and his colleagues have moved in this direction too in their hierarchical model of the Stanford-Binet. We owe to the Structure of Intellect, a clear differentiation of hereditary based mental operations that conserve knowledge from those that extend the boundaries of the known, thus preparing the way for the development of measures of creative thinking abilities.

On the matter of qualifying gifted in the several categories of giftedness, only a small percentage of individuals (5% or less) can be said to have superior ability. However, the levels of giftedness as they relate to I.Q. may be lower in one state than another to meet differing needs of people in different situations. Judgments as to what I.Q. level determines giftedness are not often well-informed and largely political in origin.

Where psychometric measures are used, a good rule of thumb in statistical terms is to use as criterion two standard deviations (SD) or 2 SDs above the mean relative to the ability measured. If a mean standard score is 100 and the SD is 15, then a person who is highly gifted on the measured ability must have 100 + 15 + 15 (i.e., 2 SDs above the mean) or a standard score of 130. This means that anyone obtaining a score of 2 SDs or more above the mean on an ability may be considered gifted relative to the ability measured. Of course, if the selection requirements are to be more stringent and only about 1% of the people screened are regarded as gifted, then only those whose standard scores are 3 SDs above the mean on the ability measured need be taken. It is not advisable to screen for superior abilities below 2 SDs above the mean, though it is not uncommon to do so in practice.

This procedure allows one to pick superior children on one or more ability or abilities relative to the test scores derived, and relative to the group from which one intends to select them. National norms are usually given in the norms-technical manual of the test, but by using the method described, you will be able to derive local and often highly relevant norms because your group of children may not be a part of the group used by the test constructor to derive norms.

CHAPTER FIVE

Identifying Other Gifted Children

*I*NTRODUCTION

To continue with the discussion of the identification of gifted children, we now move from procedures associated with the identification of intellectual, academic, and creative abilities to a consideration of leadership potential, visual and performing arts abilities, and the multipotentiality of giftedness. Whereas more formal procedures are available and used to identify the first three USOE categories of giftedness; the same is not the case for the areas of leadership, and visual and performing arts. However, less formal instruments like those of a biographical and perceptual nature, for example, can be used to get around the problem. As John C. Gowan pointed out (1978a), the progression of identification measures that has taken us from the use of process tests to biographical inventories and observational techniques provides us with valuable alternatives.

There are a number of problems that have to be faced when identifying gifted children, such as resource limitations, practical considerations, relevant professional preparation, and priorities. Overcoming such problems is a real challenge and will take time to meet. Making matters more complicated is the problem of cultural diversity that needs to be examined if gifted minority children are to have equal opportunity for selection and education.

LEADERSHIP POTENTIAL

The ability to lead involves not only intellectual ability but other personality variables that do not, on their own, present a reasonably good picture of leadership but become relevant as the result of interaction with groups of followers, varying situations, and related variables. A considerable amount of theory and research has been accumulated over the years and has been reviewed and summarized by a number of scholars (e.g., Fleishman, 1973; Stogdill, 1974). In general the factors found to be most highly associated with leadership can be classified as *capacity, achievement, responsibility, participation, status,* and *situation* (Stogdill, 1974).

This list should point to the complexity of the task of identifying leadership. For one thing there is no single psychological measure that can perform this task. The published measures that are available, such as the Leadership Ability Evaluation (Cassel & Stancik, 1961) and Leadership Evaluation and Development Scale (Mowry, 1964/1965), are either inappropriate or inadequate with regard to rationale, item analysis, reliability, validity, and scaling. Even the more recent instruments such as the Inventory of Individually Perceived Group Cohesiveness (Johnson, D. L., 1977) or Gifted and Talented Screening Forms (Johnson, D. L., 1980) reflect similar problems. The same needs to be said for the Leadership Skills Development Program (Karnes, F., & Chauvin, 1985) and the Leadership Training Program (Roets, 1986) that were developed on the basis of a diagnostic-facilitation model. Cecil A. Gibb's observation that, "Psychological research has never been able to identify or assess leadership ability" (Gibb, 1972, p. 1148) is to the point and continues to have a high degree of relevance.

The recognition by the USOE that leadership ability is another area of talent that needs identification in the selection process for programs of the gifted continues to present a real problem. There is no single adequate means for identifying such talent, as there is in the case of intellectual academic achievement or creative thinking abilities. Attempts to develop a single measure must be considered, at best, exploratory (e.g., Karnes, F., & Chauvin, 1985; Roets, 1986). However, there is a real need for development of adequate procedures to identify leadership ability and, in the absences of appropriately constructed instruments, some interpolation from the general findings of leadership research may offer fruitful direction.

Stogdill's Leadership Categories

The six categories of characteristics associated with leadership presented by Stogdill (1974) appear to offer comprehensive clues for the development of identification procedures that may be used in schools. First, we will take each category in turn and examine the possibilities of using not only the psychometric approach but also other resources we have, such as anecdotal data; observations of parents, teachers, and peers; and case histories. Then, we will examine a "Leadership Assessment Record" as an alternative procedure for the identification of leadership ability in the classroom.

Capacity

Capacity relates to intelligence, alertness, verbal facility, originality, and judgment. A measure of general or multifactor intelligence may be used to derive information regarding all these characteristics except originality. For this last characteristic, we shall have to use a measure of originality or creative thinking abilities that will give information on abilities such as fluency, flexibility, and elaboration. Group and individual tests of intelligence and creative or divergent thinking abilities may be used. It should not be difficult to find and use this information, which is generally already available in student records. Where these records are not available, arrangements need to be made to select and administer measures appropriate to the information needed. With respect to the level of intelligence, the search should be among those who might be classified as bright, normal, and above average, depending on the group that is to be led. Hollingsworth (1942) observes that, among children with a mean I.Q. of 100, the I.Q. of the leader is likely to fall between 115 and 130. The leader is likely to be more intelligent but *not too much more* intelligent than the average of the group led. The situation is of some relevance to the identification of the ability level of a leader in the regular classroom. We must take note of this.

Achievement

Achievement relates to scholarship, knowledge, and athletic accomplishments. In the achievement dimension, some consideration needs to be given to the kind of leadership intended for identification. As leadership relates to task performance of an academic nature, scholarship and knowledge go together. Good achievement tests and student performance in class assignments should provide the necessary information. As in the case of intelligence, the achievement level may not need to be extremely high, but for the leader, certainly higher than the achievement level of followers. Because leadership relates to groups organized for games and athletics, information about physical prowess, knowledge, skills, and experience are the key factors to be identified. The most reliable information of this kind can be obtained from direct observation of the individual who possesses these qualities, and the way he or she uses them in the group activity. All of this considered, the psychometric approach alone is still not the answer to the identification of leadership in this area.

Responsibility

Responsibility relates to dependability, initiative, persistence, aggressiveness, self-confidence, and the desire to excel. Direct observation (either by teachers or peers) and a personality inventory may be used to advantage in identifying this dimension of leadership. Of particular relevance is the Khatena-Torrance Creative Perception Inventory (Khatena & Torrance, 1990a), whose components not only provide information on creative perceptions of individuals but also the qualities of *initiative, persistence, self-confidence, the desire to excel,* as well as many other traits, not mentioned, that also contribute to leadership. Direct observation of qualities exhibited by students in their everyday classroom and playground activities should provide valuable information. Where spontaneous situations do not provide sufficient data, then situations that do evoke the manifestation of those qualities not easily observed may be arranged. Projects that invite group work, involve monitorial duties, or require special study or construction tasks can be arranged for that purpose without difficulty. Relative to direct observation, some written record of observed data can be most helpful.

Participation

Participation refers to activity, sociability, cooperation, adaptability, and humor. As in the case of responsibility, direct observation and an inventory may be used to collect data. Qualities in more than one of these dimensions may be found in a single inventory. For example, humor, cooperation, adaptability, sociability, as well as activity (in this sense, energetic) are characteristics that are found in What Kind of Person Are You?—where self-perceptions may range from the creative to the socially desirable. Adaptability can be associated with flexibility, which is a quality found in Something About Myself, and which is also identified as one of the creative thinking abilities on the Guilford or Torrance measures.

Status

Status relates to socioeconomic position and popularity. Concerning socioeconomic status, leaders as compared with nonleaders tend to come from backgrounds that range from superior (although not in the extreme) to average. Such information can easily be found in school records or by knowing the student well. Popularity can best be identified by direct observation.

Situation

Situation relates to mental level, status, skills, needs and interests of followers, objectives to be achieved, and so on. One of the best ways to identify these characteristics is to create a situation in the class in which a task needs to be performed. Thus, the achievement objectives of the group can be listed and the skills and interests of the various members as they relate to different aspects of the task can be identified. Then, discussion among members of the group can follow. All this may preface a *sociometric analysis* of relationships in this group, as the group will relate to the task at hand. Analysis of the resulting data should give clues to whom the leader (or leaders of the group) might be as the group approaches the task (or subtasks) at hand, as well as how it might relate to the other variables mentioned. The examiner may stop here or follow the analysis up with the organization and activitation of the group or subgroups to work on the specific task and, thus make direct observations. This will, in all probability, provide the information on personality-situation interaction and other variables as they relate to leadership.

Relative to mental level as it involves *social aspects of intelligence*, the best source of information is Guilford's measures of the behavioral component of the Structure of Intellect. These terms are Structure of Intellect abilities in the behavioral domain. Here, behavioral content relates essentially to nonverbal information involving attitudes, needs, desires, moods, intentions, thoughts, and the like, that occur in human interactions. These functions, especially in relation to the divergent thinking operation and the product dimension of the Structure of Intellect, provide reasonably good clues to one dimension of leadership. Take for instance behavioral content as it relates to divergent thinking situations.

> *Behavioral Units*—For example, Expressing Mixed Emotions, which requires a listing of many different things that individuals might say if they were both disappointed and jealous; or Alternate Picture Meanings, which presents a line drawing of a face that has a somewhat ambiguous expression and individuals are asked to list alternate interpretations of the psychological meanings of the expression.
>
> *Behavioral Classes*—For example, Multiple Behavior Grouping, which presents either a list of statements that need to be classified in different ways or line drawings of faces, hands, or other body parts

from which one selects small groups of drawings, each possessing common attributes of the psychological disposition indicated.

Behavioral Relations—For example, Creating Social Relations, which contains pictures of people—usually two—with some possible connection between the members of each picture.

Behavioral Systems—For example, Creating Social Situations, which calls for several story plots, when given three characters: (a) fearful woman, (b) angry man, and (c) unhappy child. (A sample response may be: (c) brings home a poor report card; (b) the father is angry with (c); and (a) the mother is afraid that (b) will hurt (c).)

Behavioral Transformations—For example, Multiple Expression Changes, which presents a number of faces, all of the same sex, each with a different expression and with three related events given, such as: "A man trips a lady who is walking; the man apologizes to the lady; the lady becomes angry." (The task lies in the selection, in turn, of sets of three faces for the man to go with each step in the series of events. Furthermore, each set selected after the first requires a revision or transformation of the man's sequence and attitudes.)

Behavioral Implications—For example, Suggested Feelings and Actions, which is a test that presents a situation, like "Late at night when A and her family are in their mountain cabin, she hears over the radio that a forest fire is raging a few miles away." (The task requires the thinking of different emotions and corresponding actions arising from the situation.)

Plan for Assessing Leadership

If some assessment procedure for leadership ability can arise out of the preceding discussion, perhaps it might be organized as it is here in a "Leadership Assessment Record" developed by the author.

Leadership Assessment Record

1. Socioeconomic Position:
   _____ Superior
   _____ Above Average
   _____ Average

2. Intelligence (Wechsler):
   _____ Verbal I.Q.
   _____ Performance I.Q.
   _____ Composite I.Q.

(S-B 4th ed.):   Standard Age Scores
or I. Q., Equivalents

_____ Verbal Reasoning

_____ Abstract/Visual
Reasoning

_____ Quantitative
Reasoning

_____ Short-Term Memory

_____ Composite

3. Creative or Divergent Thinking Abilities: Flexibility   Source

_____ (Figural)

_____ (Verbal)

Originality

_____ (Figural)

_____ (Verbal)

Other

_____

_____

4. Academic Achievement: _____   Source

_____

_____

_____

5. Personality Traits:

_____ Intelligence (bright, normal, or above average)

_____ Alertness and keen awareness of environment

_____ Verbal facility (fluency of speech)

_____ Originality (novel, clever, remote ideas)

_____ Judgment

_____ Scholarship

_____ Dependability

_____ General knowledge

_____ Specialized knowledge

_____ Initiative

_____ Persistence

_____ Aggressiveness

_____ Self-confidence

_____ Desire to excel

_____ Active (energetic)

_____ Sociability (participates in group activities)

_____ Cooperation

_____ Adaptability

_____ Humor

_____ Popularity

_____ Prestige

Note: Information for this inventory may be generated by the teacher; by the pupil reporting about himself or herself, or about someone else the pupil knows; and by the parent.

6. Sociometric Data: Generate information on the individual in relation to the group in which he is a member, so that the *stars* of the total group and/or *clique* can be identified as potential leaders. How to do this can be found in, for instance, *Sociometry in the Classroom* (Gronlund, 1959).

7. Multitalent Perception Inventory:

   (Khatena & Morse—KMMPI)   _____ Leadership

                                           _____ Versatility

8. Case History: Collect as much information about the individual from a variety of sources including direct observation of the individual in formal and informal settings (e.g., in the classroom and playing field).

9. Information from Other Sources: Any information derived from anecdotes or from the observations of parents, teachers, and peers about the behavior of the individual that will give insights on his or her leadership potential is also of value.

10. Summary Assessment: This assessment is to be based on all the information obtained from the above categories (1–9).

11. Comments or Remarks: Direction can be given to the educational placement of individuals, showing leadership potential, in special programs designed for them.

Source: J. Khatena, Multitalent Assessment Records. Copyright © 1988 by J. Khatena. Reprinted by permission.

VISUAL AND PERFORMING ARTS ABILITIES

Identification of talent in the performing and visual arts areas is not an easy matter. We have to face the many categories of talent present and lack good and suitable instruments to measure them. This situation is further complicated by the differential manifestation or presence of observable talent at different age and grade levels, and the specialized knowledge and skills relative to each talent that may have been acquired and mistaken for real talent. Theory and research suggest that generally talented individuals in the performing and visual arts are bright, that creativity is a significant energizing factor in talent, and that specific to each art form exists highly specialized abilities that require the language and skills peculiar to that art form for their expression. Hence, any approach at identification of talent in the areas of performing and visual arts must recognize and handle these variables.

The procedures for the identification of two areas of talent, music and art, will be discussed here. Several components are involved in each of these areas of talent. Two of these components, intelligence and creativity, can be considered to be common to all areas of talent. However, talent does not involve mental abilities alone and, depending on the area of talent, its identification will hinge on what specialized abilities, personality traits, and productivity are sought. Screening books on measurement inform us that there are a few measures unique to the area of music abilities although, with the exception of probably two or three, the measures are generally poor indicators of musical talent.

In addition, there are even fewer measures of art talent; and none of them are really appropriate for spotting talented students in the elementary and secondary schools. Certainly no measure of talent for drama exists.

Consequently, if psychometrically appropriate and sound instruments are not available, identification of the gifted in the areas of the performing and visual arts will have to depend on observational approaches. In practice, identification of musical and art talent is done by *audition,* an observational form that requires an individual to demonstrate by performing before, or presenting a *portfolio of products* to, an expert who subjectively determines the extent of talent the individual possesses. This evaluation then acts as the predictor of future talent growth. Such experts should be alerted to seek out not only superior ability to reproduce a style or technique, but also the ability to be innovative, with the tendency to break away from the more conventional nature of the art form.

Music Abilities

To identify a child who is gifted musically, we must recognize that we are looking for someone in possession of musical aptitude rather than someone who has acquired musical knowledge and skill, although some of this knowledge will be considered as part of the screening operation. Definitions of music talent are many and include the ability to retain, recognize, and reproduce a short musical phrase; to have absolute pitch;

to recognize intervals; to have a feeling for tonality; to love music; or to have general intelligence. But no clear definition of musical talent exists (Lehman, 1968).

Then, there is the theoretical orientation that regards musicality as something made up of a *hierarchy of talents,* many of which are independent of one another (Seashore, 1938); or that regards a talent for music as comprising a number of elements subsumed under a *general factor of musicality* (Mursell, 1932).

Lehman differentiates between tests that are designed to measure *capacity* for musical learning, even though no such learning may have taken place (i.e., aptitude tests), and tests that are designed to measure how much has been *learned* or accomplished at a particular time (i.e., achievement tests). He also points out that musical ability includes both aptitude and achievement even though neither includes the other. Hence, musical aptitude tests must be so constructed that the musical training an individual may or may not have received will not affect the results in any way.

Among the many tests of music talent available is the Seashore Measures of Musical Talents (Seashore, 1938; Seashore, Leavis, & Saetviet, 1960), which is the oldest. Others are the Kwalwasser-Dykema Music Test (Kwalwasser & Dykema, 1930), the Standardized Tests of Musical Intelligence (Wing, 1939, 1961), the Drake Musical Aptitude Tests (Drake, 1954), the Musical Aptitude Profile (Gordon, E., 1965), and the Measures of Musical Ability (Bentley, 1966).

Common to most measured elements of music, are *tone, rhythm, pitch, time,* and *intensity.* Other elements measured by one or another music test relate to *quality, consonance, melodic taste, timbre,* and *harmony.* Nearly all these published measures are deficient; few report technically sound information. The best among them are probably those constructed by Bentley, E. Gordon, and Wing. The author's preference is for Gordon's Musical Aptitude Profile because it gives relatively more complete information on musical aptitude.

Musical Aptitude Profile

The Musical Aptitude Profile (Gordon, E., 1965) is an objective measure of basic musical aptitude designed for use with students from Grades 4 to 12. It does not concern itself with historical or technical facts about music. The basic factors measured by the test are

Tonal Imagery   Part I: Melody
                          Part II: Harmony
Rhythm Imagery   Part I: Tempo
                          Part II: Meter

Musical Sensitivity Part I: Phrasing
                    Part II: Balance
                    Part III: Style

The complete battery of seven tests includes practice songs and directions given on recorded tape. The tests are made up of original short selections for violin and cello composed by E. Gordon and performed by professional artists. Subjects are asked to compare a selection with a musical answer to decide whether the two are alike or different, or exactly the same or different, or determine which is the more musical performance. Total testing time is 1 hour 50 minutes. Each of the three main divisions of the battery may be administered during the time limits of a regular class period.

To distinguish students who have the potential musical talent to create new music from those who have the potential to perform the music of others, measures of divergent or creative thinking abilities developed by Guilford, Khatena, and Torrance may be used, especially Creativity Tests for Children (Guilford, 1973), Thinking Creatively with Sounds and Words (Khatena & Torrance, 1990b), and the Torrance Tests of Creative Thinking (Torrance, 1974b). Further, creative personality characteristics can be identified by using the Khatena-Torrance Creative Perception Inventory (Khatena & Torrance, 1990a). It is of value to refer to the less widely known, but nonetheless important, attempt of Margery Vaughan (1971) to develop a measure of creative music talent. Her approach may give clues to the design of badly needed measures of music talent.

Other behaviors that pertain to musical performance and production may best be identified by direct observation.

Plan for Assessing Musical Talent

If some assessment procedure for musical talent can arise out of the preceding discussion, perhaps it might be organized along the lines of this "Musical Talent Assessment Record."

Musical Talent Assessment Record

1. Musical Aptitude: _____ Tonal Imagery
   (E. G. Gordon Scale)   _____ Rhythm Imagery
                                        _____ Musical Sensitivity

2. Creative or Divergent: Flexibility
   Thinking Abilities: _____ Figural
   (Torrance—TTCT)   _____ Verbal
                                         Originality
                                         _____ Figural
                                         _____ Verbal

   (Khatena & Torrance—TCSW)   Originality
                                         (auditory/verbal)
                                         _____ Sounds and Images
                                         _____ Onomatopoeia and Images

3. Creative Personality: Creative Index
   (Khatena & Torrance—KTCPI)
   Something About Myself   _____
   What Kind of Person Are You?   _____

4. Musical Achievement (if any):   _____

5. Musical Behavior Traits:

   _____ Is able to hum or sing in tune

   _____ Knows how to make a tune loud or soft for effects

   _____ Shows awareness of difference between production of good from
   bad sounding notes

   _____ Has a sense of rhythm

   _____ Can keep time to a tune

   _____ Can beat different time with rhythm changes in a tune

   _____ Knows when to accent different beats for effect

   _____ Is able to vary loudness and softness of beat for effect

   _____ Can hum or sing in harmony with another person without the
   aid of musical notes

   _____ Remembers tunes easily

   _____ Remembers rhythm easily

   _____ Quick to learn a new tune

   _____ Quick to learn a new rhythm

   _____ Can sing another tune that resembles a known but not an identical tune

   _____ Can dance to a tune

   _____ Can dance to tunes with different rhythms

_____ Sings, dances, or plays an instrument every day

_____ Given an incomplete melody can add a tune to complete it

_____ Makes own tunes

_____ Plays an instrument by ear

_____ Can read simple music

_____ Can write a simple tune

_____ Has a good voice

_____ Enjoys listening to music

_____ Likes producing music with others

Note: Information for the inventory may be generated by the teacher; by the pupil reporting about himself or herself, or about someone else the pupil knows; and by the parent.

6. Multitalent Perception Inventory:

(Khatena-Morse—KMMPI)   _____ Music

                                   _____ Versatility

7. Case History: Collect as much information about the individual from a variety of sources including direct observation of the individual's musical talent exhibited in formal (i.e., audition) and informal settings.

8. Information from Other Sources: Any information derived from anecdotes or the observations of parents, teachers, and peers about the behavior of the individual that will give insights about his or her musical potential is also of value.

9. Summary Assessment: This assessment is to be based on all the information obtained from the above categories (1–8).

10. Comments or Remarks: Direction can be given to the educational placement of individuals, showing musical talent, in special programs designed for them.

Source: J. Khatena, Multitalent Assessment Records. Copyright © 1988 by J. Khatena. Reprinted by permission.

Art Abilities

Identification of students who have ability in art is also difficult. There are no completely satisfactory tests of aptitude in art, especially ones that can be administered during school years.

Guilford (1968) has described some figural abilities that are important to artistic ability—ideational and expressional fluency, spontaneous and adaptive flexibility, and elaboration—in the divergent production dimension of the Structure of Intellect. These abilities are measurable as follows:

Divergent Figural Units—For example, Sketches, which present a simple basic figure to which is to be added just enough detail to make a recognizable object; Monograms, which require arrangement of such letters as *A, V,* and *C* to make many different monograms as if they were initials of a name.

Divergent Figural Classes—For example, Alternate Letter Groups, which present a set of capital letters, such as *AHVTC,* for the formation of subgroups, each of which makes a class that are all straight lines according to the figural properties of *AHVTC.*

Divergent Figural Systems—Emphasis is on organization of visual elements into wholes, for example, Making Objects Test, which requires the use of two or more of several given simple geometric forms to construct a named object.

Divergent Figural Transformations—These are concerned with adaptive flexibility and are in line with the emphasis on shift, for example, Planning Air Maneuvers, which involves the planning of sky writing two capital letters in succession as efficiently as possible with an airplane pilot given instructions as to start, finish, and turns of the airplane.

Divergent Figural Implications—For example, Decorations, in which outline drawings of common objects, such as pieces of furniture and articles of clothing, are each repeated two times with instructions for filling them in with decorative additions.

These figural abilities have been included and modified in Guilford's Creativity Tests for Children (1973) comprising the 5 verbal and 5 nonverbal items described earlier in this chapter. It is a test that can be used both for the identification of divergent thinking abilities (taking the 10 items together) and for the identification of art abilities (taking items 1–5, i.e., Making Something Out of It, Different Groups, Making Objects, Hidden Letters, and Adding Decorations).

Another very useful measure for this purpose is the figural forms of the Torrance Tests of Creative Thinking (Torrance, 1974b), from which information about the figural fluency, flexibility, originality, and elaboration abilities of a student—all abilities important to art talent—can be derived. This measure comprises three subtests that require students to use their imagination to use the various shapes, lines, and circles given to produce pictures no one else would think of drawing. Scoring the test using the published scoring guide gives fluency, flexibility, originality and elaboration scores in the figural dimension that should tell us about the individual's potential to be creative. However, if the drawings are looked over with care, some indications of art talent may also be observed, although subjects are not asked to produce pictures that can be considered as meeting particular artistic standards. Important elements of creativity and art talent may be identified at one and the same time.

There are not many specific art ability measures. Among the ones that require the production of drawings for the purpose of assessment of art potential are the Horn Art Aptitude Inventory and the Knauber Art Ability Test. The Advanced Placement Program in Studio Art offers identification of art potential for college placement. The Meier Art Judgment Test and the Meier Aesthetic Perception Test—of little concern to us here—measure the ability to judge art but require no drawing abilities. Except for the Placement Program in Studio Art, the other four art measures mentioned earlier have psychometric problems that complicate their use (Clark & Zimmerman, 1984).

In brief, the Horn Art Aptitude Inventory, suitable for high school seniors, does not concern itself with advanced skills in art, but rather with predicting future success in artistic activities. It requires subjects to draw simple pictures; then they are to compose more elaborate pictures using a few given lines as clues. The scoring is subjective but uses various works of quality as criteria.

The Knauber Art Ability Test, a much older test constructed in 1930, requires subjects' actual drawings and rearrangement of pictorial compositions. Responses are scored for quality according to the key that is provided.

Advanced Placement Program in Studio Art

Early attempts to assess artistic aptitudes were based on measurement of art judgments or preferences between *good* or *bad* compositions of well-known works of art (e.g., Meier Art Judgment Test). Unlike these attempts, the Advanced Placement Program in Studio Art (Dorn, 1976) is designed to appraise the quality of studio art performance by recognizing all the highly subjective elements used in the creation of an art work.

A *portfolio*—comprised of four original art works of a specific size and several slides (2 x 2 inches) that document other works—is submitted with the help of the subject's school to Educational Testing Service in Princeton, New Jersey. The examination consists of three sections:

Section A: The student's four original compositions of a given dimension are evaluated for quality.

Section B: The student's group of slides or film that shows work over an extended period in an area of concentration is evaluated.

Section C: Two slides submitted by the student, each showing proficiency in four broad areas—spatial illusion, drawing, color and organization of three-dimensional materials—are also evaluated.

The judging is done by experts in the field who rate the components of the portfolio according to agreed upon criteria of quality, giving emphasis to uncommon responses in art. Judgments are made with great care. The reliability of evaluations is ensured by training the judges to use the criteria set before and during their reading of all three sections of the evaluation. This evaluation procedure of studio art performance of the gifted, although not yet perfect, is considered a step in the right direction, providing some measurement of the ability of high school students to benefit from a college education in art.

Art Abilities, General Intelligence, and Creativity

To identify a student who is gifted in art, some consideration needs to be given to intelligence. Students who are highly talented in art are generally quite bright. Creative thinking abilities, especially as manifested in the visual-figural dimension should be taken into account. Attention should also be given to talent specific to art, which can be identified not only through psychometric tests (if available), but also through the student's artwork.

One of the surest ways to spot children gifted in art is by the frequency and level of productivity they have attained. Talented children are often seen communicating their ideas and feelings nonverbally in drawings, paintings, and other art forms. Visual narrative—a quality that is considered a catalyst, or a basic and primary element that activates other aspects of artistic giftedness—is observable in the works of young children (Wilson & Wilson, 1976). The Wilsons cite Alan Garner, Julian Green, and C. S. Lewis as examples of writers who used "visual narrative as children until they were able to use words with sufficient facility to convey the subtlety and complexity of the worlds they were busily creating" (pp. 432–433). It is also visual narrative that leads gifted children to produce a vast number of drawings.

> For gifted young people [visual] narrative is the train engine which pulls with it the freight cars of tension and relief, emotions and feelings, repressions and sublimations, symbolizations and expanding aspects of reality. (p. 435)

The teacher, who is involved in the difficult job of identifying the child gifted in art, needs to become familiar with the personality characteristics and some important observable behaviors of such creative children. To derive information concerning traits of the creative personality, the teacher could use the Khatena-Torrance Creative Perception Inventory.

Plan for Assessing Art Talent

If some assessment procedure for art talent can arise out of the preceding discussion, perhaps it might be organized along the lines of the "Art Talent Assessment Record."

Art Talent Assessment Record

1. Figural Abilities (Guilford):

   Fluency
   _____ Ideational
   _____ Expressional
   Flexibility
   _____ Spontaneous
   _____ Adaptive
   Elaboration

2. Creative or Divergent Thinking Abilities:

   (a) Creativity Tests for Children (Guilford)

   _____ Verbal
   _____ Figural

   (b) Tests of Creative Thinking (Torrance)

   Figural
   _____ Fluency
   _____ Flexibility
   _____ Originality
   _____ Elaboration

3. Creative Personality Traits:
   (Khatena & Torrance—KTCPI)

   Creative Index

   Something About Myself

   _____

   What Kind of Person Are You?

   _____

4. Art Achievement:

   Rating

   (a) Advanced Placement Program in
   Studio Art

   _____

   (b) Interview

   _____

5. Art Behavior Traits:

   _____ Scribbles earlier than most other children in the class

   _____ Produces many ideas in drawings or paintings

   _____ Initiates drawings

   _____ If given a situation, takes it to develop new ones

   _____ Unusual and interesting visual imagery in drawings

   _____ Drawings show imagery expanding in chain reaction

   _____ Sensitive use of art materials

   _____ Sensitive handling of techniques

   _____ Highly developed sense of movement in drawings

_____ Highly developed sense of rhythm in drawings

_____ Great feel for color

_____ Sensitive to order and organization

_____ Varies organization of elements to suit different situations

_____ Interest content

_____ Tells a story

_____ Expresses feelings

_____ Shows confidence when undertaking a drawing

_____ Intense personal identification with experience depicted

_____ Produces many drawings

_____ Enjoys expressing self in art

_____ Likes adding details to basic idea

_____ Flexible in use of art materials

_____ Innovative in selection and use of art materials

_____ Tends to want to draw unusual situations

_____ Has unusual ideas for pictures

Note: Information for the inventory may be generated by the teacher; by the pupil reporting about himself or herself, or about someone else the pupil knows; and by the parent.

6. Multitalent Perception Inventory: _____ Art Talent

   (Khatena-Morse—KMMPI)   _____ Versatility

7. Case History: Collect as much information about the individual from a variety of sources including direct observation of the individual's art talent exhibited in formal and informal settings.

8. Information from Other Sources: Any information derived from anecdotes, observations of parents, teachers, and peers about the behavior of the individual that will give insights on art potential would also be of value.

9. Summary Assessment: This is to be based on all the information obtained from the above categories (1–8).

10. Comments or Remarks: Direction can be given for the educational placement of individuals, showing art talent potential, in special programs designed for them.

Source: J. Khatena, Multitalent Assessment Records. Copyright © 1988b by J. Khatena. Reprinted by permission.

MEASURES OF MULTIPLE BEHAVIORAL DIMENSIONS

So far we have looked at identification instruments relative to each of the five USOE categories of giftedness. Several instruments of the inventory or rating scale type have been constructed on the assumption that behavioral characteristics of the gifted and talented are measurable by a single biographical instrument comprising multiple scales (anywhere from 4 to 10).

Among these instruments are the Biographical Inventory Form U (Taylor & Ellison, 1983), Gifted and Talented Screening Form (D. L. Johnson, 1979), Scale for Rating the Behavior Characteristics of Superior Students (Renzulli & Hartman, 1971), and its later extension in Scales for Rating the Behavioral Characteristics of Superior Students (Renzulli, Smith, White, Callahan, & Hartman, 1976), the Guidance Institute for Talented Screening Instrument (Male & Perrone, 1979), and the Kranz Talent Identification Instruments (Kranz, 1981).

The best researched of these instruments is the one constructed by C. W. Taylor and R. L. Ellison. This instrument is a careful outgrowth of their earlier biographical inventories, and their attempts to provide indices in the major talent areas of creativity, academic talents, leadership, and artistic potentials. The other instruments mentioned vary in purpose and use, so much so that identification may be leveled at educational placement or guidance, and the tests may be taken by the student or by an adult for the student. Generally, the tests are loosely put together; the work done in providing evidence of essential psychometric properties, especially in the areas of reliability and validity, is insufficient. Furthermore, there is either an absence of appropriate normative data, or when these data are available, they are poorly defined and described. Nearly all these scales may be said to be in various stages of development and definitely in need of considerable refinement.

Another instrument that has been recently developed is the Khatena-Morse Multitalent Perception Inventory (Khatena & Morse, 1987, 1990; Morse & Khatena, 1988). It is designed to assess individuals from 10 years of age to adulthood in five broad areas of talent, namely, art, music, leadership, creative imagination, and initiative. The instrument is a self-report inventory consisting of 50 items and it comes in alternate forms. Individuals take from 10 to 20 minutes to complete the inventory depending on their age level. Children younger than 10 years of age can take the test with the help of an adult who knows them well.

Five factor orientations provide scores for art, music, leadership, creative imagination, and initiative, and the total score gives a versatility index that represents these several areas of talent. Norms, for both regular and gifted students of school age and adults, have already been generated. All raw scores obtained from the instrument can be converted to *T*-scores; standard scores and percentile ranks by reference to conversion tables provided. The measure is psychometrically sound and supporting technical information can be found in the test manual (Khatena & Morse, 1991).

NOMINATIONS AND PRODUCT APPRAISAL

Screening procedures relate to *nominations* and *product appraisal*.

Nominations

Nominations may be made by oneself (mainly applicable to students in the junior and senior schools) and others (i.e., fellow students, teachers, and parents). To assist in the nomination process, some form of an inventory, checklist, or rating scale may be used to guide the nominator in identifying traits that are indicators of a variety of talents or abilities. Information derived from the measures that have been discussed so far may also be used by the nominator as such a guide, though one would expect that nominations are frequently based on more informally derived information. In any case, the nomination process is sharpened by using agreed upon criteria as a frame of reference. It must be realized, though, that even with the help of the inventory, checklist, rating scale and like criteria, subjective variance is high. This balance makes the nomination process quite imprecise. However, when used as an initial screening device for clues about talent and abilities, nomination can be very useful when no tests are available for purposes of identification. The nomination process should be used with caution and should be supplemented with more formally derived information.

Product Appraisal

Product appraisal involves the evaluation of student achievements in art, music, science, poetry, and performance. The appraisal may be done either by a single person (most frequently a teacher), or by a group of people (by way of a panel of judges). Appraisals may be done formally or informally. However, it is important that the element of subjectivity be minimized and the judgment of more than one judge be shaped and expressed consistently. To ensure that there is consistency in the evaluations, appraisal must be based on a commonly accepted set of criteria that includes an agreed-upon definition of creativity and the extent to which the generation of the "new" is given its proper place, in keeping with a sense of beauty and good taste.

The advantage of product appraisal over nomination is the fact that in the latter some tangible manifestation of talent is required and present. Establishing appropriate criteria to act as touchstone to talent appraisal is essential, for it will serve to keep in proper place expected subjectivity that may threaten the validity of the process. It is important to have an informed team of judges evaluating products as, for instance, in the manner suggested by Theresa M. Amabile (1983). To adapt her method of consensual assessment of artistic creativity for the screening of talented children may be a step in the right direction.

IMPLEMENTATION PROBLEMS

Identification of the several categories of giftedness present many problems that hinge on theoretical issues that are far from settled and on practical considerations that make full implementation of measurement very difficult, if not inhibitive. It should come as no surprise to learn that although many states have accepted the USOE categories of giftedness, they have not included all these areas in their screening operations. As we have seen, we do not yet know all that needs to be known to allow for the development of suitable instruments for adequate identification of these five areas.

With the five USOE areas of giftedness, finding measures that can identify intellectual abilities, creative or productive thinking, and specific academic aptitude can be done with relative ease, although some disagreement persists about the precision of these instruments. The remaining two areas—leadership and performing and visual arts (music and art)—do not have similar traits that can be identified by locating measures. As a consequence, many practical problems arise in terms of administration, time, and cost, necessitated by the use of alternative screening procedures. To avoid these problems, screening plans, by and large, focus on the use of I.Q. and achievement measures and, to a much smaller extent (confined to relatively few states) focus on creativity measures.

With these factors in mind, we are in a better position to understand the reluctance of many states to throw themselves into attempting to identify all five categories of giftedness. Their reluctance is not so much because of an unwillingness to recognize the varieties of giftedness, but rather because sufficient uncertainty and instability can enter into screening operations, calling into question judgments in the selection of gifted students.

Another factor of some importance concerns the influence that the trained personnel who run the testing units for the state have on the testing procedure. By professional preparation, they veer toward testing for I.Q. and using achievement measures. Because we do have an acute need for well-trained personnel in the screening and advisement of students in several categories of giftedness, a re-education of those in office and appropriate preparation of those now in training appear to be increasingly necessary. We must recognize these problems and prepare ourselves to deal with them. It is unlikely that the search for better and different identification procedures will slacken. In fact, there is every indication that this need will continue to grow over the years.

CULTURAL DIVERSITY

An important contribution to our understanding of human beings and their behavior comes from the works of social anthropologists Ruth Benedict (1935), Clyde Kluckhohn (1970), and Margaret Mead (1930), among others. In attempting to find answers to questions concerning some of the problems faced by individuals growing up in an American environment, these social scientists chose to study the institutions and behavior patterns of less complex social groups in this country and elsewhere in the world. Almost without exception, these scholars concluded that many of the problems experienced by our youth arise from cultural shaping and conditioning.

Cultural Diversity in America

The cultural diversity observable among the different peoples living in the United States can be attributed to cultural variance. Language differences contribute to the complexity of cultural variability in other lands, as they do in this country. The English used by subcultural groups in this country is not altogether the same language. Variation not only exists in the spoken tongue but also in the denotation and connotation of word meaning as well as word usage. To complicate matters, fresh waves of Spanish-speaking immigrants and those speaking languages of Asian countries continue to enter the United States, adding to its cultural diversity. They are referred to by John U. Ogbu (1988) as *voluntary minorities* to distinguish them from the native Americans and African Americans, whom he calls the *involuntary minorities.*

The United States has long been well known as a "melting pot" of peoples from many parts of the world. Many of the cultural differences which these people bring with them have been absorbed into a common American culture comprising a number of subgroups. Some of these subgroups are, as well, nondominant, generally have low socioeconomic status. They include native Americans, African Americans, Mexicans, Puerto Ricans, Chinese, Vietnamese, Indians, and other

Asian subgroups. All share a common American education and culture, while still maintaining some aspects of their own cultural heritage, which makes for cultural diversity in this country.

Cultural Diversity and I.Q.

The American school system is geared toward educating the average student. It is a repository of the middle-class culture and value system, which operates as a major educational influence shaping the lives of students. For years, the educational design has included learning and testing as important elements. The growing recognition of individual differences in ability and needs has manifested itself in the rise of the testing movement and in the provision of a differential curriculum. Students have been tested for achievement over many years, mainly to evaluate learning outcomes. Sometimes I.Q. information is also used for educational placement.

At the time that advocates for special education were being heard, and federal or state legislation was passed to provide opportunities for exceptional children (one might include the gifted as a category of *exceptionality* although the latter term seems generally to be applicable to those students with handicaps or disturbances), identification of general intellectual ability, as measured by I.Q. tests, was commonly practiced. Children would be categorized, for the purposes of education, along a continuum that includes the educable mentally retarded, the average, and the highly intelligent. Using a frame of reference that is uniquely white, middle class, both in terms of test items and norm groups, traditional I.Q. measures compare the performance of students from culturally diverse groups with the performance of students of the dominant white group for which the tests were really designed. Consequently, the results show culturally diverse students as deficient. These students are then called culturally deprived, disadvantaged, or different.

H. H. Goddard (1908, 1911) first used an American translation of the Binet and Simon measure in institutional settings, but cultural bias showed this approach to be unsuitable. Terman's design of an American version of the Binet measure proved to be more productive. It is ironic that, whereas the Stanford-Binet recognized the need to construct a measure of intelligence that would reflect the cultural difference and uniqueness of this country, it limited itself to America's dominant white middle-class population and their culture.

In addition, the underlying assumption that the Stanford-Binet is an instrument relevant for use in the cases of all Americans without regard to cultural diversity and socioeconomic factors is faulty. Comparison of different groups of people to norms that do not apply to their groups violates good measurement rules and, without question, introduces extraneous variables that contaminate the results. It is to be expected then that readings on the measures for people who are different from the norm group and for whom the items of the test were not designed, by way of language idiosyncrasies and content, would not be correct and more than likely show deficits.

Clearly, such people, rather than being called disadvantaged, should be regarded as being *at a disadvantage.* Much of the controversy over the mental capacity of blacks versus whites as measured by I.Q. scales (e.g., Gage, 1972; Jensen, 1969; Shockley, 1972) could have been avoided had the thrust of the arguments been directed toward the cultural diversity of the population rather than the deficits among blacks, using a biased frame of reference as the criterion.

A very telling argument about this controversy and related factors has been made by John U. Ogbu (1988). He distinguishes between the cognitive behavior and degree of cultural adaptation among members of the white dominant Western culture and minorities who came to this country voluntarily (migrants from Asia and Europe) and that of the people who were involuntarily imported (blacks from Africa) or subjected (native Americans). Furthermore, he suggests that culturally biased measures are not the only root to the problem of lower test scores attained by the involuntary group. Conscious or unconscious "resistance" to test-taking by the involuntary minority, perceived by Ogbu as a defense of their culture and personal well-being, is an important part of the problem that needs to be recognized and addressed.

The Problem of Definition

Of the many problems that confront us when we are trying to make up our minds about special groups, the problem of *definition* obtrudes. In selecting a word to name a group relative to certain attributes, we are sometimes not fully aware of the connotations of the word that is assigned to it. Although in some respects the denotative meaning of the word communicates those attributes that fit it, in other respects emotive implications and overtones may be inherent in the usage of the word.

It is of value then, to take a second look at such words as *deprived, disadvantaged, different,* and *diverse.* These are words commonly used to describe the culture of minority groups. The first two words have negative connotations: *deprived* suggests deliberate withholding, whereas *disadvantaged* suggests lack. Both words indicate deficit conditions that attend a present state of being and imply comparison to a frame of reference expected to apply to the whole referent population.

In addition, it is of importance to remember that, when we refer to the culturally *different* and *diverse,* we mean to include ethnically different groups about whom the word *disadvantaged,* especially, loses its meaning. For the scion of a Jewish or oriental immigrant family, even though poor, may not be culturally disadvantaged (Gowan, 1979e; Ogbu, 1988). Rather, the alien cultural tradition may actually give advantage in terms of a rich cultural background, which may account for the rapid rise of many descendants of immigrants to managerial and professional positions.

Gowan (1979e) also asks us to note how Cuban émigrés with similar handicaps as Mexican-American families (Ogbu's voluntary minority), customarily regarded as culturally disadvantaged, have made rapid adjustments to American life, while the Anglo-Saxon Kentucky people living in the hills, a subgroup of the dominant white group, have failed to adjust. Further, Gowan considers that the word *disadvantaged* is ostensibly related to poverty and low socioeconomic status in the family and goes on to define *disadvantaged* not so much in ethnic terms but rather as being outside of the economic and cultural mainstream.

The selection of one or another of the four terms (*deprived, disadvantaged, different,* and *diverse*) to denote a minority group will vary depending on whether the user's perspective relates to differences among a variety of cultural groups or to differences between a group and some standard relative to a trait or behavior pattern. The problem posed by this distinction has led many to question the validity of the deficit terms *deprived* and *disadvantaged* and to suggest the use of *different, diverse,* or *minority,* as examples, as more appropriate terms (Baldwin, 1978; Frasier, 1979; Fuchigami, 1978; Torrance, 1977b).

We have already discussed the concept of giftedness and its multifaceted nature, which is equally as relevant to the minority gifted (Fuchigami, 1978), the culturally diverse gifted (Baldwin, 1978; Frasier, 1979), or those considered "different" (Torrance, 1977b). Cultural and socioeconomic factors tend to veil the talent potential of these gifted groups, consequently hindering true readings and proper identification (Baldwin, 1987).

A recent important contribution to assist us in our understanding of the subject, is the *National Report on Identification* (Richert, Alvino, & McDonnel, 1982). Among other issues discussed in this report is one that focuses attention on current practices of identifying the disadvantaged. These practices tend to underrepresent the underachieving poor and minority gifted children who are in most need of programs designed to develop their potential; creative or divergent thinkers whose abilities are not tested by standardized intelligence tests or grades; and other groups including the learning disabled or handicapped gifted.

The report makes the point that these groups, rather than being inherently disadvantaged, are put at a disadvantage when measures of academic achievement are used exclusively or given inordinate weight in the identification process (Richert, 1985).

The Problem of Identification

The selection of students for participation in gifted programs or projects in and out of school brings into sharp focus the problem of identification. We have already discussed the general narrowness of identification approaches that rely on I.Q. and achievement. The growing recognition that there exist varieties of talent that must be taken into account in the identification-selection process has led to some embarrassment. It has been found that appropriate procedures are not available to identify some areas of talent. This problem appears to be further complicated by cultural diversity factors so that not only is there the problem of designing instruments or procedures for the identification of a multiplicity of gifts, but also the problem of making these approaches relevant and meaningful for the many cultural groups that constitute American society.

Of the many well-known discussions on the important issues of identification and nurturance of the culturally different gifted (e.g., Chambers, Barron, & Sprecher, 1980; Clark, K. B., 1965; Fantini & Weinstein, 1968; Gallagher & Kinney, 1974; Riessman, 1962), there are three that merit special notice. One, by R. J. Samuda (1975), focuses attention on issues pertaining to the measurement of abilities of minority groups; another, by Bruch (1975), examines issues that involve the assessment of creativity in the culturally different. To these must be added Torrance's (1977b) discussion, which deals not only with major issues and trends in the discovery and nurturance of giftedness in the culturally different, but also provides a unique concept—using creative positives both for purposes of identification and education.

Both Samuda and Bruch note the inadequacies inherent in the idea that test measures, constructed for use with members of the majority culture, are just as appropriate for use with members of diverse subcultures. They also ask questions on the relevance of item content, reliability, validity, and related psychometric procedures as well as on their administration and interpretation for cultural minorities. Another issue explored in common is the need for measures to take into account the influence of experience and differences of language usage in the context of cultural diversity. Both Samuda and Bruch see the need for training testers and developing test administration procedures that reflect an orientation toward a difference model and that point away from a deficit model.

Samuda's observations concern the need for the development of new measures for diagnosis and prescription that incorporate the special language characteristics of minority groups and serve as open-ended probes that include atypical patterns and varieties of learning. As departures from traditional testing and deficit models, Samuda's concepts have neglected to emphasize a multitalent approach and a search for the abilities that are especially encouraged by culturally different groups (Torrance, 1977b).

Bruch offers a more future-oriented and balanced summary of the issues. However, she includes the need for assessment procedures that go beyond I.Q. so that multiple talents and creativity can be identified, and that recognize the value of identifying such talents by more informal observation procedures, taking into account environment, experience, and cultural diversity. Her conceptualization of the problem is in line with Torrance's (1977b) emphasis on the need for a nonpsychometric approach whose rationale is to identify the talents of the culturally different by means of creative positives.

About the best, most comprehensive and forward-looking discussion on the discovery and nurturance of giftedness in the culturally different, is Torrance's (1977b) monograph whose purpose, in the main, is to provide a resource book of alternatives. The problem is perceived as complex; it pivots mainly on issues of the identification and development of giftedness. Torrance points to the inadequacies of traditional tests that, for instance, deny culturally different students special educational opportunities; prevent access to higher education; incorrectly place minority children in programs for mentally retarded students (Astin, 1975; Goolsby, 1975); and, by means of the issues and consequences associated with test usage, thwart the discovery of giftedness among the culturally different (Bruch, 1975; Kamin, 1974; Miller, 1974). (The ineffectiveness of educational programs for culturally different children and the need for different alternative education relevant to them are pointed out by many, for example, Coleman, 1973; Jencks, 1973; Torrance, 1977b.)

On the matter of identification, there have been attempts to correct inadequacies of traditional measures. These have included translations (e.g., Spanish and English versions of the Wechsler Adult Intelligence Scale and the Inter-American Series: Test of General Ability) as well as scoring refinements that tend to highlight the specific strengths of culturally different and disadvantaged groups (e.g., Bruch's work with the Stanford-Binet, 1971; Mercer and Lewis's System of Multicultural Pluralistic Assessment, 1978).

To these may be added measures with no verbal content, minimal instructions, and no time limits (for some measures) that can be adapted for use with culturally different children (e.g., Arthur-Point Scale, [Arthur, 1947]; Chicago Non-Verbal Examination [Brown, 1963]; Institute for Personality and Ability Testing Culture-Fair Intelligence Test: Scales I, II and III [Cattel & Cattel, 1963]; Test of General Ability [Flanagan, 1960]; Raven's Progressive Matrices [Raven, 1947]).

Torrance (1977b) considers that most of the instruments described, regardless of various adaptations, appear to have racial and sociocultural biases. He suggests that only two instruments that are useful in the identification of giftedness lack cultural bias—the Torrance Tests of Creative Thinking (Torrance, 1966, 1974b) and the Alpha Biographical Inventory (Taylor & Ellison, 1967). The latter can be used to discover talent in minority groups but is not as yet commercially available.

Other possibly unbiased approaches to the identification of culturally different children are, for instance, Thinking Creatively with Sounds and Words (Khatena & Torrance, 1990b), the Khatena-Torrance Creative Perception Inventory (Khatena & Torrance, 1990a) (both require students to use or report their own cultural background and thus are culture relevant), and the Structure of Intellect Learning Abilities Test (Meeker, M. N., 1979b; Meeker, M. N., Meeker R., & Roid, 1985).

An approach that turns away from the traditional culture-free to culture-specific procedures to assess ability is the Black Intelligence Test of Cultural Homogeneity (R. L. Williams, 1972b, 1972c), a measure that consists of 100 multiple-choice questions to be answered as blacks would answer them. Two other measures are the Black Awareness Sentence Completion Test (R. L. Williams, 1972a) and Themes Concerning Blacks (R. L. Williams, 1972d). R. L. Williams's basic idea is now used in several developmental projects and may eventually give rise to the construction of measures for identifying giftedness in other minority groups (Torrance, 1977b).

Torrance observes that creativity measures can be used to advantage in the identification of the creative potential of minority children. The open-ended nature of the measures permits students to respond in terms of their own experiences regardless of what these may have been. Besides, the testees can use whatever language or dialect they find most comfortable.

For instance, the Torrance Tests of Creative Thinking were designed to be used with children, youths, and adults from the kindergarten through graduate and professional school levels. Thus far, it has been translated and used in 25 different languages. The many studies that Torrance cites support the relevance of his measures for identification of talent in minority groups. In particular, studies have found that the Torrance Tests of Creative Thinking appear to assess abilities that are little influenced by heredity (Pezzulo, Thorsen, & Madus, 1972; Richmond, 1968), but are most susceptible to the influence of experience (Davenport, 1967). The same may be said of Thinking Creatively with Sounds and Words, which has already been used either in the English version or in translation in a dozen countries abroad.

Continued refinements of the Torrance Tests of Creative Thinking by Torrance and his associates have resulted in the construction of a streamlined scoring procedure for the figural components of the battery.

Not only can the measure provide a creative index that is a better indicator of giftedness than can standard scoring, but it also gives additional information about strengths that can be used in the planning of learning activities consistent with the concept of emphasizing creative positives. Other facilitating conditions for effective testing of minority groups relate to appropriate warm-up, the use of language or dialect in which students are most comfortable, and the quality of test settings.

The expanded conception of giftedness has not only made us aware of the multidimensional nature of giftedness, but also brought into sharp notice the deficiencies of psychometric procedures, if not their inappropriateness, for the discovery of varieties of talent. Torrance says this realization prompted him to consider nontest ways of identifying the creatively gifted (1962b), which he saw as being more urgently needed for talent identification and development among economically disadvantaged and culturally different students (Torrance, 1973, 1974a). His efforts found expression in a more comprehensive system for both discovery and nurturance of talent. Torrance (1976a, 1976b, 1977b) discusses how each *creative positive* may be discovered in turn—its importance, its evidence among the culturally different, its use in the curriculum, and its use in developing careers.

According to the streamlined scoring procedure for the figural forms (Torrance, 1989a), a list of 13 criterion-referenced measures supplement the norm-referenced measures of fluency, flexibility, originality, elaboration, and resistance to premature closure. For instance, they include abilities to express feelings, to improvise, to use expressive speech, to be responsive to the concrete and kinesthetic, to have a sense of humor, and to be problem-centered and original. (The complete list can be found in Chapter 4.) The list serves as the rationale for *creative positives* and is indicative of talent among the culturally different (Torrance, 1977b, p. 26).

Two other approaches for identifying the culturally diverse gifted merit some consideration. One refers to testing-of-limits and the other to learning potential assessment device (Sattler, 1988).

Testing-of-Limits

The *testing-of-limits* approach (Sattler, 1988), attempts to go beyond the standardized testing procedure so as to obtain additional information about a child's abilities. Procedures that do this include the giving of additional cues to the child, using the child's method of test-taking, providing additional time limits, and using an alternative scoring system.

Learning Potential Assessment Device

The Learning Potential Assessment Device was invented by R. Feuerstein (1979, 1980). It is a dynamic assessment approach used with low functioning children to give them a better chance to show their potential ability. The same procedure has promise with culturally diverse children. It uses a pretest-training-posttest design in which the examiner, after the initial screening, evaluates the extent to which a child can benefit from instruction by a posttest. In this way, the examiner becomes a teacher-observer and the examinee becomes a learner-performer.

However, Sattler (1988) indicates that although some children are found to improve in test performance following training, more information may be needed about how this training generalizes to other tasks, particularly those related to classroom activity. Despite this observation, the Learning Potential Assessment Device is a worthy addition to approaches to identify talent in the context of cultural diversity, and if judiciously used can prove to be very useful.

The *National Report on Identification* (Richert, 1985; Richert, Alvino, & McDonnel, 1982) indicates that in order to eliminate inequity, a variety of identification methods needs to be used, because giftedness has many dimensions, including abilities, personality factors and environmental influences, that affect them. Besides, one instrument or procedure measures one of many facets of giftedness. We need to go beyond measurement of academic achievement in order to find students whose abilities are not indicated by test or school performance. However, formal and informal information about giftedness must be used for the purposes intended to ensure their validity.

Additional information on cost of administration, reliability, validity, and the like are also given in the report. Richert (1985) goes on to indicate specific questions that the panel suggests should be asked by the test user prior to using the recommended instruments—questions that relate to

1. abilities sought for each category of giftedness;
2. the assessment of these by the test chosen;
3. the cut-off scores to be used that may or may not exclude creative and/or disadvantaged students; and
4. the use of the test at an appropriate stage of identification.

CONCLUSIONS

It is generally thought that intelligence plays an important role in most of the other categories of giftedness. It is well known that academic aptitude or achievement is very positively related to general intelligence, as measured by I.Q. or, currently, with standard age score (SAS). A moderate level of intelligence appears to be required for creativity to function well. In the area of leadership, the intelligence level of the leader is expected to be higher than the average intelligence of the followers. It has been observed that high levels of performance in the performing and visual arts may require above average or well above average general intelligence; depending on the level of creativity involved in the activity, creative thinking abilities of above average to well above average are also needed. High levels of creativity are most pervasive, for instance, in musical composition and art; creativity is present wherever the art form requires a breaking away from tradition or the production of a new form.

The energizing functions of creativity may enter into most categories of giftedness. Where mental operations and behavioral correlates of each of the talent areas call for innovation or the production of the new, creativity becomes a prerequisite.

Another factor of high relevance relates to cultural diversity and the problems associated with identification. Selecting measures that are not heavily verbally weighted and are culturally relevant is an important consideration. Furthermore, it may become necessary to use nontest measures, at least for purposes of initial screening, in the circumstance of the nonavailability of more culturally relevant measures. However, where tests are available, an adaptation of these measures for use with a cultural minority by way of testing-of-limits and learning potential assessment approaches can prove to be very useful. Cognizance must also be given to the presence of an expanded conception of intelligence that recognizes a variety of talents and their implications for the culturally diverse.

In attempting to identify a gifted child, a fruitful and less expensive approach would be to obtain initial information from those who are close to the child—parents, teachers, coaches, and peers—about one or more of the child's gifts. These inquiries may be followed up with screening that can include observations of the child by trained personnel and, when available, by the administration of tests. What measures are selected will depend on the circumstances, resources, personnel, and set criteria. When teachers are asked to do the screening because they are qualified to do so, they should not delegate it to others. Certain measures may only be administered by trained professionals. If this is the case, then their services must be sought.

In general, a useful approach to screening students for superior abilities would be to obtain information regarding the student's level of (a) general mental ability (preferably verbal and nonverbal), and/or structure of intellect abilities; (b) creative thinking abilities; (c) achievement in school subjects; (d) specialized information relative to a talent area in which the student is expected to show excellence, and where no measures are available for this, a checklist may be used as a guide for gathering observational data; and (e) abilities relative to formal and/or informal measures that take into account cultural diversity and its socioeconomic correlates.

CHAPTER SIX

Gifted Children Growing Up

*I*NTRODUCTION

Although much has been written about the development of the intellect, the focus point of most of this writing is the general population. Relatively little has been done to generate information regarding the developmental patterns of the gifted intellect. The works of Lewis M. Terman and his associates provide the single best source of information on the gifted as they grow up to mid-life and beyond.

Much of the information on the developmental aspects of intellectual functioning as it relates to general intelligence and its factor components is derived from the Stanford-Binet, Wechsler scales, and like measures of intelligence. Although Guilford (1967) discusses intellectual development as it relates to abilities identified through the factor analysis of L. L. Thurstone and T. Kelley, he has done very little to generate empirical evidence that indicates intellectual growth patterns. Thurstone and Kelley's findings are related to a number of abilities similar to those of Guilford's Structure of Intellect, but Guilford's model itself was not used to study the developmental patterns of the complex intellectual abilities of the gifted.

Approaches to the study of intellectual development in the general population and the gifted may be categorized as *quantitative* (i.e., having roots in measurement) and *qualitative* (i.e., having roots in developmental stage theory). The *quantitative* approach can be traced to the construction and use of the Stanford-Binet in the 1920s, and the application of the measure in Terman's *Genetic Studies of Genius,* as it relates to the gifted. To these instruments may be added those tests that used other measures of intellectual functions, especially the Wechsler scales. Interest in finding information about the developmental patterns of creative thinking abilities can be traced to the measures developed by E. P. Torrance, J. Khatena, and their associates.

The *qualitative* approach to the nature of the intellect as it relates to age has its roots in Jean Piaget's developmental stages, and more recently, in J. C. Gowan's model and G. Land's model that is related to creativity. On the one hand, development of the intellect is conceived as continuous and related to the quantitative approach; on the other hand, development is conceived as discontinuous and related to the qualitative approach.

The picture that emerges from all these contributions is relatively sketchy and to some extent confusing and even incomplete. This lack of definition, in part, can be attributed to an expanding concept of intellect and a number of other variables. For instance, the extent to which intelligence is predetermined or subject to change; the effects of a changing environment; the appropriateness of test items in a measure for all age levels; sampling and related psychometric problems; and in some ways, the lack of empirical study and the general speculative nature of developmental stage theory are all to be noted.

Development is the product of maturation and nurture. *Maturation* is the unfolding of a design that is essentially innate, and there is nothing external that has the power to influence it. *Nurture* is the influence of the environment (e.g., physical, educational, social) as it interacts with innate growing-up patterns to facilitate their fullest expression. The term *growth* is used to describe the measurement of development and is concerned with increment and decrement; *maturity* indicates the attainment or completion of a particular stage of development in preparation for the next stage (Olson, 1959).

These terms refer to the quantitative changes that are expected to take place in *chronological age,* where growth (the measured consequences of these changes) is regarded as continuous. They also refer to qualitative changes that occur as an individual leaps from one sequence of development to the next higher level of maturity. Gowan has described these changes—from one sequence of three stages to two others in triadic sequence (1972)—as being discontinuous. It would be appropriate to note that the view of intellectual development as being continuous derives its logic and force from psychometrics; the view of development as being discontinuous derives its rationale and energy from observation, the clinic, and philosophical speculation.

INTELLECT AND CREATIVE DEVELOPMENT

To understand development as *continuous*, we need to examine the work of Terman and his associates, who used the Stanford-Binet and Concept Mastery Test (a measure constructed by Terman for use with high school students) in studies of gifted children. The measures were used to identify precocious children from Grades 3 to 8, and to study their intellectual growth, behavior, and personality characteristics as they increased in chronological age until mid-life.

Terman's group, when compared with the general population, continued to maintain their intellectual superiority; with few exceptions, the superior child became the superior adult (Oden, 1968). In the 12-year interval between the two administrations of the Concept Mastery Test to 768 gifted subjects (422 men and 346 women), Terman found that, contrary to the notion of "early ripe early rot" (Bayley & Oden, 1955), these subjects actually increased their scores in adulthood. (A fuller account of Terman's highly gifted students as they grew up to mid-life can be found in Chapter 2.)

Mental growth takes place gradually and continuously from birth to maturity, but at what age this growth ceases is a matter for debate. For instance, the slowing down in rate of growth for most mental functions that takes place during the early teens reaches its peak in the middle twenties (Bayley, 1949; Wechsler, 1966). But evidence from the Harvard Growth Studies shows intellectual gains up to nearly 30 years of age (2% taking place after the age of 21 or 22). As this relates to the 768 gifted individuals whose mental growth was measured longitudinally by the Concept Mastery Test (a measure that calls for a knowledge of symbols and abstractions and the ability to use these relations to each other), Bayley and Oden (1955) see, in the gains made on the test, implications for the improvement of this kind of knowledge and ability in superior adults through 50 years of age at least. Owens (1953) longitudinal study provides corroborating evidence.

The conflicting evidence about the amount of decrement and the time when these changes begin has been attributed to the nature of the measures used (Bayley & Oden, 1955) and the instruments' lack of power to differentiate changing abilities at the upper levels of intelligence (Shock, 1951).

The relationship between age and scores on a measure of general intelligence appears to be one of gradual but accelerating decline (Jones & Conrad, 1933) and is consistent with Wechsler's (1966) observation that human capacity, after initial growth attains a maximum, begins to decline slowly at first and more rapidly later. He illustrates this in a general curve of average decline in mental ability of people aged 16 to 75 (Figure 6.1).

Figure 6.1 Curve of Average Decline of Mental Ability with Age (Ages 16–75)

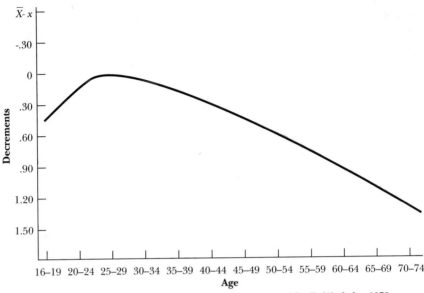

From *The Measurement and Appraisal of Adult Intelligence* (p. 202) by D. Wechsler, 1958, Baltimore, Md.: Williams & Wilkins. Copyright © 1958 by D. Wechsler. Reprinted by permission.

Age effects mental functions in different ways, as can be measured by the individual subtests of the Wechsler scales. The curves formed on these scales show the same characteristic form as the generalized curve of mental ability illustrated in Figure 6.1 (Wechsler, 1966, pp. 202–205). For instance, vocabulary scores are found to be higher at age 60 than at age 20, but nonverbal reasoning scores appear to decline substantially by age 50 (Foulds & Raven, 1948). But not all intellectual functions decline with age. The scores for knowing, vocabulary, and information show continuous increases into later adult years (Berkowitz, 1953; Corsini & Fassett, 1953; Owens, 1953).

Wechsler (1950) discusses the growth of children's intelligence and indicates that various levels of mental maturity are reached at different periods of children's lives. For instance, a 15-year-old child attains mental maturity between 5 years 6 months and 15 years 6 months. Mental growth relating to memory span for digits, for example, shows rapid increase to age 11 and little thereafter; memory improves rapidly to age 14; and vocabulary shows a more gradual and steady growth.

Generally, growth curves for most intellectual abilities resemble the vocabulary growth curve. This curve is characterized by a rapid rise in test scores during the first few years and a gradual slowing down as age 15 is reached—except for a brief spurt that occurs between the ages of 10 and 12. An exception to this pattern is the age curve for memory span of digits—the line connecting mean scores at successive age levels consists of a series of risers connected by plateaus of varying breadths. This result suggests that growth is discontinuous for some mental abilities (Wechsler, 1950).

The problem of changes in intelligence with age is summed up by Wechsler (1966) as follows:

> General intelligence as evaluated by pragmatic criteria appears to maintain itself unimpaired over a much greater portion of adult life and to decline at a much slower rate than do the mental abilities by which it is inevitably measured. Our general answers have been that sheer ability enters as only one of several factors of intelligence, that factors like drive, interest and motivation also operate in varying degree as determinants and that learned responses, stored information and general experience may substitute for or better serve the individual than original aptitude. To these may be added the fact that at different ages different skills or abilities contribute varying amounts of whatever is needed for effective performance. (p. 142)

BEYOND TERMAN'S LONGITUDINAL STUDIES

Mathematical Precocity — Stanley

The special case of mathematical intelligence has been studied by Julian Stanley and his associates (Stanley, Keating, & Fox, 1974; Stanley, George, & Solano, 1977). Stanley's work is perhaps the only other longitudinal study of the intellectually gifted youth (albeit his subjects are those with special ability in mathematics).

According to Stanley, the Study of Mathematically Precocious Youth (SMPY) project, begun in September 1971 at Johns Hopkins University, is developmental and longitudinal but not retrospective. Seventh- and eighth-grade students who are already superior mathematical reasoners are identified. Their development, under the influence of the program, is then observed in ensuing years. SMPY is concerned mostly with capitalizing on its participants' already evident high-level reasoning ability and motivation, rather than on some presumed underlying potential that has yet to manifest itself. However, SMPY does have great interest in the nature of mathematical talent as it develops and unfolds, especially from about age 12 and on, and of how intellectual prodigies turn out.

Stanley's (1977c) approach, unlike Terman's, is experimental, using the case study model to discover the effects of his intervention program.

His longitudinal study at Johns Hopkins University concerned itself with the identification and acceleration of mathematically precocious youth. The model consists of three sequential aspects, namely, discovery, description, and development.

The identification of mathematically precocious youth takes place in the *discovery* phase of SMPY. The Scholastic Aptitude Tests of Educational Progress, an achievement battery of the College Entrance Examination Board, provides supplemental information about the youth. This phase is followed by the *descriptive* phase, when the most talented are tested further and studied a great deal. Once enrolled in the program, these youth are exposed to a smorgasbord of activity based on accelerated learning. In this *developmental* phase of SMPY, the participants are, in addition, continually helped and counseled to choose from a variety of educational opportunities offered to them. Acceleration allows them to move rapidly ahead from beginning to advanced mathematics, skipping what they already know to take advantage of advanced courses in calculus, linear algebra, and differential equations, among other areas. "Fast-paced" learning, encouraged by the teacher in the stimulation of a class of the participant's intellectual peers, has been found to produce astoundingly good results.

Another feature of the SMPY model is *diagnostic testing*, which provides instruction on specific points previously unknown to the participant. To facilitate and advance the learning experience in mathematics, SMPY emphasizes educational and vocational *counseling* and *tutoring* of the individual by a team of mathematically gifted youth who belong to the program.

Among the many benefits derived by SMPY participants during a five-year period (1971–76) are the following:

1. Increased zest for learning and life
2. Reduction of boredom in school with better attitudes toward education and other activities
3. Enhanced feelings of self-worth and accomplishment
4. Reduction of egotism and arrogance
5. Better preparation in mathematics specifically and in other subjects generally
6. Better preparation for entrance to the most selective colleges
7. Admission to college, graduate school, and a profession earlier with more time and energy for creative pursuits
8. More opportunities to explore different specialties and hobbies
9. More time to explore various careers before marriage
10. Less expense to parents and/or students
11. Greater chances of college professors wanting to be their mentors
12. Expectation of greater professional and personal success in life

In comparing his studies with Terman's, Stanley (1977c) indicates similar and dissimilar relationships between the two.

The studies were *similar* in the following ways: both (a) select the ablest 1 in 200 youths in the main, (b) use standardized tests for the purpose of identification, (c) conduct statewide screening over a period of several years, (d) study extensively male and female participants longitudinally, and (e) report the results in books, articles, and speeches.

Stanley's study was *dissimilar* in that it (a) helps participants educationally through various and vigorous interventions; (b) screens these students (mostly with Stanford-Binet I.Q.'s of 140 or above) initially by a difficult mathematical reasoning test rather than an intelligence test; and (c) works intensively with 250 youths (whereas Terman starts with more than 1,500), and counsels a secondary group of 1,800 (upper 1.5% of the age groups with respect to mathematical aptitude). Furthermore, participants are, in general, academically aggressive; mathematically oriented; self-confident; and 11 and 12 years old in Grades 7 and 8 (Terman's groups range across all school grades).

Stanley indicates that although he does not expect SMPY to locate or produce a Nobel laureate, much less a successor to Gauss or someone of the caliber of Norbert Wiener, several of the participants have distinguished themselves by their achievements. For instance, one young man, on his 16th birthday, as a sophomore in college, began important research in electrical engineering; another, at age 19, did original research in mathematics; and a third, at age 17, solved an important problem in computer science.

According to Stanley, study of the achievements of participants of SMPY will be on-going for at least 20 years. Presently, though, he considers the program as being of great help to a number of young men and women who would not progress as well without the intervention. For him and others involved in the project, it is sufficient to enhance talent rather than create genius.

> We might have been able to help a lonely, awkward person such as Wiener use his great talents better at an earlier age, and probably Einstein would have scored quite high in a contest like ours had he deigned to enter it, but those two men are examples of persons who somehow achieved magnificently anyway. . . . We suspect that many classrooms also serve as premature tombs for mathematical talent. (Stanley, 1977c, p. 107)

Structure of Intellect — Guilford

Guilford (1967) observes that the age at which an individual reaches the maximum score on a measure of intelligence varies from test to test. Because we cannot be sure if the ceiling of a test is high enough to measure higher levels of ability or abilities, we really do not know if the test actually measures the maximum of an average person. Furthermore, just because the average person reaches a maximum level of growth at a certain age does not mean that all members of the population cease to grow at that age. In fact, each individual's growth curve is unique because within the context of upward development there may occur periods of little or rapid change relative to different rates of development in different intellectual abilities. Guilford's findings have important implications for the gifted, whose mental growth curves can be expected to show many more idiosyncratic features than those of the general population.

McVicker J. Hunt (1964) cites W. Johannsen, the Danish geneticist, as making a distinction between the *genotype* (inherited) intelligence of an individual, which cannot be measured, and the *phenotype* (inherited × environment) intelligence, which is intelligence that interacts with various circumstances and experiences and can be directly observed and measured.

According to Johannsen, intelligence needs interaction with the environment to develop and manifest itself. D. O. Hebb (1949) makes a similar observation in terms of two kinds of intelligence, namely, *Intelligence A*, or the capacity for development (not measurable); and *Intelligence B*, or the product of *Intelligence A* interacting with the *environment* (measurable, however imperfectly, by tests). Both Hunt and Hebb recognize the importance of experience in the development of innate potential.

For a model of intelligence that incorporates the interactive elements of innate ability and environmental influences, we have to go to the Structure of Intellect (Guilford, 1967). Its five mental operations, *cognition, memory, convergent production, divergent production,* and *evaluation,* are predetermined or inherited. These mental operations are designed to act on an information-based dimension whose roots lie in the environment, and comprise the *contents* (input) and *products* (output) faces of the cube model of intellect. Intellectual activity based on this model involves the processing of information, either as input or output, by heredity-based mental operations. Development of intelligence occurs as a result of the interactions of these three dimensions of intellect.

According to Guilford (1967), the child, in his or her development,

> learns how to bring together the three aspects as represented by the parameters of the Structure of Intellect in the various combinations, each combination being unique. How well any particular combination develops depends upon how much and how effectively he exercises that combination, and these circumstances depend upon what his environment offers to him and the needs he has for coping with these offerings. Individuals differ with respect to how much they have exercised each kind of combination, by necessity or by incidental involvement. (p. 417)

Guilford rejects the *Garrett hypothesis* (Garrett, 1946), which favors a single general intellectual ability prevailing in infancy and early childhood over the many factor abilities of the Structure of Intellect. However, Guilford is not certain if his model applies morphologically to individuals of an early age as extensively as it does to adolescents and adults. Besides, there is the difficulty of constructing tests that measure such abilities.

All in all, there are no direct studies of either the general population or the gifted on the rate of growth of abilities related to the Structure of Intellect. Guilford (1967), however, cites a study by L. H. Stott and R. S. Ball (1963) that identifies 31 intellectual and 5 psychomotor factors (without *g*) by analyzing items from a number of test batteries for infant and preschool children. Guilford cautiously relates these factors to Structure of Intellect abilities. The 31 factors, he says, represent the 5 mental operations, 4 content, and 5 of the 6 product categories—with "classes" as the missing product category.

Creative Thinking — Torrance and Khatena

One of the Structure of Intellect mental operations, *divergent production*, has stirred up considerable interest. It has led to a number of studies on the creative development of American children as measured by the Torrance Tests of Creative Thinking (Torrance, 1974b). What has emerged from cross-sectional studies is a generalized developmental curve (Torrance, 1967b). This curve (Figure 6.2) shows decrements in creative thinking just before entry into Grade 1 and in about Grades 4, 7 and 12, with growth peaks occurring between Grades 3 and 4, and again in about Grade 11 (Andrews, 1930; Torrance, 1962a, 1963, 1965c, 1967b).

Of the several drops in creativity, the worst seems to occur at about the fourth grade or at age 9. Torrance has called this the *fourth-grade slump* in creative thinking abilities. It has been observed that it is at this time that children experience the greatest amount of personality disturbances, behavior problems, learning difficulties, and the like.

Torrance's (1968) 4-year longitudinal study on developmental aspects of creative thinking abilities of 100 children, corroborates these findings. On the average, he found that slumps in fluency, flexibility, originality, and elaboration occur at the fourth-grade level. However, he also found that, although 45% to 61% of the children showed decline, a few children did show increase in creative thinking abilities. In general, children were found to improve their scores in the fifth grade, although the scores they obtained were relatively lower than those in the third grade.

He also explored the *fourth-grade slump* in creative thinking abilities cross-culturally (Torrance, 1967b). The evidence of this extensive study led him to conclude that, although development is relatively more con-

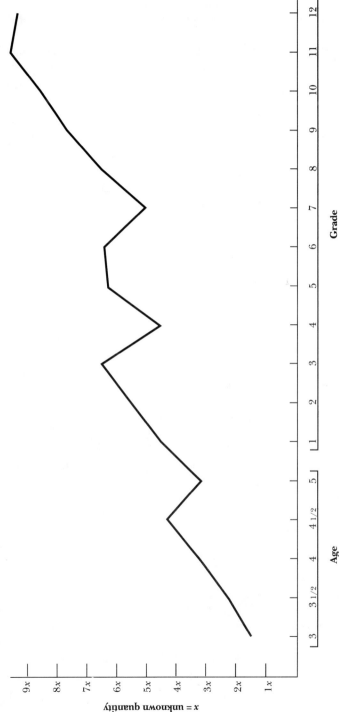

Figure 6.2 Generalized Developmental Curve of the Creative Thinking Abilities in the Dominant Culture of the United States

From "Understanding the Fourth Grade Slump in Creative Thinking," by E.P. Torrance, 1967. Unpublished manuscript. Copyright © 1967 by E.P. Torrance. Reprinted by permission.

tinuous in some cultures than in others, there is little noticeable growth during the elementary school years. Most cultures, however, show discontinuity in the development of creative thinking abilities. Generally, discontinuities in growth of creative thinking abilities occur at the end of the third grade or at the beginning of the fourth grade, although, with some groups, such discontinuities did not appear until the 6th grade. Torrance (1967b) attributes the fall in creative thinking abilities to stress and demands made on children.

> There are a number of indications that these discontinuities occur within a culture whenever children in that culture are confronted with new stresses and demands. When Christian missions and similar groups establish schools in underdeveloped areas, they apparently bring both a stimulating and disrupting influence on development, producing discontinuities in creative development. (p. 301)

In attempting to find out if the same conditions applied to the production of original verbal images, the children's versions (Form 1A and Form 1B) of Onomatopoeia and Images (Khatena & Torrance, 1990a) were administered to 1365 children (680 boys and 685 girls) between the ages of 8 and 19. These children attended schools in Georgia, Ohio, and West Virginia. It was found that these children experienced two slump periods in their ability to produce original verbal images. This decrement manifested itself around the fourth and fifth grades or at the ages of 9 and 10. The recovery that followed this drop was overtaken by another slump at the 10th grade or at age 15. Small sex and age fluctuations do not alter the basic pattern, and these findings are congruent with Torrance's research on the subject (Khatena, 1971a).

The earlier manual of Sounds and Images (Cunnington & Torrance, 1965) also includes some data on the *fourth-grade slump* as determined by Form 1 of the measure (now Form 1A). However, a number of the Minnesota subjects at the third-grade level are not differentiated by sex. For the sake of comparison, fourth-grade data for boys and girls were combined. The mean difference between the third and fourth grades was found to be highly significant. Consequently, a study designed to find out if the same developmental pattern occurs in the production of original verbal images was carried out (Khatena, 1972). In this study, Form 1A and Form 1B of Sounds and Images (Khatena & Torrance, 1990b) were administered to 665 children (352 boys and 313 girls) selected from several West Virginia schools. It was found that girls experience a slump in ability to produce original verbal images in response to sound stimuli at age 11, although this was found to be statistically significant. At age 9, girls show lower means than at age 10. Boys seem to do better at age 9 but with increasing age the differences even out. Both boys and girls experience a spurt in their productivity at age 12 with a leveling off at the age levels that follow and reach their peak at ages 14 to 19.

These two studies of children's production of original verbal images generally indicate drops in children's originality especially in the upper elementary grades (Grades 4 to 6) or between the ages of 9 to 11. When this was checked by a longitudinal study (Khatena & Fisher, 1974) using Onomatopoeia and Images to measure the production of original verbal images with a group of 8-year-olds over a 4-year period, it was found that loss in originality occurred in children between the ages of 9 and 10 or at about the fourth-grade level. There was some gain at the age of 11.

Similar patterns presented themselves in recent analyses of original image production by gifted and regular school students on Sounds and Images and Onomatopoeia and Images cross-sectionally and longitudinally (Khatena & Torrance, 1990b). These and related findings described earlier lend further support to Torrance's observations concerning the fourth-grade slump in creative thinking abilities.

Other longitudinal studies using the Torrance test batteries (verbal and figural), were done for the purpose of establishing predictive validity of the measures. Among these are two short-range (1 week to 9 months) predictive studies (Torrance, 1963; Weisberg & Springer, 1961), and long-range (5 to 12 years) predictive studies (Torrance, 1972b; Witt, 1971).

Short-Range Prediction

The first study (Weisberg & Springer, 1961) was of 32 intellectually gifted (i.e., high-I.Q.) fourth-grade children. It showed that the high creatives of this group, when compared with the rest, reflected more creative self-acceptance, greater self-awareness, an internal locus of evaluation that allowed for greater independence from environmental influences, and greater readiness to respond emotionally to the environment. That is, these creative preadolescents behaved more sensitively and more independently than less creative but equally intelligent children.

The second study (Torrance, 1963) investigated some of the social-interaction behaviors of highly creative children, 25 each from Grades 2 to 6. Each class was divided into five subgroups on the basis of their scores on the Torrance Tests of Creative Thinking. Children were required to discover intended and unintended uses for a box of science toys. Observation focused on techniques used by the groups to control its most creative members. The findings showed (a) that the highly creative children made outstanding contributions, despite obvious pressure exercised by groups to reduce their production and originality; (b) that although most of the creative members (68%) produced more ideas than other group members, few (24%) were credited by the others with making the most valuable contribution to the success of the groups; and (c) that the creatives counteracted group pressures by being compliant, by showing counter aggression, by exhibiting indomitable persistence, by apparently ignoring criticism, by showing silence and apathy, by inconsistent performance, and by filling in the gaps when others faltered (Torrance, 1972b, pp. 237–238).

Long-Range Prediction

Two of several of the long-range prediction studies are of special relevance. The one by Witt began in 1965 and extended over a period of 6 years (1971). This study was done with 16 highly creative disadvantaged children in Grades 2 to 4 from a ghetto school in New Haven, Connecticut. Twelve of these children were also in an out-of-school program designed to develop their creative strengths. The other study, conducted by Torrance (1972b), spanned a period of 7 to 12 years, depending on the participant (1959–71) and involved 392 students, the total enrollment of the University of Minnesota High School in Grades 7 to 12.

The findings of the Witt study showed that of the 12 children attending an out-of-school program, 10 demonstrated superior creative talent. They achieved high-level performance, receiving awards in one or more of the art forms (e.g., music, art, and drama) and winning competitions in citywide contests, science and arts camps, and the like. They also won scholarships to excellent private schools for children; three children also demonstrated superior verbal creativity in science and other areas as indicated by the honors they attained (Torrance, 1972b, p. 244).

The 7-year follow-up of Torrance's (1972b) major long-range prediction of the original 69 students in the 1960 class found significant relationship between their scores on the Torrance Tests of Creative Thinking and their achievements in the following areas:

Poems, stories, songs written
Poems, stories, songs published
Books published
Radio and television scripts or performances
Original research designs developed
Philosophy of life changed
In-service training for co-workers created
Original changes in work situation suggested
Research grants received
Business enterprises initiated
Patentable devices invented
Literary awards or prizes received for creative writing, musical composition, art, and so on

The 12-year follow-up study of 236 (of the original group of 392) students was conducted in 1971 when subjects were between 25 and 31 years old. Torrance's findings give some credence to the belief that the creative achievements of women are less predictable than those of men; that the creativity measures (Torrance Tests of Creative Thinking) used were consistently better predictors of women's adult creative achievement than the measure of intelligence (Lorge-Thorndike Intelligence Tests) used; and that, although originality was a good predictor of quantity and quality of creative achievements as well as creative aspirations of students in Grades 9 through 12, it did not predict the same for those in Grades 7 and 8. Torrance attributes this last finding to a variety of complex factors: a slump in the subjects' creative thinking abilities (which was expected to occur); and the fact that a large proportion of these subjects at the time of the follow-up testing were in military service, were still in college, had undergone a period of rebellion and exploration, and only recently regained an achievement orientation to life without attending college or seeking success through other routes. Torrance concludes that

> although the subjects of the 12-year validity study were fairly advantaged and most of them had ample opportunities and freedom to develop their creative abilities, the results do indicate that creativity tests administered during the high school years can predict real-life adult creative achievements. It is doubtful that such favorable results would be found for a population severely limited in opportunity and/or freedom. The subjects of this study now range from 25 to 31 years, and we do not know whether these results will continue to hold up at the end of another 12 years. An examination of the clues provided by the detailed responses of the subjects, however, suggests that the creative achievement differences between the more creative and less creative subjects are likely to widen as time elapses. (1972c, pp. 250–251)

The information generated from these several longitudinal studies on career patterns of creative high school students led Torrance (1972c, pp. 87–88) to conclude that

1. young people identified as creative during the high school years do tend to become productive adults.
2. at least twelve years after high school graduation appears to be a more advantageous time for a follow-up of adult creative achievements.
3. the unusual occupations [ex]pressed as choices by highly creative high school students tend to become realities.
4. highly creative high school students tend to develop careers [that] involve detours for relevant but unusual combinations of training and/or experience. More of them include study or work in a foreign country as part of their career development than do their less creative peers.
5. creative achievements in writing, science, medicine, and leader-

ship are more easily predicted by creativity tests administered in high school than are achievement in music, the visual arts, business, and industry.

6. young adults identified as highly creative in high school more frequently than their less creative peers attain their peak creative achievements in writing and surgical discovery, dissertation research, musical composition, style of teaching, and human relations organization. The low creatives tend to report as peak achievements "cop out" or "drop out" experiences unaccompanied by constructive action, while many of their more creative peers reported withdrawal experiences either for periods of renewal or for creating a new and more humane life-style.

Torrance (1971b) indicates that the main problem of the creatively gifted lies in the search for an *identity*. They resolve this problem in three basic ways; that is, they choose conformity, rebellion, or creative individuality. Those who stop short in the search are, at best, self-made men and women. More often, they lack identity, are miserable, become delinquent, suffer from alcoholism or drug addiction, and are prone to suicide or insanity.

Reflecting on the more than 200 cases in this study, Torrance seems sure that because a period of wandering appears necessary, the creatively gifted child must be given the freedom to wander, to experiment, to risk, to find out what's possible, to discover limits, and to decide what *fits*. Furthermore, creatively gifted children reflect in their lives the dynamic and creative paradox of being unique yet universal at one and the same time. Although they are different from anyone else, the creatively gifted strive to be the same as everyone.

A third interesting observation relates to the African-American, native American, and Chicano children who are creatively gifted and who not only want to belong to their respective ethnic group but also want to be recognized as individual human beings.

Discussing careers, Torrance (1972d) observes that creatively gifted young women are permitted by society to fulfill themselves in many ways. However, they do face obstacles. Those who are deterred by obstacles deliberately sacrifice their creativity for other rewards. Some recognize and accept obstacles, deliberately choosing to avoid conformity-demanding institutions while seeking to attend or work within institutions that do not require the sacrifice of their creativity. Others reject traditional achievement routes (e.g., doctorates, publication), commit themselves to diversity, and remain open to alternatives for creative achievement and fulfillment. Among those who reject traditional routes are those who, although they do not attain success and recognition, continue to be creative in a variety of ways. Still others see child rearing and caring for a family as great creative challenges that provide fulfillment. Torrance concludes that it is difficult to predict which careers creative women will choose, not so much because of the limitation of choice but because of the variety open to them.

The findings of the 22-year follow-up study of elementary students who were first pretested in 1958 (Torrance, 1980, 1981b, 1989b), based on the use of real-life creative achievements as criteria, confirm those of the earlier longitudinal studies. Creativity test predictors significantly correlate (p .01) with all creative achievement criteria. Torrance's (1980) conclusions on the results of this longitudinal study are as follows:

> I believe the data from the 22-year longitudinal study demonstrated that it is possible to predict, to a significant degree, adult creativity from the performances of children during the elementary school years. Much of the variance or individual differences in adult creativity are unexplained by childhood test performances. Having a future career image that persists, being in love with something, and having a mentor or having teachers who value creativity all make significant differences. The struggle to maintain one's creativity is an unceasing one and the battle may be won or lost at almost any age. Central to this struggle is finding successful strategies for finding opportunities for playing the game in one's own way and being willing and able to walk away from the games that others impose. (p. 158)

DEVELOPMENTAL STAGES

Wechsler (1950) observes that the growth curve for memory span of digits, unlike other growth curves (e.g., vocabulary and information), consists of a series of risers connected by plateaus of varying breadths. The shape of this curve may be, in part, due to units of measurement that are too large or insufficiently discrete. Or it may be due to certain mental abilities that are, contrary to current views, *discontinuous* functions, so that increase or decrease can only occur by certain amounts or *quanta*. This discontinuity is in keeping with thought on the subject of growth in terms of developmental stages.

About 400 years ago, William Shakespeare in his play *As You Like It*, compares man's life stages to different acting roles. A man lives the life of an infant, schoolboy, soldier, judge, old man, and a final role to complete his life cycle. Sigmund Freud talked about the five developmental periods of sexual libido nearly a century ago; and Abraham Maslow (1954), Jean Piaget (1950) and Harry Stack Sullivan (1953) have all stated that there are qualitatively different developmental stages, each with different specific emphases.

Piaget (1950) identified five cognitive developmental stages (sensorimotor, preoperational, intuitive, concrete operations, formal operations), which John Gowan (1972) expanded to eight by adding creativity, psychedelia, and illumination.

Erik Erikson (1950) named eight affective developmental stages (trust-mistrust, autonomy-shame and doubt, initiative-guilt, industry-inferiority, identity-role diffusion, intimacy-isolation, generativity-stagnation, and ego-integrity).

Lawrence Kohlberg (Kohlberg & Mayer, 1972) presents eight stages of moral development (premoral, preconventional 1 and 2, conventional 1 and 2, postconventional 1 and 2, and commitment-development mutual obligation.

William G. Perry (1970) describes eight stages of conative or purposive development (basic duality, multiplicity-prelegitimate, multiplicity subordinate, multiplicity correlate-relativism subordinate, relativism correlate-competing or diffuse, commitment foreseen, initial commitment, and orientation in implications of commitment and developing commitments).

The ninth stage of development, described as agape-love (Erikson), cosmic knowledge (Gowan), expanded identity (Perry), and moral responsibility-ability-desire (Kohlberg), becomes fused into unity (Simpson, 1977).

That the concept of developmental stages holds great importance for education today has been well expressed by S. K. Bailey (1971).

> It seems clear to me that the most liberating and viable educational reforms of the next several years will come through the building of curricula and other educative activities around some of the developmental insights of men like Piaget, Bruner, Erikson, Bloom, and Maslow. Although much separates these scholars in terms of analytic style and specific fields of concentration, they all seem to hold to the idea that human beings go through fairly discrete stages of development and that each stage calls for rather specific educational treatment. And all of these men seem to be united in their belief that the maximization of human potential within the constraints of each life stage is the best way of preparing for succeeding stages. (p. 14)

The Gowan Periodic Developmental Stage Model

Of these several descriptions of developmental stages, the model provided by John Gowan (1972, 1974), which incorporates the theories of both Erikson and Piaget, serves us best, and will be discussed further.

Gowan (1972, 1974) has combined the eight affective stages of Erikson and the five cognitive stages of Piaget with three of his own, namely, creativity, psychedelia, and illumination, in a model of periodic developmental stages (Table 6.1). This model focuses attention on a *periodicity* of three that results in similarities among Stages 1, 4 and 7; Stages 2, 5 and

Table 6.1 The Erikson-Piaget-Gowan Periodic Developmental Stages

		Attentional Modes	
Developmental Levels	*Latency* 3. It, They The World	*Identity* 1. I, Me The Ego	*Creativity* 2. Thou The Other
Infant Erikson (affective)	Trust vs. Mistrust ①	Autonomy vs. Shame and Doubt	Initiative vs. Guilt
Piaget (cognitive)	Sensorimotor vs. Chaos	Preoperational vs. Autism ②	Intuitive vs. Immobilization ③
Youth Erikson (affective)	Industry vs. Inferiority	Identity vs. Role Diffusion	Intimacy vs. Isolation
Piaget-Gowan (cognitive)	Concrete Operations vs. Nonconservation ④	Formal Operations vs. Schizophrenia ⑤	Creativity vs. Authoritarianism ⑥
Adult Erikson (affective)	Generativity vs. Stagnation	Ego-Integrity vs. Despair	(Agape-Love) ⑨
Gowan (cognitive)	Psychedelia vs. Conventionalism ⑦	Illumination vs. Senile Depression ⑧	

Note. From *The Development of the Psychedelic Individual* (p. 51) by J. C. Gowan, 1974, Buffalo, N.Y.: Creative Education Foundation. Copyright © 1974 by J. C. Gowan. Reprinted by permission.

Table 6.2 Gowan's Periodic Table of Developmental Stages

		Latency (The World: It, They)	Identity (The Ego: I, Me)	Creativity (The Other: Thou)
Infant	1.	Thing oriented Sexually latent relative to individual with his world of experience World percepts (0–1)	2. All about "me" Finds his identity Negativism (2–3)	3. Deal with love relations Expansion from self-love to love of parents (4–6)
Youth	4.	Size, shape, form and color of things and what one can make of them (7–12)	5. Redefines his identity in terms of what he can do as a young adult Clamor for independence Idealism Attitude and action anathema to authority figure (13–17)	6. Generalized heterosexual love to love one person of opposite sex (18–25)
Adult	7.	World of significant others such as child Broaden to world of ideas, formulas, production, art creations and other mental children (26–40)	8. Again redefines his identity in terms of meaning of his life and death in the world (40–onward)	9. Love all mankind (Buddha-Christ type)

Note. From *The Creatively Gifted Child: Suggestions for Parents and Teachers* (p. 102) by J. Khatena, 1978, New York, N.Y.: Vantage Press. Copyright © 1978 by J. Khatena. Reprinted by permission.

8; and Stages 3, 6, and 9. It reinforces the concept of *escalation* (components of discontinuity, succession, emergence, differentiation, and integration). Furthermore, the model deals with the significance of *dysplasia* or malformation in development (i.e., splitting of cognitive and affective stage levels in malfunctioning individuals). Gowan emphasizes self-actualization as the outcome of escalating to higher developmental stages.

According to Gowan (Table 6.2), an individual goes through three stages of development (latency, identity, and creativity) at each of three levels of growth (as infant, youth, and adult).

A paraphrase of Gowan's (1972) description of these nine developmental stages follows:

1. Latency (Stages 1, 4, and 7)

    For the infant (0–1), this is the period when he gets to know the things around him, to experience the "thing" character of the world.

    As a youth (7–12) he begins to know things for their size, shape, form and color, and what one makes of them.

    As an adult (26–40) he is concerned with others who are important to him, such as children, their productions, art creations, and other "mental children."

    Common to the infant, youth and adult, is his immersion in the world of senses. Things get done, changes occur, no self-consciousness is felt, very little time is left to assess feelings or to be concerned with the questions of "Who am I?" Accomplishments strengthen and prepare the person to search for his identity.

2. Identity (Stages 2, 5, and 8)

    The infant, youth and adult are concerned here with questions like: "Who am I? Why do I exist? How am I in relation to others? What happens to me when I die? Will I be saved?

    During these times the person searches within himself for answers, withdraws rather than returns, defies authority rather than obeys it, and "marches to the music of a different drum."

    At each stage, he tries to come to terms with himself: as an infant he searches for his identity, as a youth he redefines it in terms of the meaning of his life and death in the cosmos.

    Others find it difficult to live with an individual passing through these stages—the infant with his negativism, and adolescent with his idealism, demand for independence and rebellion against authority both by his attitudes and actions.

    During this time of turning into himself and away from the world it is easy for him to believe that no one understands him, often spending too much time in self-examination, forgetting the real world outside himself leading to moodiness resulting from the discrepancy between what he wants to be and what he finds he can be and do.

3. Creativity (Stages 3, 6, and 9)

    During stages 3 and 6, which deal with love, the person passes from love of self through love of parent of the opposite sex to generalized love of people of both sexes and to love of one person of the opposite sex. Stage 9 may very well exist where love is for all mankind given in the way of Buddha and Christ (Agape-Love).

Gowan sees love as required for creation, both physically and mentally. That is why stages 3 and 6 are important. Creativity first develops during stage 3 when a person gains control of his environment through affectional relations with the parent of the opposite sex such that "boys" who are affectionately close to their mothers and "girls" who are unusually close to their fathers, during 4 to 7 years, tend to become more creative than others of similar ability. It is during this period that warm affection given by the opposite-sex parent freely enlarges the bridge between the fantasy life and real world of the child.

Again in stage 6, adolescent creativity is normally enhanced through the inspiration of loving and being loved by a person of the opposite sex. However, in some cases of adolescent love, consummation involving physical relations tends to reduce the high energy potential aroused but when delayed or partly prevented from being used, great art, music, and literature result.

Love in our lives is seen as central to creativity so that if we want to be creative we should put more love in our lives. Although the developmental process of stages 3 and 6 naturally emphasizes creativity, it is not completely absent at the other stages of development. Love and creativity may enter into our lives environmentally at any time and the degree to which love is abundant is the degree to which creativity is likely to be present. However, a good start in stage 3 is expected to give the best assurance that creativity will occur again in stage 6.

Escalation

Within each of the three stages, development occurs through cycles of escalation (Gowan, 1972, 1974). The purpose of escalation is to facilitate the emergence of an individual's creativity. Escalation, or the raising of the level of action by discrete jumps—much like moving up an escalator or a flight of stairs—is described as an aspect of developmental process that is increasingly complex. It embraces five different, but interrelated, attributes of development: *succession, discontinuity, emergence, differentiation, and integration* (see Table 6.3).

1. Succession—Succession implies a fixed order within a hierarchy of developmental stages. The rate of succession from one stage to the next (i.e., the extent of development at any one stage) is relatively flexible and dependent on the nature of the organism and its environment. Piaget calls this *hierarchicization*. It leads to developmental spread or *decalage,* which is dependent on personal and cultural idiosyncrasies.

Table 6.3 Components of Escalation

Component	Description	Piaget's Nearest Term	Relevant Material
Succession	A fixed order of hierarchical stages	Hierarchicization	Decalages (cultural and personal lags)
Discontinuity	A discrete succession of discontinuous equilibration	Equilibration	Each stage has characteristic properties and tasks
Emergence	The budding and making of the implicit, explicit	Consolidation	Budding
Differentiation	Fixation and shift in emphasis	Integration	Fixation Metamorphosis
Integration	A gestalt of structures d'ensemble	Structuring	Summation structures d'ensemble (parts which assemble to make a whole)

Note. From *The Development of the Psychedelic Individual* (p. 63) by J. C. Gowan, 1974, Buffalo, New York: Creative Education Foundation. Copyright © 1974 by J. C. Gowan. Reprinted by permission.

2. Discontinuity—Discontinuity involves an ordered and discrete sequence of equilibria, like a series of stairs—termed *equilibration* by Piaget—so that any attempt to escalate from one level to the next requires additional input of energy.
3. Emergence—Emergence involves budding and the making of the implicit, explicit in the flowering of characteristics unseen before. It is the debut of new powers—called *consolidation* by Piaget. At this time a given stage is simultaneously a summation of the accomplishments of previous stages and a preparation for the tasks of the next stage.
4. Differentiation—Differentiation refers to the attribute that clarifies, fixates, and metamorphoses the emphasis in successive developments. Take for instance the teenager who seems to have outgrown the family and regards himself or herself as a prisoner with only the telephone as a lifeline to age mates. Piaget has no word that exactly fits this description. According to Gowan, the nearest Piagetian word to this is *integration* (i.e., restructuring and coordination).
5. Integration—Integration sums up the other attributes into a higher synthesis with greater complexity and unites them into a gestalt which Piaget calls *structuring*. This is very much like driving a car

on an open road in overdrive with feelings of freedom and elation that come from the sense of using the automobile to the utmost for which it was designed. Accordingly, Gowan considers the Piagetian term structuring as fitting his definition better since Piaget's concept of integration means reemphasis.

By this process, the environment may have maximum or minimum effect on the individual, depending upon the individual's position in the cycle. Continual environmental stimulation, however, is required for escalation into the higher or self-actualizing levels.

Dysplasia

Gowan (1974) describes *dysplasia* as a lag, arrest, or slowdown of some part of an individual's development relative to the time it should occur. When one aspect of the psyche (e.g., affective) continues to escalate while the other (e.g., cognitive) does not or becomes arrested, Gowan calls it *relative dysplasia*. *Absolute dysplasia* is the disparity between the stage of development at which the individual, relative to age, ought to be and the stage at which the individual actually is.

When *relative dysplasia* occurs between the affective and cognitive stages, it is the cognitive that tends to lag behind in most cases. Exceptions to this condition may occur when, for example, (a) a 10-year-old girl with an I.Q. of 150 is in Stage 4 (industry) affectively but is in the cognitive stage of formal operations, and hence reasoning in syllogisms; (b) a brilliant youth, aged 14, although still in Stage 5 (identity), has already escalated into cognitive Stage 6 (creativity) and is producing original works of music, poetry, or mathematics; (c) a bright idealistic young adult of 23 has escalated into cognitive Stage 7 (psychedelia) although affectively is only in Stage 6 (intimacy).

There are three higher cognitive stages than those named by Piaget (Flavell, 1963). They go with Erikson's three affective stages—intimacy, generativity, and ego-integrity—and are *creativity, psychedelia,* and *illumination* (Stages 6, 7, and 8). These stages of development, because they involve expansion of the mind beyond formal operations (convergent thinking), are increasingly rare, even in intelligent, healthy adults. Facilitation of escalation into these stages by using various kinds of techniques: education, therapy, sensitivity training, and meditation, among others, is in the process of becoming a major movement for superior adults.

Periodicity and Transformation

Gowan (1974) asks us to observe an important happening in nature and in human life that he relates to a *transformation of energy* taking place from one stage of development to the next higher stage of development. This transformation he calls *periodicity,* which "occurs when the same pattern of events is seen to run through higher development as has been contained in a corresponding pattern from a lower sequence" (p. 49)—something that seems to have escaped the notion of human development theorists.

The answer to questions such as "Why should there be developmental stages at all?" or "Why cannot development, like growth, be one smooth accretion?" lies in the critical aspect of energy transformation in the individual. *Transformation* and focusing of energy are essential to the development and the creative processes. Because the amount of energy available for use is not enough to be expended on Gowan's three areas—the world (it, they), the ego (I, me), and the other (thou)—simultaneously, energy must be focused through attention, and expended on first one and then each of the other of these three aspects. It is this process that leads to the three-phase *periodicity* of the developmental stages.

One of the unnoticed consequences of the periodic nature of the developmental stages is that the first barriers to accomplishment of the tasks of a given developmental stage are the *negative polarities* of the previous stage (i.e., the stage, three back from a specific developmental stage). Thus, as examples, for children in Stage 4 (industry) mistrust is the barrier to concrete operations. In Stage 5 (identity), shame and doubt plague young adolescents in their identity crises; in Stage 6 (intimacy), guilt and immobilization keep individuals from happiness in sex or joy in creative performance; in Stage 7 (generativity), inferiority makes individuals feel inadequate for the grandeur of generativity and psychedelia; in Stage 9 (ego-integrity), role confusion prevents ego-integrity.

Developmental stage theory can be regarded as carrying the discontinuity principle of *quantum theory* over to behavioral science. Escalation is the jump from one riser to the next on the developmental staircase. Energy from the organism is required for each jump, but certain freedoms are gained as a result. We ask, "What is escalating?" One answer appears to be that it is the ego strength that helps control and develop the creative imagination, illustrated by a comparison of the horrors and dread of night terrors in the child and the beauty and simplicity of a musical or mathematical product as conceived by the adult. Developmental process centers around stabilizing and controlling the creative imagination and harnessing it to constructive, not destructive use. As we shall see later, this activity is related to the functions of the preconscious.

Escalation Versus Acceleration

The importance of *acceleration* (or moving at a faster rate through schooling) in *escalating* individuals to higher levels of mental functioning is little known. Such questions as, "Can acceleration of gifted children in any developmental stage produce escalation?" or "Do gifted children automatically escalate to higher developmental stages at an accelerated pace or do they need educational intervention to bring escalation about?" are to the point. Although evidence of the positive effects of acceleration in learning is available (Gowan & Demos, 1964; Stanley, Keating, & Fox, 1974), no clear-cut research evidence exists indicating that acceleration in fact produces escalation (Epstein, 1977). (Note that brighter individuals have the advantage of moving more quickly through successive stages; although precocity across stages is clearly present, it may not be as pronounced within stages; and advance organizers are facilitative of children's acceleration from the preoperations level to the concrete level [Ausubel, 1978; Lawton, 1976; Lawton & Wanska, 1976].)

Studies by P. Arlin (1975) and J. Weinstein and A. Altschuler (n.d.) corroborate earlier views on development by psychologists such as Jean Piaget (cognitive stages), Erik Erikson (affective stages), and Robert J. Havighurst (developmental tasks). Arlin (1975) predicts a developmental cognitive stage that follows Piaget's formal operations stage and calls it problem solving (Gowan's creativity stage). H. T. Epstein (1977) considers Arlin's observation a prediction of a hitherto unknown stage. That Piaget did not formulate this problem-solving stage and other stages beyond formal operations can be, perhaps, attributed to the unwillingness of Piaget's children to continue to submit themselves to the daily drudgery of observation (Gowan, 1974).

Four of Weinstein and Altschuler levels of self-knowledge bear an interesting resemblance to Gowan's Stages 4, 5, and 7. As observed by Gowan (1979d, pp. 52–53), their analysis of student stories led to the identification of four developmental stages with relevant descriptions as follows.

Concrete Operations (Stage 4):
  Stream of consciousness reporting of separate images with no causality, nothing but separate feelings, and no overall start and finish.

Formal Operations (Stage 5):
  Report of feelings with start and finish of story and a moral, causal outcome; however, no pattern across situations.

Creativity (Stage 6):
  Strong personal feelings in report of personality characteristics and personal style of which the story is an example, but outcome is fatalistic, working out the same across different situations.

Psychedelic (Stage 7):
  Choice, responsibility, and autonomy enter reports, with the individual able to change his response pattern.

Although some differences exist between Gowan's, and Weinstein and Altschuler's informational categories, the developmental trend of these stages clearly follows periodic developmental stage theory.

Koplowitz (1978) proposes that two higher stages beyond the usual Piagetian cognitive ones exist, namely:

Systems Stage:
> The individual understands complementarity, homeostasis, and interdependence (resembling Gowan's creativity stage 6).

Unitary Operational Thought Stage:
> The individual understands that the manner in which the universe is perceived is only one of several possible constructs (resembling Gowan's psychedelic stage 7).

This view is consistent with the current one that there may exist higher cognitive stages beyond Piaget's formal operations stage (e.g. Gruber, 1973; Vygotsky, 1974).

The Preconscious and Creativity

In his discussion of developmental stage theory, Gowan (1974, 1975) indicates that much of the source of creativity lies in the *preconscious,* a term originating with Sigmund Freud, who divided the mental life of a person's psyche into *unconscious, preconscious,* and *conscious.* Harry S. Sullivan (1953) explains Freud's formulation more simply as the bad-me, not-me, and good-me.

Bad-me (the unconscious) refers to that part of our mental life that stores ideas and drives that cause us too much pain, anxiety, or guilt if we are conscious or aware of them. We store these ideas and drives in the unconscious to defend the self (ego), for instance, by pushing the ideas aside (repression) or using other Freudian defense mechanisms (e.g., sublimation or rationalization). Of course, these ideas and drives remain active in our unconscious and, without our awareness, are the cause of some of our behaviors. Sometimes we notice them when our defenses are relaxed, as in dreams, slips of the tongue, or when we are under the influence of alcohol or drugs.

Good-me is that part of our mental life that we are aware of and that can be called the conscious positive self-concept.

Not-me is the part of our mental life where frightening and uncanny experiences occur, for example, those we meet in dreams and nightmares. According to Sullivan (1953)

> the personification of the not-me is most conspicuously encountered by most of us in an occasional dream while we are asleep; but is very emphatically encountered by people who are having a severe schizophrenic episode, in as-

pects that are to them most spectacularly real. As a matter of fact, it is always manifest . . . in certain peculiar absences of phenomena when there should be phenomena; and in a good many people . . . it is very striking in its indirect manifestation (dissociated behavior) in which people do and say things of which they do not and could not have had any knowledge, things which may be quite meaningful to other people, but are unknown to them. . . . This is a very gradually evolving personification of an always relatively primitive character—that is organized in usually simple signs in the parataxic [experiences received as images] mode of experience, and made up of poorly grasped aspects of living, which will presently be regarded as "dreadful," and which still later will be differentiated into incidents which will be attended by awe, horror, loathing . . . or dread. (pp. 162–163)

It is the preconscious or not-me area of our mental life that is the source of much of our creativity, and in a series of analogies Gowan (1975) explains that the preconscious can be considered

as an ever refilling well wherein all creative men have learned to dip their bucket, or as a great computer, containing in its data banks all knowledge, and creativity is but the process of operating the terminal console. Or it can be considered as a great collator, chewing up the events and ideas of the day, and rearranging them into other forms and patterns, or like an enlarged fluid container, with a permeable membrane through which (by osmosis) creative ideas are leaked into consciousness. (p. 301)

Gowan (1974) illustrates this last analogy by comparing the preconscious to an *enlarged fluid container* through whose permeable membrane creative ideas leak into the consciousness (Figure 6.3).

Gowan (1974) also tells us that the *preconscious* is the source of human creativity, especially if it is strengthened, protected, and enlarged through regular use and through increased mental health. At first creative persons make intuitive use of their preconscious—when leaks occur through the permeable membrane, as it were, by osmosis—which manifests itself in works of art of one kind or another. At a higher level of creativity (psychedelia or state-of-mind expansion that takes place naturally without the help of drugs), the barriers that separate the *unconscious* and *conscious* are thought of as doors that swing open to let in the resources of the preconscious for cognitive processing and production. In the final state of wholeness and holiness, the barriers completely disappear such that the conscious and preconscious become one.

If the preconscious becomes open to persons in the way Gowan describes, then they become creative. In another analogy, Gowan (1975) explains this process as the *printing of a new edition of old newspapers.* He compares the preconscious to an editor who obtains the material needed for the new edition from the archives of the unconscious, which contain

Figure 6.3 Development of the Preconscious

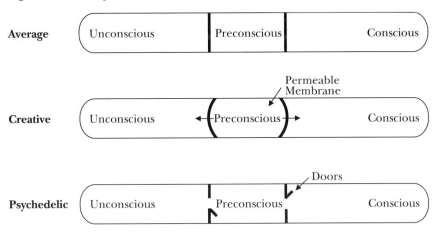

From *"The Development of the Psychedelic Individual"* (p. 83) by J.C. Gowan, 1974, Buffalo, New York: Creative Education Foundation. Copyright © 1974 by J.C. Gowan. Reprinted by permission.

all the editor's past experience in chewed-up and digested form—a vast assortment of biological impulses, taboo acts, rejected compromises, affected pains and pleasures, remembered facts, personal feelings, horrifying nightmares, and a host of other material. What the new edition is to be will depend on the extent to which the editor finds the unconscious accessible.

Stage 6 of Gowan's periodic table (Tables 6.1 and 6.2) stresses an *intuitive* kind of creativity that prepares a person for the *psychedelic* creativity of Stage 7 when the resources of the preconscious become available, not so much by chance but almost at will.

> The preconscious, like fire, makes a good servant but a bad master. The developing relationship between the individual and the preconscious starts as a scary and traumatic encounter, but becomes more humanistic through the parataxic procedures of creativity. It is like the developing relationship between a young child and a young colt. At first the child is afraid of the horse, and cannot ride him; the horse is skittish, unbroken and unpredictable. Eventually through many intermediary stages, the child learns to ride the horse and the horse is taught to accept the rider, until finally the man is complete master of the animal, now fully amenable to his commands. (Gowan, 1978c, p. 219)

DEVELOPMENT FOR TRANSFORMATION

That we understand that intelligence consists of many abilities possibly defined by the Structure of Intellect is not enough. We need to recognize that ability is one dimension of the multimodal construct, to which is to be added energy (derived from emotive-motivational fields of forces). Ability needs to be energized before it can become active and operable.

The conceptual model of developmental stages as it relates to the periods of an individual's life when verbal and nonverbal creativity can be most effectively activated holds significant implications for the gifted. In addition, any attempt at educational facilitation has to bear in mind the achievement of potential ability.

Attempts made over the past 25 years to understand these and related issues, especially as they relate to the gifted, include designing theoretical constructs, models, or plans. Examples of such structures or systems can be seen in Guilford's Structure of Intellect model (Figure 3.5), the Erikson-Piaget-Gowan periodic developmental stage chart (Table 6.1), and the Holistic Model for Educating Gifted Children (Figure 3.1).

Recently, the search for models and plans was intensified, and attempts have been made to discover constructs that would allow for conceptions of greater order and generalizability. Seeing principles in patterns for the derivation of even higher levels of order has attracted no small attention and has given rise to some extremely valuable contributions to thought.

Theoretical speculation rooted to, and deriving insights from, such disciplines as biology, physics, chemistry, mathematics, and psychology has produced a way of thought called *general systems*. Derald Langham (1974), originator of the Genesa model, prefaced his version of *general systems* with the following questions:

> If you had a magic key that would fit all makes of truth would you use it? If it revealed principles and made them available to you, would you use them? If it unveiled answers to your problems, would you be happy? (p. 177)

In the past few years, drawing from the advances in scientific and mathematical thought, Stuart Dodd, Derald Langham, George Land, John Gowan, and several others have each attempted to find *general principles* to explain existence and behavior. Interacting with one another by mail, visits, and meetings (such as the Creative Problem Solving Institutes of 1974 and 1975 held in Buffalo, New York), they attempted not only to convince one another of the significance of their systems but also to find a *system of systems*. Gowan and Dodd (1977) observe that because general systems is about generalities and not specifics, it is difficult to explain. However, Land (1973) tells us that the idea of general systems is not complicated but just the opposite—simple, for its purpose is to *dis-*

cover the fundamental laws of nature that apply in theory and practice to everything. Relevant to the concepts of growth and development are Gowan's *developmental stage theory* and Land's *transformation theory*, both of which will be discussed as systems.

Land's Transformation Theory as a System

Land prefaces a discussion of transformation theory with several highly relevant observations about systems (Land & Kenneally, 1977, pp. 12–17) paraphrased as follows:

> In a system, it is important to differentiate the parts of the system from the whole system and to see their relationship to each other as well.
>
> Things move from states of disorder to states of order and from these states of order to disorder before attaining higher states of order.
>
> The scientific method encourages partialistic thinking through analysis to a solution—solving always creates new problems because the part affects the whole.
>
> Systems may be seen as subsystems of larger systems.
>
> A whole system may be identified by its organization; by its boundary, which sets it apart from its environment (where it takes in things from and puts things out into its environment); and by its synergetic character (because a mature system is more than the sum of its parts).
>
> The self-regulation of a system must have more than negative or positive feedback. It must have "feedforward," or shared regulation, so that new information derived from the environment continuously provides for proper connection and adaptation to the system's changing environment.

Then comes the key concept of his theoretical model—*growth*. Land defines growth as the process by which things become connected with each other and operate at higher levels of organization and complexity, and as that which guides all systems and subsystems.

Land and Kenneally (1977) summarize and extend these basic concepts to form Land's transformation model. According to the model, a general system moves from no order to the establishment of order; connections are made among various entities to form an orderly pattern by which it derives identity. The relationship among the entities at this point is one of *control* (Stage 1). Like entities in the environment connect to produce similar patterns, moving from a relationship of control to one of *influence* (Stage 2). When the number of like entities in the environment available to form similar patterns are used up, further growth requires the use of different entities, and the relationship becomes one of *mutual sharing* (Stage 3). The sharing of differences leads to new same-ness, and the system prepares to break down to establish a new identity at a higher level (Stage 4), and the growth process goes on.

These are, in essence, Land's three distinctly different forms of growth. The first three stages he labels *accretive, replicative,* and *mutu-alistic*. The fourth he calls *transformational;* it represents a transition to a new and higher level of development. Land and Kenneally (1977) illus-trate these processes rather well using the analogy of a child playing with Tinker Toys—constructing, disassembling, and reconstructing various objects.

The creative process in Land's Transformation Theory—which in-cludes four different kinds of creativity, directly related to his four stages of growth—is described in the following terms:

1. The most primitive level of creativity simply produces enlarge-ment of an idea or concept—a change in scale creating a "super-market from a grocery store" (*accretive stage*). [Both J. P. Guilford and E. P. Torrance have identified this as the ability to elaborate.]
2. The next level of creativity makes modifications in the form of the pattern but not in its basic function—modification that could lead to the improvement of something, making it lighter, stronger, more efficient, and so on (*replicative stage*). [This formulation is similar to Alex F. Osborn's use of these categories to induce shifts in creative thinking. E. P. Torrance, for instance, has called think-ing of this kind *flexibility.*]
3. Creativity at the next higher level relates to the making of high-level combinations, analogies and metaphors (*mutualistic stage*).
4. At the fourth level, creativity relates to invention or the recom-bination of the old concept at a higher level of relationship to the environment involving destructuring and reintegration (*trans-formation*).

The Lands' (Land, A. G. & Land V., 1982) concept of *oscillation* be-tween divergent and convergent thinking has direct parallel in the men-tal creativity and physiological-biochemical evolution process. Such os-cillation is possibly the simplest and most general of nature's principles, and in terms of ordering-disordering for the emergence of a higher order, it constitutes the underpinning of Land's transformation theory. What mental creativity and physiological-biochemical processes share in common are mutation and hybridization.

Mutation involves the random rearrangement, substitution, and addi-tion or deletion of small parts of genetic DNA in whose modus operandi is unconsciously mimicked the random ideation technique occurring in brainstorming. We are reminded of Alex F. Osborn's (1963) approach to improving something without changing its essential characteristics found in his principles of adaptation, modification, substitution, addition, multiplication, subtraction, division, rearrangement, reversal, combination, and so on.

Hybridization relates to innovation and invention, and at the mental level uses paradoxical metaphors or oxymora to deliberately "force-fit" opposites, a process used in Synectics (Prince, 1968) to generate analogies. In the *unity of opposites*, high levels of creative thinking evolve. This principle can be illustrated by two overlapping circles that share differentness while producing a synergistic new. A. Rothenberg (1976) has called the psychological basis of such mental activity *Janusian thinking*.

Periodic Developmental Stage Theory as a System

Gowan's contribution to *general systems* comes from his developmental stage theory. Like Land, he perceives growth as an essential feature of his system but prefers to regard it as development. He makes a distinction between the two when he says that development is to growth as quality is to quantity—the apple enlarges but it also ripens.

Although Land's *evolutionary process* approach and Gowan's *developmental process* approach are different, they obey the same laws of nature. A dialogue between Gowan and Land in 1976 at the Creative Problem Solving Institute in Buffalo, New York, attempted to find common ground for their systems. It led to creative insights for bonding their models, the implications of which have yet to be worked out. Gowan was led to reiterate that the developmental cycle is discontinuous and not continuous as previously believed. (However, in later dialogue with the author, Gowan was willing to concede that an inherent continuity within each development stage, which permits the welling up of energy to precipitate escalation to higher levels, exists. Thus discontinuity in the developmental cycle is established.)

Gowan's Periodic Development Stage system pivots on the development of the creative individual. Hence it concerns itself with those stages of development optimal to creative interactions of the inner and outer worlds of the individual. Land calls this the mutualistic stage of his transformation model, when creative processes operate.

Transformation in Land's model differs little from Gowan's *periodicity*. Both preface the entry into the next higher level of growth or development. The highest level of the creative process, in both models, allows for transformation involving the function of analogical and metaphorical brain activity and the tapping of the preconscious. At present, some would refer to this as right-brain functioning or the function of the creative imagination and its imagery correlates.

Briefly, *creative imagination imagery* may be said to be the province of Land's mutualistic stage and Gowan's creative and psychedelic stages, all of which are related to high levels of psychological functioning. It is at these stages that high-level combinations and connections are made by analogy and metaphor, at which time the preconscious is tapped. To re-iterate, transformations occur when movement taking place at a lower level of order moves to a higher level of order through the process of destructuring and reintegration.

SOCIOCULTURAL EVENTS AFFECTING DEVELOPMENT

So far, development has been viewed as an individual phenomenon. It has been discussed as continuous and discrete, as it relates to the intel-lect and creativity. D. K. Simonton (1978) and Silvano Arieti (1976) have emphasized that development cannot be treated as isolated from its *so-ciocultural* origins. Both question why creative geniuses appear at one time and place in history and not at another; both attribute this phenom-enon to certain sociocultural events that significantly affect the creative development of individuals. Like others before them, they recognize that the appearance of men of eminence takes place irregularly and in clusters.

Developing Creativity for Eminence

Simonton (1978) focuses attention on conditions that facilitate or hinder the emergence of creative giants. In addressing the historical circum-stances responsible for the emergence of such geniuses as Aristotle, Shakespeare, Michelangelo, and Beethoven, Simonton examines the events that influence creative people and makes a critical distinction be-tween two phases of their lives: (a) the sociocultural events that may have influence on the *period of a creator's productivity* (e.g., warfare and its aversive impact on a person's output at a certain career point); and (b) the sociocultural events that may have influence on the creator's *developmen-tal period*. Of the two, according to Simonton, it is the latter phase that is far more important to the *emergence of eminence*.

> Perhaps a special set of political, cultural and social conditions is most con-ducive to the development of creative potential in a youthful genius. In adult-hood, that creative potential then becomes fully actualized in the form of prolific and significant creative productivity. Thus, it is quite conceivable that the creative genius is either made or broken during childhood, adolescence, and early adulthood. So, complete knowledge of the historical forces behind a creative genius requires that productive and developmental period influ-ences be carefully segregated. (Simonton, 1978, pp. 187–188)

To Simonton, the *developmental periods* of childhood and adolescence through adulthood tend to be more significantly affected by external events than do *specific periods* of productivity. The latter periods enjoy immunity to external events, with the exception of physical illness and war. He identifies seven variables that have influence on the creative development of individuals: formal education, role model availability, zeitgeist, political fragmentation, warfare, civil disturbances, and political instability.

Formal education is an important influence on the individual's creativity while growing up, but, beyond a certain point, it can inhibit creative development by enforcing an overcommitment to traditional perspective.

Availability of eminent creators as *role models* for emulation is of great importance to the emergence of other eminent creators. So the more role models there are for emulation during the developmental period of genius, the greater the increase in creative potential. Generally, it is to be expected that emulation occurs in the same discipline. For instance, precocious musicians will be influenced by an eminent musician rather than by someone in the scientific or literary fields. If a precocious musician is influenced by someone in another discipline, the impact may not always be beneficial, as can be seen in the negative effects of religious activity (requiring a high degree of conformity) on philosophy and creativity. To this may be added the adverse effects of role model availability on creative development when the presence of an excess of role models may lead a potential genius to make a premature commitment to a particular school of thought that makes a disciple of him or her rather than a leader.

On the matter of *zeitgeist*, Simonton indicates that major minds in the history of ideas are neither ahead nor representative of their time. Instead, they tend to be behind their times. He explains that, unlike lesser thinkers, eminent thinkers are most influenced by the zeitgeist dominating the intellectual scene during their development period. In this way, they are lead to be preoccupied with elaborating the ideas to which they were most exposed and to act as synthesizers. That is, they make prior accomplishments into a single unified philosophical system.

Political fragmentation, or the existence of many independent states within a civilization, engenders cultural diversity that significantly affects creative development more than it does creative productivity. Diversity shapes the content of the creator's intellectual base, promoting an openness to experience, change, individualism, and material welfare.

Constant warfare, however, in the lifetime of the youthful creative genius has the opposite effect on his or her creative development by discouraging those intellectual qualities that are shaped by political fragmentation.

Civil disturbances (i.e., popular revolts, rebellions, and revolutions) have a potent influence on creative development although, at times, exposure to such events can have a negative impact.

Of all these influences, *political instability* is the most detrimental to creative development. To be creative, an individual must find the world somewhat predictable and controllable; personal efforts must have some prospect of eventual fruition.

Simonton's conclusions about the significance of sociocultural conditions on creative development not only explain the rarity of eminence in our times but also direct our attention to those shaping influences in our society responsible for facilitating or hindering the development of creativity during the formative years of our young and growing gifted. Perhaps our overemphasis on the formal aspects of education to the near neglect of providing opportunities for emulating eminent men and women should command our notice and guide us to make changes that would benefit the gifted. It should be our aim to prepare the gifted to push to the frontiers, and this we can do by including and integrating creative habits of mind and ways of learning. There is an abundance of material to assist us in facilitating the creativity of our gifted and in the development of their creative abilities, imagination and imagery, and right-brain processing (Feldhusen & Treffinger, 1980; Gowan, 1978b, 1978c, 1980; Grady, 1984; Guilford, 1977; Khatena, 1978a, 1979a, 1984; Meeker, 1969; Renzulli, 1973; Torrance & Myers, 1970).

Individual Creativity and Creativogenic Society

We now turn our attention to the work of Silvano Arieti (1976). His interest in creativity as individual and societal led him to examine social theories on the subject. A. Kroeber (1944), for instance, catalogues the occurrence of geniuses in the various disciplines of science, mathematics, music, literature, and so on, with no explanation for the clustering of such eminence.

Following in his wake, C. E. Gray (1961, 1966), compiled a creativity curve for Western civilization that agreed with Kroeber's main findings on the emergence of genius in clusters. According to them, the blossoming of genius occurs several times during a civilization. Such peaks are rare and do not characterize most of civilization's course, nor are they of equal duration. Gray advances an *epicyclic theory* that views history as a series of concurrent cycles—economic, social, and political. Each cycle passes at different rates through formative, developed, florescent, and degenerate stages. It is at the coincidence of the florescent and developed stages of the three cycles that clusters of creativity occur. Gray's analysis of history, in terms of the *epicycle theory*, indicates that favorable economic, social, and political factors promote creativity.

Arieti (1976) points out that there exist a number of differing views on whether genius shapes culture or is shaped by it. On the one hand, there are those who would give nearly all the credit to culture. Such views regard highly creative individuals not as rich personalities but as measures of cultural expression (Kroeber, 1944), as indices of the growth of their culture (Gray, 1966), or as passive representatives who express their times (L. A. White, 1949). On the other hand, there are those who would attribute to these geniuses either the making of culture (Galton, 1870) or the remaking of culture by them before they are made by it (James, 1880).

L. A. White (1949) reached two significant conclusions: (a) Invention or discovery would occur only if culture makes available materials and ideas necessary for the synthesis; and (b) if this were the case, invention or discovery would become inevitable under normal conditions of cultural interaction. However, Arieti points out that the capacity of the individual who makes the significant synthesis must not be overlooked, as was done by L. A. White, because *the significant synthesis is the creative process* itself, the significance and unpredictability of which appear *magical*.

Analysis of the works of Kroeber, Gray, L. A. White, and others led Arieti to conclude that

1. individual possibility for genius is much more frequent than the occurrence of genius.
2. potentiality for creativity exists.
3. creativity can be activated.
4. some cultures promote creativity (creativogenic cultures).

Arieti regards the potentially *creative person* and the *creativogenic culture* as two essential components of creativity. Individuals, he suggests, make roughly two contacts with culture. One contact relates to individuals' use of their biological equipment to understand their environment and satisfy their needs. The other contact relates to individuals' acquisition of things already present in the culture that are mediated by interpersonal relationships. Both the individual and culture are perceived as *open systems;* the individual gives to culture and takes from it.

When a culture is *creativogenic*, it makes available to an individual creative elements that are perceived or accepted as such if similar characteristics exist within the individual. This, then, prepares the way for a *magic synthesis* that will produce innovation, which, in turn, is offered to, and becomes a part of culture. A creativogenic society offers the individual the possibility of becoming great, but it does not make the occurrence of greatness automatic.

Arieti points to nine conditions that exist in a society that will facilitate and foster greatness and creativity. According to him they are as follows:

1. Availability of cultural means (an elite to preserve these cultural means; accessibility to equipment, materials, etc.)

2. Openness to cultural stimuli (cultural stimuli are present, requested, desired, and made easily available)
3. Stress on becoming, not just being
4. Free access to cultural media for all citizens without discrimination
5. Freedom—or even retention of moderate discrimination—after severe oppression or absolute exclusion is an incentive to creativity
6. Exposure to different and even contrasting cultural stimuli
7. Tolerance for, and interest in, diverging views
8. Interaction of significant persons
9. Promotion of incentives and rewards

Both Simonton (1978) and Arieti (1976) recognize that geniuses have the potential to become eminent and that actualization can occur through creativity. Simonton, who makes distinctions in creative productivity at certain times in a person's life, sees creativity as a part of development in an individual's formative years, and identifies those cultural conditions that facilitate or hinder creative development. Arieti, however, looks at creativity as a dynamic exchange of two open systems, the individual and creativogenic culture, with certain conditions that facilitate the emergence of eminence. While Arieti emphasizes the conditions in a culture that can be expected to foster creativity, Simonton examines cultural conditions that affect creative development. The combination of the two views can only enhance our understanding of creative development still further.

MORAL DEVELOPMENT

Moral development is the consequence of the interaction of individual potential with sociocultural influences and events. In so far as moral development involves intellectual abilities and processing capabilities, inherited operations play a significant role. However, moral development is related to behavioral correlates of the individual living in a group. Its *raison d'être* is society, which provides a frame of reference for individual behavior. Without the group, the individual has no need for morality, because the term implies a system of rules to govern behavior of social beings to preserve the integrity and unity of a society. The reader is referred to a Holistic Model for Educating Gifted Children (Figure 3.1), which places in context the process of individual development—morality being one aspect of it—relative to the interactive relationship of the Individual, Environment, and Interventions components.

The *system of rules* under which a society lives and operates may be referred to as *sociocultural tradition*. The whole history of events, circumstances, dealings, beliefs, rituals, and practices of a group gives rise to a set of patterns that become incorporated as the group's way of life. What emerges are its manners, mores, and, in a large measure, its culture. Intrinsic to a culture is an *established* and *evolving code of behavior*. That which is established relates to tradition, whereas that which is evolving relates to the ever changing component that admits exceptions. With these changes a new formulated tradition emerges. This code of behavior determines what is right or wrong and just for individual members of the group. It forms the ethics of a people, which make living together possible. When the ethics of a group become linked to a religious belief system, monotheistic or polytheistic in origin, ethics become morality, and a socially based system acquires divine force.

People are born without morality. They have to learn to be moral, first, from their parents; later, from age mates and other mates, from other adults around them, and from social and educational agencies. Such learning is a lifetime undertaking. Its acquisition evolves as the individual learns how to behave according to rules that have a built-in mechanism for change, governed by necessity and consensus.

The individual growing up applies what he or she has learned in a variety of ways. Each person is guided by the general and specific principles of behavior that were experienced in the growing up process, and the inherited intellectual operations that assist the individual in making judgments essential to appropriate responses. However, before judgments can be made, the individual goes through the processes of understanding the set of events and remembering how they should be dealt with (either by the example of others or personal experience). These experiences prepare the individual to consider one or several behavioral alternatives that then have to be evaluated before a decision to act is made.

These processes are the mental operations incorporated in Guilford's Structure of Intellect model. As we know, informational content and products may vary, whereas mental operations, because they are inherited, do not. In the case of making *moral judgments*, evaluative thinking abilities apply themselves to a behavioral information frame of reference rooted to morality, and the reasoning involved for this, whether convergent or divergent, can be called *moral reasoning*. Hence, the Structure of Intellect, by its very nature, can be harnessed to effect educational intervention, generally, and moral education, specifically.

Relevance of Attitudes and Values

Attitudes and values have important roles to play in an individual's moral development. They are closely linked to the formation of an individual's moral frame of reference and must be taken into account when considering the nature of moral development. They give further dimension to the intellect as it searches for appropriate culturally approved behaviors.

An *attitude*, in its simplest form, is a feeling complex, visceral in origin. It is indirectly organized by repeated occurrence as an emotive-intellectual attachment to one phenomenon or another. In time attitudes cluster to form an *attitudinal system* that determines the way an individual views the world. Such a system will have a decided effect on an individual's selection of all kinds of behaviors, including moral ones. The extent to which an individual will be properly governed by a moral frame of reference will also depend on an individual's attitudes to it. Attitudes are formed directly as the individual interacts with the physical-sociocultural universe; they may also be formed indirectly by imitation or learning. Morality is learned; the individual acquires and internalizes it, so that as it is manifested, it is a consequence of intellectual and attitudinal processing. Because this is an on-going activity throughout a person's life, it must be taken into account in any view of moral development.

Another essential to moral development is the acquisition of *values*. In its simplest form, a value is an *appraisal of worth* of something or someone. We are born with no values. They develop with experience and example to become a repertoire as we grow older. Value formation, unlike attitude formation, is cognitive not emotive. Judgment has to be exercised. Evaluative thinking abilities are brought to bear in the matter of appraisal. However, to judge or appraise, there must be *criteria*; at first we acquire them as the result of the experience and explanation of others, and later, when we become more knowledgeable, we formulate them ourselves. We establish touchstones, as it were, to guide us in appraisals.

Most of our values are assimilated from tradition and the social groups that we are members of. An individual's system of values places differential worth on various aspects of prevalent morality. Consequently, a certain *relativity* enters into individual moral reasoning, judgment, and consequent behavior. That is why we have those who deviate from society's norms and a system in place to correct such deviations. *Deviant behavior* as it relates to tradition may be thought of as a consequence of the *tension between individual autonomy and social stability* (Rich & DeVitis, 1985). A society sets up behavioral norms and values for its members. When there is a lack of consensus on these, social disorganization predicates the increase of deviance and violence. That is why a society establishes acceptable norms, compelling goals, and consistent procedures for achieving them, manifested in the institution of effective socialization practices.

Two different but complementary orientations have been proposed by Andras Angyal (1965), namely, the striving for increased individual autonomy in the context of a healthy form of heteronomy that he calls *homonomy*. "The person behaves as if he were seeking a place for himself in a larger unit of which he strives to become a part" (p. 12). In this way, both individual autonomy and social stability co-exist.

Emile Durkheim (1961), writing on the subject of the competing interests of individual autonomy and social stability, identifies three basic elements in the internalization of moral values: the spirit of authority and discipline, attachment to social groups, and autonomy or self-determination.

According to Durkheim *authority and discipline* are moral imperatives that perform the important function of character formation, specifically, and personality, generally. They safeguard social stability and create possibilities for individual autonomy.

Individual attachment to the group is the prerequisite for moral development, for without social life there would be no purpose for morality. Couched in terms of an evolutionary relationship, Durkheim (1933) indicates that

> family, nation, and humanity represent different phases of our social and moral evolution, stages that prepare for, and build upon, one another. . . . Just as each has its part to play in historical development they mutually complement each other in the present. (p. 399)

Autonomy or self-determination is essentially linked to morality in that moral behavior of an individual presupposes the opportunity for choice of decision. Moral reasoning and judgment belong to the individual operating in the context of rule sets. It is such autonomy that allows for differences in behavior that eventually may lead to the setting of new rules of conduct.

Hershel D. Thornburg (1973) indicates that the *locus of an individual's value system* is within the family, such that during childhood there is a high degree of consistency between values and behaviors. As the individual grows older, discrepancies occur between values and behaviors. When values control behaviors, the inconsistencies produce guilt, anxiety, shame, and so on. When behaviors affect values, the inconsistencies produce value shifts. Maximum shifts occur during adolescence, when the individual forms his or her own value system. These shifts prepare the way for the maximum value-behavior consistency that facilitates the functioning of a well-adjusted adult. Drawing from the research of Jean Piaget, Lawrence Kohlberg, and others, Thornburg conceptualizes the developmental nature of the consistency between values held and behaviors expressed by the child growing up to adulthood, providing approximate age ranges for their occurrence (see Figure 6.4).

In one way or another, theories of moral development (Rich & DeVitis, 1985) concern themselves with the individual growing up, the so-

Figure 6.4 From Consistency Through Inconsistency to Consistency

Primary Influences	Consistency Range	Stage	
Society	Behavior ⟶ Values	Adulthood (27 on)	Consistency
Peers/Society	Behavior ⟵ – – – ⟶ Values	Young Adulthood (20–26)	Toward Consistency
Peers	Behavior ⟵ – – – ⟶ Values	Adolescence (14–19)	Inconsistency
Parents/Peers	Behavior ⟵ – – ⟶ Values	Preadolescence (9–13)	Toward Inconsistency
Parents	Behavior ⟵ ⟶ Values	Childhood (1–8)	Consistency

From "Behavior and Values: Consistency or Inconsistency" in Contemporary Adolescence: Readings (2nd ed.) (p. 102) by H. D. Thornburg, 1973, Monterey, Cal.: Brooks/Cole. Copyright © 1973 by H. D. Thornburg and Libra Publishers, Inc. Reprinted by permission.

ciocultural group of which the person is a member, and the consequences of membership in that group. Despite the fact that different theorists (e.g., Sigmund Freud, Alfred Adler, Carl Jung, Erik H. Erikson, and Jean Piaget) give varying emphases to these components of moral development, they recognize that the development of a sense of morality is not totally individual. Most theories of moral development take life from the larger models of human development. Furthermore, because inherited predispositions, unlike culture patterns, are less variable, there is the view (e.g., Sigmund Freud, Carl Jung, Jean Piaget, and Lawrence Kohlberg) that certain traits are universal. There is also a learning component (e.g., conscience development, role modeling, or social behavior) inherent in moral development constructs. All individuals living with others must learn the rules that govern behavior, indirectly through the parents or directly through the extended family and various social groups. As has been indicated, in moral development the individual has to struggle and come to grips with the problem of being subject to the *collective will* while maintaining personal autonomy. As Carl Jung observes, the critical aim of all moral life is to learn how to emerge as an individual while maintaining harmony with the totality of life that surrounds existence.

Although many theoretical positions on moral development have been advanced, discussions of them in textbooks tend to be limited to a few, with those proposed by Piaget and Kohlberg receiving particular attention. However, for a better perspective, we should not omit recognition of the contributions of Sigmund Freud (psychoanalytic), Carl Jung (neoanalytic), Erik H. Erikson (sociocultural synthesis), and Robert Sears (behavioral).

Robert J. Havighurst includes two of his ten *developmental tasks* for adolescence under moral development. These tasks are desiring and achieving socially responsible behavior, and acquiring a set of values and an ethical system as a guide to behavior. Developmental tasks are by definition performance-based and reflective of the contributions of the several theorists mentioned, and for our purpose will not be elaborated on. However, some attention will be given to the contributions of Freud, Jung, Erikson, and Sears before dealing with those of Piaget and Kohlberg (Rich & DeVitis, 1985).

Freud's Psychoanalytic Model

Freud's discussion of moral development is particularly relevant to the developmental stages of early childhood. His well-known constructs of the id, ego, and superego (Freud, 1923) are pivotal to his theory of moral development and directly related to the unconscious and conscious processes of human functioning. The *id*, primitive or animallike instinctive tendencies, governs a child's behavior almost entirely at first. The *ego*, conscious, more rational thought processes, regulates the id as the child grows up to maturity. As frame of reference for its operation, the ego is controlled by the *superego*, consisting of rules initially learned from parents and later from social others, from which emerges the *ego-ideal* and *conscience*. The ego-ideal and conscience regulate the moral development of the child, the former providing models for identification, and the latter operating through a sense of guilt provides the touchstone to social sensitivity. Together, they prepare the way for socially approved conduct and represent the functional qualities of a well-adjusted child.

Essential to the preservation of human integrity are *defense mechanisms*, two of which have significant relevance to the process of moral development. These are *repression* and *sublimation*. Repression provides a balance between id impulses and cultural demands, and sublimation transforms id predispositions into socially acceptable behaviors—often expressed in one art form or another. A balance is continually sought between the demands of society and the assertions of individual autonomy.

Jung's Fantasy to Reality Model

According to Jung (Storr, 1983) moral development is a *lifelong process* whose ultimate goal, to be achieved by very few individuals, is self-actualization. Like Durkheim, and Freud, Jung perceives the moral maturation of a child as an inner struggle to resolve the almost *irreconcilable conflict between individuality and collectivity*—the problem of how to emerge as an individual in harmony with the totality of surrounding life.

It is interesting to note that whereas Freud's concept of the unconscious is individual, Jung's is collective—a position drawn from anthropologically based evidence. So the heart of the struggle begins at the unconscious level, where primordial roots are at one and the same time individual and collective. To Jung moral development is rooted in the unconscious, whose elements must be made to surface for conscious processing so that an individual can become self-regulated. For the child, a gradual shift from fantasy (unconscious related) to reality (conscious related) and the ability to distinguish between the two realms occurs.

Intervention procedures of education advance moral growth. These procedures move from *early education*, where the individual learns from parents by example, to *collective education*, where general rules and principles are learned from society and adhered to without crushing unique individuality. These two stages prepare the way for *individual education*, which involves the subordination of earlier learned rules and behavioral codes to the growth needs of autonomy, especially as shown by gifted individuals. However, moral development includes not only individual assertion in collectivity, but also an obligation and sense of responsibility to the human species, a task so great that few persons are capable of its realization.

Erikson's Stages of Identity Crisis and Resolution

The five Freudian stages of development (oral, anal, phallic, latent, and genital) are extended by Erikson (1950) to eight *psychosocial stages* stretched over the *total life span* of individuals. In this way, sociocultural perspectives are added to an otherwise individual psychology of development: the individual relates to and finds a place in the larger social context that is both cultural and transgenerational.

Of particular relevance to moral development is Erikson's fifth stage: Acquiring Identity While Overcoming a Sense of Identity Diffusion—A Realization of Fidelity. During this stage, adolescents have the crucial task of resolving fundamental problems or conflicts to establish an identity so as to face the challenges of the adult world.

Adolescents expend their energies in establishing an *ideology*—a systematized set of ideas, ideals, and imagery—that unifies the striving for psychosocial identity. In addition, they develop the ability to sustain loyalties despite the contradictions of value systems and, in so doing, confirm their ideology. They are assisted by the process of *ritualization* in which ceremonial habits of daily behavior allow them to lead balanced and adaptive lives affirmed by their peers. However, such rituals of ideology may become transformed into a total zealous devotion to black-and-white standards of right and wrong in the name of a fanatical ideal.

In distinguishing morals from ethics, Erikson indicates that morals refer to infantile and adolescent morality, while ethics refer to a mature morality that no longer holds to such puerile values as righteousness and prejudice. He advocates a more mature and universal form of ethics that disclaims moralistic fanaticism—as seen in the behavior of those who make deals with their own consciences. In the main, he suggests that ethical development occurs in three distinct areas: *moral learning* in early childhood, *ideological experimentation* in adolescence, and *ethical consolidation* in adulthood. The most mature description of the ethical realm for Erikson is expressed in a *universal sense of values* that is agreed upon by major religions, generally, and by those of the Judeo-Christian tradition, particularly, and exemplified in the several socially based commandments summarized as "love thy neighbor as thyself." Erikson reformulates this governance to mean, in an ideal sense, *mutualism* between the doer and the other.

Sears's Behavioral Perspectives of Child Rearing

Of all the behaviorists and social learning theorists, Robert R. Sears (Sears, Maccoby, & Levin, 1957) has presented us with perhaps the most detailed account of how moral growth processes are embedded in *child-rearing practices*. Sears's model calls for the use of psychological cues to direct behavior, and upon modeling, primarily after the mother figure. Furthermore, he advocates the use of positive and negative modeling. In the former instance, the mother encourages the child to acquire the behavior of others he or she admires (older brother, sister, school or neighborhood peers, fictional or public heroes, or parents themselves), and in the latter, disciplinary measures are diligently and consistently applied. The child is to learn how to relate actions to their consequences; to facilitate this learning task, specific rewards and punishments are to be meted out for good and bad behavior respectively.

Sears's model also incorporates two very important principles of moral development that reflect psychoanalytic and behavioral concepts. These are the development of self-control or *conscience*, and *identification*. The development of conscience involves shifting control by others to control by self, even in the absence of others. Identification occurs without instruction and is an instance of informal or incidental learning, when the child casually begins to copy adult attitudes and interests, and the self-regulating sanctions of parents. Sears calls this role practice, whereby the child observes the behaviors of others and pretends to be the persons he or she observed. A secondary form of identification occurs when the child internalizes inhibiting and restricting attitudes exhibited by the same-sexed parent.

Piaget's Cognitive Basis for Moral Behavior

Of all the theories on moral development, Piaget's is perhaps the only one that is *cognitively* based—consistent, as it is, with his early discussion of the subject in *The Moral Judgment of the Child* (1930). For Piaget, cognition is innate, invariant, hierarchical, and culturally universal.

As we saw earlier, morality is a culturally based phenomenon that provides the individual with the framework for making decisions of a moral nature. At least two interdependent functions are involved in moral reasoning and judging. There is the function of *cognition*, which is an intellectual process; and there is the function of *moral content*, upon which cognition works in the act of arriving at a solution. Piaget does not separate the two in his handling of the subjects within which the implicit questions of cognitive processes are intertwined with explicit issues of morality. This treatment is not altogether different from the way theorists of intelligence, with the exception of J. P. Guilford, have handled conceptions of abilities, combining intellectual operation and content as ability.

Three of the four Piagetian characteristics of cognition described earlier relate to the intellect. As far as the fourth condition is concerned, that cognition is culturally universal, Piaget must mean that the intellectual process is to be found in all human beings despite their specific cultures. Variation in sociocultural content is what exists; intellectual processes are brought to bear to handle such content.

Like Emile Durkheim, Piaget's approach to cognitive-moral stages of development attempts to show the individual operating in the context of sociocultural authority and restraint, then moving on toward autonomy, cooperation, and equality. The individual achieves moral maturity in two stages. At first, the very young child bases moral judgment on unilateral respect for authority figures (like the parent, teacher, and other adults) and the rules they make. Here the child is constrained to behave morally, a stage which Piaget calls *heteronomous morality*. The individual, in middle childhood and adolescence, begins to develop a personal or subjective moral sense that leads to the establishment of a morality based on autonomous and reciprocal relationships. This morality of cooperation and equality Piaget calls *autonomous morality*. Piaget considers a sociocultural group, whose individuals can move from a heteronomous to an autonomous morality so that cooperation and equality pervades, mature.

Kohlberg's Theory of Moral Development

Cognitive stages were discussed earlier in the section on development as discontinuous; the relationship between Erikson and Gowan's contribution to a person's development was illustrated in the Erikson-Piaget-Gowan Periodic Developmental Stage Chart. For Piaget, developmental stages stop with Formal Operations, at a time when the logical thinking functions of adolescents reach maturity. Gowan suggests that the next stage should be creativity, and goes on to expand the model to find cognitive parallels for the Eriksonian affective stages of development (Table 6.1).

Kohlberg (1966), consistent with a *life-span theory of cognitive development* and on the basis of the Piagetian cognitive stage theory, extends Piaget's model to include postadolescent stages omitted from his theory of moral development. These stages are (a) preconventional, (b) conventional, and (c) postconventional (1)—autonomous or principled. The tie-in with Piaget's moral development stages are presented in Table 6.4.

The model is similar to Table 6.1 in that it presents nine stages set up in a three-by-three matrix of stages and levels. The three stages (latency, identity, and creativity) that an individual goes through at one level are repeated twice more (infant, youth, and adult). Table 6.4 illustrates a comparison between Piaget's (1930) and Kohlberg's (1966) moral development stages. Let us take each level in turn and see how each relates to Piaget's and Kohlberg's moral development stages.

Table 6.4 Piaget-Kohlberg Cognitive-Moral Developmental Stages

Developmental Level		*Attentional Modes*	
	Latency 3. It, They The World	*Identity* 1. I, Me The Ego	*Creativity* 2. Thou The Other
Infant			
Piaget (Cognitive-Moral)	*Sensorimotor (0–1)* Rules—purely motor and individual —received unconsciously, not coercive Play leading to ritualized schema	*Preoperational (2–3)* Egocentric Receive codified rules and imitate them No regard for codified rules Plays alone or with others such that everyone can win (2–5)	*Intuitive (4–6)* Creative fantasy
Kohlberg (Moral)	*Premoral (0–1)* Good is what is pleasurable Bad is what is painful or fearful	*Preconventional (1) (2–3)* Obedience and punishment Physical consequences of action determine its "goodness" or "badness" Rules obeyed to avoid punishment	*Preconventional (2) (4–6)* Hedonistic orientation Right is satisfying one's own needs Conformity to obtain rewards Naive egalitarianism Exchange and reciprocity orientation
Youth			
Piaget (Cognitive-Moral)	*Concrete Operations (7–12)* Competence in "tool world" manipulation Cooperation—each plays to win	*Formal Operations (13–17)* Logical thinking and hypothesizing	

Concerned with mutual control and unification of rules (idea still vague) (7–8)
Codification of rules
Fixed in detail and known to whole society
Rules are sacred, untouchable, lasting forever
Rules as law by mutual consent, alterable only by general opinion (11–12)

Postconventional (1) Autonomous, Principled (18–25)
General individual rights
Standards agreed upon by society
Majority rule
Social contract obligations

Kohlberg (Moral)

Conventional (1) Role Conformity (7–12)
Good-boy orientation
Whatever pleases others and is approved by them
Conformity to win approval

Conventional (2) (13–17)
Law and order orientation
Authority
Doing one's duty
Pulling one's weight
Maintain fixed order—social or religious

Postconventional (2) (26–40)
Universal principle orientation
Right is defined in accordance with self-chosen ethical principles
Universality
Respect for dignity of human beings
Expanded Identity
Moral responsibility

Adult   Kohlberg (Moral)

Postconventional (2) (40–)
Continuation and expansion of Stage 7
Reverence for life

Emphasis on equality and mutual obligation
Rules used to reach consensus

Infant

The first stage (latency), Piaget calls *sensorimotor* (0–1 year), a stage that is purely motor and individual and characterized by motor handling of objects (e.g., marbles). It is a time when rules are received impersonally and without any conscious effort, learned, as it were, from the mother's knee, when the baby is almost altogether passive. In play activity, the baby learns to ritualize the patterns absorbed. Play at this stage is purely individual and can only be referred to under "rules"; it is motoric rather than collective-based. For Kohlberg, this is the *premoral* stage, a time when what is good gives pleasure, and what is bad gives pain and is feared.

The child then moves on to the next stage (Identity) called *preoperational* (2–3 years) by Piaget. At this stage, receipt of rules occurs with the child's awareness. Examples of codified rules are learned by imitation, though at this time the child has no regard for them. During this period of egocentrism, the child plays alone without bothering to find playmates. Even if the child plays with others, the child is really playing on his or her own with no intent of winning. A parallel to this, is Kohlberg's *preconventional (1)* stage, within which the orientation is obedience and punishment. As Kohlberg describes it, there exists a deference to superior power and a trouble-avoiding set. The physical consequences of an action determine whether it is good or bad.

The *intuitive* (4–6 years) or third stage of this level (see Table 6.1) is designated by Gowan as the fantasy or creative stage (see Table 6.2). At this point there is some overlap of Piaget's second and third stages—the egocentric stage extends itself to the present one and beyond into the first stage of youth. The parallel play of the previous stage is gradually transformed into an incipient cooperation in Stage 3 and the one at the next level (7–8 years), where the child plays to win. For Kohlberg this advances the previous stage to *preconventional (2)*, within which the orientation of the child is naively egoistic and hedonistic: Action that satisfies one's own needs is right. The child conforms to obtain rewards and obeys rules to avoid punishment. Exchange and reciprocity are tied to a naive sense of egalitarianism.

Youth

The first stage of this level is Piaget's *concrete operations* (7–12 years). During this period the child exhibits cognitive command of the concrete and practical, gaining competence in the handling of the "tool" world. The moral aspects of this stage of development are a carryover from the previous stage of incipient cooperation and competitiveness that leads to a concern for mutual control and unification of rules (7–8 years). At this time, agreement that may be reached about a set of rules for one game, for instance, does carry over to other games. Ideas about rules in general are quite vague at this time. Several years later (11–12 years), rules, by mutual consent, become codified, fixed in detail, and known to the whole society. Parallel to this stage is Kohlberg's *conventional role conformity (1)* with its good-boy orientation, when pleasing and helping others are goals, and conformity is accepted as a way of winning others' approval.

Piaget's period of *formal operations* (13–17 years), with its logical thinking and hypotheses-forming, comes next. At this time, the moral development of the adolescent reaches its peak with the internalization of the product of mutually agreed upon rules and the emergence of an autonomous conscience. Morality, which was once a mystical respect for rules coupled with a rudimentary knowledge and application of their contents, is now dependent on rationality for its effective application. Kohlberg's *conventional role conformity (2)* parallels this stage. This stage's orientation stresses adhering to authority, maintaining social order and laws, doing one's duty, and pulling one's weight.

Piaget goes no further in his discussion of either cognitive or moral development. Kohlberg, however, viewing moral development as a lifespan phenomenon, continues, as illustrated by the remaining stages in the matrix. The third in this level is *postconventional (1)* (18–25 years), within which the orientation is contractual-legalistic. It is a period when the individual has autonomy, and the relative freedom to choose from those moral principles and standards set by the sociocultural group of which he or she is a member. At this stage, we have the case of individual right within the demands of majority rule. Emphasis is on equality and mutual obligation within a democratic order, within which procedural rules provide the basis for reaching a consensus.

Adult

Postconventional (2) (26–40 years) is a continuation of the process begun at the previous level, and reflects a universal principle orientation that not only refers to actually ordained social rules but to principles of choice involving appeal to logical universality and consistency. That is to say, the rightness of an action is determined by conscience in accordance with self-chosen ethical principles that subscribe to mutual respect, trust, and human dignity.

The next stage of the adult level, *commitment-development-mutual obligation* (beyond 40 years), is a continuation and an expansion of the preceding stages, and reflects a reverence for life.

Very rarely does an individual attain Stage 3 of the adult level. The few who attain it exhibit saintlike qualities and are examples of moral perfection. Such individuals do things not for gain or benefit but for the common good. Their love (agape) is for all mankind and their actions reflect this.

PROVIDING MORAL EDUCATION

In the previous discussion on moral development, we have encountered several different viewpoints whose commonality admit of the individual and society and interaction between the two. The affective and cognitive functions of the individual on the one hand, and the sociocultural content of a society on the other hand, provide the bases for the development of a moral being. Moral development occurs as a result of the socialization process; the stages the individual passes through move him or her from a passive to active assimilation of behavioral codes and rules for processing and action. With maturity, the individual develops the autonomy and the intellectual capacity to make choices with greater degrees of freedom, which a morally mature society allows, thereby paving the way for the establishment of new behavioral rules and codes.

Much of moral learning takes place informally, beginning in the home with parents and other members of the family; then in play with fellow age-mates; and later in school through interaction with others, example of teachers, and the writings and actions of contemporary and historical figures. Planned instruction that can produce a morally better informed person is desired by both parent and teacher, because nearly all social interactions in an individual's personal or professional life call for rule-guided behavior. However, a system of moral education that can be regarded as appropriate for all has yet to be designed. Religious and cultural biases make the teaching—in a classroom setting—of moral content very difficult. In addition, there is also the problem of resolving the conflict between the existing morality of a society, or moral consensus, and the morality of a personal ideal, or individual moral sense, before a personal autonomy can emerge.

Several Models of Moral Education

One of the best discussions on moral education is by F. K. Oser (1988). He brings to our attention the existence of six models based on an action theory of caring, judging, and acting—rationale-building, consideration, values clarification, values analysis, cognitive moral development, and social interaction models—before he presents his own model. These models represent differing fundamentals, goals and educational methods (Hersh, Miller, & Fielding, 1980).

To Oser's models may be added T. Lickona's (1983, 1985) educational strategies for parents, which are based on a concept of gradual natural development. The strategies proposed by Lickona include fostering mutual respect, setting a good example, teaching by telling, helping children to think for themselves and take on real responsibilities, balancing independence and control, and loving children. R. T. Hall (1979) also presents strategies applied to the topics of justice, property, truth, integrity, and personal relations, for fostering moral learning. Yet another source is a German-language teaching handbook edited by K. Schneid (1979) that presents methods to deal with areas such as values transformation, moralization, personal decision-making help, and stimulation of self-education. These several approaches present a variety of perspectives, discuss different teaching methods and learning materials, and provide appropriate and practical appraisal.

Kohlberg's Stimulating Moral Development Model

Kohlberg (1966) suggests that moral education in school should be properly planned to go far beyond classroom management, which mainly concentrates on moralizing about trivial disruptive behaviors. Kohlberg does not question the value of moral education in school, but rather points out the problems that attend the formulation of its aims and content. Moral education may be perceived as (a) a state-, school-, or teacher-derived system imposed upon the individual, (2) a systematic approach (used in Russian schools) to moral indoctrination supported by moral sanctions, or (3) a stimulation of the moral development of the child, rather than, for example, the current American system of moralizing about infringements of minor administrative regulations or teacher-annoying behaviors by individual teachers and principals.

Kohlberg proposes that a system that stimulates the natural development of a child's moral judgment and character instead of one that teaches fixed virtues can be the effective goal of moral education in school. Such an approach would require the participation of the total peer group, social integrates as well as isolates. Methods for attaining this goal would involve the creation of a classroom atmosphere that encourages participation rather than direct teacher influence.

The expected result is *moral maturity*. A morally mature individual will exhibit the ability to make moral judgments and formulate moral principles rather than conform to adult-framed moral judgments. The more the individual is able to show autonomy in this respect, the more the individual will exhibit a greater morality. Moral judgments of this kind tend to be based on principle; are universal, inclusive, and consistent; and are grounded to the objective, impersonal, and ideal. To become morally adult is to have learned to make decisions on the basis of principle and to have accepted this as one's own standard.

Stimulating moral development involves the debate not only of immediate and real-life issues of a classroom, but also of morally real and challenging conflict situations. For in such circumstances, the adult answer that discourages a child's way of thinking about moral matters may not be found. It is this sense of uncertainty that paves the way for the handling of genuine and difficult moral conflicts, and encourages the appearance of new cognitive elements.

Moral judgment is only one part of moral character development. It must be accompanied by the abilities to guide and appraise action. The stimulation of a moral development approach can facilitate the capacity not only to make moral judgments, but also to evaluate application of personal moral judgments.

Oser's Moral Discourse Model

Fitz K. Oser (1988), as mentioned earlier, presents an approach to encompass different elements of moral learning that he titles *moral discourse,* an approach that echoes Kohlberg's system of debating morally real and challenging conflict situations. It is a model that refers to an interactive ideal discussion about problems of justice; in the course of discussion the individual has the freedom to develop a personal point of view while considering the point of view of others.

Central to the notion of moral discourse is the presentation of moral knowledge. Following a discussion of a moral or value problem, questioning the right way of action, the teacher encourages the group to think about the discussion in such a way that they can better see its underpinnings and better their understanding and judgment.

Moral discourse in an educational situation is designed to allow students to affect positively each other's moral actions, cognitive structures, values, and moral emotions. Students learn to use rules and principles regarding justice and respect in such a way that personal success can be deferred in favor of another person, a community, or society. Competence gained in moral discourse leads to the use of moral principles and rules in the process of decision making.

The moral discourse model makes a distinction between values education in general and moral education. Whereas the former teaches social, political, religious, aesthetic and related values, the latter teaches a universally oriented conception of justice. Values relate to worth that an individual may place on one field of human interest or another, while morality involves universal human principles that in moral discourse must often be reconstructed before judgment is made. In moral discourse, fresh perspectives are developed through a cognitive restructuring that brings about a transformation of an individual's whole belief system.

In moral discourse, a moral problem is given to a single student or group of students by the teacher. The problem must be understood relative to four ethical principles: justification, fairness, consequences, and universalization. The discourse that follows relates to seven different contextual elements of educational moral situations, the end results of which should lead to better understanding. Oser (1988, p. 921) indicates that discourse should be

> directed to the *moral* conflict and to the stimulation of a higher level of moral judgment
> directed towards moral *role taking* and moral *empathy*
> oriented to *moral choice and action*
> directed toward *shared norms* and to a moral community (positive climate)
> oriented toward the student's own reasoning and attitude change and psychological disposition (coping and defending)
> directed towards one's theoretical moral knowledge (e.g., moral psychology, moral philosophy)

By and large, moral discourse teaches students to weigh complementary aspects of morality in order to effect its transformation into a more balanced and mature morality. Moral discourse has no hidden curriculum and does not indoctrinate. It helps students to generate rational arguments and gives them a chance to practice morality. By this process, students learn to justify their actions without the pressure of time limits and within a nurturing educational climate. The approach is holistic. Because students share views as they come to grips with moral issues with better understanding, they develop a moral sense or personal morality in the context of moral consensus or group morality.

Vare's Confluent Model for the Gifted

Not much had been written on the subject of morality and the gifted child. Barring the contributions of Jonathan V. Vare (1979) who attempts to link the emotional and cognitive dimensions of gifted individuals in a moral education program, and Conchita Tan-Williams and D. Gutteridge's (1981) work on the role of creative thinking and moral reasoning of academically gifted adolescents, little else has been written. The latter study is inconclusive in its findings. It indicates that the relationship between moral reasoning and creativity is far more complex than hitherto assumed and requires a more sophisticated model of investigation. The Vare paper, which ties in with previously discussed theories, offers instructional strategies that merit our attention.

Vare's approach, described as a *confluent model* of moral education, emphasizes the necessity of taking into account both the cognitive (Piaget) and affective (Freud-Erikson) needs of gifted children so that the children can attain the personal autonomy of Kohlberg's Postconventional (1) level (described in Table 6.4). Rather than relying on a hidden curriculum of moral education, by which the structure of the school, the way decisions are made, and the nature of discipline are transmitted by imitation, infection, or internalization, Vare proposes that we design a

Figure 6.5 Diagram Showing Why Gifted Child Is More Likely to Be Verbally Creative

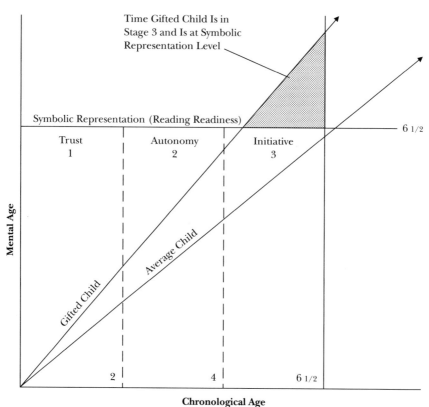

From *The Development of the Creative Individual* (p.58) by J.C. Gowan, 1972, San Diego, Cal.: Robert R. Knapp. Copyright © 1972 by Robert R. Knapp. Reprinted by permission.

systematic program of moral education. Such a program should allow children to explore life's events as they happen outside the classroom in a guided learning situation, akin to Oser's moral discourse approach. In this way, children will be allowed to question, examine, and propose alternatives to dilemmas of a moral nature, such as those often reported in newspapers but left unresolved.

Gowan (1971) has pointed out to us that gifted children, by reaching the stage of symbolic representation (reached by the average child at about 6 1/2 years of age; Stage 3 of Table 6.1), can intellectually negotiate experience or communicate it. In being able to do this, gifted children discover that their experiences are not altogether unique and uncanny but common to others, a realization that precedes consensual validation. He illustrates this information in the diagram (Figure 6.5).

We are reminded of Gowan's (1971) observation that gifted children tend to reach Piaget's formal operations stage earlier and therefore are capable of exercising moral reasoning and judgment earlier. Consistent with this observation is Vare's comment that the gifted, by virtue of their superior abilities and unique emotional needs, have the potential for more mature moral reasoning at an earlier age than most other children. They reach the formal operations level of thinking, indicative of an autonomous level of intellectual functioning characterized by abstract reasoning and logical-rational thought, earlier than their peers of the same chronological age. That is to say that gifted children are ready for a moral education that is based on principalistic ethics, at which time self-choice is permitted in moral reasoning.

The confluent model of moral education proposed by Vare has as its goal (similar to Durkheim, Kohlberg, Oser) the achievement of *moral autonomy*, which relies on productive thinking in the form of decision making according to moral reasoning and ethical principles. Its *cognitive goals* include logical-rational evaluation and critical-analytical thinking; and its *affective goals* include empathy, openness and trust, and tolerance or acceptance. Specifically, Vare offers instructional strategies that involve

1. *discussion* (Socratic peer discussion of dilemmas and values clarification, and related discussion techniques such as debates, written discussion of value positions, and responses to moral dilemmas in essays or editorial discussion, action, investigation)
2. *action* (role playing, simulation and games, and creative dramatics)
3. *classroom investigation* (jurisprudential model as a means of inquiry, group investigation, and classroom meetings of teacher and students)
4. *total environment* (a just community school that stresses solving of school issues in a community meeting using the Socratic moral discussion method)

The classroom and school climate should focus on solving problems (concrete or hypothetical) in such a way that reasoning is done according to principles of fairness in a democratic atmosphere of openness, tolerance, and concern for others. In such a context the gifted student's autonomous development, within a principles frame of reference, can be best facilitated.

MORAL RESPONSIBILITY AND THE GIFTED

We have so far concerned ourselves with the nature and nurture of moral development as they relate to children growing up to adulthood.

Because, by and large, the characteristics of development are universal, they are applicable to the gifted as well as the general population. However, as was pointed out in the preceding paragraphs, gifted children, by virtue of superior abilities, reach the Piagetian formal operations stage ahead of other children of similar age. Besides their affective development tends to be more sensitive to the social world around them; this sensitivity creates needs that go beyond those experienced by other children. This is especially the case for children who are developmentally in the creativity stages of the periodic model presented by Gowan (Table 6.1).

Manifest creativity of gifted children, and later of adults, is essentially linked to the social world. In a *creativogenic society*, a *magic synthesis* occurs between individual creativity and society's support of it (Arieti, 1976). Hence the gift of individual creativity, if it is to have meaning, must be closely related to the sociocultural world in which it is expressed.

There is the expectation that individual creativity levels itself at production for the general good of the community of which the individual is a member. However, this is not always the case, for although creative acts and productions have been initiated for this purpose, distortions do occur with disastrous end results. Nowhere have we seen this more clearly expressed as in advances in science and technology—we stand with bated breath as we consider the future of mankind and the potential for nuclear holocaust (Gruber, 1985).

This concern led Howard E. Gruber (1985) to point out the relevance and significance of *moral responsibility*, especially as it relates to the gifted among us who are capable of generating the new. What is the point of a great gift if its owner is not appropriately connected to the world? For the survival of the human species depends on a creativity that not only produces but also sees in the production the implications for responsible use and application.

Reasoning and judgment are thinking events. If these are qualified by morality, then the thinking is done within a moral frame of reference, whereby the individual and society are not antagonistically but mutually bonded. Unlike reasoning and judgment, which are inherited mental operations, responsibility is an acquired propensity. It is both individual and social at one and the same time, and has a frame of reference for presenting one's "true account" as well as the rightness or wrongness of one's choices that become subject to evaluation. Placed in the context of morality, responsibility acquires meaning in terms of society's rules and codes that set limits on an individual's autonomy.

In an attempt to relate moral development and giftedness, Gruber considers the possibility of a domain of moral giftedness and creativity, and the extent to which creative achievement in other domains relate to the problem of moral responsibility experienced by creative individuals.

About the former, he questions whether or not it would be useful to think of moral responsibility as a frame of mind or special sort of intelligence, perhaps like one of Howard Gardner's (1987) multiple intelligences. The latter idea involves analysis of the relationship between moral responsibility and giftedness, and is contingent on recognition by gifted individuals of relevant moral issues associated with their creations.

Gruber's ideas of moral responsibility as exhibited by a morally gifted person are as follows:

1. Moral reasoning and universalism are shown by a morally gifted individual in the higher stages of moral reasoning.
2. Cognition and moral responsibility are shown by an individual who is well informed about the world in which action must take place, and capable not only of intense involvement in it, but also of taking positive action to solve problems of major threat to human survival.
3. Initiative is shown by the gifted responsible person who avoids distractions of daily life, envisions need for dealing with a cause, and finds a way to do something about it.
4. Moral passion accompanies thought and action of the morally responsible gifted person committed to work for the cause.

According to Gruber, the most prominent developmental stage theories are not suited to explain extraordinary moral responsibility. Such theories are meant to explain development in a relatively stable environment where things are predictable. With the gifted and creative, focus must be given to the atypical and innovative in recognition of evolutionary divergence. Stage theories are appropriate for the general population; because they show development as proceeding along a single line or *unilinear* path, they need to be modified for the gifted and creative to permit *multilinear* paths. We need to reconceptualize development as being open and capable of producing totally new adaptations to totally new conditions to deal with a rapidly changing world in which survival means adaptation. Consistent with this view is D. H. Feldman's (1980) position that if we are to have a viable and complete theory of development we must move away from the concept of universality in cognitive development to accommodate the unique and idiosyncratic in an evolving relationship.

CONCLUSIONS

The psychometric approach used to describe developmental characteristics of intellect emphasizes continuity of growth and age, with a decelerating rate of growth that peaks between 16 and 28 years. Everyone does not agree with this theory nor with the time at which decline occurs. As measures of creativity developed, an emphasis on creative growth as continuous emerged. A noticeable decline in creative thinking abilities was found to take place during several periods of a child's life. These declines were seen to be especially severe during the middle elementary school years, but there was some recovery at age 11 or in Grade 5. Wechsler makes the interesting observation that, after a rapid growth of the first few years, there is a gradual slowing down of development in intellectual abilities as age 15 is reached, with the exception of a brief spurt between the ages of 10 and 12 when the decline and catch-up in creative thinking abilities appear. Is it possible that there is some relationship between the quickened growth of certain intellectual abilities at the expense of others? Could it be that continued emphasis in the first few years of schooling on left-brain activity (e.g., reasoning, logical thinking, knowing, and remembering) has an effect on the development of certain intellectual abilities at the expense of creative thinking abilities?

Developmental stage theory and transformation theory both subscribe to and emphasize discontinuity in growth and development. Rather than considering growth as occurring at a rising but decelerating rate with age, both models speak of rising from one level of development to the next higher level of development. Where Gowan describes growth in terms of escalation from one age period to the next in the repeated triadic cycle of infancy, youth, and adulthood, Land describes growth in terms of rises to higher levels of functioning in triads not necessarily contained by chronology. Both models imply the attainment of peaks in functioning within any one stage of development in preparation for the entry into the next higher level of development. Instead of decline in growth, Gowan speaks of dysplasia relative to a model of growth that has united the cognitive and affective in its design, and of healthy development, necessitating the growth of both cognitive and affective components at each stage and level. If the growth of one component, cognitive or affective, takes place without the other, dysplasia occurs. Growth for Land relates to survival so that, when the mutualistic stage is reached, a transformation must take place to a next higher level for the recurrence of a similar pattern of growth that prepares for the next transformation to occur at an even higher level than the one before—otherwise death follows. Grow or die is central to his model.

Creativity is essential to growth in both models. Gowan sees its energy and its source of productivity in love. Land sees creativity as being part of mental functioning from the lowest level of accretive growth to its highest forms, at which time destructuring of the order is essential for a reintegration or transformation to a higher order. It is at the mutualistic stage that creativity makes use of high-level combinations, analogies, and metaphors, whose province lies in the preconscious and right-brain functioning.

Quantitative growth is specifically related to the intellect; qualitative growth is related to the interactive effects of intellect and affect, and is characteristic of growth of nearly all kinds of life. Finally, whereas the psychometric approach derives empirically based data for growth curves from average scores, with considerable individual variation, the developmental stage approach derives data from observation, speculation, and clinical and scientific findings.

The sociocultural origins of creativity and its development in individuals add another dimension to creative development. Simonton identifies five of seven sociocultural conditions that appear during the lifetime of youthful geniuses as facilitative of their creative development toward eminence in adulthood, with the remaining two having strong educational implications. However, he suggests the reduction of an overcommitment to formal aspects of education beyond a certain point, and an increased emphasis on making available role models of eminence for emulation. Arieti conceives of genius acquiring eminence by creative transactions with a creativogenic society. The conditions that determine such a society not only provide an explanation for the occurrence of a renaissance but also suggest the possibility of precipitating such an outcome by appropriately arranged conditions. The nine conditions he proposes may very well find application in schooling and help develop a more effective and fruitful educational climate, which will maximize the creative development of young gifted children toward eminence in adulthood.

To place these views in proper perspective, we have to consider, for instance, the theorizing of Gowan and Land and the empirical research of Torrance and Khatena on the development of the creative person. These theories emphasize the importance of the individual as compared with Simonton's view, which emphasizes cultural conditions as shaping the creative development of an individual. It is Arieti who sees, in the dynamic relationship and creative exchange of the individual and society, a magic synthesis that leads to invention, discovery, and eminence.

Most of the studies and discussions about intellectual development have centered in general on all children as they grow up. There is a substantial gap in our knowledge about the intellectual development of gifted children. Although it is not difficult to interpolate findings concerning children in the general population and apply them to gifted children—some of these findings may be highly relevant—studies peculiar to the gifted are needed. The many hypotheses about development, especially from the approaches of developmental stage theory and general systems, are yet to be explored and validated. In these approaches lie some potentially fruitful directions for the study of the intellectual development of gifted children. In addition, work needs to be done to find specific applications of the sociocultural origins of creative development in educational settings so that our gifted will become by "magic synthesis" men and women of eminence.

Any discussion of moral development must include affective, cognitive, and behavioral learning approaches. Each of these approaches has something to teach us about moral development of all children with attitudes, values, conscience, reasoning, judgment, responsibility, and the like, as consequence. Any framework of morality is socioculturally rooted and necessarily includes the individual in the shaping process. Of course a democratic society, in its endeavor to shape the individual, fosters moral growth toward autonomy, so that the individual can make choices in the context of a moral code of ethics.

Moral education of children begins from birth, first informally at the mother's knee, facilitated by imitation, modeling, and reinforcement; external controls then have to be internalized to become a person's conscience. Children are taught morality, and as their mental life grows and expands to maturity, they become increasingly capable of using intellectual functions to reason and judge moral matters. An informal incidental moral education in school is, in addition, linked to school discipline. But this education is not enough and must give way to a systematic educational program of moral development. Such education, in a democratic society, does not limit itself to indoctrination, rather it strives for a deliberate presentation of issues, even if controversial in nature, for discussion and evaluation under guidance in a nurturant classroom environment. These discussions will prepare children to be more aware of and sensitive to the moral world in which they live, and equip them with the tools to deal with problems as they crop up. A systematic approach to moral education should familiarize all children, the gifted in particular, with the affective and intellectual resources at their command. Furthermore, these resources must be used in dealing with moral matters so as to foster a healthy value system, a greater awareness of social obligation in the context of individual enterprise, and an acute sense of social and human responsibility for the things created.

CHAPTER SEVEN

Gifted Children Have Problems

*I*NTRODUCTION

We have been reminded many times by anthropologists that it is not the individual who shapes culture but culture that shapes the individual (e.g., Benedict, 1935; Kluckhohn, 1970). This is not to say that the individual has no influence in determining culture or modifying it with the passing of years. In fact, a culture emerges because recurrent individual behavior in groups leads to the emergence of common behavior patterns that become known as customs or traditions. These traditions in turn are responsible for the unique traits and qualities that distinguish individuals in a group, and one cultural group from another.

Individuals depend on the physical and sociocultural universe to bring to flower and full bloom the inherited abilities and behavioral predispositions given to them by their parents and ancestors. Shaping forces operate through the individual's sensory-psychic system to establish the dynamics of a people's way of life. These forces originate from the larger environment or may be generated by the sociocultural group. The former stems from nature and the latter is humanly contrived (see Figure 3.1).

People are products of their environment. They will be shaped by nature, and, if living with others, may be shaped by fellow human beings. The shaping may be informally done as the individual interacts daily with others, observes and gets to know the customs of the group, and adopts its way of life. Formal shaping is done by institutions of learning, religious or secular. There is information to be communicated, and a curriculum that is the embodiment of the culture that produces it to be taught. In shaping an individual, a culture intervenes by way of education (Figure 3.1). It creates a delivery system that is aimed at arranging for the acquisition and processing of information, and provides support, confirmation, and direction to facilitate this aim.

Whether the interventions are informal or formal, resistance to change is ever present. Individuals have to give up something of themselves to achieve the commonality and unity that identify them as members of a cultural group. The pressure required to bring "sameness" out of difference is tremendous. Some persons easily succumb to it. Others, who find it hard to come to terms with the sacrifice of their individuality, put up a fight, thereby coming into conflict with the cultural group. Such conflict is most likely with highly creative individuals, whose nonconforming predisposition distinguish them from other gifted people. It has prompted Torrance (1962a) to emphasize the importance of recognizing and guiding creative talent, and Arieti (1976) to advocate the need for a "creativogenic" society in which individual creativity is meshed in "magic synthesis" with cultural endorsement and support.

We have already discussed the effects of sociocultural influences on children as they grow to adulthood. However, let us take note that the wrong kind of formal education can prevent the individual from realizing his or her full potential. Furthermore, the struggle and instability of one or more sociocultural groups can also act as potent inhibitors, which create problems for individuals and thereby hinder the full realization of their talents.

In the early years of the gifted movement, beginning with Lewis Terman's work with geniuses in the 1920s, a major concern revolved around the problem of identification and its measurement correlates. Studies of gifted children as they grew up by Terman, Oden, and others (e.g., Terman & Oden, 1947) focused on the highly intelligent individual who generally attended the city schools of California. Today we enjoy the advantage of having many measures available; Terman had to develop instruments from scratch. He had little by way of prior contributions on the gifted to guide him; he was the major initial contributor to this branch of knowledge. To most of us, he is recognized as the "father" of the gifted movement.

Terman did not take into account socioeconomic factors—something we are concerned with today in research and practice—when developing his measures and using them on gifted children. Nor did he pay proper attention to the gifted population living in rural areas. It is only because we have been made more acutely aware of the significance of these shaping influences by the contributions of others who followed and built on Terman's work that more and more of us take into account these factors when becoming involved in identifying, educating, and guiding the ablest.

Having expanded our conception of giftedness, we are strongly inclined not only to look for the high I.Q. gifted but also to look for other dimensions of giftedness. We cannot rely on I.Q. tests alone to identify the gifted; we have to turn to other identification procedures that will assist us in discovering the creative individual, leader, talented musician, nonverbally gifted, and gifted others. Much of giftedness has to do with innate abilities, but it also has to do with the interactive influences of the physical-sociocultural environment and their psychological correlates, which shape and direct the variety of ways that abilities manifest themselves.

Consequently, any approach to identify, educate, and guide the gifted must take into account the effects of these mediating variables. It means, for instance, that we have to reassess the suitability of available measures to identify the gifted among those who have not had the same intellectual, social, and psychological advantages as those for whom certain measures were designed. We are referring to the culturally diverse gifted, those who are often penalized by identification instruments whose content and idiom are not designed to identify them.

Other groups affected by environmental-cultural shaping influences and related press factors are those who do not do as well in school as their high potential should allow or who prematurely discontinue schooling. This failure to continue schooling may, for example, be attributed, on the one hand, to interference and retardation because of emotional difficulties and adjustment needs or physical handicaps or, on the other hand, to sex bias, which could arrest, retard, or divert the development of potentially gifted girls toward actualization.

Interference with normal development by culture, the socialization process, and education are the root causes of the gifted individual's problems. Hence we must assist the individual in making needed adjustments to such pressures, in order to avoid the dire results of repressing creative needs; to deal with underachievement in the narrow sense—inadequate performance in school; to overcome physical and emotional disabilities that interfere with the use and manifestation of talent; and to recognize and handle cultural diversity so as to facilitate the realization of full potential. All these factors, including the developmental arrest of girls as they grow up, inhibit the proper realization of the promise of our superior individuals, and may be viewed and treated as different facets of underachievement.

ADJUSTMENT NEEDS OF GIFTED CHILDREN

From the Terman studies discussed earlier (e.g., Terman & Oden, 1947), we learned that gifted children as they grow up to mid-life are generally physically and intellectually healthy, stable, emotionally mature, socially and sexually well-adjusted, and maritally happy. They are also achievers at superior levels. However, not all gifted individuals are free from problems or altogether successful. Some who are highly gifted are prone to emotional and social difficulties (Hollingsworth, 1926; Terman, 1925), often having to deal with the problem of synthesizing their personal life and existence as creative human beings (Kenmare, 1972). Adjustments do not come to them easily. According to L. Burnside (1942), social maladjustment of the gifted child begins in the preschool years:

> The brilliant child is yet too immature to learn the lesson of "suffer fools gladly." Here begins the emotional maladjustment of isolationism. They [sic] are friendly and need companions of their own age who can understand and reciprocate their efforts at social contacts. Failure to achieve this may lead to a life of phantasy or disillusionment and bitterness of chicanery. (p. 224)

Walter Barbe (1954) notes that although gifted individuals are ahead of their age-mates in mental capacity, they are not necessarily made to feel like misfits. Problems arise when they are rejected because other children do not understand them. Failure in making their age-mates recognize and accept them for what they are may lead them to become stereotyped bespectacled introverts.

Considerable attention is given by Torrance (1962a, 1965a) to problems that gifted children face in their conflicting interaction with the sociocultural environment. The creative energizing force that dominates the lives of highly gifted children sets them up in a position of independence and nonconformity in their relationships with the group of which they are members. This position often leads to confrontations of one kind or another that require them either to learn to cope with arising tensions or to repress their creative needs, the former impelling them toward productive behavior and mental health; the latter, to personality disturbances and breakdown.

Gifted children are generally subject to more stress than their age-mates, just because they *will* march to their own drum and do their own thing. Often their independence sets up an antagonistic relationship with their sociocultural group. Variation from the norm is frequently not tolerated and gifted children bear the consequences of their deviant behavior. That is why gifted children need to be provided a "refuge" by the system so as to assist them in making the kinds of adjustments that allow them to maintain their uniqueness without incurring penalties (Torrance, 1979c).

Society is still harsh in its treatment of creative persons, especially children. Almost inescapably, the creative child will come into conflict with the "authorities" in the system or establishment. He [she] will experience frustration and must have a source of encouragement and support. He [she] must have a right to fail without being ostracized or ruined. (p. 367)

PROBLEMS OF UNDERACHIEVEMENT

Underachievement has been generally defined as a deficit condition in schooling and, more specifically, as poor performance and low grades in school subjects. However, it would be preferable to regard it more broadly, that is, not only as achievement below expected performance in school subjects but also as below expected achievement in terms of expressed talent potential and productivity.

Underachievement, in another sense, can and should be regarded as dysplasia or development arrest, where either or both cognitive and emotive components of the psyche do not escalate to higher levels of development towards self-actualization (Gowan, 1972). In this respect, we should consider the special case of the gifted girl who may never achieve full realization of intellectual potential as an adult owing to arrest in cognitive but not affective development. If actualization of potential is realized, it may occur much later in life than expected.

A certain looseness attends usage of the term *underachievement*. Its meaning appears to depend on whether we are comparing the achievement of an individual with that of a group, or whether we are comparing an individual's actual performance with what I.Q. says he or she is capable of doing. Our earlier discussion of intelligence has indicated that I.Q. beyond prediction of scholastic achievement is questionable. I.Q. is generally known to predict academic performance especially if there is a match between the abilities measured and those required to do certain school subjects, such as language and mathematics. I.Q. does not predict performance as well in such areas as music and art, or with subject matter that requires creative ways of learning. Besides, variables such as interest, motivation, and attitude toward learning may have much to do with how well a person performs in all school learning situations. Consequently, an understanding of the concept of underachievement is relative, owing to the complex nature of motivation, and the difficulty inherent in precisely defining the concept (Gowan, Khatena, & Torrance, 1979).

Gowan (1955), writing on the subject of the underachieving gifted child, defined underachievement as performance that is one standard deviation or more below ability level. When applied to gifted children, the term refers to performance in the middle third of scholastic rank, and with severe underachievement, to performance in the lowest third of scholastic rank. Another definition (Shaw, 1960) states that

> the underachiever with superior ability is one whose performance, as judged either by grades or achievement test scores, is significantly below his [or her] high measured or demonstrated aptitudes or potential for academic achievement. (p. 15)

Both definitions are appropriate, though Gowan's reference to percentile rank divisions operationalizes underachievement.

Such definitions, however, reflect the more traditional view of underachievement as it relates to I.Q. and scholastic achievement. Apart from the fact that we are beginning to be more accepting of varieties of giftedness, we have also begun to recognize the importance of bringing to greater fruition the creativity of gifted individuals. Divergent thinking, as an underlying dimension of intellectual functioning, acts as a catalyst to productivity and is considered as significant to achievement (McGuire, Hindsman, King, & Jennings, 1961). According to Gowan and Demos (1964), C. McGuire on achievement, J. P. Guilford on intellect, E. P. Torrance on creativity, and J. W. Getzels and P. W. Jackson on creativity and intelligence, a different perspective of achievement is needed.

> Formerly, a discrepancy between narrow-spectrum measures of intelligence and achievement in school marks was laid to motivational aspects (the "over" and "underachiever"). But if narrow-spectrum tests do not measure all of the intellect, and if creativity is an important part of what is missing in tests, then the research of Getzels and Jackson on the ability of youngsters to achieve as well as narrow-spectrum tested gifted children, makes considerable sense. If we broaden our measurement of ability to wide-spectrum testing which includes more of the Guilford factors, we may considerably lessen the variance necessary to assign to motivational factors. The intelligent underachiever may underachieve because he is not creative rather than because he is not motivated. (Gowan & Demos, 1964, pp. 298–299)

Any definition of underachievement must include the discrepancy between actual and expected levels of attainment. Such levels must not be limited to scholastic achievement as predicted by I.Q. but must go beyond such achievement to other dimensions of talent and their realization. Therefore, we should ask questions such as the following:

Are persons identified as having extraordinary gifts in art or music expressing their talent at a level compatible with their identified talent, if not above it?

Are the individuals who show a superior capacity to lead others actually fulfilling their anticipated promise?

If we are to conceive these achievement levels in statistical terms, we should be able to expect that in whatever area of talent a person has been identified as superior, for instance, in intellect, music, art, or leadership, that person should express the talent in ways considered superior and, if measurable, at two or more standard deviations above the mean. Of course, measuring such performances may not always be easy or even practical to do. However, an expanded concept of underachievement must be cognizant of this difficulty so that efforts to find ways and means to make such an approach possible will continue. Underachievement, it must be emphasized, is relative, especially in terms of a multivariate concept of giftedness, and measurement with statistical tools must accommodate this variability.

CAUSES OF UNDERACHIEVEMENT

Many studies on the subject have identified causes of underachievement, centering on the consequences of the individual's transactions and interactions with the immediate family, school, society, and the larger environment (e.g., Angelino, 1960; Butler-Por, 1987; Delisle, 1982; Gallagher, 1985; Rimm, 1986; Strodtbeck, 1958; Whitmore, 1980).

The reasons behind its causes have been classified in a number of different ways, for example, McIntyre's (1964) proposed physical, sociological, economic, and psychological causes, alone or in combination. It is well known that many physical illnesses have a detrimental effect on the studies of bright individuals although, on occasion, physical problems spur a student to high levels of attainment (Anastasi, 1958). Common problems of sight, hearing, infection, disease, malnutrition, and the like, may hold students back, limiting their enthusiasms, interests, and capabilities, thus leading to underachievement (Baum, 1984).

The debilitating effects of adverse socioeconomic conditions are significant factors in underachievement, and pivot on poverty, low-level aspiration, motivation, language deficit, ethnic difference, and cultural variation (Bonsall & Stefflre, 1955; Frierson, 1965). Causes of underachievement, as they relate to psychological factors, include various kinds of mental ill health and emotional disturbance, often rooted in home and family climate; and stress interactions with parents and others (Ford, 1989; Gallagher, 1985; Gowan & Demos, 1964; McIntyre, 1964; Morton & Workman, 1978; Rimm, 1986).

Whitmore (1980) suggests that underachievement, as it relates to gifted elementary underachieving students, can be described in terms of three distinct behavioral syndromes: (a) the aggressive gifted child; (b) the withdrawn gifted child; and (c) the erratic, less predictable gifted child who vacillates between aggression and withdrawal.

Recently, Rimm (1986) made the observation that underachievement is not inherited, and can occur by imitation and modeling of parent behaviors, in particular. Essential elements of the underachievement syndrome either singly or in combination include the following:

1. Underachievement patterns initiated early in life and associated with attention addiction derived from being exceptional or ill, with carryover effects to school
2. Acquisition of excessive power directed toward manipulating others to avoid responsibility rather than to move toward accomplishment
3. Inconsistency of and opposition by parents in the early years, the one creating instability; the other, deprivation of an achievement model for identification rather than competition
4. Inability to cope with healthy competition
5. The impact of social changes related to family, education, competitive pressure, and mass media

Home and Family Dynamics

Achievement has much to do with a child's upbringing. It depends on the kind of relationships shared with father, mother, and siblings. Stability of parents' relations, such that family life is not continually torn by disagreements, fights, and other disruptions that may lead to separation or divorce, is required. The parents' educational level and a stimulating home environment facilitates achievement. High levels of aspirations, affectional support, and reinforcement all contribute to achievement. In addition, appropriate achievement models are needed. When these conditions do not exist, the potential to achieve is threatened and underachievement can be expected.

Studies have attempted to identify the extent to which underachievement can be attributed to the relationship of bright children with their father or mother. Strodtbeck (1958) suggests that, if the power of the father is great (the higher the socioeconomic status, the greater the father's power), the son can be expected to be less achieving than the dominant father. Certainly, the level of aspiration on academic matters of father and son can be expected to be similar. When the aspiration level of the father is low, underachievement can be anticipated for the son (Shaw, 1960).

Underachieving boys appear to identify not with their fathers but with other male figures, for instance, a teacher, an uncle, or a minister, probably because of negative feelings toward the father (Kimball, 1953), generated by the father's hostility to and rejection of the son (Karnes, McCoy, Zehrbach, Wollersheim, Clarizio, Gostin, & Stanley, 1961). If parents are too autocratic or authoritarian, developmental arrest and consequent underachievement follow (Gallagher, 1985; Gowan, 1957).

When the parent in question is the mother, there appears to be some difference in the way the son and the daughter are affected. That is, when father and mother are both highly authoritarian and low in acceptance, the son shows poor academic performance; when mother is low authoritarian or laissez-faire, the daughter tends to show poor academic performance (Drews & Teahan, 1957; Pierce & Bowman, 1960).

Underachievement is discussed by McIntyre (1964) as a passive trait disturbance, more commonly found in boys than girls. Briefly, the characteristics of passive-aggressive children include dawdling, stubbornness, pouting, sullenness, procrastination, inefficiency, and daydreaming. Such children behave in the following ways:

They are sometimes cocky and obnoxious.

They do not fight back directly and outwardly but rebel through a form of inaction.

They want freedom but cling to dependency, caught between the desire to be nurtured and the refusal to be dominated.

They have difficulty accepting reality or having to face it.

They appear calm and without anxiety outwardly, but seethe with resentment.

They may appear disinterested, unmotivated, lazy, self-sufficient, unsociable, and lonely.

McIntyre points to the observation that parents of such children tend to confuse the aggressive activity involved in learning, achievement, and success with aggression related to hostile and hurting impulses (Grunebaum, Hurwutz, Prentice, & Sperry, 1962). Consequently parents may not actually want their sons to achieve in school because to achieve is to hurt.

According to McIntyre, when parents do not share executive functions in the home, one parent may be dominant and the other submissive. A boy whose mother is dominant and father submissive is overprotected and infantalized by her. When the father is dominant and the mother is submissive, the son perceives it to be dangerous to be a man. In either case, the son is a pawn in the game and transfers the anger and resentment felt for the parents to the teacher. He mistakes the parents' disinclination that he learns in school for a demand for high performance. Consequently, he may try to get even with them by underachieving in school.

Furthermore, a girl in such a family, being generally passive, dependent, and nonassertive, is less likely to resent her parents' neurotic demands. Her parents become upset only when she starts to fight back. Passive-aggressive girls appear lazy and uncaring and, unlike boys who often hide their feelings, are more willing to share their feelings with others and are anxious to discuss their upsetting experiences.

Underachievers appear to come from homes where parents are either overindulgent and overprotective or indifferent and rejecting. In such homes, there is less identification with and more rejection of parents. An unstable climate exists because of parental disagreement concerning child-rearing practices. This situation prevents the child from establishing standards of behavior leveled at excellence (Gowan & Demos, 1964). Against such a familial background, it is not easy for a growing child to move from one stage of development to the next higher stage as described by the Gowan-Piaget-Erikson Periodic Developmental Stage model (Tables 6.1 and 6.2). Developmental arrest or dysplasia can be expected, with consequent detrimental effects on the student's achievement level.

According to Gowan and Demos, underachievement, viewed as failure in one or more developmental tasks, can lead to an internalization of conflict involving hostility, resentment, aggression, projection, regression, overdependence, fear, withdrawal, and escape tendencies. For instance, children who experience developmental arrest do not learn the joy of real work and accomplishment to assist them to find status among their peers and authority figures. Instead, they derive satisfaction from earlier developmental stages. Besides, boys, being slightly less mature than girls, sometimes find their parents expecting more of them than necessary. This may cause a more problematic introduction to cultural demands (Gowan, 1957).

Some of the major causes of underachievement as failure in certain developmental tasks according to Gowan and Demos (1964, pp. 306–307) include the following:

The child's own difficulties with the task.

The lack of skill of parents in handling early relationships, such as trust, toilet training, industry, independency training, etc.

Psychotic or neurotic involvements of the child.

Failure of the school properly to stimulate the child.

Lower parental socioeconomic status, which interferes with the intellectual component of developmental task attitudes, especially at higher levels.

Lack of parental socioeconomic status, which interferes with the intellectual component of developmental task attitudes, especially at higher levels.

Environmental and sub-cultural attitudes, which similarly impede intellectual development tasks at their highest level.

Parental environmental and cultural attitudes, which (a) reinforce clannishness and inhibit the breakaway for the child, and (b) promote authoritarianism and dependence on fate and supernatural authority and inhibit the "do-it-yourself," entrepreneur, risk-taking "reasonable adventurer" type individual.

Parental attitudes of over-protection and over-indulgence, which prevent children from having early independence experience and do
not put enough stress into the environmental background.

Parental, environmental, and school attitudes of antiintellectualism,
lack of respect for scholarship and hard work necessary to attain it.

School Dynamics

Focus on the underachiever in the school setting is necessary. When we
talk about underachievement, we refer to students who do not do as
well in school subjects or obtain the kind of grades their I.Q.s predict.

Underachievement may be general or specific (Raph, Goldberg, &
Passow, 1966). If underachievement is *general*, it is more likely related to
personal difficulties that are psychological in nature. If it is *specific*, its
occurrence is probably precipitated by difficulties in the acquisition of
knowledge and skills in subjects such as reading or arithmetic at the elementary school levels, and language or mathematics at the upper levels
of schooling. Often, underachievement may be a misapplication of intellectual abilities to learning; inadequate learning of the fundamentals
may hinder the mastery of more advanced learning.

Psychological disturbances and specific learning difficulties, however,
are not independent of one another but related causes of underachievement. Home and family problems are not left behind when the child
comes to school. In fact, they preface all activities in school, hindering or
facilitating the child's progress in academic and nonacademic areas alike.
This is not to say that psychological disturbances do not occur in the
child's life at school owing to the demands of others (e.g., teachers,
peers) and the pressure of learning. But a child who is relatively free of
serious home and family problems comes to school with a mentally
healthy predisposition to benefit from educational experiences. We must
also recognize that the difficulties a child encounters in learning a school
subject may cause disturbances. However, these disturbances are less
likely to jeopardize the child's achievement if the difficulties are symp-
tomatic of specific learning content rather than personal problems.

Generally, most studies of and discussions on underachievement concentrate on non-school-related variables, such as personality characteristics, adjustment, self-concept, peer attitudes, and parental background,
rather than on classroom behaviors, study practices, and the school environment (Gallagher, 1985; Raph, Goldberg, & Passow, 1966). Several
recent works (Baum, 1984; Butler-Por, 1987; Rimm, 1986; Whitmore,
1980), however, give special emphasis to scholastic underachievement
as well, and offer approaches to remedy the problem.

Studies of school-related variables of underachievement (Dowd, 1952;
Frankel, 1960; Granzow, 1954; Lum, 1960; Westfall, 1958; Wilson & Morrow, 1962) find college and high school underachievers dislike the courses

they take and the professors who teach them. They spend fewer hours on their studies, do less homework, use poorer study techniques, and have lower grade aspirations than achievers. Furthermore, underachievers are poorly adjusted to school rules and procedures. When assignments are too long or difficult, underachievers become easily discouraged. However, if they are inclined to go to school or college, they are less apt to plan taking college courses in the pure sciences and liberal arts. They commonly withdraw from school work, often engaging in nonverbal activity in another area than the one studied. This is especially the case with mathematics. Underachievers' main problems rest not on the mechanics of study but on motivation and attitude.

School-related causes of underachievement have also been observed by others (Bricklin & Bricklin, 1967; Butler-Por, 1987; Goldberg & Passow, 1959; Rimm, 1986; Strang, 1960; Willard, 1976). These causes include changing of schools and poor preparation due to a lack of basic instruction, the result of frequent absences or irregular attendance. Other factors that contribute to underachievement are poor, laborious, and discouraging study habits; bad teaching, unsympathetic and insensitive teachers; drill classes, busy and boring work; and overemphasis on competition. Other contributory conditions include a curriculum that fails to interest and challenge the learner to high endeavor; educational pressures and unrealistic expectations at home that may lead to rebellion; a teacher who is satisfied with adequate rather than capacity performance; attitudes that destroy the incentive to achieve; and rigid and narrow classroom activities that inhibit productive learning or allow creativity to wither before it matures.

Gowan's (1957) comments on underachievement as the result of interference with creative learning and expression and consequent lack of approval are to the point. The gifted underachiever he says

> appears to be a kind of intellectual delinquent who withdraws from goals, activities, and active social participation generally. As a child, his [her] initial attempts at creative accomplishment may not have been seen by others as "worthwhile" but only as "queer" or "different." The blocking of this avenue of rewarding behavior by others, tending as it does to reinforce his [her] often overcritical appraisal of the disparity between his [her] goals and achievements, may blunt his [her] work libido, stifle his [her] creativity, and consign him [her] to a routine of withdrawal and escape as the most tolerable method of insulating his [her] ego from hurt in an alien and uninterested world. (p. 101)

In an interesting paper, R. M. Roth and A. H. Meyersburg (1963) lay the responsibility of underachievement on the student. They suggest that poor achievement does not arise from the student's incapacity but from the choice of not preparing for the kinds of academic performance that will be evaluated. According to them, the possession of poor academic skills is an outgrowth of previous choices for poor achievement. Such choices may be expressed as "overall limited achievement" or as "achievement in deviant channels." The patterns of poor-achievement choice are enduring and do not undergo spontaneous change; they are related to personality or character traits.

Whitmore (1980) makes an interesting observation about the differing perceptions by teachers, parents, and pupils as to who is to blame for underachievement:

> Teachers perceived the problem as the child's attitudes and behavior, often relating that to inadequacies of the home. Parents perceived the problem first of all as the school's lack of responsiveness to the educational needs of their child, and secondly as the child's stubbornness in wanting things his [her] way and unwillingness to try hard enough to do better. The children blamed the school or, more often, themselves. All of them, to varying degrees, had integrated the feedback from teachers, parents and peers to conclude that they were the problem—something was wrong with them since school was "okay" for everyone else. (pp. 86–87)

School Settings

Two empirically/experimentally based discussions of underachievement that command our notice relate to the DeWitt Clinton High School project in New York (Raph, Goldberg, & Passow, 1966), and the Cupertino Elementary School Experimental Program in California (Whitmore, 1980). Both of these projects deal with gifted underachievers and present valuable insights for our consideration.

DeWitt Clinton High School

A most persuasive discussion on gifted underachievers comes from the DeWitt Clinton High School for boys in New York. As underachievement pertains to school dynamics J. B. Raph and her coresearchers identified self-concept, self-ideals, motivation, and adult models as significant factors. They found that a positive self-concept consistently related to scholastic mastery more than it did to intelligence. In W. W. White's (1959) competence-motivation construct, they saw a plausible explanation for their findings that young underachievers, regardless of geographical location or socioeconomic level, realistically appraised the discrepancy between their ability and their scholastic performance. At the same time, the authors recognized the problem of finding a theoretical justification for a self-concept that was either the cause or effect of scholastic attainment. This led them to suggest that

> applied to school achievement, White's [1959] focus would postulate that later academic skill and satisfaction in mastery might well be related to the pleasures derived from such competencies. Put more concisely, "I can do" be-

comes "I am," in that satisfaction in mastery becomes linked to the self-concept. (Raph, Goldberg, & Passow, 1966, p. 182)

Raph and her associates found, from interviews of underachieving boys of the DeWitt Clinton High School, that underachievers tended to minimize their ability, evaluating themselves as "pretty average," "about like others," and so on, to avoid both social ostracism from their peers and the more stringent demands of adults. Their finds are corroborated by the observation that the peer culture does not support outstanding school attainment (Coleman, 1961; Tannenbaum, 1960), and that the gifted child is, in the first place, a minority of one (Torrance, 1962a).

On the subject of self-ideals, Raph and her fellow researchers found that underachievers did not appear to see the discrepancy between poor class performance and future professional aspirations or desired status. Insofar as underachievers are able to see this gap, they perceive the narrowing of this discrepancy in terms of doing more than achievers. However, if they are unable to bridge the gap, they may experience greater stress, which leads them to use defensive maneuvers in order to reduce the dissonance felt. Furthermore, underachievers may meet this discrepancy by withdrawing entirely from the demands of school, becoming truants and, eventually, school dropouts.

Continuing with the discussion, Raph and her colleagues found that underachievers of the DeWitt Clinton High School attributed their success or failure to particular teachers. The researchers explain the excessive responsibility placed on the teacher by these gifted adolescents by way of their dependency on extrinsic motivation (e.g., good grades, parental and teacher approbation). That is why when no reward was available their reward-seeking behavior shifted to blame. These underachievers also blamed themselves for poor school performance, citing inappropriate study time, laziness, and the like; justifying their lack of application to being unable to live up to their good intentions when the time to do so came. The authors recognized the complexity of explaining such irrational factors but perceived in attempting such an explanation possible clues for understanding the disparity between ability and performance.

Need-achievement theory (McClelland, Atkinson, Clark, & Lowell, 1953) offered another plausible explanation for underachievement. It conceptualized two dispositions being activated in a performance situation, namely, achievement-motive and motive to avoid failure (J. W. Atkinson, 1960):

[Atkinson] postulates that these two opposing tendencies, to approach and withdraw, are inherent in any activity when the behaving individual expects that his [her] performance will be evaluated and that the outcome will be either a personal accomplishment or a sense of incompetence. He bases a number of predictions on this model, [one of which is] that individuals whose need for success is stronger than their fear of failure will try harder and perform better than individuals with the reverse pattern, i.e., those whose fear of failure is stronger than the need for success. (McClelland, Atkinson, Clark, & Lowell, 1953, p. 188)

The problems concerning adult models were also given attention. The DeWitt Clinton High School project also found that fathers of underachievers made frequent reference to their own college aspirations and not to those of their children, whereas mothers seemed to be more concerned with their boys' school performance (Raph, Goldberg, & Passow, 1966). Furthermore, academic failure and hostility toward a family member who demanded success were related (Kirk, 1952). Besides, for the development of a high need-achievement, a boy needed more autonomy from his father and a high degree of involvement from his mother, including both reward and punishment (Rosen & D'Andrade, 1959).

Cupertino Experimental Program
Another interesting account of the gifted underachiever in the context of schooling grew out of Whitmore's (1980) concern for elementary school problem students. These students were excluded from special classes provided by the Cupertino Extended Learning Program because they did not score high enough on the Stanford-Binet to be considered intellectually gifted. Whitmore felt that they might be gifted despite their test results and decided to work closely with several of them, because problem behaviors and lack of achievement often command teachers' attention and conceal mental giftedness.

Working with these students confirmed that they were gifted. The handicaps most commonly shared were learning disabilities directly related to perceptual-motor skills. Whitmore attributed the underachieving gifted child to one of four etiological types:

1. Learning disabled (e.g., a student of extremely high abilities involving abstract thinking and verbalization with a disability that is caused by perceptual-motor deficits)
2. Behaviorally disordered or emotionally disturbed (e.g., a student who is, because of perceived academic and social failure in school, severally disturbed)
3. Neurologically handicapped or minimally brain damaged (e.g., a highly creative child with a wide range of abilities—some high and others low, such as gross motor and visual-motor coordination—who is impulsive and emotionally responsive without discipline of thought or action)
4. Paralyzed perfectionists (e.g., a student unable to make headway because of an irrational need to be perfect, aggravated by disturb-

ing immaturities, who is in need of self-understanding and self-esteem based on a realistic self-concept)

Such classification, she felt, would indicate the source of the students' learning or achievement problems, which in turn would help to determine appropriate individual treatment programs.

Whitmore studied 29 underachieving gifted during the period from 1968 to 1970. They gave her clues about the nature and possible sources of their problems, and also about several useful remedial and/or preventive directions that could be taken to ease these problems. These directions involved (a) the need for early identification of the gifted so that emphasis is placed on potential for superior performance rather than on actual achievement, and (b) the importance of providing preventative intervention or early remediation before negative attitudes and counterproductive habits become firmly established and resistant to influence.

She is emphatic that specific handicaps of schooling make gifted children underachievers. These handicaps of schooling include a dull, meager curriculum that destroys motivation to achieve in school; inappropriate teaching strategies that are incompatible with learning style; and a lack of adult assistance to handle socioeconomic conflict, gain self-control, and set realistic self-expectations. Her conclusion is underscored by her underachievers' observations that the development of their negative feelings, problem behaviors, and underachievement can be traced to the following factors:

1. A perceived lack of genuine respect for them as individuals
2. A competitive social climate
3. Inflexibility and rigidity in expectations of student performance, curriculum choices, and sequence of learning experiences; and a lack of time and opportunity to pursue individual interests
4. Stress on external evaluation
5. Predominance of the failure syndrome and criticism
6. An unrewarding curriculum

Whitmore's educational philosophy sees no difference in the educational programs provided for the achieving or underachieving gifted, except in the amount of teacher time and effort directed toward such objectives as enhancing self-esteem, developing social skills, and remedying academic deficiencies. Consequently, she considers the educational program provided for the underachieving gifted in Cupertino appropriate for gifted achievers as well. Such a program, although designed for elementary school students, can be modified, according to Whitmore, for students of the secondary school. Evaluation of this experimental program at the end of 2 years has indicated the tentative effectiveness of such an approach. The 1972 and 1975 follow-up evaluation studies have indicated lasting program effects resulting in improved attitudes and behavior throughout the elementary school years. Whitmore expects these results to give direction to efforts to provide educational alternatives for gifted underachievers.

We have already made the point that it is easier to identify the causes of underachievement than it is to develop procedures to prevent, correct, or cure them. The roots of underachievement are primarily psychosocial and scholastic, with an interactive dimension that increases their complexity. The psychosocial aspects of underachievement are perhaps less amenable to prevention or cure than are the scholastic. It is perhaps easier to operationalize learning problems and plan remedial action. Whitmore has suggested how we may set about dealing with underachievement and has outlined detailed instructional procedures that she has tried out with a good measure of success in her Cupertino project.

As previously mentioned, the causes of underachievement have been investigated with great success; the development of the procedures used to correct or cure it has not followed quickly (Gowan, 1979a). Human nature and society, being what they are, will probably not allow the condition to be eliminated (Newland, 1976). However, at least two recent serious attempts to remediate or cure underachievement, one by Nava Butler-Por (1987) and the other by Sylvia B. Rimm (1986), have been made.

Scholastic and Psychosocial Approaches

Butler-Por (1987) discusses underachievement in the context of schooling. Although she discusses various issues relating to underachievement, she gives special focus to scholastic underachievement and intervention procedures that can be used to remedy it. Her emphases are on the following:

1. Catering for individual differences
2. Recognizing the need for behavioral change of patterns associated with school difficulties
3. Emphasizing the importance of teacher belief in students' ability to make changes coupled with realistic expectations of the students' progress
4. Accepting personal responsibility as a means to effect change, so that the locus of control becomes internal
5. Assuming personal responsibility in planning strategies to improve the school situation with less dependence on tangible rewards
6. Recognizing the importance of feedback and positive reinforcement in the change process

Classroom strategies recommended for implementation are well known in the education of children generally. The educational objectives attend to intrinsic and competence motivation with appropriate feedback and reinforcement. The development of thinking skills and provision of stimulating creative and intellectually challenging learning situations are encouraged. Furthermore, the acquisition of social skills, awareness, and responsibility are to be facilitated by appropriate social learning experiences. These experiences are to be complemented by teacher efforts to assist students in social and emotional adjustments in the context of a supportive classroom.

Attention is also given to the classroom climate; organization; basic and differentiated curriculum and its enrichment; and teaching methodology that takes into account individual interests, inquiry, creativity, and social skills' development. The approach is consistent with good practice in the education of all children generally, and the gifted specifically, with every intention to remedy underachievement.

Rimm (1986) discusses underachievement more broadly, leaning towards the psychosocial rather than the scholastic. She proposes a *trifocal model* to cure underachievement. The model involves parents, teachers, and students. It consists of six steps; the first five—assessment, communication, changing expectations, role model identification, and correction of deficiencies—apply to all underachievers. Step 6, modifications of reinforcements (at home and in school), consists of three categories: (a) dependent conformers and nonconformers, (b) dominant conformers, and (c) dominant nonconformers. One of these three categories of underachievers is to be selected for attention and cure by the teacher or parent. Rimm says that because it takes time to effect a cure, patience and perseverance are needed.

The causes of underachievement as identified by Rimm—initiating situation, excessive power, inconsistency and opposition, inappropriate classroom environment, and competition—have already been described. To cure underachievement stemming from these sources, Rimm presents 12 laws that summarize her position on the subject. These laws seem pretentious as stated; nonetheless Rimm expects them to predict the effectiveness of her approach to the problem (Rimm, 1986, pp. 303–308).

> Children are more likely to be achievers if their parents join together to give the same clear and positive message about school effort and expectations.
>
> Children can learn appropriate behaviors more easily if they have an effective model to imitate.
>
> Communication about a child between adults (referential speaking) dramatically affects children's behaviors and self-perceptions.
>
> Overreactions by parents to children's successes and failures leads them to feel either intense pressure to succeed or despair and discouragement in dealing with failure.

Children feel more tension when they are worrying about their work than when they are doing that work.

Children develop self-confidence through struggle.

Deprivation and excess frequently exhibit the same symptoms.

Children develop confidence and an internal sense of control if power is given to them in gradually increasing increments as they show maturity and responsibility.

Children become oppositional if one adult allies with them against a parent or a teacher, making them more powerful than an adult.

Adults should avoid confrontations with children unless they are sure they can control the outcomes.

Children will become achievers only if they learn to function in competition.

Children will continue to achieve if they usually see the relationship between the learning process and its outcomes.

Dropout Problem

A major outcome of consistent underachievement is eventual withdrawal from school. This is commonly referred to as the dropout problem, one which causes serious waste of our talent resource.

Generally, the symptoms and causes have been listed and categorized as primary factors and other related factors (Kowalski & Cangemi, 1974). The information is presented as Table 7.1.

Robert D. Strom (1967), writing on the general population of dropouts, points to several factors that cause students to drop out of school. One relates to the culture of poverty and its family tendencies, which seem to foster dropouts. Another places incorrect emphasis on grades as indices of learning. A third focuses attention on an antiquated secondary school curriculum that has been designed for the cultured few and hardly recognizes the differing needs of individuals. Furthermore, there is the imposition of "nonsensical" experience that goes under the name of education. It is not surprising to find that the general population of dropouts' perception is that they are not learning anything of value.

On the matter of high incidence of dropouts, Strom prefers to consider it to be more a symptom of the education system's chronic disorder than the individual's. In a series of questions, he reminds us of some very pressing problems associated with the reasons why students drop out of school, and concludes that until we help individual potential dropouts to succeed, schools will collectively fail (Strom, 1967, p. 31).

Do we not overwork the language or doctrine of individual differences and yet seldom employ this practice in teaching and evaluating children?

Table 7.1 Symptoms and Causes of Youngsters Leaving School

Primary Factors	Other Related Factors
Low reading ability	Low scholastic aptitude
Low I.Q.	Dislike of school
Low socioeconomic status	Unhappy family situations
Parents formerly dropouts	Home pressures
Pregnancy	Performance below potential
Frequent absence and tardiness	Feels rejected by the school
Retention	Poor work habits
Broken homes	Perception of school as a hostile un-
Alienation	happy place
Avoiding participation in extracurric-	Lack of self-confidence
ular activities	Lack of self-knowledge
Pupil–teacher relationships	Lack of self-acceptance
Consistent failure to achieve in regu-	Lack of self-control
lar schoolwork	Feelings of insecurity
Frequent changes of schools	Sex problems
Record of delinquency	Is resentful, defiant, and rude
Desire to find employment	Shows rebellious attitude toward
	authority
	Daydreaming; excessive fantasy
	behavior
	High needs for love, acceptance,
	and attention
	Disinterested in school
	Low self-esteem
	Poor social adjustment
	Fatalistic attitude
	Emotional maladjustment
	Immaturity

Note: From "High School Dropouts—A Lost Resource," by C. J. Kowalski and J. P. Cangemi, 1974, *College Student Journal 8* (4), p. 72. Copyright © 1974 by College Student Journal. Reprinted by permission.

Do we not insist that children remain in school because it is good for them when, in fact, for those whose history of failures is constant this is socially sadistic?

Do we not tell the student he ought to choose what's right and yet limit his right of choice by giving him no alternative within the curriculum? Is tyranny a word for events on foreign soil or does it include the practices of some public schools?

It takes little perceptiveness to recognize the relevance of these questions for the highly able dropout as well. There is no doubt that the whole area of underachievement and its culmination in dropping out of school is a very complex one indeed. The variables are many, interactive, and cumulative (French, 1968; Gallagher, 1985; Gowan & Bruch, 1971; Strom, 1967; Whitmore, 1980).

Sometimes the bright student may drop out for reasons related to personality patterns, personal adjustment problems, sex roles, cultural expectations, and limited programs in schools. For girls, additional reasons for dropping out may include marriage or pregnancy.

There is also the struggle for individuality as adolescents seek to find themselves and to assert their independence in an environment that demands strict adherence to rules. It is not that they reject learning, rather they protest the conformity required in a school setting. Dropouts are concerned that their schools do not prepare them for the real world, and that teachers tend to be unfeeling and insensitive to their needs.

John McLeod and Arthur Cropley (1989) offer that there is good reason to believe that dropouts are as a group gifted. They often become disenchanted with schooling that holds them back; a lockstep curriculum whose emphasis is on excessively boring practice exercises. Disenchantment leads some to become involved in drugs and other forms of delinquency. Those who make it to the university find that leisurely study habits developed in the secondary schools' mixed ability classes are inadequate to meet a more intellectually challenging academic environment. Although many gifted students survive the shock, some wastefully drop out.

HANDICAPPED GIFTED

Other dimensions of underachievement relate to handicaps of one kind or another, for instance, physical disabilities, or emotional disturbances. Handicapped students often pass unrecognized as potentially gifted—their disabilities conceal their possibilities—but today, educators and psychologists have become more aware of them.

There is the problem of a wider acceptance of the concept of handicapped gifted and the selection of appropriate programs for them, as well as the selection of proper instruments or procedures for their identification. The greater the awareness and understanding of the hindrance and obstruction that disabilities pose for these gifted, the more the idea that average or below average attainment in school is a function of the handicap and not the ability will be accepted.

Generally, underachievement is said to have occurred when a student has performed below capacity as measured by I.Q. or achievement test scores. In the case of gifted students with handicaps, it could be that because their capacity level is not known by or is inaccessible to the observer, underachievement may be mistaken for the performance of less able students and go unnoticed. In addition, the facts that other areas of talent are not identified by I.Q. or achievement test scores and that talent in the nonintellective areas may be overlooked are also applicable to the handicapped gifted. However, there is relatively little sustained research on the handicapped gifted. Although there is need for better identification methods and guidance provisions for the handicapped gifted and talented, the literature is still too spotty to offer significant direction.

Emotional Disability

Emotional factors interfere with the proper mental functioning of gifted individuals at home and in schools but receive insufficient attention. Learning is affected by emotions; emotional disabilities can lead to learning disabilities that hinder proper achievement of all children including the gifted (Ford, 1989; Morton & Workman, 1978). Learning disabilities that affected the scholastic achievement of gifted students received notice in the discussion of underachievement in the DeWitt Clinton High School and the Cupertino Experimental Program.

In the DeWitt Clinton High School, it was observed (Raph, Goldberg, & Passow, 1966) that underachievement resulting from learning disabilities is highly specific to a content area. However, if underachievement in one content area is severe enough it may affect performance in other content areas. Raph and her associates also point out that different abilities are needed for the mastery of different content areas; this conclusion anticipated Mary N. Meeker's (1967, 1968, 1969) direction on learning disabilities as they relate to the Structure of Intellect and its correlates in the Stanford-Binet and Wechsler scales.

A related observation indicates that gifted children with learning disabilities not only show an extreme range of discrepancies among their several aptitudes but also are very sensitive about these discrepancies (Gowan & Bruch, 1971). This observation further confirms Guilford's (1967) remark that we possess many different abilities, as illustrated by the Structure of Intellect, some of which are less developed than others. That is why, in part, we do not do so well in all subject areas.

Physical Disability

A physically handicapped person may be blind, hearing impaired, speech impaired, or possessed of another crippling physical disability. Little has been done, especially by way of educational programs, for the physically handicapped gifted. What training is given to teachers or to students with particular handicaps has been approached primarily from special educational opportunities for the handicapped, which do not help teachers or students to learn how to challenge the handicapped gifted (Gowan & Bruch, 1971).

There is recognition in the literature that handicapped individuals may also be gifted, especially when the handicap is compounded by adverse socioeconomic conditions (e.g., Baldwin, Gear, & Lucito, 1978; Maker, 1976, 1977; Torrance, 1977a, 1977b). Approaches at identifying talent of the handicapped gifted (Karnes, 1984; Karnes & Bertschi, 1978; Maker, 1976) and providing educational facilitation (Maker, 1977; Vantour, 1976) have also received some attention.

A recent discussion of the needs of the gifted handicapped (Davis & Rimm, 1985) points to the difficulty of identifying them, a major problem being that their gifts are concealed—often by the disability itself—to teachers and sometimes even parents. Measures like the intelligence test may be a handicap to the discovery of talents of gifted handicapped children. Furthermore, observation of the handicapped gifted child is more difficult than observation of the normal gifted child. Some of the best descriptions on the subject can be found in case studies (e.g., Pringle, 1970; Whitmore, 1980).

Pringle (1970), for instance, presents three referrals (Toby, Jack, and Martin), all gifted but physically handicapped students, and goes on to discuss the effects of their disabilities. We have read about Toby in Chapter 1. Here we shall consider case studies involving Jack and Martin.

Jack

Jack, aged 10 years 9 months at the time of the referral, had an I.Q. of 142. He was referred to Pringle by a plastic surgeon to look into the psychological aftereffects of a street accident that had left him paralyzed. Prior to the accident Jack was quite an athlete, with an outstanding record in swimming, football, and cricket. He had been a lively, active, cheerful boy, well liked by his teachers and extremely popular with his age-mates who had regarded him as a born leader.

Jack was unconscious for several weeks due to the accident that left him paralyzed and speechless. He had a badly dented skull; he required several operations, and skin grafts on his face. When Jack was recovering, he experienced an epileptic seizure that required drug treatment. Jack's well-meaning mother overprotected and overfed him to the point of obesity.

She left Jack torn by a conflict. Its sources were guilt for having caused so much anguish to a family that lavished so much love and care on him, and resentment for being "mollycoddled" or babied and deprived of independence as his condition improved. This conflict aggravated his depression over the handicap, causing increased moodiness, and sudden outbursts of temper followed by bouts of weeping and contrition.

Although he was well on the road to recovery physically, he remained psychologically disturbed, perhaps because of the delayed shock over the accident and his mother's overprotective attitude, or because of the effects of the drugs he was taking. Pringle decided that mother and son needed a break from each other and recommended that Jack be sent to a children's convalescent home. Two months there, and Jack almost regained his preaccident self, with his improving mobility enhanced by physical and game activities. His persistence in practicing those movements and skills he had lost and some correction of his obesity restored his previous personality.

Jack's schoolwork improved though he continued to be slow, a condition that was expected to clear up when drug therapy was discontinued. It was anticipated that he would eventually recover completely. He wrote poems and painted, held his own in high school, channeled his love for sports into refereeing, and won the admiration and friendship of his teachers and peers as he moved ahead into the senior year of high school with every expectation of success.

Martin

Martin, aged 5 years 11 months, had an I.Q. of 175. He suffered from intermittent deafness and bronchial trouble. An inexperienced young teacher misinterpreted his dislike for school, consequent boredom, and disillusionment as lack of ability. The principal, who considered Martin an average student taking longer than usual to settle down, thought that his mother was making too much of a fuss over the boy.

In school, the boy was described as quiet, withdrawn, and somewhat unsociable. He was good at arithmetic, below average in reading, and outstanding in spelling. Before starting school, Martin had learned to read and spell by himself using the names of street signs, labels on cartons, and captions of his favorite programs in the *Radio Times* and on television as aids. The initial joy of going to school was soon dispelled. No attention was paid to his repeated complaints that he was bored and felt that he was wasting time in school. Things went from bad to worse; by the end of the semester Martin made daily requests to be allowed to stay at home to "do real work like sums or spelling" instead of playing all the time in class. His parents were puzzled and disappointed that Martin was not taking to his education as they had expected. The mother, herself a trained teacher, was infuriated by the principal who told her not to fuss over the child, lest the child have no chance of successfully passing the secondary entrance or 11-plus examination. Of course Martin, being the exceptionally bright boy he was, passed the selection examination.

It looked as if the progressiveness of the school applied in a too rigid and unimaginative way was responsible for the problem, for the principal genuinely believed in the value of an informal, gradual approach to learning, without adaptation to suit the individual needs of children of exceptional ability. Later, on following Pringle's recommendation that Martin skip to a higher grade in the junior high school where more formal work was done in a quieter atmosphere and deafness was less of a handicap, Martin's academic brilliance became evident. Having collected an impressive number of advanced level subjects in the General Education Examinations that London University uses for admission, Martin was in an advantageous position of having to make a choice to study for a degree in psychology or medicine.

PROBLEMS OF GIFTED GIRLS

The problems that gifted girls face as they grow up go beyond underachievement viewed as a mismatch between measured ability or talent and manifest performance in school subjects. Rather, we have to view their problems in terms of perceived influences that arrest their achievement thus preventing them from escalating to the promise of higher development toward fulfillment and eminence as adults.

Although much attention has been given to the problems of gifted girls that arise from sex differences and the limits placed on their career choices, little has been done to trace the source of their problems to the developmental stages that are directly related to the normal growing up process. In the main, these problems are tied directly to underachievement. As discussed, the roots of underachievement are bound to genetics and inherited predispositions, the environment and its cultural correlates, and interactions of these dimensions. Consequently, problems affecting gifted girls relate to the main and interaction effects of these variables.

Intellect and Achievement Sex Differences

The problems of girls, beyond those associated with sex differences, have not received the attention they deserve. Earlier sources of such information can be found in the work of Terman and Oden (1947). For instance, they bring to our notice the fact that of their group of gifted child writers, seven of the most gifted were girls whereas all the eminent adult writers in the study were men. This led them to conclude that variables other than heredity must have a part in determining eminence.

On the question of sex differences and I.Q., more boys than girls registered very high I.Q.s. In a follow-up study of the Terman gifted, D. H. Feldman (1984) found that approximately 60% of the gifted group with I.Q.s of 150 and above were males, and that of the 26 who scored an I.Q. of above 180, 19 were males.

In a comprehensive review of sex differences and general ability to learn, achievement, specific attitudes, and cognitive styles in the general population, Eleanor E. Maccoby and Carol Jacklin (1974) presented the following conclusions:

1. In basic intellectual processes of perception, learning, and memory, boys and girls were quite similar.
2. Girls and boys did equally well up to the age of 10 years on verbal tests.
3. Girls did better than boys on verbal tests whose items included spelling, comprehension of complex reading material, and understanding of verbal forms of logical relations, as well as on some creativity measures.
4. There were no sex differences in quantitative ability until the ages of 9 to 13 years; during this time, boys did better even when an equal number of mathematics courses were completed.
5. During this period, differences in science achievement were also evident.
6. Adolescent boys had an advantage, which continued through high school, on tests of spatial ability.
7. On problem-solving tasks involving response inhibition or problem restructuring, boys and girls did equally well.
8. There were no sex differences on tests of concept mastery, reasoning, and nonverbal creativity, though girls, after the age of 7 years, did better on tests of verbal creativity.

From the above, it appears that, in general, boys and girls do not differ significantly in intellectual processes, though differences in visual-spatial abilities, verbal creativity, mathematics, and science achievement in favor of boys and verbal creativity in favor of girls begin to manifest themselves in adolescence.

According to Guilford (1967), variability in intelligence and intellectual operations for boys and girls do exist, however, such that shifts occur according to age levels and measures used. On the subject of sex differences and intellect, Guilford indicates that a child's intellect is linked to genes that determine the status of certain abilities, and to cultural attitudes and beliefs in connection with sex roles. Sex differences as measured by a composite I.Q. are ambiguous, favoring one gender or the other, depending on age levels at which comparisons are made and composition of the scale with sex bias. There is less ambiguity when factor ability scores are used.

Along the continuum of intelligence, males show more variability than females, with sex difference becoming observable in the extreme ends of the distribution. For instance, Terman's group of gifted individuals (I.Q. 140 and above) comprised more boys than girls at the high school level, with the reverse being the case at the elementary school level. It appears that I.Q. difference in favor of girls in early childhood shifts to a difference in favor of boys in adolescence.

Gender differences in intellect relative to some Structure of Intellect abilities can be determined by inference. According to Guilford, males tend to score higher on such tests as

Street Gestalt Completion (CFU)
G-Z Spatial Orientation (CFS-V)
G-Z Spatial Visualization (CFT)
Porteus Maze (CFI)
Arithmetic Reasoning (CMS)
Match Problems (DFT)
Gottschaldt Figures (NFT)

While females score higher than males on such tests as

PMA Reasoning (CSC)
Opposites, Verbal Analogies (CMR)
Wechsler Similarities (CMT)
Memory for Figures (MFU-V)
Digit Symbol (MSI)
Memory for Words (MMU)
Word Fluency (DSU)
Ideational Fluency (DMU)
Expressional Fluency (DMS)
Symbolic Identities (ESU)

Information from these tests allows us to make *two generalizations:* (a) males tend to excel in figural abilities (6 of the 7 tests listed for males are figural, and 1 of the 10 listed for females is figural); (2) females tend to excel in verbal abilities (of the 10 tests listed, 5 are semantic and 4 are symbolic). Guilford suggests that because *figural* abilities are associated with right-hemisphere functioning and *semantic* left-hemisphere functioning, one might predict males as having a better developed right hemisphere and females a better developed left hemisphere.

Studies of high school students show a smaller number of gifted girls than boys as underachievers when grades were used as the criterion. In college, no noticeable sex differences are discernable in achievement when grades are used as a criterion, but test scores show boys excelling (Gowan & Demos, 1964). However, Sally M. Reis (1987) makes the interesting observation that because females receive higher grades than males throughout school, underachievement for adult women must be conceptualized beyond grade indicators to include belief in what can be attained or accomplished in life.

Regarding the achievement of intellectually precocious boys and girls in *mathematics* and *science,* Camilia Benbow and Julian C. Stanley (1982) noted that there were sex differences in mathematical reasoning ability, attitudes toward mathematics and science, performance in mathematics and science, and how mathematics knowledge was considered to have been acquired. However, all these sex differences, except in ability, were considered negligible and perhaps associated with small effect size. Sex differences in mathematics achievement was particularly related to visual-spatial and mathematical ability (Fox, 1979).

In a recent paper, Stanley (1988) reports that the 1987 annual talent search, conducted by the Center for the Advancement of Academically Talented Youth established at Johns Hopkins University, screened 27,000 people using the Scholastic Aptitude Test (SAT). Of the students who scored 500 or more on the mathematics component of the Scholastic Aptitude Test or SAT-M, 19% were boys and 8% were girls, estimated to be the top 1% of their age group on mathematical reasoning ability. Furthermore, youths who scored at least 500 on the SAT-M before the age of 13 were considered exceptionally talented. Scores on this measure run as high as 800, and Stanley reports that 6% of college-bound male and 2% of college-bound female 12th-graders scored 700 or more, with the average for each group, reported by the College Board in 1987, being 500 and 453 respectively.

Stanley indicates that to score 700 or more on the SAT-M before age 13 years, must be regarded as a phenomenal feat rarely accomplished because pupils are not likely to have studied much mathematics in school. The number who scored above 700 has increased in subsequent talent searches from the two who scored that high in the 1972 Study of Mathematically Precocious Youth (SMPY). Of the 269 boys and 23 girls identified as mathematically precocious, there were 12 times as many males as females who obtained 700–800 on the SAT-M before the age of 13 years (Benbow & Stanley, 1982).

The same group's *verbal* scores on the *Scholastic Aptitude Test* or SAT-V were also far beyond the average attained relative to grade and sex, being in the upper one fourth or one fifth of the norm group with girls generally doing better than boys. It was observed that these girls tended to be appreciably more knowledgeable than the boys about the use of commas, capitalization, tense and number of verbs, and other aspects of grammar and syntax, evidence of which is corroborated by the findings of the Educational Testing Service.

As for *science,* Benbow and Stanley (1982) notes that seventh and eight grade boys and girls involved in the 1976 SMPY liked biology, chemistry, and physics, with boys preferring physics or biology and girls preferring biology and chemistry. Although these preferences were significant, no sex differences were noted in perceived performance in and learning of science. All in all, despite their wide ranges in scores on the mathematical and verbal components of the SAT, these students were remarkably alike in background, experiences, interests, and values.

Career Patterns of the Gifted

There is a sex differential in the career patterns of gifted individuals, which must be closely linked to cultural attitudes and role expectations. Take, for instance, the findings of Terman and Oden (1959) on the jobs held by members of their gifted group at age 44:

Fifty percent of their gifted women were housewives with no outside employment.

Forty-two percent of the remaining 50% of the women, held full-time jobs, whereas 8% held part-time jobs.

Twelve and one-half percent of the women (as compared to 4% of the men) of the group were teachers or administrators in elementary or secondary schools.

Twenty percent of the women (as compared to 5% of the men) were secretaries or held office positions.

Eleven percent of the women (as compared to 45% of the men) held professional positions.

Six and one-half percent of the remaining women held jobs in a number of other fields.

The decline in the professional and educational status of gifted women as a result of various personal and sociopsychological factors as well as ignorance about career development was discussed by P. L. Wooleat (1979). She calls our attention to the following:

1. Women account for about 65% of the increased labor force between 1950 and 1960, 26% of which is related to technical and professional jobs. The decline between 1950–1960 is especially noticeable in women's participation in the sciences. In chemistry, the decline was from 10% to 8.6%; in physics, from 6.5% to 4.2%; and in mathematics, from 38% to 24% (Torsi, 1975).

2. Professional and technical jobs held by women in the 1940s declined from 45% to 40%. Although the number of women obtaining the bachelor's degree remained fairly constant during 1940–1960, a decline from 40% to 35% took place in the acquisition of the master's degree, and from 15% to 12% in the acquisition of the doctor's degree (Theodore, 1971).

According to the National Science Foundation, the number of women pursuing scientific careers has increased in the past 15 years, such that the number of women scientists and engineers increased 200%. It must be noted, however, that of the 2 million American engineers, only 3.5% are women; and of the 225,000 physical scientists, only 12% are women (Dembart, 1984).

To find explanations for these differences, the various views advanced focus attention on slower maturation, emotional, and social development of boys as compared with girls. Other factors considered included socio-cultural pressures and values that assign different roles to and make different demands on boys and girls so that girls at an early age are expected to accept the status quo, whereas boys have fewer conformity requirements. In addition, the behavior of girls is more strictly regulated than that of boys. Although these views have changed, girls traditionally have been expected to become housewives and mothers rather than pursue an academic or professional life. Although achievement is perceived as essential for boys, it is not so perceived for girls (Callahan, 1980; Gowan & Demos, 1964; Havighurst, 1961; Morse & Bruch, 1970; Reis, 1987; D. Rogers, 1969).

Career Problems of Gifted Women

One of the best discussions on the problems that have implications for career guidance of gifted women is offered by Wooleat (1979). She discusses subjects such as sex typing of social roles, creativity, achievement motivation, direct versus vicarious achievement, and contingency and discrepancy factors as important variables for explaining the under-achievement of gifted women.

Sex Typing of Social Roles

One of the major contributing causes to the underachievement of girls is sex stereotyping (Callahan, 1979, 1980; Morse & Bruch, 1970; Reis, 1987). Differences in cultural expectations of males and females, which communicate to individuals their relative worth and respective roles in life, are expressed in numerous ways by the media, books, speeches, and so on. Even in school, boys vocally dominate the classroom and get more attention and encouragement than do girls; assertiveness and attention getting is expected of boys whereas ladylike and timid behavior is expected of girls (Sadker & Sadker, 1985). Consequently, boys and girls are treated differently at all levels of schooling (Schmidt, 1982).

Sex typing brings to the fore the fact that the attainment of eminence by men in the professions is a cultural expectation and, hence, looked on favorably. Similar accomplishments by women, however, are regarded as having been attained at the expense of sex-role expectations, and disapproved. When gifted women aspire to careers their aspirations are in conflict with the prevailing social image; often they are dubbed *masculine*. Similarly, men who pursue artistic interests are labeled *feminine*.

This masculine bipolar sex orientation is said to be responsible for many of the conflicts experienced by gifted women in pursuit of careers.

Creativity

Femininity and masculinity are well-known opposite-sex traits possessed by creative individuals. These people have been found to accept opposite-sex characteristics in themselves (e.g., assertiveness in women and aesthetic inclinations in men) and allow them to be expressed in conscious behavior in a way that others may repress (Bruch & Morse, 1972; MacKinnon, 1978). Torrance (1962a, 1963) used the concept of androgyny in developing divergent titles such as "A woman who swears like a sailor" or "A man who becomes a nurse" for one of his creativity tests known as The Imaginative Story.

Wooleat (1979) suggests that research may show the existence of more similarities in dominant characteristics between creative men and women than we realize. Differences existing between men and women arise primarily from socialization practices that tend to reinforce certain stereotypes—men are to achieve and women are to be nurturant. A mentally healthy gifted female adult is expected to possess quite a different set of characteristics than that of a female adult of the general population (Broverman, Broverman, Clarkson, Rosenkrantz, & Vogel, 1970).

We also have Callahan's (1979) observation that although girls earn higher grades in school, men write more books, obtain more degrees, produce more works of art, and make more professional contributions. Even in literature, where people agree that females tend to surpass their male counterparts, men are the ones shown to be more productive. Reis (1987) explains that males demonstrate more creative productivity because they have more time for work and fewer home-related duties and outlets. Females demonstrate their creativity in ways related to the family or home, and if they work outside the home they have even less time to devote to creative productions.

Achievement Motivation

D. C. McClelland and his associates define motivation in terms of strong affective association that relates goal anticipatory response to pain or pleasure (McClelland, Atkinson, Clark, & Lowell, 1953). They state that motivation for achievement can be traced to basic motivational patterns that are set early by child-rearing practices, competition relative to a standard of excellence, unusual accomplishment, and involvement over a long period of time. However, their approach to identify high and low achievers did not discriminate between high-achieving and low-achieving girls (Pierce & Bowman, 1960). It prompted M. S. Horner (1972a, 1972b) to find an explanation for this difference in a dimension that went beyond Atkinson's (1960) conceptualization of two opposing tendencies that approach or withdraw in a performance situation, namely, achievement-motive and motive to avoid failure. Although these two dispositions are considered by Horner as appropriate to an achieving man, a third motive, which she calls motive to avoid success, is also present in some women. This motive is especially evident when a woman is in competition involving both sexes; suppression of performance by a woman is perceived as necessary to avoid being labeled a failure as a woman as a result of successful achievement. This is troubling to the gifted woman who has to resolve the conflict of her dual tendencies to achieve and to act in a nurturant role.

Wooleat (1979) suggests that the psychological implications of the motive to avoid success in mixed sex competition can be found in *attribution theory* (Ickes & Layden, 1979), which attempts to explain the relationship between performance and one's perception of the causes of successful or unsuccessful performance. Causal attributes appear to fall into four categories: ability, effort, task difficulty, and luck. Generally men, as a group, tend to attribute their successes to ability (stable internal factor) and their failures to effort or luck (unstable external factors). Women, however, view their successes in terms of luck or ease of task, and their failures to lack of ability, making persistence in a task unlikely and success expectation low. Of relevance is the observation that bright girls do not anticipate success as readily as boys (Walberg, 1969). What is more, teachers nearly always attribute girls' failure to intellectual inadequacies and boys' failure to lack of effort or motivation (Dweck, Davidson, Nelson, & Enna, 1978).

Direct Versus Vicarious Achievement

Another interesting perspective concerning the career development process relates to the extent one gains status and reward through self-achievement or through the achievement of others. J. Lipman-Blumen and H. J. Leavitt (1976) term this as direct versus vicarious achievement. The traditional role of women places them in the position of obtaining status and achievement vicariously by facilitating the efforts of their husbands and children who obtain their status and achievement directly.

Wooleat, citing a personal communication from J. D. Pedro (Wooleat, 1979, p. 335), notices the relationship of direct versus vicarious achievement and planning involvement or avoidance. Pedro, she notes, reported that girls who are high on direct-achievement orientation tend to be more advanced in their career planning than girls who intend to depend on vicarious achievement; boys, allowing for some intrasex differences, are strongly direct-achievement oriented.

Thus, the process of socialization, acting on these psychological attributes, makes it more difficult for gifted women than for gifted men to achieve eminence, even though their ability potential may be equal. In addition, as Morse and Bruch (1970) observe, gifted women's career achievements may be delayed by the probable interruption of their education during child-bearing years, lack of mobility, or getting a late start in a career. With a family, even goal-directed women may take many more years to achieve their career goals.

Contingency and Discrepancy Factors

The contingency factor is another element relevant to the resolution of the conflict between career and family goals as experienced by gifted women. Wooleat (1979) points out that the marriage patterns in the United States show that men marry either below or at their own educational level, whereas women marry at or above their level. As a consequence, gifted women who delay graduate level and professional level education until a suitable husband is found discover that the "pool" of desirable husbands is not very large. Such delay by married gifted women may be related to the anticipated difficulties of finding highly specialized jobs in the same locality for both themselves and their husbands.

There is also the case of those women who slow down their educational advance so that they will not graduate ahead of their husbands because this may pose the problem of whose career comes first, with consequent painful decisions. Hence, we find such solutions as contingency planning, delaying education, or reducing the discrepancy between career and family goals. Instances of reduction of discrepancy include the choice of occupations that are compatible with the "female" or nurturant role (e.g., teaching or nursing) or participation in male professions on a part-time basis. These difficulties do not affect the career patterns of men and, therefore, do not require the use of contingency planning or reduction of discrepancy between career and family roles for men.

DEVELOPMENTAL STAGES OF GIFTED WOMEN

The underachievement of gifted women may also be looked at from a developmental standpoint. Earlier, in discussing individual development as occurring in stages, attention was called to Gowan's periodic development table, which represents a combination of the cognitive stages of Piaget, the affective stages of Erikson, and the creative stages of Gowan (Table 6.1). An individual passes through three stages of development—growing from infancy through youth to adulthood—so that, within each stage of development, the person passes through the phases of latency, identity, and creativity and each time moves toward a higher level of creativity and self-actualization. Gowan's model presents a general system of human development in the cognitive and affective domains, an approach that is generally applicable to all. Periodic developmental stages relative to women, generally, and gifted, specifically, are particulars of the whole picture. Some deviation from the ideal pattern can be expected, as pointed out by both E. Julia Simpson (1977) and Catherine B. Bruch (1972).

Gowan's Model Expanded

Applying these stages to gifted women, E. Julia Simpson (1977) expands Gowan's periodic development model to include W. G. Perry's *conative* or purposive mode (Perry, 1970) and Kohlberg's *moral* mode (Kohlberg & Mayer, 1972) in the developmental stages of infancy, youth, and adulthood. She points out that the divisions in the periodicity table are not as definite and clear cut as they appear to be, and that some overlap and continuity from one stage to the next can be expected. Furthermore, Simpson describes Gowan's terms of *escalation* and *dysplasia* (absolute and relative).

For Perry dysplasia that finds expression in terms of *temporizing* may occur. By temporizing he means the occurrence of a prolonged pause in development lasting for a year or more, allowing a person to make the next step forward. He also uses the term *retreat* to represent an active denial of the potential of a particular stage because of anxiety, resentment, passive resistance, or rebellion, allowing a person to move back to an earlier stage of reassurance and freedom before choosing to reengage in the "new" stage. Perry uses the term *escape* to describe denying or rejecting the implications for growth and being encapsulated or limited to a particular stage.

Kohlberg uses the term *horizontal decalage* to indicate the spread across the range of basic physical and social actions, concepts, and objects to which the stage potentially applies. Kohlberg's horizontal decalage, like Gowan's escalation, is more important than acceleration if healthy development to the next stage is to occur.

We are reminded by E. J. Simpson that *developmental tasks* in the affective domain are not completed in the same stage in which they are begun. Rather, a continuous process begun in one stage is more fully developed and integrated in the next two succeeding stages, and finally is completed in the fourth stage so that regression under stress may occur.

According to Simpson, many gifted women will spend more time in certain stages of development than in others so that *uneven progression* through these stages can be expected. For instance, relative to the Erikson-Piaget-Gowan Periodic Table (Table 6.1), J. Simpson suggests that women will have to spend more time in the affective domain fulfilling affiliation needs (Stage 4) and parental needs (Stage 7); in the cognitive domain at the conventional level of moral commitment (Stage 5); in formal operations (Stage 5); and in conative development (Stage 6).

These are the areas that I see the typical, traditional woman as spending most of her adult life in. I am not unbiased as to the "traditional woman's role" having spent most of my adult life as primarily wife, homemaker and mother; but I am coming to realize, more and more, that this role is not for all women for all time, and that, as needs are filled in one stage, a woman or any individual, can be freed and stimulated to move on to the next—that a woman who is reaching toward self-actualization, or ego-integrity, can fill different roles at different times of her life, perhaps more so than a man. (J. Simpson, 1977, p. 378)

To find a theoretical explanation for this, E. J. Simpson refers to Erikson's (1973) thesis concerning a productive inner body space located in the center of a woman that is superior to the missing penis. The woman who can reflect on this inner space without apology is one who can direct her own unique talents and viewpoints toward leadership in the affairs of man, moving as it were, into stages of creativity, self-actualization, ego-integrity, postconventional morality, and commitment.

At this juncture it seems appropriate to focus on Catherine B. Bruch's (1972) insightful perspective on Gowan's affective development (Table 6.1) of the creative productive woman. She indicates that currently women have many more choices, do not necessarily fit the norm, and exhibit a variety of developmental patterns, contrary to Gowan's generalizations.

> The questions raised by Gowan (1972) as to the affective relationship of girls with their fathers in the initiative stage and to the affective developments in the intimacy period and thereafter in his later elaborations of creative development, will need careful validation as to their applicability to women. Again, the Eriksonian bases for these period stages may be biased towards development in men. Women in our more emancipated age have more choices open to them for choosing whether to marry or not to marry, whether to be totally, partially, or not-at-all involved in child-bearing and child-rearing, etc. Although Torrance (1971) found some women to experience creative gratifications in child-rearing, he also cited that the number of children was negatively correlated with the criteria of creative achievement and aspiration.
>
> The Eriksonian sequence of adult development is also representative of the cultural norms, but creative persons generally do not fit these norms. Even adult developmental stages may observe several patterns of time-out for child-bearing and rearing, short or long periods, earlier or later in adult ages, with larger or smaller numbers of children so that during the generativity stage there may be no peaceful time available for access to the proposed psychedelic level of inner awareness. It is therefore anticipated that several patterns of development of various adult levels of creativity will be found in creative women, from the intimacy period onward.
>
> For example, intimacy for the woman who does not marry may mean simply learning to care deeply for another human being so that the warmth

estimated as a creative-productive characteristic may emerge. It may not lead at all to actual generativity, although this could be experienced vicariously through the contacts possible in working with the children of others. The professional woman who is married may have other patterns dependent upon the necessity for study time en route to an advanced degree, the postponement of family, or the care of children by others. The realities of financial struggles while the wife (and the husband) progress to advanced levels of study, and the wife's lowered likelihood of receiving scholarship aid, set varying sequences upon women's creative development. (Bruch, 1972, p. 8)

Self-Esteem and Identification

Another theoretical position on sex-linked differences in the developmental process relates to self-esteem and identification. Judith Bardwick (1971) wrote that, in the main, boys' self-esteem is based on achievement whereas girls' self-esteem is based on acceptance. Perhaps girls, being dependent on others for assurance and reinforcement, do not find esteem within themselves, for esteem can evolve only when an individual sets goals and achieves them.

Bardwick perceives identification as a process involving both parents. The girl identifies with the personal qualities and maternal role of the mother while identifying with her father who she loves and by whom she is loved. Should rejection of maternal-role-model-related variables occur, a girl may identify more strongly with her father's role activity perceiving herself as more capable of achieving success and self-esteem in male-oriented activities. This conclusion ties in with the observation (J. Simpson, 1977) that children who relate more to opposite-sex parents are more likely to facilitate the development of their creativity so that the development of sense of self-esteem and achievement Stages 4 and 5, which are more difficult for girls, allows an individual to move into the creativity of Stage 6 of Gowan's model (Table 6.1).

Affiliation and Achievement

Most adult women see affiliation with the nuclear family as critical to their achievement of self-esteem. Although the motives to achieve in other areas are considered important, they can be only secondary to the need for affiliation. Generally, it is only after women feel secure in the family and have esteem as females that a reemergence of achievement motivation may occur. At that time, mature women may assume multiple roles. They take for granted their family affiliation, and may go to college to extend themselves in various directions seeking higher developmental stages.

That women tend to remain in this stage of development longer than men may be attributed to feelings of security and happiness that can be a part of fulfilling the vital role of mother. Achievement motivation can and often does recur when women no longer have the need to take care of dependent children and can turn their attention to their own self-esteem by moving on to new stages of development. Those women who cannot move to the next higher stages of development experience a form of escape (Perry, 1970) or dysplasia (Gowan, 1972). This experience may be the result of their affiliative, love, productive, and care roles (affective areas of Stages 6 and 7 in Gowan's model) being the most culturally acceptable.

CONCLUSIONS

Special problems of the gifted are closely linked to various aspects of underachievement. These aspects include the interactive effects of the physical and sociocultural environment in the shaping of individuals; the discrepancy between attainment as predicted by the I.Q. index and actual performance in school subjects that is below expected level; an expanded frame of talent reference that is multivariate and far more complex than hitherto considered to ascertain underachievement; the variability of gender, in general, and those specific factors that hinder gifted girls from achieving excellence and eventual eminence; the omission from consideration of physical and emotional disability factors when making decisions regarding gifted students' underachievement of potential; and underachievement due to the developmental arrest of girls' cognitive and affective dimensions as they grow up to adulthood.

The complexity of underachievement has been generally recognized more in terms of causes that interfere with I.Q.-predicted school performance. The real problem of discovering appropriate remedies for underachievement lies in the identification of specific causes. Often, the interactive nature of a multiplicity of causes defies an adequate prescription on how to approach the correction of underachievement. What makes the correction even more complicated is that even a specific difficulty may not only have a multiple number of root causes but that the problem itself may be multidimensional. The complexity of the situation is further aggravated because underachievement may be conceived both as below par performance in school as well as poor performance in achieving higher levels of fulfillment and self-actualization.

Dealing with the problem of underachievement is a challenge. It demands a reorientation that will recognize the shaping effects of environmental and cultural factors; the multidimensional nature of talent; the usefulness of a variety of test procedures including nonpsychometric approaches; the importance of identifying specific talent strengths so that situations that are relevant to the development of such talent can be handled properly; the diagnostic value of identification for planning educational activities and experiences; the necessity for programs that are innovative, flexible, forward looking in design, and significantly relevant to the complex dimensions of underachievement—programs that include strong guidance components to ensure high levels of achievement, mental health, and self-actualization.

CHAPTER EIGHT

Learning to Cope with Problems

*I*NTRODUCTION

Recognition of individual differences falls within the discipline of humanistic psychology. As the attempt to study these differences pertains to the gifted, we are reminded of the efforts of Lewis Terman and his associates to learn more about highly intelligent individuals, and their identifications, characteristics, and behaviors as they grew up to mid-life.

Five follow-up studies were done on Terman's (1925) 1,000 superior students (Burks, Jensen, & Terman, 1930; Cox, 1926; Oden, 1968; Terman & Oden, 1947, 1959). In brief, these subjects grew up to be gifted adults who maintained their high level of intelligence, had lower mortality rates, enjoyed good physical and mental health, had minimal involvement with crime, ranked high in education and vocational achievements, were active in community affairs, and held moderate political and social views. Furthermore, their characteristic traits included interest, energy, will, and character, all of which were predictive of their superior performance and achievement as mature adults.

However, about two thirds of this group felt that they had not actualized their potential. Their attitudes found corroboration in Oden's (1968) study, which attempted to assess the relationship of genius and vocational achievement. In comparing the 100 most successful and least successful male geniuses, she found that the most successful came from families of higher socioeconomic status where, as children, they were encouraged to succeed. The most successful were ranked higher as adolescents on volitional, intellectual, moral, and social traits. They were found to have more self-confidence, perseverance, and integration toward goals. In addition, the scholastic achievement of the successful men was similar to their achievement in grade school. As for the least successful men, half graduated from college.

Though gifted individuals have problems in common with those who are less gifted, they are beset with problems that are directly related to their mental superiority and its search to express itself in socially acceptable ways without sacrificing individuality. They are generally emotionally more sensitive, and if they are creative, the conflict that results from their attempts to express themselves as individuals in society can at times be devastating to their personal, social, and educational lives. While it was commonly held that gifted children do not need help in making adjustments and adaptations, a more current, and better, understanding of their problems speaks strongly in favor of guidance (Brandwein, 1955).

GUIDANCE FOR THE GIFTED

Much that has been written about guidance has focused attention on (a) providing guidance in the areas of education and vocation, recognizing problems that children face personally and socially; and (b) on approaches taken by school counselors, teachers, and parents to effect guidance (Collangelo & Zaffrann, 1979; Durr, 1964; M. J. Gold, 1965; Hildreth, 1952, 1966).

Old and New Perspectives

That gifted children need guidance has been repeatedly emphasized. Gowan (1979a) perceived that the problem of adequately providing guidance revolved around the absence of a curriculum of guidance. Such a curriculum, according to Gowan, can be found in developmental stage theory, especially as it relates to the cognitive and affective dimensions of growing up (Tables 6.1 and 6.2).

Several years ago, Gowan (1979c) charged that guidance or counseling as practiced confuses psychotherapy with guidance. Psychotherapy focuses on the abnormal problems of adults, which require private and long-term treatment; guidance or counseling is concerned with developmental problems of normal children, which require short-term treatment.

He also charged that the practice of counseling tends to consider the concept of positive self-regard as a panacea that is not only necessary but also sufficient. This is unlike some aspects of developmental counseling (e.g., vocational), in which individual diagnosis and prescription are absolutely essential because what is needed, more than support, for instance, is specific job-opportunity information.

Finally, Gowan noted that the practice of guidance is based on a pathological medical model (e.g., psychotherapy) whose attention is crisis oriented. Such a model has been outmoded by Maslovian concepts. Therefore, the practice of guidance in school should be preventative and leveled at positive development toward the maintenance of good mental health.

Fresh perspectives for guidance are suggested by Gowan (1979a): emphasis is on counseling students with normal developmental problems associated with task performance. The goal of this counseling is to ensure appropriate cognitive and affective development. Furthermore, counseling is required to go beyond establishing counselee positive self-concept into areas of specific vocational, educational, interest, and motivational needs, providing the right kind of information for better decision making. Guidance should be preventative rather than remedial, so that conditions and opportunities can be created to assist students in achieving higher levels of creative development toward self-actualization and good mental health.

Providing guidance for all children in school is quite a recent development, taking life from the inception of vocational guidance required by the Smith-Hughes Act of 1917. Extensions of vocational guidance spread to other aspects of childhood, to developmental tasks, to the proliferation of the counselor's tools—especially testing—and to the more global and clinical aspects of the problems people encounter in their lives (Gowan & Demos, 1964).

Other developments in areas where guidance was necessary and more slow in coming included the recognition that gifted children experienced special problems (Gowan & Demos, 1964). Among these problems were (a) choosing from many attractive career and life-style alternatives; (b) being integrated into a specialized occupational structure before interests are developed; (c) handling problems of upward mobility, peer relations, and socialization; and (d) finding appropriate and genuine adult role models.

J. B. Conant (1958) had observed that for adequate development of the academically talented student, guidance was essential, and had to be comprehensive, continually available, and realistic relative to desirable educational objectives. Gowan (1979a), at a later time, reiterated Conant's observation, and pointed out that guidance for the gifted involves the application of principles of guidance, modified to provide differential guidance for developmental acceleration.

A number of years ago, Gowan and Demos (1964) had observed that with the exception of two works on guidance (Gowan & Demos, 1964;

Torrance, 1962a), no comprehensive statement about guidance for the gifted had been written. Together, the authors gave the most forward theoretical view of guidance for the gifted and creative. Although many had addressed themselves to the problem (Barbe, 1954; Hildreth, 1952; Martinson, 1961; Passow, 1957; Strang, 1958), thought on the subject had not been substantially advanced. In the main, these studies advocated the necessity and importance for guidance of the gifted in terms of their educational, vocational, and personal needs. Such guidance would involve the counselor, teacher, parent, and community.

Recent forward-looking perspectives that are germane to the development of counseling concepts and practice for the gifted add to the earlier comprehensive theoretical statement (Colangelo & Zaffrann, 1979; Gowan, Khatena, & Torrance, 1979). Among the many facets of guidance discussed in these studies are those associated with the significant on-going efforts of the Guidance Laboratory for Superior Students (John W. M. Rothney founder) at the University of Wisconsin (Madison), and the earlier efforts (initiated and supervised by John C. Gowan) of the Summer Gifted Child Creativity Classes at San Fernando Valley State College in California. Both efforts were aimed at training counselors to work specifically and differentially with gifted children (Zaffrann & Colangelo, 1977).

Zaffrann and Colangelo (1977) stated that, drawing from Gowan's theoretical model, differential guidance for the gifted from a developmental perspective involves, in particular, social and educational concerns; career and vocational concerns; concern for the problems of gifted women; and developmental arrest, dysplasia, and malfunctioning. They advocated a counseling program for gifted children that would take these concerns into account to facilitate mental health and creativity through the affective domain. Perrone and Pulvino (1977) also subscribed to the developmental stage model but emphasized the development of creative functioning in terms of right-hemisphere functioning, and what Bob Samples (1975) called the metaphorical mind. They contrasted right-hemisphere functioning with left-hemisphere functioning and the rational mind (Piaget, 1950), field-independent with field-dependent behaviors (Rotter, 1966), and divergent with convergent thinking (Guilford, 1967). In addition, they saw that creativeness was best produced by affective support and cognitive stimulation, implying that counseling should take these two elements into account.

According to Gowan, these perspectives are valuable (Gowan, Khatena, & Torrance, 1979), but need qualification. Writing on the specialized functions of the right and left cerebral hemispheres (Fischer, 1974), Gowan (1980) indicated that we need to know which of the two halves of the brain is dominant, because some people have right- while others have left-brain dominance (i.e., divergent or convergent thinking styles).

When we understand this, we are in a position to maximize the learning and mental functioning of an individual. That is why education should emphasize the development and perfection of those specific talents possessed by the gifted rather than attempt to develop talents that are present to a lesser degree. Differential learning modes are essential, therefore, to the effective nurturance of creativity and should be an important consideration of guidance.

DEVELOPMENT AND GUIDANCE

Gowan focused attention on the primary importance of using developmental stage concepts in guidance (Gowan, 1980). Developmental stage theory (Tables 6.3 and 6.4) indicated that, relative to the Structure of Intellect, divergent follows convergent thinking as creativity follows Piaget's formal operations. This relationship suggested that a stricter adherence to the order of developmental stage theory would be a more fruitful approach to the educational guidance of the gifted.

The most common form of dysplasia prevents cognitive escalation to creativity in young adults, and Gowan (1972) wrote that this problem should be the prime focus of guidance for the gifted, so that the movement of all parts of the psyche of an individual beyond the fifth developmental stage of formal operations can be toward full creativity and self-actualization.

Finally, Gowan pointed out the importance of guidance in the synergistic development of the individual because, when all aspects of the psyche are functioning harmoniously, higher levels of creativity and self-actualization emerge, and major creative works as well as continued personal development after sexual maturity follow.

Guidance of Creative Development

Creative development of an individual in terms of developmental stage theory and transformation theory have already received our attention (Chapter 6). The *growth model for transformation* (Land, 1973) has not been discussed in terms of the gifted and its guidance implications in cases where the *developmental model* (Gowan, 1972) has been shown to be relevant to the gifted with implications for guidance. Both of these areas need emphasis and relevant inferences need to be drawn for guidance of the gifted.

Moving to the conception of an individual's creativity and its interactive relationship with society we find that Arieti (1976) and Simonton (1978) have presented interesting and thought-provoking ideas. According to Arieti, the individual and society are two *open systems in dynamic energy exchange.* The extent to which society shapes an individual's creativity is the extent to which society meshes its own creative predisposition and values in an interrelationship he calls a *magic synthesis.* Simonton views *sociocultural conditions* as exercising *significant influence on the creative development* of youthful geniuses during their lifetimes to bring about the *emergence of eminence.* Together, these views represent the best attempt at a fresh conceptualization of approaches to guiding the gifted.

Periodic Developmental Stages

Briefly, developmental stage theory is based on the rationale that development is *discontinuous.* Individuals, as they grow up from infancy to adulthood and into old age, pass through three developmental stages three separate times, each time at a higher level. Developmental characteristics of individuals relate to concerns of the following: (a) nature and function of the world (latency); (b) themselves as persons (identity); and (c) creative functioning (creativity) during infancy, youth, and adulthood.

Tables 6.1 and 6.2 present details of each of these stages in a matrix that relates the affective stages of Erik Erikson and Sigmund Freud, the cognitive stages of Jean Piaget, and the creative stages of John C. Gowan. Therefore, we shall concern ourselves with *escalation* and *dysplasia* as they relate to cognitive and affective development on the one hand, and to creativity and self-actualization on the other hand.

Development occurs through *cycles of escalation,* the five attributes of which are *discontinuity, succession, emergence, differentiation,* and *integration.* Continual environmental stimulation is required for escalation into higher levels of creative functioning as the individual moves toward self-actualization. The extent to which this stimulation has maximum or minimum effect depends on the individual's position in the cycle of development. Gowan's model (Table 6.1) goes beyond Piaget's *formal operations* stage to include three additional stages that, in turn, go beyond Erikson's stages of *intimacy, generativity,* and *ego-integrity* to the stages of *creativity* (Stage 6), *psychedelia* (Stage 7), and *illumination* (Stage 8). These last three stages (6, 7 and 8) involve an increased mind expansion that is rare even among healthy and intelligent human beings.

Escalation from one developmental stage to the next is important in overcoming *developmental discontinuity.* Hence, *facilitation of the escalation process* should be one of the major concerns of guidance. A number of methods have been developed that allow superior adults to reach higher developmental levels including various kinds of educational experiences, therapy, sensitivity training, and meditation, all of which can be adapted for use with young gifted people.

Dysplasia exists when malformation occurs in cognitive and affective development. When dysplasia occurs, individuals are not in the affective-cognitive stage of development that they should be in (absolute dysplasia). Or they may develop affectively but not cognitively or vice versa (relative dysplasia). Dysplasia may be single or double. It cannot be more than double because of the triplicity of the model, since development moves to a higher level when the same stages are repeated (Table 6.1).

Dysplasia produces a block to development preventing cognitive escalation to creativity and causing some kind of neurotic dissonance (Figure 6.6). This block is a problem that gifted children may face, and is one of the prime reasons that they need guidance. The main purpose of such guidance is to assist the development of the gifted, facilitating escalation of all parts of the psyche beyond formal operations (Stage 5) through creativity (Stage 6), psychedelia (Stage 7), and illumination (Stage 8). In this way, gifted individuals can be prepared to move toward higher levels of creative functioning for self-actualization.

Discontinuity in the development of creative thinking abilities takes place during the ages of 5, 9, 13, and 17 years with the severest of the drops occurring at about age 9 or the fourth grade (Torrance, 1962a). This coincides with Stage 4 of the developmental stage model and occurs again in Stage 5 (Khatena, 1978a). Studies of the *fourth-grade slump* or discontinuity in creative thinking abilities conducted in societies abroad indicate that it also occurs as a consequence of cultural interference, Christian missionary activities, and stress (Torrance, 1967b).

It is increasingly recognized that gifted children need guidance if they are to realize their full potential. This is especially so in Stages 6, 7 and 8. However, information about developmental discontinuity in creative thinking performance indicates that an earlier handling of the problem is required. Escalation from the intuitive or creative (Stage 3) to concrete operations (Stage 4) needs to take place without loss of creative functioning. Having been alerted to the restricting, stressful, and inhibiting times of a child's life during the elementary to middle elementary school years that preface the fourth-grade slump, guidance for the gifted can focus on prevention of much of these inhibiting influences.

Guidance can remove or remedy the causes of interference that bring about discontinuity of the child's creative development. Suggestions for counteracting some of these interferences are proposed by Khatena (1978a).

We have been in search of ways and means to overcome the problem of decrements in creativity especially at a time when children seem to be very vulnerable, and Torrance and others have shown conclusively that by arranging proper stimulating conditions and opportunities for creative achievement that much can be done to prevent the fourth grade slump. Gowan has added the dimension of love which tends to prepare and predispose the person for creative thoughts and acts, and for appropriate links that may be established between the conscious and preconscious so that the ability to dip into the pre-conscious to bring back creative ideas at will is developed.

It would be very useful to help your child to be creative during the ages of 4 through 6 or stage 3, especially if you observe that he shows signs of being low in his ability to be creative. You might also give him many opportunities to be creative around the ages of 9 and 10 years which is within stage 4 of the Gowan developmental model (7–12 years). Of course you will have to be on the lookout for the times when he is exposed to much stress, and over long periods of time; so do what you can to take some of it away. Entry points into various levels of schooling do expose your child to stress and you should be particularly watchful over the pressures brought to bear upon him by his new surroundings, teachers, friends and learning. With your understanding and help he may avoid this difficult period of his life, or overcome these pressures while continuing to maintain his creativity and be productive. (pp. 106–107)

Growth for Transformation

Land's (1973) growth model, as it relates to creativity and stages of growth processes, is fundamental to his transformation theory. As the *accretive* stage relates to creative thinking, it involves enlargement of an idea or concept, or elaboration. The *replicative* stage involves modification of form or pattern while retaining similar function and may be called flexibility. The higher levels of creative thinking that occur in the *mutualistic* stage involve metaphor, analogy, imagery, and the tapping of the pre-conscious. At the fourth level, destructuring of the existing and coexisting patterns for reintegration or restructuring takes place. At one and the same time, *transformation* occurs for creative thinking at a higher level, and is preparatory to a repetition of the same cycle of increasing order.

These stages of *ever-increasing order* are not necessarily affected by chronology and may occur at any time in a person's life relative to a situation or mental event. Pertaining to the gifted, one implication for guidance that emerges is the need to assist the individual through these cycles of growth at one level of creative thinking to similar cycles of growth at increasingly higher levels.

Creative thinking has been found by many (e.g., Khatena, 1984; Parnes, Noller, & Biondi, 1977; Torrance, 1972a) to be malleable and re-sponsive to intervention or *training* procedures. Experiences can be ar-ranged that encourage individuals to pass from elaborative and flexible thinking to original thinking, which calls for the use of creative imagina-tion, imagery and analogy, and the operations of synthesis-destructur-ing-restructuring (Khatena, 1984), energized by love and facilitated by the accessibility of the preconscious through frequent use (Gowan, 1978b, 1978c).

Feedback (positive or negative) for *feedforward* are essential features of Land's (1973) transformation model. Individuals interact with the environment in constant dynamic relation so that input is received from it. Input of information is *mediated* by Piagetian processes of assimiliation and accommodation or Guilfordian intellectual operations and return to the environment as output. In the numerous transactions that occur between individuals and their environment growth takes place; each time at increasingly higher levels. Herein lies another occasion for guidance. Arrangements can be made for appropriate environmental stimulation leveled at facilitating the development of creative functioning so that positive reinforcements (feedback) can be provided for the creative development of gifted individuals. In this way, escalation to higher stages of creative functioning within the growth cycle can be facilitated.

Society and Creative Development

Simonton (1978) and Arieti (1976) both point to the importance of societal influences and conditions on the creative development of individuals. Their cogent observations provide another perspective for guidance of the gifted.

Of the seven sociocultural conditions identified by Simonton (formal education, eminent creators as role models, *zeitgeist*, political fragmentation, constant warfare, and political instability) affecting youthful geniuses during their lifetimes, six were found to facilitate creative development towards self-actualization and eminence. Two, however, have guidance as well as educational implications. These are *formal education* and creative *role models* for emulation.

As important as *formal education* is to children's creativity as they grow up, there comes a point beyond which an overcommitment to tradition inhibits creative functioning. We have seen this overcommitment as being partly responsible for the drop in creative thinking abilities, particularly at about the fourth grade, but at several other times in the schooling of children as well (Torrance, 1967b). We are also well aware of the pressures exerted on children by education to conform to prearranged educational experiences, with consequent pressures and ill-effects on their mental health (Gowan & Bruch, 1971; Torrance, 1962a). These pressures can stunt the creative development of gifted children.

Guidance can serve to encourage children to acquire knowledge needed for living without sacrificing their creativity. Children can be given guidance to circumvent restrictions imposed by society and the educational system so that they may learn in productive ways, leading to higher levels of creative development. Many have offered to help achieve this goal. In particular, it is well to note the advice given to us by Torrance and his associates (Torrance, 1962a; Torrance & Myers, 1970), Gowan and his associates (Gowan & Demos, 1964; Gowan & Bruch, 1971), and several others (Colangelo & Zaffrann, 1979; Khatena, 1978a, 1990; Webb, Meckstroth, & Tolan, 1982).

Eminent creators as *role models* for emulation appear to be very important to the emergence of other eminent creators. The effects are maximized and more predictable if emulation occurs in the same discipline, especially during the developmental period of genius. This finding has particular significance for guidance because arrangements can be made not only to bring historical and contemporary creative eminent men and women to the notice of gifted students for *emulation* but also, where feasible, to make plans for *mentoring* by bringing together eminent people with gifted children for face-to-face interaction.

Arieti (1976) views the individual and society as being two open systems in dynamic exchange. When a society offers the individual the possibility of becoming great it is, according to Arieti, *creativogenic*. Nine conditions (described in Chapter 6) that facilitate such an occurrence are present in a creativogenic society. For the gifted child, several of these conditions take on significance, and guidance plays an important role in assisting the development of greatness.

Drawing from Arieti's observations as presented in the nine conditions, the following guidance approaches are suggested:

Guidance can ensure that gifted individuals have access to other talented and gifted people with whom they can work, learn, and interact so that the individuals seeking guidance are stimulated to be more productive.

Guidance can see to it that materials, supplies, equipment, and the like, for activities and experiences needed for creative development are made available to the gifted.

Guidance can make gifted children more aware of what their culture can offer.

Guidance can provide opportunities for gifted children to receive what they desire or request of cultural stimulation.

Guidance can ensure that gifted children are exposed to different and even contrasting cultural stimulation.

Guidance can emphasize that gifted children continue to strive toward self-actualization.

Guidance can develop gifted children's tolerance for, and interest in, divergent views.

Guidance can assist gifted children to attain high levels of creative functioning and achievement.

Guidance can arrange for systems of incentives and rewards that move from the extrinsic to the intrinsic, and endorse the shift toward intrinsic reward.

Enabling the gifted to develop and realize their creative potential is of paramount significance for guidance.

We have attempted to perceive the implications for guidance of developmental stage theory, growth for transformation theory, and historical and sociocultural perspectives. In reiterating observations made for the guidance of gifted children, the following ten suggestions are presented:

1. One major concern of guidance should be to provide continual *environmental stimulation* to facilitate escalation toward higher levels of creative functioning and self-actualization. Several ways used to facilitate superior adults can be adapted for gifted children and youth. These include the provision of various educational experiences, therapy, and sensitivity training.

2. When dysplasia occurs, guidance is needed to assist the gifted to *develop as completely as possible* (i.e., cognitively and affectively), and to effect *escalation* of all parts of the psyche beyond Gowan's Stage 5 through Stages 6, 7 and 8 to creativity and self-actualization.

3. Guidance of the gifted can take the form of counteracting measures, which include the arrangement of stimulating conditions and opportunities, the fostering of love that makes accessible the preconscious for creativity, the encouragement in the use of creative imagination, and the reduction of stress, to *alleviate discontinuity* in creative mental functioning.

4. The gifted can be assisted through their creative growth cycles, *moving from lower to higher* ones, by providing them with experiences and activities aimed at developing their creative thinking abilities and using metaphor, analogy, and imagery.

5. *Appropriate environmental stimulation* to facilitate the creative development of gifted children should include effective positive reinforcements (feedback) and information that allows for escalation to higher stages of creative functioning within the growth cycle (feedforward).

6. To counteract the adverse influences of formal education that may stunt the creative development of the gifted, guidance can be given to them to acquire the necessary *knowledge and skills for living without sacrificing their creativity*. This should be done in such a manner that the gifted learn in ways that lead to productivity and higher states of creative development.

7. Guidance can be given to the gifted to *emulate* historical and contemporary eminent creators and arrangements can be made, where feasible, for face-to-face interaction with these models.

8. Eminent men and women of talent, *materials,* and *equipment* can be made accessible to the gifted for the advancement of their creative development and talent expression.
9. The gifted can be guided to an awareness of the diversity and richness of *cultural offerings* that will stimulate them to creative striving and self-actualization.
10. The gifted can be assisted to attain the highest levels of *creative achievement* so that they may obtain both extrinsic and intrinsic rewards with an appropriate preference for the intrinsic.

GUIDANCE TO MASTER STRESS

Another function of guidance as it relates to gifted students is to identify the nature and function of stress and suggest approaches to *cope with stress,* not in a remedial but in a preventative sense. This observation is consistent with an earlier one on the positive thrust of guidance as it applies to the normal development of gifted individuals.

Stress interferes with personal development toward mental health, creativity, and self-actualization. Individuals are constantly bombarded with all kinds of stress from one moment to the next in their lives. They are put in the position of having to make adjustments and adaptations to stress to avoid inevitable disorientation and breakdown.

The Terman studies (e.g., Terman & Oden, 1947, 1959) on gifted children who grow up to mid-life have reiterated that the gifted are generally *mentally healthy* individuals. However, not all of them have remained so throughout their lives and, for these, early promise has not been fulfilled. Although one may attempt to find an explanation in specific events of their lives, there is a factor that these gifted individuals have in common—their inability to deal successfully with stress. One of the most significant responses to this problem holds considerable implications for guidance of the gifted. It is the idea that mental health involves *constructive* rather than adjustive responses to stress (Torrance, 1965a).

Assessing the various *concepts of mental health,* Torrance distinguishes between those related to the perceptions of society and those related to the perceptions of professional mental health workers. He draws on his research with the Imagination Story (Torrance, 1962a), an instrument that calls on children to write original stories when given divergent titles, such as "The Monkey That Flies," "The Lion That Does Not Roar," "The Man Who Cries," "The Doctor Who Became a Carpenter," and "The Rooster That Doesn't Crow."

Let us take, for instance, a couple of stories written in response to these divergent titles, which illustrate certain kinds of problems that creative individuals experience (Torrance, 1962a).

Story 1—"The Monkey That Flies." A story by a fifth-grade African-American boy from Georgia illustrates persistence in coping with failure.

Divergent Title: The Monkey That Flies

Once there was a monkey that was very sad. He was sad because he didn't know how to fly. He said to himself, "Why can other animals fly but we can't fly?" Then he began to climb up a tree; he ate some bananas and coconuts. The monkey jumped out of the tree and began to fly. He fell down on the ground. Then the monkey climbed the tree again and began to try to fly. Again he fell to the ground. Again he climbed up and finally began to fly. (p. 116)

Story 2—"The Rooster That Doesn't Crow." A story by a girl from St. Paul, Minnesota, illustrates repression of creative needs resulting in disabling neurotic symptoms.

Divergent Title: The Rooster That Doesn't Crow

Once there was a rooster. He was quite a one too. You see he was quite a curious rooster. One day he saw a farmer chewing tobacco and he wondered about it. Another day the farmer left some out. The rooster found a piece and ate it. Then he started to hiccup. From that day on when the sun comes up, he would not cock-a-doodle-doo. He would go "hiccup." He is not curious any more.

Torrance indicates that mental health as reflected in such stories requires conformity to behavioral norms as the alternative to destruction; brings relentless pressure for the well-rounded personality; emphasizes convergency because divergency is equated with mental illness and delinquency; and overemphasizes sex roles so that any deviation from appropriate masculinity and femininity is also associated with mental illness and delinquency.

From the findings of the stories, Torrance (1965a) constructs a picture of what a mentally healthy person in our society is like.

First he must conform to the behavioral norms of his society. He must be well rounded and must work hard to correct any irregularities in development. If some aspect of development has lagged, he must neglect all else and achieve the expected standard. If some function or skill has been developed to an unusually high level, he must deliberately neglect further development along this line or suppress it. Individuals whose behavior is "different" are usually labeled as mentally ill (crazy, wild, etc.) or delinquent (naughty, bad, etc.). Regardless of natural inclinations and talents, the mentally healthy person according to this dominant position must conform to his society's concepts of masculinity or femininity. (p. 9)

There have been many attempts by professionals to define mental health. They have varied from simplistic single-sentence definitions to comprehensive and multiple-criteria listings of the well-adjusted person. Of these definitions, M. Jahoda's (1958) approach appears to be highly relevent. She suggests that *appropriate adjustment toward mental health* involves the following:

Attitudes of an individual toward his or her own self (accessibility to consciousness, correctness, feeling about the self, and sense of identity)

Growth, development, or self-actualization (self-concept, motivational processes, and investment in living)

Integration (a balance of psychic forces in the individual, a unifying view of life, emphasis on the cognitive aspects of integration, and resistance to stress)

Autonomy (regulation of behavior from within and independent behavior)

Perception of reality (perception of need distortion and empathy [social sensitivity])

Environmental mastery (ability to love; adequacy in love, work, and play; adequacy in interpersonal relations; efficiency in meeting situational requirements; capacity for adaptation and adjustment; and efficiency in problem solving)

It is not so much a lack of agreement among professionals as to what constitutes mental health as it is the difficulty of expressing, in words, a multivariate and complex phenomenon. Some words identify units of the construct, other words classify and systematize these units into large categories, and yet other words omit detail in favor of a global construct.

Torrance (1965a) defines *mental health* as "the healthy, complete functioning of the mind" whose proper operation may suffer interference from many forces within individuals as well as from the external environment. He labels this interference *stress*. It is in the use of individual potentialities as resources to cope constructively with stress that offers guidance significant direction.

Behavior Under Stress

Drawing information from survival research, Torrance (1965a) identifies the *stressful physical conditions* that can lead to death (e.g., water or food deprivation, extreme heat or cold, sleep deprivation) and the *stressful psychological aspects of these conditions* (e.g., shock, mental confusion, inefficiency, apathy, suicide) as they affect healthy mental functioning. He adds *other stressful conditions* that bear no threat to life (e.g., interpersonal irritations, failure to achieve ambitions).

When these conditions are severe he observes that such behaviors as overcompensation, heroism, increased speed, efficiency, planning, and the use of higher levels of intellectual functioning to approach full potential, are called for, so that death or breakdown can be prevented. The function of mental health professionals is to *prevent the occurrence* of such breakdowns and *help* individuals in their lives, studies, and career aspirations.

Stress can be regarded as an interference with the normal and full functioning of mental abilities that assist individuals to cope with their problems. Torrance conceives behavior under stress as a process through which *specific stresses,* mediated by *duration, intensity,* and the *state of the organism,* elicit a variety of possible responses. Specific stresses stem from situations that involve person, family, learning, and environment generally. They may take the form of conflict, hostility, love, deprivation, disability, failure, and developmental changes, which may cause a variety of negative or positive behaviors (Figure 8.1).

Stress Duration and Intensity

When stress occurs and lasts for a *short period* of time, mastery of it is more likely to take place than if the duration is *prolonged.* Prolonged stress often leads to ineffective coping and eventual collapse, regardless of the ability level or emotional condition of the individual.

If *stress is mild,* improved performance, increased activity, learning, and so on, result. However, if *stress is intense,* deterioration of performance and eventual breakdown can be expected. Furthermore, *mild but prolonged stress* is even more damaging; more breakdowns stem from this than from brief intense stress.

It is important to know what the *process of adaptation* as it relates to normal functioning that suffers interference from stress is so that breakdowns can be prevented. The onset of stress causes *shock,* which temporarily adversely affects both intellectual performance and emotional control. This *arrest* is followed by rapid *overcompensation and maximum effort,* which restore proper intellectual performance and emotional control and, in turn, are followed by *recovery,* a return to continued normal functioning.

Should stress continue over a prolonged period, fatigue with decreasing mental efficiency and emotional control sets in. This ultimately leads to *collapse* and *breakdown* (Figure 8.2).

State of Person

Another mediating variable between stress and its behavioral consequences is the *state of a person* and the great variability that exists among

Figure 8.1 Typical Stresses Encountered and the Mediation of Their Effects

Stresses	Mediating Variables	Consequences
Conflictual hostile family conditions; broken home; crowded living conditions; poverty	Duration	Cheating, lying
Hostile and delinquent neighborhood; high-class, competitive neighborhood		Stuttering, nervousness
Deprivation of love in family and among peers, lack of friends, peer rejection		Excessive daydreaming
Failure in studies, athletics, friendships, dating	Intensity	Apathy, laziness, neurasthenia
Intense motivation or pressure to succeed, unfair or too stiff competition, no chance to succeed		Anxiety
Deficient basic skills for learning—reading, arithmetic, spelling	State of Organism	Withdrawal, timidity
Physical handicaps and developmental abnormalities	(ego strength, spontaneity, ability, skills, etc.)	Chronic fatigue
Excessive outside activities		Alcoholism, drug addiction
Uncertain or inconsistet discipline		Truancy, stealing, vandalism
Physiological growth processes and new requirements of maturation		Sexual promiscuity, homosexuality, rape
Unstable environment		Thoughts of suicide, suicide
		Homicide, destructiveness
		Hostility and defiance
		Overcompensation
		Heroism, all-out effort
		Increased speed and efficiency
		Planning and cooperation
		Mutual support and assistance
		Creativity

From *Constructive Behavior: Stress, Personality, and Mental Health* (p. 20) by E. Paul Torrance, Copyright © 1965 by Wadsworth Publishing Company, Inc. Reprinted by permission of the publisher.

Figure 8.2 Conditions of Stress and Their Consequences

Stress Condition	Consequence	Theoretical Curve
1. Performance under stress over time	Mastery	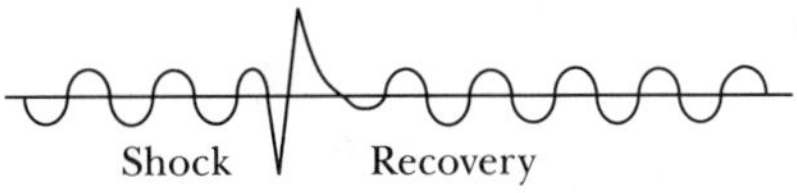 Shock Recovery Normal Overcompensation Continued adaptation
2. Performance under continued stress	Collapse	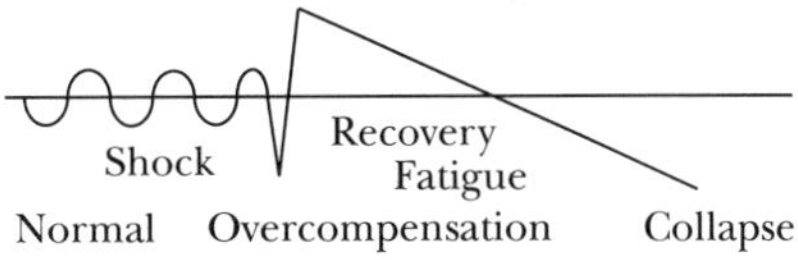 Shock Recovery Fatigue Normal Overcompensation Collapse
3. Performance under stress over time with prolonged shock of resistance and: (a) inadequate over-compensation	Collapse	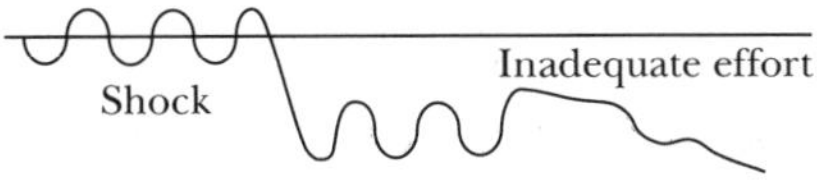 Shock Inadequate effort Normal Overcompensation Collapse
(b) inability to rise to the occasion	Collapse	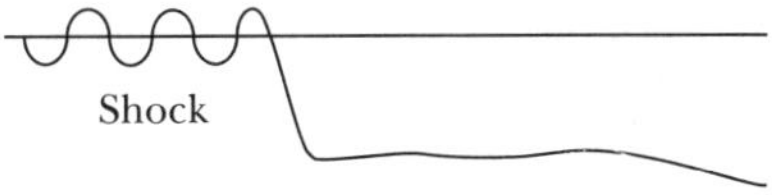 Shock Normal Inability to rise to occasion Collapse
4. Performance: (a) typical under increasingly intense stress	Collapse	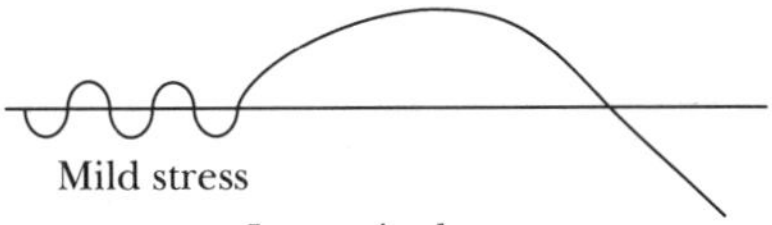 Mild stress No stress Increasingly intense stress Collapse
(b) unsuccessful increasingly intense stress	Collapse	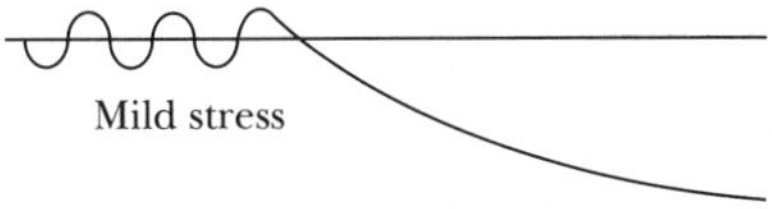 Mild stress No stress Increasingly intense stress Collapse

From *Constructive Behavior, Stress, Personality, and Mental Health* (p. 22-27) by E. Paul Torrance, Copyright © 1965 by Wadsworth Publishing Company, Inc. Reprinted by permission of the publisher.

individuals relative to this state. The extent to which an individual achieves *mastery* over a stressful situation depends on a great number of variables, including the presence or absence of coping skills, specific relevant ability, physical disabilities, and prior experience or training for dealing with the stress. The mediation of ego-strength has much to do with the slowing down, speeding up, or prevention of the stress adaptation process described earlier.

When *failure to cope* with a stressful situation occurs, it means that the stress is more than the individual can handle. Generally, when an individual is unable to adapt to stress it is because, to some degree, he or she is experiencing a loss of anchor in reality (i.e., contact with the environment) or a lack of structure. The disorientation that ensues causes further stress and makes necessary a successful adaptation to stress.

Included among a variety of factors that bring about *disorganization and disorientation* of an individual are the strangeness or instability of the situation, with demands for handling it in ways unfamiliar and non-habitual to the individual; threats to the individual's central value system; changes that occur too rapidly for efficient processing; or inadequate skills for coping with overwhelming requirements. For mastery of the stressful situation, the individual needs help in reorganizing or restructuring the situation in order to establish appropriate anchors in reality (Figure 8.2).

Gifted Students Experiencing Stress

Gifted students, like others, experience stress as well. An interesting account of how stress caused by *academic failure* affects the gifted and the process by which the *adaptation* is achieved is given by Torrance (1967a).

> Let us consider the gifted student who suddenly encounters academic failure. When the stress (failure in a school subject) is suddenly encountered, there is first shock and lack of adaptation. Perhaps there is resistance to accepting the reality or seriousness of the failure. The student may wonder if some mistake has been made, blame the teacher or some other external source, or reason that he "just slipped up" or that "the test was no good." In successful adaptation [Figure 8.2, 1], there will be rapid overcompensation, improved methods of study, increased energy in studying longer hours, etc. With recovery there will be a levelling off of performance and the restoration of emotional control; but if the teacher persistently refuses to recognize the improved performance and holds on to his original assessment of [the] student's ability and achievements, we can envision the consequences [Figure 8.2, 2]. The frequency of breakdowns among gifted students under such conditions is well known to anyone who has worked very long with gifted students.
>
> Let us say that our mythical gifted student, after the first shock and accep-

tance of the seriousness of his failure, puts forth a maximum effort [Figure 8.2, 3a]. At first he succeeds, but the course and the standards of the instructor become increasingly more difficult. He is pushed to use more expensive coping devices. He may increase his speed of reading and writing, obtain expert help, work with another student, or exercise greater ingenuity and creativity. If these expensive energies continue to be required by his academic program and there is no let up in the demands, some kind of breakdown will occur eventually. The result may be withdrawal from school, delinquency, thoughts of suicide or even suicide. He may react by cheating and deceit, excessive daydreaming, apathy, hostility and defiance, etc.

In another case, our gifted student may be unaccustomed to challenges that require "all out" performance. His attempt to rise to the occasion may be weak and inadequate and his collapse may come rapidly [Figure 8.2, 3b]. Some gifted students consistently fail because they never find anything they consider worth their best efforts. Others keep thinking that they can "get by" with less than their best efforts.

In still another case, our gifted student may fail altogether to recognize the seriousness of his failure. He makes no effort to overcompensate or "go all out" and immediate collapse follows. He simply waits until it is too late [Figure 8.2, 4a]. In another situation, he may be so surprised, shocked or hurt by the failure that he will panic, become apathetic, and is unable to take any constructive action [Figure 8.2, 4b]. Such behavior may be seen in withdrawals from school, serious misbehavior, and the like. (pp. 4–5)

We have just seen how a gifted student who experiences the stress of academic failure may respond to it in a number of different ways, which could result, under varying conditions, in mastery of stress or collapse or breakdown.

Other stressful conditions that lead to a variety of problems for the gifted (Gowan & Demos, 1964; Rothney & Koopman, 1957) include the following:

Numerous educational and occupational opportunities available to them and wise choices they have to make, occasionally before they are ready to make them

Unusual need that they develop specialized interests that go with certain professional occupations, even if their true interests lie elsewhere

Appraising and conceptualizing themselves at higher levels than their age merits

Early awareness of developmental tasks before they are physically ready to attempt them

Unusual pressures exerted on them by parents, teachers, and peers

Confusing experience over the dual norm group that leads to their inability to discriminate between situations applicable to all persons regardless of ability and situations that apply more closely to those who are gifted, for which different expectations may be held

Lack of educational challenge, especially from elementary school curriculum

Failure to find friends of the same age

Lack of occupational information

Lack of motivation

Impatience with routine learning and dull classrooms

Independence in thinking and judging

Resistance to conformity

Hypersensitivity and vulnerability to criticism

Desire to excel coupled with perfectionist tendencies

Passion for truth and desire for meanings beyond the obvious, which may lead to disillusionment and rebellion against "irrelevent" society

Uneven pattern of intellectual abilities

Physical and emotional handicaps

According to Torrance (1962a), *society applies coercive influences* on divergency and even on outstanding performance. Individuals who use creative talent often alienate themselves from friends. They are under tremendous pressure to be well rounded. There exists a misplaced emphasis on sex roles, with efforts to establish sex norms during early childhood that are reinforced throughout the education of these individuals. School may disallow or even retard individuals from learning on their own. There is a lack of awareness that creative individuals have the desire to attempt difficult and even dangerous tasks, seek to discover their potentialities, and realize their self-concepts creatively. People may also be unaware that creative individuals possess different values from the norm. Many often misinterpret the motivations of high creatives who cannot seem to stop working, and who create difficulties for themselves by deliberately trying to be different while searching for their uniqueness. High creatives even reject their society's demand that they surrender their individuality. They are, consequently, often in psychological isolation and estrangement from parents, teachers, and peers.

All these situations bristle with stress-inducing conditions that call for effective adaptive and adjustive behaviors if they are to be mastered. Maladaptive behavioral patterns can only lead to collapse and breakdown; these patterns are not only tied to the *intensity* and *duration* of stress but also to the *mediating* variable of individual differences and to *coping* reactions. The problems gifted individuals face arise from their creative needs in transaction with society and the external world, the consequences of which may not be entirely satisfying.

Problems may lead to the *repression of creative needs*. If repression is prolonged and adjustment maladaptive, neurosis or even psychosis may occur (Khatena, 1973b, 1978a).

> Repression of his creative needs may lead the highly creative child to become outwardly conforming, obedient and dependent, with damaging consequences to his concept of self. It may also lead to serious learning disabilities and behavioral problems. In preferring to learn by authority, he sacrifices his natural tendency to learn creatively by questioning, guessing, exploring and experimentation. As a result, he loses interest in and is resistant to learning. Development of awe for masterpieces and a spread of feelings of inadequacy from deficiency in one area of learning to other areas, where no deficiency exists, follows. Further, much of the aggressive behaviors in the classroom that the highly gifted child exhibits can be traced to his inability to use creative and scientific thinking strategies to overcome his tensions. These tensions often arise from his reactions to a school curriculum that is unchallenging, repetitive, reproductive and boring, before they become problems that result in his misbehavior.
>
> The more serious problem of prolonged enforced repression of the creative child's needs may lead to emotional problems and neurosis, and even psychosis (e.g., Gowan, 1955; Torrance, 1962a). Neurosis, as you know, is a condition generated by acute and prolonged anxiety states and can be very much the case of continued repression of creative needs especially in the context of conflict situations. Neurosis hinders rather than facilitates the functioning of the creative process, contrary to popular opinion. Kubie (1958), writing about this subject, suggests that many a creative man of the arts and sciences refuses therapy because he erroneously believes that his "creative zeal and spark" is dependent upon his neurosis; what is really essential is that the preconscious process functions freely to gather, assemble, compare and reshuffle ideas in the activity of creation.
>
> Torrance (1962a) writes of psychosis relative to maladjustment of the creative individual in a special sense. In psychosis, resulting from the blocking of creative energies, thinking is often paralyzed and the imagination functions in a way that cannot distinguish between reality and irreality. The creative individual who has his productivity blocked, may develop behavior traits similar to those of psychotics whose reaction to reality may be very much like the behavior of the paranoid personality in some respects, or his behavior might become withdrawn or schizophrenic. (1978a, pp. 89–90)

LEARNING TO MASTER STRESS

The thrust of guidance for the gifted in mastering stress should be toward *prevention* rather than cure. The many problems that gifted students face often arise from attempts to express their uniqueness. Society does not understand this, will not tolerate it, and even attempts to stifle it. Counselors must recognize this if they are to render effective service. They may begin by understanding the nature and function of giftedness and the special characteristics and needs of gifted individuals whom they will serve. It is important that they recognize conditions that are likely to thwart, obstruct, or prevent healthy development and expression of uniqueness, and provide appropriate counselor–counselee interactions.

Preventative guidance also requires that the counselor anticipate stress-inducing conditions. In this way, opportunity to develop coping skills can be given to gifted individuals to manage stress from its onset. Among the several approaches that can be taken to guide the gifted toward mastery of stress are the development of *interpersonal skills*, the use of *intellectual abilities*, and other useful *coping mechanisms*.

Developing Interpersonal Skills

Gifted individuals, in trying to be themselves and to realize their talents come into conflict with parents, teachers, peers, and the larger group, as we know. Other people feel threatened by the uniqueness of gifted individuals and, in one way or another, pressure the gifted to be like everyone else. In the counseling situation, the gifted need to understand their situation and the fact that, so long as they interact with others, they will have to cope with the pressure to conform. They will have to learn how to continue to be unique and individual without antagonizing others if they are to avoid difficult and even hostile conditions that threaten their development and actualization. Guidance, therefore, should help gifted children recognize their outstanding talents, which may be threatening to others, and to learn that one way of gaining acceptance is by using their talents to serve the larger group. In this way they can build what P. Pepkinsky (1960) has called a *credit rating*.

We are advised by Torrance (1962a) to help gifted children maintain characteristics essential to creativity while teaching them skills to avoid, or reduce to a tolerable level, social sanctions that may be leveled at them. As this advice pertains to elementary school education, he advises the following behaviors to serve as a useful *model* that guides gifted children to overcome the tendency to be obnoxious without sacrificing creativity.

> Help the gifted child maintain his assertiveness without being hostile and aggressive. He [the gifted child] must be aware of his superiors, peers and subordinates as persons. He may work alone but he must not be isolated, withdrawn or uncommunicative. In the classroom he must be sociable but not intimate. He must "know his place" without being timid, submissive, or ac-

quiescent and must speak "his mind" without being domineering. As he tries to gain a point, he can be subtle but not cunning or manipulative. In all relationships, he must be sincere, honest, purposeful, and diplomatic. In the intellectual area, he must learn to be broad without spreading himself too thin, deep without being "bookish" or "too scientific," and "sharp" without being overcritical. (p. 156)

Another important facet of this kind of guidance aims at preventing gifted children from experiencing *isolation* or *estrangement* from teachers and peers, or reducing these conditions should they exist. Gifted children have an intense need to communicate with others and sometimes may not be in a position to do so. The counselor may help them learn to tolerate some separateness or assist them in finding someone with whom they can communicate—perhaps another gifted child who has common interests.

Not enough emphasis is given in the counseling situation to gifted students' use of their many *intellectual abilities*. Usage of these abilities in dealing with others, as children grow older, make them more effective. With growing intellectual maturity, gifted individuals can more accurately perceive the attitudes, interests, and abilities of others and, thus, gain those interpersonal skills that will allow them to deal with others in more constructive ways. Just as people can become more skilled in debate with practice, gifted children, through experience, can become more skillful in their transactions with others. Counselors can arrange a variety of experiences to clarify the gifted childrens' relations with others, and increase their social competence.

Jacob L. Moreno's *sociodramatic* technique, which Torrance used as a problem-solving approach to encourage gifted children to learn in creative ways, can be used to advantage in counseling situations (Torrance, 1975b; Torrance & Myers, 1970). Problems that gifted children face may be presented and clarified and progress made toward finding a solution by means of role playing in dramatic situations.

Imagery in a sociodramatic situation may also be used to great advantage (Khatena, 1984). Take, for instance, Penelope's circumstances handled in a sociodramatic situation using imagery.

The leader presents the following problem to a sociodramatic group:

Penelope, who is 13 years old, wants to meet her girlfriends on Friday at a parking lot near a fast food restaurant. It is a hang-out for boys. Her mother objects, saying she fears her daughter will get involved with a group of undesirables, who probably drink and take drugs. In short, she fears for her daughter's safety. But Penelope argues with her that there is nothing to fear. The boys are her school mates, they are all right, and that she can take care of herself. Besides, she was only going to meet her girl friends. A heated scene follows, and Penelope goes to her room in a huff. Shortly thereafter, she returns and asks to visit her neighbor, Angela, three blocks down the street. Her mother allows her to do so, and Penelope goes to meet Angela, who convinces her to go to the car park. Penelope's mother finds out, another scene follows and Penelope is grounded for a week. She refuses to understand that her mother has her best interests at heart and deeply resents her for the unjust punishment. (p. 179)

Several exercises can be given to the sociodramatic group to help them understand and deal with this stressful problem. Let us take these four exercises in order to get a feel for the kind of activities experienced by the group (pp. 179–180).

Exercise 1: The leader presents the problem to the group and asks members to close their eyes, relax, and mentally explore the problem. The exercise then begins as follows:

Visualize Penelope, her mother and [her] friends, the parking lot with several boys standing or wandering near the restaurant.

Now image Penelope and try to picture what kind of person she is. How does she relate to her friends? How does she relate to her mother? Image Penelope and her mother talking about her intention to spend the evening out.

Open your eyes and talk about the situation. Let us hear about the different pictures you had in your mind of Penelope, her mother, friends and their relationships.

(Group members share their experiences and discuss them.)

Exercise 2: Shut your eyes again and image Penelope talking to her mother about meeting her friends in the parking lot.

What does her mother say? What is Penelope's response? Image Penelope countering the objections; her mother's firm refusal to allow her to go out. How does Penelope get around the problem? Image her convincing her mother and visiting Angela with her mother's permission. Visualize them going to the parking lot against the mother's wishes. Her mother finds out and punishes her—image this. Also image her resentment.

Open your eyes and describe the images that came to your mind and your feelings about them. Discuss the sequence of events and establish the conflict.

Exercise 3: In the next few minutes I want you image with whom you can identify. When you are ready let me know with whom you have identified: Penelope? her mother? Angela? (Pause) Are there others involved with whom you have identified? Let us try to act out this situation.

Exercise 4: We now have several who will take the roles of Penelope, the mother, Angela, and other roles you identified. Before we begin, sit back for the next few minutes and visualize yourself in a chosen role. When you are ready, describe your role in the event and the setting for it.

Once the action is set in motion creative thinking techniques like analogy and synthesis-destructuring-restructuring may be used. Furthermore, dramatic techniques such as soliloquy and double-role and role reversal techniques may be used to creatively attack stress-inducing situations with a view to finding behavioral solutions.

The outcome of these techniques may be discovery of the true causes of the problem as well as alternative behaviors that can be adopted to prevent or avert the problem. In these ways, factors that cause stress may be identified and become apparent to the gifted child, with the purpose of preparing him or her to anticipate antagonistic stress-inducing behaviors and circumscribe them, using alternative behaviors that may produce more tolerant and nurturing reactions from others. As these interpersonal skills are acquired, gifted individuals are more likely to experience little or no stress; if stress occurs they will be knowledgeable enough to master it and maintain normal and healthy mental functioning. In developing interpersonal skills, gifted individuals understand that they possess intellectual resources. Knowing how to use these resources will help them to cope with stressful problems.

Using the Intellect

As children grow older and develop increasing command of their *intellectual abilities*, they learn to substitute intellectual approaches for the more primitive strategies they used to cope with emergency situations. Torrance (1965a) emphasizes the importance of using intellectual resources to create *constructive behavior* when dealing with *stress*. He examines these resources in terms of the mental operations of the Structure of Intellect, namely, *cognition, memory, convergent thinking, divergent thinking,* and *evaluation*. According to Torrance, the first three entail the least expenditure of energy while the last two require the most. This leads him to suggest that cognition, memory, and convergent thinking, if first called into play, often allow some energy to be held in reserve, making possible productive and evaluative mental operations to handle stress when necessary.

However, it is quite appropriate to consider these five mental operations working together in a problem-solving format handling stressful situations (Guilford, 1967), although each mental operation is presented as handling stress separately. Furthermore, it should be noted that, consistent with the Structure of Intellect model, the *content* and *product* dimensions are also involved in any stress-handling activity.

The source of stress lies in the perceived mismatch created by information coming from the physical and sociocultural environment as it interacts with the individual who is in the act of processing it (Figure 3.1).

If guidance is to be useful in mastering stress and attaining good mental health, intervention by a counselor is necessary (Figure 3.1).

Let us consider the use of each of the five mental operations in turn to see the extent to which the intellect can be used to master stress, remembering that problem solving may occur each step of the way.

Cognition

Cognition can assist a person in recognizing when a situation becomes serious enough to require some adaptive action to avert disaster before it is too late. Often, many of us experience stress in a situation because we are not familiar with it. Knowing something about a situation before actually experiencing it helps reduce anxiety and permits more efficient functioning.

Related to this recognition is the identification of the components of a problem or its structure, allowing an individual to know the situation as well as possible for what it is. In this way, not only does the situation become familiar, but the course of action to be taken also becomes apparent. Knowing the causes and anticipating the consequences of certain actions will more than likely lead to successful adaptation to situations. (Remembering the nature and structure of past experiences and the plans of action devised to handle them, and evaluating these actions and their consequences, come into play as well.)

Cognition can also be used to ensure that one thinks well of oneself and expects to succeed. Furthermore, it allows for the understanding of feedback information relative to performance under stress so that behavior can be rapidly adapted to improve the chances of success. Having the proper information provides the essential basis for problem-solving behaviors and appropriate decision making.

As indicated, cognition calls for the expenditure of less energy than some of the other functions. Therefore, understanding the situation and knowing what to do allow persons to handle a large number of stressful situations. Energy thus conserved can be used to solve problems needing productive and evaluative thinking, enabling the individual to recover more quickly from the shock of stress. Thus, return to normal functioning can be effected. A fuller awareness of self and the environment with attendant excitement and joy will, in turn, increase mental health.

Memory

Memory abilities are very important in relation to stress. These abilities allow a person to recall experiences that were stressful and examine how the stress was handled, whether the strategies used succeeded or failed, what modifications were made in the process of successful adaptation, and how the stress was eventually mastered. Thus, memory of previous stresses and how they were handled provides a frame of reference for handling current stressful situations.

Implied in this process is the use of evaluative thinking abilities. Stress experiences are appraised to determine the extent to which previous successes in dealing with them can pave the way for decisions for coping with new stress.

Stress may also be related to lapses in memory. Such lapses may not only give rise to discomfort but also hinder effective coping in emergency situations. It is important, then, to arrange conditions that will facilitate appropriate storage for retrieval.

Memory of oneself, of one's liabilities and assets, of the use of personal resources to cope successfully with stressful situations, and so on, is important because it reminds individuals that they are not without means to cope with emergencies.

Remembering one's acquired knowledge and skills and their availability for use can assist an individual when coping behaviors are required.

Remembering how one interacted with others is also important; it should not only help one cope with stress but also circumvent stress by providing examples of appropriate interpersonal behaviors.

Furthermore, memory provides an individual with a frame of reference to structure or prestructure situations as the need arises for successful adaptation.

Convergent Thinking

Convergent thinking is considered important in coping with life's stresses as well. In general, it requires less of an expenditure of energy than other thinking operations. It is usually the easiest and quickest way of coming up with answers.

For persons who have limited abilities, it is the most efficient method on which to rely to plan actions that are in line with the thoughts of others. Convergent thinking, then, can be used by individuals to cope with stress in ways that conform with the thinking of the group. In this way, additional stress is less likely to occur.

Sometimes, however, trying to arrive at the one best or common solution is not without difficulty and can lead to an accumulation of stress that may become overwhelming. Nonetheless, coming up with the same answers as others brings with it social approval, satisfaction of certain needs, and rewards. It allows convergent thinkers a rapport with others and with their environment. By establishing this rapport, tension is reduced for convergent thinkers and the groups to which they belong.

Divergent Thinking

The role of divergent thinking in coping with stress involves developing the ability to deal with the excessive rate of change in our world. We cannot rely on a single solution to a problem; it may be obsolete as soon as it is identified. Rather, we must rely on the capacity to produce many alternative solutions in keeping up with change.

If tried solutions to a problem prove to be unsuccessful repeatedly, frustration can be avoided by using divergent thinking to produce fresh approaches and strategies for handling the problem.

Fatigue, which sometimes sets in during a coping situation, can be removed by divergent thinking, because some wild, exciting idea, with the promise of fresh possibilities, can revitalize and energize a person to increase his or her efforts toward successful adaptation.

A reserve of many ideas and possible solutions to a problem increases the prospects for making better decisions; when better decisions are made the confidence that one will successfully overcome the problem also increases.

In addition, generating a number of possible alternative solutions prepares a person to anticipate the many possible outcomes that are less likely to be stressful. Using the many solutions approach can increase one's hopes for successful coping.

Divergent thinking frees the individual in terms of his or her own uniqueness. It allows the individual to be more comfortable with her- or himself, and to be a more authentic person with consequent benefits in relations with others and the world.

Evaluative Thinking

Evaluative thinking requires the most expense of energy. Its role in coping with stress is an important one.

It is essential for a person to recognize the seriousness of a situation. This realization, however, not only calls for the operation of cognition and memory but also for an evaluation of the situation so that a decision can be made for adaptive action. Evaluation entails maintaining contact with the environment and structuring the situation to anticipate the consequences of action. These steps are taken to prevent shock.

In appraising a situation while preparing to make a decision, individuals learn to recognize and accept their limitations. In this way, they can reduce the number and seriousness of the errors that become a part of their plans to cope with the situation effectively.

Biases—unconscious motivations—that interfere with evaluation abilities in the making of decisions can also be corrected so that coping with stress can be done more successfully. By the process of evaluation, a mass of data can be given simple structure and proper emphasis for easier use in coping with stress in a situation. Furthermore, evaluation is important for the testing of the reality and efficacy of the divergent thinking used in producing solutions to problems.

Other Coping Mechanisms

Torrance (1965a) also offers several useful coping mechanisms or strategies that he has drawn from approaches people have used to cope with life. These mechanisms, used to cope with stressful situations, involve *risking or avoiding, mastering or failing, overloading or unloading, denying need or making peace,* and *encouraging the continued fight.* These strategies when used with gifted children can be expected to aid them develop more effective ways of dealing with such common stresses as (a) curricular and career choices; (b) realistic self-concept development; (c) pressures exerted by peer group, school, and society; and (d) changing patterns of nonachievement and delinquency.

Risking or Avoiding

All individuals at one time or another find themselves in the position of having to make decisions. In school, students have to make decisions about educational or vocational choices. If gifted, they have many more alternatives from which to choose.

Decisions also have to be made on student's developmental tasks as well as their relations with others. The more unfamiliar the situation, the greater the hesitancy to make decisions. Often, an appeal for help is made to the counselor, teacher, or parent.

The person providing counsel must resist the temptation to make the decision for the student. Instead, the cause of the student's hesitancy needs to be found. The student can then be assisted in obtaining adequate information about the problem. Familiarity with the situation is more likely to lead the student to attempt or risk making a decision.

We do know that the highly gifted individual is often a risk taker. Yet, there may be times when a situation may so overwhelm the student that some reassurance needs to be given so that there is some reduction in the risk before a decision is made.

The student may test a tentative decision before going on to make a final decision. This will give him or her a second chance to make changes that will alter the course of action before it ends in failure. The technique of limited commitment (Cooper, 1961) may be tried when an action can be divided in such a way that only limited resources need be committed to the action until the student can make up his or her mind. Or, the situation can be simulated on a small scale to try out an action plan before the plan is adopted for implementation.

Gifted students should be encouraged to take risks when coping with the problems that face them, even if, in some instances, risk taking may lead to failure. Some preparation in risk taking should keep to a minimum the expense of wasted resources.

If it is evident that the student is avoiding making a decision, finding out the cause of insecurity is the proper corrective action. If the cause is deep rooted psychologically, it may be beyond the teacher's or parent's ability to help.

One approach that may be taken is to let students avoid making decisions about where they stand on issues until they are ready to make them. This may help them determine the extent to which they can use their judgment. In addition, students should be well informed about the decisions they have to make and encouraged, even pressed, to make preliminary or trial decisions. The success of their trial decisions may persuade them to move farther along in the decision-making process.

Counselors can assist gifted individuals in learning the strategies of risking or avoiding making decisions. In addition, counselors can show the connections between conduct and consequence; they can give dramatic examples and offer criticism and encouragement to help individuals define the limits of a situation; or they may define the limits for them (Redl & Wattenburg, 1959). In addition, counselors can help students to cultivate the habit of thinking of as many causes and consequences of a person's behavior as possible (Torrance, 1965a).

Mastering or Failing

Many individuals are unwilling to take risks or are reluctant to make changes in their lives because they are afraid of the unknown. Learning and occupational choices may also be inhibited by this fear. Highly gifted students face a wide array of choices, which can sometimes overwhelm them and result in indecisiveness.

The counseling situation can help to alleviate this problem in a number of ways. Students may be helped to understand the situation that faces them. Where possible, some actual preliminary experiences can be planned for them. When a choice of occupations is involved, for example, arrangements can be made for some on-the-job experiences at several locations. Such learning experiences should be preceded by some preparation; the students should be informed about what to expect in job-related situations.

Role playing can be a very valuable technique in making the unknown familiar. It can be used in place of actual experience or as complement to it. Structuring and restructuring an experience are also extremely valuable methods that assist students in obtaining as much information as needed for a new or forthcoming experience.

By using these methods, students can learn what the specifics of a given situation are, enabling them to judge whether their academic, personal, and special talent resources meet them. If they cannot meet these requirements, they can assess what else needs to be done to develop the necessary resources to master the situation.

If a situation is too big or difficult to handle, some restructuring may be needed; students may require assistance to understand the situation. They can turn to their peer groups for support and encouragement so that appropriate decision making can follow.

In the event of failure to cope with the situation, the counselor would do well to help students recognize what went wrong so that, where possible, they can correct their errors. If students do not have the skills to do so, the counselor will need to help them develop them.

It is important that students learn the virtue of admitting mistakes. Counseling can help them do this more easily; by learning to make such admissions, students will find themselves in a learning set that will reduce the chances of further errors and prepare them for fresh solution finding and appropriate verification. Such an approach will prevent students from collapsing under the stress of failure; help them profit by their mistakes; and prepare them for renewed attempts to cope, with greater probability of success and mastery.

Overloading or Unloading

Overloading is caused by an accumulation of stress that becomes burdensome to individuals. Release must be found for this stress before individuals can give their attention to learning and career goals or be able to recognize the seriousness of a situation.

The process by which such release can occur has been described as unloading, relieving oneself of tensions. The counseling situation affords individuals the opportunity to unload their pent-up feelings. Just the opportunity to gripe about things or talk things over will free individuals and help them clarify their position and see the stress for what it really is. Then, they can begin to make a more accurate appraisal of their needs and decide on a course of action that should lead to achievement of their goals.

Structuring and restructuring the situation applies here as well. Once unloading has taken place, individuals are better able to handle their situations. The counselor can then give them the guidance necessary to create a structure that will facilitate effective decision making.

The problem of overloading is often related to the availability of time and its economical use in terms of the way activities are organized. Unloading can be accomplished by taking a task perceived to be much bigger than it really is because of the limited time available for its accomplishment and breaking it down in terms of the content of the task and the time available to handle it into smaller and more manageable units. A plan of how best to handle each unit in turn until the task is completed is then devised.

The counselor can give valuable guidance in this respect to students who are overwhelmed by the magnitude of preparing for an important final examination, for example. By reducing anxiety, the counselor will make it possible for students to attack the problem successfully. Some practice in the use of these techniques should help students prevent the occurrence of future overloading.

Denying Need or Making Peace

Conflicts between the needs of individuals and the demands of situations (e.g., frustration, fatigue, hostility) interfere with the effective functioning of evaluative thinking abilities and result in bad judgments. Hence, the counseling situation should assist the gifted student in resolving these conflicts before encouraging them to make better decisions.

The aids that Torrance (1965a) suggests to resolve these conflicts involve counteracting the threats in some way. Threats can be counteracted by using objective information, allowing time to pass so that the odds may change, enduring and not surrendering, recognizing that the problem may need more mental effort or expensive energies, and practicing strategic withdrawal.

Decisions that involve others must also be accepted by them. Their acceptance can be more easily won if the decisions are congruent with their interests, intentions, and goals.

Encouraging the Continued Fight

A valuable aid in coping with a problem that begins to become too much for an individual is the encouragement and support of a group of which the individual is a member to persevere and not give up the fight. The counselor's awareness of this powerful source of coping energies is important, because arrangements to create this climate can be made in the counseling situation.

Occasionally, students need to be aroused or spurred to greater effort by being countershocked out of their apathetic, paralyzed, or surrendered state. They are then able to learn, with counselor assistance and support, how best to make full and better use of their personal resources (e.g., religion, values, sense of humor, acceptance of support from others).

The use of expensive mental energies like divergent thinking or evaluation, which over a long period will lead to breakdown, must be recognized by the counselor. However, to continue the fight, the use of expensive mental energies may be necessary and, for a time, its value in helping students to overcome their predicament cannot be emphasized more. In addition to the use of expensive mental energies, students may be counseled to keep busy and plan activities for continued stimulation, because such activities improve their chances to continue the fight with every possibility of eventual success.

COUNSELING ROLES

We have approached guidance of the gifted from two theoretical positions. One relates to creative development, and the other relates to stress management. We have also touched on personal, academic, and career counseling as means to cope with developmental changes and stress. This section will look at academic guidance of the gifted student more closely, and indicate what applications this approach may have for career guidance of the adolescent student.

So far, guidance has been discussed in terms of the counseling situation. Although we have referred to *counselors* as the ones giving guidance, *teachers* and *parents* should also be thought of as having important roles in the counseling situation. There are some areas of counseling that can best be handled by teachers. These include not only the educational but also career and personal aspects of guidance. There are other areas of counseling that parents can handle best, such as problems of very young children and some types of personal problems.

Ideally, a counselor should be available to children in both elementary and secondary schools and continuity of counseling should be the goal. However, this does not happen in most educational situations. That is why it is so important that counselors, teachers, and parents work closely together to complement one another so that guidance works at an optimal level (Landrum, 1987; Zaffran, 1978). Hence, it seems more appropriate to emphasize counseling as being determined by *situation* rather than *role*.

The counselor must be thought of as someone who provides service to students and to those who work with students, for example, parents, teachers, and administrators. While counselors *give counsel* to student clients, they *act as consultants* to parent, teacher, and administrator clients (Zaffron, 1978).

As for counseling gifted students, counselors concern themselves with education (e.g., study skills, reading difficulties, overtesting, and examination preparation), career (e.g., multipotentiality, familial-social-gender expectations), and personal needs and problems. As consultants, counselors give expert advice on personal, educational, organizational, orientational, and attitudinal matters, thus paving the way for collaborative efforts in guiding the gifted.

An interesting model for counseling parents of gifted students was proposed by David F. Dettmann and Nicholas Colangelo (1980). It consists of three approaches which, while not mutually exclusive, are primarily different in focus. The three approaches are *parent-centered, school-centered,* and *partnership* (Figure 8.3).

The *parent-centered* approach relies almost exclusively on parent moti-

Figure 8.3 Three Approaches Counselors Can Take in Working with Parents of Gifted

Counselor

Knowledge of specific needs of gifted
Knowlege of specific needs of parents of gifted

Parent-Centered Approach

Assumptions

- Parents are responsible for intellectual & affective development of child
- Home environment is most important to development of gifted
- Parents should seek outside experts or provide for enrichment activities if they feel child needs them

Role of Counselor

- Essentially provide information and advice as to what parents can do
- Encourage parents to actively seek suitable experiences for child

Role of Parents

- Very active in providing for their child
- Role is as active as financial sources and parent interest will allow

School-Centered Approach

Assumptions

- School is responsible for intellectual & affective development of child
- School environment is most important to development of gifted
- School should establish appropriate gifted programs

Role of Counselor

- Expert in providing for needs of gifted
- Help parents see that needs of gifted can be best met through experts and school programs

Role of Parents

- Passive participants
- Not seen as a teacher for their children
- Role of parents essentially confined to parent/school organizations, etc.

Partnership Approach

Assumptions

- Counselors have expertise that can be beneficial to parents of gifted
- Parents of gifted have knowledge and expertise that the counselor & school need to understand child
- Parents are partners with educators in meeting educational and affective needs of gifted
- Parents, with help of counselor, can be actively involved in the learning process of their child

Roles of Counselor and Parent

- Counselors and parents work as a team
- Counselors provide information to parents and elicit information about child
- Parents and counselor make joint decisions on best direction to meet educational needs of gifted

From "A Functional Model For Counseling Parents of Gifted Students" by D.F. Dettmann and N. Colangelo, 1980, *Gifted Child Quarterly*, 24(4) p. 160. Copyright © 1985 by Gifted Child Quarterly. Reprinted by permission.

vation and resources. Central to the approach is the parent role in developing the intellectual and affective components of their gifted children.

The *school-centered* approach provides long-term ongoing educational programs for many gifted students—something the parents, dealing with one or two of their own children, cannot do. Other trained experts, such as a psychologist or counselor, can be called on to give assistance. But the school-centered approach unilaterally sets priorities and may not always have the resources to adequately provide for the gifted. In addition, parents are not often involved by teachers and counselors in making educational decisions, which is unfortunate, for parents, by providing extensive information about their children, can make the efforts of a teacher and counselor more effective.

The *partnership* approach is the best, for it uses home and school resources, actively involving parents and counselors in facilitating the education of gifted students and making learning a continuous process. There is no doubt that all parties benefit by the collaboration.

Academic Guidance

Some years ago, Ruth Strang (1960) differentiated the guidance of gifted children as it applied to *three school-age levels,* namely, preschool, elementary school, and secondary school.

At the *preschool* level, it is the parent who is primarily responsible for giving guidance. The areas of help needed by preschoolers relate to goals toward character formation and personality development. They include recognition of, and respect for, the rights and feelings of others; the ability to make, carry out, and accept the consequences of decisions; and satisfaction in success and the willingness to try again in the event of failure and disappointment.

Guidance of *elementary school* children becomes the responsibility of teachers as well as parents. In general, teachers take an active part in the development of the total child with special emphasis on intellect, whereas parents continue with the guidance that has shaped the child since birth, leaning more and more on teachers for the academic guidance of their children.

For the most part, guidance in the elementary school is indirect, being generally related to children's ongoing activities. In a nutshell, teachers guide as they teach. They give sensitive and continuous developmental guidance. Such guidance aims at fostering the child's "ever increasing self-understanding—understanding of what he can do well, what he might learn to do, what his limitations are, and the kind of person he is becoming" (Strang, 1960, p. 144). That is to say, teachers assume more responsibility for what the child is, does, and becomes. In addition, teachers have the responsibility of stimulating and satisfying the intellectual curiosity of gifted children, promoting academic learning, and creating a favorable learning environment that will maximize the realization of their students' talents.

Milton J. Gold (1965) suggests that it is not only in the early years of children's schooling, but also throughout their school life that an interest in academic activities for their own sake should be fostered. At the same time, an appreciation for the demands of the world requiring advanced scholastic achievement for top-level jobs should be developed. According to M. J. Gold (1965), the gifted elementary student should be given the opportunity

> to try his wings with more advanced mathematics, science, art media, musical performance and appreciation, literature, creative writing, dramatics, social sciences and industrial arts. Laboratories, shops, and studios where the youngster can work under minimal supervision provide excellent settings for such exploration. Foreign language laboratories and programmed materials may also be employed by gifted students for independent self-discovery. (p. 368)

Many (Durr, 1964; Strang, 1960; Torrance, 1962a) have indicated that where counselors are available in *elementary schools*, they should help teachers understand their pupils so that they may guide the students they teach; assist in the modification of classroom procedures, where necessary, to meet the special needs of gifted students; advise both parents and other teachers about the children's exceptionality and make them aware of special opportunities and programs available to enhance their children's development and talent; act as patron and supporter of the creatively gifted; and work with the principal, administration, and committees to make conditions in school more conducive to the development of gifted children.

At the *secondary school* level, guidance generally rests with the counselor, although the teacher can, and sometimes does, assist the adolescent. Parents can also play an active role to complement the work of both counselor and teacher.

Academic guidance for the gifted, at this juncture of schooling, pivots on adequate and appropriate preparation for advanced work that will facilitate college studies. Furthermore, it affords the opportunity to identify the students' special talents and make arrangements for the suitable development of these preferences to the accelerated levels that gifted students are capable of achieving (e.g., mathematics, science, foreign languages, and art).

Such guidance also makes available and accessible information about special programs and projects designed for gifted students. These include the Study of Mathematically Precocious Youth at the Johns Hopkins

University in Baltimore, Maryland; the Learning Lodge of the Talcott Mountain Science Center in Avon, Connecticut; the Program for the Academically and Creatively Talented administered by the Anchorage School District in Alaska; the Quest for Advanced Intellectual Development housed in Hanover School of Bethlehem in Pennsylvania; and the Governor's Honors Program run by the states of Georgia and North Carolina, among others.

The fact that gifted students have a variety of interests and strengths makes choosing a school curriculum quite difficult. Counselors have the special task of helping gifted students focus on their selection of areas of study so that these areas contribute to the distinctive development of their intellectual assets and they achieve academic excellence and actualization.

The counselor ought to be able to *communicate* effectively with parents, teachers, and school administrators about their precocious students who require special support, attention, and acceleration, and be persuasive enough in doing so to assist them in fulfilling their students' needs.

It may be possible for enterprising and dynamic counselors to initiate *curricula changes* that will provide the optimum intellectual stimulation to the gifted or, when this cannot be done within the school, to arrange for similar exposure to relevant subject matter by using the resources of a neighboring university or the larger community.

It would be of immense value to have qualified counselors who are flexible with gifted students; counselors should not be surprised to find that many gifted students do change their minds about what they want to do, which necessitates a review of goals and a replanning of students' directions.

Counselors may also be faced with the need to guide gifted students to choose study areas that will prepare them for the many *alternative* means of higher education because such students have been known to change courses several times in college or to revise their study plans at the point of college entry.

In their discussion of *intellectual adjustment*, Gowan and Demos (1964) advise counselors to bear in mind that *continuous guidance* of youth is necessary at all stages. Furthermore, they suggest that counselors can foster an aura of expectancy about going to college (as if everyone needs it and each one will receive a scholarship).

They point to the value of the subject teacher as having a *predisposing relationship* (Brandwein, 1955) with the gifted student, a relationship within which a general willingness to spend time and show pains exist; motivation to succeed in the curriculum is planned and reinforced through a system of rewards; and failure can be faced and authority questioned.

To these conditions, Gowan and Demos add the need to provide gifted youth with the opportunity to thrash out, in senior seminars, some basic questions regarding problems and fears that beset everyone, themselves included. This arrangement is expected to allow gifted students to experience intellectual adjustment in a give-and-take situation. Such experience is aimed at reassuring students, providing them with some emotional experience and the opportunity to be involved in a verbal exchange while under some tension beyond that of a routine classroom experience.

Furthermore, the plight of *very upwardly mobile youth from low socioeconomic backgrounds* should receive the counselor's attention. It will be helpful to listen to the problems of young, perhaps cynical, persons who are uncertain about the problems that lie ahead and ambivalent about the environment that they are leaving and offer some explanations. In addition, it will be helpful to expose them, as part of a group, to activities (e.g., cultural, social, or work related events) which they may soon be experiencing. These students may be shown information about scholarship possibilities, other financial resources, or part-time jobs, and assisted in applying for them.

Where *parental rejection* exists, the counselor needs to find alternative adult models. If the counselor is not the model, then, it could be other professional men or women of breadth and culture. Gowan and Demos also emphasize the need for such students to have a *patron,* a parentlike person who gives without expectation of return. Students will find in such patrons or mentors examples of the ability to help and nurture others worthy of emulation.

Career Guidance

Career guidance, until very recently, went under the heading of vocational guidance. It is, in the main, the concern of the secondary school, although sometimes it is offered in the elementary school years. Career guidance, in close association with educational guidance, emphasizes the creation of conditions in the school setting within which gifted students can be assisted to recognize their abilities and potential and see possibilities for use and realization of these talents. On the one hand, guidance may show the way to *suitable occupations* that often require special training. On the other hand, guidance may assist in the *planning of a program of studies* that leads to a college education. Such guidance may postpone definite career choices to the sophomore or junior years in college, especially of the intellectually gifted.

Many academically gifted students are often not ready to select a career while in secondary school (M. J. Gold, 1965) because career choices for them are complicated by numerous *alternatives* to be selected. *Indecision* must not be regarded as weakness. Gifted students must not be pressured to select a career just because others are doing so at the time. In this respect, they may need counselor assurance that delay in making a choice is quite all right. Intellectually able students may need to be made aware that such indecision should not preclude their selection of a college education. In fact, they should be guided and encouraged to consider advancing their education in college, where, during the first two years, they can select a curriculum that is a part of the general studies requirement. Thus, there is little or no loss to their academic or professional training when more highly specialized areas of study are required in preparation for their chosen career.

Furthermore, the counselor can advise students on the *selection of a college* relative to talent, interest, availability of scholarships, and related opportunities. They can also provide students with information, for instance, on college admission academic requirements and appropriate times for admission and enrollment.

According to Gowan and Demos, *summer jobs* or *experiences* are of value to gifted students. These activities help students understand what it is they want to do. The counselor can use students' experiences as clues for appropriate guidance. There is something to be said for *growing into a career choice.* Although this can be frustrating to all concerned, it is better that gifted youth know themselves and to what they aspire before plunging into a career that can lead to a dead end, with little room for growth and eventual self-realization. Proper *matching of aptitudes and interests* is important to effective career guidance of able youth.

> Where aptitudes and interest are both high in an area, the counselor could point this out. Where interests are strong and aptitudes weak, he may warn against it; and this may be a useful form of elimination. Where aptitudes are strong and interest weak, he had better keep silent, for fear of prejudicing the client against it. Finally, where both aptitudes and interests are weak, he can generally get the youth to agree that this area is out at once. (Gowan & Demos, 1964, p. 261)

Curriculum guidelines on *career education* for the gifted and talented are presented in several papers that emerged as results of a federally funded project (Hoyt & Hebeler, 1974). In dealing with issues of career education, the writers recognize the *multifaceted nature of giftedness.* They place more emphasis on priming individuals for the world of work (for which individuals should be primed) than on the needs of growing individuals to make career choices. Although some attention is given to individual students (e.g., characteristics, identification, career needs), the orientation of the work is toward public education and the community, whose responsibility it is to provide job information and to cultivate work values for incorporation in the individuals' personal value systems (Hoyt, Evans, Mackin & Mangum, 1974).

> Career education is the total effort of public education and the community to help all individuals become familiar with the values of work-oriented society, to integrate those values into their personal value system, and to implement those values into their lives in such a way that work becomes possible, meaningful, and satisfying to each individual. (p. 15)

Special concerns about career development of the gifted have focused attention on issues pertaining to social expectations; school and parental pressure; adult role models; social isolation; multipotentiality; availability and exploration of many career options relative to intellectual capacity; and investment of self, money, and time (Fredrickson, 1979; Herr & Watanabe, 1979; Jepsen, 1979; Sanborn, 1979). Career development is a lifelong process involving one or more of these factors at one time or another.

Counselors, in assisting gifted students to make career decisions, need to take a *multipotential approach,* according to Ronald H. Fredrickson (1979). This approach consists of five sequential phases: readiness, awareness, exploration, reality testing, and confirmation.

> *Readiness* is the first stage in career decision making. It assumes that to make and implement choices the individual must have reached a stage of emotional maturity that allows him or her to assume responsibility for the career decision.
>
> *Awareness* is the next stage in career decision making. It assumes that the individual has developed self-awareness and awareness of the work world, with the latter serving to motivate and captivate the individual's interest in acquiring appropriate attitudes and skills needed for the development of a meaningful career.
>
> *Exploration* involves a systematic plan of inquiry that requires extensive review and examination of alternative occupations.
>
> *Reality-testing* relates to finalizing occupational choice on the basis of examining the risks, resources, and personal drive involved; it also involves simulated or even real job experience.
>
> *Confirmation* is the final stage that leads to the making of a career decision; the decision followed up by appropriate preparation for the acquisition of career-related knowledge and skills.

To effectively achieve the *making and implementing* of career decisions, it is essential that the counselor involves parents and teachers. As it involves the gifted student, the counselor will have to tailor counseling to the student's needs, providing *individualized counseling.* Although there are differences in opinion about *group counseling,* there is a place for it, especially as a way of having gifted students share their feelings and perceptions about their development, counteracting their feelings of social isolation and loneliness (Zaffrann & Colangelo, 1977). The end result of career selection, in this counseling approach, will not only meet the needs of the individual but also the expectations of society.

Counseling Intervention Strategies

In presenting *guidelines* for implementing a *guidance or counseling program* for gifted and talented students, Mary S. Landrum (1987) brings to our notice many available counseling strategies that can be used to serve the uniquely specific needs and problems of the gifted. These strategies include the use of humor, learning styles, bibliotherapy, group dynamics, observation, parental contact, interviewing, group discussions, values clarification, creative dramatics, puppetry, and sociodrama.

Landrum also suggests other counseling strategies that have been used to help gifted students found to be most effective in either preventing difficulties or resolving problems and groups them according to personal-social, academic, and career or vocational goals. Examples of these strategies include individual and group conferences, teacher-assisted classroom guidance activities, cooperative efforts of school professionals, location of special referral services, provision of values clarification experiences, and coordination of the total guidance program.

CAREER COUNSELING MODELS

Concern for providing the best career counseling for gifted students has produced a variety of *career guidance models* (e.g., Ginsberg, 1951; Walz, Smith, & Benjamin, 1974). This concern has found expression in two more recent models. The first, the Guidance Institute for Talented Students or GIFTS, was developed at the University of Wisconsin (Madison) Guidance Laboratory. This model approaches guidance from a holistic developmental-motivational position (Perrone, Karshner, & Male, 1979). The second model, developed by Torrance (1979b) of the University of Georgia, is based on group dynamics and uses *sociodrama* in career education.

A Holistic Developmental Model

The *GIFTS career model* (Perrone, Karshner & Male, 1979) provides a theoretical rationale for the career development of gifted students that aims at making them understand different career patterns. It draws upon Eriksonian *developmental stage theory* and Maslowian *need-motivation*

Table 8.1 Maslow-Erikson Theoretical Constructs

Gifts Career Development Model	Security/ Safety	Social Acceptance/ Love	Self-Esteem/ Achievement	Self-Actualized
Self-awareness and under-standing	Trust of self to mistrust of self	Self-accep-tance to rejection of self	Competent to incom-petent	Integrated to compart-mentalized
Social aware-ness and understanding	Trust of others to mistrust of others	Accepted by others to rejected by others	Competence seen by others to incompe-tence seen by others	Integrated to compart-mentalized
Action orientation (organizing/ planning)	Risk to non-risking	Toward others ac-ceptably to toward others un-acceptably	Pro-active to reactive	Meaningful to irrelevant
Goal attain-ment (action/ evaluation)	Self-confi-dence to self-protec-tion	Achieve member-ship to re-jection of membership	Goal achieve-ment to goal failure	Integrity/ generativity to despair/ stagnation

Note: From Career Development of Talented Persons (p. 5) by P. A. Perrone, W. W. Karshner, and R. A. Male, 1979. Unpublished manuscript.

theory. The model that is presented has two dimensions: one dimension consists of awareness of self and others, action orientation, and goal attainment; the other dimension consists of safety, love, esteem, and self-actualization needs (Table 8.1).

The selected concepts from Erikson's developmental stage theory and Maslow's need-motivation theory that are integrated in the GIFTS model are considered to be important dynamic, energizing qualities that explain differential *career development patterns*. Each cell of the 4 x 4 matrix (Table 8.1) has an implied continuum that shows the dynamics of the structure of an individual's orientation toward career development.

The authors of the GIFTS model assume that (a) each column represents a *world orientation* based on the individual's interaction with the environment; (b) each row represents *change and growth*, moving from security to self-actualization (and the reverse for regression); and (c) people will operate from one or more *developmental levels* at different times of their lives owing to personal and environmental reasons.

In brief, concerns related to career guidance found in case study examples of talented individuals include the following:

A mistaken notion that the talented are capable of attaining anything to which they aspire

The difficulty that the talented experience in reconciling their value systems with society's value system

A premature commitment to career choices based on school subjects in which the gifted attain distinction, with the hazard of remaining perpetual students

The search for a career as a principle means of support

A conflict between achieving excellence and settling for acceptance

A great need of the gifted for mastery and thoroughness, which causes them to fixate on detail at the expense of obtaining a good *gestalt*

The severe delay of certain psychosocial needs resulting from an expectation of an extended education

An extension of the dependence-independence conflict, resulting from a prolonged preparation for career entry

The significant changes in the individual and nature of the work that occur during the student's extended preparation for a career

The perception of many gifted women that marriage and careers are mutually exclusive, leading them to make unnecessary compromises in career planning

The ability to adapt and adjust to new peer referent groups as the gifted move from high school to college

The need to redefine themselves as gifted and talented in new contexts, and to adjust or adapt their behavior accordingly

The GIFTS model underscores the authors' conception of career guidance as an *ongoing lifelong process,* beginning in early childhood and proceeding throughout the life of the person. This conception differs from the more limited view of educational and career guidance as preparing children, through appropriate education and counseling, to move toward jobs or careers.

The model sees career directions in the whole context of the person's life. It takes into account their needs, motivations, goals, and interactions with others at each phase of their lives. Viewing career guidance in this way builds on dimensions and gives greater significance to earlier theories of educational and vocational guidance.

A Sociodramatic Model

Another valuable approach to career guidance is *sociodrama*, a technique that combines the strengths of *role playing* in dramatic situations with the *group creative problem-solving process.*

Sociodrama was first developed in the 1940s by Jacob L. Moreno (1946). He and others in the field later refined and elaborated on the technique (e.g., Haas, 1948; Klein, 1956; Moreno, 1952; Moreno & Moreno, 1969). It was later shown that the problem-solving process in sociodrama can be as deliberate and disciplined as any other creative problem-solving approach (Osborn, 1963; Parnes, 1967a; Torrance & Myers, 1970). Torrance (1975c) has described, for instance, how sociodrama may help us cope with everyday problems that may confront us in the future as well.

Torrance (1976b) discusses how the *principles and techniques of sociodrama* may be applied to career education. He formulates a methodology that combines role playing, creative problem solving, and career education objectives in sociodrama. Role playing, although a popular method in career education and intrinsic to relevant instructional and curricular materials developed for the purpose, does not help students know their abilities and career interests, nor does it take into account career education objectives. In addition, role playing does not have well-defined procedures for moving the creative process toward creative problem-solving outcomes, whereas sociodrama as applied to career education does.

Sociodrama is primarily based on an educational methodology that has a *preventative* rather than therapeutic focus. It is group or *social-problem-centered* and can be used in almost any physical setting, including the classroom. The intent of sociodrama is to give guidance by educating the individual in a group setting. As applied to career education, its prime focus is on a problem or conflict that is expected to arise in a career, especially when the conflict is related to the application of knowledge or acquired skills.

The *problem or conflict* may be handled by the creative problem-solving process in a sociodramatic situation. The *steps* taken, which are similar to those of the Osborn-Parnes method of creative problem solving, include the following:

1. Defining the problem
2. Establishing a situation (conflict) in operational terms so that deferred judgment is used
3. Casting characters (protagonists), keeping in mind that participation is voluntary and not prearranged
4. Briefing and warming up actors and observers by the director for possible alternatives; some preparation of the acting situation and setting
5. Acting out the situation by using a variety of production techniques to dig deeper into the problem in a psychologically safe atmosphere, where freedom to experiment with new ideas, behavior, and problem-solving techniques are provided

6. Cutting the action whenever actors are no longer in character or are unable to continue, when the episode comes to a conclusion, or when the director perceives the opportunity to stimulate higher levels of thinking by moving to a different episode
7. Discussing and analyzing the situation, the behavior, and the ideas produced; evaluating, according to some agreed-upon criteria, the alternatives generated, as a way of working toward selection of an effective solution
8. Making plans for the further testing and implementation of ideas for new behaviors that are similar to the selling, planning, and implementing stage in creative problem solving

The fact that sociodrama calls for the use of both *rational* and *emotive* techniques in processing the problem makes it a viable approach to career education. To put this in neuropsychological terms, both the right and left hemispheres of the brain are required to function so that linear thought (e.g., analytic, logical, verbal, sequential thinking) and nonlinear thought (e.g., global, creative, nonverbal, imaginative thinking) are combined and directed toward the solving of a problem sociodramatically.

A *sociodramatic session* involes a director, one or more actors or protagonists, and a group as the participating audience. The subject of the drama is a problem or conflict situation that needs definition, examination, exploration, and clarification by way of arriving at a solution. The creative problem-solving steps by which this may be accomplished have already been described.

There are several ways of approaching the creative handling of a situation. These are described as *production techniques.* Drawing from Moreno (1946), and his own works, Torrance (1975c, 1976b) suggests 14 sociodramatic production techniques that may be applied to career education. Among these techniques are the soliloquy, double, multiple double and magic net.

Production techniques used in sociodrama for career education may involve one or more of the following:

Applying knowledge of subject matter and subject-related skills, for instance, to career problems, conflicts, uncertainties, and predictions

Encouraging the incubation of original ideas and fresh insights

Discovering new problems in applying information to career problems

Exploring role requirements in different careers as well as the personal qualities and learning necessary for those careers

Making effective decisions, accurate observations, and being aware of the feelings of others

Encouraging deliberate predictions as well as planning future implementation of decisions and exploring ways of changing behavior to prepare for future decision-making

Experiencing different occupational roles and constructing life-styles
associated with various career choices and future conditions

Predicting consequences of career decisions and new life-styles

Elaborating alternative courses of action and evaluating decisions

The *audience* also plays an important role in sociodrama. Because this approach involves the creative problem-solving process, the audience may play research and problem-solving roles not ordinarily found in sociodrama. Members of the audience may be asked by the director to identify with the protagonist and supporting actor (auxiliary ego), to act as observers, to serve as public opinion, to analyze the action at any stage of the creative problem-solving process as deemed relevant, to play a purely supportive role for the protagonist or auxiliary ego, or to act as a consultant. Any one of these roles may be taken by the audience as they relate to core objectives and specific career education needs of the group at the time.

Although Torrance does not mention the gifted in discussing socio-drama as applied to career education, the use of creative problem-solving in sociodrama is highly relevant to the education of the gifted as it is to all students. The *multipotentiality* of gifted students makes career choices extremely difficult; sociodrama offers a viable approach to helping gifted students explore and discover *career direction* that will both match their abilities and interests and place problems attendant to their choices in the appropriate context. The creative problem-solving process as used by gifted students in dramatic situations not only assists them in applying their knowledge of various careers and the career-related skills they have acquired but also offers them the opportunity to test the validity of this knowledge in a participating group. The group is expected to assist them in identifying and clarifying the problems they may face, generating ideas and hypotheses that need to stand the test of supportive scrutiny, and eventually arriving at some sound decisions.

It is more likely, at present, that gifted students will find themselves in heterogeneous class settings rather than in one comprised of other gifted students. In either setting, heterogeneous or homogeneous, socio-drama can be expected to operate effectively. The *heterogeneous setting* provides the context of a social group similar to the one with whom the student is likely to interact in the world of work. Besides, this setting may provide an atmosphere more congenial to career education. The *homogeneous setting* provides a stimulating social context of peers who are probably facing similar problems that need resolution. Furthermore, in the latter setting gifted students have the opportunity to experience in sociodramatic circumstances career possibilities and attendant conflicts.

COUNSELING THE CULTURALLY DIVERSE GIFTED

Some attention to the culturally diverse gifted has been given in this text in terms of (a) the shaping influences of the larger environment, including the physical and sociocultural universe; (b) a discussion of the richness of cultural diversity and the deprivation experienced by subcultures in a larger or majority cultural group; (c) attendant measurement and identification problems, and (d) underachievement. It is pertinent at this point to say that everything said so far about counseling gifted students generally is applicable to the culturally diverse gifted. However, differences in culture have special implications for counseling and deserve further attention.

Special Needs

That cultural diversity is an important factor to be taken into account in counseling the gifted has been endorsed by many (Colangelo, 1985; Colangelo & Lafrenz, 1981; Frasier, 1979; Marion, 1981). Counseling needs of such students include the following:

Recognizing that they are gifted
Establishing an identity with their own subcultural group
Making social adjustments between their own culture and the dominant culture
Facing and resolving their interpersonal conflicts
Coping with peer pressure that discourages success in the majority culture
Dealing with their weakness in verbal and semantic skills
Relying on visual rather than auditory styles of learning
Handling the lack of ability to be introspective
Making appropriate academic and vocational decisions

The counselor who is aware of these special needs can help the culturally diverse gifted to deal with them so that these gifted can get on with the important task of realizing their potential.

Mary Frasier (1979) suggests that the counselor can assist by finding appropriate *mentors* for these students, by encouraging a *creative questioning attitude* that will allow them to recognize and explore many possible answers to a problem. The counselor can assist them to get around the problem of becoming *alienated* from peers of their own culture. Like Gowan and Demos, she recognizes the *upward mobility* problem culturally diverse gifted students face, bringing with it emotional turmoil, which counselors can alleviate by alerting these students to the source of the problem and developing internships for valuable direct "hands-on" and "minds-on" experiences. Furthermore, she suggests that the counselor develop students' *awareness of alternative paths* by means of activities that expose them to options—activities that include the use of mental imagery and guided fantasy to facilitate imaginative exploration of current and future opportunities.

Coping Models for Emotional Needs

Herbert A. Exum (1979), in addressing the *emotional needs* of gifted black students, proposes a Black Identity Facilitation model or BIF which is an extension of the Deliberate Psychological Education model or DEP (Mosher & Sprinthall, 1971).

Deliberate Psychological Education Model

The DEP Model has five objectives: (a) increasing interpersonal skills; (b) encouraging divergent thinking, especially in laboratory sessions; (c) matching interests of students and teachers through team teaching and laboratory experiences; (d) decreasing isolation and increasing sensitivity to problems faced by other than black students, and complementing their altruistic needs; and (e) affording a positive match of content, experience, and behavioral style that implies a oneness between the observer and phenomenon being observed.

The model usually offers *courses,* the core of which is cognitive, with attention focused on human development. Its purpose is to facilitate identity formation at the secondary school level, encouraging students to grow toward the formal operations-conventional moral reasoning stage of development.

In addition to course work, students are exposed to a variety of *laboratory-related activities* whose main purpose is to allow students to experiment with new roles in different settings. Students in the laboratory setting engage in peer tutoring and counseling fellow students.

The three phases of the counseling laboratory include making *tapes* of their attempts at helping peers and parents; comparing their perceptions of what is going on with perceptions of the counselor; and taking a realistic look at their expectations, goals, and development of commitment. The model uses a *team-teaching* approach involving staff, schools, community, and social service agencies.

Black Identity Facilitation Model

Since the DEP model does not focus deliberately on the *meaning of the black experience* under oppression or related awareness, Exum (1979) considers it incomplete and proposes the BIF model for that purpose. BIF requires that the cognitive part of the curriculum represents a psycho-historical examination of the black experience and the examination of crosscultural interactions. It includes as subjects both gifted and non-gifted individuals.

Themes of the core courses are self-esteem, values and ethical behaviors, sexuality, and assertiveness. The *laboratory sessions* on teaching and counseling are concerned primarily with the development of communication skills. Paraphrasing, reflecting feeling, and appropriate use of self-disclosure may be effectively learned through the use of videotape/role-playing sessions. Furthermore, by using a developmental approach, significant experience, and careful inquiry, a deliberate blending of real experience and process and content, action and reflection, doing and thinking, can be brought about.

Team teaching is also used to present cognitive information for modeling proper communication skills as well as teaching/counseling behaviors in laboratory settings; and to provide individual and/or group sessions with students who serve as peer tutors and counselors, within which individual attention to issues arising from course experience is given.

Counseling in Black Families

Concern is also expressed for the counseling needs of the *families* of black gifted students. In this respect Exum (1983) defines the family as *nuclear* (husband, wife, and their own children with no other members present), *extended* (other relatives of family members), and *augmented* (members not related to the family head sharing the same household living arrangements of the nuclear family). More than two thirds of black families are nuclear in structure, one quarter are extended, and one tenth are augmented.

According to Exum, it is inaccurate to consider black children as coming from the stereotypical single-parent female family. Besides, because the immediate family of black children may vary greatly in number, available space for family conferences or interviews with the head of household will have to be taken into account by counselors.

The counseling process should involve as many of the family members as possible. The counselor would do well not to assume that those in authority are the students' biological parents, for other family members may play just as important a role in the counseling situation.

Psychosocial Family Orientation

The psychosocial orientation of the family is also an important consideration. This orientation relates to four *styles of adjustment to racism:* pre-encounter, encounter, immersion, and emersion. Each has important implications for counseling.

Preencounter

The counselor may find the family worldview dominated by Western and Protestant ethics, which are accepted without question. Besides, the family may be prowhite or even antiblack, both of which contribute to the disharmonious feelings and pressure of variance that black students experience with the family and the outside world.

Encounter

The counselor may find that the family is working through the process of reinterpreting the world—a process triggered off by negative experiences—and is preoccupied with rediscovery of itself in relation with its black legacy. Such a family will be in disarray and students will not understand it, and perhaps unjustly blame themselves for this state of affairs and their failure to resolve it.

Immersion

The family involved in immersion has antiwhite feelings, perceiving all whites, including the counselor, as inferior. Their objections to counseling services do not include services that can be offered by the black counselor. The discomfort that the family may cause the rejected white counselor is compensated by students' heightened ethnic esteem. Consequences of this esteem may be very positive for the students, bringing in its wake a high degree of creativity and academic achievement.

Two unproductive sets of outcomes may occur for the family if it does not move beyond immersion, namely, disappointment and rejection on one hand, and continuation and fixation on the other. With regard to the first set of outcomes, students of the family experiencing immersion may become frustrated to the extent of adopting a nihilistic, hopeless, and even antihuman world view. As for the second set, students develop a hatred for whites and are said to have a pseudoblack identity. In either case, a white counselor will have great difficulty communicating with the family and may do well to refer it to a black or Afrocentric counselor.

Emersion

The counselor, where possible, can assist the family to work through the first three states of dysfunction to a fourth, based on positive interaction or emersion. A family experiencing this style of ethnic operation will have diminished antiwhite feelings. The family and children consequently develop an interest in actively participating in the community for the purpose of making the world a better place for all people. They cherish and value both their own heritage and the culture of others.

Knowing the states of families to be dealt with, counselors will be better positioned to provide the kind of guidance needed for black gifted students. It goes without saying that students will absorb and reflect the characteristics and orientations of the families in which they live. Hence it is essential for counselors to take into account the family when planning to counsel gifted black students (Exum, 1983; Marion 1981). They can do this be increasing their knowledge about the community they serve, heightening their visibility in the black community, scheduling appointments flexibly, being aware of the parents' need to belong and communicate, and maintaining family-school relations.

CONCLUSIONS

Fresh perspectives on guidance of the gifted has focused on (a) counseling normal children to help them overcome problems of development, moving them in the direction of self-actualization and good mental health; (b) facilitating the creative development of gifted children, (c) preventing stress from interfering with normal functioning by developing strategies to master it to prevent breakdown; and (d) using counseling in preventative and situational ways. All these goals have strong theoretical roots, which have invigorated approaches to guidance of students in general and the gifted in particular.

A growth and developmental psychology that includes creativity as an essential component, the psychology of stress and its mastery through the use of the intellect and the development of interpersonal skills, and a social psychology that brings into sharp focus the dynamics of group creative problem solving and role playing in dramatic situations call into play a multiplicity of resources for guidance. These psychologies hold great significance and high relevance for personal, academic, and career guidance, providing explanations for many of the problems connected with underachievement and the problems of special groups, such as gifted women and the culturally diverse.

The literature has made it evident that there is a lack of good counseling in schools, either because the education system is unable to support sufficient numbers of professional school counselors to make their work effective, or because school administration adulterates counseling functions by assigning counselors to other than counseling duties. For example, the effectiveness of professional counselors is dissipated by the overwhelming press of students for academic advisement, leaving little time or energy for real contact with individual students who may be reluctant to go to the counselor for help.

Any administrative arrangement or model guidance program for the gifted cannot neglect to take into account the essentials of creative development, the variety of stress factors that impinge on the individual and affect behavior, the preparatory work that must go into equipping the individual with coping skills, the individual counseling circumstances, the arrangement of situations so that problems can be brought into the open to work toward solutions through the use of sociodrama, and the special influences of cultural diversity upon the individual in family context.

Counselors should get to know counselees intimately, not only for course work placement (often done with a superficial acquaintance of students and in the context of preparing them for the next higher grade); but also to develop a better understanding of their abilities, talents, interests, hobbies, motivations, interpersonal relations (schoolmates, teachers, family, and others), and the kind of problems they are prone to experience. Certainly, the counselor needs to work in close cooperation with teachers and parents as well as with other counselors who may also know student counselees.

The counselors should not be oriented toward treating symptoms in crisis situations, but toward expecting to improve the mental health of students. Frequent association with students, coupled with a thorough understanding of the students, will allow him or her to operate effectively. It is of the utmost importance for students to feel that the counselor is approachable and accepting. They must feel that the counselor is someone whom they can trust and with whom they can communicate freely; someone who is there when needed and who can be depended on to provide direction when necessary; someone who will stand aside and permit growth when it is about to take place.

CHAPTER NINE

Nurturing Creative Intellect

*I*NTRODUCTION

The study of creativity has focused mainly on developing creative measures and the problems involved in their development, nurturing the process for productive thinking and expression, identifying creative potential in exceptional and superior individuals, and understanding societal, ethnic, and cultural controls and influences. Although much has been learned about creativity to date, little has been done to explore the relationship between creative imagination and its imagery-analogy correlates. In recent years, however, some substantial research has been done on imagery and the creative imagination (Ahsen, 1982; Durio, 1975; Forisha, 1978; Khatena, 1984, 1987; Rockenstein, 1989).

For many years, *process learning* has been emphasized in education generally (e.g., Bruner, 1960). It gained renewed vigor and specific direction from an operational-informational theory of intelligence based on the Structure of Intellect, and brought into play both act and content in a comprehensive way, with significant implications for school learning events (Guilford, 1972). Divergent thinking, creativity, creative imagination, intuition, and related dimensions of brain functioning have become important foci in the arrangement of educational experiences. These focus points have led educators of the gifted to suggest approaches to learning, such as acquisition of various thinking and creative problem-solving skills, engagement in sociodrama, and involvement in the use of intuition, that are expected to maximize intellectual development. As a result, the gifted can move toward the intellectual frontiers and become not just conservers of knowledge but producers of it.

CREATIVE IMAGINATION

In an attempt to put creative imagination and its imagery correlates in a broader perspective, the author proposed the Multidimensional Interactive Creative Imagination Imagery Model (Khatena, 1984). The model has been described earlier as consisting of three major dimensions: Environment, Individual, and Cosmos. (In an earlier version, Figure 3.1, the Cosmos Interventions and Outcomes dimensions were left out.)

Information received from the physical and sociocultural universe (Environment) is transmitted to the brain via the senses and neurophysiological pathways. The electrochemical impulses take the form of images that are codified for individual mental processing and emerge in some communicable form or another for processing by the intellect and creative imagination (Individual). In creative activity, the imagination is rooted to the intellective-emotive system of the individual, drawing, during peak experiences, from nonordinary reality and the supernatural (Cosmos).

The magic and mystery of the imagination set in motion by creative energy have given articulation to the world, transforming reality to dreams and dreams to reality. Mercutio of Shakespeare's *Romeo and Juliet* explains that those who experience imaginative fantasies are visited by Queen Mab who presides over the birth of fairies.

> she gallops night by night
> Through lovers' brains, and then they dream of love;
> O'er courtiers' knees, that dream on curtsies straight;
> O'er lawyers' fingers, who straight dream on fees,
>
> (1.iv.55–92)

Cosmic Imagination

The Romantic poets deified imagination, describing it as some force outside themselves that is responsible for creative experiences and works. This force, which sets in motion their creative acts, had been characterized by the Greeks as the *Muses.*

William Blake describes imagination as *spiritual energy* in whose exercise we experience, in some way, the activity of God. For the Romantic

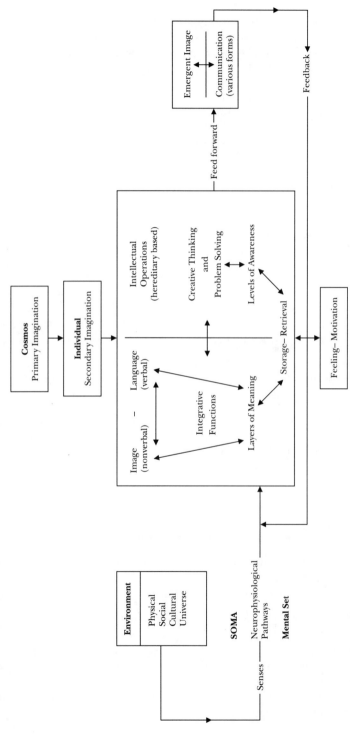

Figure 9.1 Multidimensional Interactive Creative Imagination Imagery Model

From *Imagery and Creative Imagination* (p. 41) by Joseph Khatena, 1984, Buffalo, N.Y.: Bearly Limited. Copyright © 1984 by Joseph Khatena.

poet William Wordsworth, imagination is another name for *absolute power* identified with *clearest insight, amplitude of mind,* and *Reason in her most exalted mood.* Wordsworth (1888) expresses an affinity for this omnipresence of imagination in his poem "Tintern Abbey" (composed in 1798).

> And I felt
> A presence that disturbs me with the joy
> Of elevated thoughts; a sense sublime
> Of something far more deeply interfused
> Whose dwelling is the light of setting suns,
> And the round ocean and the living air,
> And the blue sky, and in the minds of man;
> A motion and spirit, that impels
> All thinking things, all objects of all thought.
>
> (p. 94)

Imagination has also been called *an ability of prime importance* by Samuel T. Coleridge (1817), because human beings, in their creative activity, simulate the creative act of God. Coleridge considers imagination as *seminal* rather than perceptual. According to Coleridge, imagination is both divine and human. The divine aspect of the imagination he calls *primary:*

> The primary imagination I hold to be the living power and prime agent of all human perception, and as a repetition in the finite mind of the infinite mind of the creation in the infinite I AM.

For Johannes Brahms, creative imagination, which he associated with musical composition, was felt as *vibrations,* the source of which was a divine *awe-inspiring experience.* When he had the urge to compose, he invoked his Maker to provide him with inspiration:

> I begin by appealing directly to my Maker. . . . I immediately feel vibrations which thrill my whole being. . . . In this exalted state I see clearly what is obscure in my ordinary moods; then I feel capable of drawing inspiration from above as Beethoven did. (Brahms cited in Abell, 1964, pp. 19–21)

Brahms then relates that while he is in a trancelike state these *vibrations* take the shape of distinct mental images, which precipitate the flow of ideas that give birth to musical composition.

> Those vibrations assume the form of distinct mental images. . . . Straightaway the ideas flow in upon me, directly from God, and not only do I see distinct themes in the mind's eye, but they are clothed in the right forms, harmonies, and orchestration. Measure by measure the finished product is revealed to me when I am in those rare, inspired moods. . . . I have to be in a semi-trance condition to get such results—a condition when the conscious mind is in temporary abeyance, and the subconscious is in control, for it is

through the subconscious mind, which is a part of omnipotence that the inspiration comes. (Brahms cited in Abell, 1964, pp. 19–21)

Gowan (1977a), in an analysis of high creativity experienced by musical composers in the act of composition, identifies three phases of the process: the prelude ritual, conscious or unconscious, that often ends with an invocation; the altered state of consciousness or creative spell (e.g., trance, dream, or revery) inducing vibrations leading to mental images that generate ideas to be finally clothed in some form; and the postlude of positive emotions experienced by participants.

Imagination as Intuition

Closely allied to cosmic imagination is *intuitive imagination*. It provides a link between cosmic energy and the individual's grasp of it for creative use. Zoa Rockenstein (1988) has operationally defined *intuition* as "an open channel to universal sources of knowledge and wisdom that transcends the boundaries of time, space, the senses, and the logical-rational mind" (p. 78). Intuition occurs without conscious awareness or rational thinking, is instaneous and comes as an *insightful* flash or *illumination*, and patterns information and understanding as wholes (Isaack, 1978; Rockenstein, 1989).

Clark (1988) discusses three levels of intuition: *rational intuition* (contradictory but needed for the realignment and reintegration of known information for new insights); *predictive intuition* (enlarging the previous level to incorporate new information into existing patterns, encouraging fresh insights, hunches, best guesses, solution-finding, and forecasting—a process some call creativity; and *transformational intuition* (deified, transcendental information, ideas received in dream states and visions).

These descriptions of intuition are very much related to Coleridge's primary and secondary imagination (see "Imagination as Intellect" following), and Wallas's incubation-illumination process in problem solving. The testimonies of peak experiences of writers, musicians, artists, and scientists explain the intuitive phenomenon of creativity. *Intuitive imagination* is not something that occurs in and of itself. It operates, as Figure 3.1 shows, in a holistic and interactive framework of human-cosmic functioning, sometimes better attributed to the level of the individual; at other times, attributable to the individual activated by cosmic-deified energies, visions, vibrations, and inspirations.

Imagination as Intellect

Imagination as thinking is the individual's "mind activity." It requires mental processing of information and mind events that break up an existing order to reorganize it into a new order at a higher level, thereby effecting transformation. Coleridge (1956) calls this the *secondary imagination*, which coexists harmoniously with its divine counterpart, the *primary imagination*.

> The secondary imagination I consider as an echo of the former, co-existing with the conscious will, yet still as identical with the primary in the kind of its agency, and differing only in degree, and in the mode of its operation. It dissolves, diffuses, dissipates, in order to recreate; or where this process is rendered impossible, yet still, at all events, it struggles to idealize and to unify. It is essentially vital, even as all objects (as objects) are essentially fixed and dead. (p. 167)

Coleridge's secondary imagination anticipates R. W. Gerard's (cited in Ghiselin, 1955) and C. M. Bowra's (1969) recent definitions of imagination as *mind action*. Such action is leveled at producing new ideas and insights or generating new hypotheses for problem solving.

According to Gerard, creative imagination is "an action of mind that produces a new idea or insight" (p. 226), or "the heat of mental work transforming the soft ingot of fancy into the hard steel of finished creations" (p. 227). Bowra explains imagination as problem-solving activity aimed at producing ideas and insightful solutions:

> When we use our imagination we are first stirred by some alluring puzzle which calls for a solution, and then by our own creations in mind, we are able to see much that was before dark or unintelligible. (p. 7)

On the subject of imagination, Peter McKellar (1957) suggests two kinds of thinking, namely, *R-Thinking* and *A-Thinking*. R-Thinking relates to reasoning, logic, and reality-adjustment, whereas A-Thinking relates to dreaming, fantasy, and mental events prominent in psychosis, the creative process, and the creative act.

Creative imagination, according to Harold Rugg (1963), involves problem solving (Wallas, 1926), feeling, and logical thinking in the act of discovery—the internal experience of knowing about an object or event and its external measurable consequence. Furthermore, creative imagination is a function of the transliminal mind in which lives all human experience and where the creative flash or illumination occurs, free from censorship. Below the level of awareness, the body and the mind function in concert, engaging in the creative process of forming and transforming information for meaningful expression. There is also the state of relaxed tension that facilitates the sudden flash of illumination. Finally, the creative imagination deals with felt-thought expressed through gesture-symbol (a prelanguage form of communication), and verbalized thought through name-symbol. Together they constitute the creative mind in the act of discovery verifiable by logical problem solving.

Imagination as Brain Activity

John Eccles (1972) sees creative imagination as brain activity. For a brain to exhibit creative imagination, according to him, it must have a sufficient number of neurons with a wealth of synaptic connections that have the sensitivity to increase their function with usage, forming and maintaining a wealth of memory patterns or *engrams*. If creative imagination is to occur, such a brain must have the unique capacity for continual activity, combining and recombining these patterns in novel ways. Eccles considers creative imagination as the most profound of human activities, one that is responsible for the occurrence of new insights and illumination.

Furthermore, Eccles speculates that this theory of imagination and creativity is based on secure evidence concerning the specific way information is conveyed to the cortex, making his interpretation possible.

According to Khatena (1973a, 1975a), creative imagination is the chemistry of mental processing, allowing intellectual and emotive forces to participate in stimulating, energizing, and propagating the creative act. Others have attempted to explain different modes of mental functioning in terms of the left and right hemispheres of the brain (de Bono, 1971; Olson, 1977; Samples, 1975; Sperry, 1974). R. Ornstein (1972), for instance, indicates that

> although each hemisphere shares the potential for many functions, and both sides participate in most activities, in a normal person the two hemispheres of the brain tend to specialize. (p. 51)

The *left brain* specializes in handling incoming perceptual information and processing it by means of language into logical-analytical thought and decision in the continual stream of internal discourse that accompanies consciousness. By removing left-hemisphere functions by means of relaxation, meditation, hypnosis, fantasy, daydreaming, sensory deprivation, or similar states, right-hemisphere imagery can occur.

The *right brain* is spatial, holistic, simultaneous in nature, and capable of handling informational complexity. It specializes in the handling of divergent thinking operations, intuition, insight, invention, metaphor, analogy, and the production of creative imagination imagery. The cerebral hemispheres, while having specialized functions, are not independent; they complement one another in an integrative alliance.

To illustrate this let us take Thinking Creatively with Sounds and Words (Khatena & Torrance, 1990b), a measure of originality consisting of two components: Sounds and Images and Onomatopoeia and Images. The test, in the context of right-brain and left-brain activity, invites interesting speculation about processing auditory-visual-verbal stimuli as input for output as verbal images. Sounds and Images presents auditory stimuli alone; Onomatopoeia and Images presents stimuli that are at once auditory, visual, and verbal.

The listener receives information with instructions to be imaginative and produce original verbal images. When, for example, Onomatopoeia and Images is administered, both right-brain and left-brain activity is induced because of the multidimensional stimuli. As input data the auditory-visual components of onomatopoeic words (e.g., *boom* or *crackle*) stimulate the production of right-brain images, while their verbal aspects set in motion the decoding processes of the left brain, which act with right-brain productively, almost simultaneously.

Image activity, the province of the right brain, follows. It includes the use of the imagination in the destructuring, reintegration, and transformation processes, which leads to the emergence of new imagery for transference to the left brain for encoding in language that is ready to be recorded in verbal written form on the response sheet. Because it requires the symbiotic relationship of both halves of the brain in creative endeavor, such activity is of great value; it calls for the exercise of verbal and image functions that are rooted in creativity (Figure 9.1).

Julian Jaynes (1976) locates creative imagination imagery in the Wernicke area of the right cerebral hemisphere. Imagination goes on there all the time, although it is overlaid most frequently with left-brain or dominant hemisphere cognitive activity. Gowan (1978b, 1978c) has likened this activity to static of a radio receiver; it interferes with right-brain signals associated with creativity. When the cognitive activity of the left hemisphere abates, some type of resonance phenomena is set up, the first evidence of which is *vibrations,* followed by the occurrence of imagery.

PROCESS OF INCUBATION

Incubation is that stage of creative thinking and problem solving when mental events, set in motion earlier by deliberate and intensive preparation, are energized, becoming autonomous, so that fruitful *insights* that lead to good *solutions* to problems can occur. The time this process takes may vary from a moment to days or months and is beyond the awareness of the creator. Potentiality, when in use, it taps the *preconscious* (Gowan, 1978b).

Coleridge (1956), for instance, prior to composing the poem "Kubla Khan" had been working with various technical devices and reading Samuel Purchas's *Pilgrimage.* On falling asleep from the effects of an anodyne (an opium derivative) taken to relieve him from "a slight indisposition," Coleridge experienced a dream-vision that found poetic expression.

In consequence of a slight indisposition, an anodyne had been prescribed from the effects of which he fell asleep in his chair at the moment that he was reading the following sentence, or words of the same substance, in Purchas's *PILGRIMAGE:*
"Here the Khan Kubla commanded a palace to be built and a stately garden thereunto. And thus ten miles of fertile ground were inclosed with a wall."
The Author continued for about three hours in a profound sleep, at least of the external senses, during which time he has the most vivid confidence, that he could not have composed less than two or three hundred lines; if that indeed can be called composition in which all the images rose up before him as THINGS, with a parallel production of the correspondent expressions without any sensation or consciousness of effort. On awaking he appeared to himself to have a distinct recollection of the whole, and taking his pen, ink, and paper, instantly and eagerly wrote down the lines that are here preserved. (p. 181)

Gowan (1978b), on the subject of incubation, likens it to the mental analog of physical gestation whereby an ovum develops into a baby. It is a process of metamorphosis during which right-brain imagery serves as the vehicle for the production of creativity. Gowan indicates that *preparation* (academic discipline) is the necessary condition and *incubation* (relaxation) the sufficient condition for creative insights to emerge. In addition, he suggests that by incubation is meant

> any technique of relaxation of the conscious cognition (left cerebral hemisphere function) such as, but not confined to dreams, day-dreaming, fantasy, hypnosis, meditation, diversion, play, etc., which allows subliminal processes (right hemisphere functions) to operate. (p. 23)

The main characteristics of incubation can be summarized as follows:

Incubation depends much on intensive and careful preparation.
It requires no conscious or voluntary thinking of the problem in hand.
It functions (under optimum conditions) either through relaxation or rest with no interference from conscious thought about the problem or, when attention is given to solving other problems, through a series of incubations.
It facilitates right-hemisphere or creative imagination imagery for the occurrence of creative solutions.

Incubation in Problem Solving

Henri Poincaré (cited in Ghiselin, 1955), the French mathematician, tells us that incubation (or the work of the unconscious mind) was present when he was involved in analyzing difficult problems. Wallas (1926) identifies the involvement of four distinct steps in the problem-solving process. Wallas's steps are *preparation, incubation, illumination,* and *verification,* the steps of his famous creative problem-solving paradigm, incubation being the stage when a person is not deliberately involved in conscious thinking about a problem. Earlier, in the nineteenth century, Helmholtz formulated the first three steps (preparation, incubation, and illumination).

Although there have been recent discussions on incubation (e.g., Dorsel, 1979; Guilford, 1979; Khatena, 1979a; Parnes, 1988; Schubert, 1979; Torrance, 1979a), there are relatively few studies of the subject. These studies provided mixed results about the existence of an incubation process in experimental situations (Olton, 1979). However, two experiments on specific associative priming of relevant associative elements on the incubation of creative performance was found to be effective (S. A. Mednick, 1962; M. T. Mednick, S. A. Mednick, & E. V. Mednick, 1964).

Testimony about the incubation process providing the basis for insights and illumination is not lacking. Besides, a number of studies have reported that creative people experience, and even deliberately use, the process of incubation prior to poetic composition (Patrick, 1955). Their conclusions are consistent with what has been reported about Coleridge's composition of "Kubla Khan."

Incubation and Reflective Imagery

Images may occur when an individual is in a state of rest. During these times conscious control fades and attention shifts to an internal frame of reference where images freely flow.

Images in this situation are *reflective* and are the kind experienced prior to composition of literary and artistic endeavors (Khatena, 1984). Reflective imagery occurs in the absence of a problem. Such imagery is not deliberate and controlled but autonomous and free flowing. An example of the reflective state in poetic composition has been cited in the composition of "Kubla Khan." While in a dream state Coleridge experienced images that were later synthesized in this poem of great beauty and depth of meaning.

Incubation and Energy Fields

James Vargiu (1977), on creativity, suggests that the function of imagination may be thought of in terms of *creativity energy fields* that are both mental and emotive. Drawing on the analogies from physics, he tentatively defines the creative process as a large number of simple *mental elements* within the boundary of a *creative energy field* whose properties are such that each mental element will respond to the influence of the creative field, and all mental elements can interact with one another. To illustrate this, he describes the well-known behavior of a thin layer of iron filings in the presence of a magnet.

> At first, the field is too weak to set the iron particles in motion. They are held in position by friction. As the intensity of the magnetic field increases, some of the iron particles overcome friction and begin to move, interacting with the nearby granules in a way that increases the overall magnetization. This in turn sets other particles in motion, accelerating the process and starting an "avalanche" EFFECT or CHAIN REACTION which causes the pattern to suddenly form itself, independently of any further approach of the magnet. (p. 23)

By analogy, mental events pass through the stages of preparation, frustration, incubation, illumination, and elaboration. The suddenness of *illumination* is explained as *avalanche effect*.

> Thus the "illumination" comes to our consciousness as something new, something unexpected. It is produced by the creative field, of which we are not aware, and when it occurs it is beyond our conscious control. So it generates in us the unique and paradoxical impression of an unknown source that leads to deeper knowing, of a blinding flash that leads to clearer vision, of a loss of control that leads to greater order. (p. 24)

Incubation precedes illumination. Vargiu suggests that incubation is not a statistically random ordering of mental elements. Rather, it is the dynamism involved by the creative energy field that, in the initial stage of the creative process, passes through the stages of preparation, confusion, and frustration to lay the groundwork for the occurrence of incubation and illumination.

> The initial part of the creative process—from preparatory activity to confusion and frustration—can thus be seen as having a three-fold purpose: supplying material on which the creative field can play; overcoming friction by setting this material into motion, thereby making it more responsive to the influence of the creative field; and providing conceptual "seeds" through which the creative insight relates to the problem. It is common knowledge among creative people that the intensity of the preparatory stage often determines how closely the insight will fit the problem. The stage of confusion and frustration have only a subsidiary function, but are psychological means we may need to justify saying what amounts to THE HELL WITH IT, and turning our attention elsewhere. We then move on to the incubation stage, the crucial and delicate period during which the often very weak creative field can act on the mental elements without the disturbance of our conscious manipulation, and therefore in the cumulative, coherent fashion that leads to illumination. (p. 27)

Figure 9.2 Intellectual Abilities Activated by Energy Fields

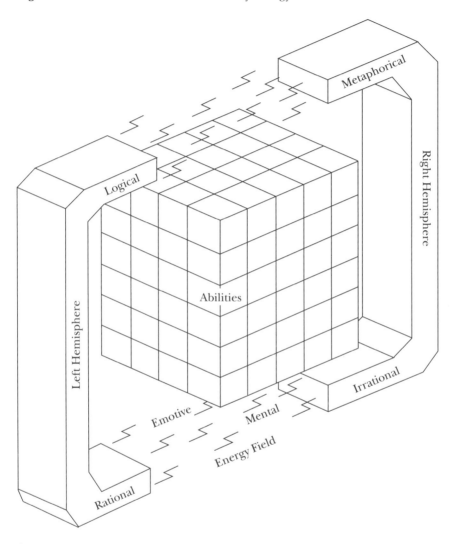

From *"Teaching Gifted Children to Use Creative Imagination Imagery"* (p. 6) by Joseph Khatena, 1979, Starkville, Miss.: Allan Associates. Copyright © 1979 by Joseph Khatena.

Vargiu expands this model to include the *emotional field* that runs intact with mental elements. The emotive tends to organize these mental elements into configurations that correspond to the emotive's own energy patterns. It is this interaction between the mental elements and the emotional field that constitutes the very essence of imagination, enabling images to be formed in the mind and energized by feelings.

Creative imagination involves *intellectual abilities* as well as *energy fields*. These elements operate together in various ways to lead to incubation, creative imagery, and illumination in the creative process. Synthesizing Guilford's model of intellectual abilities, and Wallas's and Vargiu's thoughts on creativity and the problem-solving processes, we can construct a model that illustrates that abilities energized by magnetic fields of mental and emotive forces are central to the workings of creative imagination. Activity set in motion by imagination causes these forces to act and interact with each other and with intellectual abilities. This activity may be deliberate or ongoing without our full awareness. However, if processing this activity presents a problem, incubation is induced, producing imagery that leads to illumination and problem solution (Figure 9.2).

IMAGINATION IMAGERY

Some of the most beautiful things we say derive their energy and effectiveness from creative imagination and the images they produce. It is creative imagery that often provides the artist or poet with the central idea for a picture or poem (Richardson, 1969). For instance, Wordsworth's (1888) lamentation for someone whom he loved is expressed in the lines of one of his "Lucy" poems, composed in 1799:

> A violet by a mossy stone
> > Half hidden from the eye!
> > Fair as a star when only one
> > Is shining in the sky. (p. 115)

The image of a violet against the background of a mossy stone is naturally beautiful in color, texture, and vitality. It presents the girl (implied in the four lines) as being alive and within reach, although she may pass unnoticed (i.e., "half hidden from the eye"). Just like the flower, she is delicate, fragile, and transient. The second image of the girl as a star shining alone in the sky reiterates her beauty, but this time as gemlike, something beyond compare and remote although permanent. The imagery of these lines, congruent with the central notion of someone beautiful, once alive but now dead, transforms fact into poetry (Khatena, 1978b).

Imagery as Language of Discovery

Much of brain activity, as it relates to creative imagination, has to do with imagery or the reexperiencing of images and their language corre- lates. According to Eccles (1972), the image, by association, is evocative of other images and when these images of beauty and subtlety blend in harmony and are expressed in some language—verbal, musical, or pic- torial—they evoke transcendent experiences in others. Thus, we have artistic creation of a simple or lyrical kind. Furthermore, an entirely dif- ferent order of image making provides illumination that gives new in- sight or understanding. As it relates to science, image making may take the form of a new hypothesis that embraces and transcends an older hypothesis.

Imagery is the *language of discovery*. We have only to read from the tes- timonies of geniuses involved in the creative process to realize the im- portance of imagery in discovery and invention, for instance, Charles Darwin's theory of evolution. Friedrich Kekule von Stradonitz's imagery experience just prior to and part of the insight that led him to the discov- ery of the structure of the carbon ring, which became the foundation of organic chemistry, is worth considering.

> I turned my chair to the fire and dozed. Again the atoms were gamboling be- fore my eyes. The smaller groups kept modestly in the background. My men- tal eye, rendered more acute by visions of this kind, could now distinguish larger structures, of manifold conformations, long rows sometimes more closely fitted together, all twining and twisting in snake-like motion. But look! What was that? One of the snakes had seized hold of its tail and the form whirled mockingly before my eyes. As if by a flash of lightning I awoke. (Kekule von Stradonitz cited in Koestler, 1964, p. 118)

Albert Einstein tells us that images, primarily visual and motor, not words or language, served him as elements of thought. The principle of the rotating magnetic field—a discovery that revolutionized electrical science—appeared to Nikola Tesla in images that were as sharp, clear, and solid as metal or stone (Ghiselin, 1955).

Moving from science to music, we have, for instance, the testimony of Wolfgang Amadeus Mozart. In a letter to a friend, Mozart indicates that ideas came to him when he was cheerful and altogether alone, whether in a carriage or during a period when he was unable to sleep at night. At those times his ideas (as images) flowed most abundantly, with the most appealing ones stored in memory to take shape, at heightened mo- ments, as musical composition.

Another testimony comes from William Wordsworth, the poet. He communicates the image-discovery process in his poem I Wandered Lonely as a Cloud (composed in 1804). In moments of tranquility, he recollects illuminating images of an earlier experience of natural beauty, charged with feeling.

> For oft, when on my couch I lie
> In vacant or pensive mood,
> They flash upon the inward eye,
> Which is the bliss of solitude!
> And then my heart with pleasure fills
> And dances with the daffodils. (p. 205)

Imagination imagery is the province of Land's (1973) mutualistic stage, and Gowan's (1974) creativity-psychedelic stages. These stages relate to higher levels of psychological functioning. It is at these stages that higher combinations are made by destructuring and reintegration; by analogy and metaphor tapping the preconscious to effect transformations needed for the occurrence of illuminating images (Khatena, 1979a).

Function of Imagery

In psychology, an image is defined as a perception in the absence of an external stimulus irrespective of the sense modality in which it occurs. Rosemary Gordon (1972) tells us that when she speaks of an image she speaks of

> the perception of forms, or colors, or sounds, or smells, or movements, or tastes in the absence of an actual stimulus which could have caused such perception. This does not mean that such external stimuli did not present themselves in the past nor that the image is independent of such past experiences. But it does mean that at the time the perception of the image no such stimulus is present. (p. 63)

An individual perceives the external world through his or her senses and records messages about the world in the brain as images that are later retrieved from storage in the absence of the original stimulus event. These images can be photographic, without the mediation of emotive-motivational processes unique to each individual, but this is unlikely. Images can be expected to differ from one person to the next even when the original stimulus events are the same.

The image is important because it gives coherence to a multitude of sensory input information about the world (Khatena, 1979b). It orders events, experiences, and relationships. In addition, it links the past and present, and projects the future. Furthermore, it is the repository of experiences, needs, and frustrations, projecting the uniqueness of individual personality and providing information about the inner life or private world of the individual. Finally, it is the key to humankind's creativity.

R. Gordon (1972) examines at length the privacy and exclusiveness of

the image world of each individual. That our image worlds are so different from one another is natural because a great many variables affect
them. Among these variables are dimensions of informational content,
sense modality, flexibility-rigidity, divergency-convergency, autonomy-
control, and activity-passivity. These dimensions are further affected by
the extent to which a person's imagery is predominantly reconstructive
or constructive and inventive. Gordon suggests that perhaps these factors are the distinguishing features of the artist or creative person versus
the nonartist or critic. She includes the world of synaesthesia, where
"visual images evoked sounds and tastes, and tones mixed up with colors
of touch sensations" (p. 66) to these different dimensions of imagery.

Edgar Allan Poe, in a poem, *hears* and *feels* the approach of darkness.
Furthermore, he describes sensations that accompany death as E. Wilson (1931) cites in his study.

> Night arrived; and with its shadows a heavy discomfort. It oppressed my
> limbs with the oppression of some dull weight, not unlike the distant rever-
> beration of surf, but more continuous, which beginning with the first twi-
> light, had grown in strength with the darkness. Suddenly lights were brought
> into the room . . . and issuing from the flame of each lamp there flowed un-
> brokenly into my ears, a strain of melodious monotone. (p. 13)

Different artists need different kinds and combinations of imagery.
The playwright, filmmaker, and theatre director, for instance, need imagery that includes both visual and auditory images, whereas the painter
needs imagery that is primarily visual, and the musician needs imagery
that is primarily auditory. These differences in imagery also vary for artists in different cultures. For example, the Chinese artist sketches a London that looks more like a city in China than England. Furthermore,
Shakespearian costumes were particular to Shakespearian England
rather than to the times in which the plays took place. Rosemary Gordon
concludes that although the image world of an individual is personal
and private it is open to influence and change. Arieti (1976), on the subject of art, the individual, and society, perceives in their *magic synthesis*
individual discovery and invention.

Perception Imagery and Art

By visual arts, we mean drawing, painting, sculpturing, designing, and
related production of art forms that appeal to the eye; by performing
arts, we mean music, dance, oratory, drama, and all other related forms
of art that require performance. Persons engaged in the production of
such works of art have to possess certain talents that allow them to perceive the ordinary world with an uncommon eye. It is an eye that stores,
as images, sensory impressions that go beyond the visual, auditory, and
kinesthetic. Sensory boundaries are crossed so that, for instance, what is

heard is seen, what is touched is visualized, and so on. To these sensitivities may be added a sensitivity to rhythm and a depth of feeling that, when energized by the creative imagination, brings about a magic synthesis of the elements that result in an image precursory to a work of art (Khatena, 1979b, 1984).

Arieti (1976) says that individuals may paint what they see, like a tree, a human being, or an animal. In this case they rely on *perception*. Or they may paint by memory rather than by looking at what they see. In the latter case, they resort to imagery, as earlier artists who painted in caves in the absence of their animal subjects did. Artists who rely on imagery have first to perceive the object before they can evoke it through imagery (Figure 9.1). Such images may be checked by referring to the objects that gave rise to them prior to use. In this way, they reexperience the original perception as cave dwellers probably did in the course of painting.

Perception of an object is affected by thoughts, feelings, and past experiences so that the inner representation of the outer object is not an exact replica (Figure 9.1). Paul Cezanne, for instance, did not wish to reproduce nature in mirrorlike fashion, as was conventionally done, but to represent his view of it. After a long period during which realism was the fashion, his art opened the door to *subjectivity,* which grew in importance, leaning as it did more toward the primary rather than the secondary process. That is, there was greater reliance on imagery and imagination than on perception and memory, thereby allowing a fuller and more profound expression of the human spirit. As a result, artists are no longer bound by the dictates of the retina. They can soar in the realms of fantasy propelled by emotions. They can symbolize rather than describe or narrate. In a more general sense, humans have found that through art forms they can break the seal that locks them fast to their inner world, allowing them to communicate, with minimum distortion, the essential nature of the original message (R. Gordon, 1972).

Gowan (1975) sees art as the final product of experiences of the numinous or primary imagination received as images (parataxic). Art permits the individual to find an external form for fears, fantasies, and psychic tensions constructively. In so doing, the artist achieves catharsis while producing objects of social value, beauty, and delight. The production of a masterpiece is explained by Gowan as

> the long journey from the collective unconscious (archetypes) to the personal unconscious (icons) through creativity to the personal preconscious, and finally to external collective display (art). (p. 227)

On art as *image-magic,* Gowan draws our attention to the *parataxic* mode, which is characterized by the production of images that first served as magic elements (symbols)—the origin of visual art—then as signs (icons), and finally as pictures (modern art). In creating images that find expression in some form of art, humans gain autonomy, purpose, and security. This therapeutic magic finds expression in Pablo Picasso's reaction on seeing the first exhibition of African art in Paris.

> Men had made those masks and other objects for a sacred purpose, a magic purpose, as a kind of mediation between themselves and the unknown hostile forces that surround them, in order to overcome their fear and horror by giving it a form and an image. At this moment I realized that this was what painting was all about. Painting isn't an aesthetic operation; it's a form of magic designed as a mediator between this strange, hostile world and us, a way of seizing power by giving form to our terrors as well as our desires. When I came to that realization, I knew I had found my way. (Picasso cited in Collier, 1972, p. 174)

IMAGERY AND CREATIVE IMAGINATION

Imagery has been classified as *after-imagery, eidetic-imagery, memory-imagery,* and *imagination-imagery* (Hilgard, 1981; McKellar, 1972; Richardson, 1969).

After-imagery is imagery that is the most dependent upon actual sensory stimulation conditions and least dependent upon centrally aroused processes. Visual afterimages occur most frequently although they may appear in other sense modalities. Instances of these include seeing a flash of lightning in the dark, feeling the pressure of a hat on the head after its removal, or experiencing the vibrations of plane travel immediately after the trip.

Eidetic-imagery relates to the formation of preceptlike images. They are different from afterimages in that they last longer and do not require a fixed gaze for their formation. The eidetic image is three dimensional if the original is three dimensional. It is nearly always visual with the imager clearly knowing that the image is a mental representation and not a physical object. The eidetic image is closed to change though open to correction toward the original eidetic. Examples of eidetic images include single images of father at work or father in the evening, mother in communication with father, members of the family or mother experiencing various feeling states, quarreling images of parents, or someone playing the piano or in song.

Memory-imagery is the retrieval from storage of images associated with past, present ongoing, and future anticipated events, experiences, thoughts, and actions. Typically it resembles a hazy etching, is often incomplete and unusually unstable. It is of short duration, indefinitely localized, and open to arbitrary change. Major dimensions of the memory-image are vividness and controllability. Take for instance a memory image of a hammer in a garage lying on top of an old bookcase, or someone slipping on a banana skin into a nearby drain, or the anticipated pleasure of a scientist receiving the Nobel prize at next week's award ceremony.

Imagination-imagery has no particular context, occasion, or personal reference. Although the images are recognized as things, they are not perceived as anything in particular. They tend to be novel, substantial, brightly colored, sharp, and the product of fantasy. Examples of imagination imagery relate to dreams or hallucinations, or image experiences prior to artistic and scientific composition.

There is general agreement about what constitutes the first three image labels. Some nonsignificant difference in labeling the elements of imagination imagery exist, and for the present purpose the names given to these elements by Allan Richardson (1969) will be used. They are as follows:

Hypnogogic imagery—imagery that comes in the semidream state between sleep and wakefulness

Perceptual isolation imagery—imagery that occurs when external stimuli are radically reduced under controlled conditions like being put in a dark soundproof room where sensory cues are minimal

Hallucinogenic drug imagery—imagery chemically induced from such drugs as LSD, peyote, and mescaline

Photic stimulation imagery—imagery evoked by any relatively slow, rhythmic visual stimulation that induces a trancelike state or drowsiness

Pulse current imagery—imagery induced by electrical impulses that are externally applied to the temples to stimulate the appearance of imagery

Non-drug-induced hallucination imagery—imagery like that experienced by schizophrenics, mystics, and shamans

Creative imagination imagery—imagery like that experienced by writers, artists, musicians, scientists, and inventors in the creative act

Common to all these forms is the reduction of external stimuli impinging on individuals to a level that frees them to attend to an inner world of stimulus events for the experience of imagination imagery. However, unlike the first five imagination imagery categories, creative imagination imagery involves a constructive fantasy that brings about transformations.

Stimulating Creative Imagination

Creative potential is well known to be responsive to nurture. This responsiveness is based on the assumption that creative thinking is the heritage of all human beings whose mental functioning is not obstructed or impaired by nature or environmental forces (Maslow, 1959; Osborn, 1963; Rossman, 1931; Royce, 1898). Developmental acceleration of creative mental functioning through planned environmental enrichment has been claimed and generally substantiated by compendia of research on the creative imagination (Khatena, 1984; Osborn, 1963; Parnes, 1958, 1960, 1988; Parnes, Noller, & Biondi, 1977; Torrance, 1972a; Youtz, 1962). On the whole, improvements in creative performance as demonstrated by measures of creative thinking confirm the view that much can be done to help individuals realize their creative potential more effectively.

Training Procedures

A variety of training procedures have been used to improve creative behavior and mental functioning with great success. These have included principles of creative problem solving, brainstorming, idea-generating techniques, free association, incubation, and the like (Feldhusen, Treffinger, & Bahlke, 1970; Maltzman, Bogartz, & Breger, 1958; Mansfield, Busse, & Krepelka, 1978; S. A. Mednick, 1962; Parnes & Meadows, 1959; Torrance, 1965b). There has been recent extension of the Osborn-Parnes verbally driven creative problem solving model by way of a more intuitive imagery-driven approach (Parnes, 1988). Otherwise, there has been very little direct attempt to explore the effects of stimulating the creative imagination to produce original imagery (Khatena, 1984).

Creative imagination engages in constructive fantasy for transformation, organizing the intellective-emotive systems in various ways to process informational content as images. These processes include divergent thinking, breaking away from the obvious and commonplace, transposition, synthesis-destructuring-restructuring, and analogy and metaphor (Khatena, 1984, 1987).

Divergent Thinking Processing Images

Of the five mental *operations* of the Structure of Intellect (Figure 3.5), it is divergent thinking (Figure 4.3) that is primarily involved in creative imagination activity. An essential dimension of *secondary imagination,* the inherited capacity of divergent thinking deals with information received from the environment in novel and unique ways. The *content* dimension of the Structure of Intellect indicates that information in its raw or primary form comes to us from the environment in one of four forms: figural, symbolic, semantic, and behavioral. This information is organized by the intellect in six different ways—units, classes, relations, systems, implications, and transformations—for mental processing, the outcome of which is the *product* dimension. Products in language (verbal codification of images) or nonlanguage (images) form can also serve as a secondary or processed source of information input. If the information is received in verbal form, a process of the intellect decodes the language to reproduce the original or near-original image experience. Information concerning behavior of the individual or group may be both verbal and nonverbal; on its receipt the intellect records the experiences verbally or converts them to images.

We have been told emphatically by Guilford (1967) and Meeker (1980a) that the best guarantee for developing intellectual abilities generally and divergent thinking specifically is to expose individuals to experiences that call for their use. Nourishment of divergent thinking, a function of creative imagination, will strengthen it and facilitate it so that it grows as near as possible to full potential.

Divergent thinking consists of 24 modes of operation (Figure 4.3), each of which can be developed in the service of creative imagination. In planning experiences for this purpose, symbolic and semantic content can be combined, thus reducing divergent thinking to 16 modes of operation. The author has presented a series of exercises involving divergent thinking as it processes images, and has indicated that the image content may be both of a general nature and specific to school learning (Khatena, 1984). No matter which is chosen, it is the exercise of divergent thinking that improves the function of creative imagination for productive manifestation.

Let us take two examples of divergent thinking processing images. One relates to figural content and the other to symbolic-semantic content (Figure 9.3).

Divergent thinking processing images, used in school learning, is illustrated by the following excerpt (Khatena, 1984).

> Divergent Production of a Behavioral Relation (DBR)
> The exercise calls for the image exploration of relations among different people: mother, father, siblings, friends, employer, employee, teacher and student. It can be used to study relationships in different situations among people who are to become characters in literary compositions. Some good prose depicts people and their relations with one another, examples of which are abundant in the works of Charles Dickens, Emily Bronte and D. H. Lawrence, to mention a few. Students can be introduced to the relationship Heathcliff and Cathy share in Emily Bronte's *Wuthering Heights* or that Paul Morrel has with Miriam or his mother in *Sons and Lovers* by D. H. Lawrence. Suitable passages can be identified, read and imaged by students who can be led to note the finer points of language and figurative expressions that simulate vivid and meaningful images. A collection of such experiences becomes preparatory to more serious writing in the higher grades of the senior high school. (pp. 195–196)

Breaking Away from the Obvious and Commonplace

We have seen that information from the environment on its way to the brain is filtered by the mental set of previous experiences, including some quite common ones that key our behavior to them (Figure 9.2). For us to be creative, we need to break away from inhibitory experiences. To

Figure 9.3 Divergent Production of Contents and Products

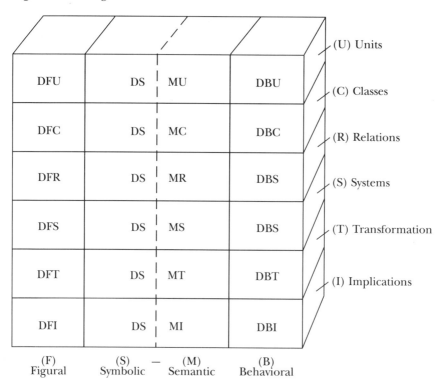

DFU	DS ¦ MU	DBU	(U) Units

From "Imagery and Creative Imagination" (p 118) by Joseph Khatena, 1984, Buffalo, N.Y.: Bearly Limited. Copyright © 1984 by Bearly Limited. Reprinted by permission.

do this we need to consciously apply the strategy of *breaking away from the obvious and commonplace.*

The strategy requires a person to deliberately think in nonhabitual or noncustomary ways. The person must be open to clever, unusual, and novel forms of thinking and doing. To illustrate this strategy, individuals may be given a square, for instance, with the task of breaking away from the mental set of square to produce another but unique nonsquare response. The stimulus set is square; the breakaway may result in the drawings that move away from a square-shaped clock or window to a student smoking a pipe (Figure 9.4).

As a verbal stimulus, the word *roar* can be given. Examples can be set up for comparison, and a response that is definitional, is considered commonplace. However, *roar* can be imaginatively processed to give responses like *talk noisily.* A response of greater imaginative strength would be *blood gushing out of a wound.*

Figure 9.4 Breaking Away from the Obvious and Commonplace

A useful tool to encourage the breaking away from the obvious and commonplace is Thinking Creatively with Sounds and Words (Khatena & Torrance, 1990b). Both of its components, namely Sounds and Images and Onomatopoeia and Images present recorded auditory or visual-auditory-verbal stimuli that call for a breakaway from commonplace thinking to produce original images.

As illustration, let us take a look at some of the original verbal images produced in response to stimuli (in parenthesis) on Onomatopoeia and Images by creative adults and children

Adults
Sunny car in hell (ouch)
An ant walking on the icing of a cake (murmur)
Crickets in harmony (jingle)
Horrid housewife in a hot kitchen (whisp)
Squash of bugs on cement (flop)
Introduction to confusion (zoom)
A frog with an insect stuck on its tongue (stutter)

Slushing watermelon through my teeth (fizzy)
Children
A bird landing heavily on her nest (crackle)
Fly-catching plant closing pores (buzz)
A tree growing out of its bark (moan)
A handful of fingernails scratching on a blackboard (growl)
Violin on a dog's nerves (ouch)
Eraser tearing paper by mistake (groan)
Barber cutting a man's hair fast (jingle)
A frightened lizard (zoom)
A witch melting (fizzy)

A few original images produced by creative children in response to each of the four sounds (in parenthesis) of Sounds and Images are given as follows to illustrate the breaking away from the obvious and commonplace.

Tearing of cloth in an echo chamber (thunder)
Cow with stomach trouble (electronically processed cymbal roll)
Seeds of a watermelon hitting foil (reverberating spring in echo chamber)
Someone's thoughts while robbing a bank (blend of assorted abstract sounds)

Transposition

Transposition is taught in terms of the transference of an existing structural or functional relationship of a phenomenon from one mode of expression to another.

As a figural stimulus, two circles are presented, one being larger than the other. Simple instances of transposition are made in terms of space, music, algebra, and linguistics (Figure 9.5).

The verbal stimulus *thunderstorm* representing the disequilibria of natural elements is the expression of a heard relationship. The point being made is that, in transposing this heard relationship of disequilibria to disequilibria in another sense modality (sight, taste, touch, smell), the individual shows imaginative strength. One example of such a transposition that expresses disequilibria in terms of explosion in the sense modality of taste is a *grape-drenched palate*. Recall what was said about synaesthesia earlier in the discussion, and Edgar Allan Poe's perception *melodious monotone* issuing from the *flame* of each of several lamps brought into a dark room on the arrival of night. Poe's perception is another example of transposing from one sense modality to another.

The two components of Thinking Creatively with Sounds and Words can also serve as tools in effecting transpositions. For instance, if to the sound of thunder came the response *advancing red upon retreating beige,*

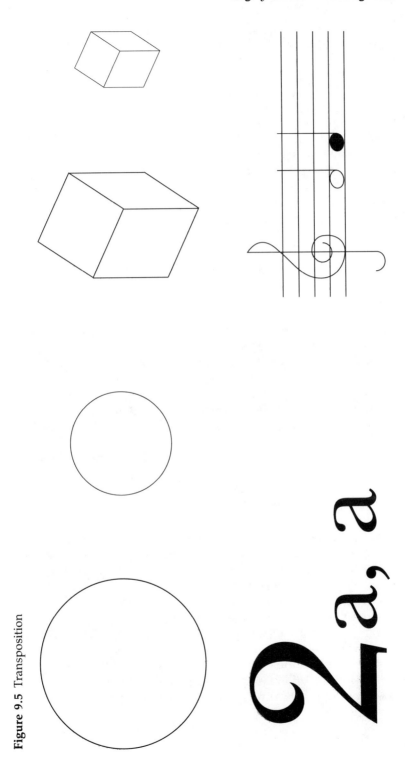

Figure 9.5 Transposition

or to the onomatopoeic word *groan* came the response *flowers seeing their fellows plucked away.*

Synthesis-Destructuring-Restructuring

The activity involved in *synthesis-destructuring-restructuring* is an evolutionary process and calls to mind Land's (1973) transformation theory, which relates to the establishment of an order and the need for breaking up of this order to establish a new and higher order. What the creative mental process and physiobiochemical processes of evolution share in common is *mutation* and *hybridization* (Land & Land V., 1982). *Mutation* involves the random rearrangement, substitution, addition or deletion of small parts of genetic DNA, unconsciously mimicked in creative ideation (Osborn, 1963); *hybridization* is concerned with innovation and invention whose mental dimension is metaphor and paradox.

The process of synthesis-destructuring-restructuring in the context of imagery and creative imagination has received attention in the author's earlier works (e.g., Khatena, 1984). Information retrieved from memory storage as images is synthesized in unique ways by creative imagination. This synthesis gives a certain order that appears to be appropriate at the time of production. However, the time comes when the existing order is no longer satisfying or relevant. The need for a new order arises, determining the separation or destructuring of the elements making up the old order. A recombination or restructuring follows. In the emergence of the new structure or order lies *transformation*—the result of creative imagination activity.

Creative imagination engages in the activity of *synthesis*, through which experiences are organized into unique form. The act of synthesis permits considerable freedom in the manipulation of information for creative expression. It puts together elements that hitherto have not been combined so that something unique can be produced. Because synthesis begins the three-dimensional creative process of synthesis-destructuring-restructuring, it has primary importance, for by it unrelated information acquires order and first form. *Restructuring* implies *destructuring*—a breaking up of the product of synthesis to its elemental composition takes place. This destructuring prepares the information for its reorganization into another unique product of greater quality.

Exercise in the use of the process may involve different kinds of content: figural, verbal-semantic, and behavioral. Presentation of various materials should lead to the exercise of the process. Participants may be asked to deal with the information with or without reference to imaging. Let us take an example of the process using figural and symbolic-semantic information.

Figural Information

Participants construct a human figure with three triangles, four rectangles, and four semicircles presented on a flannel board (synthesis). The geometrical shapes are then pulled apart (destructuring) and reassembled as an automobile (restructuring). The participant is now instructed to pull apart the same pieces to be put together into a different unique picture (destructuring-restructuring). Other pictures may be made in like manner and in this way the process to effect transformations continues.

Symbolic-Semantic Information

A picture of the *Three Wise Men of Gotham* is shown to participants, who are encouraged to ask questions that cannot be answered by merely looking at the picture, guess why events in the scene are taking place and what the consequences of these events are. These activities are a means of "warming up." They are followed by instructions to the participants to identify the main elements of the picture. These participants then select three elements of the picture, perhaps the three wise men, the bowl, and the sea, to put together in a unique way to make an unusual and interesting story (synthesis). At this point a fresh element can be introduced, a bird, shark, or magic bottle, for example. The elements that make the story are separated (destructuring) in readiness for the inclusion of the fourth element. A fresh combination of the elements then leads to the composition of another story (restructuring). And so the process of synthesis-destructuring-restructuring can go on to produce other transformations.

No mention of the use of imaging in these exercises has been made so far. It takes little effort to activate imagery in either activity. Participants can be instructed to image the elements separately, together, or combined to make a whole (synthesis). Breaking up the new imagery into its component parts can also be imaged in the same way (destructuring) to preface their reintegration into something entirely new (restructuring) thereby effecting transformation. Imaging may be done with eyes closed or open. Image activity with closed eyes is often more restful, since it reduces awareness of external interfering stimuli and induces concentration on image events. With sufficient experience, participants can image very well with eyes open.

ANALOGY AND IMAGERY

Analogy and metaphor have been the subjects of much discussion and research over the past decade (e.g., Khatena, 1984, 1987; Khatena &

Khatena, N., 1990; MacCormac, 1986; Pollio & Pollio, 1979; Wheeler, 1987). These discussions have centered on such topics as identification, developmental patterns, sense modality correlates, psychotherapy, poetics, motifs, and creative imagination in art. A major function of analogy and metaphor is to find likeness in dissimilar things, to introduce meanings beyond the objects of comparison themselves. According to Akhter Ahsen (1982), such meanings in a state of poetic incompletion suggest the existence of others.

Analogies have been described by the Synectics group (W. J. J. Gordon, 1961) in terms of creative problem solving. To communicate thoughts, feelings, or experiences that do not easily lend themselves to expression, a search for some familiar situation to which the thought-feeling complex can be related ensues. This search involves the process of *making the strange familiar* or *making the familiar strange* thereby producing insights of hitherto concealed relationships. These mechanisms are involved in the making of creative analogies and have been presented in Synectics as personal analogy, direct analogy, symbolic analogy, and fantasy analogy.

In *personal analogy* a relationship is found between the person making the comparison and some other phenomenon with which this person and others are familiar. Suppose a person wants others to know how thin he is without having to give a lengthy description, he may say, "I'm as thin as a stick." Or, suppose a person wants to tell someone that she is very happy, she may say, "I'm as happy as a lark."

Just as in personal analogy, *direct analogy* finds a relationship between two unlike phenomena, but without self-involvement. To produce a direct analogy, the "I" of the earlier comparison may become *she* or *Jean* thus reading, "Jean is as thin as a stick." Another direct analogy relative to being fat is, "John is as fat as a pig." And if the activity is focused on eating habits, the analogy becomes, "John eats like a pig."

In *symbolic analogy*, a sign or symbol that has as many similar characteristics as the phenomenon itself is found for the phenomenon to be described. For instance, if there is need to describe someone as dependable, strong, stable, consistent, and so on, without using too many words, the selection of some phenomenon (animate or inanimate) that approximates these qualities may be made. For example, the Rock of Gibraltar has been traditionally known to have such qualities: the Rock can serve as a sign or symbol of the qualities possessed by the person in mind. Using symbolic analogy, she may then be referred to as, "the Gibraltar of my life."

Where *fantasy analogy* is concerned, at least the comparison object or subject must be imaginary. Myths, legends, allegories, fairy tales, and the like, are all rich sources of imaginary materials for comparison: the Devil, Medusa, Pandora's box, Ariel, rainbows, dragons, the Garden of

Eden, paradise, Sugar Candy Mountain, Jekyll and Hyde, and so on. Suppose the information to be conveyed is that someone is very wicked, evil, and murderous: such a person may be compared to Hyde, "John is Hyde himself" or "Leonora's whispers stirred the Hyde in John."

In making these analogies, several well-known figures of speech based on agreement, similarity, or resemblance may be used. These are simile, metaphor, personification, and allusion.

Figure of Speech

A *simile* is a form of comparison between two things that often uses the words *like* or *as* (e.g., John is as *fat* as a pig.).

A *metaphor* is a figure of speech that attempts to relate two things different in kind as if they were both similar or even identical (e.g., John is a pig.).

Personification is a form of comparison that attempts to give lifeless objects or abstract things attributes of life and feeling (e.g., Time marches on.).

Allusion is a form of comparison that makes use of familiar phenomena in literature, mythology, legend, present-day happenings, and so on to explain or describe something that is well-known (e.g., She proved to be the Good Samaritan.).

Imagery can be described as mental pictures or images that have organized themselves into a pattern. One thing this does is to make some sense of the world for the persons making images. They are very much like artists in the act of creating the world the way they see it: in the canvas of their mind, there appear images as they react to the world they see and, like artists in the act of painting a picture, they give organization and meaning to these images. How they depict their worlds, what details they include, the choices they make of colors, the style they choose, and the extent to which they allow their emotions to become involved are all dependent on their emotional-intellectual makeup and the creative energizing forces at work at the time.

In the preceding text, analogy was used to compare imagery with painting: the mind is the canvas on which perceptions of the world are painted. Imagery could have been compared to a painting with no attempt at elaboration, but the choice was made to add further details to the basic image—the individual is compared to an artist whose mind is a canvas. Thus, by extending the comparison, or making it more elaborate, the images are combined to make a more complex image pattern. To put it in another way, "Imagery is a painting on the canvas of one's mind." This is a complex image pattern. Simple and complex image patterns can be used in the act of comparison. The more highly imaginative a person is, the greater the tendency to use more complex images.

Figure 9.6 We the People

Whether personal, direct, symbolic, or fantasy analogies are created, imagery is used. More often than not, analogies with complex patterns tend to be more interesting and provocative than simple image patterns. (Compare "Mary sings like a crow" with "Mary sings like a featherless crow on a winter's day," for example.)

An example of the use of symbolic analogy and imagery is found in a work by Nelly Khatena entitled "We the People." This is one of more than 80 art compositions in the "Egg Series" produced within an oval or egg shape. Symbols in "We the People" include an eagle, the Star Spangled Banner, the Capitol, and the Constitution of the United States, ingeniously synthesized into an original form of great beauty conveying a message of "freedom" and "democracy" (Figure 9.6).

For other examples (Khatena & Khatena, 1990), the reader is directed to "Strawberry Patch," the cover design of a recent issue of the *Journal of Creative Behavior* (1986)—a beetle and strawberries symbolically share a beautiful transformative relationship, analogously resembling a bionic spaceship headed for the stars. Another work, "Genesis," appeared as the cover art of a book entitled *Imagery and Creative Imagination* (Khatena, 1984). In this picture, a variety of myths (e.g., Judeo-Christian and Greek-Roman) symbolize the destruction and rebirth of life.

IMAGERY IN PSYCHOGENICS

Another creative approach using imagery in a variety of circumstances, particularly leveled at discovery and healing, comes from Win Wenger (1979). *Beyond O.K.* provides psychogenic tools to help the reader generate experiences that enhance mental and bodily health. In terms of imagery or visualization, Wenger suggests two imagery production modes: directed imagery and spontaneous imagery.

According to Wenger, *directed imagery* has four main uses: discovery of information, control of the autonomic-physiological system for purposes of healing, control of external objectives and outcomes to increase the probability of their occurrence, and the integration of brain functions to increase intelligence. Directed imagery occurs when an individual responds to given instructions. These instructions promote induced relaxation and image streaming, encouraging the individual, with the help of a partner or tape-recorder or in reply to prerecorded exercises, to describe aloud observed image experiences.

The stage is set by directed imagery for the occurrence of *spontaneous imagery*. Directed imagery takes individuals to the frontiers of their image experiences and prepares the way for the participants to take the next step forward into discovery imagery. At this point, imagery, no longer in the control of the experiencer, acquires a life of its own, is free flowing; spontaneously it will show the person experiencing images of everything.

Wenger's (1979, pp. 49–51) description of *image streaming* gives us a good feel for his approach.

> Arrange to meet with a friend who is willing to explore with you and to take turns during the following [exercise] in reasonable calm, quiet surroundings where you won't be interrupted for a few minutes.
>
> (1) Ask your friend to close [his or] her eyes and to begin breathing slowly, deeply and calmly, relaxing more and more just by simply seeing how much, or how much more, he [or she] can let go *with each breath* out.
>
> (2) After a minute of this, with your partner attending only to his breathing, to how good it feels to breathe this way, and not "looking for" images, watch his closed eyes closely. Every few seconds, you will see movement of his eyes under the lids.

(3) A second or so after any of these signs—especially after you detect eye-movement under the lids, ask softly: "What was in your awareness just then?" or "What was your impression just now?" Once he is describing, let him describe. Also ask your partner to report whatever visual impressions he notices regardless of whether you happen to query him about them.

(4) A dozen or so images into the experience, center on one interesting image and draw out more and more sensory-detailed description of it. Discover what experience, in turn, this probing description leads to, find what insights result.

(5) Take turns. You will want that experience too, with its many benefits—including the benefit of improving intelligence through improved communications between left and right sides of the brain.

(6) Once you know "where to look," whenever you have a moment simply look in on your own image stream to see what's going on, what it's leading to, what your "mind's eye" is trying to show you. Your best results will occur, if, as you look at your own spontaneous images, you describe them aloud—either to a friend, or to your own tape recorder. Keeping a tape recorder set up by your own bedside, a very convenient circumstance for looking in on your spontaneous images, is an excellent idea.

FOSTERING CREATIVE PROCESS

The process approach to learning has been repeatedly proposed by many cognitivists (e.g., Bloom, 1956; Cole, 1972; C. R. Rogers, 1967) and, more recently, by advocates of creative learning (Feldhusen & Treffinger, 1980; Meeker, 1969, 1989; Torrance, 1965c; Torrance & Safter, 1990; F. E. Williams, 1972) because learning pertains to most children attending regular schooling. With the growth of the gifted movement, especially over the past 30 years, and the search for better ways to facilitate the intellectual growth and advancement of gifted students, recent advocates of process learning have turned their attention to the relevance of some of these approaches for the gifted.

The rationale of the process approach sees learning in the control of each individual and related to intellectual abilities and emotive or affective correlates. It finds expression (1) in techniques that familiarize individuals with their own capabilities, and (2) in strategies that call for the use of these capabilities in learning strategies that can be effectively adapted to the needs of changing circumstances. Furthermore, it implies the growth of abilities in the conducive and facilitative climate of *psychological safety* and *psychological freedom* (C. R. Rogers, 1967) that foster the occurrence of higher levels of mental functioning leading to productive consequences.

Many approaches to training people to think in creative ways have been tried. Torrance (1972a), in reviewing the effects of training procedures and related variables on creative thinking (as measured by the Torrance Tests of Creative Thinking), categorizes these approaches as problem solving, creative arts, media and reading programs, curricular and administrative arrangements, teacher influence and classroom climate, and motivational mechanisms.

Several creativity training programs appraised for their effectiveness (Mansfield, Busse, & Krepelka, 1978) provide another good source of information. The programs appraised include the following:

1. Productive Training Program. The productive training program is a self-instructional program for fifth- and sixth-grade students aimed at developing creative problem-solving abilities and favorable attitudes toward problem solving (Covington, Crutchfield, Davies, & Olton, 1974).

2. Purdue Creative Thinking Program. The Purdue Creative Thinking Program is designed for fourth graders to foster divergent thinking abilities in verbal and figural fluency, flexibility, originality, and elaboration (Feldhusen, Speedie, & Treffinger, 1971).

3. Osborn-Parnes Creative Problem-Solving Program. The Parnes Creative Problem-Solving Program is designed for adults (Parnes, 1967a, 1967b). It uses many techniques derived from Osborn (1963), with a particular focus on brainstorming. Brainstorming is a three-step process involving fact finding, idea finding, and solution finding. It has two important underlying principles: the production of many ideas increases the chances of more good ideas, and deferred judgment does not permit criticism until all ideas have been produced.

4. Myers-Torrance Workbooks. The Myers-Torrance Workbooks are designed to foster the creativity of elementary school children through practice in activities requiring the perceptual and cognitive abilities that are presumed to underlie creativity (e.g., Myers & Torrance, 1964, 1968).

5. Khatena Training Method. The Khatena Training Method, designed for both children and adults, provides instruction and practice in five creative thinking strategies: breaking away from the obvious and commonplace, transposition, analogy, restructuring, and synthesis (e.g., Khatena, 1970, 1971c).

6. Other Methods. A variety of other little-researched training programs include the use of divergent production abilities, games, experiences from the visual and auditory senses, principles of general semantics, self-instruction to modify what persons say to themselves during problem solving, focusing on reformulating feelings, and synectics.

The major question posed by the appraisal of these approaches is whether the creativity gains made by means of exposure to any of these programs would actually affect real-life creativity. The answer about the effects of such training on developing creative adult professionals is uncertain because their creativity may depend on the joint occurrence of a number of cognitive, motivational, and personality characteristics as well as on situational factors.

Furthermore, it is recognized that at nonprofessional levels the training, when integrated with instruction in a particular subject area, is more likely to lead to productivity. Take, for instance, the writing of original stories or the conducting of original science projects. The appraisal makes mention of the value and enjoyment that training has for students although its effects on attitudes are uncertain. It also discusses the relative effectiveness of the training programs and arrives at the conclusion that the Osborn-Parnes Program and the Khatena Training Method have the most convincing records, having in common breadth of training without being linked to a fixed set of materials.

One thing worth noting about these several approaches is that, by and large, they are targeted at the general population with only an occasional study aimed at the gifted. On the whole, the picture is quite well sketched by the review although it is not complete in terms of the different training programs or materials available for consideration (Feldhusen & Treffinger, 1980; Karnes & Collins, 1980), or in terms of the supporting research, some of which needs updating.

But these are not of concern here. What we need to examine are the generic roots of these and related approaches, which can be identified, mainly through the (1) Structure of Intellect, (2) creative problem solving of current or future problems with its sequential steps or systems approach, and (3) sociodrama, to which must be added (4) imagery and creative imagination (discussed earlier in this chapter).

Structure of Intellect

One viable approach to the use of process in education is the Structure of Intellect Model (Guilford, 1967). Another is Benjamin S. Bloom's taxonomy of educational objectives (Bloom, 1956). Bloom's taxonomy of educational objectives (knowledge, comprehension, application, analysis, synthesis, and evaluation) is *hierarchical;* Guilford's model of the intellect is three dimensional (operations, contents, and products) and *interactive.* In terms of the intellectual functioning of the learner, Bloom's taxonomy has its most direct parallel in the operations aspect of the Structure of Intellect. The lack of emphasis on information content and the generation of products makes his taxonomy quite incomplete. Besides, because there is no empirical validation by factor analysis, the philosophical basis of the categories have the status of untested hypotheses (Guilford, 1972). However, we shall see shortly how Bloom's taxonomy is made an integral part of Frank E. Williams's Cognitive-Affective Interaction Model (F. E. Williams, 1972).

The Structure of Intellect (Guilford, 1967, 1988) is an informational theory of intelligence that depends on the environment for its materials. These may take any one of four forms of *content:* figural (visual-auditory), symbolic, semantic, or behavioral. Content may be organized as *products* in any one of six ways: units, classes, relations, systems, transformations, and implications. Five mental *operations*—cognition, convergent thinking, divergent thinking, and evaluation—act upon both contents and products. The Structure of Intellect provides the rationale and procedures for the development of several training models that are being used in schools and special projects all over the country.

To foster intellectual development, Guilford (1972) suggests that we have four goals. The first goal relates to the development of skill. The second goal relates to the stockpiling of specific items of information. In this way, possession of information (cognition) and its use (production) are emphasized. Two additional goals involve the evaluation and retention of information. These goals are dependent on achievement relative to other mental operations (Guilford, 1967).

Abilities are operationalized by the Structure of Intellect. Thus theory informs practice in a way that not only permits the arrangement of exercises that use these abilities and facilitate continued development, but also directs the planning of curricula to activate the function of these abilities. In addition, knowledge of Guilford's model can assist in designing teaching methodology requiring the use of Structure of Intellect abilities. The model provides a frame of reference for the development of assessment procedures to measure these abilities.

Guilford (1977) considers it important to *exercise these abilities* so that intellectual development can be maximized. He points to the fact that first-rate musical performers or golf players, for instance, do not reach peak form without engaging in hours of special exercises. Likewise, practice of each intellectual ability is expected to promote its performance potential. This practice can be facilitated once children are aware of the resources they possess.

Training of intellectual skills does not have to be limited to formal exercises especially designed for that purpose. With proper emphasis, such training can be achieved while using regular class learning material. Teaching can be redirected to emphasize not just the formation of concepts weighted to the cognition of semantic units but also to the remaining five semantic products (classes, relations, systems, transformations, and implications) in whose involvement units of information acquire significance, meaning, and usefulness. Furthermore, in the selection of a curriculum, provision should be made both for the development of general skills as well as for their immediate and special uses. The more courses allow Structure of Intellect abilities to be "exercised," the more transfer benefits can be expected to result from them (Guilford, 1967, 1977).

A rationale for the development of many training procedures, especially as they relate to exercises in creative thinking (e.g., Davis, 1970; Renzulli, 1973; Schaefer, 1971) has been provided by the Structure of Intellect. Insofar as the *development of models* is concerned, two are of particular interest to us. The first (Meeker, 1969) is a direct application and extension of the structure to education. The second (F. E. Williams, 1979) augments the Structure of Intellect Model with concepts borrowed particularly from the taxonomy of educational (cognitive and affective) objectives (Bloom, 1956; Krathwohl, Bloom, & Masia, 1964) and cognitive development (Piaget, 1967).

Both of these models were conceived for students in general; their application in instructional settings is broadly based. The fact that these models were developed for general use does not mean that they have no relevance for gifted students. In fact, they have much to offer to the intellectual development of gifted students. They put in students' hands tools that will allow them to cope with the details of ever-expanding curricula.

Mary N. Meeker and Frank E. Williams have attempted to slant their models to meet the needs of gifted students. Meeker (1979a) shows the relevance of the structure approach used in individualized education programs, but does not say much more than she had previously about the potentiality of the model. F. E. Williams (1979) finds common ground between the strategies used in his model and those of Renzulli's enrichment triad, but does not get away from the model's original intent to reach all students in any specific way.

Meeker's Instructional Materials

Meeker, more than anyone else, has applied Structure of Intellect concepts to educational problems in general, and the problems of remedial education specifically. Consistent with Guilford's thoughts on the development of intellect through educational experiences, Meeker (1969) observes that teaching a person how to use an ability is as important as the mastery of prescribed content. That is why there is the need to go beyond measuring I.Q. to identify which abilities are more developed than others. This identification will provide the basis for diagnosing intellectual strengths and weaknesses, allowing educational experiences to be planned according to the learner's needs.

She believes that emphasis should shift from strengthening and enriching curriculum, and developing acceleration approaches and teaching techniques, to utilizing the learning process itself. The Structure of Intellect is seen by her as a way to circumvent the philosophical problem of keeping pace with the continuous expansion of knowledge. Because it is stable, it provides a frame of reference for the *fashioning of learning* experiences beyond curriculum content.

The Structure of Intellect is also regarded as the basis of a *cognitive therapy* that concerns itself with assisting students in overcoming failure attributable to the lack of development of the requisite abilities for success. A differentiated measure of abilities is the key to the identification of deficiencies, and the Structure of Intellect can provide this differentiation. In this way, many intellectual failures can be avoided through the development of prerequisite intellectual skills.

By providing a practical thrust for Guilford's theoretical model, Meeker offers the practitioner an instrument that, if understood and properly used, can give the learning situation greater meaning for the learner. Theory is made operational in the form of small learning components that recognize the interactive nature of ability and information and ways they are organized. Organization permits a structuring of learning experiences that, at one and the same time, can identify abilities and facilitate their development. One major outcome of this early work was the development of the *Structure of Intellect Abilities Workbooks* (Meeker, 1980a; Meeker, Sexton, & Richardson, 1970). The goal of these workbooks is to train children to use Structure of Intellect abilities.

The *Structure of Intellect Abilities Workbooks* evolved from the theory-based curriculum of Meeker's (1969) earlier work. The workbooks are organized into five components, each is based on one of the five mental operations of the Structure of Intellect. Exercises in the workbooks call into play within the context of curriculum materials known interactive content and product dimensions.

The approach is *prescriptive*. It *individualizes instruction* based on a diagnosis of intellectual responses on an I.Q. measure such as the Stanford-Binet or the Wechsler Intelligence Scale for Children. With the assistance of a psychologist who uses prepared templates, the I.Q. is translated into Structure of Intellect *profiles*. The psychologist then prescribes tasks necessary to the development of certain abilities.

If a teacher does not have the assistance of an intellectual profile, Meeker and her associates suggest that the workbook material be used to teach an ability at the *units* level if a deficit exists or if a weak ability needs to be tied to a stronger one. The teacher would then go to the *classes* level—the beginning of concept formation. *Relations* and *systems* may be taught together. Finally, instruction that deals with *transformations* and *implications,* high-level abstract abilities associated with creative experiences, follows. It should be noted that this approach has (a) general and specific objectives that are clearly stated, (b) materials and instructions that are outlined separately to assist teachers in finding the individualized materials related to the objectives, and (c) procedures for evaluation and reinforcement.

Tasks are set up in a small-step-structure approach. Each task fits a defined Structure of Intellect ability and serves as an example of the instruction to be selected when shaping other similar tasks. The importance of approaching learning in this way is emphasized by the authors of the workbooks. Meeker in her introductory remarks says:

> Education, if based on the premise that it is necessary to teach children how to learn rather than [to teach them] content, or if based on the premise that we need to develop thinking abilities rather than subject matter, may manage to survive during this century. The clamor to train children in affective abilities [may] be best heard when we show that we can develop cognitive abilities for then it will be demonstrated that somehow, magically, thinking does relate to affective growth (Meeker, Sexton, & Richardson, 1970, p. viii).

Guilford, time and again, has pointed to the need for the development in school of two very much neglected mental operations of the Structure of Intellect: the *divergent* and *evaluative thinking* operations. In school, instructional materials require that students use cognition, memory, and convergent thinking operations. Tests are designed to measure intellectual potential associated with cognition, memory, and convergent thinking. It is not surprising that many educators have constructed their own training procedures or recommend others that encourage the use of the two neglected abilities, placing more emphasis on divergent and creative thinking.

The intellectually gifted student generally uses creative thinking abilities less frequently than the creatively gifted. In seeking the best of the *Structure of Intellect Abilities Workbooks* to use in educating the superior student, it would appear that we should be selective; we would most frequently choose the *Divergent Production Workbook* (Figures 9.7 and 9.8).

To be consistent with Meeker's prescriptive approach, however, a Structure of Intellect profile may be obtained to give information on what abilities need to be developed. The Structure of Intellect Basic Test (Meeker, 1980b) is needed for this. The test is an adaptation of adult measures Guilford and his associates have developed (Guilford, 1967), scaled down in format, content, and response mode for use with students in Grade 2 through Grade 12 (Meeker, 1979b). It incorporates 24 of the 90 subtests designed to measure identified abilities relative to creativity and school learning, especially in reading, arithmetic, and writing. The measure may be administered to an individual or in groups. (Instructions are available on a cassette.) An accompanying manual provides scoring keys and instructions for developing teaching strategies.

Such an approach leads to the prescription of exercises needed to de-

Figure 9.7 Divergent Production of Symbolic Implications

Child's Name   Cell _____

                                 Subject _____

                                 Grade _____

Objective:
To develop the ability to produce unusual, remote or clever responses involving reinterpretations or new emphasis on some aspect of an object or situation.

Recommendation to Teacher	
Materials: Short story—verbally or visually presented Sample story: (lower grade) Three men built houses. One man built his house on the sand and no foundation under it. Everyone thought he was very foolish. Another man built his house on the dirt with no foundation. The third man built his house on a great flat rock. The house built on sand lasted only a week, for the winds blew it down. The house built on the dirt lasted six months and the house built on the rock is now 200 years old!	Instructions general: Present the story to the student. Explain proverbs—give examples. Make the stories more sophsiticated for junior and senior high-school students. Specific: After reading and/or hearing the short story students are assigned the task of making up their own proverbs as homework. Evaluation of progress: The proverbs will be read in class. Students will guess the interpretation.
Reinforcement techniques:	Task: Proverbs

From *SOI Abilities Workbooks: Divergent Thinking* (p. 480) by M.N. Meeker, K. Sexton, and M.O. Richardson, 1970, Los Angeles: Loyola-Marymount University. Copyright © 1970 by M.N. Meeker. Reprinted by permission.

Figure 9.8 Divergent Production of Semantic Transformation

Child's Name   Cell _____
                                      Subject _____
                                      Grade _____

Objective:
To develop the ability to produce varied implications from given symbolic
information.

Recommendation to Teacher	
Materials: Pencil Duplicated exercise <table><tr><td>Math</td></tr><tr><td>Name_____ Date_____ Write new equations using these letters. The new equations must be based upon the equations. *Example:* Given: A + B = C *New Equations:* C – B = A B + A = C 1. Given: D + F = E *New Equations:* _____ _____ 2. Given A – B = C New Equations: _____ _____</td></tr></table>	Instructions general: Specific: Follow the directions on the exercise. Evaluation of progress:
Reinforcement techniques:	Task: Equations

velop certain intellectual abilities. These exercises can be effectively implemented using a specific series of tasks organized in Meeker's workbooks. (This diagnostic-prescriptive approach also applies to reading
and arithmetic [Meeker, 1979a] and will be dealt with in the next chapter.)

If there is weakness in the Structure of Intellect approach, it lies in the
overt emphasis of the model on thinking functions. Also, there is the
tendency for schools, because of the way the workbooks are designed,
to teach the skills in isolation. They do not teach the skills using Shakespeare's plays or physics experiments, for instance; instead they rely on
dull pencil-paper exercises. Those of us who perceive the need to nurture the whole individual prefer to include feeling and other nonintellective factors (e.g., Gowan, 1978c; Khatena, 1984). Guilford (1972, 1977)
also recognizes this problem with the Structure of Intellect. Though, he
does not include feeling in the model, affective characteristics may lie
within the behavioral content component of the Structure of Intellect.

We should quickly note the intent of the model, which is to present to
us the *nature of thinking* in the first place, and in the second place, the
nurture of thinking, to advance intellectual development to its fullest potential. The Structure of Intellect as advocated by Meeker may not be the
answer to the total development of individual intellect. But it is the most
significant operational approach available for the enhancement and
growth of those abilities within the structure. As other dimensions of
intellectual functioning, outside the model, are perceived to be in need
of development, exercises can be designed to complement the basic tenets of the structure.

Williams's Cognitive-Affective Interaction Model

Another approach that claims relationship to Guilford's theoretical
model is the Cognitive-Affective Interaction Model (F. E. Williams, 1969,
1972). Williams's three-dimensional model (Figure 9.9) is modified to
substitute meaningful content to the teacher (Curriculum), strategies
teachers use (Teacher Behaviors), and cognitive-affective activity of students (Pupil Behaviors) for contents, operations, and products. However,
the dimensions of Williams's model are neither altogether parallel nor
interchangeable with the Structure of Intellect, nor are they meant to be.

The cognitive-affective model concentrates on divergent production
operations without using specific Structure of Intellect terminology (e.g.,
divergent symbolic transformation [DST]; divergent figural implications
[DFI]). Instead, for the cognitive dimension, it uses broader factor categories (fluency, flexibility, originality, and elaboration) which are similar to
those used in the Torrance Tests of Creative Thinking (Torrance, 1974b).

Williams uses *cognitive* to mean creative thinking abilities, and *affective*
to mean four personality traits: curiosity, risk taking, complexity, and
imagination. His model gives focus to curriculum strategies and to teach-

Figure 9.9 A Model for Implementing Cognitive-Affective Behaviors in the Classroom

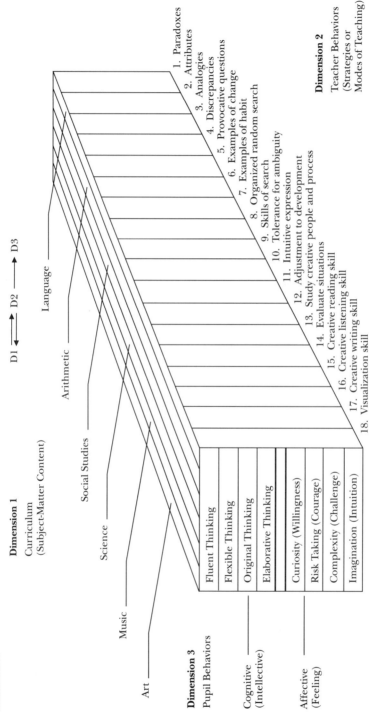

From "Assessing Pupil–Teacher Behaviors Related to a Cognitive–Affective Model," by Frank E. Williams, 1971, *Journal of Research and Development in Education* 4(3), p. 17. Copyright © by Journal of Research and Development in Education. Reprinted by permission.

ing strategies, both of which were not the original intent of the Structure of Intellect, although Guilford (1967) perceived them as having important educational implications relative to his model. These implications were later translated into classroom practice by Meeker (1969, 1980a).

One face of Williams's structure (Dimension 1) deals with curriculum (subject-matter content) as it relates to art, music, science, social studies, arithmetic, and language. A second face (Dimension 2) deals with teacher behaviors (strategies or modes of teaching) as they relate to paradoxes, attributes, analogies, discrepancies, provocative questions, examples of change, examples of habit, organized random search, skills of search, tolerance for ambiguity, intuitive expression, adjustment to development, study of creative people and process, evaluative situations, creative reading skill, creative listening skill, creative writing skill, and visualization skill. The third face (Dimension 3) deals with pupil behaviors (cognitive and affective).

One of F. E. Williams's (1969) first remarks on the subject of finding a suitable model for encouraging creativity in the classroom identifies the inadequacy of taxonomical models, such as Bloom's (1956) taxonomy of educational objectives in the cognitive domain. To this he adds Piaget's stage theory of intellectual development (Flavell, 1963), and Krathwohl's taxonomy of objectives in the affective domain (Krathwohl, Bloom, & Masia, 1964).

According to F. E. Williams, taxonomies are deficient because (1) their components are conceived in hierarchical order; (2) they hold that the creative process (defined by many as synonymous with such mental processes as hypothesizing, synthesizing, inventing, associating, and transforming) is only found within the higher stages or levels of the taxonomies; and (3) they rest on the erroneous assumptions that children are incapable of higher level thinking before the earlier levels are mastered and until they reach the adolescent stages of development.

F. E. Williams maintains that there is also a need to include the affective dimension of cognitive functioning in process models (Krathwohl, Bloom, & Masia, 1964; Piaget, 1967). Furthermore, he observes the need for a *morphological* rather than a taxonomical model to take into account both the cognitive and affective behavioral dimensions. Guilford's structure model describes an interrelated classification of intellectual abilities in the cognitive domain but leaves out the affective domain. And although the cognitive-affective model proposed by Krathwohl, Bloom, and Masia (1964) includes thinking and feeling, it is one-dimensional. Hence, F. E. Williams considers a morphological interaction model of cognitive and affective behavioral dimensions related to curriculum and teaching strategies as necessary. This conclusion became the rationale for his cognitive-affective interaction model.

The model expresses itself in the Total Creativity Program (F. E.

Williams, 1972). The program comprises five books, two poster sets, two audiotapes, a teaching strategies packet, and an instructor's manual. It is designed to give practical assistance to teachers in almost any classroom. No large-scale innovative or drastic changes and no expensive materials or equipment to supplement methodology in current use are needed. Pupils are encouraged to want to be involved in creative learning experiences. In addition, the program can be used to train teachers, in both regular and in-service programs, about the principles of creativity and their effective application to school learning. The program has been very favorably reviewed (Cole & Parsons, 1974) as an elaborate and well-designed instructional system that serves as a good example to educators, researchers, and curriculum developers.

We have seen so far that both Meeker and F. E. Williams have adapted the Structure of Intellect for use in the classroom, the one arranging for learning across the five mental operations and the other including the dimension of divergent thinking. Both approaches are three dimensional and interactive. Meeker's approach is directly related to the structure cells of Guilford's model. F. E. Williams draws more broadly from the factorial components of divergent thinking; Krathwohl's affective categories; and creative personality research of, for instance, D. W. MacKinnon (1978), F. Barron (1969), and E. P. Torrance (1979b).

Although Williams recognizes the importance of the affective roots of intellectual abilities and their functioning, he separates them in his model. Meeker's approach, however, omits affect altogether, unless one reads affective characteristics into the behavioral content category. Both advocate the development of teacher competencies, and a means of facilitating an effective use of their approaches with children and adolescents. Direction for the use of these models with gifted students can be extrapolated from direction for their use with all students. If the development of creative mental functions in gifted children is the primary goal, then either model can serve the purpose.

Creative Problem Solving

Creative problem solving is an important process approach that can be effectively applied to day-to-day living and, specifically, to education. Evidence about the complexity of problem solving can be found in the literature of general psychology, animal psychology, factor analysis, and psychobiology.

1. General Psychology—General psychology contributes experiments involving the use of a variety of problem-solving tasks, such as Maier's (1930) string-and-hatrack problems and Luchins's (1942)

water-jars problems. Syllogisms, mechanical puzzles, and concept attainment are other problem-solving tasks used.

2. Animal Psychology—Animal psychology provides us with other evidence derived from problem-solving situations involving mazes, puzzle boxes, discrimination tasks, and detours, as well as field-configuration problems (e.g., Kohler, 1927; Thorndike, E. L., 1932; Tolman, 1948).

3. Factor Analysis and General Systems—Another important source of information on problem solving can be traced to factor analysis. Its finding that problem solving is factorially complex has led to the construction of a generic problem-solving model based on the Structure of Intellect, from which other problem-solving models can be derived (Guilford, 1967).

4. Psychobiology—Yet another generic problem-solving model has emerged from transformation theory, a psychobiological process approach to understanding the universe (Land, 1973).

One can view problem solving as a sequential-steps process. Among those who have contributed to and have had an impact on the further development of this approach are John Dewey (1910), Graham Wallas (1926), W. J. J. Gordon (1961), and A. F. Osborn (1963). Nearly all such models call for the use of facilitative strategies by way of attribute listing; questioning; brainstorming; morphological analysis; and metaphor, analogy, and imagery.

The unique application of the principles of creative problem solving to sociodrama provides yet another approach (Torrance, 1975a). It is an approach that uses the stage as metaphor, allowing participants to function as both audience and protagonist in the resolution of conflict.

Alternatively, creative problem solving may be viewed as a process rooted to larger systems. A systems approach to creative problem solving was proposed by Guilford (1967) and Land (1973), the former using intellectual operations, and the latter using biopsychological and transformative processes.

Sequential Steps

Dewey's (1910) problem-solving steps are (a) sensing a difficulty, (b) locating and defining it, (c) suggesting possible solutions, (d) considering consequences, and (e) accepting a solution. Others who followed him made minor modifications to these steps or elaborated on them.

The steps proposed by Rossman (1931) were derived from a study showing how 700 inventors solved problems. He also used Dewey's steps but added two more—the surveying of available information and the formulation of new ideas.

Table 9.1 Several Sequential-Step Approaches to Creative Problem Solving

John Dewey	Joseph Rossman	Graham Wallas	James Vargiu
Difficulty felt	Need or difficulty observed		
Difficulty located and defined	Problem formulated		
	Available information surveyed	Preparation or information collected	Preparation Frustration
		Incubation or on-going unconscious activity	Incubation
Possible solutions suggested	Solutions formulated	Illumination or emergent solutions	Illumination or solutions avalanche
Consequences considered	Solutions critically examined	Verification or testing and elaborating solutions	Elaboration
Solution accepted	New ideas formulated New ideas tested and accepted		

The steps proposed by Wallas (1926) omit Dewey's first two and begin with preparation (information gathering) and incubation (unconscious workings of the mind). They go on to two others, which are similar to Dewey's fourth and fifth steps. Wallas called these final two steps illumination (emergent solutions) and verification (acceptance).

Theorizing on the problem-solving aspects of creativity led Vargiu (1977) to propose problem-solving steps similar to Wallas's. The difference between these two models lies in Vargiu's addition of frustration as a step following preparation, and his change of verification to elaboration, which, in any case, is included as part of the process of solution testing.

These four approaches are shown in Table 9.1. As we shall see, they are taken into account by the Structure of Intellect and the Biopsychological and Transformational Process Models. These problem-solving steps form the basic principles of creative problem-solving models, two of which will be discussed in the following sections.

Osborn-Parnes Creative Problem-Solving Model   The principles of creative problem solving are discussed in *Applied Imagination* (Osborn, 1963). The well-known procedure for group-think, better known as brainstorming, has four basic ground rules, which are said to lead to effective creative problem solving. Osborn advocates that *criticism* be ruled out, *freewheeling* be welcomed, a *quantity of ideas* be desired, and the *combination and improvement of them* be sought.

In describing the principles and techniques of deliberate idea finding, Osborn offers two significant approaches to creative problem solving: *deferment of judgment* and *quantity breeds quality*. To these he adds yet another significant contribution to the principles of brainstorming—the application of a three-step process in creative problem solving (Osborn, 1962, p. 20).

1. *Fact finding*
   Problem definition: Picking out and pointing to the problem
   Preparation: Gathering and analyzing the pertinent data
2. *Idea finding*
   Idea production: Thinking up tentative ideas as possible leads
   Idea development: Selecting from resultant ideas, adding others, and reprocessing by means of modification, combination, rearrangement, substitution, and so on
3. *Solution finding*
   Evaluation: Verifying the tentative solutions by tests and in other ways
   Adoption: Deciding on and implementing the final solution

In this way, Osborn (1962) incorporates the alternation between creative and evaluative thinking (elsewhere described as *green-light* and *red-light* activity) and the principle of deferred judgment.

Parnes and his associates applied and extended these principles in courses at State University College of New York at Buffalo, in annual national and regional meetings of the Creative Problem Solving Institute, and in several publications (Parnes, 1967a, 1967b; Parnes, Noller, & Biondi, 1977).

His illustration (Figure 9.10) of the creative problem-solving process (Parnes, 1967a) indicates that a problem situation appears to the experiencer as unclear or a fuzzy *mess,* so that the definition of the problem at this point cannot relate to the real problem at hand. As a result of careful exploration to uncover the facts contingent on the problem, *fact finding,* sufficient clarity may result and recognition of the real problem, *problem finding,* occurs. This should lead to *idea finding* via brainstorming (often encouraged as a group process) and the production of many alternative solutions, the *solution-finding* step.

To facilitate the generation of ideas, criticism must be deferred and freewheeling welcomed, for wild or silly or impractical ideas may spark other ideas that lead to a practical solution. At this time, the presentation of any number of ideas is encouraged on the theory that *quantity breeds quality.* A number of procedures may be used to facilitate this improvement of ideas, including hitchhiking on the ideas of others; asking

Figures 9.10 Typical Flow of the Creative Problem-Solving Process

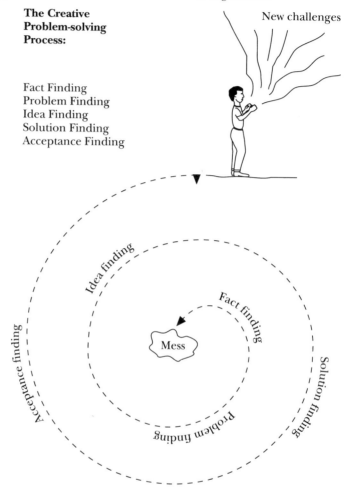

The Creative Problem-solving Process:

Fact Finding
Problem Finding
Idea Finding
Solution Finding
Acceptance Finding

New challenges

Idea finding

Fact finding

Mess

Acceptance finding

Solution finding

Problem finding

Every goal man reaches provides a new starting point
and the sum of all man's days is just a beginning."
Lewis Mumford

From "*Creative Behavior Workbook*" (unpaginated) by Sidney J. Parnes, 1967, New York: Charles Scribner's Sons. Copyright © 1967 by Charles Scribner's Sons. Reprinted by permission.

idea-spurring questions (e.g., Put to other uses? Adapt? Modify? Magnify? Minify? Substitute? Rearrange? Reverse? Combine?); and encouraging the use of free association, analogies, various sense modalities, and so on. Once several solutions are identified, they may be subject to evaluation according to some agreed-on relevant criteria (e.g., cost, time required, usefulness, social acceptance). Evaluation may be followed by *acceptance-finding to determine* the most appropriate solution for a successful plan of action.

Parnes and his associates added the following mechanisms to their creative problem-solving approach:

1. The *dynamic-delicate balance* between *judgment* and *imagination;* between open awareness of the environment through all the senses and deep self-searching of the layer upon layer of data stored in memory; between logic and emotion; between the processes of making it happen and of letting it happen; between the insights and the action

2. The presence of *sensitivity, synergy,* and *serendipity* to illuminate the creative process that requires divergent thinking (*Sensitivity* implies great awareness through all senses. *Synergy* occurs when two or more elements, on becoming associated, bring about an emergent element that transcends its parts. *Serendipity* results from an awareness of relevancy in accidental happenings.)

3. The practice in *coping behavior* that programs nurturing creativity give

4. The productive consequences of *stimulating the brain* with such processes as deferred judgment and various idea-stimulating techniques

5. The *challenge of keeping creativity alive* through creative calisthenics to prevent the atrophy of talents and to develop the creative muscles through exercise; the excitement of self-discovery through a creative education that provides its own reason for being and its own self-stimulation, so that a person's entire life can be built around the intense desire to learn

The variety and diversity of the Creative Problem Solving Institute's experience, teaching, and research led Parnes (1975) to reformulate some of his thoughts on creative problem-solving processes and procedures through his activities with the Creative Education Foundation. Although reaffirming the basic tenets of the Osborn-Parnes system, Parnes underscores that the basic philosophy of the Creative Problem Solving Institute emphasizes continued development—*growing* and *becoming* (Land, 1973)—rather than simply to *become.* The Institute's eclectic program not only includes the five-step process—fact, problem, idea, solution, and acceptance finding—but also interlaces processes derived from synectics, sensitivity training, art, fantasy, meditation, body awareness, and so on; hence, it subscribes to the concept of *balanced growth*. Parnes (1975) comments on the problem-solving process as follows:

> Thus the problem solving process becomes one of opening up the self to the fullest possible awareness of the storehouse of energy and resources within oneself—in one's vast mental library of life experience—as well as in the vast data of the external world. Problem solving becomes the task of finding the greatest number of interconnections and interrelationships among these vast resources, including the layer upon layer of primary information stored in our brain cells from birth and even from embryonic states. One searches for the kinds of synergistic connections that one can make toward the solution of one's problems, one's goals, one's wishes, one's aspirations, one's hopes, one's dreams—for oneself, one's family, one's group, one's society, one's world, one's universe. (pp. 26–27)

A shift of emphasis by Parnes and his associates on the use of the imagination and judgment—from its sequential occurrence to its more generalized occurrence through all the creative problem-solving steps—has taken place. Thus, there is an unleashing of the imagination, which is to be gradual while the judicial abilities are concurrently strengthened; a stretching of the imagination to all creative problem-solving stages rather than restricting it to the idea-generation stage; and a continuing effort to acquire a multiplicity of viewpoints of the problem in the problem-definition stage. This changing emphasis is what Parnes and Biondi (1975) term the *delicate balance*.

Two pertinent questions are brought to mind by this: "How loose can a person stay before falling apart?" and "How tight can one remain before freezing up?" The authors say that if judgment is no longer to overwhelm the imagination in decision making, we shall have to maintain the "deferjudice" stance that will allow us to oscillate comfortably between "nojudice" and "prejudice," "looseness" and "tightness," with full awareness that nothing is final.

Parnes extends the concepts of the Osborn-Parnes creative problem-solving method by emphasizing the *importance of imagery*. What was implicit in the earlier problem-solving system is made explicit in two works. In the first, *The Magic of Your Mind* (1981), Parnes begins to use *intuitive imagery*, within the context of the logical Creative Problem Solving Model (first-generation deliberate creativity development). (A second-generation method stressing the use of *spontaneous imagery* processes was discussed in the chapter on incubation and autonomous imaging.)

His next work, *Visionizing* (1988), presents the third generation of creative problem solving, which combines the first and second, and within which the *explicit use of imagery* is recommended. Here, spontaneous imagery processes that facilitate dreaming-wishing and visioning as techniques for solving problems of current import or future relevance are presented in a five-session program. Parnes defines *visioning* as the *actualization of a dream*, the activity involved in making a dream come true. Creative problem solving assists in the expansion and amplification of dream-related opportunity-objectives to bring about their partial or complete fulfillment.

The remainder of the book places visionizing in the context of the Osborn-Parnes method of creative problem solving. The five-session program itself includes instructions on *relaxation;* encouragement to describe *image-flow verbally*, in great detail, and participate in *image-streaming*, in which individuals work in pairs describing to each other the images that each experiences in a session (Wenger, 1985); use of tapes, music, and other devices. Many useful, interesting activities are presented in the sessions as a means of training participants to actualize their dreams in a creative problem-solving way.

Synectics Creative Problem-Solving Model   Another viable approach to creative problem solving is synectics, which has its origins in the works of W. J. J. Gordon (1961) and G. M. Prince (1968). In the main, Gordon and Prince have operated as Synectics Incorporated, serving the needs of business and industry.

Synectics is a term borrowed from the Greeks meaning the *joining together of different and apparently irrelevant elements.* W. J. J. Gordon tells us that synectics attempts to integrate individuals from different backgrounds (e.g., physics, mechanics, biology, geology, marketing, or chemistry) into a problem-stating-solving team. Members of the synectics team make conscious use of the preconscious to increase the probability of success in stating and solving problems.

Part of the time the group, which is composed of about six members, attacks problems to find out their origins. Part of the time, the group devotes itself to the implementation of concepts directed at the development of solutions (i.e., building working models, conducting experiments, investigating market potentials), an activity considered most important in a synectics project. The several functions of the group include keeping in touch with ongoing projects, learning how others overcome specific problems to understand more about the invention process, and teaching select candidates from client companies to use the synectics method.

The theory of synectics is based on the assumption that people can increase their creative efficiency if they understand the *psychological processes* that set it to work, and that the *emotional or irrational* is more important than the intellectual or rational. The creative process is defined by synectics as the *mental activity in problem stating that results in artistic or technical invention.*

Among the *psychological states* considered necessary if a successful inventive effort is to take place is the ability to tolerate and use attitudes, information, and observations that do not appear to be relevant to the problem in hand. A companion state involves the ability to play—to sustain a childlike willingness to suspend adult disbelief. Such "playfulness" includes the following:

Play with words, meanings, and definitions, involving transposing a specific invention problem into a general word or statement

Play in pushing a fundamental law or a basic scientific concept out of phase

Play with metaphor

Two very important creative processes in synectics are *making the strange familiar* and *making the familiar strange*. The first relates to the need to understand the problem, whereas the second requires a new way of looking at the known world. Four mechanisms, each metaphorical in nature and identified with *making the familiar strange*, are personal analogy, direct analogy, symbolic analogy, and fantasy analogy (explanations of which were given earlier in the chapter). Analogies are essential to successful problem solving because through them we are consciously able to tap the preconscious.

Personal analogy results from the personal being identified with elements of a problem, which releases the individual from viewing the problem in terms of its previously analyzed elements. Take, for instance, the story of Frederick Kekule von Stradonitz identifying himself with a snake swallowing its tail. This vision developed an insight into the benzene molecule as being a ring instead of a chain of carbon atoms.

Direct analogy is a mechanism that describes the comparison of parallel facts, knowledge, or technology. It has been found that a biological perception of physical phenomena can produce generative viewpoints. For example, Alexander Graham Bell's perception of the human ear led to the invention of the telephone.

Symbolic analogy uses objective and impersonal images to describe a problem. It is a compressed description of the function or elements of a problem expressed in qualitative rather than quantitative terms. It is immediate and complete in a blurt of association. Take for example the problem of inventing a jacking mechanism to fit into a 4" x 4" box yet extend out and up three feet to support four tons. After approaching analogies that allowed him or her to look at jacks in a new way, a member of a Synectics team came up with the idea of The Indian Rope Trick: "The rope is soft when the guy starts with it. He shows it to everybody. The whole magic is how to make it hard so he can climb up on it" (W. J. J. Gordon, 1961, p. 46). The related ideas that followed refined the symbol to make it work. A model was later built based on the Symbolic Analogy of the Indian Rope Trick that functioned exactly as described in the session.

Fantasy analogy involves wish fulfillment; imaging can lead to all kinds of magical solutions that prepare the way for their translation into practical terms. For instance, the problem of inventing a vapor-proof closure for spacesuits was solved by imaging a skinny demon as a wire pulling together, imbedded springs in rubber, or stitching with steel.

Analogies evoke imagery as they make comparison or associative connections (as discussed earlier in this chapter) and should be considered as related to the synectics descriptors and rationale.

Application of these principles in a synectics problem-solving session is discussed by Prince (1968) as a series of steps that flow into one another, an excursion that leads to a point of view about a potential solution to a problem, which, if not satisfactory, prepares the way for other excursions through the same process.

Fresh insights from synectics research led Prince (1975) to present a theory of thinking and problem solving called *mindspring*. It is a theory that is both cognitive and emotive, drawing strength from playfulness, ambiguity, analogical relationships, imagination, and related variables.

Over the years, the overemphasis on precise, accurate thinking has restricted and repressed approximate thinking, which is so essential to learning. Consequently, Prince suggests the need for balance between *precision* and *approximation*. A person should be able to oscillate between tolerance for approximation and a wish for perfection as well as swing from the logical and rational to the nonlogical and irrational. Prince calls these *thinking attitudes.* The swing here reminds us of Parnes and Biondi's (1975) concept of a delicate balance of imagination and judgment.

Mindspring theory comprises five elements—wishing, retrieving, comparing, transforming, and storing—that are cyclic in operation. *Imaging* is important to each of the five elements.

Wishing is useful and is another form of exploratory thinking. Because it is not concerned with reality, it can open a person's eyes to new possibilities. Wishing gives temporary freedom from reality and can be beneficial when used in problem solving. A problem can be redefined through wishing. Because every problem is loaded with implications and facets, a series of wishes that deal with them can enrich thinking and evoke fruitful images in preparation for unexpected retrieval opportunities.

Retrieving brings to notice the astonishing inner resources possessed by individuals, the memory or experience bank with billions of bits of information that cover or are relevant to nearly every human activity or problem. The difficulties in gaining access to some of these data relate to the expectation that our retrieval service is poor, to our intolerance of approximations, and to the belief that we should steer clear of problems when we lack the precise knowledge to solve them. Some strategies that can assist us when we have a problem with retrieval are idea getting, use of analogy and paradox, picture making, and cloud watching.

Comparing presupposes standards and the learned response of applying them to everything. Ideas are aborted if they do not appear perfect; and because wishing, imaging, and transforming are so repressed, their work is invisible to us. Actually, we are in command of the Muse who allows us to push ideas around at will. Comparing does not have to be a negative activity if we are able to assume the stance of looking out for the positive or the pro qualities in an idea. An idea is not a simple monolithic proposition but a spectrum of implications, which, when sorted, range from the acceptable to the unacceptable.

Transforming, if it is to be useful, depends on an intense awareness of one's freedom to retrieve, image, and mutate anything in any way one wishes. An idea in its final form may bear no discernible relationship to the form it took when initially retrieved. It may, through successive approximations, move in the direction of a solution.

Storing involves taking possession of the new by connecting it to approximations we have already made. For example, relating the new experience of the needles of a pine tree to the stored experience of hair calls forth a childlike response: "That tree is hairy." This technique leads to the bold guessing habit or approximate retrieving that will make us better learners.

Lateral Thinking Problem-Solving Model   Edward de Bono (1967, 1970) offers *lateral thinking* as another approach to thinking and problem solving. He observes that there are two fundamentally different sorts of thinking: *vertical thinking* and *lateral thinking*.

Vertical thinking is like digging the same hole, going deep and proceeding rigidly along the path of highest probability. *Lateral thinking* proceeds imaginatively along a variety of low-probability paths in the hope of generating new and better approaches to the problem. There is a need in lateral thinking to let go of the obvious; there is the danger of being trapped by it. Lateral requires that we avoid proceeding carefully from stage to stage, freeing ourselves so that a more imaginative step can at some point emerge.

According to de Bono (1970), the mind does not behave in the ideal logical way. In the act of solving a problem, the efficiency of logic may lead a person in the wrong direction. Thus he suggests that there is a need to shift attention from problems themselves to the way the mind tackles them. In addition, de Bono emphasizes the importance of a *problem approach* rather than efficient *problem follow-up*. He points out that the approach selected has much to do with habit, attitude of mind, or even emotion.

Repeatedly, de Bono (1975) emphasizes that *thinking is a skill* and, like any skill, it can be developed and improved. This accounts for his great insistence that it is necessary to *practice* thinking skills.

Unlike the attempts of F. E. Williams (1972) or Meeker (1969) to incorporate the teaching of thinking skills into a school's regular curriculum, de Bono is of the opinion that *practice in thinking* can be provided most effectively outside regular subject courses and content specific to one or another area of human interaction or occupation. In this respect, his orientation is similar to the Osborn-Parnes and Synectics models of creative problem solving, for instance.

According to de Bono (1985), people from all backgrounds and educational levels can improve their thinking, eventuallly becoming *masterthinkers*. A *masterthinker* is one who has developed thinking skills to a high degree. The approach taken by a *masterthinker* is exploratory and objective, constructive and cooperative. Such a thinker knows that human emotions, feelings, and values are essential to thinking and uses them in making choices and decisions. Furthermore, a *masterthinker* knows that thinking is the ultimate human resource upon which the world depends for its future.

To be a *masterthinker* a person must want to become one, must focus on thinking, must set aside some time for thinking, must know some thinking techniques, and must practice thinking. De Bono facilitates this by making available a handbook and accompanying audio cassettes (de Bono, 1985) that provide the learner with exercises directed to thinking. By using this resource and the *Five-Day Course in Thinking* (de Bono, 1967), which offers intriguing and enjoyable ideas and exercises to test and complement the acquisition of new thinking skills, the learner can become a *masterthinker.*

However, we should recall the distinction made between *content* and *process* in Khatena's Multidimensional Interactive Creative Imagination Imagery Model (Figure 3.1), or Guilford's Structure of Intellect Model (Figure 3.5), and the point that different kinds of content are processed by the same inherited mental operations. What this means is that informational content may be *generic* as de Bono, Osborn-Parnes, and Synectics have posited, or informational content may be *specific* to school learning as F. E. Williams and Meeker have advocated. Both positions are legitimate in the context of the larger perspective offered by Guilford's generic problem-solving model (Figure 9.13) and Khatena's creative imagination imagery model (Figure 9.1).

In his *training program* de Bono (1974, 1976) provides practice in developing skills of *elaboration.* The problem-solver lists the requirements for a product or solution in order of importance and uses the list as a guide to work out a solution. De Bono considers this procedure important because an idea that does not fulfill the requirements of a situation can have little value.

De Bono's *Thinking Course for Juniors* (1974) instructs an adult to talk to a child about the child's creative problem solving, using the following sequential steps: *praise, clarification, criticism,* and *amplification.* The first two steps are expected to encourage children to open up to themselves and the problem and prepare them to evaluate their work critically in terms of the requirements set when first encountering the problem or during the clarification process. Moving on to the amplification step allows children further opportunity to open up to modifications, additions, elaborations, future plans, and so on.

If we compare these problem-solving steps to those offered in Table 9.1, we can see that de Bono's first step (praise) is unique because, unlike the other steps, attention is given to the problem of getting the process started. That is, a kind of warming up is encouraged and receives positive acknowledgment at the start. This opening up of problem-solvers increases their chance of resisting premature closure and generating better solutions.

Other aspects of de Bono's (1970, 1971, 1975, 1976) *training procedures* relate to the use of such devices as chance, humor, synthesis, diversion, and fantasy. They encourage the problem-solver to avoid easy acceptance of alternatives immediately as they occur; to foster the careful consideration of both sides of issues; and to search for new and unusual perspectives on problems. All of these recommendations are central to *lateral thinking.*

Attention is also given by de Bono to the training of the problem-solver in the use of different ways *to conclude* or bring about closure, and to differentiate whether a conclusion is tentative, changeable, or definite.

De Bono also considers *emotions* as most important to lateral thinking. Emotions, he says, come before thinking. However, if thinking occurred first, then emotions would give it power. Because emotions may be either *facilitative* or *inhibitory,* it is important for problem-solvers to know if emotions are affecting their thinking at the time of problem-solving activity.

Furthermore, de Bono favors *drawing* as a medium for training children to understand better the problem-solving process. He uses it, almost exclusively, as a method of instruction in his problem-solving course, and is himself a highly effective user of this technique in his lectures.

Sociodrama

Another effective group approach to creative problem solving is *sociodrama* (e.g., Torrance, 1975c, 1976b; Torrance & Myers, 1970). It is a technique that attempts to solve not only present-day problems but also those that might occur in the future. Sociodrama, as applied to career guidance, has been the subject of an earlier discussion (Chapter 8). It

places the principles of creative problem solving in a deliberately contrived, living, and dramatic context such that a group or social problem
is examined with the assistance of various production techniques. In a
sense, it combines the principles of creative problem solving and synectics with that of drama. The metaphor is the stage, and the play is the
drama of real life.

Sociodrama, viewed as a creative problem-solving technique, can be
used to bring about a unity of opposites. In this respect, it echoes Moreno's (1946) theory of the unity of mankind reflected in his works on
psychodrama and sociodrama. Torrance (1979b), citing the research
findings of Barron (1969) and D. W. MacKinnon (1978), tells us that
highly creative individuals incorporate many sets of opposites in their
personality so that at one and the same time, they tend to be

More masculine and more feminine
More independent in their thinking and, yet, more open to sugges-
   tions and information from others
More conforming and more nonconforming
More playful, more serious, and more hardworking
More humorous and graver than their less creative counterparts

The creativity that emerges from a *collision of these opposites* appears to
highlight the essence of the problem in whose resolution unity of these
opposites is attained.

The *basic conflict* is brought to the *surface* when the problem is defined
in a sociodramatic setting. This setting requires that decisions be made
for the selection of roles that best illustrate the conflict, with the experiences of the sociodramatic group giving clues for these decisions. The
following are a few examples of individuals in conflict: parent versus
parent, parent versus child, child versus teacher, patient versus physi-
cian, and employee versus employer.

Group consensus on the selection of conflicting roles that bring out the
greatest number of aspects of the conflict is followed by the casting of
characters and the establishing and enacting of the conflict situation. In
this way, a highlighting of each conflicting role is effected, even to the
point of exaggeration at times, to increase the chances of obtaining a
creative solution to the problem.

Torrance (1975c) tells us that it is not often that initial confrontation in
a sociodrama results in a solution that will bring about a unity of opposites. It may be necessary to use some special production techniques,
such as the aside and soliloquy, to effect a resolution. Torrance also emphasizes the usefulness of *double* and *multiple double production techniques*
as effective in bringing about a unity of opposites and promoting interdisciplinary thinking, resulting in a variety of viewpoints to the problem.

One production technique that Torrance used successfully with young and disadvantaged children to help them overcome their shyness in expressing themselves and their lack of self-confidence is the *magic net game.* Pieces of nylon net in various colors (36" x 72") serve as the magic net. Torrance and Myers (1970) describe the magic net game as follows:

> In the "Magic Net" game, about ten children were given pieces of net and invited to choose whatever role they desired. They were then asked to "feel" themselves into these roles in various ways. Next, the entire group would be invited to make up a story, using the roles chosen by the actors wearing the "Magic Net." The story is enacted as it is told by the audience. Usually, one story teller begins a story and others continue it. In some cases, it has been found helpful to give the story teller a "Magic Net" to overcome his self-consciousness and to identify him clearly. (p. 89)

Torrance and Myers point out that an interesting feature among younger and older disadvantaged children is the tendency to choose roles similar to those selected by their peers, indicating a strong need for support by peers for coexperiencing roles. When a child dared to choose a unique role, reinforcement sometimes observed to be necessary was provided by other children taking similar roles.

For instance, Pamela, a 6-year-old, extremely timid girl chose to be a bear in a princess story. But she did not act the role despite the magic of the net and the director's encouragement until three aggressive boys were selected by the director to play supporting bear roles. Then, she became a bear with zest.

Here are a graduate student's observations about Pamela's behavior that day.

> Pamela had been so quiet and had not been a part of the creative drama, dance, song, or play until today. Then she was given a magic net and decided to be a bear. She was too timid and withdrawn to be a good bear even with encouragement. Dr. Torrance, realizing this, reinforced her with some more encouragement. She became an excellent bear. She overcame some of her shyness and began to interact with the group, not just in play acting. Her success seemed to change her whole self-image. Pamela in her quiet voice entered into the group problem-finding game and gave some very intelligent problems. She was anxious to participate and contribute to the group. . . . I saw a sense of achievement in her approach.
>
> Earlier I could not get her to concentrate and study when she did the Picture Interpretation Test. She would answer questions without studying the picture. But, today, she would look at pictures and study them. She was able to make up an entire story of "Smokey Bear" from the pictures. I was amazed that she knew so much.
>
> Her self-image is very poor, maybe because of her sense of failure in the first grade. But the feeling of success at being a bear and Dr. Torrance's congratulations changed her self-opinion. She found today that she is far more

intelligent than I had dreamed. She lacks confidence and being unsure and inhibited can be taken for signs of a low I.Q. But when the inhibition is broken, you can see that she is not dull but too afraid to exert and show her abilities. (pp. 89–90)

Sociodrama can be used not only as a procedure for creatively solving present problems, but also as an approach to *project oneself into the future* by assuming a variety of roles in numerous situations. One can perceive that relevant problems will arise, and then brainstorm ways of dealing with them. Futurists have developed disciplined ways of studying the future (e.g. Hencley & Yates, 1974) so that anticipation of probable events will minimize surprise, and choices made now may influence the shaping of the future.

In keeping with this thinking, Torrance (1975c, 1979b) advocates (among other techniques) the use of the *audience techniques* of sociodrama to give *glimpses of infinity* and to help people attain a future orientation to a given problem. He suggests using the *future projection technique*. This technique requires actors to show how they expect a conflict will shape up in the future. Intense warm-up and communication of known particulars of the situation are regarded as essential, and, generally, involve *dyadic brainstorming* between the director and the protagonist. Sometimes the audience may also participate in constructing the future situation, drawing from the acquired information about the future. This production technique may tap various states of consciousness to include daydreaming, expanded awareness, internal scanning, and stored memories.

Systems Approach

A systems approach to creative problem solving offers a larger conceptual model of organized information on the subject. It takes into account many related variables, positioning them in sequential processes that, on the one hand, are both interrelated and interactive and, on the other hand, forward moving to a point where the completion of one problem-solving activity is looped to the inception of another.

Two such approaches come to mind, the one arising from the Structure of Intellect (Guilford, 1967), and the other from processes of biopsychological origins (Land, 1973). Both models are designed to show the relationship of a person in the act of processing information to solve problems to his or her environment. Guilford's approach (Structure of Intellect Problem-Solving Model) focuses on intellectual functioning. Land's approach (Transformation Problem-Solving Model) gives conceptual focus to biopsychological connectedness of the internal processing and problem-solving systems. In addition, both models are *self-regulatory* and dependent for success on positive and negative feedback as well as feedforward or shared regulation, because newly generated data would feed the system continuously for adaptation and adjustment to an ever-changing environment.

Transformation Problem-Solving Model   The Transformation Problem-Solving Model proposed by Land (1973) has already been discussed in an earlier chapter on development (Chapter 6). It would be well to refer back to what was said on the subject at this juncture, for Land's transformation theory is directly related to his approach to problem solving.

In the Transformation Problem-Solving Model, the function of biological processes and systems as they occur within human thinking and problem solving is represented by the same steps that living organisms follow.

1. Searching for available knowledge and information
2. Analyzing, breaking down, and digesting the data
3. Manipulating the information through imagination into new synthesis, into a hypothesis or idea
4. Internally projecting the use of the idea
5. Evaluating the solutions for their "fitness," that is, their potential effect and value and the probable feedback that will be received (Land, 1973, p. 103)

The satisfactory completion of the *internal processing* of a problem leads to transfer into the primary growth system and its tryout in the external world. Land suggests that the *brains* of human beings may be, in fact, *miniature evolutionary laboratories* where, through experience, each one of us can observe the evolution, mutation, and selection processes as they proceed in our minds at any one time.

Structure of Intellect Problem-Solving Model   Guilford (1977) considers that the best place to see the components of the Structure of Intellect working together is in problem solving and creative thinking. A problem is encountered when it becomes necessary to go beyond the items of information that we have already structured. Then, a need arises for new intellectual activity that goes beyond comprehension or understanding to include productive thinking.

He sees the necessity for a general problem-solving model that not only serves creative production but also takes into account the traditional models of problem solving, the Structure of Intellect categories, and related conditions. The Structure of Intellect Problem-Solving Model, having roots in theories of intelligence and high relevance for education, is presented as Figure 9.11.

The model as shown in Figure 9.11 is a *communication system* (also called an informational-processing model), which shows the events of a problem-solving episode that are spread out in time, from start to finish, with input from the *environment* (E) and input from the *soma* (S). The

Figure 9.11 Structure of Intellect Problem-Solving Model

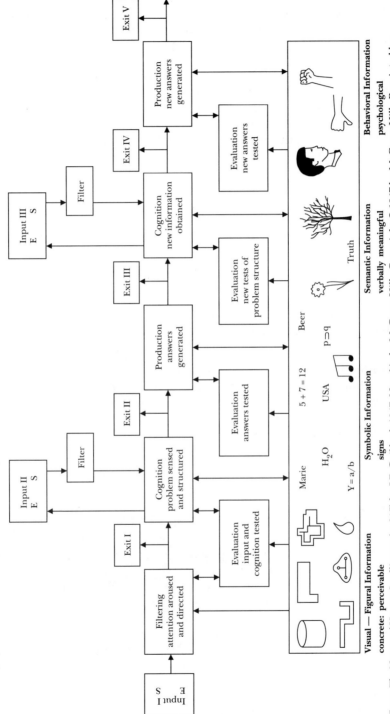

From *The Nature of Human Intelligence* (p. 315) by J.P. Guilford, 1967, New York: McGraw-Hill. Copyright © 1967 by McGraw-Hill. Reprinted by permission.

latter (S) is concerned with body parts and includes feeling and motivational states of an individual. The *arrows* in the figure show that information flows, at times, in a one-way and, at other times, in a two-way direction.

All Structure of Intellect *operations,* with the exception of memory, are involved, as indicated in the rectangles of the problem-solving model. Examples of different kinds of Structure of Intellect *contents,* organized as units—systems with some relations—and implications can be found in *memory storage* at the base of the model. Information transmitted from memory storage to *cognition* and *production* operations may at times pass through the filtering function of *evaluation,* but at other times, it may be transmitted directly to the mental operations for processing, as in the case of *suspended judgment. Evaluation* is ongoing at every step of the problem-solving process.

The other *input sources* (Input II and Input III) relate to an individual's active search for further information from the environment. This process is indicated by the upgoing arrows from cognition to input stations; relevant filtering by evaluation to and from memory storage is also indicated.

The several *exit stations* indicate cessation of problem-solving activity. Take for instance the following:

Exit I: The problem is completely ignored or rejected.

Exit II: There is recognition that the problem is not important, that it is impossible to solve, or that problem solving should be postponed for the time being, possibly with intention to renew the activity following incubation.

Exit III: A satisfactory solution is reached.

An important feature of the model is the generous allowance for *looping* that involves *feedback* information (e.g., for each cognitive and memory phase, there is the loop from cognition to production, which can be repeated many times). It is this looping that allows some flexibility with respect to the order of events; for instance, the need for backtracking to earlier stages of the problem-solving process or even going back to the environment for additional fact finding when we discover our failure to solve a problem is due to having wrongly diagnosed it. What follows are a *restructuring the problem* and a new round of problem-solving operations, thus focusing attention on the fact that there may be more than two cycles of problem-solving activity before the goal is attained.

Creative activity in the Structure of Intellect Problem-Solving Model is said to occur whenever *divergent production* takes place. The problem must not only be creatively solved but creatively structured as well. Besides, transformation comprises creative production and *convergent production* functions.

The *production stations* of the model (Figure 9.11) represent both diver-

gent production and convergent production operations, because, in re-
calling information some element of transfer is involved in both operations. Differentiation of divergent or convergent production must be
specified in the required response. Take, for instance, the many names
that can be given when an individual is asked to name American writers
of the first half of the twentieth century (*divergent production*) versus giving one name when asked to name the American who wrote the story of
a certain archbishop (*convergent production*).

Guilford reiterates that his model is *generic* and may not fit any particular episode of problem solving. That is why other special flowcharts
of models, specific to the needs of certain types of problem solving, may
have to be developed. Furthermore, he brings to our notice *helping* and
hindering variables in creative thinking and problem solving (Guilford,
1977, pp. 165–169). Paraphrased here, they include the following:

Environmental influences of family, home and society

Motivation, whose primary source is intrinsic and associated with
achievement, competence, and cognitive congruence; and whose
secondary source of satisfaction lies in the approval of others, the
desire to be different and avoid the trite and banal, the preference
for complexity; in addition, are those dimensions of interests in different kinds of thinking (e.g., reflective, logical, autistic versus realistic, convergent, divergent, and tolerance for ambiguity)

Informational-memory store that assists in the generation of ideas not as
a sufficient but as a necessary condition for creative production

Flexibility (a ready shifting from class to class, transformations in divergent production activities, and redefinition or transformations
in convergent production) versus rigidity or the blocking of these
processes

Group thinking or *brainstorming*, mainly at the Structure of Intellect
problem-solving step of production but also at other places

Ruling out of criticism during the idea-generation session to avoid reduction in creative output

Attitudes and emotions tending to suppress the flow of ideas (e.g., sex
roles taken too seriously, too much attention or pressure to norms;
emotional states, like prejudice, fear, anxiety, envy, negativism,
apathy, and complacence; respect for authority figures, attempts to
please others to "get ahead," and lack of self-confidence)

To Guilford's list must be added those strategies and tactics designed
to promote increased effectiveness in problem solving. They include the
following:

Broadening the problem
Breaking the problem into subproblems
Asking questions

Suspending judgment
Extending effort to generate ideas
Listing attributes
Forcing relationships
Brainstorming
Attempting morphological analysis
Allowing for incubation
Enducing altered states of consciousness (e.g., visual thinking, relaxation, meditation)
Inducing transformations (e.g., adapt, modify, substitute, magnify, minify, rearrange, reverse, and combine)
Establishing criteria for evaluation

Intuitive Imagination

If *intuition* can synthesize disparate ideas and combine them in ways hitherto different, presenting them as a new whole, configuration, or pattern (Isaak, 1978); if *intuition* is a function of mind that permits exploration of the unknown as a way of sensing fresh possibilities and indications (Jung, 1921); and if *intuition* is related to the various facets of creative imagination (Khatena, 1984), then it can be cultivated and enhanced (Bruner, 1960).

The language of discovery or *imagery* is the language of *intuitive imagination*. As a human function it can be fostered and trained, just as other facets of the creative imagination dealt with in this chapter. Various techniques proposed for the purpose of educating *intuition* (Clark, 1988; Markley, 1988; Rockenstein, 1988, 1989), include one or more of the following conditions: preparatory relaxation exercises, imagery, focusing of attention, incubation-illumination phases of problem solving, internal blockbusting to insight formation, visionizing, and exploring current and future possibilities.

Let us take for instance Zoa Rockenstein's (1989) technique for Training the Creative-Intuitive Mind, a system that relates intuition to creative thinking and problem solving. Rockenstein sets this up as a Taxonomy of Educational Objectives for the Intuitive Domain which consists of four levels.

Level 1: Awareness. Expanding an awareness of intuition is the first step. To achieve this goal we need to (a) become familiar with terms related to intuition, such as *precognition* and *imagery*; (b) reflect on intuitive events in our past; (c) learn about intuitive experiences of others; and (d) project a more futurelike intuitive image of self.

Level 2: Comprehension. Comprehension involves integrating intuitive thinking, an integral part of the creative process (e.g., preparation, incubation, illumination, and verification), with other forms of thinking.

Level 3: Development. Here we seek to construct new or expanded thought networks of mind, whose foundations are the first two levels. Imagery helps to fine-tune intuition at this level; it is facilitated by relaxation, focusing, and meditation, which quiets the mind to center its energy on a problem or area of interest. Other aids are to be found in guided imagery, dream exploration, and precognition.

Level 4: Individuation. This term refers to the continued development of the intuitive potential of an individual seeking self-realization.

O. W. Markley (1988) brings to our notice a number of methods available to develop the intuitive mind that are particularly suitable for application in three broad areas: *creative problem solving* and *psychotherapy* (used to circumvent resistance and produce helpful insights); *strategic planning* (used to cultivate an inspiring sense of vision, produce a statement of mission, and innovative strategies appropriate for current and emerging conditions); and *policy analysis* and *futures research* (used to explore possible, probable, and preferable future conditions).

Visionary (imagery) and transpersonal (ego transcendence and expanded awareness of perceptual thought) knowledge processes are brought into play by these methods. Effective use of these methods requires skills that call for *voluntary suspension of judgment* and *passive volition* or letting go to allow the desired phenomena to happen. To facilitate the use of these methods are needed either (1) an experienced, skilled, and flexible guide; or (2) mastery of skills by the participant.

The several methods presented by Markley include (1)focusing on current concerns, (2) experiencing alternative futures, (3) revisioning current concerns for transforming perceived problems into opportunities, and (4) experiencing alternative futures.

According to Markley, these methods can be used independently or, for better results, sequentially or recursively. They have been found to be very useful in a wide variety of situations calling for decision making in the face of uncertainty and risk.

CONCLUSIONS

It is clear from the foregoing discussion that the creative imagination with its imagery correlates is complex, multidimensional, and interactive. It relates to the whole spectrum of life. By its nature and purpose, creative imagination brings about the birth of the new and beautiful. When we understand its sources and interactivity, we are in a better position to create, control, and direct individual potential to manifest itself to the full.

The power to achieve this understanding comes from our increased awareness of creative processes at work in the act of invention and discovery. This awareness has led to the design of training approaches that simulate actual creative experiences, which encourage productive ways of learning and prepare us for the real task of the creative effort, the eventual outcome of which is the emergence of high-level original work.

Much has been said about the value and development of creative imagination and creative thinking abilities, especially over the past quarter century; various procedures have been designed for this purpose. Some procedures concentrate on the mechanisms of the creative process, while others find application of these processes in curriculum materials.

Almost any system of process education, if it is to be viable, will have elements of the productive, either by way of thinking operations or their application in problem-solving modes. These elements are of particularly high relevance to the gifted. Not only should our concern be to assist gifted students in becoming independent planners of their own acquisition of knowledge and skills, but also assure that they do so in ways that capture these skills for storage. Such storage must be in forms that lend themselves to alternative means of retrieval so that the gifted become less regurgitators of the old and more producers of the new. Consequently, educators are encouraged to make more use of the creative imagination and creative problem solving to prime the gifted to process information at increasingly higher creative levels for original and useful production.

Learning for Excellence

*I*NTRODUCTION

Our understanding of the gifted has been enhanced by many developments that have taken place in the field of education. Research recognizes a variety of potential talents that awaits release for full manifestation. It has become increasingly important for us to become knowledgeable about the nature of intellect and creativity and the technical know-how to facilitate their achievement. Further, we are better informed about the problems gifted children face and the many ways counseling can prevent or even alleviate these problems.

By becoming better acquainted with intellectual and creative processes used in the act of invention and productivity, we have been able to develop approaches that can be taught to people in general and the gifted in particular. These approaches have been refined to the point of expressed strategies that can be incorporated in thinking toward creative ends. Exercising the processes of creative thinking generally prepares for application both in learning school material, and in cultivating a productive intellectual life-style.

Schooling can provide adequate nurturance of the intellectual processes so that all children, including the gifted, will derive full benefit

is placed more on the devel-
strategies that have become
gful school curriculum could
e. Besides, command of abil-
ike the Structure of Intellect
currence of greater transfer
implifies learning in another

s to accomplish the best for
s are found to be more work-
to be more effective. How-
nould have the power to ex-
n of intellectual and talent
nany available techniques are
acceleration and enrichment, individualized education models, teaching to Structure of Intellect abilities, self-directed learning, and mentor facilitation toward self-actualization.

Relatively little has been written on motivation as it pertains to the gifted. Perhaps, motivation, on the one hand, is universally operative, but on the other hand, is specifically different for the gifted. For, when compared to others in society, the gifted have the predisposition to be intrinsically motivated—both by latent ability and talent, and by compelling curiosity and creativity—to discover and produce the new and valuable. However, motivation is significant in producing commitment and goal direction toward achievement at the highest levels. Systems of motivation that appear to hold particular relevance for the gifted are those related to achievement through competence, the principle of incongruity-dissonance, growth motivation toward higher levels of self-fulfillment, and motivation inherent in creative learning.

ACCELERATION AND ENRICHMENT

Acceleration and its related facets, as a way of speeding up the growth and manifestation of intellect in school, have provoked considerable interest, discussion, and even disagreement over the years (e.g., DeHaan & Havighurst, 1965; Gallagher, 1985; George, Cohen & Stanley, 1979; Gowan & Demos, 1964). Whether acceleration directly concerns itself with the highly gifted or with students generally, schooling does not, by and large, provide the individual development of intellect that is appropriate for everyone. Educators find themselves frustrated in the day-to-day learning situation by obvious unevenness of student intellectual growth.

Acceleration as Enrichment

By using enrichment activities teachers have tried to express students' potential more fully and with a better measure of success. In fact, it has been suggested that there is no apparent dichotomy between enrichment and acceleration (Meister & Odell, 1979). After all, gifted children naturally have enriched experiences, insights, and interests. However, according to researchers, the gifted cannot grow to full potential by self-direction alone. They need planned enrichment. Conceptualizing acceleration in the broader terms of enrichment of content and methodology, educators gave some direction to

   innovations with diverse grouping procedures that arrange and rearrange, relative to project assignments, the larger classroom groups to facilitate learning of the basics and of other specific school subjects (e.g., Feldhusen, Vantassel-Baska & Seeley, 1989)

   learning materials and texts, making them more orderly, interesting and attractive as well as providing related materials directed toward making a more appealing classroom environment to enhance learning (e.g., Passow, 1979)

   the larger methodology of various plans (e.g., Dalton and Winnetka Plans) and methods (e.g., Project, Center-of-Interest, and Playway), frequently experientially based and intended to provide for individual and group development, harks back to the attempts of the progressive education movement of the 1930s (Ingas, 1979)

   the recent manifestations of progressive education specifically designed for gifted students described as theoretical models (e.g., Barbara Clark's Integrative Education Model, Calvin W. Taylor's Multiple Creative Talents and Knowledge, and Abraham J. Tannenbaum's Enrichment Matrix Model) (Renzulli, 1986)

The emphases on individualizing educational experiences are either behavioristically oriented (e.g., Operant Conditioning and its application in Programmed Instruction) or cognitively-affectively based (e.g., Taxonomy of Educational Objectives, Structure of Intellect or self-directed learning).

Acceleration can be thought of as *horizontal* and *vertical enrichment*. Horizontal enrichment provides more same-level educational experiences, whereas vertical enrichment offers educational experiences of increasing levels of complexity. Such kinds of acceleration are the province of individual classrooms, which can generalize to other similar individual school units.

Recent application of the accelerative-enrichment approach for gifted students in pull-out arrangements, for example, has led to the establishment of a center located in one school to serve one or more schools in a district. The centers are either state supported efforts or federally funded special projects. Although some variation in the practice exists at different levels of schooling (elementary, middle, junior and senior high schools), the thrust is generally the same because the plan operates within the lockstep of grade levels. In such acceleration, such practice should be functional and not limited to providing grade advancement. In fact, acceleration should be facilitative of intellectual development toward levels beyond the confine of grades.

Acceleration as Grade Skipping

Grade skipping, another form of acceleration (Bowman, 1955; Gowan & Demos, 1964; Stanley, 1977a), is fraught with the danger of causing gaps in the acquisition of learning and may bring psychosocial developmental problems. However, intellectually able students, eager to move ahead at rates faster than the conventional lock-step schooling system will allow, are less likely to be affected (Daurio, 1979).

If grade skipping is used as the accelerative procedure, special attention and care should be made for the times chosen. That is, students at certain grade levels will feel less shocked by the change educationally and psychosocially than at other grade levels. Anticipated gaps in learning can be overcome by special preparatory educational experiences.

A more fruitful approach, however, appears to be accelerative learning without gaps. That is, a student continually progresses in certain subject areas in nongraded schooling, and emphasis is placed on learning accomplishments, not on grade chronology. What remains important is that, as rapidly as their capacity will permit, students advance in their acquisition of knowledge and skill to the highest levels of achievement. Acceleration, thought of in this way, can lead to the most productive results. However, the constraints of administrative arrangements pose problems, and much needs to be done to discover ways to overcome them.

Stanley (1977b) of the Study of Mathematically Precocious Youth (SMPY) at Johns Hopkins University reminds us of a number of different options for gifted student acceleration, as follows:

early entrance into school, preferably at the kindergarten level
early exit from school by skipping the senior year to attend the first year of college as a substitute
skipping grades, preferably the last one prior to moving from one school level to the next (i.e., skip grade 6 and go to grade 7, or skip grade 9 and go to grade 10)
taking courses required in the senior year in grade 10 and grade 11 (and for some even earlier)

completing two or more years of study in a subject in one year

using special mentors to pace, stimulate, and tutor brilliant students through various courses

obtaining credit through college board examinations or college departmental examination on entry into college to validate previously acquired learning

taking correspondence courses at high school or college levels from a major university

using self-paced (including programmed) instruction (not recommended by SMPY)

attending private schools with distinct social or athletic advantages over public schools (not recommended for students of I.Q. 140 and above by SMPY)

Mathematically Precocious Youth Project

Although research has generally supported acceleration (e.g., Daurio, 1979; Elwood, 1958; Gallagher, 1966; Klausmeier, 1963; Pressy, 1949; Ripple, 1961; Terman & Oden, 1947), it is not as widely practiced as enrichment (George, Cohen & Stanley, 1979; Stanley & Benbow, 1986). Education favors enrichment over acceleration, and many parents are not only hesitant to accept acceleration for their children (Newland, 1976) but also wholeheartedly conspire with educators to restrain able children from moving ahead at accelerated paces natural to them (Stanley, 1977a).

According to Stanley and Benbow (1986), there are logical and empirical reasons for the choice of educational acceleration over enrichment. SMPY relies on pacing educational programs that are responsive to the capabilities and knowledge of the individual student, which are based on three principles derived from developmental psychology (Robinson, 1983).

1. Learning is sequential and developmental.
2. Large differences in learning status among individuals at any given age exist.
3. Effective teaching assesses the student's learning status, and poses problems slightly above the level already mastered. As for programs for SMPY participants, Stanley and Benbow (1986) indicate that adaptation of existing curricula made available to younger students is more productive than designing new ones.

Stanley and Benbow (1986) assert that SMPY did consider educational enrichment, namely, busy work, irrelevant academic enrichment, cultural enrichment, and relevant academic enrichment. They believe that cultural enrichment is beneficial to mathematically precocious youth, though it does not fulfill the aims of curricula in mathematics or other academic subjects. Stanley describes and comments on each of the four kinds of enrichment as follows:

Busy work—keeps the bright students occupied with a great deal more of the subject they already know so well

Irrelevant academic enrichment—provides brilliant students with a special academic course (like high level social studies) that is not congruent with the direction of their academic tendency or may provide them with essentially new academic work like games or creative training separate from subject matter

Cultural enrichment—provides certain "civilized" experiences (e.g., music appreciation, performing arts, and foreign languages) beyond the usual school curriculum, which, although they may prevent boredom, do not meet students' specialized academic needs

Relevant academic enrichment—provides students with seven or eight years of special academic experience, followed by participation in the usual type of academic experiences. Such enrichment needs to be sustained to prevent boredom and frustration. For instance, even though such enrichment consists of a superb 13-year mathematics program (i.e., from kindergarten through 12th grade), it is insufficient unless backed up by a strong provision of college credit

Stanley (1977a, 1986) concludes that any kind of enrichment (except cultural) without acceleration is a deficit to the brilliant student. Consequently, he advocates a three phase approach to acceleration, which SMPY uses as follows:

Phase 1-Discovery—In this phase, young students of high mathematical reasoning ability, generally between the ages of 12 and 13, are selected for the project (Stanley, 1977a; Stanley, Keating & Fox, 1974). The principle measure used is the Scholastic Aptitude Test since the mathematical component was found to be excellent for identifying high-level mathematical reasoners among seventh and eighth graders. The verbal (reasoning) component of the measure, when administered to high scorers on the mathematical component, was found to be of great value for predicting radical mathematical accelerates. This measure is also used with an achievement test like the Sequential Tests of Educational Progress.

Phase 2-Description—During this phase, the most talented of these students are tested further.

Phase 3-Development—In this phase, mathematically precocious youth are continually helped and encouraged. Each is offered a smorgasbord of educational opportunity from which to choose, whatever combination the individual finds suitable, or nothing. They are encouraged and provided with the educational opportunity to study mathematics beginning with a course titled "Algebra I." Or they can skip to more advanced courses in mathematics like calculus, linear algebra, and differential equations (Stanley, 1979).

Special features of the SMPY program are *diagnostic testing,* and the ensuing *specific teaching* of just those points not known to the student, as Stanley (1977a) explains:

> For example, many seventh- or eighth-grade youths who reason extremely well mathematically can score high on a standardized test of knowledge of first year high school algebra even though they have not yet studied a school subject entitled "Algebra I." If, for example, such a student can answer correctly thirty out of forty items on Form A of Educational Testing Service's Cooperative Mathematics Algebra I Test in the forty-minute time limit, he has scored better than 89 percent of a random national sample of ninth graders did after studying Algebra I for a whole school year. Then the youth is handed back the test booklet, told which ten items he missed, and asked to try them again. If he still misses, say, six items, they are examined carefully and he is helped by a tutor to learn quickly those points that he did not know. After suitable instruction on just those points and on any points in the test about which he was unsure (e.g., items guessed right), he takes Form B of the test under standard conditions and his success is studied. In this way an able youth can often go on to Algebra II within a few hours, rather than wasting nearly all of a long, tedious 180-period school year on Algebra I. He already knows most of the material of the first course or can learn almost any not-yet known point almost instantaneously. This type of diagnostic testing and teaching of superior mathematical reasoners makes so much sense that we cannot understand why it is tried so seldom. SMPY has formalized the procedure into a day-long "Algebra Tutorial Clinic." (p. 6)

In addition, SMPY has developed a team of mathematically talented youths as *expert tutors* of other talented youths. These youths work on a one-to-one basis resembling the tutorial system of Oxford and Cambridge Universities. This approach is proving to be the fastest and best way to swiftly accelerate highly able youths in the study of mathematics. Mathematically gifted students are also offered much *educational and vocational counseling* along with memoranda and individual letters as well as a newsletter titled the *Intellectual Talented Youth Bulletin.* Since the inception of SMPY in 1971, communication has been directly with the youths themselves.

An offshoot of SMPY is the development of a program at The Johns Hopkins University for verbally gifted youth (Stanley & George, 1980). Three of the liberal arts departments (Writing Seminars, Classics, and

German) at the university were helped to set up special 2-hour courses on Saturdays during the academic year for verbally gifted participants of the SMPY talent search. Courses offered included Expository Writing, Greek, Latin, and German. The writing course was designed to improve students' expository writing skills in preparation for the English Composition Test of the College Board. The Greek and Latin courses were expected to "enrich" students' vocabulary and influence their verbal scores on the Scholastic Aptitude Test. There was also the expectation that the German course would lead to high school credit and, relative to the best students, college credit through the two Advanced Placement Program examinations in German.

Despite practitioners objections about the academic acceleration of gifted children, which warn of the potential social and emotional harm to student development (Southern, Jones & Fiscus, 1989), accelerative approaches have been found to be effective. According to Linda E. Brody and Camilla P. Benbow's (1987) study, acceleration was not found to be harmful either emotionally or socially to intellectually gifted students. They indicate that acceleration provided many more options to meet individual needs than any other program. It can be used as a supplement to a challenging program without the expense and effort of a specially designed curricula. Acceleration also offers the promise of encouraging the gifted to achieve at a younger age thereby becoming more productive members of society for a longer life period.

A Purdue University Perspective

Acceleration in terms of advanced placement of precocious children in general was advocated by John F. Feldhusen, Theron B. Proctor, and Kathryn N. Black (1986). It is a method available to every school despite limited resources, small student populations, or both. These researchers claim that advanced placement may be the primary means for educational programs to meet the educational and socioemotional needs of intellectually or academically gifted and talented youth. Wise practice of this kind of acceleration was found to maintain student interest in school, to encourage students to excel academically, and to complete higher levels of education for their own and society's benefit.

According to Feldhusen and his associates, grade advancement decisions should be based on comprehensive individual assessment related factors. To achieve proper grade advancement they offer guidelines that include

a comprehensive psychological evaluation of the child's intellectual functioning, academic skill levels, and social-emotional adjustment

an I.Q. of 125 or above, or a level of mental development above the mean for the advanced grade levels of academic skills compatible with the advanced grade, with private tutoring provided as needed to correct skill deficits

freedom from social and emotional adjustment problems, with a demonstrated high degree of persistence and motivation

good physical health, with some attention given to body size if engagement in competitive sports in later years is important to the child

no undue parental pressure felt, but rather governed by child's own desire to advance

positive attitudes toward the accelerated child by the teacher

concern about child's social-emotional maturity by public school teachers with parental and psychological verification

advanced grade placement made at the beginning of the school year and backed up by similar advancement at mid-year

grade advancement arranged on a trial basis, perhaps over a period of six weeks with the availability of counseling services

flexible levels of advancement for those who may not do so well and those who excel at the designated levels

acceleration of precocious children to dispel the myth of social-emotional difficulties and to avert the occurrence of problems of poor study habits, apathy, lack of motivation, and maladjustment

Another form of acceleration advocated (Proctor, Black & Feldhusen, 1988) is early admission of children who are both ready and able to begin their formal schooling at a chronological age younger than the officially approved entering guide. The research available supports this position (Daurio, 1979), though many school systems, according to Proctor et al. fail to implement the suggestions of the findings. School systems, in part, operate with the mistaken notion that younger children placed in advanced programs may develop achievement and adjustment problems later in life. The failure to implement such programs may also be due to the scarce research on the benefits of early admission. Besides, school personnel in general are biased against early admissions, with many school administrators favoring a uniform entrance age. In addition, uninformed parents who fear the ill effects of early admission on the social and emotional development of their children, do not press for it.

According to Proctor and his associates, early admission of intellectually advanced children is highly desirable. In one respect, such children can receive instruction at a level and pace compatible with their own levels of readiness. For another, early admission facilitates learning by providing needed mental stimulation, challenge and opportunity for high level intellectual work. Besides, intellectually gifted children admitted earlier to school have been found to do better or as well academically as their older classmates, with their academic standing increasing as they move on through the grades. Other advantages include the prevention of underachievement, the acquisition of better study habits as challenges are to be met, generally better development socially and emotionally as it keeps pace with intellectual development rather than chronological age, and less likelihood of adjustment problems. All in all, benefits are derived not only by the individual, but also by the school, teacher, and society.

Enrichment Triad Model

In another currently viable and popular view of enrichment, Renzulli (1979a) questions the value of the principal activities of programs serving gifted and talented students. As an alternative, he offers an enrichment model aimed at guiding the development of the qualitatively different, and creating defensible programs for able students. Two program objectives are offered as follows:

1. For the majority of time spent in the gifted programs, students will have complete freedom to pursue topics of their own choosing to whatever depth and extent they so desire; and they will be allowed to pursue these topics in a manner that is consistent with their own preferred style of learning. (p. 112)
2. The primary role of each teacher in the program for gifted and talented students will be to provide each student with assistance in (1) identifying and structuring realistic solvable problems that are consistent with the student's interests, and (2) acquiring the necessary methodological resources and investigative skills that are necessary for solving these particular problems. (p. 114)

These two objectives form the basic tenets of the Enrichment Triad Model (see upper right hand corner of Figure 37). The model comprises three different types of enrichment.

Type I—general exploratory activities,
Type II—group training activities, and
Type III—individual investigation of real problems.

The first two are appropriate for all learners and the third—the major focus of the model—is for gifted students. Type I and Type II Enrichment deal with strategies for expanding student interests and for developing the thinking and feeling processes. Thus they represent logical input and support systems for Type III Enrichment. It is the interrelationship of the first two types of enrichment with the third that is emphasized in this model.

The underlying assumptions of enrichment in the model relate to (a) experiences or activities that are above and beyond the so-called regular curriculum, (b) activities (with the possible exception of some Type II ones) that must show respect for the learner's interest and learning styles and require the learner's sincere desire to pursue a topic or activity of his or her own choosing, and (c) location of in and out of school enrichment and time as needs dictate.

Briefly, Type I Enrichment consists of exploratory activities and experiences designed to assist students to become familiar with topics or areas of study expected to generate genuine interest. The students' interests will give clues to determine a Type II Enrichment activity and to facilitate Enrichment activities that will facilitate Type III activities.

Guidelines for Type I Enrichment
Three guidelines are suggested for Type I Enrichment activities as follows:

Exploratory activities for students must be purposeful and lead to alternative suggestions for further study.

Students should be exposed to a wide variety of topics or areas of study from which they can select problems for in-depth investigations [e.g., (a) by developing interest centers in social sciences, physical and life sciences, mathematics and logic, music, the visual and performing arts, writing, philosophy, ethics, social issues that are stocked with appropriate books, old newspapers, documents, maps, and related materials; (b) by field trips; or (c) by inviting resource persons—local historians, poets, dancers, architects actively engaged in contributions to the advancement of knowledge—to make presentations to gifted students].

Teachers should find direction from these kinds of enrichment for planning Type II Enrichment activities.

Guidelines for Type II Enrichment
Type II Enrichment activities emphasize training exercises for developing thinking and feeling operations or processes that can enable the learner to deal more effectively with content. Various general terms like critical thinking, problem solving, reflective thinking, inquiry training, divergent or creative thinking, sensitivity training, and awareness development have been used to describe these processes. To these must be added such specific terms as brainstorming, analysis, synthesis, flexibility, originality, values clarification, and commitment.

Renzulli (1979a) suggests using B. S. Bloom (1956) and D. R. Krathwol, B. S. Bloom & B. B. Masia (1964) taxonomies of educational objectives, and J. P. Guilford's (1967) Structure of Intellect as models that incorporate these thinking and feeling processes. He also indicates several sources of new curriculum materials that emphasize process rather than content objectives that can be used for Type II Enrichment. He notes that process may not always have content relevancy, and that such activities can be appropriate without content focus. However, Type II Enrichment must lead to Type III Enrichment so that practicing process leads to actual use of these activities in real inquiry situations. It must be remembered that Type II Enrichment activities should be purposefully selected to represent a logical growth of student interests and concerns that can bind Type I and Type III Enrichment components of the model to provide a defensible rationale for its use.

Guidelines for Type III Enrichment

Type III Enrichment activities require the student to become an investigator of real problems. In this component of the model, the teacher has the responsibility of ensuring that the student (a) identifies and focuses on solvable problems, (b) acquires needed methodological resources and investigative skills, and of special importance, (c) finds appropriate outlets for products.

Triadic Revolving Door System

A later development of the enrichment triad is its link up with the revolving door concept (Renzulli, 1984, 1986), expressed as The Revolving Door Identification Model or RDIM (Renzulli, Reis & Smith, 1981). RDIM is based on the assumption that we cannot predetermine which students are or are not gifted. The strict labeling approach is avoided by substituting a somewhat different aim for special programs designed for advanced level learning and creativity. The RDIM is a flexible identification model designed for education. Students are identified with a program in mind. The program may already exist or has to be specially designed for the purpose, taking into account individual needs relative to local conditions and resources.

Establishing the Talent Pool

RDIM begins by identifying a group of students in the top 15–20% of the school population in general ability or any and all specific performance areas of high priorities in a given school's overall programming efforts to form the Talent Pool. Three research based reasons are given for the selection of such a Talent Pool.

This group can be expected to ultimately engage in creative productivity and manifest gifted behaviors.

Most activities typically used in gifted programs for the top 2% or 3% generally work effectively with this larger group.

This group is capable of showing high degrees of mastery of regular curriculum compacting including the advanced coverage of regular curriculum. Compacting of curriculum makes available to students varying amounts of time for a wide variety of enrichment and acceleration experiences.

Renzulli defines *first level identification* as the establishment of the Talent Pool. Instruments used for this purpose include those that provide *psychometric, developmental, sociometric,* and *performance information.* So as not to exclude potentially gifted students from being selected for the pool of talent, a final check is made in the form of *special nominations.* This obviates instrumentation discrepancies, and follow-up reviews provide opportunities for entry into the program after the initial selection process. All this is done in a step-by-step format.

Second level identification assesses the talent pool students in regular and special program activities. The service provides performance based learning experiences that help determine which of the participating individuals or small groups should *revolve* into more advanced levels of learning according to their interests in special topics or problems. At this point careful assessment of student interests, learning style, and learning strengths are made, especially in programs using the Enrichment Triad and RDIM.

A student in the Talent Pool is "revolved" into the advanced level enrichment experiences of individual or small group investigations according to *action information*—the dynamic interactions that take place when a student shows extreme interest or excitement over a topic, area of study, issue, idea, or event taking place in or out of school. Interaction in learning occurs when a student comes into contact with or is influenced by another person, concept, or piece of knowledge. The interaction becomes dynamic when a strong and positive influence encourages further exploration and involvement. Action information is "productivity oriented" and prepares the way for intensive investigation that is expected to lead to the development of a creative product.

Indicators of Creative Information

Four major characteristics serve as indicators of creative information (Renzulli, Reis & Smith, 1981), and these are presented as follows:

1. Action information cannot be gathered at the beginning of a school year by questionnaires, rating scales or checklists.
2. Action information is always something that grows out of the interest of children.
3. Action information is more subjective than status information and is highly dependent upon the intuitive thoughts, reactions, and observations of the teacher.
4. There is not one "best" situation in which action information can be observed.

Action information is gathered through observation of students, and recording for communication of such information is done on a form titled *Action Information Message* (AIM) symbolized as a light bulb to highlight its role in RDIM. Information contained in AIM assists in revolving students into advanced level enrichment and/or accelerative experiences. It is the action information feature in RDIM that makes it uniquely different from other identification and programming models.

A word more about the Enrichment Triad and its conjunctive use with RDIM is in order. The Triad is used to facilitate enrichment of all students. For the gifted identified for RDIM, Type I Enrichment serves as an *invitation* to more advanced levels of involvement for individuals and small groups of the Talent Pool. Students of the pool select areas of special interest and excitement for intensive investigative study, revolving from Type I Enrichment to Type III Enrichment activity. Relative to Type II Enrichment, arrangements are made for Talent Pool students to participate in activities designed for all students in the regular classroom. Such activities are selected by the Enrichment Team that most closely relates to the regular curriculum. Students of the Talent Pool are motivated to think of Type II Enrichment activities as a step toward Type III Enrichment—a stage where they can participate in investigative activities aimed at generating a creative product. All involved in the education of these students are prepared with an orientation that facilitates the goals of RDIM and the Enrichment Triad.

Escalation from Enrichment and Acceleration

Stanley and Renzulli have expressed apprehension about the looseness of enrichment as generally practiced. On the one hand, Stanley generally avoids general enrichment approaches and moves toward a more precise focus of acceleration by narrowing the concept to the *accelerative-enrichment* of mathematical talent. On the other hand, Renzulli recommends tightening enrichment into a *triadic enrichment model* that is given fresh focus by an *identification-revolving door* operational system levelled at making the learner a competent and producing investigator.

The thrust of Stanley's program lies in the acceleration of highly specialized ability toward highest achievement in mathematics and related areas; the thrust of Renzulli's model is toward fuller preparation and development of the gifted individual's cognitive and affective resources for more open-ended but well-organized learning situations. Acceleration as perceived by Stanley, may be the effective route for the rapid actualization of mathematical talent of gifted junior high school students; the research supports this position. However, the multidimensional nature of talent may require different approaches for different talents as well, and Renzulli's approach seems to have taken this direction.

We have already discussed Frank E. Williams's model, and it would be appropriate at this juncture to refer to it again, indicating the link it has with Renzulli's model. Note that F. E. Williams's model concerns itself with a creativity program, whereas Renzulli's model encompasses all of school learning.

Williams's Cognitive-Affective Interaction Model

F. E. Williams (1979) attempts to find a relationship between the Enrichment Triad Model—which is aimed at differentiated education for gifted students—and his own Cognitive-Affective Interaction Model—which is designed to promote better and creative education for most students. According to him, the two models complement each other well so that the Enrichment Triad Model serves as a guide for the goals of student development and the Cognitive-Affective Interaction Model serves as a multi-strategy approach on how to meet the goals. However, in the light of the RDIM contribution, Renzulli is more explicit in terms of approach, and worked in conjunction with the enrichment triad, the total system operates quite effectively.

Neither model is taxonomic or hierarchical. Instead the Enrichment Triad Model is morphological and the Cognitive-Affective Interaction Model is interactive. Although conceptual differences exist, similarities between the two are illustrated by F. E. Williams (Figure 10.1).

To show how the models are complementary in operation, one of two examples given by F. E. Williams (1979) relates to an ungraded lesson idea in mathematics for a whole class that begins with Type II Enrichment activities:

> A teacher should randomly select five objects in the classroom for measurement. Length of room, height of ceiling, area of table, volume of box, and circumference of opening in wastebasket are some suggestions. Divide the class into smaller work groups, three to four students, asking each group to choose a recorder. This person records the group's measurements. Students should be told there will be two tasks for them to become involved in, both requiring group activity.
>
> The first task is for each group to estimate or predict measurements of the five selected items in the room without use of any specific measuring instruments. No rulers are allowed at this time. Only improvisations are accepted, and groups are told they are to create clever ways to predict measurement of the five things. Watch groups and observe what happens (divergent productions). If at this moment students do not know how to obtain area, volume, or circumference measurements, now is the perfect time for a teacher to step in and present such facts.
>
> After all groups have guessed by improvisation some ways for predicting the five measurements and have them recorded, pass out a yard or meter stick to each group. The second task is to arrive at actual measurement of the

Figure 10.1 Williams's Strategies Orchestrating Renzulli's Triad

Type I Activities Using Exploration Strategies	
Paradoxes	Self-contradictory statement or observation
Attributes	Inherent properties, traits, or characteristics
Analogies	Similarities or situations of likeness
Discrepancies	Unknown elements or missing links
Provocative questions	Inquiries bringing forth exploration or discovery
Examples of change	Exploring the dynamics of things by alterations, modifications or substitutions
Examples of habit	Sensing rigidity and habit-bound thinking
Type II Activities Using Training Strategies	
Organized random search	Organized structure randomly leading to a production
Skills of search	Skills of historical, descriptive or experimental search
Study creative people and process	Analyze traits and study process of eminent people
Evaluate situations	Setting criteria, deciding, critical thinking
Creative reading skill	Idea generation through reading
Creative listening skill	Idea generation through listening
Creative writing skill	Self-expression through writing
Visualization skill	Expressing ideas in visual form
Type III Activities Using Production Strategies	
Tolerance for ambiguity	Tolerating open-ended situations without forcing closure
Intuitive expression	Sensing inward hunches and expressing emotional feelings
Adjustment to development	Developing from rather than adjusting to experiences or situations
Evaluate situations	Deciding upon solutions and productions by consequences and implications
Creative writing skill	Self-expression through written production
Visualization skill	Expressing ideas in visual form

Note: From "Classification of Williams Strategies Across Renzulli Type Activities" by F. E. Williams, 1979, *Gifted, Creative and Talented Magazine*, 9, pp. 2–10. Copyright © 1979 by *Gifted, Creative and Talented Magazine*. Reprinted by permission.

five things in some definite units of mea
sets of recordings have been obtained, the
the second by actual measure. This gives eac
work on further.

The task at hand now is for each group to design so
tem representing a comparison between improvised g
combinations thereof. If the class has had no training in grap
now is the time to present such information. Sophistication o
sion and graphic representation of the two sets of comparative da
pend on prior knowledge, experience and grade level of the groups (R
Type II training activities using two Williams strategies organized rand
search and evaluate situations, cuing for both divergent and convergent pro
ductive thinking).

Students motivated by such training activity could be challenged to move
on into Type II production activities. Some may become intrigued with ideas
for designing an original graphic system by comparing subjectively predicted
data arrived at under improvised conditions against objectively accurate data
arrived at under measured conditions. A few most inquisitive [students]
might wonder how to arrive at area or volume of an irregularly shaped object
such as the trapezoidal form of a wastebasket. At this time they should be
introduced to the principles of calculus and, if they so desire, allowed to pursue work in higher mathematics as an individual or with a small accelerated
group (Renzulli Type II activity applying Williams strategy adjustment to development). (pp. 5–6)

Acceleration is important, but it is not the same as *escalation* (Gowan,
1979d; Renzulli, 1979a). *Acceleration* places emphasis on the use of abilities to acquire content at a swifter rate compatible with abilities potential. *Escalation* places emphasis on growth to higher levels of mental
functioning. The rate at which intellectual development is facilitated by
acceleration does not ensure *transformation* to higher intellectual functioning levels (Tables 6.1 and 6.2). Each stage of development prepares a
student for the welling up of energies needed for intellectual leaps. Escalation to higher levels of intellectual functioning is the key to fulfillment
of potential and promise in the gifted. Where acceleration is the movement toward such an end, escalation effects transformations. The question to ask is not so much what we are accelerating the student to, but
whether acceleration will produce escalation to the next stage of intellectual development.

INDIVIDUALIZING EDUCATION

Thoughtful educators have repeatedly questioned traditional education
for its ineffectiveness, emotional harmfulness, undemocratic nature, un-

ıman needs (e.g., Con-
ı, 1970). Further, tradi-
meet the challenges of a
:ated people who are re-
vive change and turn ad-

ıstruction (which is often
rather than at the *individ-*
ving from such factors as
ıool terms and poor pupil
ching materials, and little
emergence of the graded-
∍nth century. According to
∍ one of the greatest inhib-
ıllowed in the wake of the
ıs a variety of graded curric-
to freeze the subject content

ula and standardized .... for each grade.

The Dalton Plan, Winnetka Plan, and Gary Plan (Bahner, 1979; Ingas, 1979) reacted against the rigidity and stereotyping of schools and allowed greater attention to the needs of the individual student. All of the plans initially were steamrollered out of existence by traditional education. Edward Ingas (1979, p. 3), describes these three plans as follows:

> The Dalton Plan—This system developed principally by Helen Parkhurst in Dalton, Massachusetts was a reaction to the conventional system which paid no attention to individual variables in learning. The curriculum was divided into monthly segments. A pupil could not start a module until he finished a prior one. Children were to set their own work schedules. This system had a number of "contracts" between children and their advisers. The concept of contracts and units still exists.

> The Winnetka Plan—Developed by Carleton Washbourne, a school principal in Illinois, this plan directed pupils to their goals. It was up to the child to achieve the goal, such as "write a friendly letter." After the child felt that he was ready, he was asked to take a test to see if he had, indeed, achieved his goal: if so, then he went on to a new "goal."

> The Gary Plan—This system was more ambitious in intent than the prior two, in that it represented an attempt at a totalistic education in which children learned to play, to socialize, to study and to work. Developed by William A. Wirt the school ranged from kindergarten through high school, and consisted of a complex of buildings in which a wide variety of activities took place 12 months a year.

To these plans must be added the less formalized approaches of the Playway Method, the Project Method, the Center-of-Interest Method, and the Activity and Experience Method. All these approaches emerged in the 1930s as the Progressive School Movement, spearheaded by the philosophy and efforts of John Dewey (1910). Similar reactions found expression through behaviorism (Operant Conditioning) in the Teaching Machine and Programmed Instruction Methods, Team Teaching, and the Non-Graded School Approaches.

Additional approaches for individual schooling included programs for grouping and ranging students along the dimensions of time and homogeneity (Gowan & Demos, 1964). Segregation of individuals according to grouping procedures varied from temporary part-of-the-day work groups—engaged in a certain specified task—to more permanent arrangements that would keep the same individuals together for a whole year's education program. The grouping of students of diverse mental abilities and achievement levels relied on the evaluation of the basic subjects (reading, writing and arithmetic), multiple interests, a variety of handicaps, and the like. These approaches sought to reduce heterogeneity among students on one or more variables and to discern individual differences and needs for more effective instructional management.

However, various studies on the effectiveness of homogeneous grouping (grouping according to ability) proved inconclusive (Gold, 1965; Gowan & Demos, 1964). The studies did suggest that grouping was not as important as the rationale and accuracy of grouping purposed to differentiate content, method, and rate of learning (Eash, 1961; Exstrom, 1961).

Further, the observation made on the incompatibility of ability grouping and individualization by writers of the *National Society for the Study of Education (NSSE) 1962 Yearbook on Individualizing Instruction* compels us to look to other pertinent efforts at individualizing learning. Among these are the procedures developed for Individually Guided Education (IGE) levelled at all children (Bahner, 1979; Klausmeier, 1975), Individualized Education Programs (IEP) levelled at the gifted (Meeker, 1979a; Renzulli & Smith, 1979b), self-directed learning (Treffinger, 1975) and Mentor facilitation (Gold, M. J., 1979; Runions, 1980; Torrance, 1984).

Individually Guided Education

John M. Bahner (1979), the chief designer, describes Individually Guided Education (IGE) as a comprehensive and systematic approach at managing the learning environment in a school or related setting. The IGE system is applicable to all types of curriculum from the standard to the humanistic, which emphasizes the critical roles of the teacher and support persons (parents, school board members and administrators). The approach was developed in the 1960s by the joint efforts of the Institute for Development of Educational Activities (an affiliate of the Charles F. Kettering Foundation) under the leadership of John M. Bahner and the Wisconsin Research and Development Center for Cognitive Learning led by Herbert J. Klausmeier. However, the alliance broke up and each organization went its own way to develop separate IGE programs.

To follow Bahner's efforts, we find that the theoretical foundations of the IGE consists of two dimensions, namely, (1) learning and its logical relationship to the teaching act, and (2) teacher and teaching roles. According to Bahner (1979, pp. 66–70) IGE is applicable to all learners, and its learning constructs state that learning is increased when learners are

> clear about what is to be learned
>
> involved in keeping to defined objectives and activities to achieve those objectives
>
> in a supportive environment with at least one instructor particularly concerned with enhancing their self-concept and sharing accountability for their learning program
>
> given constructive feedback almost immediately with their involvement in the assessment analysis
>
> provided opportunity to apply immediately their initial knowledge and understanding, with appropriate critique and preparation for further application

Teaching in IGE extends beyond the classroom. It includes planning and evaluating before, during, and after the teaching act; the relationships of all teachers in the building; and outside-the-school support. In IGE, the teacher has to work with the change process relative to the school, the problems of the school, and the supportive peer reference group, as Bahner (1979) explains.

> The individual school is the strategic unit of educational change.
>
> Each school needs a process by which it can deal effectively with its own problems if it is to maintain continuous improvement.
>
> Basic changes in the effects of schooling (e.g., reading achievement, attitudes toward school) are lasting only when such changes include support of the administrative hierarchy and school board, when organizational structures are revised in response to the needs of the changes, when new modes of operation are assumed by the teachers involved, and when students modify their behavior appropriately.
>
> Most schools are not strong enough to overcome the inertia against change built into the school district and, therefore, require a supportive peer reference group.
>
> Teachers learn new roles best when the principles of learning discussed above are followed. (70–74)

In practice, this form of IGE has 35 outcomes that are identical for all levels of schooling, with differences occurring from school to school in the application and emphasis of outcomes. Based on the listed constructs, IGE concerns itself with academic and nonacademic curricula, student evaluation, counseling, discipline, and administrator, teacher, parent, and student roles.

Gifted and Individualized Education Programs

The Individualized Education Program (IEP) represents a systematic approach to long standing traditional instruction (Treffinger, 1979). In recent years, it has received considerable attention, mainly due to the requirements of Public Law 94-142 relative to educating the handicapped. IEP has derived direction from earlier theories on individualization and established procedures that are inherent, for instance, in the IGE program (Bahner, 1979) and its adaptation in IGE-Multi-Unit School (Klausmeier, 1975), in Individually Prescribed Instruction or IPI (Weisberg, 1971ab), and in texts on modular instruction (Russell, 1974).

These individualized program packages are based on sound rationale and procedures, and are just as relevant for gifted students as they are for average and handicapped students. Several fundamental principles of the IEP, as a useful tool for planning education for any student, proposed by Donald J. Treffinger (1979) include (a) sound instructional design and accurate assessment information for instructional decisions, (b) learning not necessarily in isolation, (c) provision for different learning outcomes according to individual needs, (d) a variety of learning activities, (e) cooperative planning with input from many sources, and (f) many ways of implementing the individually based learning approach.

As these apply to gifted, talented, and creative students, S. M. Butterfield (1979) and Donald J. Treffinger (1979) caution us to be sure that the IEP *truly* differentiates instruction *qualitatively* rather than quantitatively and by rate of learning alone. This observation was made earlier on the subject of guidance and nurture of the gifted, and is equally significant in the design of IEPs for the gifted.

To this we must add that there is a need to re-focus individualized programs for gifted students from instruction to self-directed learning. We must realize that there is a need to move away from teacher-directed to *student-directed* learning whenever feasible (Jeter & Chauvin, 1982). Flexibility and change mechanisms are essential built-in devices for the occurrence of evolution within what appears to be preset conditions of learning. There must be no mistake that the program component in an IEP does not mean conditioning, but suggests some tentative directions for gifted students to follow. It should be of concern to us that some educators, engaging in IEPs, may mistake the fundamental precept of individualization of learning experiences for excessive structure, and in so doing put the gifted in a learning straitjacket.

According to Treffinger (1979), the basic principle of an IEP plan is not detailed prescription of each activity, but a flexible contract of services with the student. He makes the following specific recommendations to teachers planning IEPs for the gifted so as to produce effective instructional management tools. Teachers should recognize the uniqueness of the individuals interests and provide motivation and styles of learning, while attending to the various purposes of instructional components with provision for openended learning. Further, methodology should subscribe to problem-solving, inquiry, and research, with students involved in the planning. Individually based learning integrates the resources of the school, home, and community, coupling regular with special educational programs. In addition, continuous monitoring and revision of programs to ensure the flexibility of individually based learning is necessary. Such an approach to learning, if it is to be successful, requires systematic evaluation relative to the objectives set.

Currently, there are not many published accounts of IEPs specially developed for the gifted student. Among the ones that have been designed on the basis of sound conceptual models are those by Renzulli and Smith (1979b) specifically related to Renzulli's Enrichment Triad and its Revolving Door application, Treffinger's (1986) Individualized Programming Model, and Meeker's (1979a) Structure of Intellect Individualized Education Program. For the present purpose, we will consider the models by Renzulli and Smith (1979b) and Meeker (1979a), as instances of individualizing learning programs for the gifted.

Enrichment Triad IEP Model

The IEP model, based on the Enrichment Triad, has two major goals (Renzulli & Smith, 1979a), namely, (1) to provide teachers and administrators with a practical approach to individualization that includes both material and procedural steps for its implementation, and (2) to provide a valid rationale in support of such programming. J. S. Renzulli and L. H. Smith's IEP approach involves the following:

1. *Three supporting models*—derived from research and theory of learning and instruction (i.e., a characteristics model of gifted and talented students, a learning process model that matches students to learning environments, and an enrichment model that attempts to integrate regular curriculum experiences with those more appropriate to the gifted
2. *Practical considerations*—(i.e., identification of strengths from various sources, buying time for recommended higher level experiences, cognitive-affective development, integration with the regular program, total faculty in-service training, and the development and organization of learning experiences that represent *true* differentiation)
3. *Management*—(i.e., a system of organizing and implementing the theoretical and practical aspects of the model)

These three components of Renzulli and Smith's IEP system are interactive in nature. The model's global function in individualizing learning for the gifted is illustrated as Figure 10.2.
This model (Figure 10.2) assumes the following:

the capability of the gifted to master the regular curriculum at a much faster rate and at higher levels of proficiency than their non-gifted peers

the provisions of special opportunities for the gifted to identify and pursue advanced-level areas of study of particular attraction to them through procedures described in the Enrichment Triad Model

the focus on individual strengths (both general and specific, as these relate to higher levels of thinking, creativity, task commitment) with provision for their development in learning situations that are relatively unstructured

Renzulli and Smith call attention to instruments that have been developed to facilitate the enhancement of the strengths of the gifted, namely the Strength-A-Lyzer, Interest-A-Lyzer, Learning Style Inventory, and Compactor.

Strength-A-Lyzer (Renzulli & Smith, 1978a)—used to record information about the gifted and their abilities derived from various test sources (intelligence, aptitude and creativity); their interests and learning styles; and teacher ratings and end-of-the-year grades in the various subject-matter areas. The end result should lead to recommended action to guide the design of an individual program.

Interest-A-Lyzer (Renzulli, 1977b)—used to find students' individual present and potential interests so that educational experiences can be built around them. The four steps recommended for interpretation of student responses are (a) sharing of responses in small-group discussions to discover each student's pattern of interest, (b) the grouping of students according to common interests that may lead to group or class projects, (c) the follow-up studies and discussions on the feasibility of activities to be carried out in terms of cost, time, availability of resource persons and materials, and the like, thereby ensuring realistic parameters for the activity, and (d) problem focusing (probably the most important and complex of the four steps), an in-depth treatment of which can be found in Renzulli's (1979a) Enrichment Triad Model. The information thus obtained is recorded in the interest section of the Strength-A-Lyzer.

Learning Style Inventory (Renzulli, 1978)—used (with its accompanying teacher version) to find out both the strategies a student prefers when interacting with particular bodies of curricular materials

Figure 10.2 Individualized Educational Programming Model—Gifted/Talented

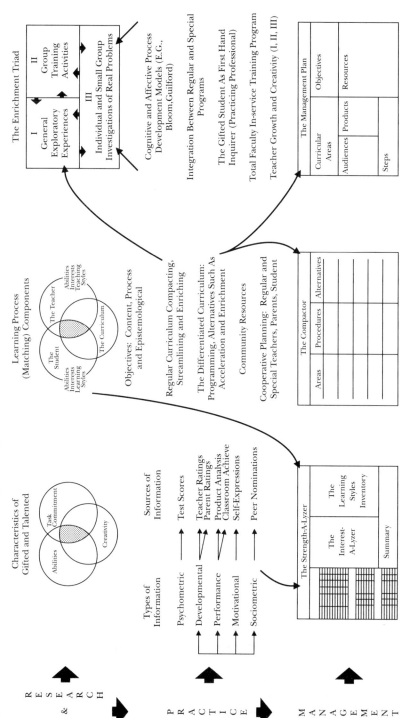

From "*A Practical Model for Designing Individualized Education Programs (IEPS) for Gifted/Talented Students*" by J.S. Renzulli and L.H. Smith, 1979. Unpublished Manuscript. Copyright© 1979 by J.S. Renzulli. Reprinted by permission.

(projects, drill and recitation, peer teaching, discussion, teaching games, independent study, programmed instruction, lecture, simulation) and the instructional strategies most frequently preferred by the teacher to facilitate a closer match between learning and teaching styles. Information thus derived is recorded in the appropriate section of the Strength-A-Lyzer.

Compactor (Renzulli & Smith, 1978b)—a systematic plan for compacting and streamlining the regular curriculum so that (a) competencies for later achievement are assured and the boredom of doing unchallenging work in the basic skills areas is relieved, and (b) the time saved can be used by students to pursue acceleration and enrichment activity. Information from the Strength-A-Lyzer gives direction to the compacting of certain curricular areas and to basic materials for acceleration and enrichment activities that are recorded respectively in the three columns shown in Figure 10.2.

The description of developing management plans for individual and small group investigations attempts to provide the guidance necessary to implement the third component of Renzulli's Enrichment Triad, which requires inquiry and solving of real problems aimed ideally at adding to present knowledge or at creating a relatively new artistic product, including consideration of possible audiences and outlets.

As Renzulli found greater meaning for his Enrichment Triad Model— linking it with his Three Ring Conception of Giftedness, Revolving Door Identification Model, and recent theoretical information generated by Sternberg and Gardner—he progressively refined some of his earlier illustrations to incorporate these developments. The most recent manifestation that applies these developments is the School-wide Enrichment Model (Renzulli & Olenchak, 1989), which instigates measurable educational and attitudinal change (Olenchak & Renzulli, 1989). The model is presented as Figure 10.3.

Participants of the study included 11 elementary schools consisting of 1,698 students in grades K–6, 236 elementary grade teachers, 120 parents and 10 principals. The study showed positive changes in student and teacher attitudes toward education of the gifted, high levels of creative output, large increases in student-centered enrichment activities, self-selected interests, greater cooperation between classroom teachers and gifted education specialists, and more favorable parental attitudes toward special programming for the gifted.

Structure of Intellect IEP Model

Credit goes to Meeker (1979a) for designing the Structure of Intellect IEP model, whose major purpose is to tailor curriculum to fit an individual pattern of intellectual abilities based on a theory of individual intelli-

Figure 10.3 Overview of the School-Wide Enrichment Model

Self
Actualization

Creative
Productivity

Service Delivery Components

Type III Enrichment

Individual and Small Group Investigations
of Real Problems

Type I Enrichment	Type II Enrichment
General Exploratory Experiences	Cognitive and Affective Development Learning How to Learn Skills Research and Reference Skills Communication with Audience Skills

Personal Support System

Interest and Learning Styles Assessment	Counseling * Understanding Camaraderie * Emotional Suport Teacher as: Advocate, Patron, Defender, Confidant and Friend

Curriculum Compacting

Organizational Components

Staff Development Activities

Simulation Situations (SIMSITS)	Network Newsletter	Training Institutes
Flexible Identification Procedures	Schoolwide Enrichment Team	Directory of Model Users Video Tape Series	Confratute
Evaluation Instruments	Taxonomy of Process Skills	Bibliography of Methodological (How-to) Books	Categorized Process Materials Directory
Parent and Student Orientation Materials	Curricular Prototypes	Planning Guides for Service Delivery Activities (Action Forms)	

The Goals

Expand Services to a Larger Proportion of the School Population	Integration With Regular Curriculum General Faculty Participation	Minimize Elitism–Label the Services Rather than the Students	Promote a Radiation of Excellence Throughout the Entire School

Rationale
(Research Theory)

Research Underlying the Three Ring Conception of Giftedness (Renzulli, 1978, 1986)	Recent Studies by Sternberg, Garner, and Others

William James	Alfred North Whitehead	John Dewey	Jerome Bruner	Paul Torrance	Virgil Ward	Philip Phenix	Albert Bandura

Validation Studies on the Model - See Technical Report

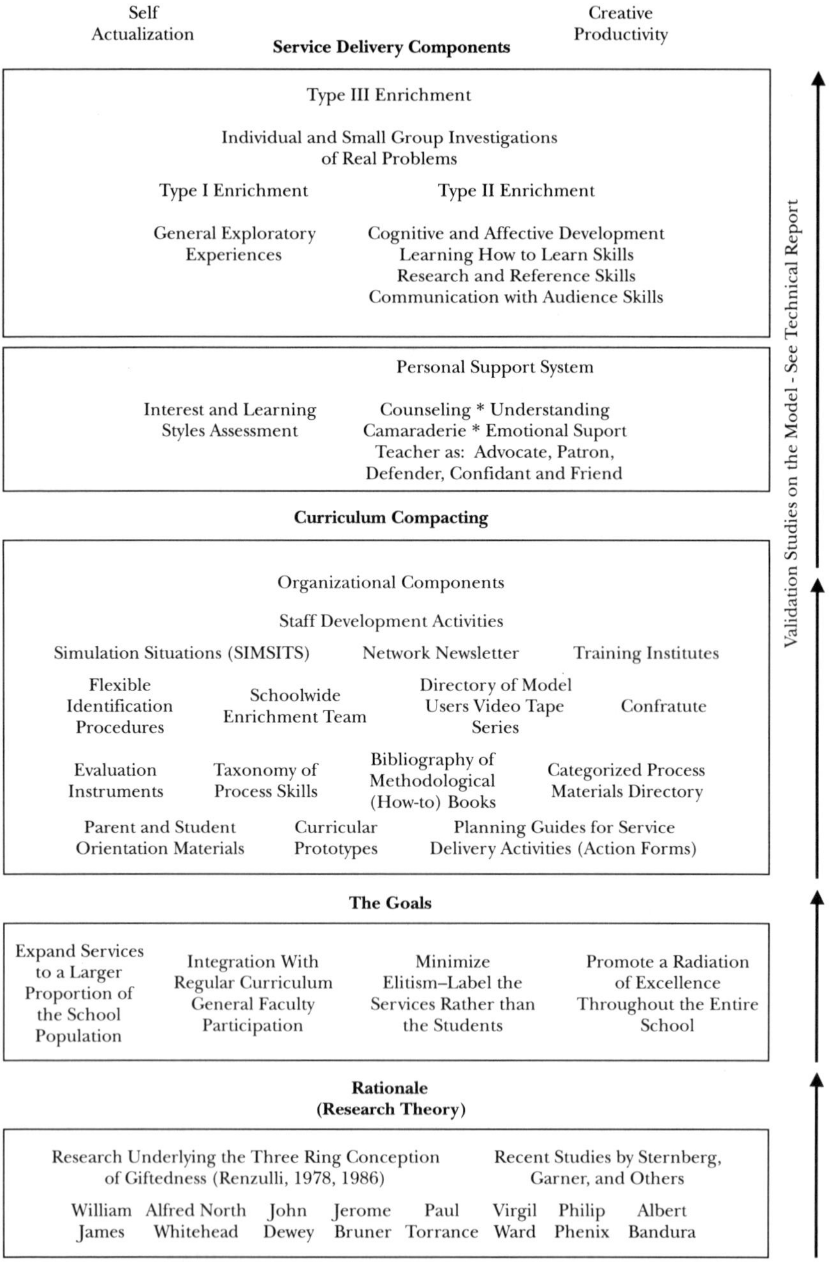

Note: From "The Effectiveness of the Schoolwide Enrichment Model on Selected Aspects of Elementary School Change" by J.S. Renzulli and F.R. Olenchak, 1989, *Gifted Child Quarterly*, 33(1), p. 36–46. Copyright © 1989 by *Gifted Child Quarterly*. Reprinted by permission.

gence. The model is closely linked to Meeker's earlier work on Structure of Intellect abilities (1969) and the revised workbooks first generated in 1970 (Meeker, 1980a). In the IEP model Meeker indicates that a knowledge of the Structure of Intellect model, and training in its use and interpretation, assists teachers to perceive students as individuals with multi-varied intellectual aptitudes and faculties; this perception helps to identify individual and group strengths and weaknesses precisely. Consequently, a prescriptive Structure of Intellect program can be developed to strengthen areas of relative weaknesses and enhance areas of identified strengths. In this way, students in programs that use the Structure of Intellect IEP approach can be expected to experience a curriculum that is pertinent to both their abilities and basic educational needs.

To implement this model, Meeker developed the Structure of Intellect Learning Abilities Test or SOILAT (1979b). The measure consists of 24 of the 120 predicted Structure of Intellect abilities. These abilities form clusters that diagnose reading readiness (Cluster A), reading accomplishment (Cluster B), arithmetic readiness (Cluster C), and creative potential (Clusters D, E, and F). The relationship between these Structure of Intellect abilities and subject matter (Meeker, 1979a) is presented as Figure 10.4.

An IEP, using the Structure of Intellect Model, begins with an analysis of the raw scores of the SOILAT 24 subtests. Responses to the test items may either be manually or machine scored. The results are then presented as profiles of relative strengths and weaknesses. The administration and scoring procedures are to be found in the test manual that describes two strategies for prescribing learning tailored to the individual.

The first strategy is based on individual patterns of learning with targets specifically keyed to individual abilities. The second strategy is a more general grouping of individual strengths and weaknesses.

Once *diagnosis* has taken place, *prescription* of an IEP for a gifted student follows, based on the materials developed by Meeker and her associates (Meeker, 1980a; Meeker, Sexton & Richardson, 1970). The Structure of Intellect IEP was highly commended for its effectiveness by C. Hedbring and R. Rubenzer (1979), and is currently widely used.

Meeker (1979b) puts the assessment by SOILAT in the broader context of *total human functioning* in a paradigm shown as Figure 10.5. Her interpretation of the paradigm relates to different kinds of giftedness designated as Area I (academics, intelligence and language), Area II (affective), and Area III (physio-neurological).

She comments on each of the three areas as follows:

> The academically gifted are, of course, performing at a gifted level in Area I. Typically they are excellent convergent producers with gifted memory abilities that bring them to the attention of their teachers. Individual Educational

Figure 10.4 Relationship Between Structure of Intellect Factors and Subject Matter

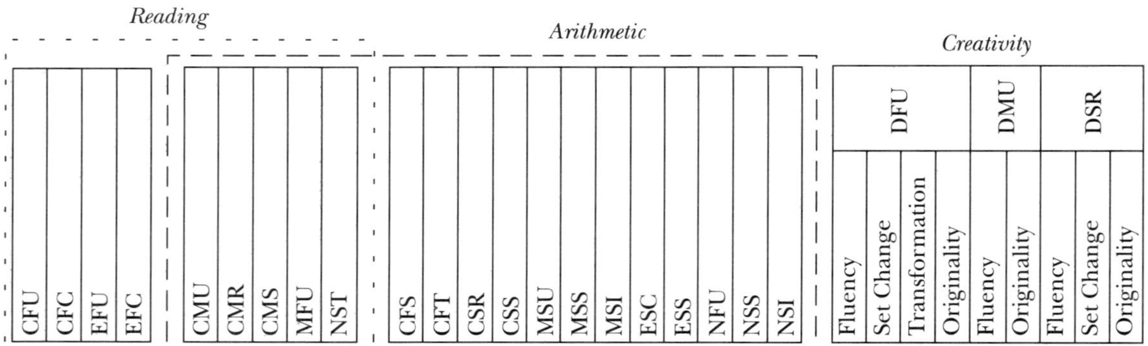

Reading (Foundational abilities)

- CFU – Visual closure
- CFC – Visual conceptualization
- EFU – Visual discrimination
- EFC – Judging similarities and matching of concepts
- MSU – Visual attending
- MSS – Visual concentration for sequencing

Reading (Enabling skills)

- CMU – Vocabulary of math and verbal concepts
- CMR – Comprehension of verbal relations
- CMS – Ability to comprehend extended verbal information
- MFU – Visual memory for details
- NST – Speed of word recognition

Writing

- NFU – Psycho-motor readiness

Arithmetic

- CFS – Constancy of object in space (Piaget)
- CFT – Spatial conservation (Piaget)
- CSR – Comprehension of abstract relations
- CSS – Comprehension of numerical progressions
- MSU – Auditory attending
- MSS – Auditory sequencing
- MSI – Inferential memory
- ESC – Judgment of arithmetic similarities
- ESS – Judgment of correctness of numerical facts
- NSS – Application of math facts
- NSI – Form reasoning (logic)

Creativity

- DFU – Creativity with things (figural level)
- DSR – Creativity with math facts
- DMU– Creativity with words and ideas

Note: From "IEPS: Diagnosing and Matching Curriculum to Cognitive Patterns (p. 29) by Mary N. Meeker, 1979, Los Angeles: N/S LTI on the Gifted and Talented. Copyright © 1979 by Mary N. Meeker. Reprinted by permission.

Figure 10.5 Meeker's Paradigm for Assessing Three Major Areas of Human Functioning

Area I — Cognitive/Academic Functioning								Area II — Social/Emotional Functioning					Area III — Physio/Neurological Functioning						
Linguistics	Cognition	Memory	Evaluation	Convergent Production	Reading	Arithmetic	Divergent Production	Environment	Emotional Adjustment	Social Skills	Social Adjustments	Motivation	Nutrition	Maturation	Visual Performance	Auditory Acuity	Perceptual-Motor Visual-Auditory	Integration	Neurological Referral
Observation, Speech	•CFU, •CMU, •CFS, •CFT, •CFC, •CSR, •CSS, •CMR, •CMS	•MSU V & •MSS V. •MSU A. •MSS A. •MFU, •MSI	•EFU, •EFC, •ESC. •ESS	NFU, •NST, •NSS, •NSI	Standard Achievement test (CMU & NST)	Standard Achievement test (CMU & NSS)	DFU, DMU, •DSR	Case study: home, school	•Projective psychological tests	Observation	Projective psychological tests	•Observation, performance, Piers Harris	•Medical tests for allergies and nutrition	•Medical tests gross motor skills	•Visual tests (SOI Developmental Vision Form)	Medical examination, Hearing Blocks MSU & MSS Aud	•Psycho Neurological •Neurological tests NFU	PORCH, LINDAMOOD, ITPA, SOI-LA. MSU & MSS	Bender Gestalt, NFU

Reading Related

Math Related

Curriculum can be based on findings within each of the columns above.

• Area 1—emcompasses language, structure of intellect learning abilities, and academic performance, Scholarship and creativity show up here with high functioning.
• Area II—encompasses social and emotional functioning; sometimes called affective functioning by educators. Leadership shows up here.
• Area III—emcompasses physiological and neurological functioning. Talent shows up here.

From "Using SOI Test Results: A Teacher's Guide" by M.N. Meeker, 1979, p. 18.
Copyright © 1979 by M.N. Meeker. Reprinted by permission.

Plans (IEPs) can be made for all students in each one of the Area I columns using the SOI Sourcebooks, Task Cards, and standard curriculum.

We tend to equate giftedness with academic giftedness but there are gifts and talents in the other two areas as well. Area II giftedness can be assessed as well as Area I. An Area II giftedness is usually reflected in school leadership, social leadership, and interpersonal relations. Many Area I gifted need support in Area II.

In some ways Area III is the most neglected and yet any serious problem here will affect performance in Areas I and II. The best kind of education we can provide today would begin with excellent diagnosis in Area III. The earlier the diagnosis here, the better the chance of avoiding special education placement and long-term failure in average classrooms for students who enter school with Area III deficiencies. Many Area I potentially gifted are severely hampered by Area III problems which often go undetected. Area III giftedness is best described as talent and is shown in athletic, musical, dancing, artistic, and skill-craft talent. In other words, the Area III talents depend upon motor functioning which is at gifted level—how the artist sees, how the musician hears, how the athlete coordinates body with eyes and ears. For example, the talented vocalist shows Area III giftedness; if the vocalist also creates the music, then that is a demonstration of Area I Divergent Symbolic Production and Memory in Area I, as well as in Area III where body movements communicate to the audience exactly what is expected to be interpreted from the action. The quarterback on a football team has Area III giftedness, but his decisions and changes in plays on the spot demonstrate Area I (Figural and Evaluation) giftedness. Area III giftedness is the motor skill underlying the Cognition overlay. In other words, giftedness, talents, [and] leadership are human functions which are extremely outstanding performances in any one or more of the three areas. At the same time, any gifted person can be nongifted in any of the other column functions in the paradigm.

Our search for giftedness will be more humane with the understanding that giftedness is certainly differential and may, for any individual, be confined to one area of special aptitude—that the identification of giftedness in one area should not carry with it the expectation that the person will be gifted in all areas. This is especially meaningful for the gifted whose greatest needs are in Area II, the social-emotional area. Since the gifted have a tendency toward acute sensitivity, feelings of being different, and loneliness (except for Area II gifted), their motivation is easily diminished or extinguished when they are locked into an environment at home or school and that environment is neither supportive nor accepting. Equally damaging to the gifted are parents and teachers whose expectations approach perfection during childhood, and just as damaging is the forced competitiveness for "A's" in all subjects. Occasionally this perfectionism does stem from the student, and in these cases, support and teaching tolerance for failure becomes most important. Many of our potentially gifted students fail to perform in Area I when their Area II needs are not met.

The paradigm reminds us that human functioning is multifaceted and while we may emphasize one aspect or another in nurturing development, we should not lose sight of the total human profile. The diagnosis of SOI abilities as they relate to the learning of school subject matter should be made on every student entering school. We talk about basic education—we forget that basic intelligence training is just as fundamental a part of education as is basic skills training. (pp. 15–16)

Self-Directed Learning

Another important methodological dimension of individualizing education is *self-directed learning*. The discussion so far has indicated that the emphasis in individualizing education for the gifted and talented has not been placed so much on learner control but on educator control of learning. However, the discussion acknowledges that IEGs, IEPs, and related arrangements do take into account, or provide for, abilities, interests, styles of learning, and even, to some extent, active participation of the individual student in the planning of the programs.

From all accounts (e.g., Bahner, 1979; Renzulli, 1986) we must note that the major construct of individualized educational arrangements provides students with the choice of learning alternatives, an aspect also emphasized by Robert L. Fizzell (1980). Yet what emerges from the methodology of the IGE and IEP is the tendency to have both educator dominance and design of student learning. The extent to which the student gains control of learning according to felt needs, motivations, interests, and aspirations—where the full compass of his or her abilities and talents can operate and be energized by personal commitment—is the extent to which individualized education becomes self-directional, a position also reiterated by several others (e.g., Betts & Neihart, 1986; Dirkes, 1988; Renzulli, 1986; Treffinger, 1978).

Researchers and educators who consider self-directed learning the most suitable approach for gifted students also acknowledge the practical problem of students who have been consistently programmed by general public schooling to develop responsive rather than initiatory learning habits. Placed in a gifted program where self-directed learning is an immediate requirement can be threatening, and even, anxiety producing. Students, who during nearly all their educational life have had their learning mapped out for them, are unlikely to know how to cope with a sudden change that puts them in total charge.

Several educators (e.g., Betts, 1985; Renzulli, 1977; Treffinger, 1975, 1978) develop curriculum models that focus on the goal of facilitating self-directed learning growth recognize that gifted children do not automatically shift from teacher-directed to student-directed learning, since they do not have the skills needed to achieve the shift that requires them to take command of their learning.

For instance, Treffinger (1975) is correct in perceiving the need for gradual transfer of such powers. According to him, self-directed learning or "responsible autonomy" can be attained more effectively through teacher and parent efforts. His proposed plan of self-directed learning is worthy of serious consideration and recalls characteristics of self-directed learning:

organized

supportively structured (according to students' abilities, interests, needs, etc.)

individualistic, yet cognizant of social outcomes

unselfish in addressing itself to learning goals and objectives

involved in a variety of cognitive and affective processes and outcomes

necessitates good evaluation procedures that take into account evidence that goes beyond passing judgments on student efforts to include every conceivable evidence through planned instructional experiences

requires the student's active participation in every phase of the learning process

In a later discussion of self-directed learning, Treffinger (1978) offers parents and teachers some initial and tentative guidelines.

1. Admonitions are inadequate, since telling a child to be independent and direct his own learning will not help very much.
2. Don't assume what children know or do not know, but find out through informal assessment or more formal diagnostic work all you can about students' strengths and skills, so as to determine their needs.
3. Don't smother self-direction by doing for them things they can do (or can learn to do) for themselves but exercise patience for self-direction to emerge.
4. Adults must have or develop an attitude of openness and support for self-directed learning so that they do not impose their will on what and how students must learn but clarify their goals and facilitate independent and creative learning.
5. Learn to defer judgment when dealing with children so that their curiosity, inquiry, and independence is not inhibited or stifled by premature, excessive, or arbitrary evaluation.
6. Emphasize the continuity of problems and challenges whereby students can integrate information acquired in their studies so that they learn to view problems and issues in many different ways, and to grasp that solutions introduce new problems and challenges.
7. Provide systematic training in problem solving and the skills of

independent research and inquiry. By getting command of these methods, students actively learn to assess their interests, diagnose their needs, develop a plan of action, locate resources, carry out appropriate activities, present results, and verify their total effort.

8. Treat difficult situations at home or school as opportunities to use new skills and meet real everyday problems.
9. Be alert to audiences that are appropriate for sharing children's efforts, or for opportunities to create such audiences so that they may have their works exhibited, recognized or appreciated, and even rewarded.
10. Help students learn how to direct their own learning gradually— don't expect it to happen all at once! You can avoid frustration, disappointment, or even abandonment of effort to institute independent or self-directed study, as well as prepare the students to assume greater responsibility for planning and conducting their own learning.
11. Create! Be a model of self-directed learning in your own life, thereby giving your students the opportunity of observing you occupied productively in independent inquiry. (pp. 15–19)

A couple of interesting models of independent study, which exemplify self-directed learning, are proposed by George T. Betts (1985) and M. Ann Dirkes (1988). The first model discussed emphasizes the *autonomy* of the individual in the learning situation, and the second model emphasizes *thinking* in the curriculum. Both serve as examples of efforts to develop self-directed learning models.

Autonomous Learner Model

The Autonomous Learner Model developed by George T. Betts (1985, 1986) provides individualized learning opportunities, development of skills in independent learning, training in thinking and feeling, and learning that allows for different interests and learning styles. The model consists of five dimensions—orientation, individual development, enrichment activities, seminars, and in-depth study. (See Figure 10.6.)

> *Dimension I-Orientation*—provides students with a basic understanding of giftedness, and information about their interests, abilities, and the program.
>
> *Dimension II-Individual Development*—designed to assist students to acquire those skills and attitudes (e.g., problem solving, decision-making, creative thinking, study skills, computer research skills, interviewing group process, leadership, personal responsibility, and acceptance of others) needed for self-directed learning.

Figure 10.6 Betts's Autonomous Learner Model

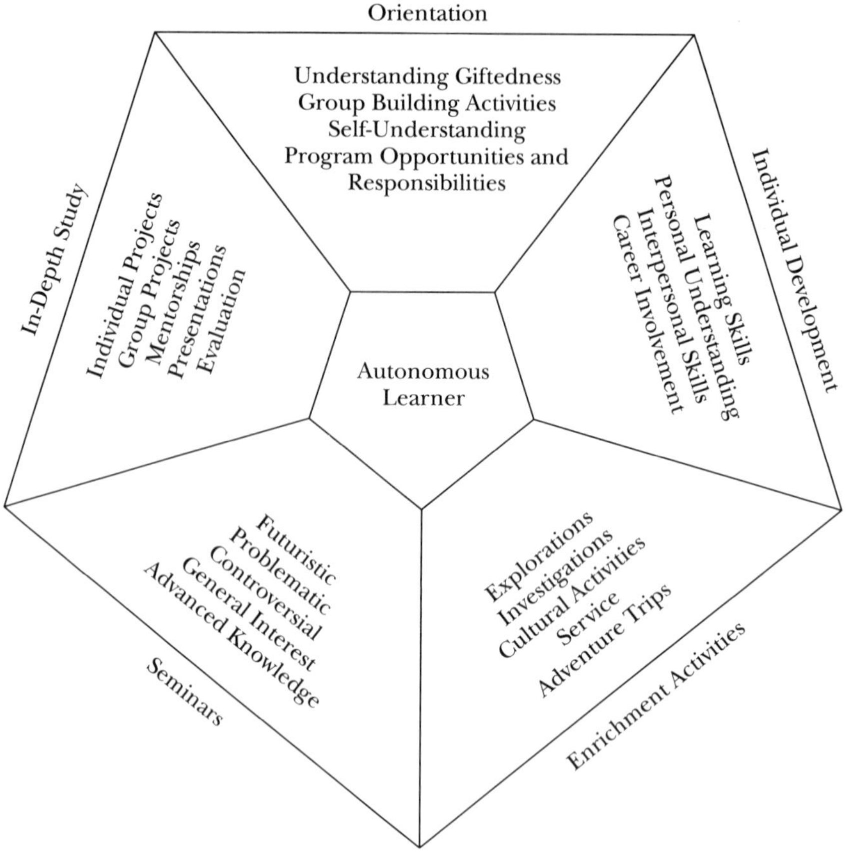

Orientation

Understanding Giftedness
Group Building Activities
Self-Understanding
Program Opportunities and
Responsibilities

Individual Development

In-Depth Study

Individual Projects
Group Projects
Mentorships
Presentations
Evaluation

Learning Skills
Personal Understanding
Interpersonal Skills
Career Involvement

Autonomous
Learner

Futuristic
Problematic
Controversial
General Interest
Advanced Knowledge

Seminars

Explorations
Investigations
Cultural Activities
Service
Adventure Trips

Enrichment Activities

From *"Implementing Self-Directed Learning Models for the Gifted and Talented"* by G.T.
Betts and Maureen Nerhart, 1986, *Gifted Quarterly Press*, 30 (4), p. 174-177.
Copyright @ 1986 by *Gifted Quarterly Press*. Reprinted by permission.

Dimension III-Enrichment Activities—designed to provide students
with experiences in many content areas in preparation for the in-
depth studies that they will eventually opt to do.

Dimension IV-Seminars—emphasizes idea production projects in small
groups (3–5 members) whose outcomes are presentations to appropriate audiences.

Dimension V-In-Depth Study—requires that the student select a topic,
design a learning plan with goals included, discover needed resources and materials, plan a time-line or schedule, determine
evaluation criteria, and actively participate in the final evaluation
of the project. The teacher serves the student as a facilitator.

The Autonomous Learner Model designed for gifted and talented students also may be used with curriculum in a regular classroom in the secondary and elementary school levels. At the secondary level, the model is offered as an elective course attended by students on a daily basis. The model can serve as a pull-out program or resource room of an elementary school, where students can work sequentially through various dimensions of the curriculum model and their gifted program.

By following the *Autonomous Learner Model* students gain independence because they develop their own interests. Self-directed learning eventually results in the completion of a product which is then presented to an audience.

Betts and Neihart (1986) recommend that before developing a program for the Autonomous Learner Model and other similar models (Renzulli's and Treffinger) the following guidelines should be considered:

> development of appropriate skills, concepts, and attitudes for lifelong self-directed learning
>
> provision for opportunities to integrate the cognitive, emotional, and social development
>
> assessment of learning styles and development of strategies to foster integrative growth
>
> knowledge about the use of the entire area of high level thinking skills that include analytic, creative, and evaluative thinking
>
> support provided for the role shift that students have to make from "student" to "learner"
>
> assistance for students to develop techniques for discovering the topic for study and methodology for implementing it to its final conclusion with appropriate reinforcement of the entire process
>
> opportunity to begin and complete an in-depth study in an area loved by the student
>
> inclusion of the student in the decision-making process of program selection
>
> shift in teacher role from "dispenser of knowledge" to that of "facilitator of the learning process"
>
> allowance for time, patience, opportunity, and guidance to foster self-directed learning

All in all, conclude Betts and Neihart, to individualize instruction requires educators to change their philosophies, attitudes, and methods. Further, the transition from traditional educational approaches require flexible educators who are open to change and who are willing to take risks with curriculum.

Betts and Neihart apply their model to Renzulli's and Treffinger's approaches to individualizing learning and this pairing produces learning self-direction. Here the similarities among the three learning methodologies become apparent. All three models stress training gifted students to acquire knowledge and skills needed for self-directed learning. The models also recognize the importance of assessing and respecting the child's interests and learning style. Further, the methodologies recommend that a variety of instructional approaches (e.g., small group, individual, large group, and pairs) be used, and suggest modifications to the learning environment that will facilitate self-directed learning. However, unlike the first two, the Autonomous Learner Model includes a strong affective component, addresses career development, and offers guidance to achieve these ends.

Self-Directed Thinking

Another self-directed learning model emphasizing self-initiated thinking to maximize learning of school curriculum is proposed by M. Ann Dirkes (1988). She considers self-directed thinking a factor of Sternberg's (1984b) conception of intellect as *metacognition*. We have already described metacognition, one of three components of Sternberg's *triarchic theory of human intelligence,* as a higher executive process used to determine the nature of a problem and select a strategy for solving it. According to Dirkes, metacognition enables students to recognize learning opportunities and to design plans for thinking and creative production so essential to self-directed thinking. In recognizing, assessing and monitoring their potential to think, gifted students can predict the uniqueness of their contributions.

Dirkes (1988) offers a plan to implement self-directed thinking in the school curriculum, which consists of the four following dimensions (pp. 93–94):

1. A general plan for self-directed thinking on ways to develop metacognition
2. Instruction for self-directed thinking involving scoring of idea production, decision making by students about assuming responsibility, reinforcing independent thinking, listing on the wall as a reminder to students to initiate specific thinking strategies, monitoring students' thinking strategies and interests by use of brief questionnaires, and charting the purpose in the form of a problem statement that includes objectives to direct what they do, outlines, idea-organizing diagrams, and summaries to develop understanding
3. Implementing the plan (e.g., using self-directed thinking to plan a composition on the habits of birds)
4. Evaluating student performance by using measures to evaluate thinking strategies used, student ratings of their own work accord-

ing to specific criteria, and teacher-made tests to measure thinking and planning to emphasize the importance of self-direction

It is worthwhile to note that Dirkes's emphasis on self-directed thinking is similar to the emphasis on developing various dimensions of the intellect and thinking proposed by Guilford (1972, 1977), Meeker (1980a, 1989), F. E. Williams (1972), and de Bono (1985) with or without curriculum materials. The only difference is that these researchers have not overtly advocated self-direction in the effective use of thinking operations or skills, but imply it in their models.

The several contributors to self-directed learning emphasize its importance for inclusion in almost any educational experience or program for gifted students. Self-directed learning or thinking requires careful thought on the part of the planner and should include adequate preparation for effective implementation. Preparation includes knowing the background of the learner and the entire learning situation. Furthermore, the planning relationship of the educator and learner must be interactive and ongoing.

To plan the learning experience, a brief written plan of action or proposal that specifies the problem, expected outcomes, and the methodology is helpful. Flexibility and open-endedness are desirable and should be included in the planning so that certain kinds of changes become allowable in the course of learning without destroying the plan's original integrity.

MENTORING

Closely associated with individualized and self-directed learning is *mentoring*, which is a service delivered by a counselor, teacher, or mentor. A person serving in a mentoring role is one with high-level expertise and competence in at least one area of knowledge, for instance, in science (e.g., astronomy, particle physics), mathematics (e.g., exponential functions, statistics, computer language), communication (e.g., eastern or western languages, comparative philology), aesthetics (e.g., music, art, drama), social and behavioral science (philosophy, psychology, social anthropology), and so forth.

Mentoring has been defined in many ways but the origin of the word can be traced to Mentor, the faithful friend of Ulysses (Odysseus). According to the myth, while fighting in the Trojan Wars the Greek King Ulysses entrusted Mentor with the education of his son Telemachus.

> Mentor was an old friend of Odysseus, to whom the king had entrusted his whole household when he sailed, with orders to defer to the aged Laertes and keep everything intact.

To Telemachus, Mentor was everything. Mentor served as a surrogate father, a guide, confidant, teacher, friend. Above all else, Mentor aimed at assisting Telemachus grow up to be the prince and royal successor of his father's domain.

To us, a *mentor* means someone primarily responsible for the education of a student. Personal involvement and affectionate attachments are highly desirable. Where such a relationship exists, it illuminates an otherwise impersonal student-teacher relationship. Frequently, the *mentor* regards the *tutee* as someone who will one day be his successor and assume leadership in the field. That is why, unlike the regular teacher, a mentor brings all of his skills to learning. This teacher-student relationship is considered a lifelong relationship and commitment, one consequence of which will be the student becoming someone else's mentor, and perhaps simultaneously serving as tutee and mentor.

Primarily, the parent is initially the gifted child's mentor. However, with the onset of schooling, teachers, learning experiences, growth of intellect, and the emergence of new powers, the parent-child mentor relationship soon shifts to a mentor away from home, which is not always easy to find.

A mentor is not necessarily a professional educator. In fact a mentor can be anyone in the professional community who exemplifies brilliance and success, like the scientist, poet, politician, bank manager, business tycoon, and so on. A mentor-tutee relationship of this nature can provide an effective link to the efforts of both parent and teacher, and may initiate self-directed learning. The nonprofessional educator, in a one-to-one relationship of common interests and goals, is more likely to be nondirective in approach, enthusiastic, and in command of unique resources for the development, progress, and productivity of the gifted student.

According to B. R. Frey and Ruth B. Noller (1983), this relationship is symbiotic. The mentor draws new challenges, a sense of contribution, and a means of remaining youthful, whereas the tutee finds support, encouragement, a sense of achievement, and career advancement. To be a mentor, says S. B. Rivchun (1980), is to leave behind a legacy.

Guiding Creative Talent

In the opening chapter of *Guiding Creative Talent* (1962a) Torrance expresses the need to properly assess and guide creative talent growth. He also advises teachers and administrators to take a counseling role by becoming a patron or mentor to the creatively gifted person. As such, one provides a refuge to the highly creative individual, helps the person understand his divergence, allows him to communicate ideas, sees that creative talent is recognized, and helps the individual's parents to better understand their child.

Torrance's (1983) twenty-two-year longitudinal study on the effects of mentoring on creative achievement discloses that mentors were primarily adult subjects' professors, employers, or notable persons in their occupations. Of the 212 adults studied, 46% (40 males and 57 females) had mentors. He found that mentors affected the quality of their creative achievement, future career image, number of creative achievements, and number of creative style-of-life achievements. Length of schooling was greater for those who had mentors. Besides, females tended to value mentor encouragement and praise while males valued mentor business and professional expertise. About 20% of the group valued their mentors for having taught them "to play the game."

Some guidelines on how mentoring can be improved are presented by Torrance (1984, pp. 56–57). Mentors can help gifted mentees in a number of ways:

> Encourage them to be unafraid of "falling in love with something" and to pursue it with intensity, for love will motivate them to do their best.
> Help them learn to know, understand, and take pride in practice, and to use, exploit, and enjoy their greatest strengths.
> Teach them to free themselves from the expectations of others and to walk away from the games that others may impose on them.
> Let them free themselves to play their own game in a way that makes the best use of their strengths, and to follow their dreams.
> Guide them to find great teachers so that they may attach themselves to them.
> Counsel them to avoid wasting expensive and unproductive energy in trying to be well-rounded.
> Lead them to learn skills of interdependence and to give freely of their infinite strengths.

Bruce Boston (1976) offers some insights about the mentor who combines the role of counselor, advisor, and companion. His analysis of the relationship between the mentor and student includes the following:

> mentor expectations of students—involvement in a total learning experience that gives equal place to doing and thinking, willingness to explore and experiment, feedback for more effective learning experiences, demonstration of the acquisition of new skills, and growth orientation
> mentor responsibilities to students—being a personal and cultural role model, able to organize and give direction according to student needs, teaching by indirection, giving realistic appraisal of

progress and dealing with conflicts, and creatively guiding the student through creative problem-solving steps

conditions for effective mentoring—arranging for the program to be experientially based, matching with care the student and mentor, making learning more open-ended, and ensuring that both learning and evaluation are competency based

Mentorship Programs

Some researchers suggest that mentorship in gifted education is lacking supervision and standardization (e.g., Boston, 1976; Gold, 1979). Perhaps, as noted by Gallagher (1985), infrequent use of mentoring in education is mainly attributable to the inconvenience of implementing it administratively. However, among the several attempts to initiate mentor programs, four are worthy of special notice. They are the Executive High School Internship Program (Hirsch, 1976), Mentor Academy Program (Runions, 1980), Mentor Connection (Beck, 1989), and Double Mentoring (Clasen & Hanson, 1987).

Executive High School Internship Program
The Executive High School Internship Program is considered by Marvin J. Gold (1979) as a major organized mentor effort in the United States. In his discussion of this program Gold explains that

> the program aids local school systems in developing plans in which high-school students are given released time from their formal studies and are put in contact with volunteer community leaders in business, industry, and the professions. Although this plan is not for the exclusive use of gifted and talented children, its value to them is of some magnitude. The period of released time is usually a semester, but may vary according to local conditions. In one school system a student might be released for a day per week during the second semester of the senior year, while a student in another system might be released for an entire six-week period or longer, and still another system might opt for two afternoons per week for the entire year. (pp. 275–276)

Mentor Academy Program
Another such program is the Mentor Academy Program, which T. Runions (1980) describes as an alternative high school enrichment credit program for high-achieving students, motivated to explore and expand their interests with mutually interested members of local schools, universities, professional agencies, and community services. Runions suggests that the Mentor Academy Program is different from other mentor type programs:

[It] totally integrates the mentor-training process by encouraging personal development of academic, career, and avocational knowledge and skills, while developing leadership/service skills through mentoring a high-achievement elementary school student, and the initiation of a life-learning process by the student that is self-supporting, self-directed, and self-transcending. (p. 156)

The Mentor Academy Program (Runions, 1980) does not confine its attention to arranging for the matching of the self-directed learner with a suitable mentor. In fact, it is a formalized system of mentoring that consists of three interactive phases.

The first phase, the Basics Workshops, is a series of workshops designed to facilitate learning basic thinking skills, creative problem-solving skills, self-directed learning skills, academic research skills, aesthetics, leadership/service skills, mentorship contract skills, futuristics, and entrepreneur skills. During this month-long focus, the student also contacts academic, career and avocational mentors to negotiate mutually agreeable conditions for sharing interests, identifies and begins to mentor an elementary school student, and designs a mentorship contract for an area of study.

The second phase, the Synergistic Seminars, is a practicum lasting approximately three months. Weekly seminars are held which are open to the whole school, and serve to introduce the students to a holistic approach in an area of study, update information about an area of study, and explore new developments in learning. The student also applies skills from the Basic Workshops in managing and monitoring a mentorship contract, and meets with a program facilitator on a regular basis.

The third and final phase, The Mentor Exchange, lasts approximately one month and is the time when students and mentors come together to share their learnings from the mentorship with interested members of the local communities and schools, organized and directed by the student mentor.

Over the five-month period, the student as mentor integrates learning with six different mentors—a professor at the local university or community college, a career person, a senior citizen, an elementary school teacher, a high school teacher in the area of study, and the program facilitator who assists and supports the student in individualizing the program, linking up self-support systems, and anticipating post-program development. (p. 156)

Mentor Connection

The Mentor Connection Program (Beck, 1989) is a mentorship program designed to investigate the personal, academic, and career benefits of its participant, as well as benefits to gifted students. The mentorship program also looks at benefits gained from two types of mentoring experiences, supplemental classroom support, and mentorship itself. The overall program lasts for eighteen weeks and consists of four integrated phases, namely, the phases of Selection, Orientation, Preparation Lab, and Mentorship.

> *Phase 1-Selection*—Junior or senior year high school students are selected for the program on the basis of ability, creativity, motivation, perseverance, and interest in a specific area to be pursued with the help of a mentor.
>
> *Phase 2-Orientation*—Students, accepted into the program, participate in formulating a plan for investigating their interest area, select and meet with an appropriate mentor, and discuss possible projects.
>
> *Phase 3-Preparation Lab*—Students meet for three weeks as a class with the Mentor Connection Instructor to prepare for their interaction with mentors, and to improve their communication and independent learning skills.
>
> *Phase 4-Mentorship*—Students meet their mentors and implement their learning plan. The phase lasts for fourteen weeks, during which each student spends eight hours per week working on a project, observing the mentor in work situations, and exploring special interests within the field. An additional two hours per week is spent in group discussions, which provide a forum for the exchange of ideas and perspectives, as well as a check-in and group building time for the class as a unit.

To explore the effects of the program over its three year history, a follow-up questionnaire entitled the Mentorship Inventory, constructed by Lynne Beck, was sent to all participants. Their responses were categorized in terms of personal benefits, academic benefits, and effects on career development. Beck found positive results for the program in all three areas, with career development most affected by it. Further, females were found to feel more strongly than males that the mentorship program helped them look at ways to integrate career and family. Beck proposes that mentorship experiences should be included in high school gifted education programs with a more systematic inclusion of a career guidance component in the curriculum, and the recruitment of more female mentors.

Double Mentoring

Double Mentoring was conceived by Donna Rae Clasen and Marilyn Hanson (1987) as a way to counteract mentorship approaches that occasionally falter or fail because students require cognitive and affective support beyond what the mentor can provide. Two mentors—an expert who focuses on his or her discipline to assure maximum academic or skill growth, and a teacher who assesses and attends to the developmental needs of the student—serve to maximize the benefit derived from the mentorship program.

Clasen and Hanson suggest seven basic steps for establishing and applying Double Mentoring: (a) establishing student commitment, (b) promoting student self-assessment, (c) making the mentor contract, (d) determining the conceptual contract, (e) developing a work plan, (f) establishing double mentoring, and (g) realizing a final product.

Clasen and Hanson are convinced that the psychological and emotional support provided by the expert and teacher mentors throughout the mentorship is perhaps the key to the student's final success. The researchers suggest six primary principles to guide the expert and teacher mentor to help the student to experience successful mentorship both cognitively and affectively, and to realize a final product or performance to the mutual satisfaction of all concerned.

The primary principles of Double Mentoring are (a) raising the student's level of expertise, (b) developing the student's ability to question effectively, (c) developing interpersonal and communication skills, (d) connecting the student with the larger world, (e) establishing time perspective (priority setting, effective time management and a sense of balance), and (f) providing psycho-social support. By following these principles, Double Mentoring insures the development of the whole student.

MOTIVATION

The subject of motivation of the gifted thus far has focused on academic underachievement and related factors, such as sex, socioeconomic and ethnic differences, school environment, and familial and societal influences and models (e.g., Alpert, 1965; DeHaan & Havighurst, 1965; Gold, 1965; Raph, Goldberg & Passow, 1966). Some attention has also been given to personality and perception variables (e.g., Fleigler, 1965; Gold, 1965) and to the ability to generalize quickly in the context of internal and external motivational events (Newland, 1976). In the main, motivation, as it relates to the gifted, is conceived as *intrinsic* so that external shaping and confirming influences *internalized* become essential components of the inner controls of behavior.

Generally, there still exist different conceptions of motivation (Bindra & Stewart, 1971; Littman, 1958). Part of the problem lies in the fact that motivation is a logical scientific construct with no immediate sensory referent (Underwood, 1949). In scientific terms, motivation is derived from animal and human studies that see external or internal forces impelling an organism to behavior or action.

According to Dalbir Bindra and Jane Stewart (1971), the concept of motivation entered English and psychological thought in the 1880s and continues to interest psychologists today. Motivation, initially understood as instinctive and extended to voluntary behavior that impelled one to goal-directed action of a particular type, later became associated with the principles of pleasure and pain that became the basis of predictable behavior according to reward-punishment and reinforcement systems. More recent studies have focused attention on neural mechanisms of motivation, the influence on hypothalamic activity, and the process of chemical coding of motivational actions.

At least two important appraisals of motivation recognize the need for reinterpretation (Hunt, 1960; White, 1959). They see weaknesses in a theory claiming that all behavior is motivated toward reduction or elimination of stimulation or excitation of the nervous system. Sources of such excitation or drive are traced to internal stimuli that arise either from homeostatic imbalances and needs or as a result of intense and painful external stimulation.

The concept of homeostatic imbalances and needs is implicit in the traumatic notion of anxiety in psychoanalysis, and in the conditioned or learned drive in behavior theory; in either case, activation of the organism is not expected to occur without the imbalances and needs. Certain theories of behavior help to explain the imbalances and needs. Concepts of fixation or conditioning—where gratifying or frustrating experiences coupled with positive or negative reinforcement—explain why some behaviors recur and others do not repeat. Although homeostasis, conditioned drive, and conditioned fear are sound in their basic assumptions, they contradict fact and call for reinterpretation.

Competence-Effectance Motivation

The primary drive theory, according to W. W. White (1959), does not explain exploratory behavior, manipulation, and general activity. W. W. White considers that a more satisfactory explanation lies in the organism's effective interaction with the environment, which he calls *competence*. Competence is significant to growth and life itself because it implies the acquisition of tremendous power to bring the environment into the service of the organism.

The motivational aspect of competence White calls *effectance*. He assumes it to be neurologic in origin; its energies are simply those of the living cells that comprise the nervous system.

In *effectance motivation*, the organism continues a transaction with the environment and achieves satisfaction or feeling of efficacy in a trend behavior rather than a goal directed behavior (drive). Effectance motivation is stimulated by conditions that produce various novel responses. Interest is sustained when the action affects the stimulus to produce different kinds of well-known responses and wanes when the action no longer presents new possibilities.

Incongruity-Dissonance Motivation

J. McVicker Hunt (1960) does not find primary drive theory adequate and suggests that living things are open systems of energy exchange that exhibit activity intrinsically and upon which stimuli have a modulating rather than initiating effect. This view implies that not all activity is leveled at reducing or avoiding stimulation. However, under conditions of low and unchanging types of stimulation for a time, increases of stimulation become reinforcing. In addition, certain types of stimulation, although intense and exciting, are positively reinforcing. Further, Hunt suggests that motivational correlates of fear and anxiety are not the products of conditioning alone but also *maturation* and *cognitive dissonance* (i.e., disturbances arising from the mismatch or incongruity between acquired central patterns of past experiences and present ones).

Drawing from various systematic theories that incorporate the *incongruity dissonance* principle in one form or another (e.g., Piaget's accommodation-assimilation system; Festinger's theory of cognitive dissonance; Roger's discrepancy between the phenomenological field and perceived reality), Hunt notes the value of making motivation and reinforcement intrinsic to the organism's information processing system. A built-in feedback mechanism indicates discrepancy between present receptor inputs and residues of past experiences or stored information as the basis for anticipating the future. In this way, motivation and reinforcement are not extrinsic to information processing, and hence, need not be the responsibility of others, namely, teachers, parents, and others in authority.

Although White and Hunt indicate that the dominant view of motivation does not explain everything about the subject, and although they suggest alternatives (*competence* or *incongruity-dissonance*) in their reinterpretation, they do not deny the relevance of drive, habit, reinforcement, and the like. However, they have questioned their underlying assumptions, which appear to be couched in all-or-nothing terms.

Prepotency of Needs Motivation

Another theoretical position of interest to us is based on *prepotency of needs*—Abraham Maslow's (1970) well-known theory of human motivation. Maslow recognizes the fundamental priorities of needs so that the ones most basic to life and survival (physiological and safety needs) take precedence over intermediate needs, which relate to living and doing things with others (loving, belonging, and esteem needs). The higher needs (self-actualization, desire to know and understand, and aesthetic needs) occur when the more basic ones have been satisfied. Of course, the attainment of higher needs does not preclude the recurrence of the more basic ones.

For most "normal" people, needs are only partially satisfied, which is probably realistically described by Maslow (1970) as decreasing percentages of satisfaction as we go up the hierarchy of prepotency. Also, as implied by the model, the hierarchy of needs is not a fixed order and some reversal is not uncommon. For instance, the need for self-esteem seems more important than love for some, or the need for self-actualization seems more important to creative people than other needs.

Another essential aspect of Maslow's (1968) theory is that it is a growth model. Thus when deficiency needs (lower four in the hierarchy, namely physiological, safety, love and belonging, and esteem needs) are satisfied, a striving for the satisfaction of higher being needs (self-actualization, knowing and understanding, and aesthetic needs) follows. This behavior is characteristic of healthy children who enjoy growing and moving forward, gaining new skills, capacities, and powers.

Maslow also makes a distinction between good choosers and bad choosers. He points out that many people, if allowed freedom of choice, appear consistently to make good choices. However, most tend to make choices that are self-destructive. The good choices tend to be made by people who are given the opportunity when higher needs emerge. Maslow perceives growth as occurring in the context of a never-ending series of situations that provides free choice between the attractions and the dangers of safety and growth. He suggests that those concerned with children's growth can assist in the gratification of their basic needs so that they can feel unthreatened and autonomous, and make the growth choice more attractive and delight producing.

Creative Acts Motivation

The creative act has its own rewards, which, in turn, motivates the generation of other similar acts. In addition, evaluation of creative products has also been found to be motivating (Amabile, 1983). Torrance (1965b), on motivating gifted children with school learning problems, advocates the following:

giving them a chance to use what they learn as tools in their thinking and problem solving

providing them with a chance to communicate what they learn

showing an interest in what they have learned rather than in their grades
giving them learning tasks of appropriate difficulty
according them the chance to use their best abilities
offering them the chance to learn in their own preferred ways
recognizing and acknowledging many different kinds of excellence
providing genuine purpose and meaning to learning experiences

In later discussions of the subject (Torrance & Myers, 1970; Torrance, 1975b), it is shown that creative ways of teaching have built-in motivations for achievement. Some of the essential characteristics of educational methods for facilitating creative ways of learning are identified as follows:

incompleteness or openness in motivating achievement
production of something and then doing something with it
having pupils ask questions

An even more powerful motivational force is a person's vision or future image of himself or herself. Expectations of what persons will become, relative to what they are in the present, are considered powerful determinants of behavior (Torrance, 1979b; Torrance & Hall, 1980). Futurists, like F. L. Polak (1973), B. D. Singer (1974), and A. Toffler (1974) are strong advocates of such imaging by individuals. They believe that persons' images of themselves in the future can only lead them to strive for their actualization.

Motivating the Gifted

Several theoretical positions, except the motivation function of creativity, have all people in mind. Hence, any discussion of their relevance for the gifted must be by way of extrapolation. Certain *extrinsic* factors—praise, recognition, and reward, or the physical arrangements in the classroom—can and do have positive and facilitative effects on gifted children. However, the major positive effect appears (1) to lie with *intrinsic* factors that relate to cognitive-affective processes brought to bear, for instance, by parents, peers, teachers, significant others, schooling, and reward systems used, whose influences are internalized, and (2) to their *interaction* with the internal environment relative to such factors as abilities, information-processing mechanisms, affective conditions, needs, and desires.

Generally, the gifted depend more on internal than external control. They are generally autonomous, self-directed, and growth oriented. Their possession of superior mental abilities and talents can aid them gain more effective command of their environment. Besides, they have extraordinary potential to move towards productivity and self-fulfillment. However, various interferences can obstruct this expected pattern and may call for some temporary external intervention and control as we have seen in the problems that underachieving gifted students face.

Apart from creativity and future imaging of oneself, motivational controls for the gifted may be found in systems proposed by White (*competence-effectance*), Hunt (*incongruity-dissonance*), and Maslow (*prepotency of needs*). The motivational principles of *competence-effectance* and *incongruity-dissonance* operate, for instance, in both Land's (1973) Transformation problem-solving model and Guilford's (1967, 1977) Structure of Intellect problem-solving model.

These problem-solving systems are information-processing models that, in the problem-solving process, engage in transactions with the external environment. As self-regulated systems, they provide feedback to the processing operations for the production of appropriate solutions to problems which are then internalized as stored information to provide the basis for handling other problems. The more efficient or competent persons become in the handling of these operations and the greater the success they experience in arriving at solutions with attendant achievement satisfactions or feelings of efficacy, the more they are likely to repeat such acts.

Inventors have spoken of the exhilaration and mastery of successfully overcoming problems connected with a new invention. They also express a desire to seek new problems, overcome them, and discover solutions to re-experience similar feelings and satisfactions (Rossman, 1931). Experiencing and participating in problem solving, as these inventors profess, is in itself rewarding. Problem-solving activity is inherent in research and has been advocated for gifted students (Renzulli, 1979a; Torrance, 1965c).

Maslow's growth motivation model has also relevance for the gifted as it relates to esteem needs, self-actualization, knowing and understanding, and aesthetic needs.

Just as there is an intrinsic reward factor associated with problem solving leading to a creative solution, product, or invention, there is self-satisfaction for individuals in the act of discovery boosting their self-esteem. If self-esteem is to be enhanced, an individual's solutions to problems and products must be appreciated or esteemed by others. In winning the acceptance and approbation of others, individuals achieve added self-esteem and the praise of others.

The importance of rewarding creative performance has been stressed by Torrance's (1965c) and, in a somewhat related focus, by Renzulli's (1979a) advice to arrange for outlets and exhibitions of the gifted child's products (outcome of Type III Enrichment). Esteem of self and by others are very closely intertwined and may be considered two faces of the same factor. Esteem can be accepted as a strong energizing or motivating force that may determine quality and direction of performance.

Self-actualization encompasses the notion of fulfillment of potential in its broader sense. In a narrower sense, however, self-actualization must include the successful accomplishment of singular expressions of potential, the cumulative effect of which must ultimately lead to realization of self. This operational definition of self-actualization is implemented in the many successful outcomes of creative endeavors of the gifted, in their creations of various art forms, and in their scientific discoveries and inventions.

Knowing and understanding in both cognitive and affective dimensions are needs more apparent in the gifted than in others. These needs are pervasive to their intellectual and affective states, and motivate the gifted to get to know the world around them and to prepare for breaking new ground, stepping to the frontiers and beyond, and making new discoveries.

Aesthetic needs are yet other forces that activate the gifted to be producers or consumers of the beautiful and true. These needs are essential to potential talent and its productive expression, especially in the literary, visual, and performing arts.

Although arrangement of events and appropriate support can facilitate the realization of these needs (and this must be emphasized), the real needs come from within the individual. These must be recognized as the prime movers or motivators to the actualization of self. They have paramount importance for the gifted, and perhaps dictate special facilitative provisions. In the "magic synthesis" (Arieti, 1976) of individual and societal needs the best can happen for our gifted.

CONCLUSIONS

Nurture has been, and will continue to be, the prime concern of formal education. In simplistic terms, although educators may want to know how gifted students are to be identified, they want to hurry on with the business of teaching them. What must be realized is that identification and its measurement correlates are no longer regarded as ends in themselves but as means to prescriptive education, where strengths and weaknesses in abilities provide the clues for designing instructional materials and procedures. Further, the emphasis on teaching in the traditional sense has declined, in favor of arranging conditions that will take into account student abilities, interests, and intentions to facilitate learning toward productive development of potential unique to the individual.

Individualization of nurturing practices has become the key to superior educational opportunities for the gifted. Enrichment provides a fresh application of acceleration. For instance, when a special aptitude for the language of mathematics is determined early, enrichment programs direct the student toward fullest development. Similar implications exist for special aptitudes for language or other symbolic and visual systems of the literary, scientific, visual, and performing arts fields.

Enrichment conceived as accelerative, productive, and transformative requires the establishment of conditions to maximize individual growth potential. Programs for individualizing learning experiences for ability development—with special emphasis on divergent thinking and affect—organize learning to a specific need. Acceleration as cumulative provides the opportunity for optimum development within a certain area of learning. Transformation allows acceleration to become the catalyst for growth from lower levels to higher levels of mental functioning (escalation).

Any view of educational opportunities for gifted children must distinguish between provisions for all students and those specially designed for the able. Educators have developed numerous approaches for the individualization of learning. Recent advances in program development for the gifted have focused on learning content and rate in the context of students' unique abilities. Individual differences and needs are assessed by diagnostic-prescriptive methods leveled at identifying strengths for enhancement and identifying weaknesses for alleviation. For instance, while Meeker's individualized approach uses specific curriculum content to educate singular components of the Structure of Intellect, Renzulli's more general approach hinges on his Enrichment Triad and Revolving Door principles leading to inquiry, problem-solving, productions, and outlets for recognition. Further, the importance of self-directed learning and mentorship program models must not be viewed as separate individualized approaches to learning for the gifted, but as closely interactive components for productive learning and ferment.

Although of high significance, motivation is the most nebulous aspect of learning. We have seen the power of motivation in shaping and maintaining behavior when systems of rewards and reinforcements are applied. This practice has merit for certain kinds of learning and for people at certain intellectual levels, but it is not the whole answer to the question of how best to energize gifted people in particular to learn. We are reminded of the inadequacy of external manipulation as the prime and only mover in learning. Further, the place of homeostatic imbalance, anxiety, and related drive-inducing states are questioned.

The gifted, by nature and potential, possess energies that characterize them as initiators of learning events. Motivation for them is generally intrinsic. When these energies are suppressed by influences of family, peers, society, school, and the like, gifted students become low achievers and cause for concern. If these influences and controls serve as positive sources, needs, abilities, information-processing systems, and future imaging can occur, and the gifted will move toward the highest levels of accomplishment and self-realization.

Issues on motivation are far from settled, and continue to generate interest and research. Among the most relevant approaches for the gifted are competence-effectance motivation, incongruity-dissonance motivation, and growth motivation related to esteem by self and others, self-actualization, knowing and understanding, and aesthetic needs. In addition creative ways of learning and future imaging are powerful motivators of gifted students.

CHAPTER ELEVEN

Learning Designs

*I*NTRODUCTION

Learning must be considered a shaping and interactive force that determines unique sociocultural groups. Some of the forces that impinge upon individuals—like those determined by nature—are quite beyond control; other forces—like those contrived by society—are relatively within control. The latter aspect is comprised of informal and formal education.

Informal education includes all experience from the sociocultural universe that is encountered in daily living. In *formal education* the sociocultural group serves to teach the individual to function as a member of society and as an individual. Formal education also provides knowledge and skills considered necessary for living productively and effectively.

The Holistic Model for Educating Gifted Children (Figure 3.1) identified formal and informal education in terms of the *individual, environment, interventions, outcomes,* and *communication.*

1. Current opinion supports the education of the *whole individual,* such that we pay attention not only to a person's intellect and the various ways it can be organized to process and produce information, but also to a person's emotional and motivational systems that may facilitate or hinder such education.

2. We are also better aware of the developmental aspects of the whole individual. We attempt to provide more adequate conditions in the

specific *environment* of the school for healthier growth so that learning is facilitated and mind expansion is nourished.

3. Our command of learning approaches has improved as we see more clearly their link with various philosophical, psychological, and sociological theoretical positions that directly or indirectly assist in the designing of many *intervention* procedures involved in providing formal education.

4. *Outcomes* of learning stemming from the intervention procedures include not only achievement but self-actualization and good mental health.

5. Further, effective *communication* of learning by the student, its ideational and imaginative expression, and recognition and reward consequences by the educator require attention.

Closely connected with the education of the whole individual is the provision of a whole school intervention approach. In this context, learning is not solely dependent on predetermined curricula to be organized for the learner but also relies on dynamic and living curricula in an ever changing environment, whose fundamental source lies not totally in accumulated knowledge and wisdom but in nature. William Wordsworth (1888) pertinently expresses this as he counters his friend's question "Where are your books?" in a poem composed in 1798—"The Tables Turned":

Enough of Science and of Art;
Close up those barren leaves;
Come forth, and bring with you a heart
That watches and receives (p. 85).

The agents of this dynamic transmission are the school and the teacher. Both have important roles to play in bringing about learning. The school provides location, management, and resources, whereas the teacher selects the most beneficial knowledge and dynamically delivers the sum total of human experience for intellectual germination and continual growth.

As a consequence, education, especially for gifted students, refers to learning according to and beyond the daily curricula and includes special projects (e.g., Study of Mathematically Precocious), programs (e.g., Four School Enrichment), and even schools (e.g., Roeper School), which will be discussed later in the chapter.

Over the past two decades many approaches to educate the gifted have emerged. These have included acceleration and enrichment, individual or self-directed study, and identification-diagnostic-prescriptive learning procedures, using the confines of regular school curricula to produce several differential education models for the gifted. Furthermore, special perspectives have been advanced in recent years that account for cultural diversity, futuristic education for the gifted, or educational provisions in ideal circumstances. These have important implications for designing school curricula.

PHILOSOPHY OF GREAT EDUCATORS

Our discussion of the gifted, their identification, development, problems, predisposition to counseling, and learning has so far emphasized psychological and sociological considerations. However, we have also inherited much that is philosophically based from Plato, Comenius, Locke, Rousseau, Pestalozzi, Froebel, Montessori, and Dewey, who have earned honorable places in the history of education (Rusk, 1957).

Each philosophy of education relies on the intellectual and social tendencies of their times. Although historical in nature, these theories influence today's educational practice for the gifted in particular. Too often we regard current contributions without reference to their origins and to know these will enhance our understanding of the present in terms of its generic forms. In this way, we will not only find greater meaning and relevance in current educational practice, but also find ourselves in a stronger position to propose new ones.

We will now consider the doctrines of eight great educators (Rusk, 1957) whose influence continues to this day and contributes to the design of gifted education.

Plato (circa 427–347 B.C.)

Education, to Plato, was of the utmost importance, and had to be the major concern and responsibility of parents and the state. For proper education of children was the surest way of ensuring the health, continuity, and productivity of the country.

Plato discusses education in two of his major works: the *Republic* (Campbell, 1902) and *Laws* (Rusk, 1957). In the *Republic,* education is restricted to those who by nature were suited to lead or govern the country. In *Laws,* Plato views education as universal and compulsory, equally applicable to males and females.

Education in the *Republic*
Plato describes natural endowment as an important factor in determining diversity among individuals, and he believes that division of labor, in an *ideal state,* should take this into account. To do this, citizens of the state had to be separated into two classes: the industrial or artisan class and the guardian class (consisting of military and governing subclasses).

Rather than dicussing the education of the industrial or artisan class, Plato concentrates on the general education of the guardian (military and ruling) class. Education of the guardians is governed mainly by the principle of *imitation*. In this theory, education begins with music and continues with gymnastics: the development of mind precedes the development of body.

Plato stresses educating the child as early as possible. Further, since the young child is highly impressionable, the tales that were told had to be models of virtuous thoughts. The appropriate stories for the young place high value on truth, and commend obedience and self-control over sensual pleasures. Where necessary, fables concerning heroes and others should agree with these principles, such that wickedness and injustice should not be shown to lead to happiness and profit.

The music selected should foster temperate and courageous characteristics of the citizen, not effeminate and convivial traits. Further, rhythms were to be determined by the nature of words. Plato considers training in terms of harmony and rhythm a potent force that forges access to the innermost regions of the soul. Other arts and crafts must impress the good in their productions, as well. Emphasis is on the *ethical*. Artists, in Platonic theory, discern truth and beauty to ensure that the young grow morally and intellectually healthy.

Plato advocates a healthy and simple environment for children, who would become the future guardians of the state. Such an environment would facilitate the assimilation or *imitation* of those elements related to good character formation.

In the *Republic* Plato mentions that gymnastics should, like music, begin in the early years and continue throughout life. Further, although he recognizes the need for gymnastics in education, he maintains that a whole life devoted to gymnastics alone would generate uncivilized behavior. However, he emphasizes that a good soul improves the body rather than body excellence improves the soul.

However, Plato also advocates that several higher education subjects should be presented to the young person, not as something forced but as preparation for the study of *philosophy* or *dialectic*, inviting the search of ideas and developing clear thinking. Compulsory learning would be harmful, since the mind would not retain it. Instead he stresses that early education should involve play by which the natural bent and interests of the learner could be discovered. However, the education of children should be carefully monitored throughout to ensure the success of the system producing future guardians of the state.

Education in *Laws*

In *Laws*, Plato takes another look at education from the vantage of old age as he considers the characteristics of the perfect citizen-ruler and the method that would best serve to shape such a person. The idealism of the earlier treatise finds practical application in this work, and the education he proposes is as relevant to women as it is to men. For although women were physically weaker than men, they were nevertheless equal to men in politics and government. Further, unlike the early education proposed for young children, higher education was to be considered compulsory, as much as possible. At this stage of education, individuals belong to the state rather than to their parents. Hence the state, for the general good, was to have primary charge for shaping these individuals.

Early education of potential guardians of the state continues until age sixteen and extends into higher education to be pursued throughout life. Young students between 17 and 20 serve in the military. The best among them would undergo ten years of special training in mathematics as preparation for dialectic. At this time, students are chosen for the study of dialectic for a period of five years. After this stage, students return to practical life for those between 35 and 50 years, and assume positions of command in the military and hold offices of state. Beyond 50 years, rulers would spend their time contemplating the good and mainly engaging in philosophy, so that they could serve as model rulers of the state for the public good when called upon to do so.

As subjects for study he includes arithmetic, plane and solid geometry, astronomy, and theories of music or harmonics. These areas of learning prepare for the highest of the sciences, namely philosophy or dialectic. The principles determining these areas of study lead to reflection and have universal application.

John Amos Comenius (1592–1670)

Comenius, in contrast to the narrow view that education should be provided for the ruling classes alone, advocates universal education. For he believes that infinite possibilities could be realized by sound education. Not only does he propose education for all boys and girls, but he also devised teaching methods and wrote books that would facilitate this.

Comenius stresses an education strongly based on the religious beliefs of the times; in Europe Christianity dominated. The scholars serving as educators were, for the most part, clerics operating from monasteries. Relatively few people were in a position to benefit from available education. Those who could take advantage of this rather limited educational opportunity were comprised mainly of male offsprings of the nobility, a few preparing for life or office in the church, and others with adequate means. Consequently, education for people then was quite restricted.

In *The Great Didactic* (Keatinge, 1910), Comenius proposes educational reforms inspired by religious motives as well as by a great interest in a scheme of universal knowledge aimed not so much at making men learned but at making them wise. He advocates the education of all boys and girls without exception. They should become learned quickly, pleasantly, and thoroughly in the sciences. They would be trained to be morally pure and pious in ways that would prepare them for life.

He emphasizes the value of public schooling over home instruction by parents who had neither the competence nor the time to teach their children. Large classes were preferred because they provided better and more pleasurable results, and young children especially would benefit more by imitating others than by precept.

A common school for all averts the creation of class distinction among the young. Students would be promoted according to their ability, with more stringent admission requirements for those attending the university. Those who could not reach advanced levels of education should become apprentices in suitable occupations regardless of social status.

Comenius also contributed to the consistency of instructional method, facilitative school environment, and acquisition of knowledge from its original source before its symbolic or language referent. In the primary school learning is encouraged through the mother tongue or vernacular. The common school curriculum should prepare students to become, as adults, wise, virtuous and pious. Students should master the principles, causes, and uses of the most important things in the universe. Further, order, whose source was to be found in nature, is regarded as something of great importance, and should enter into all aspects of education.

To such traditional maxims of teaching method as proceeding from the easy to the difficult, and the particular to the general, Comenius encourages education from the general to the particular. Studies should be relevant to age and mental capacity, and interrelated and integrated. Emphasis is placed on inductive method of teaching. Further, he advises the proper selection of text books that would foster virtue or good morals. Comenius commends dialogue and discussion of controversial topics, presence of men holding civil office and managerial positions at disputations kindling zeal of scholars by being present at public performances, praise and reward, and emulation as stimulants to school pupils. Finally, he condemns corporal punishment especially if it is given to pupils who lack readiness to learn, for the fault often lay with the teacher for not making the pupil receptive.

John Locke (1632–1704)

John Locke does not consider the need for comprehensive education for all children: educating the many is not his primary concern. Instead, Locke asserts that education should reflect class differences, whereby children of noble birth or of good breeding were to be provided with an education to prepare them to become gentlemen (or ladies if necessary). He considers home training, under an appropriate tutor, as quite a sound approach. Further, Locke assigns education the responsibility of developing virtue, wisdom, and breeding with learning of least importance, since development of character and personality was to come before development of culture and intellect. These and other thoughts on education are expressed by Locke in two works, namely, *Some Thoughts Concerning Education* (Quick, 1895) and *Of the Conduct of the Understanding* (Fowler, 1901).

Locke was an empiricist. For him, external experience is paramount to the shaping of the individual mind, a process he refers to as the "historical plain method." The mind is like a blank sheet or blank surface—a *tabula rasa*. For the most part, impressions of the outside world, formalized as education, shape people. However, Locke recognizes that innate individual differences make the contributions of education negligible.

Consistent with his thoughts on innate individual differences, he does not support formal training of memory or reasoning for transfer of training effects. To him the effects of practice are not general but specific. Language is best learned through conversation not grammar. Mathematical reasoning was the ideal method for reaching truth. According to Locke, since a sound mind and sound body are essentials, appropriate physical education is advocated.

Further, he emphasizes that everyone should learn to read and write. Students should gain command of their native tongue—English. To express themselves with facility, clarity, and elegance, students of English should practice its use daily. In the study of languages, English should take precedence over Greek and Latin. To this study Locke adds the arithmetic, astronomy, geometry, geography, chronology, history, ethics law, and natural philosophy. Further, students should acquire the skills of dancing, music, and wrestling. He recommends that they learn a trade as well. In order to complete their education Locke includes travel.

Locke stresses educational methodology. Teachers should use procedures that facilitate learning, stimulate curiosity, and improve through exercise the analytical and organizational faculties of mind. Chief among these procedures is learning through play. The right psychological moment for learning a task would take into account the aptitude and interests of students. Relevant learning, to the advantage of students, should provide delight to maintain student attention. Besides, teachers should convey to students that they are loved to ensure that they heed and enjoy the learning. Certainly corporal punishment was to be avoided at all cost.

Jean-Jacques Rousseau (1712–1778)

For Rousseau, the primary aim of education is the cultivation of virtue. All else should give way and be postponed to virtue and this responsibility belongs to the tutors.

Rousseau emphasizes the common nature of people rather than their individual differences determined by inheritance. Direct study is the best method of discovering the most important traits of children. According to Rousseau, man is a free agent but is also responsible for his own actions. He places high priority on spiritual values, and links freedom to man's progress or self-improvement.

Education of children is solely the responsibility of the state, not the home. However, in *Emile,* he indicates that parents have an important part to play in the education of their children; through them children would acquire those values that would make them good citizens. Further, children should be provided with a common public education that is consistent with public interest.

Although Rousseau addresses the education of a single child of ordinary mind at home in *Emile* (Rousseau, 1672) he (in reality) presents a universal education scheme that became the source of democratic education. Here he distinguishes three phases of education: natural (nonsocial) or negative (anti-social) for children up to adolescence, social or moral for the youth, and civic or political thereafter. Rousseau requires that potentialities of every stage be fully exploited before proceeding to the next stage.

He recommends the inclusion of physical exercises for moral value and social training derived from participation in common games. Rousseau does not mention intellectual studies. A complete abandonment of a predetermined curriculum shifted the emphasis from curriculum-centered to child-centered learning. Education was to be effected entirely through activity and first-hand experience.

Rousseau indicates that education comes from nature, men, and things. Education should determine the relationship of man to the physical and social environment. However, Rousseau emphasizes the need for children to live according to nature, for to do so would be to live according to the rational principle of the universe, or to reason. Children follow their natural and inherited capacity for proper growth. For education that followed the order of nature did not interfere with this growth, but education that was social in origin did.

Students would become interested in what they learned when provided with tasks that matched their capabilities. Focus on this proper match of task and ability—to generate interest in learning—provides the basis of unifying work and play as two faces of the same thing.

He prefers to call the tutor a master who provides guidance, not instruction. The role of such a person consists of making the student want to learn. For the student who detested what was to be learned would learn nothing. The student should have the right to happiness and the learning situation facilitates it.

Further, Rousseau would prescribe a trade for the student. By having a trade, economic independence could be maintained in the face of changed fortune. Besides, dignity of labor, being socially valued, could be ensured. Training to acquire a trade would aid generally in training the mind.

Boys and girls required different kinds of education since they were to be prepared for different vocations. Girls' education was planned in relation and subservient to boys' education, so that they could take their rightful place in society. In general, Rousseau asserts that boys study the useful and become specialized, whereas girls should have a broad education to prepare them for the many duties they would have to assume by virtue of their socially determined role.

Education, to be complete, must include travel for the student to become familiar with people in other countries and, in so doing, know mankind generally.

J. H. Pestalozzi (1746-1827)

Education for all, regardless of economic, class, ethnic, or national factors, guided Pestalozzi in his attempt to formulate a practical educational scheme. He states that everyone is entitled to the acquisition of useful knowledge, and the development of their physical, intellectual, and moral capacities. Ultimately, education is not an exercise for perfect achievement but a proper preparation for life.

Parents should have their children work on tasks of their immediate interests. Ideally, well-educated mothers supervise a home education. Pestalozzi stresses learning that has contact with reality. In *How Gertrude Teaches Her Children* (Pestalozzi, 1907), he advocates instruction that incorporates activity and experience, rather than a method based solely on words alone. Furthermore, children should be taught that in every occupation of life accurate and intelligent observation of common things and nature forces is necessary.

Pestallozi also states that education should be based on love. Reciprocal love in itself is insufficient; love has to be coupled with training for independence. Love for a subject should be balanced by many faceted interests.

Pestalozzi sought a general method of instruction that would be based on the nature of teaching and on psychological principles. His approach to instruction is rooted to the concept of *Anschauung* or the immediate experience of objects and situations. The basis of all knowledge and experience extends beyond the mere awareness of objects to include the spontaneous appreciation of moral actions and immediacy of experience. Knowledge acquired through the senses, if it were to be clearly understood, involved recognition of the unit of a number of things considered: the form it took and its description or expression in the language of words. These three steps—which were to be used in the teaching of drawing, writing, arithmetic, and so on—formed the basic principles of his instructional technique.

Learning, according to Pestalozzi, is best achieved from the concrete to the abstract, from the real experience to its representation in the language of numbers or words. Hence all teaching had to take these into account. For instance, in the early phases of teaching arithmetic, actual experience with objects for formation of number concepts has to precede its symbolic referent. The same applies to reading, where the actual object or its picture is presented prior to giving it verbal representation.

Instruction should develop progressively. There should not be gaps in instruction, breaks in the sequence, or interruptions in continuity. Correctness should mark every instructional moment.

Pestalozzi's division of the educational process includes physical, intellectual, and the moral-religious elements. The physical aspect of the process requires instruction in artistic skill and technical dexterity as well as development of body prowess which, in any case, has mental correlates. The child inherits a spiritual nature and conscience from God, which should be developed for its proper and full manifestation by instruction. Pestalozzi emphasizes the equality of physical, intellectual, and developmental processes that should be coordinated by the spiritual. Each of the three dimensions should be cultivated at no expense to the others. Although Pestalozzi proposes the harmonious development of human powers and talents as the aim for education, he recognizes the presence of unique capacities and prescribes proper opportunity and guidance for these abilities.

Friedrich Froebel (1782–1852)

According to Froebel, union of the spiritual and material world is life, for without mind or spirit matter would be lifeless, formless, and chaotic. As for the mind, its unfoldment from within is predetermined. Whatever the child was to be could be contained in the child's inward to outward development, reflecting the development of the race. Such development is a continuous process that is the expression of the spiritual or divine that lies dormant within each person and which education should awaken.

The child, to Froebel, is innately good, and the ideal of education should be passive and should not interfere with the original nature of the individual. For Froebel, good education should call forth the best in the individual. Consequently, education should be adapted to the child's nature and needs, calling for cooperation. Froebel expresses these and other ideas on education in *The Pedagogics of the Kindergarten* (Froebel, 1910) and *The Education of Man* (Froebel, 1909).

Froebel stresses the importance of continuity of development. One stage of development should prepare for the next stage, otherwise ensuing difficulties would be impossible to overcome. Froebel identifies the four stages of development: infancy, childhood, boyhood, and youth. Infancy is a period of sensory development, and youth is a continuance of the boyhood or adolescence developmental phase.

For Froebel, childhood is the most important time in the total development of mankind, and boyhood offers a significant educational contrast to it.

1. *Childhood*

   This stage includes the emergence of language to express the inner world of the child. Focus is given more to the education of the mind than to the body. This stage is also a time for speech training. The value of play is most important in this stage and is not considered a purposeless activity but a well-ordered learning material, aimed at advancing natural development. Education in this stage of development was child-centered and found in Froebel's Kindergarten.

2. *Boyhood*

   Whereas learning in childhood is geared to play, learning in boyhood or adolescence is characterized by work. Child-centered education is replaced by curriculum-centered education. The internal world of boyhood is made external. This stage emphasizes the product not the process of learning; the childhood practice of activity for its own sake is replaced by activity that results in production from a self-selected activity. Further, boyhood activities resemble projects, where finding solutions to practical problems involves cooperative effort and provides moral and intellectual training. Another quality of boyhood education is instruction relative to matters and conditions outside the human being.

Froebel proposes various educational occupations relative to the student's life and development. He also provides an independent and systematic treatment of curricula that is considered not only as ends in themselves but also as means to full personality realization. The school curriculum also includes manual instruction, drawing, nature study, and gardening. Froebel insists on the all-around development of students and delineates an educational curriculum that would include instruction in areas of religion, natural science, mathematics, and art.

Maria Montessori (1870–1952)

Montessori used an approach based on the environment for education. Unlike other educators, she came from a medical background with considerable experience in the training of mentally defective children. She was entrusted with the organization of the infant school of model tenements in Rome, known as the House of Childhood. Children placed there were those of parents involved in reconstructing their tenements. There, she applied the educational methodology she had used with mentally defective children to train normal children. This approach later became known as *The Montessori Method* (Montessori, 1912).

Her method of educating young children is based on several principles.

1. Children should be trained to be independent of others in activities of their daily lives.
2. Appeal is made to the senses rather than the intellect, and of particular importance is the use of the sense of touch.
3. The educative process should be relevant to the mental development and interests of the child. It is not to be curriculum directed or teacher determined. According to Montessori, education should bring about the normal expansion of the child's life.
4. In her method of education, the *psychological moment* occurs when the child consciously cognizes need. This moment would be the critical time to meet the need.
5. No prizes should be given for achievement because the highest reward is in the student's sense of mastery.
6. Errors are corrected by didactic materials, not the teacher, thus making auto-education possible for each child.
7. Her method allows freedom for the child to develop according to the laws governing his own nature. Such freedom requires independent action and self-discipline.
8. Both instruction and environment should be adapted to the developmental needs of the child such that provision of scientific apparatus provides for the freedom of auto-education.

The *Montessori Method*, in practice, provides exercises of practical life (learning to do things for oneself), exercises in sensory training (particular emphasis being given to training of the tactual, auditory and visual senses), and didactic exercises (as these related particularly to the teaching of writing, reading and numbers). The training in these three areas is directed to the individual. As such, this system of instruction is not only significant in itself, but it lay the foundation for modern educational practice.

John Dewey (1859–1952)

More than anyone else, John Dewey dominated the first half of the twentieth century as an educational philosopher focusing and reflecting on the progressive leaning of the times in America. Education to him was not static but ever changing, ever evolving, and closely connected to the realities of everyday life. However, in *How We Think* (Dewey, 1910) he expresses the need for stability, recognizing that thinking in different contexts, if it were to serve as the standard frame of reference, had to remain the same to be of value.

Dewey regards everything as provisional rather than ultimate and knowledge is a means to an end, never an end in itself. In this respect, knowledge is instrumental. Further, Dewey is also pragmatic in orientation, though he does not subscribe to the concept of activity for activity's sake. Instead, he interpreted the need for constant and effective interaction of knowledge and practice, where practice inspired theory and direct experiences originated and determined educational ends. Further, Dewey considers the experimental method—a definitely planned procedure whose stages are those of any logical induction (identification of problem, setting hypotheses, testing them and formulating principles)—as key to the generation of new knowledge.

The curriculum of *The Dewey School* (Mayhew & Edwards, 1936) was pragmatic and based on the premise that life and everything associated with serving man's chief needs provides the fundamental experiences for the child's education. In addition, he observed that intellectual control, through significant curriculum, would avert the bad effects of freedom, and urged the progressive schools of his day, of which he was the chief advocate, to adhere to this by providing a new kind of subject matter. Further, Dewey's laboratory school provided the basis for future directions that directly influenced gifted programs, incorporating qualities such as school organization and curriculum flexibility, placement of students in classes according to interests and abilities, and utilizing community resources for the advancement of the student learning.

UNIFIED PHILOSOPHY OF EDUCATION FOR THE GIFTED

A composite of the educational philosophy of the eight great educators cited consists of ten major areas (Table 11.1). The columns of the table

Table 11.1 Ten Major Areas of Educational Philosophy

Educational Philosophy	Great Educators							
	Plato	Comenius	Locke	Rousseau	Pestalozzi	Froebel	Montessori	Dewey
1. Inherited ability	×							
2. Developmental stages	×			×		×		
3. Nature of education				×	×	×		×
4. Education for everyone	×	×		×	×			
5. State responsibility	×	×		×				
6. Elitist education	×		×					
7. Moral education	×	×				×		
8. Vocational education		×	×	×				
9. Curricula	×		×	×	×	×	×	
10. Teaching methodology	×	×	×	×	×	×	×	×

indicate the contributor of each of the ten areas while the rows indicate contributions to the subjects of inherited ability, developmental stages, nature of education, education for everyone, state responsibility, elitist education, moral education, vocational education, curricula, and teaching methodology.

In one way or another the philosophies of these great educators have shaped education as we know it today. However, current educational theory and practice reflect modifications of the original ideas to accommodate the needs of the times. Let us take a look at the important details within each category.

Inherited Ability

Although people share common traits, we must recognize that each individual is different from the other; both commonality and diversity among individuals are determined by natural endowment. Individuals depend on inherited capacity for proper growth, which distinguishes their roles in society as leaders or workers.

Developmental Stages

It is important to consider education in terms of development. Children pass from one stage to the next, such that the earlier stage prepares for the emergence of the next one above it, and developmental continuity is ensured.

Developmental stages consist of infancy, childhood, boyhood, and adolescence. Infancy is a time for developing correct habits and providing proper training of emotions. Childhood, the most important stage for total development, is a time for developing the senses, wisdom, discernment and thinking through direct experience. At the boyhood stage, the nature of learning is practical and utility based—a time for training the intellect directed toward solving concrete problems. The time for moral, aesthetic, and social education is during adolescence. Civil and political education follow.

Children's development unfolds from the inward to the outward, which is the result of maturation. Language and speech training directly relate to the development of mind. This education is achieved through well ordered play activity. Furthermore, educating children for occupations is crucial to their development.

Nature of Education

Education is to adapt to the child's nature, calling for cooperation and aiming at bringing out the best in the child. Consequently, education should be passive and not interfere with the child's active involvement. The process of education includes the development of the physical, intellectual, moral, and religious capacities of the individual toward proper preparation for life. Based upon love, education provides the individual with independence, liberty, and happiness. Parents play an important part in the educational process by contributing values, eventually making children good citizens. Education is not fixed or final. Instead, it is ever changing and evolving, something closely connected with the realities of everyday life.

Education for Everyone

Education is to be made available to everyone, regardless of socioeconomic, ethnic, or class differences. It is also to be compulsory. Our educational system should be free of sex discrimination, for education is relevant to both men and women who are equally endowed with keenness of mind and intellectual grasp of knowledge. Through education men and women can be prepared for the roles they are to take in society.

State Responsibility

The state should have primary responsibility for shaping the individual with education that is consistent with public interest. Instruction in the public school is favored over instruction at home, and the state has the control to determine the kind of education individuals are to receive for the roles they have to assume as they grow to become adults.

Elitist Education

Contrary to the current view, education was also regarded as elitist, so that those of noble birth would be prepared to become leaders to govern and protect society. Higher education was reserved for the best and most superior individuals.

Moral Education

The divine or spiritual is awakened by education; so education must emphasize the moral and ethical. High value should be placed on order, truth, temperance, obedience, and self-control over sensual pleasures. These characteristics can be cultivated through the right kind of education such that children learn to become wise, virtuous, and pious as adults. The proper selection of books fosters such learning through the models of virtue, truth, and beauty depicted in the stories.

Vocational Education

Different kinds of education should be provided to individuals according to their abilities. Less capable students, regardless of social status, are to serve as apprentices in suitable occupations. Learning a trade is essential for helping a student gain economic independence, maintain the dignity of labor valued by society, and earn general training of mind.

Curricula

Independent and systematic treatment of school curricula is to be thought of not as ends in themselves but as means to full personality realization. Curriculum is concerned with education of the body and mind.

Physical education takes the form of gymnastics, which is to begin early and continues throughout life. Body education alone is not enough, for in itself it generates uncivilized behavior. So education of the mind must go hand in hand with education of the body.

Education of the mind is to take the form, at first, of music education for gaining access to the soul. Musical training consists of *harmony*, selected to make individuals temperate and courageous, and *rhythm*, determined by the nature of words.

The school is to include manual instruction, drawing, nature study and gardening, religious instruction, and instruction in the natural sciences, mathematics, and art. Travel completes education, for it makes individuals know people living in other countries specifically and mankind generally.

All knowledge and experience extend beyond mere awareness of objects to include spontaneous appreciation of moral actions and immediacy of experience. Furthermore, the curricula should include the study of philosophy or dialectics as its final goal.

Teaching Methodology

Instruction should be progressive so that there are no gaps, breaks in sequence, or interruptions in continuity. Educational methodology should seek the right psychological moment for the learning of a task. Learning occurs from the concrete to the abstract, from the easy to the difficult, and from the particular to the general. Learning should be in contact with reality and based on activity and experience. Knowledge and practice should interact constantly and effectively, whereby practice inspires theory and direct experience originates and determines educational ends.

Learning methodology includes the use of the inductive-deductive or experimental method, which is the key to the generation of new knowledge. Dialogue and discussion of controversial subjects are to be included. Language education should begin with the mother tongue or vernacular. Mathematical reasoning which cultivates logical thinking is the ideal method for reaching truth.

Education that is environment centered recognizes the importance of influences that impinge upon the individual. The environment should be considered a very significant source of information made accessible to the individual through the senses. Knowledge, if it is to be understood, is first acquired through the senses. Sensory training—particularly of the visual, auditory, and tactile senses, by means of didactic materials and related scientific apparatus for auto-education—facilitates this knowledge. Symbolic labels or referents to information, acquired through the senses in the form of words, number, musical notation, and the like, follows.

A shift to child-centered from curriculum-centered learning emphasizes the individual and utilizes the natural interests and play tendencies of the learner. Education of the individual in a child-centered curriculum situation accounts for individual differences in mental capacity and interests. Unique capacity is recognized and proper opportunity and guidance is given. Individuals are encouraged to work on things of immediate interests, facilitated by the tutor who communicates a love for the learner. In such a situation, the learner is taught to be independent. Instructional technique, in this context, is based upon the immediate experience of objects and situations of *Anschauung*.

Other aspects of educational methodology relate to the use of praise or reward, the learner's sense of mastery as the highest form of achievement, the value of specific over general practice, and the positive effects of imitation and emulation on learning.

Most of these ten areas of educational philosophy apply to all children and have guided the emergence and continuance of progressive education, which has emphasized the significance of environmental influence in the context of child-centered education, development, thinking, and creativity. The various approaches, in the form of plans, projects, and even schools for more effective learning that were tried in the 1930's and beyond, paved the way for the design of special educational opportunities for the gifted then and now.

In current designs of learning, we recognize the philosophical roots inherent in the projects and plans for *educating the gifted*. The relevance of past thoughts and recent practice have given gifted education its current form and direction. Informed by the advances in psychology as well, education has been refined to the advantage of superior individuals, whose superiority is not determined today by noble birth but by high levels of abilities and talents.

LEARNING OF SCHOOL SUBJECTS

Discussion of educational provision for gifted students has so far emphasized the importance of differential nurturing. Although it is true
that there is commonality among all children, there are also differences
unique to the individual, not difficult to recognize and accept. However,
we are tempted to conceal these differences to some extent in our discussion of the gifted.

In matters of curricula there is no lack of emphasis on teaching the
basics. Curriculum content is not the subject of criticism as much as the
unbending way that teaching the basics is approached. However, many
scholars of the gifted like Clark, Meeker, Renzulli, Tannenbaum, and
Feldhusen have offered alternative ways of teaching the basics within
their models.

Schooling should not direct itself to teach gifted students only what it
predetermines. In fact, schooling should develop the students' ability—
long after formal schooling—to be critical, creative, and independent
thinkers who can generate new, unique, and valuable knowledge. The
hallmarks of curriculum development for the gifted should be a delicate
balance between depth and breadth, specificity and generality, routine
and variety, and conservation and creativity.

In pointing to the need for qualitative differences in the curriculum of
gifted children, we (Gowan, Khatena & Torrance, 1979) have emphasized the importance of including:

1. Deeper study of subjects than an average class could handle (e.g.,
   language arts—the study of phonetics, elementary philology, ety-
   mology, and so on; mathematics—the study of higher arithmetic,
   numerical permutation and combination, trigonometry and logs,
   statistics, and the like)
2. A change in teachers' function from directors to facilitators of
   learning so that teachers do not set themselves up as knowing
   everything there is to know but serve as leaders to the vast store-
   house of knowledge (e.g., in the use of libraries, in development
   and acquisition of skills, in obtaining information by means of the
   laboratory, in active participation to solve real problems, and by
   way of available outlets for resultant products)
3. Individualizing instruction (e.g., possibly with the assistance of
   computer terminals on shared time, with other learning devices
   like Individually Guided Education, Individualized Education Program or Individually Prescribed Instruction, to get around the accelerative consumption of curriculum materials by gifted students)
4. Greater processing opportunities of curriculum materials to go be-

yond Structure of Intellect operations of cognition, memory and convergent thinking, to extend to divergent thinking and evaluation, requiring decision making (e.g., to be accomplished by curriculum games, simulations or creative production by way of poems, paintings, and other art forms)

5. Intentional or purposive use of curriculum materials to develop creative thinking

It is not within the parameters of this book to go into the curriculum of each subject area. Many sources of information on matters of curricula can be found in the writings of experts in subject teaching fields. Among the many curriculum aids useful to the reader are those described in the National Educational Association publications relative to mathematics, social studies, foreign languages, English, music, and art. Another source would be the periodic curriculum issues of the *Review of Educational Research*.

Some valuable curriculum planning approaches for mathematics, science, creative writing, reading, foreign languages, art, music, and drama can be found in many publications (e.g., Fliegler, 1961; M. J. Gold, 1965; Gowan and Demos, 1964). More recent modifications of curriculum offerings in the content areas of mathematics, science, social studies, language arts, art, and music are offered, for instance, by B. Clark (1986, 1988), Feldhusen, Van Tassel-Baska & Seely (1989), Gallagher (1985), Maker (1982), and Parker (1989). Furthermore, current information on curriculum particularly designed for the gifted can be found in various articles in journals on the gifted (e.g., *Gifted Child Quarterly*, *Journal for the Education of the Gifted*, and *Roeper Review*).

Gallagher (1985) makes some important observations about several curriculum areas as follows:

Mathematics is not a static subject area where everything is known and the task is merely to master it, but a dynamic ever-expanding field dependent for its continued growth on creative and innovative ideas of gifted students, scientists, and mathematicians.

Science for gifted students is understanding its true nature and the search for truth. The acquisition of skills and methodology permit these.

Social Studies curricula should pivot on the proper study of man. To accomplish this, gifted students must be helped to understand the basic concepts of economics, sociology, and psychology. They must also be introduced to controversial ideas and be taught to use the tools needed for analysis as well as for the acquisition and evaluation of additional information so that they can arrive at unbiased viewpoints.

Language Arts for gifted students should emphasize the understanding of ideas of great complexity and the systems of knowledge in that content field. Learning should extend beyond grammar and syntax and make use of literature for the appreciation of past cultures. In addition, the study of values, as a basis for making intelligent judgements about conflicting ideas, should be included.

Viewing the development of more complex units and materials—based on advanced conceptualization of curriculum—is progressive, germane, and consistent with contemporary thought on the subject. Gallagher (1979a) stresses the importance of having actual curriculum content at the heart of any differentiated program, regardless of the particular learning environment in which it is to be delivered. He focuses attention on the value of developing curriculum units around central seminal ideas much like J. Bronowski's technique used in the television series based on his book *The Ascent of Man* (1973). His reference to the importance of integrating curriculum content with learning process is consistent with Meeker's, Renzulli's, and F. E. Williams's educational models.

Gallagher (1979a, 1985) expects teachers to have difficulty providing direct services to gifted students because of the paucity of organized curriculum resources to draw from, although conditions and resources are better today. However, if the training of teachers leads to proper command of these various processes, they will have little trouble using them in the study of curriculum. Ideally, curriculum resources should incorporate the process-content approach. This approach would simplify the task for teachers of the gifted as they make the transition from education for the average to education for excellence. Teachers of the gifted have to be resourceful and work with others, if necessary, to shape new dimensions in content.

We must not overlook the valuable contributions of Ward (1961) and Newland (1976). In a more traditional sense, Ward writes about curriculum in terms of experiences designed to promote civic, social, and personal adequacy; emphasizes intellectual activity and creativity; and includes the foundations of civilization, the study of the classics, and the instruction of ideal moral behavior in his study.

Newland defines curriculum in a broader sense to include content of subject matter extending beyond the school to all life's experiences, many of which can be tapped by educators to facilitate learning. He expects the gifted, because of their superior capacity for learning, to use verbal symbols and functions conceptually as well as metaphorically. The gifted are to expand their lives beyond the learning space of the present social context, but to be a part of the past and the future. In this manner, all human experience and knowledge are unified.

FUTURISTIC AND UTOPIAN PERSPECTIVES

Of the several recent progressive discussions of gifted education (Collangelo, 1985; Gallagher, 1979a, 1979b; Goldberg, 1986; Passow, 1979, 1986; Renzulli, 1980, 1988; Sisk, 1980; Willard, 1986), few truly provide vision for future educational nurturing of the gifted. Among those that do are Torrance, (1977c) and Gowan (1979b, 1980). Torrance foresees educational practice for the gifted in the twenty-first century, and Gowan envisions educational practice in an imaginary and idyllic state.

Education in the Year 2002 (Torrance)

Viewing established education practice for the gifted in the year 2002, Torrance (1977c) envisions schools with interdisciplinary curricula activities. Process and generic strategies of learning in schools of the past, which were sporadic or conducted in isolation, are integrated as a curricula system in 2002. In this way, research methodology, for instance, will serve as an important component of the curriculum through which students learn the scientific method and its application in the study of real everyday problems that people face.

Various techniques to solve problems—the Osborn-Parnes creative problem solving method, Gordon-Prince synectics approach to problem solving, and Moreno-Torrance sociodramatic problem solving procedures—are learned and used to gain greater command of the environment. The Delphi technique (originating from the Oracle of Delphi of Greek mythology) is a procedure that was originally used to make future predictions for consensus attainment and now serves as a productive way of handling learning and its application. In addition, the metaphorical, mechanical, and mathematical analogues, as well as simulation games, and a combination of teaching and learning techniques hold merits that are unquestioned.

Education in Utopia (Gowan)

Schools in Utopia, according to Gowan (1979b, 1980), emphasize developmental stages and escalation of gifted students toward self-actualization. Students develop from dependence on formal operations or convergent thinking to usage of creativity or divergent thinking in their intellectual activities at the secondary level. At this time, secondary school students study, as models, the biographies of geniuses and creative persons analyzing their outstanding lives relative to critical developmental stages, environmental pressures that impinge upon them during their lifetime, and the successful coping strategies they used.

Curriculum in Utopia includes mini-courses, reflecting a dynamic view of humankind seen in the process of change and becoming. They are similar to those found in

energetics (use of life energies including some we do not understand)

ecology (for better appreciation of Earth and conservation of its resources)

utopias (from Plato to Huxley)

futuristics (study of and planning for the future)

species evolution

social policy

historics (history from a dynamic point of view after Toynbee and Spengler)

glass bead game (a witty method for developing memory and ingenuity among students and musicians later becoming a method for the development and expression of ingenuity and invention in language, mathematics, and so on, that uses analogies and correspondences)

creativogenic society studies (where social institutions maximize creative talent)

creativity and its application to school learning (a solid part of the curriculum directly taught)

Further, *somatics* (a term nearest to, yet different from physical education) is taught, not as group skills leading to aggressive behavior and team rivalries, but as individual bodily exercises to reduce stress and thereby contribute to good health.

In the domain of the normal state of consciousness are mini-courses in science (e.g., astrophysics, particle physics, and astronomy) that can be understood by nonscience majors, mathematics (e.g., emphasizing exponential functions, binary notations and logs, computer and artificial languages), scientific ethics (emphasizing probability function attached to truth-value theories), and history (from perspective of historical progression of ideas liberating humankind regarded as more important than historical progression of laws liberating humankind). These mini-courses are thought of as important curriculum units of the future.

Communication theory comprises verbal and nonverbal study. Verbal study includes phonetics, comparative philology, foreign languages, and student made artificial languages with emphasis on their extensional and intentional use. Nonverbal study includes gesture, body expression, dancing, empathy, intuition, archetypes, images, dream ritual, and art. These components of communication are taught instead of language arts as we know them.

Use is made of the intensive journal method for creative writing. Flexibility of thinking is developed by the study of *metasymbolic calculus* in which symbols acquire several meanings and running prose conveys double or triple meanings.

Another important curriculum innovation involves the learning of techniques of relaxation, meditation, time distortion, and the like, so that incubation can be encouraged for occurrence of imagery. The curriculum also includes the development of a repertoire of theories rather than beliefs, the study of *general systems*, and the study of *neotics* or the analysis of the mind and consciousness.

PROGRAMS AND PROJECTS

On the matter of programs and projects, we come face to face with the many attempts, over the years, at providing special ways to help gifted students grow educationally in the broadest sense. Approaches have been numerous and have found expression at both the elementary and secondary levels as integral components of the regular classroom or as satellites to it in specially assigned centers. These centers cater to students of the school alone or act as host to students from several neighboring schools.

Programs

A variety of programs, in the form of innovative projects—peripheral rather than central to regular schooling, and supplemental rather than basic—are offered. Occasionally, these approaches are expressed as special schools that have been, and may continue to be, private. If it were difficult to give a complete account of programs and projects existing in the United States over the past two decades or so, it would be impractical to attempt to do so now because of the proliferation of programing all over the country, vitalized by the relative availability of financial support, both from public and private sources.

What stands out, however, is the fact that, with a few exceptions, not many new programs today are really much different from those of prior years. In the main, practices have not veered much from what may be regarded as traditional innovations. However, there are several major exceptions.

> Programming currently relates to a reconceptualization of acceleration and enrichment which is differential in level, purpose, and direction. Re-conceptualized acceleration, considered as the consequence of enrichment, is preparatory to advanced study, particularly in mathematics and language, of precocious youth both in

high school and university. Enrichment, conceived as accelerative, is re-conceptualized as vitalizing the development of thinking skills and acquisition of scientific methodology to be applied to individual investigation, production, and communication outlets.

Programming currently relates to the development of many intellectual abilities and processes, and the acquisition and use of creative problem solving and affective skills.

Programming relates to the identification-diagnostic-prescriptive approach attending learning events associated with curriculum, and the individualization of this approach to adequately meet the needs of gifted students.

Two overviews of programs for the gifted (Cox, Daniel & Boston, 1985; Fox, 1979) present good summaries of the various ways that have been or are still being tried with variable measures of success. Some of these approaches have received attention and documentation by many earlier sources (e.g., DeHaan & Havighurst, 1965; M. J. Gold, 1965; Gowan & Demos, 1964; Passow, 1958).

Gallagher (1979a) has pointed out that modification of existing programs to meet the needs of gifted children, as was done for exceptional children generally, can be brought about in three major areas—*content*, *special skills*, and *learning environment*.

1. *Content modifications*—include changes within established subject areas like mathematics or history; inclusion of new content areas hitherto unavailable like ethics, and value systems; more complex curriculum units and materials based on advanced conceptualization of a subject and developed around central seminal ideas; integrating content with attention to process; and individual and small group investigation of real problems.

2. *Special Skills inclusion*—developing problem solving, divergent and creative thinking skills; using the discovery method of learning; and using creativity as it relates to something.

3. *Learning Environment establishment*—includes creating a facilitative environment that may range from having a special meeting with the gifted a few hours a week to establish a special school for the gifted; and giving special attention to the needs of underachievement and cultural difference.

(*Note:* Current American special-education philosophy proposes the least restrictive environment that moves a child out of the regular program only if absolutely necessary and returns the child to the regular program as soon as the special needs are met. Further, special schools or classes for the gifted are not looked on with favor, especially if it is felt that the same results can be achieved through a part time special class or with the addition of a resource teacher in a regular classroom.)

To the three areas, a fourth was added by Fox (1979) which she calls rate of instruction. In commenting on content versus rate, she brings to our attention the need to consider modes of instruction as well, where (a) acceleration (defined as the adjustment of learning time to meet individual abilities of students), and (b) enrichment (defined as the provision of learning experiences that develop higher processes of creativity in a subject area) should complement one another. Both are necessary to meet the learning needs of gifted individuals. Further, on the subject of mode of instruction, she emphasizes that diagnostic-prescriptive teaching and its relevance for self-direction (self-paced learning) is the most useful strategy for fostering acceleration of learning rate.

She expands learning environment to include (a) appropriate equipment and facilities with essentials like computer terminals, science-of-language laboratories, and video-taping; (b) internship experiences as they relate to community and government agencies for older students; (c) homogeneous grouping; (d) well-trained teachers; and (e) development of an atmosphere of mutual trust, respect, and commitment to self-improvement.

On the subject of delivery systems, Fox includes special schools with the compromise of satellite schooling or the school-within-a-school and learning centers or laboratories. Fox also includes early admission to school and college or admission with advanced standing, grade skipping, telescoped programs, subject-matter acceleration, accelerated and enriched classes, nonaccelerative enriched classes, individualized study, tutors, mentors and internship, within-class individualization, and mainstreaming as aspects of delivery systems.

Fox concludes that no single concept of programing can effectively meet the needs of all gifted students. We can observe in currently operating projects or those put in operation during the latter half of the 1970s subscription to one or several of these delivery systems, which must include differential emphases within the instructional mode. Much of what Fox has brought to our attention is also discussed by Maker (1982) as content, process, and environment. Further it is reiterated by a more recent study on programs and promising practices funded by the Richardson Foundation (Cox, Daniel & Boston, 1985).

Projects

Currently, there are two good sources (Cox, Daniel & Boston, 1985; Juntune, 1981) of published information on special projects for gifted students. The many projects covered by both sources are representative of efforts around the country that provide educational opportunities that are not expected in regular school learning. They have features that may be linked to recent thought and to state guidelines.

Many projects include recent thought on identification, nurture, and delivery in an additive rather than conceptual way. Examples of projects that are based on some broad conceptual model include the identification-diagnostic-prescriptive Structure of Intellect Model (Meeker, 1969, 1979a) the Study of Mathematically Precocious Youth at Johns Hopkins University (Stanley & Benbow, 1986), and the Revolving Door Identification Model (Renzulli, Reis & Smith, 1981). Details of these conceptual approaches can be found elsewhere in the text. In contrast to these models are those which use a variety of enrichment procedures with no central frame of reference to give them sustained coherence.

Juntune (1981) provides information on the location, title, and administrative agency of the most successful 72 projects described. These projects tell us something about the increasing vigor of participation in innovative approaches on the one hand, and the absence of participation of some, on the other hand. On the basis of this data, we see that 15 participating states have from 2 to 10 projects at various stages of development. It is important to note the shift in programing from an approach dominantly cognitive to one massively diversified. This shift is in keeping with an expanded concept of giftedness focusing on the many ways a person can be gifted (Jackson, 1979). Of the 72 projects, 15 are selected for discussion as they relate to identification, instructional mode of learning, delivery system, and evaluation, all of which reflect the shift to an expanded concept of giftedness (Table 11.2).

Identification

The procedures used to identify gifted students for a project generally followed state guidelines. But, most projects use individual or group I.Q. measures as the major identification criterion. Of the 15 projects listed on Table 11.2, nine use I.Q. measures (e.g., Advanced Instruction Module or AIM (San Diego, CA); Quest for Advanced Intellectual Development or QUAID (Bethlehem, PA)).

However, the practice then was to use multiple criteria in the selection process to include achievement and creativity tests [e.g., Identifying and Developing gifted and Talented Students (Sandy, UT)] as well as less formal observational-inventory or nomination types of indices so that psychologist, teacher, parent, and peer might all be involved in the identification process. For instance, the Program for Academically and Creatively Talented or PACT (Anchorage, AK), the Learning Lodge of Talcott Mountain Science Center (Avon, CT), the Four-School Enrichment Program (Boise, ID), and the Primary Gifted Education (Lawrence, KS) projects all used multiple-assessment procedures. Of particular interest is the SOI Demonstration Center Project (San Diego, CA) which used Structure of Intellect measures (Meeker, 1980b) in preparation for the development of those abilities by the Meeker *SOI Abilities Workbooks* (Meeker, 1980a).

Generally, test information provided the main selection criteria, although most projects depended on nominations and observations as well. All available identification information was carefully examined when selection of students for gifted and talented programs was made.

Instructional Mode of Learning

The instructional mode of learning, at times, might directly arise from a theoretical model like the Structure of Intellect, as Meeker interpreted or F. E. Williams has modified it. At times, the instructional mode of learning might include creative problem-solving processes by using the Osborn-Parnes approach and its related derivatives. The synectics approach is less frequently used.

Content and Special Skills

Often, projects combine a number of process models including not only the ones mentioned but also Bloom's Taxonomy of Educational Objectives, Piagetian concepts, and C. W. Taylor's Multiple Talent (1978) approach integrated in the curriculum. It was not unusual for a project to concentrate its central efforts on process, particularly as process related to creative or divergent thinking and problem solving, as well as on activities that were not necessarily curriculum based. However, it was less frequent to see the application of such thinking operations to curriculum.

The most popular methodological approach is Renzulli's Enrichment Triad model, now closely linked to his three-ringed conception of giftedness (Renzulli, 1986). In terms of cognitive-affective creativity and their curriculum correlates, F. E. Williams (1972) Total Creativity Program for Elementary School Teachers was another model that had won great acceptance. The more loosely conceived concept of general enrichment that pervaded many of the projects was less effective than its more precise relative, the Enrichment Triad-Revolving Door approach. Acceleration, another feature of several projects, had found more precise focus in the Study of Mathematically Precocious Youth (SMPY) Project initiated by Julian Stanley at the Johns Hopkins University. Unlike the general accelerative features of the enrichment triad, Stanley's project encompassed acceleration to higher levels of accomplishment in a subject area (e.g., mathematics) related to special abilities. Thus, SMPY pos-

Table 11.2 Identification, Instructional mode of learning, Delivery System, and Evaluation of 15 National Special Projects

Locale	Title of Project	Administrative Agency	Grade Levels	IQ	Cognitive Abilities	Creativity (CPS)[1]	Academic Achievement	Nominations	SOI[2]/SOILA[3]	Other	Time
Alaska (Anchorage)	Program for Academically and Creatively Talented (PACT)	Anchorage School District	K–8		×	×	×	×			3 hours per week
California (San Diego)	Advanced Instruction Module (AIM)	Mt. Diablo Unified School District	K–6	×						×	6 hours per week
(San Diego)	SOI Demonstration Center	San Diego Unified School District	2–6						×		—
(Whittier)	Developing Divergent Modes of Thinking in Mentally Gifted Minors (MGM) Children	ESEA[5] Title III Project	1–8	×						×	Once a week
Connecticut (Avon)	Learning Lodge	Talcott Mountain Science Center ESEA[5] Title III & ESEA[5] Title IV-C Project	4–12	×		×	×	×			Week days, Saturdays, Summer
Idaho (Boise)	Four-School Enrichment Program	Boise School District	K–6	×		×	×	×			6 weeks interschool workshop
Iowa (Ankeny)	Ankeny Gifted and Talented Education (AGATE)	Ankeny School Board	K–8	×		×	×			×	3 hours per week
Kansas (Lawrence)	Primary Gifted Education	ESEA[5] Title IV-C Project	K–2	×			×				2½ days per week
Maryland (Baltimore)	Accelerated Mathematics for Gifted and Talented	Howard County Public Schools & Ellicott City Schools	7–8		×		×				Saturday (32 two-hour sessions)
New York (North Merrick)	Widening Interest Through New Experiences for Gifted Students (WINGS)	North Merrick School	4–6	×		×				×	1½ days per week
Oklahoma (Guthrie)	Exemplary Program	Guthrie School District	K–12	×				×			School year
Pennsylvania (Bethlehem)	Quest for Advanced Intellectual Development (QUAID)	Hannover School	4–6	×				×	×		School year
Texas (Alice)	Talented and Gifted Students	Alice Independent School District	8–12				×	×			5 days per week
Utah (Heber City)	Gifted and Talented Program	Wasatch School District	6–11			×	×			×	School year
(Sandy)	Identifying and Developing Gifted and Talented Students	Jordan School District	2–6								School year

[1]CPS = creative problem solving.
[2]SOI = structure of intellect.
[3]SOILA = structure of intellect learning abilities.
[4]IEP = individualized education program.
[5]ESEA = Elementary and Secondary Act.

| | Instructional Mode of Learning | | | | | | | | | | | Delivery System | | | | | | | | | | | | | Evaluation | | | | | | | |
| | Content | | | Special Skills | | | | | | Environment | | | | | | | | | | | | | | | Tests | | Observation | | | | | | |
Curricula (Regular)	Curricula (Special)	Other	Critical Thinking	Creative Thinking/CPS[1]	SOI Abilities (Meeker)[2]	F. E. Williams's Strategies	Enrichment Triad (Renzulli)	Other (Bloom, Parnes, C. W. Taylor)	Peers (Homogeneous)	Class (Heterogeneous)	Self-contained Class	Special School	Learning Center/Lab	Grouping (Cluster, Homogeneous)	Grade Skipping	Enrichment (General)	Acceleration	Individual Study	IEP[4]	Tutor/Mentor	Mainstreaming	Teacher Oriented	Other (Pull-out)	Cognitive Abilities	IQ	Torrance: Guilford	Achievement	SOI[1]/SOILA[3]	Product	Renzulli	Parent/Teacher/Peer	Informal Records
X						X										X	X	X					X	X		X						
X				X	X	X		X					X	X		X	X						X				X	X				
											X							X														
																	X		X													
							X				X			X									X									
				X	X	X					X			X				X								X		X			X	
X	X			X	X	X		X					X																			
X																X	X	X					X								X	
X																		X									X					
		X						X			X		X	X														X			X	X
X	X		X	X					X		X																					
X	X				X						X																					
		X	X	X		X	X	X										X	X							X			X		X	X
X								X		X			X			X		X					X								X	
X				X						X											X											

sessed an unquestionable power of its own. There was no doubt that the need for different instructional modes of learning existed, not only according to abilities and special aptitudes but also according to age levels and developmental advances of gifted students.

Some states, such as Louisiana, require Individual Education Plans (IEPs) because gifted education is included under special education. However, regarding the 15 projects selected for discussion, one finds few of them deliberately attempting to provide IEPs. Hence, there is a definite need for IEPs that range from teaching individual abilities and talents by means of accelerative procedures in various content areas to interest-determined projects.

On reviewing the projects, one finds few of them deliberately attempting to provide IEPs. Some exceptions are the Individualized Progress Program of Madrona Elementary School (Seattle, WA), the Individually Guided Education Program (Stevens Point, WI), the Structure of Intellect Demonstration Center Project (San Diego, CA), and the Quest of Advanced Intellectual Development Project (Bethlehem, PA) which uses the Structure of Intellect diagnostic-prescriptive approach. However, it must be noted that 9 of the 15 projects listed include individual study like the Program for Academically and Creatively Talented (Anchorage, AK) and Talented and Gifted Students Project (Alice, TX).

One of these projects, a mainstream approach to educating the gifted and talented, provided gifted education to all children in the regular classroom with the Wasatch School District of Herber City (UT) as the administrative agency. The project emphasized C. W. Taylor's Teaching for Multiple Talents approach based on the rationale that individuals had many talents which could be developed. The approach focused on Thinking Centers that could develop into Talent Centers where students became involved in working across various areas of knowledge. The project also used, for the purpose of identification, the *Biographical Inventory Form* developed by C. W. Taylor and R. L. Ellison (1966) at the Institute of Behavioral Research in Creativity at Salt Lake City. The instrument was designed to train teachers as well as provide for the identified needs of gifted students.

Another project implemented by The Child Development Research Group Program aimed at educating highly precocious academically and intellectually gifted students whose performance on standardized tests is 4 standard deviations above the mean or better. The program for these extremely able students emphasized enrichment, acceleration, and the creative use of abilities in a way that attempted to meet individual needs.

Two other projects listed operated in the Yakima School District of Washington State and the Vestavia Hills School District of Alabama. In Washington, the Futuristic Learners Program stressed development for the futures and leadership elements in its instructional model. In the

Vestavia Hills School District, the Confluent Model attempts to provide gifted students with moral education through cognitive and affective processes to facilitate the acquisition of moral autonomy (Piaget-Kohlberg) for individual self-reliance and inner direction.

Learning Environment

Learning environment is another facet of the instructional mode. Learning involves both theory and practice which provide structure and rationale for the educational provisions of projects. Environment includes the content of surroundings and includes

location, teacher, teaching style, teacher-student relationship, and the like

materials, equipment, and other essentials like audio-tape and video-tape facilities, teaching machines, language or science laboratories, calculators, and computer terminals

events and activities in the teaching-learning situation

community resources, including experts in the field made available on the school site

internships, essential to career education, providing on-the-job experiences for acquisition of preliminary know-how and perspectives to aspiring youth

classroom climate and interpersonal relationships

We are reminded of these essentials by both Gallagher (1979a) and Fox (1979). Most of these environmental conditions are a part of good school practice in any case.

The projects that have been discussed so far give proper attention to learning environment, emphasizing different aspects described according to project rationale, available resources, delivery system used, and related factors. The majority of the projects recognize the need and importance of providing in-service training for their teachers. If the project is well designed its theoretical rationale will provide the basis for proper implementation. Most projects focus on providing enriched environments in nearly all areas of the school curriculum. Some focus on those areas that enhance specific abilities of particular gifted students. The chief thrusts have been directed at providing general or accelerative enrichment to the intellectually or academically gifted student. Generally, projects are not designed to enhance talents especially in the areas of dance, music, drama, and the visual arts.

Delivery System

The method by which programs are implemented is another factor of relevance. School programs are offered by both the regular and special school through a *delivery system*. Delivery systems include administrative arrangements, learning centers, laboratories, tutors, mentors, and internships.

School Programs

For many years, the most common method of program delivery has been the school. The delivery of special educational opportunities in the classroom may be through individualized instruction aimed at catering to intellectual talent and interests of gifted students. Besides, grouping together highly able students in a single school for special learning events can also be provided although, at the higher levels of ability, only a few students are likely to qualify.

In the elementary school, these procedures may be practiced with several classes that are at either the same or different grade levels, whereby a special room can be set aside for activities that the gifted can engage in together. Procedures may vary in the secondary school when the nature and organization of learning events lend themselves to individualization of education. However, by and large, the same procedures used in the elementary school can be implemented in the secondary school with careful thought and planning.

Several schools can be combined with a home base or a common area (learning center) can be established in a single school. Each school can take its turn to serve as the home base. A good example of this is the Four-School Enrichment Program (Boise, ID) for gifted students from Kindergarten to grade 6 with a meeting place or open house located in each of the four schools on a rotating basis. It caters to the specialized interests of gifted students in high schools, with each of the four schools designated as a center of specialization in areas of mathematics, sciences, modern languages, and visual-performing arts. In this way, students with special abilities can benefit from the specialized training they obtain from these schools.

Examples of secondary programs for mathematically precocious youth are the Howard County Public Schools and Ellicott City Schools in Maryland for seventh-graders and eighth-graders following the Study of Mathematically Precocious Youth model established by Julian C. Stanley at The Johns Hopkins University.

A variation particularly suitable for secondary school students is the school-within-a-school arrangement. In principle it is much the same as the honors school. The school-within-a-school arrangement provides gifted youth with instruction in academic subjects by teachers especially assigned the task. At times, these students participate with the rest of the student body in social events and in learning nonacademic subjects. The same gifted students may operate as a homogeneous group and together undertake projects that may provide a public service or that may serve simply as a vehicle for them to interact with one another (Bristo, 1956; Fox, 1979).

Furthermore, several schools may participate in a program, much like the Four-School Enrichment Program (Boise, ID), which caters to the specialized interests of gifted students in high schools. In this program, each of the four schools are designated as centers of specialization in such areas as mathematics, the sciences, modern languages, and visual-performing arts. In this way, students with special abilities can benefit from the specialized training they obtain from these schools.

Now we can present the ideal delivery system—the school specially designed for the gifted student. In schools for the gifted, the best materials, resources, and teachers are available in one place. Highly able students learn and interact with other highly able students in a wealth of experiential situations.

Schools solely for gifted students may be interpreted as incompatible with the philosophy of American public education and, hence, have relatively little or no support. However, several states, Illinois, Louisiana, and North Carolina, for example, have such state schools. Two of these are relatively new.

The best *public* efforts in this direction have found expression in the special schools of Baltimore, Philadelphia, New York City, and in a few other large metropolitan areas. Generally, however, it is the specialized high schools in the country that cater to the needs of older gifted students.

The often cited Hunter College Elementary Laboratory School and the Speyer School, both in New York City, were earlier manifestations of schools for the gifted provided by public education. Among more recent efforts are the Illinois Mathematics and Science Academy in Aurora and the Louisiana School for Mathematics and Science and the Arts in Natchitoches. Other public efforts are in the Governor's School in such states as Georgia, North Carolina, and Pennsylvania. The latter are state supported schools for the gifted during the regular academic year. In contrast, Governor schools function during the summer rather than all year round.

Several other schools providing education to the gifted are *privately* owned and managed. Among them are the Mirman School for the Gifted, Roeper School for the Gifted, Calasanctius School for the Gifted, and Interlochen Arts Academy.

Summer Schools

Schools offering summer programs, to some extent, can be considered schools for the gifted for the duration of their programs. Such schools enroll various categories of superior students for educational enrichment and acceleration. Students are identified and brought to a particular location where materials, equipment, and related resources generally surpass those that are available in regular schools. Further, teachers in these programs are better prepared and selected for their special strengths or talents in the areas of the visual and performing arts. Instruction is decidedly superior and innovation thrives.

Perceptive educators have advocated the provision of special opportunities in the public school by means of summer programs in which it is much easier to bring together high ability students in an atmosphere of innovation. Such innovation can become incorporated in regular schooling the rest of the year. Besides, the scope for elective programs can be considerably broadened to meet individual needs and inclination (Conant, 1958; Gowan & Demos, 1964; Merry, 1935).

In fact, summer schools have become an important vehicle for the delivery of programs for the gifted all over the country and may be offered jointly or separately by a college and school system. Often, we find school districts or centers of learning including "summer" programs in activities for the gifted during the rest of the year, on school days, or on Saturdays. However, in the Governor's School of the various states we find sustained efforts to provide education for gifted students during the school year. The San Fernando Valley State University and the San Bernadino City Schools summer offerings are well-known provisions for gifted students. In addition, there are the Learning Lodge for Gifted Science Students at the Talcott Mountain Science Center (Avon, CT), and the flagship summer programs offered by the Guthrie Public Schools (Guthrie, OK).

Governor's Schools

One of the earliest attempts, for instance, that proved successful and enduring is the Governor's School of North Carolina. Initiated in 1963 under the sponsorship of Governor Terry Sanford and with the assistance of the Carnegie Corporation of New York and business foundation interests, this school is an important extension of public education of North Carolina. It operates under a special Board of Governors and is administered by the North Carolina State Department of Education.

In a thoughtful discussion of the school, Ward (1979) briefly describes student selection, instruction, and related information.

> Some 400 senior high-school students, selected by competition in academic areas, and by auditions in the fine and performing arts, are brought each summer to the school site at [Winston]-Salem [State] College in the Old Salem community of Winston-Salem for a seven-week period. There they pursue a program of study supplementing but not supplanting their studies in their

home communities, in a curricula pattern geared as closely as possible to their respective aptitudes and interests. Tuition is free. There are no grades in the usual sense. The faculties for the various areas are meticulously selected for competence and distinction within their respective curricula fields, and they come from secondary schools and colleges in North Carolina and in other states.

The Governor's School is a prototype in differential education for the gifted, the first of such institutions among several that were to follow with similar concepts of purpose and program. Initially, it provided occasion for some exciting and adventurous thought on the part of its progenitors. And while a succession of able faculties and administrative personnel have made notable contributions in the operation of the program and in the substance of curricula activities over the intervening years, the character of the school has remained remarkably true to the original concepts as to the organization of the program and the structure of the curriculum. (pp. 209–210)

The success of the Governor's School at Winston-Salem led to its replication at the beautiful campus of St. Andrews Presbyterian College in Laurinburg. Each summer, the Governor's School operates on both campuses.

An interesting development was the emergence of an experimental school for the gifted. Privately funded, the St. Andrews College for Kids or SACK follows the guidelines set by the North Carolina Department of Education. The school began in November 1979 and is patterned after the British open classroom of multiage grouping of students. The school has at least one full-time teacher and a student intern. College professors, working in the program, are assisted by the teacher and student intern who provide follow-up activities and assignments for the full academic year.

Compared with the fewer subject offerings in grades 5 to 9 of the public schools, SACK offers 13 to 16 different subjects. The instructional mode between the two differs as well, in that students are encouraged to learn as much as they want through individual study. Small group activities are included to give students the skills they will require for in-depth study, and self-learning is emphasized. Two years' exposure to this program should accelerate students to early college admission. Generally, SACK rationale is based on Renzulli's Enrichment Triad. The school is unique in that it is primarily research oriented, involving the direct participation of college faculty in the instructional process.

Private Gifted Schools

We now move away from schools that operate for the most part during the summer or are experimental in nature to consider several of the relatively few private schools for the gifted that function on a regular basis to provide enhanced programs. Among these are the Mirman School for the Gifted (Santa Monica, CA), Calasanctius School for the Gifted (Buffalo, NY), Roeper School for the Gifted (Detroit, MI), Interlochen Arts Academy (Interlochen, MI), Oaks Academy (Houston, TX), School for Creative and Performing Arts (Cincinnati, OH), and North Carolina School of Science and Mathematics (Durham, NC).

Mirman School for the Gifted

The Mirman School for the Gifted was designed to cater to the needs of the academically gifted of I.Q. 130 and above. Beginning in the home of Norman and Beverly Mirman in 1965, the school moved to a new location in the Santa Monica Mountains in 1970. In 1979 the school had an enrollment of 185 which has continued to grow.

The school carefully selects teachers to work with their gifted students in programs from kindergarten to grade 8. There are at least 14 full-time and part-time teachers who use a variety of enrichment procedures to enhance educational development. These procedures include an accelerative and varied curriculum with appropriate support equipment and other facilities. Both individual and group work are encouraged and attention is given to building good self-esteem and providing creative activities in the arts and sciences. The school also produces a newsletter and has strong parent support.

Teachers shift subjects according to the mood of the class. Art, history, French, science, and music combine with Greek mythology, new mathematics, literature, English and cursive writing. Sudden spurts of tangential interest in mid-lesson redirect discussion toward political problems, accomplishments in art, electronics, science fiction, and creative writing. The Mirmans told *McCall's Magazine* (Finder, 1970):

> We don't consider the lesson plan a straitjacket. In the middle of Dante's IN-FERNO, for instance one class wanted to create the circles to hell as an art project. So they did. During the study of Greek mythology, the children decided to study the Greek language. (p. 88)

There is, however, nothing undisciplined, fuzzy, or abstract about this approach.

> We try to teach our children how to think, to analyze, to evaluate. They're so glib verbally, it's very important that somebody pin them down. (p. 88)

The Mirman School for the Gifted appeals to its teachers, parents, and children for different reasons. Teachers delight in the small class size, their creative role in curriculum development, and the satisfaction of working with bright kids who give good feedback. The parents are attracted to the school because, according to Mirman (Finder, 1970), parents are often desperate that their children get quality education. As far as the children are concerned, their reasons for glee are apparent in their voracious appetites for learning that go unchecked by anyone but themselves.

The Roeper School for the Gifted

The Roeper School for the Gifted in Bloomfield Hills near Detroit was founded by George and Annmarie Roeper in 1956. It admits highly motivated children with I.Q.s of 120 and above after careful screening. The motives of parents for bringing the child to the school, their attitudes toward special education, and the home environment are also scrutinized.

The school consists of two organizational units—a lower school with an enrollment of approximately 300 students in a nongraded, multiage, open classroom environment and an upper school with an enrollment of approximately 200 students in grades 7 through 12 with each unit having a head person. A Board of Trustees is the governing body and establishes policy for the entire school. It is a nondenominational school with a scholarship program. The scholarship supports, in part, many students of different socioeconomic backgrounds. Vital to the school's continuance are its guiding principles that focus on the dignity of all people and their right to enjoy free and honest expression, to share in our cultural heritage, and to participate fully in the family of man.

Like the Mirman School for the Gifted, programs of the Roeper School are conceptualized in terms of enrichment by means of the arts and science curricula, which are expected to accelerate the intellectual development of the students in a variety of settings common to all good schooling. The school derives its strength from competent and innovative full-time instructors (including university professors), enthusiastic parents, and superior facilities and equipment. The Roeper School has a fine newsletter, *Parent Communication,* as well as a journal, *The Roeper Review.* Both these reflect not only the school's activities but also contribute to thought on gifted education.

The Calasanctius School for the Gifted

The Calasanctius School, as described by its founder, Father Gerencser (1979), began as an experiment in the education of gifted and talented children from grade 5 to the college level in 1957, and expanded to include children from age 5 and up. Located in Buffalo, New York, the school serves the needs of people of all socioeconomic levels. Students are admitted mainly on the basis of I.Q.s of 130 and above and interest in the programs.

Father Gerenscer explains that the curriculum of the school was not designed as a copy of other curricula or the so-called enrichment and acceleration methods to be used. Instead, the program was to be a unified one, built around the psychological and sociological needs of gifted children. Important features of the school's program include:

planning for a six-year sequence of basic curriculum, usually after the fourth grade or fifth grade level, in preparation for the rigors of college-level study

exposure, early in schooling, to a variety of learning experiences in clearly circumscribed fields so that, during the first three years, all courses are required, except for the choice of foreign languages and in some areas of the creative arts

college-like scheduling of a variety of courses, namely, 10 to 15 subjects per week rather than the usual 5 per day, is a challenge that gifted students seem to prefer

the notion that creativity is a natural consequence of a broadened range of experiences in memory storage

Uniqueness of the program lies in integrating the previously mentioned program features, for instance, in three kinds of activities.

1. *Seminar Program*—This program is an independent research/study program under the guidance of a proctor to culminate, after three consecutive years of work, in the presentation of a serious paper or creative art work.
2. *Field Study Trip:*—This component lasts from two to three weeks or less for younger children, and lasts the school year for the others. The program's objectives include coordinating and integrating school learning experiences with real life situations, to open the minds of students to the variety of natural beauties around them and to the best of American achievements, and to nurture an understanding of the American experience.
3. *Phenomenon of Man Program*—The program consists of a cluster of courses taken in the fourth, fifth, and sixth levels of study for one to four semesters. It aims at introducing students to the richness of a history of ideas underlying culture.

Students are finally evaluated not for the time spent in a course but for actual knowledge acquired in an area.

The program at the Calasanctius School, for students between 5 and 9 years of age, is built on a combination of three psychological theories: (a) Jean Piaget's developmental stages, (b) Carl Jung's archetypical approach regarding content, and (c) the richness of children's eidetic imagery. Another feature of the program for the young is the teaching of foreign languages, including Japanese.

The complicated nature of the program requires the assistance of a large number of highly informed teachers, which include the cream of the academic community, who complement the full-time highly competent faculty. Continuous in-service training and visits to other schools help the faculty to remain up-to-date and highly effective in the role of teaching the gifted. The school supports itself by tuition and fees, donations, and contributed services. Its important service to the gifted was recognized in 1976 when, in honor of its 20th anniversary, Calasanctius Day was proclaimed in Buffalo and Erie Counties.

Interlochen Arts Academy
The Interlochen Arts Academy, located in Interlochen, Michigan, began in 1962 as the country's first high school to emphasize the arts and academic subjects equally. It is the natural outcome of the early efforts of Joseph Maddy, who pioneered the idea that music education should receive full credit in the nation's schools, as well as the National Music Camp, founded in 1928, which expanded offerings of dance, drama, and art in the years that followed.

The Academy is a special high school that provides talented students of grades 9 to 12 with comprehensive training in music, dance, theater, literary arts, and visual-performing arts in addition to other subjects of the school curriculum aimed toward college preparation. The structure of the program allows as much latitude as possible to students, within sound educational standards for college admission requirements, to arrange their own academic study. It offers small classes with highly qualified teachers, individualized instruction, tutorials, opportunities for the explorations of topics of interest on an individual or group basis, and promotion whenever students are ready. The faculty work together to integrate the academic and fine arts curricula.

The school depends on tuition fees and contributions for support. It has a scholarship and financial aid program that makes it possible for highly talented but needy students to attend the academy. In addition, the school operates as a day and residential school, catering to an important need in Michigan.

Oaks Academy
The Oaks Academy is a private school in Houston, Texas founded in 1980 by Lila Macaluso. By 1984, the school's enrollment rose from 13 to 150 gifted students between the ages of 3 and 11 years or kindergarten to sixth grade. Macaluso predicts that the academy will eventually serve as a laboratory school for teacher training.

Psychologists carefully screen students for admission using an I.Q. and development or achievement test. Additional information on school age students is obtained from a referring school.

Curriculum at the Oaks Academy is eclectic including the use of basal readers for the development of reading skills and language experiences that are based on literature for the expansion of vocabulary. This program is facilitated by parents, teacher aids, and student discussions. A number of foreign languages are taught beginning with Spanish in the preschool. Other languages include Latin and French, and when instructors are available, German and Russian. New math is incorporated in the school curriculum, shifting to a more traditional approach to the subject at the upper levels of schooling.

Parents are involved in the screening process and actively participate in the school program at Oaks Academy. They provide additional information about their children in an admissions interview and consequently participate in the instructional program. In addition, students are encouraged to share their talents in special lessons given to their peers.

School for Creative and Performing Arts

In Cincinnati, Ohio the School for Creative and Performing Arts caters to gifted students of grades 4 to 12. Students from all over the city compete for admission to the school not through I.Q. measures but through auditions relative to one or more subjects in the arts. The school is also open to a few learning disabled students who are placed in an academically slow class but find expression of their special talents in the arts program.

The School for Creative and Performing Arts has been found to motivate many of its aspiring young artists to complete a high school education. Students here study more daily than most students in other schools in the area, with the majority of graduates going on to college.

Curriculum of the school consists of forty-eight course offerings in the arts including the general areas of the visual arts, ballet, modern dance, music, drama, and creative writing. The school encourages specialization at an early age. Although the emphasis of the school is placed on the arts, the academic subjects are not neglected; in fact, standard subjects receive equal attention, such that about a third of the collegebound graduates major in various areas of the liberal arts, and professional fields like engineering, pre-medicine, architecture, and computer science.

North Carolina School of Science and Mathematics

The North Carolina School of Science and Mathematics is a public school with significant private support designed to cater to youth precocious in science and mathematics. The school was established in 1978 by Governor James B. Hunt for eleventh and twelfth graders selected on the basis of high scores on standardized tests like the *Scholastic Aptitude Test*. Several other selection criteria include personal recommendations, samples of writing, participation in out-of-class science fairs, and related projects. Screening of students for admission to the school is stringent.

The curriculum of this school for gifted students emphasizes science, mathematics, and such subjects as astrophysics, calculus, chemistry, and microbiology. Furthermore, inclusion of courses in the humanities provide an all-around education pertinent to high school and state graduation requirements. The main thrust of the curriculum is not to offer one or more courses or to assign projects, but to develop abilities and sets of skills in writing, speaking, analyzing, computing, synthesizing and evaluating that are essential in university education and throughout life.

An active mentor program involves numerous businesses, universities, and research agencies in the vicinity of the school. Students serving as interns obtain practical experiences under expert guidance. The location of the school in the vicinity of Duke University in Durham, North Carolina State University at Raleigh, and the University of North Carolina at Chapel Hill adds an exceptionally enriched educational environment to the mentor program.

The school sponsors summer teacher institutes to encourage innovations in curriculum and teaching methodology. Further, the school influences other public schools in the state by stimulating healthy competition and teaching advances in science and mathematics, and by bringing renewed attention to the superior students of the state.

Pyramid Project

The Pyramid Project (Cox, Daniel & Boston, 1985) is an education model that provides gifted education in the regular classroom and special classes of the public school, and special schools (Figure 11.1). This five year project, initially supported by the Richardson Foundation, caters to students of the Dallas/Fort Worth metropolitan area. Participants are the Cedar Hill, Birdville, Arlington, and Fort Worth School Districts with student populations of 2,300, 16,300, 36,900, and 65,000, respectively. The project is run by a steering committee of teachers and administrators.

The Pyramid Project serves to provide gifted education to as many able students as possible. As illustrated by the Fort Worth schools effort, adjustments are made in the regular classroom to accelerate a large number of able students (base level of the pyramid) to higher grades relative to their areas of achievement. Alternately, the system provides enrichment by portable learning centers (in the library or computer room), flexible pacing, cluster grouping, and curriculum compacting. Classroom organization for students includes block class scheduling and modular scheduling to permit cross-grade grouping.

Fewer superior students with more specialized needs (mid-section of pyramid of figure) require special provisions by way of honors classes that will allow dual enrollment (elementary-middle schools, middle-high schools, and high school-college). An even smaller number of exceptionally gifted students or those with specialized interests and talents

Figure 11.1 Pyramid Project Model

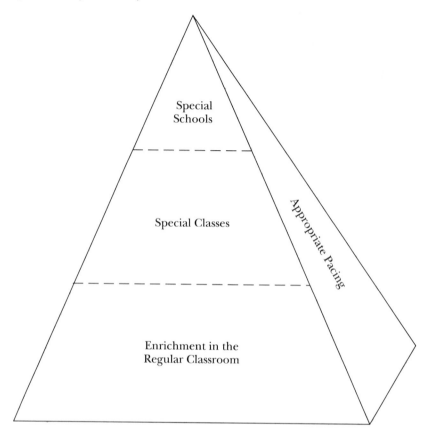

From "*Educating Able Learners: Programs and Promising Practices* by J. Cox, N. Daniel, & B.O. Boston, 1990, Austin: University of Texas Press. Copyright © 1985 by University of Texas Press.

(apex of pyramid) are channelled to special schools like the districts' existing *magnet schools,* where something like an International Baccalaureate or Visual and Performing Arts Program may be organized for them.

The Pyramid Project concept is based on students' mastery of content and skills to progress in their studies. The project includes an assessment plan to identify students' abilities and special needs for proper placement and exposure to the appropriate kind of accelerative-enrichment opportunities. A distinct feature of the project is its comprehensiveness, whereby superior students have their learning properly coordinated with the regular curriculum, and appropriate instruction is provided to them on a daily basis. The project also provides attention to levels of need within the gifted group that goes beyond providing a gifted program for all students. In addition, the project includes a provision for continuing staff development to permit longitudinal team planning, interdisciplinary planning, and cooperation among teachers, parents, and administrators.

Other Centers of Learning

Enrichment and acceleration function as the most common ways for the delivery of programs in schools. Both of these methods have received attention. Here we add the organizational elements of centers in the classroom, school or district, and mentorship or internship arrangements to our discussion. Several of the projects reported by Cox, Daniel and Boston (1985) and Juntune (1981) reflect these sources of enrichment and acceleration.

   Structure of Intellect Demonstration Center or the Creative Problem
      Solving Center (San Diego, CA)
   Resource room or resource center of many projects, including Ankeny Gifted and Talented Education (Ankeny, IO)
   Widening Interest Through New Experiences for Gifted Students
      (North Merrick, NY)
   Program for Academically Gifted Students (Mobile, AL)

Students study full-time at these centers or attend part-time in seminars, independent study or project work, creative problem-solving activities, tutorials, and the like, on a daily or weekly basis. Students are supervised or taught by a facilitator or coordinator of the gifted program.

   Acceleration may be incorporated in the activities of the centers to include advanced study of various subject areas. Acceleration certainly operates as an integral part of the individualized instruction provided by tutors, programmed materials, and individualized programs (self-directed or teacher-directed) as interpreted in diagnostic-prescriptive teaching methodology.

   We may think of acceleration in terms of telescoping programs so that (a) at the junior high school level, gifted students are placed in homogeneously grouped classes that cover three years of work in two years, or (b) at the senior high school level, gifted students eliminate or reduce the number of their electives, take courses in the summer, or earn credit by examination to graduate a year earlier, thereby completing the curriculum in three rather than four years. Early admission to kindergarten or grade 1, or reduction in the number of years spent in the junior or senior high school, or taking college courses while in high school are all facets of accelerative procedures.

Programs emphasize the function of the teacher. Whether involved in individualizing instruction in the regular classroom, serving as a tutor with expertise organized for direct instruction on a one-to-one basis, or serving as mentor with a less formalized approach, the teacher is an integral dimension of delivery programs that is crucial to schools and innovative projects providing special educational opportunities to gifted students.

Other mentor programs include the Illinois Governmental Internship Program (Springfield, IL), and Executive High School Internship Association (New York, NY), or internship arrangements illustrated by the Executive Assistant Program and the Creative Performing Arts Program (Dallas, TX), or a combination of both, for instance, in the Texas A&M University's Career Education Model. In these situations, secondary school gifted students are given the opportunity to work with experts of the community in study and on-the-job situations. They gain training and experience in their fields of interest and receive appropriate guidance. The mentor relationship and internship experience give many gifted students the necessary direction and preparation for career choices. Besides, mentors help eliminate some of the problems that naive gifted students face as they enter college because the diversity of their talents is not informed by practical experience.

We should consider program provisions for the culturally diverse. Torrance's study (1977b) on the relationship between nurture and talent among minority groups is valuable for its germane, productive, and innovative perspective. Torrance suggests three alternatives to provide selection and programming that suits specific types of giftedness. The Talent Development Center, Future Studies Center, and Creative Studies Center use this discovery and nurture of talents approach with a future focus (Torrance, 1977b, pp. 55–56).

1. Talent Development Center

For this alternative, students with some exceptional talent would be recruited. This talent might be in writing, one of the visual arts, drama, music, dance, science, politics, mathematics—even unconventional talents needed by society. All kinds of evidence would be accepted for evaluation, such as art products, musical compositions, photographs, videotaped performances, research reports, and samples of creative writing. The nature of the evidence would depend in part on the ingenuity and creativeness of the applicant. This alternative program would be designed to develop the student's particular giftedness and help the student create the kind of career he or she desires. The student would take courses in whatever departments would facilitate the development of the proposed career, including independent study under professors and specialists in the community or region. The director of this program would be an expert in the field of career development.

2. Future Studies Center

For this alternative, students gifted in future problem-solving would be recruited and selected. The special alternative admissions criteria might be performance on the future problem-solving tests developed by Torrance, Bruch, & Goolsby or some similar battery yet to be developed. The alternative program would develop abilities in future problem solving, futures research, and the like. The director of this program would be a qualified futures scholar. Students in the program would enroll in courses in whatever departments offer opportunities for developing the competencies needed in future studies or careers

3. Creative Studies Center

For this alternative, students gifted in creative problem-solving would be recruited and selected. As admissions criteria, it is proposed that the Torrance Tests of Creative Thinking and the creativity score of the Alpha Biographical Inventory be used. Both instruments are relatively free of racial and socioeconomic bias. The program would be similar to the Creative Studies Program of New York University College at Buffalo developed by Parnes and Noller and described in *Toward Supersanity: Channeled Freedom* (1973). In addition to the integrating core of creative studies, students might take some conventional major, or they might simply take courses throughout the college or university to enhance their skills as creative problem solvers. The director of this program would have special expertise in creative problem-solving and in developing creative problem-solving skills in others.

Other general approaches articulating discovery for nurturing of giftedness that expected to cater to the varying local needs of the culturally different involved

the use of creative positives or strengths to discover giftedness in the culturally different and to direct their development toward competencies required for success in the mainstream culture. Take, for instance, the program that was developed in New Haven (CT). (Witt, 1971)

the partial use of traditional criteria to select the minority gifted for exposure to an intermediate intervention program which was to prepare them to move on to high-level opportunities where their cultural strengths would be used as the basis for developing interventions [e.g., a program in the medical area known as the High School Program at the University of Pennsylvania, (Shephard, 1972)].

the discovery of giftedness and programming based on creative positives (Torrance, 1977b) to be achieved through curriculum reform in all schools and by the development of special schools in the performing and creative arts (e.g., schools in Houston (TX), New Haven (CT) and New Orleans (LA) that partially tested this approach with success [Amram & Giese, 1968; Bushnell, 1970]).

the selection of students on the basis of creative positives who performed moderately well on traditional criteria with a provision for special support programs for higher level attainment by way of cognitive therapy (Whimbey & L. S. Whimbey, 1975); an approach that made students aware of their strengths and weakness in thinking strategies and provided them with direct and specific help to improve their thinking.

the discovery and nurture of giftedness of culturally different gifted students through programs of competition that included creative writing, art, music, dance, and drama.

Additional guidelines suggested by Torrance (1977b) included a difference rather than a deficit model, a multidimensional model of giftedness, creative instructional methods and learning environment, and careful avoidance of unreasonable financial demands with the possibility of earning money to purchase educational materials. The implementation of these guidelines helped culturally different gifted students move from feelings of alienation to feelings of pride for their special strengths with opportunities for them to share these fruits with others by means of planned learning activities and administrative and classroom-management procedures. Further, arrangements were to be made for these gifted students to have sponsors—persons who could encourage and protect their rights when they were frustrated, discouraged, or abused, and who could give them a chance to succeed.

M. Fraiser and C. McCannon (1981) also suggested that instead of concentrating on deficiencies of culturally diverse students, we should pay attention to the development of strategic decision-making and learning skills that would aid students to cope with the system to advantage. On discovering their talents, they suggested that a *bibliotherapy* program would nurture them. Bibliotherapy is effective reading of books that match needs and problem areas experienced. Appropriate guidance in reading selected books could lead students to identify with characters. The same could serve as indicators of emotional or intellectual potential.

Evaluation

Of the 15 National Special Projects cited, only nine use tests or observation procedures to evaluate student progress in the respective programs (Table 11.2). Students in these projects are tested for improvement in cognitive abilities, creative thinking and achievement, divergent thinking, and achievement, and in achievement alone. However, these procedures are not necessarily a follow-up of initial screening information obtained for placement in the project, nor are they reflective of all the program goals. The same may be said for those projects that use observational procedures. To do a proper evaluation of student progress in the several areas of expected growth, similar measures need to be used both initially and finally. In this way, increments in performance may be attributed to program effects. Generally, there is an overdependence on inadequate observational procedures to provide indices of student progress. In either case, the intention of reporting fairly accurate information on student progress is partially defeated because of the lack of adequate preplanning of the measurement components of the project.

Evaluation is an essential component of any program or project, but it frequently turns out to be one of the most troublesome stages. Often those who initiate educational activities as innovative practice do not give careful attention to evaluating the planning stage of the program. And as the program reaches its final stages, there is a real need to determine if the innovative approach is effective or not. To be able to evaluate is important, for those who become involved in providing unique opportunities do look out initially for guidance.

The findings generated by a project, whether positive or negative, can be of great value in determining the direction that should be taken. It is not uncommon to find project directors frantically searching for someone or some agency to effect a rescue at a time when the evaluation component has usually become a makeshift operation. More often than not, the evaluator is unable to control the alternative explanations of change, other than those that may have occurred because of the project experience. For any appraisal to be effective, those involved should be present at the planning stage of the project. In this way, control of extraneous variables, evaluative dimensions and stages, appropriate instrumentation, correct statistical analyses, and the like, can be woven into the total project.

A distinction has to be made between a project that has been found to be significant for the education of students and has become part of an educational program or project, and a project that is in its experimental or initial phase. In the first case, it is necessary to give careful forethought to the conceptual framework of the project so that an adequate grasp of the consequences is evident. Further, it is necessary that the events, circumstances, and related conditions giving rise to the consequences relative to project related variables, become apparent. If the project is in its earliest stages it is necessary to determine if the trial run results recur when the project is in use.

To test the effectiveness of a project that is expected to change the participants, it is necessary to adhere to good design principles relative to the project's goals. The design that will control for many interferences determines the kind of computation that is to be used. The project that has been accepted as effective and incorporated into an educational program does not need such an approach. Instead, the procedure is leveled at selection of appropriate ways to assess growth, achievement, and increased competence resulting from exposure to the program.

Another consideration for innovative projects is on-going evaluation of the effects of the program components. Evaluation of this kind provides information about student strengths and deficiencies and gives important feedback data for program refinement and further program evolvement. Such formative evaluation is invaluable to the final summative evaluation of the project.

Renzulli (1975) and Renzulli and Smith (1979a) cite some pertinent evaluation research that distinguishes between formative and summative evaluation (e.g., Scriven, 1967) to describe evaluation designs used for (a) the appraisal of ongoing outcomes of a project for program refinement and evolvement, and (b) the appraisal of the consequences of the project as a whole. The combined use of the two evaluation procedures will create the most productive results. Further, the role of evaluation determines the types of data, product, process, and presage, to be generated.

A productive way of appraising the effectiveness of a project is to plan the evaluation within a study design that provides information at the outset about (a) the students' intellectual, educational, talent and creativity levels, and personality, (b) other pertinent factors that may be expected to react or interact with the program offered, and (c) performance changes that are expected to occur. The design should include feedback so that the program changes and improvement can be made at various times in the life of the project, usually at the end of each project year. A final evaluation of the total project should involve students, curriculum and related project components such as in-service training of the teaching faculty, effectiveness of expert contribution to the development of the project, parent-community related resources, and overall management of the project (Khatena, 1975b, 1977b).

Product Evaluation

Product evaluation can be regarded as the assessment of observable and measurable student outcomes, arising from exposure to program elements in a project. The derivation of such information serves to document the changes that are expected to have taken place in the student. Procedures to measure this kind of outcome present problems, especially as they relate to identifying changes of higher level processes, as for instance, in creative problem solving abilities.

Human judgment of some kind is needed, but, for this judgment to be effective, some criteria need to be established. Criterion-referenced tests that truly assess the type of learning appropriate to gifted students should be used. Information on products may be obtained by expert ratings of student products and by frequency counts through the use of school logs, checklists, or analysis of school records as these relate to the accomplishment of important program objectives. To these must be added A Consensual Assessment Technique proposed by Theresa M. Amabile (1983) to measure creative products with the participation of an expert panel of judges.

Process Evaluation

Process evaluation assesses the learning situation involving student and teacher behaviors rather than learning outcomes. Assessment of the actual dynamics of learning circumstances may prove valuable, in that strengths and weaknesses of certain teaching strategies can be identified in the formative stage to give direction to appropriate emphases or refinements. Such information will provide important data for summative evaluation reports.

The Flanders Interaction Analysis System (Amidon & Flanders, 1971) is offered as one of several assessment approaches. Another procedure suggested is the Class Activities Questionnaire (Steele, 1969), based in part on Bloom's Taxonomy of Educational Objectives, which attempts to measure the cognitive-affective dimensions of instructional climate. To this may be added the Barclay Classroom Climate Inventory (Barclay, 1978), an instrument that measures expectations in the affective and social domains of learning.

Presage Evaluation

Presage evaluation is yet another source of data. It focuses on factors assumed to have significant impact on outcomes or products, factors that relate directly to the program plan. This approach is particularly useful for the evaluation of nonproduct dimensions of a program.

An instrument developed by Renzulli and Ward (1969), entitled the Diagnostic and Evaluation Scale for Differential Education for the Gifted (DESDEG), can be used to clearly differentiate different components of a program for more careful analysis of each in an evaluation. The example given in the DESDEG (for the identification component) allows for examination of the comprehensiveness of screening and placement procedures, provides a variety of criteria used in identification, and designates the proportion of students selected at each grade level. This example forces a breakdown of information for the evaluator to see the identification system more clearly so that more meaningful questions may be asked for the making of better judgments.

For special problems encountered in evaluating a program, Renzulli and Smith (1979b) point to (a) the difficulty of measuring the effects of the program on the development of higher powers of mind and advanced levels of awareness, interest, and other affective behaviors; and (b) the highly individualized objectives, peculiar to each gifted student. Further, inaccurate readings are expected because gifted students are at the upper levels of standardized tests, because of the problem of statistical regression toward the means, and because of the low ceiling effects of tests. These problems are attenuated by the cost factor of an evaluation, the need for trained personnel who should be involved at the very beginning of the project, and the attitude of project personnel toward the evaluator because an evaluation can constitute a threat to the continuity or dissolution of the project.

These problems lead Renzulli (1975) to suggest the Key Features System (KFS) which he has found to be a particularly effective evaluation model for gifted and talented programs. KFS consists of four sequential steps, namely, (a) front-end analysis, (b) synthesis of input information, (c) data collection and analysis, and (d) file-evaluation reports.

Renzulli also suggests that, once identified, these key features can be organized in a matrix that has key features as one dimension, and sources for the collection of data as another dimension. Blank squares in the matrix can be completed according to the needs of individual programs that are to be evaluated. Further details on this model can be found in his papers (Renzulli, 1975, 1979a).

Appropriate attention must be paid to the factors that relate to an effective evaluation system of projects at the proposal stage. It would be advantageous to seek the services of knowledgeable professionals to assist in the planning and writing of the proposal so that whatever goes into the proposal belongs to the conceptual framework of the project. The discerning reader of the proposal will recognize the meaning and quality of such an approach and will be more inclined to favor the project for funding. As competition for funding continues to increase, it will become more and more necessary to attend to the relevance of this dimension of a project.

CONCLUSIONS

Designing learning is a complex task, for it does not only involve curricula but everything else required in the learning event. These elements include the learner, teacher, information and skills organized as school subjects, environment in and out of school, and evaluation of learning outcomes—all of which will have to be taken into account in the design process. To assist in this task we rely on disciplines of individual and social psychology, philosophy, measurement, and teaching techniques informed by them.

Current practice approaches education from a whole history of psychological and philosophical thought. However, it is quite common to find ourselves in the position of designing learning experiences for our students without an awareness of the sources of our ideas. The high degree of specificity in our organization of learning makes it episodic. Knowing the commonwealth of existing thought on factors attending learning puts us in the position of Ali Baba who, unlike his brother Kassim, visited the treasure cave at will knowing the correct code (Open Sesame) for treasure access.

The flexible and innovative ways we can structure and destructure for restructuring towards higher levels of integration is dependent on access to the generic pool of human experience generally, and on access to educational thought and practice specifically. Future directions can be determined and productive change initiated through these methods to create the ideal curricula.

Our task of designing learning has to consider the learner, and for our purpose, the gifted. Taken in the proper context, the gifted are similar in many ways to the general population, and hence there is much we can incorporate in our organization of learning that caters to all students. Consequently, we are tempted to modify traditional designs of learning for the gifted, rather than freshly conceptualize designs that integrate variables that are unique to the gifted population. We must keep in mind that, as far as gifted students are concerned, we are going to try our best to develop those special gifts or talents they possess, over and above general education.

The outcomes of curriculum design for the gifted manifest themselves in the special programs within the confines of the regular public school system, in numerous innovative type projects including those that provide for cultural diversity, and in private schools that are both generalized or specialized in thrusts. The better schools have built-in mechanisms for change and evolution to higher forms of learning that will ultimately result in the maximum growth of gifted individuals. The danger always exists of designing a curriculum that is static and not open to change. However, it is important to understand the design process as an ever-changing environment responsible for ensuring the proper unfolding of excellence.

CHAPTER TWELVE

Excellence in the Making

*I*NTRODUCTION

Any view of gifted education must take into account the many variables that not only comprise it but are themselves interactive. Early in our discussion, a Holistic Model for Educating Gifted Children (Figure 3.1) was presented to illustrate this interaction. If we were to begin with the "Individual" dimension of the model, we would note that the primary shaping forces rest with the "Environment." It is the Environment, in interaction with inherited life mechanisms, that is predisposed to establish human identity; it is responsible for the proper occurrence of maturation, fostering the growth and emergence of distinctly different adults.

The interaction of the Individual and Environment is integral to gifted education as it is to all education. Both have their origins in "Nature." They share a significant symbiotic partnership—what the Individual learns from the Environment allows necessary growth and greater command of the world in which he or she lives. Our observation and understanding of these mechanisms and processes have led to the development of an educational technology that, when applied, can accelerate learning.

Interventions are socially contrived to hasten the Individual's acquisition of information via the school curriculum and to determine his or her cultural identity. The procedures are meant to be facilitative but can be inhibitory. That is why those of us who serve as planners and managers of interventions need awareness and sensitivity to recognize these two forces, facilitation and inhibition, and deal with them in ways that will actualize potential.

To set all this in motion, we have attempted to study the differentials that distinguish gifted individuals and the procedures by which these differentials and, hence, these individuals can be identified. In this way, we expect to predict that if identified gifted individuals were placed in special educational programs, they would accrue maximum benefits for themselves and their society. Furthermore, we have studied factors that facilitate or hinder the development of gifted individuals with the goal of discovering the procedures that can be used to bring about positive self-realizing outcomes. We have also attended to the best ways to nurture the creative imagination of gifted individuals and optimize their learning potential.

Let us now take a brief look at what we have learned from our studies and what we can do to maximize the potential of gifted individuals.

DISCOVERING THE GIFTED

Conceptually, in the last 50 years, we have stopped viewing intelligence as "unchanging" and see it now as malleable—influenced to a large extent by experience. Furthermore, we have seen psychological theories of intelligence shift from native to informational; from unidimensional (general intelligence) to multidimensional (seven intelligences at least); and from global (verbal and performance) to a three-dimensional interactive intellect model (operations, content, and products). We have also explored the concept of componential or triarchic intelligence (metacomponents, performance components, and knowledge acquisition).

A theory that has gone beyond determining the nature of intelligence to one that sees in the nature of intelligence the potential for its development is the Structure of Intellect. As we know, the Structure of Intellect consists of three interactive dimensions: five inherited mental operations, four contents, and six product categories, which give 120 intellectual abilities (180 if figural content is viewed as comprising visual and auditory components, and operation of memory extended to retention and recording).

The inclusion of divergent production and evaluation thinking abilities as mental operations of the Structure of Intellect adds uniqueness and viability to the theory. Other theories have given no place to divergent thinking and neglected to give appropriate emphasis to evaluation in their paradigms. Furthermore, in the content dimension, the behavioral component gives due focus to an area of mental functioning that is lacking in mental testing, although earlier recognized as social intelli-

gence. Additionally, a relatively small place is given to classes of information in mental tests as well as near omission of transformation and
implication of the product dimension.

Unlike other theoretical models of intelligence that subscribe to a relatively unchanging mental function, the Structure of Intellect offers a potent frame of reference and tool for educating intellectual abilities and
maximizing their development and output. The Structure of Intellect
provides what Guilford has called a kind of grammar for thinking. Although it operationalizes intellectual functioning in a way that allows for
more systematic measurement, it does not directly provide a place for
the emotive-motivational dimension that is so important to divergent
production, more narrowly, and creative thinking, more broadly. More-
over, visual and auditory senses have now been clearly included in the
figural-content dimension and memory extended to include retention
and recording mental operations (Guilford, 1988). One can expect that in
the near future figural content may be extended to include other sensory
dimensions, especially the tactile and motoric. We have also seen the
potency of the model as its components are organized in a generic creative problem-solving model. Guilford's (1967) model more than any
other on intellectual functioning has pushed back the boundaries of
thought on the intellect; its full significance may only be realized with
the turn of the century.

We recognize now that giftedness is not to be equated with intelligence or intellectual abilities. Those committed to the gifted entered into
deliberations with the USOE in 1970 to explore the implications of this
insight. They concluded that there were at least six broad areas of giftedness, of which general intellectual ability or intelligence is only one. The
others were specific academic aptitude, creative or productive thinking,
leadership ability, visual-performing arts abilities, and psychomotor
ability (soon after discontinued from consideration as a category by the
United States Office of Education).

The federal government's recognition of these several areas of giftedness is very important, for prior to this, measured giftedness tended to
be equated with general intelligence expressed as I.Q. The expanded
concept of giftedness for specialized educational provisions has found
its way into legislation in many states, though many implementation
problems have yet to be overcome.

Let us take a look at each of these categories of giftedness in turn.

General Intelligence

Despite the fact that by 1970, 20 years had passed since the introduction
of the Structure of Intellect, federal policymakers were still clinging to
the concept of general intelligence as a major index of intellectual gifted-

ness, when it would have been more appropriate to have offered intellectual ability as an alternative index of giftedness. The use of general intellectual ability as a category of giftedness was, by that time, rooted in well-established tradition and practice; personnel were trained and available to test for it.

Still there is a need to reeducate psychometrists whose preparation limits them to perceive giftedness in terms of intelligence alone, and to provide in the curriculum of psychological training, if it is not already included, an expanded concept of giftedness and the competence to handle its measurement. The validity of sticking to general mental ability, the narrower concept of giftedness, as the sole criterion for identifying gifted children continues to be questioned. It is necessary to expand our understanding of the significance of having an operational information theory of intelligence that can reveal multiple intellectual abilities directly related to a variety of gifted dimensions.

Specific Academic Aptitude

The concept of specific academic aptitude as a category of giftedness is rooted in the recognition that Spearman (1927) gives to specific abilities in his two-factor theory of intelligence, as subsumed in the verbal-educational component of Vernon's (1951) hierarchical structure of human abilities.

Aptitude, unlike achievement, is potential, and its identification should serve as a predictor of certain kinds of learning, generally in school subjects. Achievement refers to measured outcomes of acquired learning. If it is a predictor index we want, then we should use the information derived from some measure of intellect or its relevant component. If a performance index is needed, then a standardized test in a school subject should be used.

However, what appears to be needed is some kind of prediction index that allows us to identify a gifted student with a particular academic ability and include him or her in special programs. We can do this by applying previous achievement indices developed in a certain area of specialization over time. Standardized test data, if available, may well serve the purpose. It is quite common to find, for instance, radical accelerates in mathematics identified by the mathematics component of the Scholastic Aptitude Test. What this test does is to indirectly identify aptitude through achievement. Such achievement measures may include the use of intellectual operations of cognition, memory, convergent production, and evaluation (to a lesser extent). We know that measures of achievement do not call for the use of divergent production or creative thinking.

Although achievement measures may give us information about individuals who have special academic aptitude, they will not give us information about those individuals who possess the capacity to extend the boundaries of knowledge in their areas of specialization. It is in this regard that measures of specific academic aptitude need refinement.

A reconceptualization of what abilities are to be put to work on specific curricula to reflect superior aptitude for learning in a certain subject area is wanting. In the design of instrumentation for such a purpose, due emphasis ought to be given to divergent production and evaluation mental operations as they relate to the handling of specific academic material. Furthermore, the content of this material relative to the Structure of Intellect needs to be organized in terms of classes, transformations, and implications in the product categories.

If the measures of intellectual abilities constructed by Guilford and his associates (Guilford, 1967) as they relate to the Structure of Intellect are not considered useful enough for the purpose of predicting those who have the aptitude to do well in a certain subject area, then other measures need to be constructed for that purpose.

The operational definition of abilities relative to content and product dimensions of the Structure of Intellect give more precise direction to the design of instruments that can predict more fully how well a person can handle advanced curricula. Pursuit of this approach should lead to the extension of boundaries in the identification of specific academic aptitude. Such explorations in test construction are waiting to be undertaken.

Creative Thinking

Because people do think in creative ways and traditional measures of intelligence do not provide ways to recognize this, creative or productive thinking was selected as yet another kind of giftedness. In terms of the Structure of Intellect, divergent production (creative thinking) is one of the five operations of intellectual functioning (six if memory is extended as retention and recording operations). But, divergent production is a missing dimension in I.Q. measures.

About 10 years before the federal definition of giftedness was formulated, measures of creative thinking abilities proliferated, the most comprehensive and well known of which are the Torrance Tests of Creative Thinking (Torrance, 1974b) and Thinking Creatively with Sounds and Words (Khatena & Torrance, 1990b). In addition, Guilford and his associates designed measures for testing adults (Guilford, 1967) and children (Creativity Tests for Children, 1973).

Theoretical formulations for the construction of measures of creativity took life, in the main, from Guilford's pronouncements in the 1950s about the Structure of Intellect. If we are looking for a major advance in thought on creative mental functioning, we have it in Guilford's and Torrance's development of the rationale and measurement of divergent production and creative thinking, respectively, as well as Khatena's (1984) work on the measurement of imagery and creative imagination. There is no doubt that boundaries in the field of measurement were extended by investigations of divergent production, creative thinking and their imagery, and imagination correlates; they will continue to expand as we understand more about the underlying nonintellective factors of these abilities.

The relevance and significance of the dimensions of divergent production and creative thinking, once recognized, led to studies in the 1960s that differentiated between high I.Q. and high-creative thinking abilities. The intent of these studies was more to assess the importance of including creative thinking in the identification process than to fractionalize intellect as creative and noncreative. But the findings that 70% of the top 20% obtaining high scores on measures of creativity would be missed on measures of I.Q. served almost to dichotomize the study of intellectual functioning.

If we pause to consider what mental operations are involved in creative thinking, we find that cognition, memory (retention and recording), convergent thinking, and evaluation all play their part in the process and that, as creative thinking is extended into problem solving, these several mental operations are noticeably called into action (Khatena, 1982b). Perhaps a reorientation that would pull together the separate tugs of intelligence and creativity under a model, such as the Structure of Intellect, may be productive. It may be that the traditional test format of identifying potential and aptitude would not leave out creative thinking, but would give it its due weight, providing information predictors for as many intellectual abilities as possible. The measures constructed by Guilford and his associates have already established the basic architecture to this end. It is now left to those who are innovative and competent in the field of measurement to break away from the traditional approach to testing and move in the direction of completing missing test components of the model, so as to extend the boundaries of the model as a whole.

Creative behavior is not just the result of creative thinking operations, but also the result of dynamic emotive-motivational forces—at one and the same time individual and sociocultural in origin—impinging on them. In keeping with this line of thought, psychologists engaged in measuring creative behavior have approached its identification by using biographical and self-perceptual instruments (e.g., Khatena & Torrance, 1990a). Expectations of predictive indices for the creative process, personality traits, and accomplishments must be moderated by considerations based on emotive-motivational and sociocultural factors, which must be taken into account by test constructors and their critics. Being more susceptible to variability, measures of creativity may not offer the same kind of predictive validity as measures of intelligence and their academic aptitude correlates.

Furthermore, attention needs to be given to the arrangements of conditions that will allow brief control of the dynamic properties of creative mental functioning so that as near accurate a sample of its processes as possible can be made. Because quantification is an important variable in arriving at a predictor index, there is much that remains to be done, both in refining scoring procedures to minimize subjectivity, and in seeking alternative ways to fetch, count, and explain responses to test stimuli.

Leadership

If the identification of the gifted relative to general intellectual ability, special academic aptitude, and creative or productive thinking is not free from problems—despite the advances that have been made in these areas in theory and instrumentation—identification of the gifted in the area of leadership presents even greater problems. For one thing, leadership was not linked with the study of giftedness until the USOE "recognized" the connection. For another, as a field of study, leadership had not concerned itself with identification of potential leaders with the view of enhancing their development, but with the view of using such individuals in leadership roles for specific tasks. Consequently, much of the study of leadership involved adults, and the research data that were generated concerned traits and qualities of mature individuals.

A definite step forward was taken when research recognized the complexity of the subject and turned its attention to the study of those variables that relate, on the one hand, to the dynamic interaction of the individual and group, and, on the other hand, to the individual in particular situations. Hence, leadership must be associated with person, group, and situation and their resultant interactions.

There is no single instrument available that can be used for the prediction of leadership potential. At best, we must rely on intellectual and creative ability, achievement, and personality-trait measures to give us the information we need to identify the personal dimension of leadership. For information on the social dynamics of leadership, we must rely on sociometric measures to determine an individual's relationship to the group relative to the performance of certain tasks. Furthermore, we must observe the individual in a real or simulated situation that requires leadership.

We have come a long way in our understanding of the dimension of leadership; we have had to derive much of this information obliquely, from individual and social psychology and group dynamics rather than from gifted education. However, our grasp of leadership as a category of giftedness is still incomplete and awaits rigorous investigation. We have to move away from regarding leadership as a matter of sheer ability, for not to do so would be to continue to oversimplify. Rather, we must conceive of leadership as a multidimensional phenomenon. Some work has been done, but it has led to the incomplete approach of identifying leadership by means of traits alone. Much more remains to be done to develop an appropriate rationale for the identification of leadership that includes the individual and group in dynamic relationship, and to design an effective approach for measuring this relationship.

Visual and Performing Arts

As is the case in the identification of leadership ability, abilities in the visual and performing arts are not readily measurable in terms of psychometric properties and techniques. The challenge is great and we must learn to understand the many variables involved more sensitively before we can even think of coming up with suitable approaches to measure giftedness in these areas.

Giftedness in the visual and performing arts is, by and large, not as closely related to the language of words as it is to the language system of the specific art form. When outstanding people in the visual and performing arts are administered an intelligence test that is verbally weighted to a high degree, it is not surprising to find that they show themselves to be average or normal. The reason is that they are called on by the test to show how well they think in a language system they use less frequently than in the language system of their specific art form. Besides, the mental operations that are called into action do not include creative thinking, which, for most of these individuals, is essential to their expression in one art form or another.

We are inclined to point out that much nonverbal activity occurs in the thinking and performance repertoire of artists. Although pointing this out is a way of differentiating the verbally gifted from the nonverbally gifted or talented, it does not communicate that artists use language unique to their art; that considerably more right-brain activity takes place in their mental functioning; and that much imagery occurs— especially in the visual, auditory, tactile and kinesthetic modalities—as input information for processing and as output forms of art expression.

Attempts have been made, over the years, to design measures of music and, to a lesser extent, measures of art talent, using the essentials of either of their language systems. However, these measures have yet to be proved effective predictors of talent brilliance. Furthermore, psychometric measures of other art talent are almost nonexistent. The recent shift from an awareness and appreciation of talent on the basis of product or performance to a need to identify talent potential for the purpose of providing special developmental opportunities brings with it a host of problems.

Psychometric approaches appropriate for identification of other forms of giftedness may not be as suitable for artistic talent; measures for this purpose remain to be developed. Alternative approaches must be sought that will ensure at least some elementary command of the language of the art form, the opportunity to apply this language in practice situations before assessment, and the exercise of the talent to allow creativity to manifest itself.

In general, nonpsychometric approaches to identification of talent may be the key. If this route is pursued, observational procedures containing criteria of specific relevance to the art form are needed to guide experts in the identification process. The observational approach requires close attention and study and may lead to, or be suggestive of, alternatives. The problem of effectively identifying potentially gifted students in the visual and performing arts is a pressing one that cannot be ignored if we are to provide special opportunities for them.

One of the research milestones previously referred to shows progress in the identification of human abilities using measures of intellectual processes as well as measures based on self-reports and self-perceptions of person, process, product, and press- or stress-related factors. This technique has been a major step forward, acknowledging, as it does, the credibility of autobiographical-perceptual data as predictive of present propensities (e.g., Khatena & Torrance, 1990a; Khatena & Morse, 1990, 1991; Taylor & Ellison, 1967). This approach, manifested in inventories intended to measure creativity and talent of various kinds, provides effective identification guidelines to the observer and the reporting individual. Its value has been increasingly recognized; one can expect the development of more instrumentation of this nature.

We are more inclined today to seriously consider that, beyond psychometric procedures, there may lie methods of appraising giftedness not fully investigated as yet. Individuals who do not reveal themselves and their abilities in formal measurement may be more likely to do so in informal situations. Appraisals of strengths indicative of talent can unobtrusively be made in nontest situations. Individuals can be placed in the context of a problem or social situation, for instance, with no clear-cut expectation of response, where open-endedness of response is maximized. In other words, individuals in such circumstances, freed from self-consciousness, can be themselves and engage in activity that incidentally projects their talent potential. This approach is particularly useful for the identification of culturally diverse and handicapped gifted individuals of school age.

NATURE OF INTELLECTUAL AND
MORAL GROWTH

Most of what we know about the developmental patterns of intellect and creativity has come from studies of the general population through the intelligence and factor components of the Wechsler scales. Almost no attention has been given to the development of intellect inclusive of creativity as it pertains to the gifted.

No systematic attempts have been made to study development as it relates to the Structure of Intellect. Guilford's (1967) inferences about Structure of Intellect abilities, based on the factor analytic work of L. L. Thurstone and T. L. Kelley, are the exception.

As for the study of complex intellectual abilities of gifted children growing up, almost nothing exists. It is interesting to note Guilford's (1967) rejection of Garrett's (1946) hypothesis. According to Garrett, multiple abilities develop from unitary ability of infants and younger children. Multiple abilities like those described by the Structure of Intellect appear more clearly with increasing age. Guilford disagrees with this view. He takes the position that young children have multiple abilities, which become increasingly complex with age. He does recognize that abilities related to his morphological factor model of intellect may not be the same for young children as they are for youth and adults. But as yet there are no studies on the direct rate of growth of Structure of Intellect abilities—an area open to much developmental research.

The study of intellectual and creative development may be approached in several ways. As it pertains to the individual's development, it may be regarded as continuous or discontinuous. Information about this aspect of an individual's development may be obtained from psychometrics or developmental stage theory. To study the intellectual and creative development of the individual in the context of general principles available to explain behavior, one has to go to a general systems theory, such as Gowan's (1972) on periodicity or Land's (1973) on transformation. As it pertains to the interaction of the individual and society, one can derive information from a study of historical patterns relative to the emergence of eminence (Simonton, 1978), or to the dynamic exchange between two open systems in a creativogenic society (Arieti, 1976).

What contributions have these various approaches made to the study of intellectual and creative development? The psychometric approach has shown that both intellectual and creative development can increase in adulthood, although some differentiation may have to be made among the functions of various abilities. It also points out that at the upper levels, tests do not discriminate very well, depending on test ceiling and intellectual superiority of the individuals.

That experience plays a much greater role in the development of intellect, is recognized. A fresh conceptualization of the nature and function of human abilities must follow in the wake of an information-operational theory of intelligence such as the Structure of Intellect, which facilitates a shift in emphasis from a heredity view of unitary intelligence to an interactive heredity-environment view of multidimensional abilities. Finally, the psychometric approach reveals that creative thinking abilities suffer drops at various grade or age levels. The severest of these drops appears around the fourth-grade level for children between the ages of 9 and 10; their recovery levels do not exceed the peaks attained in the third grade.

Gowan's (1972) theory of the development of creative individuals provides some corroboration for this drop in creativity. His model shows the period of the elementary school years (Stage 4) to be a time of low creative potential, when one can expect the occurrence of a slump in creative thinking abilities, whereas in the preschool years (Stage 3) creative potential is high.

Khatena's (1978a) findings of a drop in the production of original verbal imagery at about the same time as the fourth-grade slump and the earlier finding of Jaensch (1930) on the decrement of eidetic imagery of children as they grow older lead Gowan to speculate that this phenomenon may be the result of transfer from right-hemisphere processing of images to left-hemisphere processing of verbal materials. Gowan's developmental stage model extends the five cognitive stages of Jean Piaget to eight, giving emphasis to creativity in Stages 3, 6, and 9. It also gives new dimension to the Eriksonian adult stages of intimacy, generativity, and ego integrity in creativity as well as psychedelia and illumination or phase of mind expansion in Stages 7, 8, and 9.

Other contributions to thought on creative development relate to *periodicity*, a term carried over from quantum theory into behavioral science to indicate the occurrence of energy transformation that raises functioning from a lower to a higher level; to self-actualization as an escalation to higher developmental stages; to the occurrence of dysplasia or a slowing down of some part of an individual's development relative to the time it should take place; and to an emphasis on love as central to creation.

In terms of general systems as the source of some fresh insights relative to development, we turn to Land's (1973) transformation theory and Gowan's (1972) developmental stage theory. Both seek general principles to explain behavior. They perceive growth or development as occurring in triadic stages, with the attainment of one stage as preparatory to a transformation to the next higher level of development. However, whereas Gowan discusses growth in terms of escalation and dysplasia, Land speaks of it as destructuring and reintegration. Both see the involvement of analogical or metaphorical brain activity and imagery in the highest level of the creative process that prepares for transformation.

We turn to Simonton (1978) and Arieti (1976) for some fresh insights on sociocultural factors relating to the creative development of individuals. Simonton attributes greater importance to creators' developmental periods than to specific periods of their productivity; Arieti perceives creative development as emerging from the creative transactions of individuals with their creativogenic society.

According to Simonton, of the seven sociocultural influences that affect creative development resulting in actualization and adult eminence, formal education and role models have significant implications for education. Given what we know today about procedures that enhance creativity and intellectual activity, there is a good chance that we can reduce, if not prevent, the restrictiveness and narrowness of formal education.

We have already seen how misapplied formal education can adversely affect continuity in the development of creative thinking abilities, which are identified by psychometric procedures. In addition, we have learned that many approaches that offset some of the more gross aspects of misapplied formal education have been used with considerable success. It may be that with careful planning for an enlightened and stimulating curriculum as well as with the adoption of appropriate attitudes and educational stances, formal education will move in the direction of escalation and transformation, thereby helping gifted students to reach increasingly higher levels of achievement and growth toward an eminence that is so lacking in the present-day world. Good role models are hard to find, but there is nothing to prevent us from using historical figures along with our contemporaries as touchstones for our gifted, as we encourage them to strive for eminence.

The extent to which we can adapt, adopt, and even create conditions identified by Arieti as existing in a creativogenic society for use in gifted education needs to be seriously explored. These conditions may provide additional clues which help gifted children attain adult eminence.

Another condition for which we should strive is the exposure of students to all facets of culture. In this way, memory storage and retrieval of information can be transformed into creative productions by gifted individuals using creative imagination.

Education should emphasize interaction with significant people in a climate that encourages and tolerates divergent views and promotes self-actualization. After severe oppression or absolute exclusion, freedom or even moderate discrimination are conditions that are difficult to use as incentives to creativity in designing an education program. Where adverse conditions are present and release from them can be implemented, then, such conditions must be simulated to provoke creativity to function and express itself. One may see in Simonton's and Arieti's propositions for growth toward eminence within a social context many possibilities for scientific study.

It is appropriate at this juncture to consider the moral development that results from the shaping interactions of the individual and society in the growing up process. Morality arises because the individual lives in a social context. In itself, morality does not exist. Living as a group necessitates the generation of a system of rules that is integral to sociocultural tradition. The rules become codified in time to provide a frame of reference for individual behavior.

Any consideration of morality must recognize its social origins. As such, moral systems, although possessed of common elements, vary according to the sociocultural group that gave them life. A socially based system of morality acquires divinity when tied to a religious belief system, for example, behavior that is illegitimate in terms of social morality becomes sinful when judged by the precepts of religious morality.

We have learned that morality consists of intellectual and emotive components: reasoning and evaluation, on the one hand; attitudes and values, on the other. Individuals follow rules but also make choices. The tension between the two creates the evolving conditions of stability, mutation, hybridization, and return to a new stability. These conditions determine change in the social ethics of a society, which are at one and the same time fixed and flexible. What is resistant to change is divine-given morality, but even then, a society can effect change by way of reinterpreting existing moral laws.

There is no lack of theories on moral development. However, the underlying roots of such theories are similar in that their origins lie with the personal and social, often deified by religion. Different perspectives on moral development theory arise from the larger theoretical formulations of individuals who express them. The extent to which an individual can make free choices relative to existing moral codes will depend on the sociopolitical system the individual lives under. In a democratic society, a mature morality is one that allows individual growth toward autonomy in the context of a moral code of ethics.

Morality is something individuals learn from others, beginning with parents, immediate family, friends, and neighbors, and later from school and other social institutions. Consequently, morality can be incorporated in our educational plans. It is important that we recognize the informational contents of morality. For intellect operates on them in the learning and doing processes. In particular, references are made to moral reasoning and judgment with no deliberate attempt to separate mental process from moral content.

We should note that other Structure of Intellect mental operations are also involved—cognition, memory, and divergent thinking are brought into play in activity of a moral nature. What this means is that we can design moral learning experiences as we can any other learning experiences, to cultivate moral behaviors of individuals growing up. Many approaches to moral education have been suggested; it would be remiss not to remind ourselves of the power of the Structure of Intellect and its organized generic problem-solving system to effect this education as well.

Finally, as moral education applies to the creatively gifted, we must emphasize the need to design learning experiences that inculcate an understanding of moral responsibility. Many kinds of teaching methodology, from the techniques of questioning, discussion, and discourse to techniques associated with imagery and creative imagination, and sociodrama, can be used to achieve this end.

Situations and events related to moral issues can be contrived, simulated, and examined by these aforementioned and powerful educational tools. By recognizing the teachability of moral behavior, understanding, and responsibility, and being cognizant of the superior command we have today of learning-teaching machinery and technology, we place ourselves in an advantageous position to design a moral education curriculum for our gifted that can only serve to better the society in which we live.

OVERCOMING PROBLEMS OF UNDERACHIEVEMENT

The reconceptualization of abilities as being multiple rather than singular, and as having an interactive heredity-environment base rather than being solely inherited has important consequences for our thinking about the problems that gifted children face and their need to adjust to them. Many problems that gifted children face lead to underachievement—traditionally perceived as a mismatch between I.Q. potential and school achievement. However, because of a change in our perception, we now study underachievement as it relates to multipotentiality (Khatena, 1982a). A broadened concept of giftedness puts underachievement relative to multipotentiality in proper perspective.

Development Stage Theory

If underachievement were to be thought of in terms of developmental stage theory, it may be referred to as developmental arrest or dysplasia, where cognitive or emotive development do not occur together at each developmental stage. (Studying the problem of dysplasia as it applies to gifted women students, we have begun to recognize a number of developmental variables that prevent or hinder women's rise to higher levels of functioning toward self-actualization and potentiality for adult eminence.)

Unfulfilled Creativity

Underachievement has also come to be regarded as unfulfilled creativity. That is, an intelligent person underachieves not because of motivational lack but because of not having opportunities to be creative. It is more appropriate today to consider underachievement, not in the restrictive sense of lower performance level in schooling but in a broader sense that includes all areas of talent where performance is below superior level.

Handicapped Gifted

We now recognize that the handicapped gifted student's deficit functions in school subjects is not attributable so much to lack of ability as it is to the student's disability. Hence a more appropriate orientation toward disabled students' being potentially gifted can be expected.

Nonintellective Talent Factors

We also recognize that nonintellective talent must be taken into account in appraising student performance in school, for it is quite easy to neglect such talent performance when one is looking for achievement in regular school subjects. That is why achievement in school has to be screened in terms of several dimensions of talent rather than being restricted to an assessment of performance in the academic subjects of a school curriculum.

Cultural Diversity

Our better understanding of sources of cultural diversity factors in underachievement can be expected to lead to the development of better approaches to identifying talent potential. This understanding helps us when we plan experiences for growth that accentuate creative positives, and when we provide programs that are future oriented.

Developmental Arrest of Gifted Girls

As underachievement relates to developmental arrest of girls growing up, we have now begun to understand that there are many contributory factors, including role expectation, sex typing of social roles, creativity that tends to be determined by socialization, different patterns of achievement motivation, achievement that oscillates between direct and vicarious rewards, and reliance on factors of contingency and discrepancy.

Problems Directional to Research

What we know today about the problems of special groups of under-achievers, such as the handicapped and culturally diverse gifted and gifted girls experiencing developmental arrest, and underachievement as a function of misassessed potential and performance is more than we knew a few years ago. But this knowledge is only a beginning. We will need to continue to research these problems and also search for special groups of gifted not as yet identified, so that we can maximize their educational growth.

Research and practice must especially focus on problems related to the proper identification of potential in many areas of giftedness, bearing in mind the deficits of measurement that pertain to special groups, choice of criteria as appropriate predictors of achievement, selection of rationale, and planning of educational experiences that will facilitate the growth of these unique groups of individuals.

Particular attention should be paid to developmental variables as they affect escalation toward higher levels of actualization of talent, and as they test the relevance of hypotheses they generated. It will be hard to exhaust the possibilities for research and its practical application in the problem areas of giftedness. This is borne out by the special relevance of our increasing awareness of and expected support for different kinds of gifted students.

FACILITATING DEVELOPMENT

As a result of the concept that the gifted are people who can make it on their own and, hence, do not need educational and related facilitative intervention, guidance was not at first perceived to be necessary for them. When it was realized that gifted individuals could also benefit from guidance, proponents concentrated their efforts on providing gifted individuals with educational and vocational guidance. Guidance for adjustment problems, although additionally provided, was less conspicuous.

Gowan (1979a) has indicated that there was no curriculum for guidance, and charged that for rationale and procedure, guidance tends to draw on the medical model of psychotherapy. The chief concern of psychotherapy is the treatment of abnormal problems of adults on a private and long-term basis, where attention is crisis oriented. Gowan maintained that guidance should concern itself with the developmental problems of normal children involving association with them on a short-term basis. Preventative measures that would help gifted individuals attain high levels of self-actualization and mental health were advocated by him.

The importance of developmental stage theory, its creativity dimensions, and its key features of escalation and dysplasia, are emphasized as basic to guidance curricula for the preparation of counselors of the gifted. Such curricula give direction to preventative guidance aimed at helping gifted students realize high levels of creativity and attain good mental health.

The need for guidance by gifted people striving toward higher levels of creativity finds corroborative evidence in Land's transformation theory, where growth cycles in creative functioning of a lower order move on to cycles of growth of an increasingly higher order. The concepts of destructuring and reintegration at the mutualistic stage of each cycle prior to transformation for the next higher level of functioning has significance for guidance of the gifted. They provide the framework for a fresh look at success, allowing the components comprising them to be reexamined. A restructuring of the field, which includes hitherto unperceived information and alternatives for a transformation that begins a new but higher level cycle of growth, follows.

Because the gifted are on a course of accelerated development, escalation and transformation will ensure that intellectually and creatively they proceed not to single frontiers of attainment, but to multiple frontiers of increasing order. Nothing has been written on the subject of transformation theory as it relates to guidance. The application of its apparent power needs careful thought and investigation. Together, Gowan and Land offer startling new directions to guidance.

Moving from the gifted person as an individual to the gifted person in interaction with others, we recognize that there are factors in a social setting that either facilitate or hinder development. From Simonton's and Arieti's observations of conditions that foster growth of gifted individuals to eminence, we learn that guidance can make accessible historical and contemporary eminent creators as models for emulation. Where feasible, arrangements can be made for some of these eminent people to act as mentors for the gifted. In addition, guidance can make available materials, equipment, varieties of cultural exposure, and stimulation. Guidance can also apply a system of rewards and incentives to effect healthy change, moving from the extrinsic to the intrinsic, to encourage and endorse efforts toward higher levels of self-realization.

Another forward-looking approach in guidance is the inclusion of strategies that assist gifted students in coping with or mastering stress. Much of the stress experienced by the gifted arises from adjustment problems that they have to face daily in their transactions and interactions with a society that, generally, does not understand or tolerate divergence, which is often a part of striving for uniqueness. Counselors can plan a preventative rather than curative guidance program for gifted students once the origins of their stress are recognized.

Torrance's discussions of the subject have great relevance for counselors involved in the guidance of gifted students. He suggests, among several approaches for coping with stress, strategies that hinge on the development of interpersonal skills and the use of Structure of Intellect abilities organized for creative problem solving.

Movement in the field of academic guidance for the gifted has been from assisting students to plan programs of study as they relate to regular school offerings to planning accelerative learning in school subjects at more advanced levels. Counselors may also make available to gifted students many more study alternatives in areas of knowledge that are less frequently examined but that are of interest. Guidance emphasis has shifted from providing counsel for choice of school subjects to the total development of the individual. Fresh attitudes toward guidance as an ongoing process at all stages of growing up gifted is necessary. In addition, new attitudes toward guiding gifted individuals in lower socioeconomic groups also need to be adopted so that appropriate attention be given to the differential needs of the culturally diverse.

When directed toward the gifted, career guidance, unlike vocational guidance (as it was formerly known), does not only attempt to make job information and experience available but also takes into account the individual's needs, especially those needs that arise from the individual's interaction with the social environment. This involved a major shift in focus, because such guidance recognizes that addressing itself to information about the work world alone is insufficient. Individual differences must be taken into account as must transactions among individuals, the world of work, and the congruence that may emerge from the relations individuals have with the outside world.

The model proposed by Perrone, Karshner, and Male (1979) takes these and related factors into account. As a consequence, the dynamics structuring an individual's orientation of self, social awareness, understanding, and organized-planning toward goal attainment and evaluation facilitate development toward a career. Just as in other areas of guidance, career guidance is thought of as an ongoing process that begins in early childhood and continues for many years after adulthood is reached. Career guidance for the gifted takes into account needs, motivations, goals, interactions of self with others, and a variety of job opportunities that can be expected to serve them in substantial and profitable ways.

Sociodrama is a dynamic procedure that facilitates career guidance of the gifted. It is a technique that goes beyond the benefits of role playing, assisting students in understanding their abilities, interests, and feelings as these relate to careers. Aimed at clarification and solution finding, sociodrama allows the creative problem-solving process to approach the examination of potential problems in careers, calling into service the powerful dynamics of drama.

Primarily, sociodrama for educational use is preventative rather than therapeutic. It is group-centered and highly suited to the classroom. A viable approach, sociodrama assists in matching the multiple talents, abilities, and interests of gifted students with a variety of possible careers. By this method, group exploration, values clarification, fresh insights, and consensual validation of careers and their attendant problems seen in microcosm as preparation for the real thing, are encouraged and legitimized. When sociodrama as it relates to specific career choices and to more general guidance problems is seen as a valuable additional tool for guidance of the gifted, it may become more widely used and, thus, may be the occasion for research aimed at testing its effectiveness.

While all of the preceding discussion is applicable to the culturally diverse gifted, two additional propositions are of great interest to this group. One relates to Exum's (1979) model that addresses the emotional needs of gifted black students by teaching interpersonal skills, encouraging creativity in laboratory sessions, matching student-teacher interests through team teaching and laboratory experiences, decreasing isolation and increasing sensitivity to specific problems, and encouraging the perception that a oneness exists between observer and observed.

The other proposition (Exum, 1983) concerns itself with counseling black families (nuclear, extended, or augmented). As many members of the gifted black student's family as possible need to be involved in the counseling process. The counselor should have an awareness of the psychosocial orientation of the family and the four styles of adjustment to racism (preencounter, encounter, immersion, and emersion). Counseling the black gifted in the context of family is of the utmost importance. A close awareness and understanding of the special variables associated with the culturally diverse black gifted have important implications for effective counseling, if it is to establish the kind of communication that will make meaningful help possible.

NURTURING CREATIVE IMAGINATION

The study of creative imagination is rather new, but it is promising and provocative in itself and in its creative educational implications for all children. Not many years have elapsed since Richardson (1969) and Paivio (1971) observed that little, if any, serious work had been done to study creative imagination imagery. Since then, Khatena (1984, 1987) has done much to reduce the gap in this area of knowledge.

The most important happening in the 1970s relative to the study of imagery is the fact that with the resurgence of interest in imagery by psychologists of various persuasions behaviorism relinquished its 30-year hold on this field of inquiry. Their writings (e.g., Ahsen, 1977; Kaufmann, 1980; Shepard, 1978) established beyond doubt the significance of this field of study. Over the past few years there has been a proliferation of research on imagery as well as the formation of at least two national or international organizations and their journal publications, and the organization of many major conferences dedicated to the subject.

Findings from various studies on eidetic and imagination imagery have become increasingly valuable to psychotherapy (e.g., Ahsen, 1977; Shorr, 1977) and are quite extensively used by clinical psychologists and certain members of the medical profession to assist their patients in regaining their health.

Imagery's value to learning has been established by B. R. Bugelski (1970), A. Paivio (1971), and others. Nonetheless, it has not found its way, in any significant sense, into the classroom as a valuable learning tool. Translating research findings on imagery into teaching practice will require much work. For example, we have hardly begun to study one of the most important resources of the human brain, the creative imagination, in terms of its use as a tool to facilitate learning.

The study of imagery as it relates to the creative imagination has just begun and should receive strong impetus from continuing research on the brain. We have discussed how imagery, preconscious activity, and creativity are related; we have demonstrated the importance of imagery to problem solving in the incubation and illumination stages, and in visionizing (Parnes, 1988); we have encountered its use in psychogenics particularly as applied to discovery and healing (Wenger, 1979); and we have seen it presented as the language of intuitive imagination (Rockenstein, 1989). Furthermore, eminent persons in the arts and sciences have testified that they felt vibrations and experienced imagery as precursors to creative ideation, invention, or composition.

Today, better understanding of imagery processes have led to the presentation of techniques that can be used to tap this productive resource of mind. Some good approaches in this regard are available (Bagley & Hess, 1982; Gaylean, 1983; Plum, 1980). Perhaps the only work that gives particular focus to the use of imagery as it is processed by creative imagination is the one by Khatena (1984). All of these studies merit our serious consideration for use in the classroom for all children to enhance learning.

On instrumentation, we have moved from simple self-reports of imagery experiences to more complex ones. Among these are the assessment of streams of experience characterizing current everyday thinking (Klinger, 1978); and unobtrusive probing for information about imagery, cognitions, and feelings (Sheehan, McKonkey, & Cross, 1978). In addition, there are several measures of eidetic imagery, one of which uses eidetics to build on a patient's sense of reality and the pressure of fantasy and emotional history to open up many levels for developmental analysis (Ahsen, 1972).

Apart from Thinking Creatively with Sounds and Words (Khatena & Torrance, 1990b), no instruments have been used to study imagery and the creative imagination. As we know from its earlier description, the measure consists of two components, whose logic hinges on the operation of creative imagination to effect a break away from the perceptual set of audio or audio-visual-verbal stimuli to produce original images. Through this instrument, we have come to better understand those variables that are impinging on the stimulation of creative thinking on imagery, incubation-illumination imagery in problem solving, autonomous imagery, developmental patterns of imagery, and relationship of sense modalities on the production of creative imagery (Khatena, 1984). The research done so far (Khatena, 1987) only prefaces the need for further study of imagery and the creative imagination.

Gowan, Khatena, and Torrance (1979) have pointed to the importance of incubation in the problem-solving process as a sufficient condition for illumination and production of right-hemisphere imagery. Although a good repertoire of educational techniques used in preparation for creativity are available (e.g., Meeker, 1980a; F. E. Williams, 1972), equally strong techniques for incubation are hard to find, with the exception of Thinking Creatively with Sounds and Words (Khatena & Torrance, 1990b), which allows and encourages production of imagery and analogies.

On the subject of analogies Upton (1961) emphasizes the shift in the development of thinking from categorizations to analogy and finally to isomorphics, or to a study of the equivalences in analogies. Thinking by analogy and imagery can be facilitated by various incubation techniques that sever the dominance of the left-cerebral hemisphere and allow right-cerebral hemisphere activity. Synergistic cooperation between the hemispheres permits the right hemisphere to pick up the images and the left hemisphere to translate them into alphanumeric form (Gowan, 1979b, 1979d).

The importance of incubation in the creative thinking process must not be underestimated, although establishing it has proven elusive and problematic when studied experimentally (Olton, 1979). Except for brief periods that last for minutes only, it is difficult to control what subjects do during the period of incubation, other than their incubation activity (Guilford, 1979). In addition, subjects have the task of avoiding premature closure so that they may give due emphasis to the role of transformation.

However, enough is known about incubation to justify attempts to teach problem solvers to use it successfully (Guilford, 1979; Khatena, 1984). Torrance (1979a) suggests a three-stage instructional model for enhancing incubation: an introductory stage that arouses anticipation and heightens expectations, a second stage that deepens involvement and a commitment that goes beyond the superficial, and a third stage that keeps the thought process active.

Other ways to encourage gifted students to use incubation for the production of imagery have been suggested by Khatena in several books (Khatena, 1979a, 1980, 1984). Imagery and incubation properties have greatly interested the Willings International Center for Innovation in the United Kingdom to use them in therapeutic settings and with gifted underachievers for career guidance (Willings, 1988). Another viable source on incubation presents it as a teaching model (Torrance & Safter, 1990). The model guides teachers to search for their own insights so that they may lead their students to new and productive levels of learning.

Research on creative imagination imagery can be expected to continue vigorously, with special attention given to developmental factors, sensory disability and adaptations, and underachievement. Various subgroups, including the gifted and talented, culturally diverse gifted, and emotionally disabled gifted are to be included in these studies. Furthermore, the design of new instruments and scoring systems that allow creative potential and personality variations to be identified is an area that needs exploration. Construction of deliberate nurturing procedures that enhance not only educational development but also high levels of productivity is another priority.

We are at the brink of important discoveries in the field of human abilities as they relate to creative functioning. These discoveries can be expected to go far beyond the quantification of responses to given test stimuli. We expect that these studies will tell us something about the creative intellect—more far reaching than mere retrieval of information for processing by various mental operations—and give us knowledge of what, in fact, is involved in the process of metamorphosis and catalytic thinking.

Stimulating the intellect in the context of the process education advocated for the many now finds relevance for gifted students. Such an education is expected to provide individual expansion of abilities, facilitate intellectual-affective growth, turn over direction of learning to the student, and allow for adaptation of knowledge and skills acquired to changing circumstances. The early emphasis on the need for process education in the 1930s found expression in the 1960s and 1970s in the construction of various training procedures to develop thinking tools that emphasize creativity and problem solving.

The growing recognition of the added benefits of integrating process with curriculum led to the development of several good models. Of particular note are two that have as their basic rationale the Structure of Intellect—one uses all five Guilfordian mental operations (Meeker, 1980a); the other confines itself to creativity, combining it with an affective component in one dimension and teacher behaviors in another dimension (F. E. Williams, 1972). Early sequential problem-solving steps have developed into more elaborate paradigms that give greater emphasis to creativity, both in its cognitive and emotive aspects. More recently, this development has found powerful expression in the dramatic situation of sociodrama (Torrance, 1975c).

Another development in creative problem solving can be found in a systems approach (Guilford, 1967; Land, 1973). A systems-based conceptual model not only takes into account numerous variables in sequential order but also shows them as interrelated, interactive, and looped, so that the conclusion of one problem-solving activity is the beginning of another. Furthermore, a systems approach offers a generic model from which other models can take life. Emphasis is on the individual's transactions and use of the environment, with positive and negative feedback for feedforward as important mechanisms in the problem-solving process whose aim is adaptation and adjustment to an ever-changing environment.

All in all, as educators we need to come to grips with advances made in identifying processes that nurture the intellect and creative imagination. Their use in everyday life activities, in general, and in formal education, in particular, holds tremendous promise for productive, effective, and satisfying living. The least we can do is to get to know well from direct experience the mechanisms of a couple of these process approaches and to learn how to use them before planning to use them with gifted students. We also need to acquire the sensitivity to know when to use intellectual processes and resources in and for themselves, and when to apply them to curriculum content to facilitate learning that can eventually extend the boundaries of knowledge and our existence.

OPTIMIZING LEARNING

Of all aspects of giftedness, nurture is of greatest interest to professional educators because it is the business and province of experts. The professional educator should have more to say about nurture than about anything else concerning the gifted. Nurture is primarily what the demand for legislation and funds is all about, namely, the provision of special educational opportunities for gifted students. We are led to ask important questions: How different are such special provisions for gifted students in formal education than the provisions made for their less able peers? How justifiable are they? Have changes, in fact, taken place in the past 30 or 40 years that show that we have moved forward to differentiated and defensible educational programs in school for the gifted? If so, what are these changes?

For one thing, we see a broadened conceptualization of acceleration that includes enrichment emerging. Accelerative enrichment should be the key to this different approach to educational opportunity.

We have seen various kinds of acceleration methods advocated over the years, but deliberate preparation in terms of identification and study arrangements for the advanced placement of radical accelerates gives acceleration preparation a sharper focus and has begun to win convinced support in many quarters of the country for it. First tried in the area of mathematics (Stanley, 1977b), its success has led to the development of a similar accelerative program for the study of languages at advanced levels (Stanley & George, 1980). We can expect acceleration of this kind to spread to other areas of knowledge as well. The Purdue University advanced placement program is an example of this (Feldhusen, Proctor, & Black, 1986). Purdue's approach to identification is related to special aptitudes in mathematics and language that have been screened by standardized achievement tests. Such tests are used to predict academic aptitude.

The general enrichment approach as practiced is steadily giving way to a more deliberate and closely focused one that makes a distinction between exploratory activities and group-training activities suitable for many. The goal of this approach is to prepare individuals for the investigation of real problems with production and recognition as end results. This approach was presented as the "Enrichment Triad" (Renzulli, 1979a). An extension of this approach is known as the Revolving Door Identification Model (Renzulli, Reis, & Smith, 1981), through which students are identified for a program in mind. In this instance, the special use of identification is not related to a specific subject but to a program of studies for the gifted.

We should note that the first approach follows a narrow track of academic achievement by study of a content area at advanced levels, while the second aims at preparation for the acquisition of knowledge of content and process that leads to investigative competence and resultant productivity. However, what distinguishes accelerative enrichment now from earlier approaches is that it is not cumulative but transformative, so that it facilitates increasing levels of intellectual growth.

Effective nurture of the gifted involves the interplay of the many variables discussed. It necessitates the maintenance of a delicate balance among these variables to achieve the best results. We realize from experience that teaching the gifted to make use of their intellectual resources more fully requires helping them understand the processes involved and giving them practice in their use.

Process, in itself, is insufficient because it must be an integral part of learning content. Just like the interactive dimensions of the Structure of Intellect, process must react to or act upon various kinds of curricula information organized in different ways. Furthermore, especially as it pertains to gifted students, the presence of wide variations in talent potential gives greater focus to individual differences and provision has to be made for them. Consequently, there continues to be an increasing emphasis in education to individualize instructional programs. In this way, the problem of making suitable educational provisions for the individual is attacked with more precision than was possible with the earlier innovative efforts of the progressive school movement.

Individualization of learning programmed instruction based on the principles of operant conditioning is of great value for the average and below-average student. But it will not serve the gifted as well, as learning moves away from basics toward higher levels of intellectual functioning. This is not to say, however, that judicious use of the teaching machine for self-learning of the basic subjects as a means of preparation for more advanced knowledge acquisition and thinking cannot be made. But the energy lies not in extrinsic but in intrinsic motivation as competence increases.

One word of caution concerning the suitability of specific individualized instruction programs for gifted students and the extent to which qualitative differences exist is necessary. Instruction provided by the teaching machine and by programmed learning determines the efficient acquisition of basic content, whereas progressive education approaches allow greater individual freedom in learning experience. Both methods plan learning for all students.

Unlike these approaches, individualized education for the gifted as designed has built-in provisions for uniqueness of individual talent and learning style, suitable instructional procedures, and built-in conditions for flexibility and change. In addition, such individualized education reflects concern for the unknown and future as well as for the known, past and present. There is student involvement in the planning of what is to be learned. Inquiry tools and research methodology that call for the use of intellectual processes aimed at creative learning and production are also built-in requirements. Other factors in individualizing learning experiences for the gifted include careful planning, management, and evaluation relative to explicit criteria determined in advance to document student change and progress.

Conceptualization of curriculum for the gifted has moved from the strategy of imparting to students as much as is known about various areas of knowledge to that of making accessible repositories of knowledge and exciting discovery initiatives. Curriculum today deemphasizes memorization of fact and detail for quick recall in favor of productive learning of ideas seminal to higher levels of intellectual growth. The narrower use of intellectual resources directional to the known and correct has given way to the broader use of resources that are generative of the unknown and probable. From the strictures of regular school curricula to the freedoms of curricula that lead to the frontiers of knowledge are now stronger givens. There is also a move from unidisciplinary to multidisciplinary learning, and from curricula as information acquisition to curricula as tools to be used in gaining access to ever-expanding horizons of excellence.

Special provisions for the gifted are associated with organizing curricula and methodologies as programs that are expected to better meet the needs of the gifted. Innovative aspects of programs are to be seen in projects that are peripheral rather than central to regular school offerings. Programs central to regular schooling are less frequently found in public schools. Instead, they have found expression in special schools for the gifted, which tend to be private.

By and large, our schools appear to be continuing in the traditional enrichment and accelerative practices that are familiar to us. Although catchy in title, projects are not, with a few exceptions, highly innovative in conceptualization or practice. Special schools have to make considerable refinements to their curricula if they are to provide for the uniqueness of gifted students admitted to their programs. Such schools have to include and integrate in their curricula the most recent thoughts on use of intellectual resources and processes. The movement must be away from traditional enrichment and acceleration to accelerative enrichment as precursor to escalation to higher levels of intellectual growth.

Projects tend to be less stable and have more transitory provisions for the gifted. They are tryout grounds for innovative ideas. Often, however, except for those programs that have struck out in the directions of accelerative enrichment, they have not veered away from traditional innovations in practice. Deliberate development of intellectual abilities and processes, problem-solving and affective skills, and adoption of the diagnostic-prescriptive approach using a curriculum purposefully to educate abilities in the context of individualization are required if the needs of gifted students are to be adequately met.

Sadly lacking in number are projects planned to provide for the nurture and development of talent in the various areas of the visual and performing arts. There can be expected improvement of this situation in the near future. Identification procedures must not just involve administering several instruments to individuals to find out if they are intellectually gifted, as is the common practice. The intent of screening should be to discover the different talents that students possess so that they may be placed in programs that are central to talent development.

As for the number of operative projects, the past 15 years have shown a substantial increase with every indication that this trend will continue. What is highly desirable is that more and more of these projects become integrated in regular schooling rather than assume the character of satellite programs that are always threatened with financial discontinuance and consequent demise. Finally, present-day evaluation procedures not only assess predicted exit outcomes of a project relative to its objectives and design but also provide information on an ongoing basis for program refinement at various stages so that feedback becomes feedforward information for continued growth.

Another closely related aspect of nurture is motivation. As motivation pertains to the gifted, the emphasis is on the establishment of inner controls rather than outer controls, intrinsic rather than extrinsic managers of behavior and effort. The emphasis must shift from habit and conditioning to growth toward higher states and levels of functioning. For the gifted student, effective motivational forces are to be found in competence-effectance, incongruity-dissonance, and feedback for feedforward information processing. Growth needs relative to esteem, self-actualization, knowing and understanding, and aesthetics are also powerful hierarchically organized motivators. To these must be added the power of motivation that is inherent in creative ways of learning, and in the perception individuals have of what they would want to become in the future.

CONCLUSIONS

As this text comes to a close, it is appropriate to summarize our thoughts on the education of gifted students. A priority has been to make some sense of the terms *gifted* and *talented*. We have discovered that the terms are synonymous although different interpretative definitions exist. The semantics of the word *gifted* include multidimensional abilities and talents that are peculiar to the individual. We now know that environment plays a much larger part in interacting with hereditary factors to facilitate the unfolding of excellence. That social value systems determine what is or is not *giftedness* adds to the relative nature of the term. Creativity is recognized as the single most powerful energizing factor in human functioning, one that goes beyond abilities to include the interactive influences of intellective, emotive, and motivational forces. It should also be noted that goal-directed behaviors, task commitment, and operational dimensions that influence their productivity have been given much greater notice today.

Although we currently possess many assessment devices, we have a long way to go before the many categories of giftedness can be appropriately identified. Successful construction of well-designed instruments will have to be designed by those willing to invest time and effort. We must not minimize the problem of implementation, which includes training personnel whose understanding of giftedness goes beyond using I.Q. and academic achievement as indices. Nor should we minimize the problem of providing money to carry out these tasks.

One of the least explored areas of giftedness is that of development. Some data are available on intellectual and creative development but little else is available that relates to other areas of talent. Information about the development of gifted students provides important clues to what we can do to maximize their growth potential. What we know about the severe drop in creative thinking abilities is helping us to offset this problem to some extent by stimulating creative processes, alleviating stress, and providing needed support during critical developmental phases.

Developmental stage theory as extended to include creativity, certainly has great import for educational practice and counseling. Periodicity as an indicator of the transformation of energy required for escalation to higher levels of functioning is pertinent to creative leaps, which are so necessary for gifted students in their move toward actualization and eminence. Periodicity alerts us to changes in mental growth that transcend acceleration that occur among the gifted.

The triadic model of developmental stage theory is a systems approach that accounts for discontinuous growth in individuals. Transformation theory is an interesting variation of this systems approach. It cuts across chronology to account for many kinds of growth (accretive, replicative, and mutualistic), occurring at different stages and levels in triadic sequence. As the organized pattern approaches perfection, it begins to break down or destructure. Reorganization of reintegration of elements constituting the earlier structure involves the inclusion of other elements from the environment. This is preparatory to the occurrence of transformation for the next triadic movement at a higher level. Both these conceptual models have important implications for creative development of gifted students, especially as they aspire to higher levels of intellectual growth as well as when they need guidance.

The current approach to the issue of guidance involves taking into account the person as a whole. In our attempts to render help, we tend to move from crisis-oriented and therapy-rooted intervention to guidance that concerns itself with developmental problems of the normal child. This approach takes a preventative rather than a curative stance. An important feature of guidance today is the consideration of the question of individual creativity and the direction that is to be taken to facilitate its development in gifted students, enabling them to achieve high levels of intellectual functioning, self-actualization, and good mental health.

We have learned something about the nature of stress and its inhibitory and destructive characteristics, which can be reduced if not prevented by using guidance to equip gifted students with coping strategies. Guidance can be expected to continue to integrate academic and career advisement and direction on a continuing basis.

We have also become aware of the importance of the benefits of a creativogenic society to the gifted individual. However, if we cannot have such benefits in macrocosm, then we should attempt to achieve them in microcosm, so that conditions can be created to foster maximum creative growth in a school setting.

Any attempt to cater to gifted individuals must bear in mind the interests of special groups. These interests may relate to an expanded concept of underachievement and a consideration of minorities and the culturally diverse, the influence of disabilities and handicaps, and the special developmental problems experienced by girls in a society that stereotypes sex-role behaviors.

We might also look forward to increasing support from various national, federal, state, and local agencies and organizations. As more people become increasingly knowledgeable about giftedness, we can expect legislation and funding that mandate special opportunities for the gifted in all states. We can also expect many more institutions of higher learning to become responsive to the task of training teachers skilled in techniques for the education of gifted individuals.

The rich diversity of approaches that may appear separate in the nurturing process, the procedures and programs that are practiced, need to be pulled together to become integral components of curricula and central to regular schooling. Such a process, however, must have built-in mechanisms for evolving change and transformation to higher and more productive intellectual levels so that education creates open systems of energy exchange for dynamic growth.

Let us end by considering innovative or inventive attempts to achieve gifted excellence as reaching for the rainbow, even when all we can do is to imaginatively extend an outstretched hand and momentarily reach for it. The rainbow, a composite of refracted light whose beauty the artist can at best capture in fleeting imitation, perhaps serves us as a symbol of hope and promise for future educational articulation.

References

Abell, A. M. (1964). *Talks with great composers.* Garmisch-Partenkirchen, West Germany: E. Schroeder-Verlag.

Ahsen, A. (1972). *Eidetic Parents Test and analysis.* New York: Brandon House.

Ahsen, A. (1977). *Psycheye.* New York: Brandon House.

Ahsen, A. (1982). Principles of imagery in art and literature. *Journal of Mental Imagery, 6*(1), 213–250.

Allport C. W., Vernon, P. E., & Lindzey, G. (1951). *Study of values: Manual of directions* (rev. ed.). Boston: Houghton Mifflin.

Alpert, R. (1965). Motivation to achieve. In M. J. Aschner & C. E. Bish (Eds.), *Productive thinking in education.* Washington, DC: National Education Association.

Amabile, T. (1983). *The social psychology of creativity.* New York: Springer-Verlag.

Amidon, E. J., & Flanders, N. A. (1971). *The role of the teacher in the classroom: A manual for understanding and improving teacher classroom behavior.* Minneapolis: Association for Productive Teaching.

Amram, F. M., & Giese, D. L. (1968). *Creativity training: A tool for motivating disadvantaged students.* Minneapolis: University of Minnesota Press.

Anastasi, A. (1958). Heredity, environment, and the question "how?" *Psychological Review, 65*(4), 197–208.

Anastasi, A. (1988). *Psychological testing* (6th. ed.). New York: John Wiley.

Anastasi, A., & Schaefer, C. E. (1971). Note on the concepts of creativity and intelligence. *Journal of Creative Behavior, 5*(2), 113–116.

Andrews, E. G. (1930). The development of imagination in the pre-school child. *University of Iowa Studies in Character, 3*(4), 000–000.

Angelino, H. (1960, October). The low achiever: A closer look. *The Oklahoma Teacher*, p. 12.

Angoff, W. H. (Ed.). (1971). *The College Board Admissions Testing Program: A technical report on research and development activities relating to the scholastic aptitude tests and achievement tests.* New York: College Entrance Examination Board.

Angyal, A. (1965). *Neurosis and treatment: A holistic approach.* New York: John Wiley.

Arieti, S. (1976). *Creativity: The magic synthesis.* New York: Basic Books.

Arlin, P. (1975). Cognitive development in adulthood. *Developmental Psychology, 11*(5), 602–606.

Arthur, G. (1947). *Arthur-point scale.* Chicago: Stoelting.

Astin, A. W. (1975). *The myth of equal success in public higher education.* Atlanta: Southern Education Foundation.

Atkinson, J. W. (1960). Personality dynamics. *Annual Review of Psychology, 11*, 255–290.

Ausubel, D. P. (1978). Defence of advance organizers. *Review of Educational Research, 38*(2), 251–259.

Bagley, M. T., & Hess, K. (1982). *200 ways of using imagery in the classroom.* Woodcliff Lake, NJ: New Dimensions of the Eighties.

Bahner, J. M. (1979). Individually guided education. In E. Ingas & R. J. Corsini (Eds.), *Alternative educational systems.* Itasca, IL: F. E. Peacock.

Bailey, S. K. (1971). Education and the pursuit of happiness. *UCLA Educator, 14*(1), 14–18.

Baldwin, A. Y. (1978). In A. Y. Baldwin, G.H. Gear, & L. J. Lucito (Eds.), *Educational planning for the gifted.* Reston, VA: Council for Exceptional Children.

Baldwin, A. Y. (1987). I'm black, but look at me, I am also gifted. *Gifted Child Quarterly, 31*(4), 180–185.

Baldwin, A. Y., Gear, G. H., & Lucito, L. J. (Eds.). (1978). *Educational planning for the gifted.* Reston, VA: Council for Exceptional Children.

Ballard, J., Ramirez, B., & Weintraub, F. (1977). *Special education in America: Its legal and governmental foundations.* Reston, VA: Council for Exceptional Children.

Barbe, W. B. (1954). Differentiated guidance for the gifted. *Education, 74*, 306–311.

Barchillon, J. (1961). Creativity and its inhibition in child prodigies. In *Personality dimensions of creativity.* New York: Lincoln Institute for Psychotherapy.

Barclay, J. R. (1978). *Appraising individual differences in the elementary classroom: A manual for the Barclay Classroom Climate Inventory.* Lexington, KY: Educational State Development.

Bardwick, J. (1971). *Psychology of women.* New York: Harper & Row.

Barron, F. (1958). The psychology of imagination. *Scientific American, 199,* 155–166.

Barron, F. (1963). *Creativity and psychological health.* Princeton, NJ: D. Van Nostrand.

Barron, F. (1969). *Creative person and creative process.* New York: Holt, Rinehart & Winston.

Barron, F., & Harrington, D. (1981). Creativity, intelligence and personality. *Annual Review of Psychology, 32,* 439–476.

Baum, S. (1984). Meeting the needs of learning disabled gifted students. *Roeper Review, 7*(1), 16–19.

Bayley, N. (1949). Consistency and variability in the growth of intelligence from birth to eighteen years. *Journal of Genetic Psychology, 75,* 165–196.

Bayley, N., & Oden, M. H. (1955). The maintenance of intellectual ability in gifted adults. *Journal of Gerontology, 10,* 91–107.

Beck, L. (1989). Mentorships: Benefits and effect in career development. *Gifted Child Quarterly, 33*(1), 22–28.

Bem, S. L. (1976). Probing the promise of androgyny. In A. G. Kaplan & J. P. Bean (Eds.), *Beyond sex-role stereotypes: Readings toward a psychology of androgyny.* Boston: Little, Brown.

Benbow, C. P., & Stanley, J. C. (1982). Intellectually talented boys and girls: Educational profiles. *Gifted Child Quarterly, 26*(2), 82–88.

Benedict, R. (1935). *Patterns of culture.* London: Routledge & Kegan Paul.

Bentley, A. (1966). *A measure of musical ability.* New York: October House.

Berkowitz, B. (1953). The Wechsler-Bellevue performance of white males past age 50. *Journal of Gerontology, 8,* 78–80.

Betts, G. T. (1985). *Autonomous learner model for the gifted and talented.* Greeley, CO: Autonomous Learning Publications and Specialists.

Betts, G. T. (1986). The autonomous learner model for the gifted and talented. In J. S. Renzulli (Ed.), *Systems and models for developing programs for the gifted and talented.* Mansfield, CT: Creative Learning Press.

Betts, G. T., & Neihart, M. (1986). Implementing self-directed learning models for gifted and talented. *Gifted Child Quarterly, 30*(4), 174–177.

Bindra, D., & Stewart, J. (Eds.). (1971). *Motivation* (2nd ed.). Baltimore: Penguin.

Binet, A., & Simon, T. (1905). Méthodes nouvelles pour le diagnostic du niveau intellectuel des anormaux. *Annee Psychologique, 11,* 191–244.

Birch, J. W. (1954). Early school admission for mentally advanced children. *Exceptional Children, 21,* 84–87.

Bish, C. E. (1975). The academically talented project: Gateway to the present. *Gifted Child Quarterly, 19*(4), 282–289.

Bledsoe, J. C., & Khatena, J. (1973). A factor analytic study of "Something About Myself." *Psychological Reports, 32,* 1176–1178.

Bledsoe, J. C., & Khatena, J. (1974). Factor analytic study of "What Kind of Person Are You?" Test. *Perceptual and Motor Skills, 39,* 143–146.

Bloom, B. S. (Ed.). (1956). *Taxonomy of educational objectives, handbook I: Cognitive domain*. New York: David McKay.

Bonsall, N., & Stefflre, B. (1955). The temperament of gifted children. *California Journal of Educational Research, 6,* 162–165.

Boston, B. (1976). *The sorcerer's apprentice: A case study in the role of mentoring*. Reston, VA: Council for Exceptional Children.

Bowman, L. (1955). Educational opportunities for gifted children in California. *California Journal of Educational Research, 6,* 195–200.

Bowra, C. M. (1969). *The romantic imagination*. New York: Oxford University Press.

Brandwein, P. (1955). *The gifted child as a future scientist*. New York: Harcourt Brace.

Bricklin, B., & Bricklin, P. (1967). *Bright child—poor grades: The psychology of underachievment*. New York: Dell.

Bristo, W. (1956). *How New York City schools provide for gifted*. New York: New York City Schools Bureau of Curriculum Research.

Brody, L. E., & Benbow, C. P. (1987). *Gifted Child Quarterly, 31*(3), 105–109.

Bronowski, (1973), *The ascent of man*. Boston: Little, Brown.

Broverman, I. K., Broverman, D., Clarkson, F. E., Rosenkrantz, P. S., & Vogel, S. (1970). Sex-role stereotypes and clinical judgments of mental health. *Journal of Consulting and Clinical Psychology, 34,* 1–7.

Brown, A. W. (1963). *Chicago Non-verbal Examination*. New York: Psychological Corporation.

Brown, E. K., & Johnson, P. G. (1952). *Education for the talented in mathematics and science*. Washington, DC: Department of Health, Education and Welfare.

Bruch, C. B. (1968, April). *The creative Binet*. Paper presented at the Council for Exceptional Children Conference, New York.

Bruch, C. B. (1971). Modification of procedures for identification of the disadvantaged gifted. *Gifted Child Quarterly, 15*(4), 267–272.

Bruch, C. B. (1972, April). *Sex role images influencing creative productivity and non-productivity in women*. Paper presented in a symposium at the Southeastern Psychological Association Conference, Atlanta.

Bruch, C. B. (1975). Assessment of creativity in culturally different children. *Gifted Child Quarterly, 19*(2), 164–174.

Bruch, C. B., & Morse, J. A. (1972). Initial study of creative productive women under the Bruch-Morse model. *Gifted Child Quarterly, 16*(4), 282–289.

Bruner, J. S. (1960). *The process of education*. Cambridge, MA: Harvard University Press.

Bruner, J. S. (1961). The act of discovery. *Harvard Educational Review, 3*(1), 21–32.

Bugelski, B. R. (1970). Words and things and images. *American Psychologist, 25,* 1002–1012.

Burks, B. S., Jensen, D. W., & Terman, L. M. (1930). *The promise of youth: Genetic studies of genius* (Vol. 3). Stanford, CA: Stanford University Press.

Burnside, L. (1942). Psychological guidance of gifted children. *Journal of Consulting Psychology, 6,* 223–228.

Buros, O. K. (Ed.). (1972). *The seventh mental measurement.* Highland Park, NJ: Gryphon Press.

Burt, C. (1949). The structure of the mind: A review of the results of factor analysis. *British Journal of Educational Psychology, 19,* 100–111, 176–199.

Burt, C. (1962). The psychology of creative ability. *British Journal of Psychology, 32,* 292–293.

Bushnell, D. D. (1970). Black arts for black youth. *Saturday Review, 53,* 43–46, 60.

Butler-Por, N. (1987). *Underachievers in school: Issues and Intervention.* New York: John Wiley.

Butterfield, S. M. (1979). Some legal implications. In *Developing IEPs for the gifted/talented.* Los Angeles: National/State Leadership Training Institute on the Gifted and Talented.

Callahan, C. M. (1979). The gifted and talented woman. In A. H. Passow (Ed.), *The gifted and talented: Their education and development.* Chicago: University of Chicago Press. (78th Yearbook of the NSSE)

Callahan, C. M. (1980). The gifted girl: An anomaly? *Roeper Review, 2*(3), 16–19.

Campbell, D. T., & Fiske, D. W. (1959). Convergent and discriminant validation by the multitrait matrix. *Psychological Bulletin, 56,* 81–105.

Campbell, L. (1902). *Plato's Republic.* London: John Murray.

Capurso, A. (1961). Music. In L. Fliegler (Ed.), *Curriculum planning for the gifted.* Englewood Cliffs, NJ: Prentice Hall.

Carroll, H. A. (1940). Intellectually gifted children: Their characteristics and problems. *Teachers College Record, 42,* 212–227.

Cassel, N., & Stancik, E. J. (1961). *The Leadership Ability Evaluation.* Los Angeles: Western Psychological Services.

Cattell, R. B., & Cattrell, A. K. S. (1963). *IPAT Culture Fair Intelligence Test: Scales I, II, and III.* Champaign, IL: Institute for Personality and Ability Testing.

Chambers, J. A., Barron, F., & Sprecher, J. W. (1980). Identifying gifted Mexican-American students. *Gifted Child Quarterly, 24*(3), 123–128.

Chemers, M.M., & Rice, R. W. (1974). A theoretical and empirical examination of Fiedler's contingency model of leadership effectiveness. In J. G. Hunt & L. L. Larson (Eds.), *Contingency approaches to leadership.* Carbondale, IL: Southern Illinois University Press.

Clark, B. (1986). *Optimizing learning: The integrative education model in the classroom.* Columbus, OH: Merrill.

Clark, B. (1988). *Growing up gifted* (3rd ed.). Columbus, OH: Merrill.

Clark, G. A., & Zimmerman, E. (1984). *Educating artistically talented students.* Syracuse, NY: Syracuse University Press.

Clark, K. B. (1965). *Dark ghetto*. New York: Harper & Row.

Clasen, D. R., & Hanson, M. (1987). Double mentoring: A process for facilitating mentorships for gifted students. *Roeper Review, 10*(2), 107–110.

Cohn, S. J. (1981). What is giftedness? A multidimensional approach. In A. H. Kramer (Ed.), *Gifted children: Challenging their potential* (pp. 33–45). New York: Trillium.

Colangelo, N. (1985). Counseling needs of culturally diverse students. *Roeper Review, 8*(1), 33–35.

Colangelo, N., & Lafrenz, N. (1981). Counseling the culturally diverse. *Gifted Child Quarterly, 25*(1), 27–30.

Colangelo, N., & Zaffrann, R. T. (1979). *New voices in counseling the gifted*. Dubuque, IA: Kendall/Hunt.

Cole, H. P. (1972). *Process education: The new direction for elementary secondary schools*. Englewood Cliffs, NJ: Educational Technology Publications.

Cole, H. P., & Parsons, E. E. (1974). D. E. Williams total creativity program. *Journal of Creative Behavior, 8*(3), 187–207.

Coleman, J. S. (1961). *Social climates*. Washington, DC: U.S. Government Printing Office.

Coleman, J. S. (1973). Equality of opportunity and equality of results. *Harvard Educational Review, 43*(1), 129–164.

Coleridge, S. T. (1956). *Biographia litereria*. New York: E.P. Dutton. (Originally published 1817)

Collier, G. (1972). *Art and the creative consciousness*. Englewood Cliffs, NJ: Prentice Hall.

Conant, J. B. (1958). *The identification and education of the academically talented in the American secondary schools* (NEA Conference Report). Washington, DC: National Education Association.

Conant, J. B. (1977). *The citadel of learning*. Westport, CT: Greenwood Press.

Cooper, J. D. (1961). *The art of decision making*. Garden City, NJ: Doubleday.

Corsini, R. J., Fassett, K. K. (1953). Intelligence and aging. *Journal of Genetic Psychology*.

Covington, M. V., Crutchfield, R. S., Davies, L., & Olton, R. M. (1974). *The productive thinking program: A course in learning to think*. Columbus, OH: Merrill.

Cox, C. M. (1926). *The early traits of three hundred geniuses: Genetic studies of genius* (Vol. 2). Stanford, CA: Stanford University Press.

Cox, J., Daniel, N., & Boston, B. O. (1985). *Educating able learners: Programs and promising practices*. Austin: University of Texas Press.

Crutchfield, R. S. (1951). Assessment of persons through a quasi group-interaction technique. *Journal of Abnormal and Social Psychology, 46*, 577–588.

Cunnington, B. F., & Torrance, E. P. (1965). *Sounds and images: Teachers' guide and recorded text* (Adult and children's version). New York: Ginn.

Cutts, N. E., & Moseley, N. (1957). *Teaching the bright and gifted*. Englewood Cliffs, NJ: Prentice Hall.

Daurio, S. P. (1979). Educational enrichment versus acceleration: A review of the literature. In W. C. George, S. J. Cohn & J. C. Stanley (Eds.), *Educating the gifted: Acceleration and enrichment*. Baltimore: Johns Hopkins University Press.

Davenport, J. D. (1967). A study of performance of monozygotic and dizygotic twins and siblings on measures of scholastic aptitude, creativity, achievement motivation, and academic achievement. *Dissertation Abstracts International, 28*, 1968, 3865B. (University Microfilms No. 68-03350)

Davis, G. A. (1970). *Imagination express.* Buffalo: D.O.K.

Davis, G. A. (1975). In pursuit of the creative person. *Journal of Creative Behavior, 9*(2), 75–78.

Davis, G. A., & Rimm, S. B. (1985). *Education of the gifted and talented.* Englewood Cliffs, NJ: Prentice Hall.

De Bono, E. (1967). *The five-day course in thinking.* New York: Basic Books.

De Bono, E. (1970). *Lateral thinking.* New York: Basic Books.

De Bono, E. (1971). *The dog-machine.* New York: Harper & Row.

De Bono, E. (1974). *Thinking course for juniors.* Dorset, U.K.: Direct Education Services.

De Bono, E. (1975). *Think links.* Dorset, U.K.: Direct Education Services.

De Bono, E. (1985). *Masterthinker's handbook.* New York: International Center for Creative Thinking.

DeHaan, R. F., & Havighurst, R. J. (1965). *Educating gifted children.* Chicago: University of Chicago Press.

Delaney, E. A., & Hopkins, T. F. (1987). *The Stanford-Binet intelligence scale (4th ed.): Examiner's handbook.* Chicago: Riverside Publishing.

Delisle, J. (1982). Learning to underachieve. *Roeper Review, 4*(4), 16–18.

Dembart, L. (1984, March 7). Science: Social and cultural factors limit women's job opportunities. *Los Angeles Times.*

Dettmann, D. F., & Colangelo, N. (1980). A functional model for counseling parents of gifted students. *Gifted Child Quarterly, 24*(4), 158–161.

Dewey, J. (1910). *How we think.* Boston: D. C. Heath.

Dirkes, M. A. (1988). Self-directed thinking in the curriculum. *Roeper Review, 11*(2), 92–94.

Dorn, C. M. (1976). The advanced placement program in studio art. *Gifted Child Quarterly, 20*(4), 450–458.

Dorsel, T. N. (1979). Creativity: Incubation as a special case of reminiscence. *Journal of Creative Behavior, 13*(1), 53–58.

Dowd, R. J. (1952). Underachieving students of high capacity. *Journal of Higher Education, 23*, 327–330.

Drake, R. M. (1954). *Drake Musical Aptitude Tests.* Chicago: Science Research Associates.

Drews, E. E. M., & Teahan, J. E. (1957). Parental attitudes and academic achievers. *Journal of Clinical Psychology, 13*, 328–332.

Durio, H. F. (1975). Mental image and creativity. *Journal of Creative Behavior,* 9(4), 233–244.

Durkheim, E. (1933). *The division of labor* (G. Simpson, Trans.). New York: Macmillan. (Original work published in 1893)

Durkheim, E. (1961). *Moral education: A study in the theory and application of the sociology of knowledge* (E. K. Wilson & H. Schnurer, Trans.). New York: Free Press. (Original work published 1925)

Durr, W. K. (1964). *The gifted student.* New York: Oxford University Press.

Dweck, C. S., Davidson, W., Nelson, S., & Enna, B. (1978). Sex differences in learned helplessness: I. The contingencies of evaluative feedback in the classroom and II. An experimental analysis. *Developmental Psychology, 14*(3), 268–276.

Eash, M. J. (1961). Grouping: What have we learned? *Educational Leadership, 18,* 429–434.

Eccles, J. C. (1972). The physiology of imagination. In *Readings from Scientific American.* San Francisco: W. H. Freeman. (Original work published 1958)

Edwards, A. J. (1971). Individual mental testing: Part I—History and Theories. San Francisco: Intex Educational.

Ekstrom, R. (1961). Experimental studies of homogeneous grouping: A critical review. *School Review, 69,* 217–226.

Ellison, R. L., James, L. R., Fox, D. G., & Taylor, C. W. (1971). *The identification and selection of creative artistic talent by means of biographical information* (Report submitted to the USOE/HEW, Grant No. OEG-8-9-540215-4004 [010], Project No. 9-0215). Washington, DC: U.S. Government Printing Office.

Elwood, C. (1958). Acceleration of the gifted. *Gifted Child Quarterly, 2*(1), 21–23.

Epstein, H. T. (1977). Growth spurts. In J. Chall & A. F. Mirsky (Eds), *Education and the brain.* Chicago: University of Chicago Press. (77th Yearbook of the NSSE)

Erikson, E. H. (1950). *Childhood and society.* New York: W. W. Norton.

Erikson, E. H. (1973). Inner and outer space: Reflections on womanhood. In S. Berg (Ed.), *About women.* Greenwich, CT: Fawcett.

Evans, M. (1970). The effects of supervisory behavior on the path-goal relationship. *Organizational Behavior and Human Performance, 5,* 277–298.

Exum, H. A. (1979). Facilitating psychological and emotional development of gifted black students. In N. Colangelo and R. T. Zaffran (Eds.), *New voices in counseling the gifted.* Dubuque, IA: Kendall/Hunt.

Exum, H. A. (1983). Key issues in family counseling with gifted and talented black students. *Roeper Review, 5*(3), 28–31.

Fantini, M. D., & Weinstein, G. (1968). *The disadvantaged child: Challenge to education.* New York: Harper & Row.

Feldman, D. H. (1984). A follow-up of subjects scoring above 180 IQ in Terman's "Genetic studies of genius." *Exceptional Children, 50,* 518–523.

Feldhusen, J. F. (1986). A conception of giftedness. In R. J. Sternberg & J. T. Davidson (Eds.), *Conceptions of giftedness.* New York: Cambridge University Press.

Feldhusen, J. F., Houtz, J. C., & Ringenbach, S. (1972). The Purdue elementary problem-solving inventory. *Psychological Reports, 31,* 891–901.

Feldhusen, J. F., Procter, T. B., & Black, K. N. (1986). Guidelines for grade advancement of precocious children. *Roeper Review, 9*(1), 25–27.

Feldhusen, J. F., Speedie, S. M., & Treffinger, D. J. (1971). The Purdue creative thinking program: Research and evaluation. *NSPI Journal, 10*(3), 5–9.

Feldhusen, J. F., & Treffinger, D. J. (1980). *Creative thinking and problem solving in gifted education* (2nd ed.). Dubuque, IA: Kendall/Hunt.

Feldhusen, J. F., Treffinger, D. J., & Bahlke, S. J. (1970). The Purdue creativity program. *Journal of Creative Behavior, 4*(2), 85–90.

Feldhusen, J. F., Treffinger, D. J., van Mondfrans, A. P., & Ferris, D. R. (1971). The relationship between academic grades and divergent thinking scores derived from four different methods of testing. *Journal of Experimental Education, 40,* 35–40.

Feldhusen, J. F., Van Tassel-Baska, J., & Seeley, K. (1989). *Excellence in educating the gifted.* Denver: Love.

Feuerstein, R. (1979). *The dynamic assessment of retarded performers: The learning potential assessment device, theory, instruments and techniques.* Baltimore: University Park Press.

Feuerstein, R. (1980). *Instrumental enrichment: An intervention program for cognitive modifiability.* Baltimore: University Park Press.

Fideler, F. E. A. (1964). A contingency model of leadership effectiveness. In L. Berkowitz (Ed.), *Advances in experimental social psychology* (Vol. 1). New York: Academic Press.

Fideler, F. E. A. (1967). *A theory of leadership effectiveness.* New York: McGraw-Hill.

Finder, J. (1970). Living with people: The Mirman School. *McCall's, 97*(11), pp. 41, 74–75, 87–88.

Fischer, R. (1974). Hallucinations can reveal creative imagination. *Fields Within Fields, 11,* 29–33.

Flanagan, J. C. (1960). *Test of general ability.* Chicago: Science Research Associates.

Flavell, J. H. (1963). *The developmental psychology of Jean Piaget.* New York: D. Van Nostrand.

Fleishman, B. A. (1973). Twenty years of consideration and structure. In E. A. Fleishman & J. G. Hunt (Eds.), *Current developments in the study of leadership.* Carbondale, IL: Southern Illinois University Press.

Fliegler, L. A. (Ed.). (1961). *Curriculum planning for the gifted.* Englewood Cliffs, NJ: Prentice Hall.

Fliegler, L. A. (1965). Commentary on "Motivation to achieve" by R. Alpert. In M. J. Aschner & C. L. Bish (Eds.), *Productive thinking in education*. Washington, DC: National Education Association.

Ford, M. A. (1989). Students' perceptions of affective issues impacting the social emotional development and school performance of gifted/talented youngsters. *Roeper Review, 11*(3), 131–134.

Forisha, B. (1978). Mental imagery and creativity: Review and speculations. *Journal of Mental Imagery, 1*(3–4), 8–13.

Foster, W. (1981). Leadership: A conceptual framework for recognizing and educating. *Gifted Child Quarterly, 25*(1), 17–25.

Foulds, G. A., & Raven, J. C. (1948). Normal changes in the mental abilities of adults as age advances

Fowler, T. (1901). *Locke's conduct of the understanding.* Oxford, U.K.: Oxford University Press.

Fox, L. H. (1979). Programs for the gifted and talented: An overview. In A. H. Passow (Ed.), *The gifted and talented: Their education and development.* Chicago: University of Chicago Press. (78th Yearbook of the NSSE)

Frankel, E. (1960). A comparative study of achieving and underachieving high school boys of high intellectual ability. *Journal of Educational Research, 53,* 172–180.

Frasier, M. M. (1979). Counseling the culturally diverse gifted. In N. Colangelo & R. T. Zaffrann (Eds.), *New voices in counseling the gifted.* Dubuque, IA: Kendall/Hunt.

Frasier, M. M., & McCannon, C. (1981). Using bibliotherapy with gifted children. *Gifted Child Quarterly, 25*(2), 81–85.

Fredrickson, R. H. (1979). Career development and the gifted. In N. Colangelo and R. T. Zaffrann (Eds.), *New voices in counseling the gifted.* Dubuque, IA: Kendall/Hunt.

French, J. L. (1968). The highly intelligent dropout. *Accent on Talent, 2*(3), 5–6.

Freud, S. (1957). The ego and the id. In J. Rickman (Ed.), *A general selection from the works of Sigmund Freud.* New York: Doubleday Anchor. (Original work published 1923)

Frey, B. R., Noller, R. B. (1983). Mentoring: A legacy of success. *Journal of Creative Behavior, 17*(1), 60–64.

Frierson, E. C. (1965). Upper and lower status gifted children: A study of differences. *Exceptional Children, 32,* 83–90.

Froebel, F. (1900). *The pedagogics of the kindergarten* (J. Jarvis, Trans.). London: Edward Arnold.

Froebel, F. (1909). *The education of man* (W. N. Hailman, Trans.). New York: D. Appleton.

Fuchigami, R. Y. (1978). Summary analysis and future directions. In A. Y. Baldwin, G. H. Gear, & L. J. Lucito (Eds.). *Educational planning for the gifted.* Reston, VA: Council for Exceptional Children.

Gage, N. L. (1972). I.Q., heritability, race differences and educational research. *Phi Delta Kappan, 53*(5), 308–312.

Gagne, F. (1985). Giftedness and talent: Reexamining a reexamination of the definitions. *Gifted Child Quarterly, 29*(3), 103–112.

Gallagher, J. J. (1966). *Research summary on gifted child education.* Springfield, IL: Office of the Superintendent of Public Instruction.

Gallagher, J. J. (1979a). Issues in education of the gifted. In A. H. Passow (Ed.), *The gifted and the talented: Their education and development.* Chicago: University of Chicago Press. (78th Yearbook of the NSSE)

Gallagher, J. J. (1979b). Research needs for education of the gifted. In *Issues in gifted education.* Los Angeles: National/State Leadership Training Institute on the Gifted and the Talented.

Gallagher, J. J. (1985). *Teaching the gifted child* (3rd ed.). Boston: Allyn & Bacon.

Gallagher, J. J. (1986). A proposed federal role: Education of gifted children. *Gifted Child Quarterly, 30*(1), 43–46.

Gallagher, J. J., & Courtright, R. D. (1986). In R. J. Sternberg & J. E. Davidson (Eds.), *Conceptions of giftedness.* New York: Cambridge University Press.

Gallagher, J. J., & Kinney, L. (Eds.). (1974). *Talent delayed—talent denied: A conference report.* Reston, VA: Foundation for Exceptional Children.

Galton, F. (1870). *Hereditary genius.* New York: Appleton.

Gardner, H. (1987). *Frames of mind: The theory of multiple intelligences.* New York: Basic Books.

Gardner, H. (1988). Beyond the I.Q.: Education and human development. *National Forum, 68*(2), 4–7.

Garrett, H. E. A. (1946). A developmental theory of intelligence. *American Psychologist, 1,* 372–378.

Gaylean, B. C. (1983). *Mindsight: Learning through imagery.* Long Beach, CA: Center for Integrative Learning.

Gendlin, F. (1981). *Focusing.* Trumansburg, NY: Crossing.

George, W. C., Cohn, S. J., & Stanley, J. C. (Eds.). (1979). *Educating the gifted: Acceleration and enrichment.* Baltimore: John Hopkins University Press.

Gerencser, S. (1979). The Calasanctius experience. In A. H. Passow (Ed.), *The gifted and the talented: Their education and development.* Chicago: University of Chicago Press. (78th Yearbook of the NSSE)

Getzels, J. W., & Jackson, P. W. (1958). The meaning of "giftedness": An examination of an expanding concept. *Phi Delta Kappan, 40*(2), 75–78.

Getzels, J. W., & Jackson, P. W. (1960). Occupational choice and cognitive functioning: Career aspirations of highly intelligent and of highly creative adolescents. *Journal of Abnormal and Social Psychology, 61*(1), 119–123.

Getzels, J. W., & Jackson, P. W. (1961). Family environment and cognitive choice: A study of the sources of highly intelligent and of highly creative adolescents. *American Sociological Review, 26,* 351–359.

Getzels, J. W., & Jackson, P. W. (1962). *Creativity and intelligence: Explorations with gifted children.* New York: John Wiley.

Ghiselin, B. (Ed.). (1955). *The creative process.* Berkeley: University of California Press.

Gibb, C. A. (1947). The principles and traits of leadership. *Journal of Abnormal Psychology, 42,* 267–284.

Gibb, C. A. (1972). Review of Leadership Evaluation and Development Scale. In O. K. Buros (Ed.), *Seventh mental measurement yearbook.* Highland Park, NJ: Gryphon Press.

Ginsberg, E. (1951). *Occupational choice: An approach to general theory.* New York: Columbia University Press.

Glaser, R. (1966). In J. I. Goodlad (Ed.), *The changing American school.* Chicago: University of Chicago Press. (65th Yearbook of the NSSE)

Goddard, H. H. (1908). The Binet and Simon tests of intellectual capacity. *The Training School, 3–9.*

Goddard, H. H. (1911). Ten thousand children measured by the Binet measuring scale of intelligence. *Pedagogical Seminary, 18,* 232–259.

Gold, M. J. (1965). *Education of the intellectually gifted.* Columbus, OH: Charles E. Merrill.

Gold, M. J. (1979). Teachers and mentors. In A. H. Passow (Ed.), *The gifted and the talented: Their education and development.* Chicago: University of Chicago Press. (78th Yearbook of the NSSE)

Goldberg, M. J., & Passow, A. H. (1959). A study of underachieving gifted. *Educational Leadership, 16,* 121–125.

Goldberg, M. L. (1986). Issues in the education of gifted and talented children—Part 1. *Roeper Review, 8*(4), 226–233.

Goolsby, T. M. (1975). Alternative admissions criteria for college. In *Nontraditional approaches to assess the academic potential of black students.* Atlanta: Southern Regional Education Board.

Gordon, E. (1965). *Musical Aptitude Profile.* Boston: Houghton Mifflin.

Gordon, R. (1972). A very private world. In P. W. Sheehan (Ed.), *The function of imagery.* New York: Academic Press.

Gordon, W. J. J. (1961). *Synectics: The development of creative capacity.* New York: Harper & Row.

Gordon, W. J. J. (1974). Some source materials in discovery-by-analogy. *Journal of Creative Behavior, 8*(4), 239–257.

Gough, H. G. (1956). *California Psychological Inventory.* Los Angeles: Consulting Psychologists Press.

Gough, H. G. (1960). The adjective check list as a personality assessment research technique [monograph supplement]. *Psychological Reports, 6,* 107–122.

Gowan, J. C. (1955). The underachieving gifted child: A problem for everyone. *Exceptional Children, 21,* 247–250.

Gowan, J. C. (1957). Dynamics of underachievement in gifted students. *Exceptional Children, 24,* 98–101.

Gowan, J. C. (1971). The development of the creative individual. *Gifted Child Quarterly, 15*(3), 156–174.

Gowan, J. C. (1972). *The development of the creative individual.* San Diego: Robert R. Knapp.

Gowan, J. C. (1974). *The development of the psychedelic individual.* Buffalo: Creative Education Foundation.

Gowan, J. C. (1975). *Trance, art and creativity.* Buffalo: Creative Education Foundation.

Gowan, J. C. (1977a). Creative inspiration in composers. *Journal of Creative Behavior, 11*(4), 249–255.

Gowan, J. C. (1977b). Background and history of the gifted-child movement. In J. C. Stanley, W. C. George & C. H. Solano (Eds.), *The gifted and the creative: A fifty-year perspective.* Baltimore: Johns Hopkins University Press.

Gowan, J. C. (1978a). Creativity and gifted child movement. *Journal of Creative Behavior, 12*(1), 1–13.

Gowan, J. C. (1978b). Incubation, imagery and creativity. *Journal of Mental Imagery, 2*(2), 23–32.

Gowan, J. C. (1978c). The role of imagination in the development of the creative individual. *Humanitas, 14*(1), 197–208.

Gowan, J. C. (1979a). Differentiated guidance for the gifted: A dvelopmental view. In J. C. Gowan, J. Khatena, & E. P. Torrance (Eds.), *Educating the ablest* (2nd ed.). Itasca, IL: F. E. Peacock.

Gowan, J. C. (1979b). Education of the gifted in Utopia. In J. C. Gowan, J. Khatena, E. P. Torrance (Eds.), *Educating the ablest* (2nd ed.). Itasca, IL: F. E. Peacock.

Gowan, J. C. (1979c). *New counseling trends.* Keynote address at the Expressive Therapies and Creative Education Program Conference, University of Georgia, Athens, GA.

Gowan, J. C. (1979d). The use of developmental stage theory in helping gifted children become creative. In *Issues in gifted education.* Los Angeles: National/State Leadership Training Institute on the Gifted and Talented.

Gowan, J. C. (1979e). The education of disadvantaged gifted youth. In J. C. Gowan, J. Khatena, & E. P. Torrance (Eds.), *Educating the ablest* (2nd ed.). Itasca, IL: F. E. Peacock.

Gowan, J. C. (1980). The use of developmental stage theory in helping gifted children become creative. *Gifted Child Quarterly, 24*(1), 22–28.

Gowan, J. C., & Bruch, C. B. (1971). *The academically talented: Student and guidance.* Boston: Houghton Mifflin.

Gowan, J. C., & Demos, G. D. (1962). *How to enhance effective leadership.* Unpublished manuscript, California State College at Long Beach.

Gowan, J. C., & Demos, G. D. (1964). *The education and guidance of the ablest.* Springfield, IL: Charles C Thomas.

Gowan, J. C., & Dodd, S. C. (1977). General systems: A creative search for synthesis. *Journal of Creative Behavior, 11*(1), 47–52.

Gowan, J. C., Khatena, J., & Torrance, E. P. (Eds.). (1979). *Educating the ablest* (2nd ed.). Itasca, IL: F. E. Peacock.

Grady, M. P. (1984). *Teaching and brain research: Guidelines for the classroom.* New York: Longman.

Granzow, K. R. (1954). A comparative study of underachievers, normal achievers, and overachievers in reading. *Dissertation Abstracts International, 14,* 631. (University Microfilms No. 00-07563)

Gray, C. E. (1961). An epicyclical model for western civilization. *American Anthropologist, 63,* 1014–1037.

Gray, C. E. (1966). A measurement of creativity in western civilization. *American Anthropologist, 68,* 1384–1417.

Gray, C. E., & Young, R. C. (1975). Utilizing the divergent production matrix of the structure of intellect in the development of teaching strategies. *Gifted Child Quarterly, 19*(4), 290–300.

Gronlund, N. E. (1959). *Sociometry in the classroom.* New York: Harper.

Gruber, H. E. (1973). Courage and cognitive change in children and scientists. In M. Schwebel and J. Raph (Eds.), *Piaget in the classroom.* New York: Basic Books.

Gruber, H. E. (1985). Giftedness and moral responsibility: Creative thinking and human survival. In F. D. Horowitz & M. O'Brien (Eds.), *The gifted and talented: Developmental perspectives* (pp. 301–330). Washington, DC: American Psychological Association.

Grunebaum, M., Hurwutz, I., Prentice, N., & Sperry, B. (1962). Fathers of sons with primary neurotic learning inhibitions. *American Journal of Orthopsychiatry, 32,* 462.

Guilford, J. P. (1950). Creativity. *American Psychologist, 5,* 444–454.

Guilford, J. P. (1967). *The nature of human intelligence.* New York: McGraw-Hill.

Guilford, J. P. (1968). Creativity in the visual arts. In J. P. Guilford (Ed.), *Intelligence, creativity and their educational implications.* San Diego: Robert R. Knapp.

Guilford, J. P. (1971). Some misconceptions regarding measurement of creative talents. *Journal of Creative Behavior, 5*(2), 77–87.

Guilford, J. P. (1972). Intellect and the gifted. *Gifted Child Quarterly, 16*(2), 175–184, 239–243.

Guilford, J. P. (1973). *Creativity tests for children.* Orange, CA: Sheridan Psychological Services.

Guilford, J. P. (1975). Varieties of creative giftedness: Their measurement and development. *Gifted Child Quarterly, 19*(2), 107–121.

Guilford, J. P. (1977). *Way beyond the I.Q.* Buffalo: Creative Education Foundation.

Guilford, J. P. (1979). Some incubated thoughts on incubation. *Journal of Creative Behavior, 13*(1), 1–8.

Guilford, J. P. (1982). Cognitive psychology's ambiguities: Some suggested remedies. *Psychological Review, 89,* 48–59.

Guilford, J. P. (1988). Some changes in the structure of intellect model. *Educational and Psychological Measurement, 48,* 1–3.

Guilford, J. P., Hendricks, M., & Hoepfner, R. (1976). Solving social problems creatively. In A. M. Biondi & S. J. Parnes (Eds.), *Assessing creative*

Guilford, J. P., & Hoepfner, R. (1966). Creative potential as related to measures of IQ and verbal comprehension. *Indian Journal of Psychology, 41,* 7–16.

Haensly, P., Reynolds, C. R., & Nash, W. R. (1986). Giftedness: Coalescence, context, conflict, and commitment. In R. J. Sternberg & J. E. Davidson (Eds.), *Conceptions of giftedness.* Cambridge, U.K.: Cambridge University Press.

Hall, R. T. (1979). *Moral education: A handbook for teachers.* Minneapolis: Winston.

Hass, R. B. (1948). The school sociatrist. *Sociatry, 2,* 283–321.

Hassan, P., & Butcher, H. J. (1966). Creativity and intelligence: A partial replication with Scottish children of Getzels' and Jackson's study. *British Journal of Psychology, 57,* 129–135.

Havighurst, R. J. (1961). Conditions productive of superior children. *Teachers College Record, 62,* 524–531.

Hebb, D. O. (1949). *The organization of behavior.* New York: John Wiley.

Hedbring, C., & Rubenzer, R. (1979). Integrating IEP and SOI with educational programming for the gifted. *Gifted Child Quarterly, 23*(2), 338–345.

Heist, P., & Yonge, B. (1968). *Omnibus Personality Inventory, Form F: Manual.* New York: Psychological Coporation.

Henry, N. B. (Ed.). (1958). *Education for the gifted.* Chicago: University of Chicago Press. (57th Yearbook of the NSSE)

Herr, E. L., & Watanabe, A. (1979). In N. Colangelo and R. T. Zaffran (Eds.), *New voices in counseling the gifted.* Dubuque, IA: Kendall/Hunt.

Hersh, R. H., Miller, J. P., & Fielding, G. D. (1980). *Models of moral education: An appraisal.* New York: Longman.

Hildreth, G. H. (1952). *Educating gifted children.* New York: Harper & Bros.

Hildreth, G. H. (1966). *Introduction to the gifted.* New York: McGraw-Hill.

Hilgard, E. R. (1981). Imagery and imagination in American psychology. *Journal of Mental Imagery, 5*(1), 5–19.

Hirsch, S. P. (1976). Executive high school internships: A boon for the gifted and talented. *Teaching Exceptional Children, 9* (1), 22–23.

Hollingsworth, L. S. (1926). *Gifted Children: Their nature and nurture.* New York: Macmillan.

Hollingsworth, L. S. (1942). *Children above 180 I.Q., Stanford-Binet.* New York: World.

Holt, J. (1964). *How children fail.* New York: Pitman.

Horner, M. S. (1972a). The motive to avoid success and changing aspirations in college women. In J. Bardwick (Ed.), *Readings on the psychology of women.* New York: Harper & Row.

Horner, M. S. (1972b). Toward an understanding of achievement-related conflicts in women. *Journal of Social Issues, 28,* 157–175.

House, R. J., & Dessler, A. (1974). The path-goal theory of leadership: Some post hoc and a priori tests. In J. G. Hunt & L. L. Larson (Eds.), *Contingency approaches to leadership.* Carbondale, IL: Southern Illinois University Press.

Hoyt, K. B., Evans, R. N., MacKin, E. F., & Mangum, G. L. (1974). *Career education: What it is and how to do it* (2nd ed.). Salt Lake City: Olympus.

Hoyt, K. B., & Hebeler, R. J. (Eds.). (1974). *Career education for gifted and talented students.* Salt Lake City: Olympus.

Hunt, J. McV. (1960). Experience and development of motivation. *Child Development, 31,* 489–504.

Hunt, J. McV. (1964). The implications of changing ideas on how children develop intellectually. *Children, 11*(3), 83–91.

Ickes, W., & Layden, M. (1979). Attributional styles. In *New directions in attributional research* (Vol. 2).

Ingas, E. (1979). Introduction to alternative educational systems. In E. Ingas & R. J. Corsini (Eds.), *Alternative educational systems.* Itasca, IL: F. E. Peacock.

Institute for Behavioral Research in Creativity (IBRIC). (1968). *Development of the Alpha Biographical Inventory.* Salt Lake City: Author.

Isaack, T. S. (1978). Intuition: An ignored dimension of management. *Academy of Management Review, 3,* 917–923.

Jackson, D. M. (1979). The emerging national and state concern. In A. H. Passow (Ed.), *The gifted and the talented: Their education and development.* Chicago: University of Chicago Press. (78th Yearbook of the NSSE)

Jaensch, E. R. (1930). *Eidetic imagery.* London: Routledge & Kegan Paul.

Jahoda, M. (1958). *Current concepts of positive mental health.* New York: Basic Books.

James, W. (1880). Great men, great thoughts and environment. *Atlantic Monthly, 46,* 441–459.

Jaynes, J. (1976). *The origin of consciousness in the breakdown of the bicameral mind.* Boston: Houghton Mifflin.

Jencks, C. (1973). Inequality in retrospect. *Harvard Educational Review, 43*(1), 138–164.

Jensen, A. R. (1969). How much can we boost I.Q., and scholastic achievement? *Harvard Educational Review, 39*(3), 1–123.

Jepsen, D. A. (1979). Helping gifted adolescents with career exploration. In N. Colangelo and R. T. Zaffrann (Eds.), *New voices in counseling the gifted.* Dubuque, IA: Kendall/Hunt.

Jeter, J., & Chauvin, J. (1982). Individualized instruction: Implications for the gifted. *Roeper Review, 5*(1), 2–3.

Johnson, D. L. (1977). *Inventory of Individually Perceived Group Cohesiveness.* Chicago: Stoelting.

Johnson, D. L. (1979). *Social Interaction and Creativity in Communication System*. Chicago: Stoelting.

Johnson, D. L. (1980). *Gifted and talented screening form: Instructor's manual*. Chicago: Stoelting.

Jones, H. E., & Conrad, H. S. (1933). The growth and decline of intelligence. *Genetic Psychology Monograph, 13*, 233–298.

Journal of Creative Behavior (1979). Special issue on Incubation, *13*(3).

Journal of Creative Behavior (1986). Strawberry patch—cover design, *20*(2).

Jung, C. G. (1921). Psychological types. In H. Read, M. Fordham, & G. Adler (Eds.), *Collected works of C. G. Jung* (Vol. 6). Princeton, NJ: Princeton University Press.

Juntune, J. (Ed.). (1981). *Successful programs*. Hot Springs, AR: National Association for Gifted Children.

Kamin, L. J. (1974). *The science and politics of I.Q.* New York: John Wiley.

Karnes, F. A., & Chauvin, J. C. (1985). *Leadership skills development program*. East Aurora, NY: D.O.K.

Karnes, F. A., & Collins, E. C. (1980). *Instructional resources for teaching the gifted*. Boston: Allyn & Bacon.

Karnes, M. B. (1984). A demonstration/outreach model for young gifted/talented handicapped. *Roeper Review, 7*(1), 23–26.

Karnes, M. B., & Bertschi, J. D. (1978). Identifying and educating gifted/talented nonhandicapped and handicapped preschoolers. *Teaching Exceptional Children, 10*(4), 114–119.

Karnes, M. B., McCoy, G. F. Zehrbach, R. R., Wollersheim, J., Clarizio, H. F., Gostin, L., & Stanley, L. (1961). Factors associated with underachievement and overachievement of intellectually gifted children. *Exceptional Children, 27*, 167–175.

Kaufmann, G. (1980). *Imagery, language and cognition: Toward a theory of symbolic activity in human problem-solving*. New York: Columbia University Press.

Keatinge, M. W. (1910). *The great diadactic of John Amos Comenius*. London: A. & C. Black.

Kelley, T. L., Madden, R., Gardner, E. F., & Rudman, H. C. (1965). *Stanford Achievement Test*. New York: Harcourt Brace Jovanovich.

Kenmare, D. (1972). *The nature of genius*. Westport, CT: Greenwood Press.

Keyser, D. J., & Sweetland, R. C. (Eds.). (1987). *Test critiques*. Kansas City: Test Corporation of America.

Khatena, J. (1970). Training college adults to think creatively with words. *Psychological Reports, 27*, 279–281.

Khatena, J. (1971a). Production of original verbal images by children between the ages of 8 and 19 as measured by the alternate forms of "Onomatopoeia and Images." *Proceedings of the 79th Annual Convention of the American Psychological Association, 6*(1), 187–188.

Khatena, J. (1971b). Some problems in the measurement of creative behavior. *Journal of Research and Development in Education, 62*(5), 384–386.

Khatena, J. (1971c). Teaching disadvantaged preschool children to think creatively with pictures. *Journal of Educational Psychology, 62*(5), 384–386.

Khatena, J. (1972). Development patterns in production by children 9 to 19 of original images as measured by "Sounds and Images." *Psychological Reports, 30*, 649–650.

Khatena, J. (1973a). Imagination and production of original verbal images. *Art Psychotherapy, 1*, 113–120.

Khatena, J. (1973b). *Problems of the highly creative child and the school psychologist.* Paper presented at the meeting of the Southeastern Region of the National Association of School Psychologists, White Sulphur Springs, WV.

Khatena, J. (1975a). Creative imagination imagery and analogy. *Gifted Child Quarterly, 19*(2), 149–160.

Khatena, J. (1975b). *Project talented and gifted second evaluation report* (ESEA Title III, Region II, Charleston—Prepared for the West Virginia State Department of Education). Unpublished manuscript.

Khatena, J. (1976a). Educating the gifted child: Challenge and response. *Gifted Child Quarterly, 20*(1), 76–90.

Khatena, J. (1976b). *Project talented and gifted final evaluation report* (ESEA Title III, Region II, Charleston—Prepared for the West Virginia State Department of Education). Unpublished manuscript.

Khatena, J. (1977a). Some thoughts on the gifted in the United States and abroad. *Gifted Child Quarterly, 21*(3), 372–386.

Khatena, J. (1977b). "The Khatena-Torrance Creative Perception Inventory" for identification, diagnosis, facilitation and research. *Gifted Child Quarterly, 21*(4), 517–525.

Khatena, J. (1978a). *The creatively gifted child: Suggestions for parents and teachers.* New York: Vantage Press.

Khatena, J. (1978b). Identification and stimulation of creative imagination. *Journal of Creative Behavior, 12*(1), 30–38.

Khatena, J. (1979a). *Teaching gifted children to use creative imagination imagery.* Starkville, MS: Allan Associates.

Khatena, J. (1979b). Nurture of imagery in the visual and performing arts. *Gifted Child Quarterly, 23*(4), 735–747.

Khatena, J. (1980). *Creative imagination imagery actionbook.* Starkville, MS: Allan Associates.

Khatena, J. (1982a). *Educational psychology of the gifted.* New York: John Wiley.

Khatena, J. (1982b). Myth: Creativity is too difficult to measure! *Gifted Child Quarterly, 26*(1), 21–23.

Khatena, J. (1983). *Multidimensional interactive creative imagination imagery model.* Starkville, MS: Author.

Khatena, J. (1984). *Imagery and creative imagination.* Buffalo: Bearly Limited.

Khatena, J. (1987). Research potential of imagery and creative imagination.

In S. G. Isaksen (Ed.), *Frontiers of creativity research: Beyond the basics.* Buffalo: Bearly.

Khatena, J. (1988a). *A holistic model for educating gifted children.* Unpublished manuscript.

Khatena, J. (1988b). *Multitalent assessment records.* Starkville: Mississippi State University.

Khatena, J. (1989). *Music, art and leadership abilities assessment records.* Unpublished manuscript.

Khatena, J. (1990). *Creativity of gifted children:* Buffalo: Bearly.

Khatena, J., & Fisher, S. (1974). A four year study of children's responses to onomatopoeic stimuli. *Perceptual and Motor Skills, 39,* 1062.

Khatena, J., & Khatena, N. (1990). Metaphor motifs and creative imagination in art. *Metaphor and Symbolic Activity, 5*(1), 21–34.

Khatena, J., & Morse, D. T. (1987). Preliminary study of the Khatena-Morse Multitalent Perception Inventory. *Perceptual and Motor Skills, 64,* 1187–1190.

Khatena, J., & Morse, D. T. (1990). Additional evidence on reliability and validity for the Khatena-Morse Multitalent Perception Inventory. *Perceptual and Motor Skills, 70,* 1267–1270.

Khatena, J., & Morse, D. T. (1991). *Khatena-Morse Multitalent Perception Inventory: Norms-technical manual.* Bensenville, IL: Scholastic Testing Service.

Khatena, J., & Torrance, E. P. (1990a). *Manual for Khatena-Torrance Creative Perception Inventory for children, adolescents and adults.* Bensenville, IL: Scholastic Testing Service. (Originally published by Stoelting, 1976)

Khatena, J., & Torrance, E. P. (1990b). *Thinking Creatively with Sounds and Words for children, adolescents and adults: Norms-technical manual.* Bensenville, IL: Scholastic Testing Service. (Originally published by Personnel Press, 1973)

Kimball, B. (1953). Case studies in educational failure during adolescence. *American Journal of Orthopsychiatry, 23,* 406–415.

Kirk, B. (1952). Test versus academic performance in malfunctioning students. *Journal of Consulting Psychology, 16,* 213–216.

Klausmeier, H. J. (1963). Effects of accelerating bright older elementary pupils: A follow-up. *Journal of Educational Psychology, 54*(3), 165–171.

Klausmeier, H. J. (1975). IEG: An alternative form of schooling. In H. Talmadge (Ed.), *Systems of individualized education.* Berkeley: McCutchan.

Klein, A. F. (1956). *Role playing in leadership training and group problem solving.* New York: Association Press.

Klinger, E. (1978). *Modes of normal consciousness: Scientific investigations into the flow of human experience.* New York: Plenum.

Kluckhohn, C. (1970). *Mirror for man.* New York: Fawcett.

Knickerbocker, I. (1948). Leadership: A conception and some implications. *Journal of Social Issues, 4,* 23–40.

Koestler, A. (1964). *The act of creation*. New York: Macmillan.

Kohlberg, L. (1966). Moral education in the schools: A developmental view. *The School Review, 74*, 1–29.

Kohlberg, L., & Mayer, R. (1972). Development as the aim of education. *Harvard Educational Review, 22*, 449–496.

Kohler, W. (1927). *The mentality of apes* (E. Winter Ed. and Trans.). New York: Harcourt, Brace & World.

Koplowitz, H. (1978). Higher cognitive stages. *Brain/Mind Bulletin, 3*(22), 1.

Kowalski, C. J., & Cangemi, J. P. (1974). High school dropouts—A lost resource. *College Student Journal, 8*(4), 71–74.

Kranz, B. (1981). *Kranz talent identification instrument*. Morehead, MN: Morehead State College.

Krathwohl, D. R., Bloom, B. S., & Masia, B. B. (1964). *Taxonomy of educational objectives, handbook II: Affective domain*. New York: David McKay.

Krippner, S. (1967). The ten commandments that block creativity. *Gifted Child Quarterly, 11*(3), 144–156.

Kroeber, A. (1944). *Configurations of culture growth*. Berkeley: University of California Press.

Kubie, L. S. (1958). *Neurotic distortion of the creative process*. New York: Noonday.

Kwalwasser, J., & Dykema, P. W. (1930). *Kwalwasser-Dykema Music Tests*. New York: Carl Fischer.

Laird, A. W. (1971). Investigative survey: Fifty states' provisions for the gifted. *Gifted Child Quarterly, 15*(3), 205–216.

Laird, A. W., & Kowalski, C. J. (1972). Survey of 1,564 colleges and universities on courses offered in the education of the gifted. *Gifted Child Quarterly, 16*(2), 93–111.

Land, A. G., & Land, V. (1982). *Forward to basics*. Buffalo: D.O.K.

Land, G. (1973). *Grow or die: The unifying principle of transformation*. New York: Random House.

Land, G., & Kenneally, C. (1977). Creativity, reality and general systems: A personal viewpoint. *Journal of Creative Behavior, 11*(1), 12–35.

Landrum, M. S. (1987). Guidelines for implementing a guidance/counseling program for gifted and talented students. *Roeper Review, 10*(2), 103–107.

Langham, D. G. (1974). Genesa: Tomorrow's thinking today. *Journal of Creative Behavior, 8*(4), 227–281.

Lawton, J. P. (1976). *Effects of advance organizer lessons on children's use and understanding of the causal and logical*. Unpublished manuscript, University of Wisconsin, Madison.

Lawton, J. P., & Wanska, S. K. (1976). *An analytical study of the use of advance organizers in facilitating children's learning*. Unpublished manuscript, University of Wisconsin, Madison.

Lehman, P. R. (1968) *Tests and measurements in music*. Englewood Cliffs, NJ: Prentice Hall.

Lickona, T. (1983). *Raising good children: Helping your child through the stages of moral development.* New York: Bantam.

Lickona, T. (1985). Parents as moral educators. In M. Berkowitz & F. Oser (Eds.), *Moral education: Theory and application.* Hillsdale, NJ: Lawrence Erlbaum.

Lipman-Blumen, J., & Leavitt, H. J. (1976). Vicarious and direct achievement patterns in adulthood. *The Counseling Psychologist, 6,* 26–32.

Lowenfield, V., & Brittain, W. L. (1964). *Creative and mental growth.* New York: Macmillan.

Luchins, A. S. (1942). Mechanization in problem solving: The effect of Einstellung. *Psychological Monograph, 54*(6, Whole No. 248).

Lum, M. K. (1960). A comparison of underachieving and overachieving female college students. *Journal of Educational Psychology, 51*(3), 109–114.

Lyon, H. C., Jr. (1976). Education of the gifted and talented. *Exceptional Children, 43*(3), 166–168.

Lyon, H. C., Jr. (1979). A continuing account. *National/State Leadership Training Institute, on the Gifted and Talented Bulletin, 11*(2).

Maccoby, E. E., & Jacklin, C. (1974). *The psychology of sex differences.* Stanford, CA: Stanford University Press.

MacCormac, E. R. (1986). Creative metaphors. *Metaphor and Symbolic Activity, 1*(3), 171–184.

MacKinnon, D. W. (1978). *In search of human effectiveness.* Buffalo: Creative Education Foundation.

Maier, N. R. F. (1930). Reasoning in humans. *Journal of Comparative Psychology, 10,* 115–143.

Maker, J. C. (1976). *Training teachers for the gifted and talented: A comparison of models.* Reston, VA: Council for Exceptional Children.

Maker, J. C. (1977). *Providing programs for the gifted handicapped.* Reston, VA: Council for Exceptional Children.

Maker, J. C. (1982). *Curriculum development for the gifted.* Rockville, MD: Aspen.

Male, R. A., & Perrone, P. (1979). Identifying talent and giftedness: Part 1. *Roeper Review, 2*(1), 5–7.

Maltzman, I., Bogartz, W., & Breger, L. A. (1958). A procedure for increasing word association, originality and its transfer effects. *Journal of Experimental Psychology, 56,* 392–398.

Mann, R. D. (1959). A review of the relationships between personality and performance in small groups. *Psychological Bulletin, 56,* 241–270.

Mansfield, R. S., Busse, T. V., & Krepelka, E. J. (1978). The effectiveness of creativity training. *Review of Educational Research, 48*(4), 517–536.

Marion, R. L. (1981). Counseling parents of disadvantaged or culturally different gifted. *Roeper Review, 4*(1), 32–34.

Markley, O. W. (1988). Using depth intuition in creative problem solving. *Journal of Creative Behavior, 22*(2), 85–100.

Marland, S. J., Jr. (1972a). *Education of the gifted and talented: Report to the Congress of the United States* (2 vols.) Washington, DC: U.S. Government Printing Office.

Marland, S. J., Jr. (1972b). The responsibilities, activities and plans of the U.S. government for the education of the academically above-average. *Intellect, 101,* 16–19.

Martinson, R. A. (1961). *Educational programs for gifted pupils.* Sacramento: California State Department of Education.

Martinson, R. A. (1974). *The identification of the gifted and talented.* Los Angeles: National/State Leadership Training Institute on the Gifted and Talented.

Maslow, A. H. (1954). *Motivation and personality.* New York: Harper.

Maslow, A. H. (1959). Creativity in self-actualizing people. In H. H. Anderson (Ed.), *Creativity and its cultivation.* New York: Harper.

Maslow, A. H. (1968). *Toward a psychology of being* (2nd ed.). Princeton, NJ: D. Van Nostrand.

Maslow, A. H. (1970). *Motivation and personality* (2nd ed.). New York: Harper & Row.

Mayhew, K. C., & Edwards, A. C. (1936). *The Dewey School.* New York: D. Appleton Century.

McClelland, D. C., Atkinson, J. W., Clark, R. A., & Lowell, E. L. (1953). *The achievement motive.* New York: Appleton-Century.

McGarth, J. E., & Altman, I. (1966). *Small group research: A synthesis and critique of the field.* New York: Holt, Rinehart & Winston.

McGuire, C., Hindsman, E., King, F. J., & Jennings, E. (1961). Dimensions of talented behavior. *Educational and Psychological Measurement, 21*(1), 3–38.

McIntyre, P. M. (1964). Dynamics and treatment of the passive-aggressive underachiever. *American Journal of Psychotherapy, 18*(1), 95–107.

McKellar, P. (1957). *Imagination and thinking.* New York: Basic Books.

McKellar, P. (1972). Imagery from the standpoint of introspection. In P. W. Sheehan (Ed.), *The function and nature of imagery.* New York: Academic Press.

McLeod, J., & Cropley, A. (1989). *Fostering academic excellence.* New York: Pergamon.

McNemar, Q. (1964). Lost: Our intelligence? Why? *American Psychologists, 18,* 871–882.

Mead, M. (1930). *Growing up in New Guinea.* New York: Mentor Books.

Mednick, M. T., Mednick, S. A., & Mednick, E. V. (1964). Incubation of creative performance as specific associative priming. *Journal of Abnormal Psychology 69*(1), 84–88.

Mednick, S. A. (1959). *Remote Associates Test.* Boston: Houghton Mifflin.

Mednick, S. A. (1962). The associative basis of the creative process. *Psychological Review, 69,* 220–232.

Mednick, S. A., & Mednick, M. T. (1967) *Remote Associates Test: Examiner's manual.* Boston: Houghton Mifflin.

Meeker, M. N. (1967). Creative experiences for the educationally and neurologically handicapped who are gifted. *Gifted Child Quarterly, 11*(2), 160–164.

Meeker, M. N. (1968). Differential syndromes of giftedness and curriculum planning: A four-year follow-up. *Journal of Special Education, 2*(2), 185–196.

Meeker, M. N. (1969). *The structure of intellect: Its interpretation and uses.* Columbus, OH: Charles E. Merrill.

Meeker, M. N. (1979a). IEPs: Diagnosing and matching curriculum to cognitive patterns. In *Developing IEPs for the gifted/talented.* Los Angeles: National/State Leadership Training Institute on the Gifted and Talented.

Meeker, M. N. (1979b). *Using SOI test results: A teacher's guide.* Vida, OR: Structure of Intellect Systems.

Meeker, M. N. (1980a). *SOI abilities sourcebooks.* El Segundo, CA: SOI Institute.

Meeker, M. N. (1980b). *SOI-LA basic test: Technical data.* El Segundo, CA: SOI Institute.

Meeker, M. N. (1989). *How to reason: A handbook for critical thinking.* Vida, OR: SOI Systems.

Meeker, M. N., Meeker, R., & Roid, G. H. (1985). *Structure of Intellect Learning Abilities Test: Manual.* Los Angeles: Western Psychological Services.

Meeker, M. N., Sexton, K., & Richardson, M. O. (1970). *SOI abilities workbooks: Divergent thinking.* Los Angeles: Loyola-Marymount University.

Meister, M., & Odell, H. A. (1979). What provisions for the education of gifted students? In W. C. George, S. J. Cohn & J. C. Stanley (Eds.), *Educating the gifted: Acceleration and enrichment.* Baltimore: Johns Hopkins University Press.

Mercer, J. R., & Lewis, J. F. (1978). Using the system of multicultural pluralistic assessment (SOMPA) to identify the gifted minority child. In A. Y. Baldwin, G. H. Gear, & L. J. Lucito (Eds.), *Educational planning for the gifted.* Reston, VA: Council for Exceptional Children.

Merenda, P. F. (1965). Review of the Stanford Achievement Test. *Journal of Educational Measurement, 2*(2), 247–251.

Merry, F. (1935). Summer classes for gifted children. *Educational Method, 14,* 388–390.

Miles, C. C. (1960). Crucial factors in the life history of talent. In E. P. Torrance (Ed.), *Talent and education.* Minneapolis: University of Minnesota Press.

Miller, L. P. (Ed.). (1974). *Testing of black students: A symposium.* Englewood Cliffs, NJ: Prentice Hall.

Montessori, M. (1912). *The Montessori Method* (A. E. George, Trans.). London: William Heinemann.

Moreno, J. L. (1946). *Psychodrama: First volume*. Beacon, NY: Beacon House.

Moreno, J. L. (1952). Psychodramatic production techniques. *Group Psycho-therapy, 4*, 423–473.

Moreno, J. L., & Moreno, Z. T. (1969). *Psychodrama: Third volume*. Beacon, NY: Beacon House.

Morse, D. T., & Khatena, J. (1988). Evidence for validity of the Khatena-Morse multitalent perception inventory as indicated by differential performance. *Perceptual and Motor Skills, 66*, 591–594.

Morse, J. A., & Bruch, C. B. (1970). Gifted women: More issues than answers. *Educational Horizons, 49*, 25–32.

Morton, J., & Workman, E. (1978). Insights: Assisting intellectually gifted students with emotional difficulties. *Roeper Review, 1*(2), 16–18.

Mosher, R. L., & Sprinthall, N. (1971). Deliberate psychological education. *The Counseling Psychologist, 2*(4), 3–82.

Mowry, H. W. (1964/1965). *Leadership evaluation and development scale*. Knoxville, TN: Psychological Services.

Mursell, J. L. (1932). Measuring musical ability and achievement. *Journal of Educational Research, 25*, 116–126.

Myers, I. B. (1962). *The Myers-Briggs type indicator*. Princeton, NJ: Educational Testing Service.

Myers, R. E., & Torrance, E. P. (1964). *Invitations to thinking and doing*. Boston: Ginn.

Myers, R. E., & Torrance, E. P. (1968). *Stretch*. Minneapolis: Perceptive Publishing.

Nathan, C. N. (1979). Parental involvement. In A. H. Passow (Ed.), *The gifted and the talented: Their education and development*. Chicago: University of Chicago Press. (78th Yearbook of the NSSE)

National Forum. (1988a). Beyond intelligence testing. *National Forum, 68*(2), 1–48.

National Forum. (1988b). Marilyn vos Savant: Interview with the smartest woman in the world. *National Forum, 63*(2), 17.

Newland, T. E. (1976). *The gifted in socio-educational perspective*. Englewood Cliffs, NJ: Prentice Hall.

Oden, M. H. (1968). *The fulfillment of promise: 40-year follow-up of the Terman gifted group*. Stanford, CA: Stanford University Press.

Ogbu, J. U. (1988). Human intelligence testing: A cultural-ecological perspective. *Educational Forum, 68*(2), 23–29.

Olenchak, F. R., & Renzulli, J. S. (1989). The effectiveness of schoolwide enrichment model on selected aspects of elementary school change. *Gifted Child Quarterly, 33*(1), 36–46.

Olson, M. (1977). Right or left hemisphere processing in the gifted. *Gifted Child Quarterly, 2*(1), 116–121.

Olson, W. C. (1959). *Child development* (2nd ed). Boston: D.C. Heath.

Olton, R. M. (1979). Experimental studies in incubation: Searching for the elusive. *Journal of Creative Behavior, 13*(1), 9–22.

Oppen, M. B. (1970). Gifted child in a small town: A parent's point of view. *Gifted Child Quarterly, 14*(2), 92–95.

Ornstein, R. (1972). *The psychology of consciousness.* New York: Freeman.

Osborn, A. F. (1962). Developments in creative education. In S. J. Parnes & H. F. D. Harding (Eds.), *A source book for creative thinking.* New York: Charles Scribner's.

Osborn, A. F. (1963). *Applied imagination.* New York: Charles Scribner's

Oser, F. K. (1988). *Moral education and values education: The discourse perspective.*

Otis, A. S., & Lennon, R. T. (1967). *Otis-Lennon Mental Ability Test.* New York: Harcourt Brace Jovanovich.

Owens, W. A. (1953). Age and mental abilities: A longitudinal study. *Genetic Psychology Monograph, 48,* 3–54.

Oxford English Dictionary. (1982). Oxford, U.K.: Clarendon Press.

Paivio, A. (1971). *Imagery and verbal processes.* New York: Holt, Rinehart & Winston.

Parker, J. P. (1989). *Instructional strategies for teaching the gifted.*

Parnes, S. J. (Comp.). (1958). *Compendium no. 1 of research on creative imagination.* Buffalo: Creative Education Foundation.

Parnes, S. J. (Comp.). (1960). *Compendium no. 2 of research on creative imagination.* Buffalo: Creative Education Foundation.

Parnes, S. J. (1967a). *Creative behavior guidebook.* New York: Charles Scribner's.

Parnes, S. J. (1967b). *Creative behavior workbook.* New York: Charles Scribner's.

Parnes, S. J. (1975). CPSI—a program for balanced growth. *Journal of Creative Behavior, 9*(1), 23–29.

Parnes, S. J. (1981). *The magic of your mind.* Buffalo: Creative Education Foundation and Bearly.

Parnes, S. J. (1988). *Visionizing.* East Aurora, NY: D.O.K.

Parnes, S. J., & Biondi, A. M. (1975). Creative behavior: A delicate balance. *Journal of Creative Behavior, 9*(3), 149–158.

Parnes, S. J., & Meadows, A. (1959). Effects of "brainstorming" instructions on creative problem solving by trained and untrained subjects. *Journal of Educational Psychology, 50*(4), 171–176.

Parnes, S. J., & Noller, R. B. (1973). *Toward supersanity: Channeled freedom.* Buffalo: D.O.K.

Parnes, S. J., Noller, R. B., & Biondi, A. M. (1977). *Creative actionbook* rev. ed. of S. J. Parnes [1967a], *Creative behavior guidebook.* New York: Charles Scribner's.

Passow, A. H. (1957). Identifying and counseling gifted college students. *Journal of Higher Education, 28,* 21–29.

Passow, A. H. (1958). Enrichment of education for the gifted. In B. Henry (Ed.), *Education for the gifted.* Chicago: University of Chicago Press. (57th Yearbook of the NSSE)

Passow, A. H. (1979). A look around and a look ahead. In A. H. Passow (Ed.), *The gifted and the talented: Their education and development.* Chicago: University of Chicago Press. (78th Yearbook of the NSSE)

Passow, A. H. (1986). Reflections on three decades of education of the gifted. *Roeper Review, 8*(4), 223–226.

Passow, A. H., Goldberg, M. L., Tannenbaum, A., & French, W. (1955). *Planning for talented youth.* New York: Columbia University Teachers College Bureau of Publications.

Patrick, C. (1955). *What is creative thinking?* New York: Philosophical Library.

Pegnato, C. W. (1958). An evaluation of various initial methods of selecting intellectually gifted children at the junior high school level. *Dissertation Abstracts International, 19,* 1254. (University Microfilms No. 58-07298)

Pegnato, C. W., & Birch, J. W. (1959). Locating gifted children in junior high schools: A comparison of methods. *Exceptional Children, 25,* 300–304.

Pepinsky, P. (1960). Study of productive nonconformity. *Gifted Child Quarterly, 4*(3), 81–85.

Perrone, P. A., Karshner, W. W., & Male, R. A. (1979). *Career development of talented persons.* Unpublished manuscript, University of Wisconsin, Guidance Institute for Talented Students, Madison.

Perrone, P., & Pulvino, C. J. (1977). New directions in the guidance of gifted and talented. *Gifted Child Quarterly, 20*(3), 326–339.

Perry, W. G., Jr. (1970). *Forms of intellectual and ethical development in the college years.* New York: Holt, Rinehart & Winston.

Pestalozzi, J. H. (1907). *How Gertrude teaches her children* (L. E. Holland & F. C. Turner, Trans.). London: Swan Sonnenschein.

Pezzulo, T. R., Thorsen, E. E., & Madus, G. F. (1972). The heritability of Jensen's level I and II and divergent thinking. *American Educational Research Journal, 9,* 539–546.

Piaget, J. (1930). *The moral judgement of the child.* New York: Harcourt Brace Jovanovich.

Piaget, J. (1950). *The psychology of intelligence.* London: Routledge & Kegan Paul.

Piaget, J. (1967). *Six psychological studies.* New York: Random House.

Pierce, J. V., & Bowman, P. H. (1960). Motivation patterns of superior high school students. In *The gifted student* (Co-operative Research Monograph No. 2). Washington, DC: U.S. Government Printing Office.

Plum, L. (1980). *Flights of fantasy: Ideas and activities to foster the development of imagination, relaxation and self-concept.* Carthage, IL: Good Apple.

Polak, F. L. (1973). *The image of the future.* New York: Elsevier.

Pollio, M. R., & Pollio, H. R. (1979). A test of metaphoric comprehension and some preliminary developmental data. *Journal of Child Language, 6,* 111–120.

Pressy, S. L. (1949). Educational acceleration: Appraisal and basic problems. *Bureau of Educational Research Monographs*, No. 13. Columbus: Ohio State University.

Prince, G. M. (1968). The operational mechanism of synectics. *Journal of Creative Behavior, 2*(1), 1–13.

Prince, G. M. (1975). The mindspring theory. *Journal of Creative Behavior, 9*(3), 159–181.

Pringle, M. L. K. (1970). *Able misfits: A study of educational and behavioral difficulties of 103 very intelligent children (I.Q.s 120–200).* London: Longmans.

Proctor, T. B., Black, K. N., & Feldhusen, J. F. (1988). Early admission to elementary school: Barriers versus benefits. *Roeper Review, 11*(2), 85–87.

Quick, R. H. (1895). *Some thoughts concerning education by John Locke.* Cambridge, U.K.: Cambridge University Press.

Raph, J. B., Goldberg, M. L., & Passow, A. H. (1966). *Bright underachievers.* New York: Columbia University Teachers College Bureau of Publications.

Raven, J. C. (1947). *Raven's Progressive Matrices Test.* London: H. K. Lewis.

Redl, F., & Wattenberg, W. W. (1959). *Mental hygiene in teaching* (2nd ed.). New York: Harcourt, Brace & World.

Reis, S. M. (1987). We can't change what we don't recognize: Understanding the special needs of gifted females. *Gifted Child Quarterly, 31*(2), 83–89.

Renzulli, J. S. (1973). *New directions in creativity.* New York: Harper & Row.

Renzulli, J. S. (1975). *A guidebook for evaluating programs for the gifted and talented.* Los Angeles: National/State Leadership Training Institute on the Gifted and Talented.

Renzulli, J. S. (1977). *The interest-a-lyzer.* Mansfield Center, CT: Creative Learning Press.

Renzulli, J. S. (1978). *The Learning Style Inventory: A measure of student preference for instructional techniques.* Mansfield Center, CT: Creative Learning Press.

Renzulli, J. S. (1979a). The enrichment triad model: A guide for developing defensible programs for the gifted. In J. C. Gowan, J. Khatena, & E. P. Torrance (Eds.), *Educating the ablest* (2nd ed.). Itasca, IL: F. E. Peacock.

Renzulli, J. S. (1979b). *What makes giftedness?* Los Angeles: National/State Leadership Training Institute on the Gifted and Talented.

Renzulli, J. S. (1980). Will the gifted movement be alive and well in 1990? *Gifted Child Quarterly, 24*(1), 3–9.

Renzulli, J. S. (1984). The triad/revolving door: A research-based approach to identification and programming for the gifted and talented. *Gifted Child Quarterly, 28*(4), 163–171.

Renzulli, J. S. (1986). The three-ring conception of giftedness: A developmental model for creative productivity. In R. J. Sternberg & J. E. Davidson (Eds.), *Conceptions of giftedness.* New York: Cambridge University Press.

Renzulli, J. S. (1988). The multiple menus model for developing differentiated curriculum for the gifted and talented. *Gifted Child Quarterly, 32*(3), 298–309.

Renzulli, J. S., & Hartman, R. K. (1971). Scale for rating the behavior characteristics of superior students. *Exceptional Children, 38,* 243–248.

Renzulli, J. S., & Olenchak, F. R. (1989). The effectiveness of the school-wide enrichment model on selected aspects of school change. *Gifted Child Quarterly, 33*(1), 36–46.

Renzulli, J. S., Reis, S. M., & Smith, L. H. (1981). *The revolving door identification model.* Mansfield, CT: Creative Learning Press.

Renzulli, J. S., & Smith, L. H. (1978b). *The compactor.* Mansfield Center, CT: Creative Learning Press.

Renzulli, J. S., & Smith, L. H. (1978a). *The strength-a-lyzer.* Mansfield Center, CT: Creative Learning Press.

Renzulli, J. S., & Smith, L. H. (1979a). Issues and procedures in evaluating programs. In A. H. Passow (Ed.), *The gifted and the talented: Their education and development.* Chicago: University of Chicago Press. (78th Yearbook of the NSSE)

Renzulli, J. S., & Smith, L. H. (1979b). A practical model for designing individualized education programs (IEPs) for the gifted and talented students. In *Developing IEPs for the gifted/talented.* Los Angeles: National/State Leadership Training Institute on the Gifted and Talented.

Renzulli, J. S., Smith, L. H., White, A. J., Callahan, C. M., & Hartman, R. K. (1976). *Scale for rating the behavioral characteristics of superior students.* Mansfield, CT: Creative Learning Press.

Renzulli, J. S., & Ward, V. S. (1969). *Diagnostic and evaluation scale for differential education for the gifted.* Storrs, CT: University of Connecticut Bureau of Educational Research.

Rhodes, M. (1961). An analysis of creativity. *Phi Delta Kappan, 42*(7), 305–310.

Ribot, T. (1906). *Essay on the creative imagination.* London: Kagan & Paul.

Rich, J. M., & DeVitis, J. L. (1985). *Theories of moral development.* Springfield, IL.: Charles C Thomas.

Richardson, A. (1969). *Mental imagery.* New York: Springer.

Richert, S. E. (1985). Identification of gifted children in the United States: The need for pluralistic assessment. *Roeper Review, 8*(2), 68–72.

Richert, S. E., Alvino, J. J., & McDonnel, R. C. (1982). *National report on identification: Assessment and recommendations for comprehensive identification of gifted and talented youth.* Reston, VA: Education Resource Information Center.

Riessman, F. (1962). *The culturally deprived child.* New York: Harper & Row.

Rieu, E. V. (Trans.). (1957). *Homer: The Illiad* Baltimore: Penguin.

Rimm, S. B. (1986). *Underachievement syndrome: Causes and cures.* Watertown, WI: Apple.

Rimm, S., & Davis, G. A. (1976). GIFT: An instrument for the identification of creativity. *Journal of Creative Behavior, 10*(3), 178–182.

Rimm, S., & Davis, G. A. (1980). Five years of international research with GIFT: An instrument for the identification of creativity. *Journal of Creative Behavior, 14*(1), 35–46.

Ripple, R. E. (1961). A controlled experiment in acceleration from the second to the fourth grade. *Gifted Child Quarterly, 5*(4), 119–120.

Rivchun, S. B. (1980). Be a mentor and leave a lasting legacy. *Association Management, 32*(8), 71–74.

Robinson, H. B. (1983). A case for radical acceleration: Programs of The Johns Hopkins University and the University of Washington. In C. P. Benbow & J. C. Stanley (Eds.), *Academic promise: Aspects of its development*. Baltimore: Johns Hopkins University Press.

Rockenstein, Z. (1988). Intuitive processes in executive decision making. *Journal of Creative Behavior, 22*(2), 77–84.

Rockenstein, Z. (1989). *Training the creative-intuitive mind*. Buffalo: Bearly.

Roe, A. (1963). Personal problems in science. In C. W. Taylor & F. Barron (Eds.), *Scientific creativity: Its recognition and development*. New York: John Wiley.

Roebuck, M. C. (1968). *Special class programs for intellectually gifted pupils*. Sacramento: California State Department of Education. (ERIC Document Reproduction Service No. ED 042-271)

Roets, L. S. (1986). *Leadership: A skills training program ages 8–18*. New Sharon, IA: Leadership.

Rogers, C. R. (1967). *On becoming a person: A therapist's view of psychotherapy*. Boston: Houghton Mifflin.

Rogers, C. R. (1969). The facilitation of significant learning. In R. C. Sprinthall & N. A. Sprinthall (Eds.), *Educational psychology: Selected readings*. New York: D. Van Nostrand.

Rogers, D. (Ed.). (1969). *Issues in adolescent psychology*. New York: Appleton-Century-Crofts.

Rosen, B. C., & D'Andrade, R. (1959). The psychosocial origins of achievement motivation. *Sociometry, 22*, 185–195, 215–218.

Rossman, J. (1931). *The psychology of the inventor* (rev. ed.). Washington, DC: Inventors.

Roth, R. M., & Meyersburg, A. H. (1963). The non-achievement syndrome. *Personnel and Guidance Journal, 61*(6), 535–540.

Rothenberg, A. (1976). The process of Janusian thinking in creativity. In A. Rothenberg & C. R. Hausman (Eds.), *The creativity question* (pp. 311–327). Durham, NC: Duke University Press.

Rothney, J. W. M., & Koopman, N. (1957). Guidance of the gifted. In N. B. Henry (Ed.), *Education for the gifted*. Chicago: University of Chicago Press. (57th Yearbook of the NSSE)

Rotter, J. B. (1966). Generalized expectancies for internal versus external control of reinforcement. *Psychological Monograph, 80* (1, Whole No. 609).

Rousseau, J. J. (1672). *Emile*. In T. Talbot (Ed.), *The world of the child*. New York: Doubleday.

Roweton, W. E. *Creativity: A review of theory and research*. Buffalo: Creative Education Foundation. (Occasional paper No. 7)

Royce, J. (1898). The psychology of invention. *Psychological Review, 5*, 113–144.

Rugg, H. (1963). *Imagination: An inquiry into the sources and conditions that stimulate creativity*. New York: Harper & Row.

Runions, T. (1980). The mentor academy program: Educating and gifted/talented for the 80s. *Gifted Child Quarterly, 4*(3), 152–157.

Runner, K., & Runner, H. (1965). *Manual of interpretation for the Interview Form III of the Runner studies of attitude patterns*. Golden, CO: Runner Associates.

Rusk, R. R. (1957). *The doctrines of the great educators*. New York: Macmillan.

Russell, J. D. (1974). *Modular instruction*. Minneapolis: Burgess.

Sadker, M., & Sadker, D. (1985). Sexism in the schoolroom of the 80s. *Psychology Today, 109*(3), 54–57.

Samples, B. (1975). Learning with the whole brain. *Human Behavior, 53*, 17–23.

Samuda, R. J. (1975). *Psychological testing of American minorities: Issues and consequences*. New York: Dodd, Mead.

Sanborn, M. P. (1979). Differential counseling needs of the gifted and talented. In N. Colangelo and R. T. Zaffron (Eds.), *New voices in counseling the gifted*. Dubuque, IA: Kendall/Hunt.

Sattler, J. M. (1988). *Assessment of children* (3rd ed.). San Diego: Author.

Schaefer, C. E. (1970). *Biographical inventory: Creativity*. San Diego: Educational and Industrial Testing Services.

Schaefer, C. E. (1971). *Becoming somebody*. Buffalo: D.O.K.

Schaefer, C. E. (1975). The importance of measuring metaphorical thinking in children. *Gifted Child Quarterly, 19*(2), 140–148.

Schaefer, C. E., & Anastasi, A. (1968). A biographical inventory for identifying creativity in adolescent boys. *Journal of Applied Psychology, 52*, 42–48.

Schmidt, P. (1982). Sexist schooling. *Working Women, 7*(1), 101–102.

Schneid, K. (Ed.). (1979). *Erziehen in der Schule: Auftrag, Ziele and Methoden*. Munchen: Oldenburg Verlag.

Schubert, D. S. P. (1979). Is incubation a silent rehearsal of mundane responses? *Journal of Creative Behavior, 13*(1), 36–38.

Scriven, M. (1967). The methodology of evaluation. In R. W. Tyler, R. M. Gagne, & M. Scriven (Eds.), *Perspectives of curriculum evaluation*. Chicago: Rand McNally.

Sears, R. R., Maccoby, E. E., & Levin, H. (1957). *Patterns of child rearing*. New York: Harper & Row.

Seashore, C. E. (1938). *Psychology of music*. New York: McGraw-Hill.

Seashore, C. E., Leavis, D., & Saetveit, J. (1960). *Seashore measures of musical talents.* New York: Psychological Corporation.

Shaw, M. C. (1960). *Attitudes and child rearing practices of the parents of bright academic underachievers.* Washington, DC: U.S. Government Printing Office. (U.S. Public Health Services Research Project M-2843).

Sheehan, P. W., McConkey, K. M., & Cross, D. G. (1978). The experimental analysis technique: Some new observations of hypnotic phenomena. *Journal of Abnormal Psychology, 87,* 570–573.

Shephard, R. N. (1978). The mental image. *American Psychologist, 33*(2), 125–137.

Shepherd, J. (1972). Black lab power. *Saturday Review, 55,* 32–39.

Shock, N. W. (1951). Gerontology. *Annual Review of Psychology, 2,* 353–370.

Shockley, W.(1972). Dysgenics, geneticity , raceology: A challenge to the intellectual responsibility of educators. *Phi Delta Kappan, 53*(5), 297–307.

Shorr, J. E. (1977). *Go see the movie in your head.* New York: Popular Library.

Silberman, C. (1970). *Crisis in the classroom.* New York: Random House.

Simmons, W. L. (1968). Human intelligence: The psychological view. *The Science Teacher, 35*(6), 18–20.

Simonton, D. K. (1978). The eminent genius in history: The critical role of creative development. *Gifted Child Quarterly, 22*(2), 187–195.

Simpson, J. (1977). Developmental process theory as applied to mature women. *Gifted Child Quarterly, 21*(3), 359–371.

Simpson, R. M. (1922). Creative imagination. *American Journal of Psychology, 33*(2), 234–243.

Singer, B. D. (1974). The future-focused image. In A. Toffler (Ed.), *Learning for tomorrow.* New York: Random House.

Sisk, D. (1979). Gifted and talented: Three year perspective. *National/State Leadership Training Institute on the Gifted and Talented, 6*(7), 2, 7.

Sisk, D. (1980). Issues and future in gifted education. *Gifted Child Quarterly, 24*(1), 29–36.

Southern, W. T., Jones, E. D., Fiscus, E. D. (1989). Practitioner objections to the academic acceleration of gifted children. *Gifted Child Quarterly, 33*(1), 29–35.

Spearman, C. (1927). *The abilities of man: Their nature and measurement.* New York: Macmillan.

Spearman, C. (1930). *Creative mind.* London: Cambridge University Press.

Sperry, R. W. (1974, January). Messages from the laboratory. *Engineering and Science,* pp. 29–32.

Stanley, J. C.. (1974). Intellectual precocity. In J. C. Stanley, D. P. Keating & L. H. Fox (Eds.), *Mathematical talent: Discovery, description and development.* Baltimore: Johns Hopkins University Press.

Stanley, J. C. (1977a). *Educational non-acceleration: An international tragedy.* Address to the 2nd World Conference on Gifted and Talented Children at the University Center, University of San Francisco.

Stanley, J. C. (1977b). Rationale of the study of mathematically precocious youth (SMPY) during its first five years of promoting educational acceleration. In J. C. Stanley, W. C. George, & C. H. Solano (Eds.), *The gifted and the creative: A fifty-year perspective* (pp. 75–112). Baltimore: Johns Hopkins University Press.

Stanley, J. C. (1979). The study and facilitation of talent for mathematics. In A. H. Passow (Ed.), *The gifted and the talented: Their education and development.* Chicago: University of Chicago Press. (78th Yearbook of the NSSE)

Stanley, J. C. (1988). Some characteristics of SMPY's "700-800 on SAT-M before age 13 group": Youths who reason extremely well mathematically. *Gifted Child Quarterly, 32*(1), 205–209.

Stanley, J. C., & Benbow, C. P. (1988). Youths who reason exceptionally well mathematically. In R. J. Sternberg & J. E. Davidson, (Eds.), *Conceptions of giftedness.* New York: Cambridge University Press.

Stanley, J. C., & George, W. C. (1980). SMPY's ever increasing D4. *Gifted Child Quarterly, 24*(1), 41–48.

Stanley, J. C., George, W. C., & Solano, C. H. (Eds.). (1977). *The gifted and the creative: A fifty-year perspective.* Baltimore: Johns Hopkins University Press.

Stanley, J. C., George, W. C., & Solano, C. H. (Eds.). (1978). *Educational programs and the intellectual prodigies.* Baltimore: Johns Hopkins University Press.

Stanley, J. C., Keating, D. P., & Fox, L. H. (Eds.). (1974). *Mathematical talent: Discovery, description and development.* Baltimore: Johns Hopkins University Press.

Starkweather, E. K. (1971). Creativity research instruments designed for use with preschool children. *Journal of Creative Behavior, 5*(4), 245–255.

Steele, J. M. (1969). *Dimensions of the class activities.* Unpublished manuscript, University of Illinois, Instructional Research and Curriculum Evaluation Center, Urbana.

Steinbrecher, E. (1978). *The inner guide meditation.* Santa Fe, CA: Blue Feathers.

Sternberg, R. J. (1980). Sketch of a componential subtheory of human intelligence. *Behavioral and Brain Sciences, 3,* 573–614.

Sternberg, R. J. (1981). A componential theory of intellectual giftedness. *Gifted Child Quarterly, 25*(2), 86–93.

Sternberg, R. J. (1984a). Mechanisms of cognitive development: A componential approach. In R. J. Sternberg (Ed.), *Mechanisms of cognitive development.* New York: W. H. Freeman.

Sternberg, R. J. (1984b). Toward a triarchic theory of human intelligence. *Behavior and Brain Sciences, 3,* 269–287.

Sternberg, R. J. (1988). Beyond I.Q. testing. *National Forum, 68*(2), 8–11.

Sternberg, R. J., & Davidson, J. E. (1986). (Eds.). *Conceptions of giftedness.* New York: Cambridge University Press.

Stogdill, R. M. (1948). Personal factors associated with leadership: A survey of the literature. *Journal of Psychology, 25,* 35–71.

Stogdill, R. M. (1959). *Individual behavior and group achievement.* New York: Oxford University Press.

Stogdill, R. M. (1974). *Handbook of leadership: A survey of theory and research.* New York: Free Press.

Stott, L. H., & Ball, R. S. (1963). *Evaluation of infant and preschool mental tests.* Detroit: Merrill-Palmer.

Strang, R. (1958). *Guideposts for teachers of gifted children.* New York: Columbia University Teachers College.

Strang, R. (1960). *Helping your gifted child.* New York: E. P. Dutton.

Strodtbeck, F. (1958). Implication of the study of family interaction for the prediction of achievement. *Child Study, 35,* 14–18.

Strom, R. D. (1967). The dropout problem in relation to family affect and effect. In E. P. Torrance & R. D. Strom (Eds.), *Mental health and achievement: Increasing potential and reducing school dropout.* New York: John Wiley.

Sullivan, E. T., Clark, W. W. & Tiegs, E. W. (1963). *California Test of Mental Maturity* (rev. ed.). New York: McGraw-Hill.

Sullivan, H. S. (1953). *The interpersonal theory of psychiatry.* New York: W. W. Norton.

Sward, K. (1933). Jewish musicality in America. *Journal of Applied Psychology, 17,* 675–712.

Sweetland, R. C., & Keyser, D. J. (Eds.). (1986). *Tests: A comprehensive reference for assessments in psychology, education and business.* Kansas City: Test Corporation of America.

Tannenbaum, A. J. (1986). *Gifted children: Psychological and educational perspectives.* New York: Macmillan.

Tan-Williams, C., & Gutteridge, D. (1981). Creative thinking and moral reasoning of academically gifted secondary school adolescents. *Gifted Child Quarterly, 25*(4), 149–153.

Taylor, C. W. (Ed.). (1958). *The 1957 University of Utah research conference on the identification of creative talent.* Salt Lake City: University of Utah Press.

Taylor, C. W. (Ed.). (1959). *The 3rd (1959) University of Utah research conference on the identification of creative scientific talent.* Salt Lake City: University of Utah Press.

Taylor, C. W. (1969). The highest talent potentials of man. *Gifted Child Quarterly, 13*(1), 9–30.

Taylor, C. W. (1978). How many types of giftedness can your program tolerate? *Journal of Creative Behavior, 12*(1), 39–51.

Taylor, C. W. (1986). Cultivating simultaneous student growth in both multiple creative talents and knowledge. In J. S. Renzulli (Ed.), *Systems and models for developing programs for the gifted and talented.* Mansfield, CT: Creative Learning Press.

Taylor, C. W., & Ellison, R. L. (1966). *Manual for alpha biographical inventory.*

Unpublished Manuscript, Institute for Behavioral Research in Creativity, Salt Lake City.

Taylor, C. W., & Ellison, R. L. (1967). Biographical predictors of scientific performance. *Science, 155*, 1075–1080.

Taylor, C. W., & Ellison, R. L. (1983). Searching for student talent resources relevant to all USOE types of giftedness. *Gifted Child Quarterly, 27*(3), 99–110.

Taylor, I. A. (1972). *A theory of creative transactualization: A systematic approach to creativity with implications for creative leadership.* Buffalo: Creative Education Foundation. (Occasional paper No. 8)

Terman, L. M. (1916). *The measurement of intelligence.* Boston: Houghton Mifflin.

Terman, L. M. (1919). *Intelligence of school children.* Boston: Houghton Mifflin.

Terman, L. M. (1925). *Mental and physical traits of a thousand gifted children: Genetic studies of genius* (Vol. 1). Stanford, CA: Stanford University Press.

Terman, L. M. (1954). Scientists and nonscientists in a group of 800 gifted men. *Psychological Monographs, 68*, 1–41.

Terman, L. M., & Merrill, M. A. (1937). *Measuring intelligence.* Boston: Houghton Mifflin.

Terman, L. M., & Merrill, M. A. (1960). *Stanford-Binet intelligence scale: A manual for the third revision, Form L-M.* Boston: Houghton Mifflin.

Terman, L. M., & Oden, M. H. (1947). *The gifted child grows up—twenty-five years' follow-up of a superior group: Genetic studies of genius* (Vol. 4). Stanford, CA: Stanford University Press.

Terman, L. M., & Oden, M. H. (1959). *The gifted group at mid-life: Genetic studies of genius* (Vol. 5). Stanford, CA: Stanford University Press.

Theodore, A. (1971). *The professional woman.* Cambridge, MA: Schenkman.

Thornburg, H. D. (1973). Behavior and values: Consistency or inconsistency. *Adolescence, 8*(32), 513–520.

Thorndike, E. L. (1932). Reward and punishment in animal learning. *Comparative Psychological Monograph, 8*, No. 9.

Thorndike, R. L. (1966). Some methodological issues in the study of creativity. In A. Anastasi (Ed.), *Testing problems in perspective.* Washington, DC: American Council on Education.

Thorndike, R. L., Hagen, E. P., & Sattler, J. M. (1986). *Stanford-Binet intelligence scale (4th ed.): Technical manual.* Chicago: Riverside Publishing.

Thurstone, L. L. (1924). *The nature of intelligence.* New York: Harcourt Brace.

Thurstone, L. L. (1938). *Primary mental abilities.* Chicago: University of Chicago Press.

Toffler, A. (Ed.). (1974). *Learning for tomorrow.* New York: Random House.

Tolman, E. C. (1948). Cognitive maps in rats and men. *Psychological Review, 55*, 189–208.

Torda, C. (1970). Some observations on the creative process. *Perceptual and Motor Skills, 31*, 107–126.

Torrance, E. P. (1958). *Preliminary manual for Personal-Social Motivation Inventory.* Unpublished manuscript, University of Minnesota, Minneapolis.

Torrance, E. P. (1962a). *Guiding creative talent.* Englewood Cliffs, NJ: Prentice Hall.

Torrance, E. P. (1962b). Non-test ways of identifying the creatively gifted. *Gifted Child Quarterly, 6*(3), 71–75.

Torrance, E. P. (1963). *Education of the creative potential.* Minneapolis: University of Minnesota Press.

Torrance, E. P. (1965a). *Constructive behavior: Stress, personality and mental health.* Englewood Cliffs, NJ: Prentice Hall.

Torrance, E. P. (1965b). *Gifted children in the classroom.* New York: Macmillan.

Torrance, E. P. (1965c). *Rewarding creative behavior.* Englewood Cliffs, NJ: Prentice Hall.

Torrance, E. P. (1967a). Helping gifted children through mental health concepts. *Gifted Child Quarterly, 11*(1), 3–7.

Torrance, E. P. (1967b). *Understanding the fourth grade slump in creative thinking* (Final report on Cooperative Research Project No. 94, U.S. Office of Education). Unpublished manuscript, University of Georgia, Athens.

Torrance, E. P. (1968). A longitudinal examination of the fourth grade slump in creativity. *Gifted Child Quarterly, 12*(4), 195–199.

Torrance, E. P. (1970). Broadening concepts of giftedness in the 70's. *Gifted Child Quarterly, 14*(4), 199–208.

Torrance, E. P. (1971a). Are the Torrance Tests of Creative Thinking biased against or in favor of disadvantaged groups? *Gifted Child Quarterly, 15*(2), 75–80.

Torrance, E. P. (1971b, May). *Identity: The gifted child's major problem.* Address presented at the 18th National Association for Gifted Children Annual Convention, Chicago.

Torrance, E. P. (1972a). Can we teach children to think creatively? *Journal of Creative Behavior, 6*(2), 114–143.

Torrance, E. P. (1972b). Predictive validity of the Torrance Tests of Creative Thinking. *Journal of Creative Behavior, 6*(4), 236–252.

Torrance, E. P. (1972c). Career patterns and peak creative achievements of creative high school students twelve years later. *Gifted Child Quarterly, 16*(2), 75–88.

Torrance, E. P. (1972d). Creative young women in today's world. *Exceptional Children, 38,* 597–603.

Torrance, E. P. (1973). Non-test indicators of creative talent among disadvantaged children. *Gifted Child Quarterly, 17*(1), 3–9.

Torrance, E. P. (1974a). Differences are not deficits. *Teachers College Record, 75,* 472–489.

Torrance, E. P. (1974b). *Torrance Tests of Creative Thinking: Norms-technical manual.* Bensenville, IL: Scholastic Testing Service. (Originally published by Personnel Press, 1966)

Torrance, E. P. (1975a). Assessing children, teachers and parents against the ideal child criterion. *Gifted Child Quarterly, 19*(2), 130–139.

Torrance, E. P. (1975b). Motivation and creativity. In E. P. Torrance & W. White (Eds.), *Issues and advances in educational psychology* (2nd ed.). Itasca, IL: F. E. Peacock.

Torrance, E. P. (1975c). Sociodrama as a creative problem solving approach to studying the future. Journal of Creative Behavior, 9(3), 182–195.

Torrance, E. P. (1975d). The risk of being a great teacher. In E. P. Torrance & W. White (Eds.), *Issues and advances in educational psychology* (2nd ed.). Itasca, IL: F. E. Peacock.

Torrance, E. P. (1976a). Future careers for gifted and talented students. *Gifted Child Quarterly, 20*(2), 142–146.

Torrance, E. P. (1976b). *Sociodrama in career education* (Preservice Teacher Training in Career Education Project). Unpublished manuscript, University of Georgia, Athens.

Torrance, E. P. (1977a). Creatively gifted and disadvantaged gifted. In J. C. Stanley, W. C. George & C. H. Solano (Eds.), *The gifted and the creative: A fifty-year perspective.* Baltimore: Johns Hopkins University Press.

Torrance, E. P. (1977b). *Discovery and nurturance of giftedness in the culturally different.* Reston, VA: Council for Exceptional Children.

Torrance, E. P. (1977c, October). *Scenario in the year 2002.* Keynote address presented at the 24th National Association for Gifted Children Annual Convention, San Diego.

Torrance, E. P. (1978a). Dare we hope again? *Gifted Child Quarterly, 22*(3), 292–312.

Torrance, E. P. (1978b). Letter to J. C. Gowan. *Gifted Child Quarterly, 22*(2), 175–176.

Torrance, E. P. (1979a). An instructional model for enhancing incubation. *Journal of Creative Behavior, 13*(1), 23–35.

Torrance, E. P. (1979b). *The search for satori and creativity.* Buffalo: Creative Education Foundation.

Torrance, E. P. (1979c). Unique needs of the creative child and adult. In A. H. Passow (Ed.), *The gifted and the talented: Their education and development.* Chicago: University of Chicago Press. (78th Yearbook of the NSSE)

Torrance, E. P. (1980a). Growing up creatively gifted: A 22-year longitudinal study. *Creative Child and Adult Quarterly, 5*(3), 148–158, 170–171.

Torrance, E. P. (1980b). *Streamlined scoring and interpretation guide, and norms manual for figural form A, Torrance Tests of Creative Thinking (4th Revision).* Unpublished manuscript, University of Georgia, Athens.

Torrance, E. P. (1981a). *Thinking Creatively in Action and Movement.* Bensenville, IL: Scholastic Testing Service.

Torrance, E. P. (1981b). Predicting the creativity of elementary school children (1958–1980) and the teacher who made a "difference." *Gifted Child Quarterly, 25*(2), 55–62.

Torrance, E. P. (1983). Role of mentors in creative achievement. *Creative Child and Adult Quarterly, 8*(1), 8–16.

Torrance, E. P. (1984). *Mentoring relationships: How they aid creative achievement, endure, change, and die.* Buffalo: Bearly.

Torrance, E. P. (1988). *Style of learning and thinking: Administrator's manual.* Bensenville, IL: Scholastic Testing Service.

Torrance, E. P. (1989a). *Torrance Tests of Creative Thinking: Figural streamlined scoring manual.* Bensenville, IL: Scholastic Testing Service.

Torrance, E. P. (1989b). The nature of creativity as manifest in its testing. In R. J. Sternberg (Ed.), *The nature of creativity: Contemporary perspectives.* New York: Cambridge University Press.

Torrance, E. P., & Gibbs, M. S. (1979). *Norms-technical, administration and scoring manual: Thinking Creatively in Action and Movement.* Unpublished manuscript, University of Georgia, Athens.

Torrance, E. P., & Hall, L. K. (1980). Assessing the further reaches of creative potential. *Journal of Creative Behavior, 14*(1), 1–19.

Torrance, E. P., & Horng, R. (1978). *Scoring guide: Future problem solving program.* Unpublished manuscript, University of Georgia, Athens.

Torrance, E. P., Khatena, J., & Cunningham, B. F. (1990). *Thinking Creatively with Sounds and Words.* Bensenville, IL: Scholastic Testing Service. (Originally published by Personnel Press, 1973)

Torrance, E. P., & Myers, R. E. (1970). *Creative learning and teaching.* New York: Dodd-Mead.

Torrance, E. P., & Safter, T. (1990). *The incubation model of teaching: Getting beyond the Aha!* Buffalo: Bearly.

Torrance, E. P., & Wu, T. (1981). A comparative longitudinal study of the adult creative achievements of elementary school children identified as highly creative. *The Creative Child and Adult Quarterly, 6*(2), 71–75.

Torsi, L. (1975). Woman's scientific creativity. *Impact of Science on Society, 25,* 105–114.

Treffinger, D. J. (1975). Teaching for self-directed learning: A priority for the talented and gifted. *Gifted Child Quarterly, 19*(1), 46–59.

Treffinger, D. J. (1978). Guidelines for encouraging independence and self-direction among gifted students. *Journal of Creative Behavior, 12*(1), 14–20.

Treffinger, D. J. (1979). Individualized education program plans for gifted and talented, and creative students. In *Developing IEPs for the gifted/talented.* Los Angeles: National/State Leadership Training Institute on the Gifted and Talented.

Treffinger, D. J., & Poggio, J. P. (1972). Needed research on the measurement of creativity. *Journal of Creative Behavior, 6*(4), 253–267.

Treffinger, D. J., & Renzulli, J. S. (1986). Giftedness as potential for creative productivity: Transcending I.Q. scores. *Roeper Review, 8*(3), 150–154.

Turnbull, W. W. (1978). Achievement test scores in perspective. *Educational Testing Service Annual Report.*

Underwood, B. (1949). *Experimental psychology.* New York: Appleton-Century-Crofts.

Upton, A. (1961). *Creative analysis.* New York: E. P. Dutton.

Van Tassel-Baska, J. (1986). The use of aptitude tests for identifying the gifted: The talent search concept. *Roeper Review, 8*(3), 185–189.

Vantour, J. A. (1976). Discovering and motivating the artistically gifted LD child. *Teaching Exceptional Children, 8*(2), 92–96.

Vare, J. V. (1979). Moral education for the gifted: A confluent model. *Gifted Child Quarterly, 23*(3), 472–486.

Vargiu, J. (1977). Creativity: The purposeful imagination. *Synthesis, 3–4,* 17–53.

Vaughan, M. M. (1971). Music as model and metaphor in the cultivation and measurement of creative behavior in children. *Dissertation Abstracts International, 32,* 1972, 583A. (University Microfilms No. 72-11, 056)

Vernon, P. E. (1951). *The structure of human abilities.* New York: John Wiley.

Vernon, P. E. (1960). *Intelligence and attainment tests.* New York: Philosophical Library.

Vygotsky, L. (1974). The problem of age-periodization in child development. *Human Development, 17,* 24–40.

Walberg, H. L. (1969). Physics, femininity and creativity. *Developmental Psychology, 1*(1), 47–54.

Walkup, L. E. (1971). Detecting creativity: Some practical approaches. *Journal of Creative Behavior, 5*(2), 88–93.

Wallach, M. A. (1968). Review of the Torrance Tests of Creative Thinking. *American Educational Research Journal, 5,* 272–281.

Wallach, M. A. (1970). In P. H. Mussen (Ed.), *Carmichael's manual of child psychology.* New York: John Wiley.

Wallach, M. A., & Kogan, N. (1965). *Modes of thinking in young children.* New York: Holt, Rinehart & Winston.

Wallach, M. A., & Wing, C. W. (1969). *The talented student: A validation of the creativity-intelligence distinction.* New York: Holt, Rinehart & Winston.

Wallas, G. (1926). *The art of thought.* London: C. A. Watts.

Walz, G. R., Smith, R. L., & Benjamin, L. A. (1974). *A comprehensive view of career development.* Washington, DC: American Psychological & Guidance Association Press.

Ward, V. S. (1961). *Educating the gifted.* Columbus, OH: Charles E. Merrill.

Ward, V. S. (1979). The governor's school of North Carolina. In A. H. Passow (Ed.), *The gifted and the talented: Their education and development.* Chicago: University of Chicago Press. (78th Yearbook of the NSSE)

Webb, J. T., Meckstroth, E. A., & Tolan, S. S. (1982). *Guiding the gifted child: A practical source for parents and teachers.* Columbus, OH: Ohio Psychology Publishing Company.

Webster's New World Dictionary of the American Language (College ed.). (1980). New York: World.

Wechsler, D. (1939). *The measurement of adult intelligence*. Baltimore: Williams & Wilkins.

Wechsler, D. (1950). Intellectual development and psychological maturity. *Child Development, 20*(1), 45–50.

Wechsler, D. (1966). *The measurement and appraisal of adult intelligence*. (4th ed.). Baltimore: Williams & Wilkins.

Wechsler, D. (1967). *Manual for Wechsler Preschool and Primary Scale*. New York: Psychological Corporation.

Wechsler, D. (1974). *Manual: Wechsler Intelligence Scale for Children* (rev. ed.). New York: Psychological Corporation.

Weinstein, J., & Altschuler, A. (n.d.). *Levels of self-knowledge*. Unpublished manuscript, University of Massachusetts, Boston.

Weisberg, P. S., & Springer, K. J. (1961). Environmental factors in creative function. *Archives of General Psychiatry, 5*, 554–564.

Weisberger, R. A. (1971a). *Developmental efforts in individualized instruction*. Itasca, IL: F. E. Peacock.

Weisberger, R. A. (1971b). *Perspectives in individualized instruction*. Itasca, IL: F. E. Peacock.

Wenger, W. (1979). *Beyond O. K.: Psychegenic Tools relating to health of body and mind*. Gaithersburg, MD: Psychegenics.

Wenger, W. (1985). *A method for personal growth and development*. Gaithersburg, MD: Psychegenics.

Westfall, F. W. (1958). Selected variables in the achievement or non-achievement of the academically talented high school student (Doctoral dissertation, University of Southern California). *Dissertation Abstracts International, 59*, 65.

Wheeler, C. J. (1987). The magic of metaphor: A perspective on reality construction. *Metaphor and Symbolic Activity, 2*(4), 223–237.

Whimbey, A., & Whimby, L. S. (1975). *Intelligence can be taught:* New York: E. P. Dutton.

White, L. A. (1949). Genius: Its causes and incidence. In L. A. White (Ed.), *The science of culture: A study of man and civilization*. New York: Farrar Straus.

White, S. W. (1988). Opportunity and intelligence. *National Forum, 68*(2), 2–3.

White, W. W. (1959). Motivation reconsidered: The concept of competence. *Psychological Review, 66*, 297–333.

Whitmore, J. R. (1980). *Giftedness, conflict and underachievement*. Boston: Allyn & Bacon.

Willard, A. (1976). Counseling the gifted. *Focus on Guidance, 9*(1), 1–11.

Willard, A. (1986). From Goddard to Gallagher—and beyond. *Roeper Review, 8*(4), 218–222.

Williams, F. E. (1969). Models for encouraging creativity in the classroom. *Educational Technology Magazine, 9*, 7–13.

Williams, F. E. (1970). *Classroom ideas for encouraging thinking and feeling*. Buffalo: D.O.K.

Williams, F. E. (1971a). Assessing pupil-teacher behaviors related to a cognitive-affective teaching model. *Journal of Research and Development in Education, 4*(3), 14–22.

Williams, F. E. (1971b). How to you really feel about yourself? In F. E. Williams (Ed.), *Total creativity programs for elementary school teachers.* Englewood Cliffs, NJ: Educational Technology Publications.

Williams, F. E. (1972). *A total creativity program.* Englewood Cliffs, NJ: Educational Technology Publications.

Williams, F. E. (1979). Williams' strategies orchestrating Renzulli's triad. *Gifted, Creative and Talented Magazine, 9,* 2–10.

Williams, R. L. (1972a). *Black Awareness Sentence Completion Test.* Unpublished manuscript, St. Louis Center for Black Studies of Washington University, St. Louis.

Williams, R. L. (1972b, September). *The BITCH-100: A culture-specific test.* Paper presented at the meeting of the 80th American Psychological Association, Honolulu.

Williams, R. L. (1972c). *Manual of directions: Black Intelligence Test of Cultural Homogeneity.* Unpublished manuscript, St. Louis Center for Black Studies of Washington University, St. Louis.

Williams, R. L. (1972d). *Themes concerning blacks.* Unpublished manuscript, St. Louis Center for Black Studies of Washington University, St. Louis.

Williams, T. M., & Fleming, J. W. (1969). Methodological study of the relationship between associative fluency and intelligence. *Developmental Psychology, 1*(2), 155–162.

Willings, D. (1988). *The Willings International Center for Innovation.* Unpublished manuscript.

Wilson, B., & Wilson, M. (1976). Visual narrative and the artistically gifted. *Gifted Child Quarterly, 20*(4), 432–447.

Wilson, E. (1931). *Axel's castle: A study of the imaginative literature.* New York: Charles Scribner's.

Wilson, R. C., & Morrow, W. R. (1962). School and career adjustment of bright high-achieving and underachieving high school boys. *Journal of Genetic Psychology, 101,* 91–103.

Wing, H. D. (1939). *Standardized Tests of Musical Intelligence.* Slough, U.K.: National Foundation for Educational Research.

Wing, H. D. (1961). *Standardized Test of Musical Intelligence* (rev. ed.). Slough, U.K.: National Foundation for Educational Research.

Witt, G. (1971). The life enrichment activity program: A continuing program for creative disadvantaged children. *Journal of Research and Development in Education, 4*(3), 67–73.

Witty, P. A. (Ed.). (1951). *The gifted child.* Boston: D. C. Heath.

Wooleat, P. L. (1979). Guiding the career development of gifted females. In N. Colangelo & R. T. Zaffrann (Eds.), *New voices in counseling the gifted.* Dubuque, IA: Kendall/Hunt.

Wordsworth, W. (1988). *She Dwelt Among the Untrodden Ways* (1800); *I Wandered Lonely as a Cloud* (1807); *Tintern Abbey* (1798). In *The complete works of William Wordsworth*. London: Macmillan.

Youtz, R. P. (1962). Psychological foundations of "applied imagination." In S. J. Parnes & H. F. Harding (Eds.), *A source book for creative thinking*. New York: Charles Scribner's.

Zaffrann, R. T., & Colangelo, N. (1977). Counseling with gifted and talented students. *Gifted Child Quarterly, 20*(3), 305–320.

Zaffrann, R. T. (1978). Gifted and talented students: Implications for school counselors. *Roeper Review, 1*(2), 9–13.

Zettel, J. (1979). State provisions for educating the gifted and talented. In A. H. Passow (Ed.), *The gifted and the talented: Their education and development*. Chicago: University of Chicago Press. (78th Yearbook of the NSSE)

Index